THE
MACMILLAN
DICTIONARY OF
PSYCHOLOGY

SECOND EDITION

THE
MACMILLAN
DICTIONARY OF
PSYCHOLOGY

··

SECOND EDITION

STUART
SUTHERLAND

First published in the United Kingdom by
THE MACMILLAN PRESS LTD, 1995
Brunel Road, Houndmills
Basingstoke, Hants RG21 6XS, England
Companies and representatives throughout the world.

Hardcover ISBN 0333-623231
Paperback ISBN 0333-62324X

A catalogue record for this book is available from the British Library.

10	9	8	7	6	5	4	3	2
04	03	02	01	00	99	98	97	

Printed and bound in Great Britain by
Antony Rowe Ltd, Chippenham, Wiltshire

Contents

Preface vi

Acknowledgements viii

Notes on use ix

THE DICTIONARY 1

Appendix 1. Sulci and gyri of the lateral surface of the cerebral cortex 511

Appendix 2. Sulci and gyri of the medial surface of the cerebral cortex 512

Appendix 3. Brodmann's areas of the lateral surface of the cerebral cortex 513

Appendix 4. Brodmann's areas of the medial surface of the cerebral cortex 514

Appendix 5. Medial view of the brain 515

Preface to the first edition

Why write another dictionary of psychology? After all, several have been published in the last few years. The answer is that most of them despite their titles have been encyclopaedias not dictionaries, one has been more of a dictionary of psychiatry than of psychology and none have had the aims of the present dictionary. Nowadays, almost every book on psychology contains a vast number of technical terms many of which are from other disciplines, including physics, mathematics, computing science, artificial intelligence, logic, philosophy, linguistics, psychiatry, optometry, neurology, neurophysiology, neuroanatomy, neurochemistry, anthropology, and sociology. The aim of the present dictionary is to define not just psychological terms but as many as possible of those terms from related disciplines that pop out of the page whenever one reads anything on psychology. In fact, were it not that the title is awkward this volume would have been called 'A Dictionary *for* Psychologists'.

Although the dictionary contains no extended essays, I have tried to give enough material on each term to allow the reader to grasp both its meaning and its significance. Examples are provided of the ways in which many of the terms are used since these are often much easier to grasp than an abstract definition. I have, moreover, excluded all terms that are used by psychologists in exactly the same way as in everyday life. No definitions will be found of 'anger', 'rage', and 'hatred' nor – to balance the picture – of 'joy', 'delectation' and 'liking', though I have been unable to resist inserting an unorthodox definition of 'love'. Indeed, I have not hesitated to make unconventional comments on some of the more controversial terms or to censure from time to time those who invented them and those who have propagated them. I hope that anyone who believes in the wilder excesses of behaviourism, cognitive science, psychoanalysis, psychotherapy, and other disciplines will forgive the occasional streak of levity. Psychology is too important a subject to take seriously.

It is well known that the medical profession have long tried to disguise their ignorance of diseases by inventing pretentious words usually based on Latin and Greek roots. Excessive phlegm is known as 'bronchitis', while inability to have an orgasm becomes 'primary orgasmic dysfunction'. American psychiatrists have recently discovered a new syndrome for which the technical term is 'post-vacation dysphoria'. True to the medical tradition, psychoanalysts produced a massive vocabulary of their own, not all of which can be included here, though I hope that almost all the psychoanalytic terms that would be encountered in a book on psychology can be found. Psychologists have been less influenced by medicine, but as a glance at the dictionary will show, even they have not been immune from the passion to invent new terms. Social psychologists have for the most part had the sense to use English words without distorting their meanings. For this reason there are fewer technical terms from social psychology than from most other aspects of the subject. It is to their credit that there is no need for entries on 'persuasion' or 'leadership'.

I have tried to avoid 'sexist' writing, but after considerable thought I have sometimes had to resort to it in order to avoid cumbersome and distracting phrases; in particular I have used 'he' and 'him' to denote a member of either sex. Perhaps regrettably, in current English these are the unmarked form (see entry under **markedness**): this usage has historical origins and has no bearing on contemporary attitudes any more than does the sailor's use of 'she' to refer to her or his ship.

It is customary for dictionary writers to acknowledge that their work is likely to contain mistakes, and to ask readers to write pointing out any they encounter. I apologise for any errors that have crept into mine, but I beg the reader not to draw my attention to them: it was depressing enough searching out the technical vocabulary in psychology and related subjects without having to learn at the end of it all that I have got everything wrong.

NSS

Preface to the second edition

In the six years since the first edition of this dictionary was published, there has been a spate of new terms, particularly in cognitive science and the neurosciences. The increasing number of terms has been compounded by the persistent and growing belief that initials are more impressive than the expressions they stand for. To avoid readers being baffled by initials, the commoner ones are included here. Altogether I have added about one thousand new terms without deleting any of the original ones.

For the sake of readers who wish to peruse this book in bed and do not like weight on their stomach, I have used various devices to shorten the text, including running together alphabetically consecutive headwords that are synonyms and listing 'Law of X' only under 'X, law of' rather than having two entries.

Two cautions should be made. (1) There are now such a vast number of mental tests and so many computer programs in AI and computer simulation that I have had to include definitions only for those that are best known. (2) The fourth edition of the (American) Diagnostic and Statistical Manual came out in 1994, unfortunately shortly after my own revision was complete. It has only been possible therefore to include a few of the new terms from DSM-IV.

Apart from providing new terms, I have revised many of the original entries, either to improve clarity or to correct errors. In my preface to the first edition, I begged the reader not to draw attention to errors. I now wish I had not done so and am grateful to the few readers who ignored my request. I am also grateful to all those who have helped me both with this and the previous edition, but must point out that any remaining errors are their responsibility not mine.

NSS
August 8 1995

Acknowledgements

I wish to thank the following for putting me straight on various terms: Dick Cavonius, Pete Clifton, Herb Dartnall, Chris Darwin, Margaret Deuchar, Brian Everitt, Gerald Gazdar, Michael Healey, Elvira Kirchhoff, Christopher Longuet-Higgins, John Mollon, Al Parkin, Ian Russell, Gay Snodgrass, Liz Somerville, and John Willatts. I am particularly indebted to Dr Jonckheere who read all the statistical terms and most of the psychological ones and saved me from many errors. I am especially grateful to Ann Doidge (who put the dictionary onto disks) for the intuition and patience she used in interpreting my handwriting. I would also like to acknowledge the efforts of Dr David Roberts, who proved himself to be a most intelligent and conscientious sub-editor. Finally, of the many books I have consulted, I have found five recent books particularly helpful.

Robert J. Campbell. *Psychiatric Dictionary*. Fifth edition. Oxford University Press, 1981.

Raymond J. Corsini. *Encyclopaedia of Psychology*. John Wiley & Sons, 1984.

David Crystal. *A Dictionary of Linguistics and Phonetics*. Second edition. Basil Blackwell, 1985.

Robert M. Goldenson. *Longman Dictionary of Psychology and Psychiatry*. Longmans, 1984.

Arthur S. Reber. *The Penguin Dictionary of Psychology*. Penguin, 1985.

For help with terms in the second edition I wish to thank Peter Clifton, Chris Darwin, John Maynard-Smith, John Mollon, and Dai Stephens.

Notes on use

The order of headings is based on the alphabetical sequence of letters in the term, ignoring spaces, hyphens, accents, and numerals. (Thus **16PFO** is to be found between **peyote** and **PGO spikes**.)

In general, headings are not inverted, e.g. there is an entry under **ambiguous figure**, and *not* under **figure, ambiguous** (though under **figure** there is a cross-reference to alert the reader to the existence of **ambiguous figure**.) An exception to the rule of inversion is made for the various laws, methods and principles, e.g. there is an entry under **assimilation, law of**, and *not* under **law of assimilation**.

Cross-references appear in SMALL CAPITALS.

Some articles define not only the term in the heading, but one or more subsidiary terms, which appear in **bold type**, e.g. the headings **cone monochromatism** and **rod monochromatism** direct the reader to *see* **monochromatism**, where those terms are defined.

Where synonyms are in consecutive alphabetical order and are clearly connected, they frequently appear together in bold as head words with a single definition, e.g. **algaesthesia, algaesthesis**. Entries for an expression that can be abbreviated normally appear under the full expression; in cases where it is much more common to use the term's initials, the entry appears under the initials, e.g. **N-methyl-D-aspartate** is given a cross reference to NMDA where the definition is to be found.

People are usually referred to by surname only. Where confusion can arise, because there is more than one worker of the same name, initials or a first name are added.

A

A. An abbreviation for 1. AMPLITUDE; 2. AMPERE; 3. RESPONSE AMPLITUDE.

Å. An abbreviation for ÅNGSTRÖM.

A1. An abbreviation for PRIMARY AUDITORY CORTEX.

AA. An abbreviation for ALCOHOLICS ANONYMOUS.

A* algorithm. (AI) A programmable search technique based on the estimated cost (e.g. in terms of number of operations) of moving from any given node to a desired node. The program explores routes in order of these costs, starting with the least costly and proceeding towards the most costly.

A-alpha fibre. A synonym for ALPHA MOTOR NEURON.

aba. An abbreviation for ADRENERGIC BLOCKING AGENT

ABA design. An experimental design in which condition A is given first to obtain a baseline measurement, then condition B and finally condition A again to detect any possible effects of the treatment of the subject in condition B when he reverts to condition A.

A-band. See EXTRAFUSAL FIBRES.

abandoned self. William James's expression for any pattern of behaviour, thought, or feeling that a person has abandoned.

abasia. Loss or impairment of the ability to walk, due to hysteria and without organic cause.

ABC theory. Ellis's theory that when an *A*ctivating agent (e.g. a quarrel) is followed by a bad *C*onsequence (e.g. anxiety), it is not really the activating event that causes the consequence, but false *B*eliefs on the part of the person involved. The theory is part of the basis for RATIONAL-EMOTIVE THERAPY.

abducens nerve. The sixth CRANIAL NERVE; it innervates the LATERAL RECTUS muscle.

abduction. 1. Horizontal rotation of the eye towards the temple or movement of a limb outwards from the side of the body. *Compare* ADDUCTION. 2. Peirce's term for inferring an explanation for a set of phenomena, in the manner e.g. of Einstein or Hercule Poirot. It is a useful but under-used term, since it captures the distinction between inferring a theory from phenomena and inferring putative phenomena from a theory. 3. A SYLLOGISM with a true major premise and a minor premise which is only probably true.

abductor. A muscle that causes ABDUCTION (1) when contracted.

aberration. (Optics) The transmission of light through an optical system in an undesirable or distorted way. *See* CHROMATIC ABERRATION and SPHERICAL ABERRATION.

AB̄ error. The phenomenon that if an infant of about 7–11 months of age is shown an object moving from location A to location B where it is hidden, it searches for it at the original location (A). The mistake can also occur even when the object is not hidden.

A-beta fibre. A synonym for BETA MOTOR NEURON.

abience. Withdrawal behaviour.

ability. A person's current capacity to perform a task. *Contrast* APTITUDE.

ablation. Surgical removal of an organ or part of an organ.

ablative. A case of a noun or pronoun (or adjective in agreement), particularly in inflected languages like Latin. It signifies e.g. that the noun is used to indicate location at a place ('in *bed*') or that it is used instrumentally ('struck by *lightning*').

Abney effect. The phenomenon that if white light is added to monochromatic light, the hue changes slightly.

Abney's law. The law that the total luminance of radiated light containing a number of wavelengths is the sum of the luminances of the monochromatic radiations. *See also* LUMINOUS EFFICIENCY FUNCTION.

abnormal. Departing from normality, e.g. in intelligence, eyesight, etc. The extent to which some faculty or trait must depart from normality to be considered abnormal is arbitrary. The term is more frequently used for departures from normality in an undesirable direction than in a desirable one. *Contrast* NORMAL.

abnormal psychology. The branch of psychology devoted to the diagnosis, care, and treatment of the mentally ill, mentally disturbed, or mentally retarded, and to systematic research on these conditions.

aboulia. A variant spelling of ABULIA.

above-I. A literal translation of Freud's term for the SUPEREGO.

abreaction. The discharging of repressed emotions, thought by psychoanalysts to occur when the patient re-experiences a traumatic but repressed incident, usually from childhood. *Compare* CATHARSIS.

abscissa. The horizontal coordinate of a graph, conventionally called the x-axis. *Compare* ORDINATE.

absence. A synonym for ABSENT STATE.

absent qualia. *See* QUALIA.

absent state. A state, common in temporal lobe epilepsy, in which a person is largely unaware of his surroundings.

absenteeism. Unjustifiable absence from work.

absolute address. (Computing) An address in a program that specifies a storage location directly. *Contrast* VIRTUAL ADDRESS.

absolute error. (Psychophysics) The difference, regardless of sign, between a judged value and the true value. *Contrast* CONSTANT ERROR.

absolute judgement. A judgement of the intensity or quality of a stimulus made without another stimulus with which to compare it. *Contrast* COMPARATIVE JUDGEMENT.

absolute justice. The fairness of the apportionment of benefits to an individual, judged without taking into account the benefits received by others. *Contrast* DISTRIBUTIVE JUSTICE.

absolute limen. A synonym for ABSOLUTE THRESHOLD.

absolute pitch. The ability, possessed by a few people, to judge accurately the pitch of a single tone without comparing it to others.

absolute rating scale. A scale on which the strength of some quality is assessed without systematically comparing it to other examples, e.g. assigning a number from the range 1–7 to indicate how shy someone is.

absolute reflex. Pavlov's expression for an innate or unconditioned reflex.

absolute refractory period. *See* REFRACTORY PERIOD.

absolute scale. A synonym for RATIO SCALE.

absolute threshold, absolute sensitivity. The lowest intensity of a stimulus (e.g. a tone or light) at which it can be detected. The value is to some extent arbitrary, but is usually measured by determining the intensity at which the stimulus is detected on 50 per cent of presentations. *Compare* DIFFERENCE THRESHOLD.

absolute value. A number or value expressed regardless of its sign.

absorption defect. A disorder of colour vision that results in unusual matches of primaries. It is caused by unusual absorption of light by the material of the eye before the light reaches the receptors. Normal colour matching is obtained if WDW NORMALIZATION is applied.

absorption spectrum. The proportion of incident light of each wavelength absorbed by a retinal photopigment or by a group of photopigments (or more generally by any substance).

abstinence rule. (Psychoanalysis). The precept that a patient should not indulge in pleasurable activity, in order that he should come to analysis slightly frustrated and be able to keep his mind on the job without external distraction.

abstract attitude. The capacity to use general concepts and to classify individual items in terms of their different attributes (e.g. colour or shape), rather than dealing with them simply as wholes. The term was invented by Goldstein who thought the ability was impaired in brain-damaged patients.

abstract idea, abstract concept. Any idea or concept that does not refer to an individual entity but to some property, state, condition, or system, e.g. 'law', 'whiteness'.

abstract intelligence. The capacity to use abstract concepts.

abstraction. The formation of general concepts from individual instances.

abstract letter. Any letter regardless of the form in which it appears (e.g. upper case, lower case, printed, handwritten).

abstract modelling. A process thought by some to govern socialization. Instead of directly imitating others' behaviour, children are thought to formulate abstract principles of behaviour by observing others.

absurdities test. A test in which the testee has to spot mistakes or incongruities in the material presented.

abulia. The pathological inability to take decisions or initiate voluntary activity; it can occur in schizophrenia.

abundancy motive. The tendency to consume more of something that satisfies a drive than is necessary to meet the need, e.g. overeating. *Contrast* DEFICIENCY MOTIVE.

ABX paradigm. A psychophysical procedure to establish the difference threshold: two different stimuli (A and B) are presented with a third (X) that is the same as one of the other two; the subject has to determine whether X is the same as A or B. The technique is common in hearing experiments, where A and B are given first, followed by X.

acalculia. The inability to use numbers or do arithmetic, caused by brain damage (usually to the parietal lobes).

acanthaesthesia, acanthesthesia. A hallucinatory sensation of pin pricks in the skin; it can result from alcohol abuse.

acarophobia. A morbid fear of mites, and by extension other insects, worms, or small objects like needles.

acatamathaesia. Loss of the ability to comprehend or to grasp the meaning of a stimulus.

acataphasia. The use of ungrammatical or incorrect expressions, as in some aphasics.

acathexis. (Psychoanalysis) Failure to feel emotion on experiencing something that should have emotional significance.

acathisia. An alternative spelling for AKATHISIA.

accelerated interaction. Very strong emotional feelings between members of a group, particularly when caused by certain forms of group therapy, e.g. by MARATHON GROUPS.

acceleration. *See* DERIVATIVE.

accent. A synonym for STRESS (2), but used especially of the syllables on which the beat falls in verse. *See* TONE GROUP.

accentuation theory. The theory that people exaggerate the similarities between items that they place in the same category, and exaggerate the dissimilarities between items that they place in different categories.

accessibility. (Memory) The ease with which a given idea can be recalled.

accessibility theory. The theory that the evolution and ontogenesis of intelligence occurs by first developing special-purpose mental skills and then making them accessible for more general use. Thus many invertebrate species can be classically conditioned only to certain stimuli, whereas vertebrates can be conditioned to any stimulus.

accessory nerve. The 11th CRANIAL NERVE. One branch of the nerve serves the pharynx and larynx, the other serves two of the neck muscles.

accessory stimulus. A stimulus presented a very short time before (or after) the stimulus to which a subject has to respond in a reaction time task. Its presence tends to increase reaction time even if it is presented in a different modality from the target stimulus.

accessory symptoms. *See* FUNDAMENTAL SYMPTOMS.

accident proneness. The tendency to have a significantly above average number of accidents caused by one's own behaviour.

accidental alignment. In SCENE ANALYSIS, the accidental juxtaposition of lines in the projection of a polyhedron to form a VERTEX TYPE not characteristic of the 3-D structure of a 3-D corner formed by the 3-D edges. E.g. if the observer is exactly in line with two vertical surfaces of a cube obliquely presented, a T-JUNCTION will occur where a horizontal edge meets the two vertical surfaces.

accidental stimuli. External stimuli that prompt a dream, e.g. the sound of footsteps.

acclimatization. The process of adapting physiologically or psychologically to a new climate or to changed circumstances.

accommodation. 1. (Vision) The change in the curvature of the lens that brings the object falling on the fovea into sharp focus. The lens becomes less convex for far objects, more for near ones. It is not fully established whether accommodation can be used as a DEPTH CUE. 2. Piaget's term for the modification of existing concepts in the light of new experience. *Contrast* ASSIMILATION. 3. (Physiology) The decrease in a nerve cell's tendency to fire that occurs when it is repeatedly stimulated with an electric current.

accommodative distortion. The distortion of a previous memory by incorporating into it material from a more recent memory or event.

account analysis. (Sociobiology) The analysis of the way in which a person describes his actions, in order to facilitate the interpretation of the memory of those actions.

acculturation. The process by which a person learns the social habits and mores of a society (which may be the one into which he is born or one to which he moves later in life).

accumulator. (Computing) The part of the central processor that executes logical or arithmetic operations.

accuracy test. An ability test in which the score depends on the correctness of the answers rather than on the length of time taken to complete it. *Compare* POWER TEST and SPEED TEST.

accusative. The CASE of a noun or pronoun that is the DIRECT OBJECT of the verb.

acedia. A syndrome marked by apathy, listlessness, and melancholy (obsolete).

acenaesthesia, acenesthesia. Loss of awareness of one's body or more generally, a feeling of not existing.

acerophobia. A morbid fear of sour things.

acetaldehyde (AcH). One of the substances into which alcohol is broken down in the body; it is the main cause of hangovers.

ACE test. The American Council on Education test of high grade intelligence.

acetylcholine (ACh). An excitatory CHOLINERGIC neurotransmitter, probably the only one at work in the autonomic system and at the synapses of skeletal muscles, but also found in parts of the brain, particularly the hypothalamus. *See also* CHOLINERGIC RECEPTORS, MUSCARINIC RECEPTORS, and NICOTINIC RECEPTORS.

acetylcholinesterase. The enzyme that destroys ACETYLCHOLINE.

AcH. An abbreviation for ACETALDEHYDE.

ACh. An abbreviation for ACETYLCHOLINE.

achieved role, achieved status. Status acquired by a person's own efforts. *Contrast* ASCRIBED STATUS.

achievement age. The level of achievement on educational tests measured in terms of the age at which the testee's score is normally reached by others.

achievement motivation, achievement drive. The drive to succeed or to master difficulties, thought by McLelland and others to vary from person to person and from culture to culture, and to depend in part on upbringing.

achievement quotient. Achievement age divided by the chronological age of the individual.

achievement test. Any test requiring acquired skills or knowledge.

achluophobia. A morbid fear of night or darkness.

achromat. A person who sees everything in achromatic colours. *See* ACHROMATISM.

achromatic. 1. Lacking HUE; the achromatic surface colours are black, white, and grey. 2. Pertaining to a lens that is corrected for CHROMATIC ABERRATION.

achromatic interval. 1. (Vision) The range of light intensities from the ABSOLUTE THRESHOLD for a chromatic light to the intensity at which its hue can be detected. 2. (Hearing) The range of amplitudes from the absolute threshold for a pure tone to the amplitude at which its pitch can be detected.

achromatism. 1. **achromatopsia.** The rare condition of being unable to see any hues, caused by a lack of functioning cones, resulting from damage to the retina or brain. 2. Absence of colour. 3. The property of an optical system that has no chromatic aberration.

acid. 1. Any substance that when dissolved in water yields hydrogen ions. *See* pH. 2. (Smell) *See* CROCKER–HENDERSON SYSTEM.

acmaesthesia, acmesthesia. A PARAESTHESIA in which tactile stimuli that would normally cause pain are felt only as touch or pressure.

acoasm. An alternative spelling for AKOASM.

acoria. Overeating or overdrinking.

acousma. A synonym for AKOASM.

acoustic. Pertaining to sound waves.

acoustic coding. Remembering an item, e.g. a written word or a visually perceived object, by the sound of the word or of the word naming the item. *See* SHORT-TERM STORE and *contrast* ARTICULATORY STORE.

acoustic confusion. An error in perception or memory, based on confusing words that sound similar, e.g. mishearing or misremembering 'pad' as 'bad'. *Contrast* SEMANTIC CONFUSION.

acoustic cue. Any acoustic property of a speech sound that assists its identification (e.g. the spacing of FORMANTS or VOICE-ONSET TIME).

acoustic feature. Any physical characteristic of a speech sound, e.g. its fundamental frequency or its amplitude. *See also* DISTINCTIVE FEATURES.

acoustic impedance. The ratio of the sound pressure in a medium to the volume of the medium passing through a given surface area per unit time. When a sound passes from one medium to a medium of higher impedance (as when sound enters the cochlea), the amplitude of the waves is reduced; the reduction is greater for high frequencies than for low.

acoustic-mnestic aphasia. A form of aphasia that can be caused by a lesion of the left temporal lobe, and that is marked by inability to recall lists of words and to understand or repeat long sentences.

acoustic nerve. The branch of the VESTIBULOACOUSTIC NERVE that serves the COCHLEA.

acousticophobia. A morbid fear of noise.

acoustic papilla. A synonym for ORGAN OF CORTI.

acoustic pressure. The variation in the pressure of a medium as a sound is conducted through it. The human ear is sensitive to SOUND PRESSURE variations of as little as 0.0001 dyne per square centimetre and to about a millionfold range of pressures.

acoustic radiations. The pathways running from the medial geniculate bodies to the auditory cortex, which transmit information about sounds.

acoustic reflex. A synonym for TYMPANIC REFLEX.

acoustics. The scientific study of the physical properties of sound.

acoustic similarity. Any similarity between sounds, particularly speech sounds (e.g. rhyme). When it occurs in some or all of a list of words it may impair recall of the list. *See also* ACOUSTIC CONFUSION.

acoustic spectrum. A synonym for AUDITORY SPECTRUM.

acoustic trauma. Hearing loss caused by being subjected to intense noise.

acoustic tunnel effect. A synonym for HETEROPHONIC CONTINUITY.

acquiescence-response set. The tendency of subjects to respond in the way they think the experimenter or tester wants them to.

acquired. (Neurology) Caused by brain damage.

acquired characteristic. Any change in the structure or behaviour of an organism that occurs because of interaction with its environment. *See* LAMARCKISM.

acquired distinctiveness. The acquisition through learning of the ability to distinguish between two or more stimuli (e.g. faces or cars) that were initially indistinguishable.

acquired drive. Any drive that is learned, and not innate.

acquired dyslexia. DYSLEXIA caused by brain damage; the main types are DEEP DYSLEXIA, PHONOLOGICAL DYSLEXIA, and SURFACE DYSLEXIA. *Contrast* DEVELOPMENTAL DYSLEXIA.

acquired similarity. A tendency to perceive two or more items, initially perceived as distinct, as the same as a result of learning to label them in the same way. It has been proposed that variant instances of the same phoneme come to be heard as the same in this way.

acquisition. The phase during which learning takes place.

acrasia. A pathological lack of self-control.

acroaesthesia. Hypersensitivity in the bodily extremities.

acroanaesthesia. Loss of sensation in one or more of the bodily extremities.

acrocephaly. The condition of having a high, pointed head.

acrocinesia, acrocinesis. Excessive movement, which may occur e.g. in hysteria or mania.

acroesthesia. An alternative spelling of ACROAESTHESIA.

acromegaly. An illness caused by the anterior pituitary being overactive, and characterized by the extremities of the body (head, hands, etc.) being grotesquely large.

acroparaesthesia, acroparesthesia. An abnormal feeling of numbness or tingling in the extremities.

acrophobia. A morbid fear of heights. *Compare* BATHOPHOBIA.

across-fibre theory. The hypothesis that in some sensory modalities sensory quality is signalled by a pattern of neural activity in a number of nerve fibres.

ACT. 1. An abbreviation for AMERICAN COLLEGE TESTING PROGRAM. 2. A computer program containing analogies of working memory and long-term declarative and procedural memory. Nodes have different strengths and spreading activation occurs. PRODUCTIONS in the procedural memory are matched to working memory and give output through it.

ACTH. An abbreviation for ADRENO-CORTICOTROPHIC HORMONE.

actin. *See* EXTRAFUSAL FIBRES.

acting out. Impulsive and uncontrolled behaviour, usually aggressive or sexual, that may provide release from tension. More specifically, in psychoanalysis, responding in the present in a way determined by previous relationships or repressed drives. It can be defined more succinctly as any behaviour on the part of the patient of which the therapist disapproves.

actinomycin P. An antibiotic often given experimentally to animals in order to inhibit RNA synthesis, and thus discover whether such synthesis underlies learning.

action-based therapy. Psychotherapy based on getting patients to interact with one another, e.g. psychodrama or encounter groups.

action current. A synonym for ACTION POTENTIAL.

action decrement. The alleged phenomenon that while material is in the process of being consolidated in memory, it is less readily recalled than after it has been consolidated.

action potential. The change in potential across the membrane of a nerve cell (or muscle) that propagates (as an impulse) along its length. The change is from -70 millivolts to $+20$ millivolts potential difference between the outside and inside of the membrane, with the inside going from negative to positive.

action research. The attempt to improve a social system (e.g. a hospital or factory) by formulating goals, collecting data about the existing system, and modifying it in the light of the data.

action-specific energy. (Ethology) A hypothetical supply of energy that produces innate responses associated with innate drives; the energy for a particular response decreases (according to Lorenz) when the response is 'released', after which it builds up again. *See also* RELEASER and VACUUM ACTIVITY.

action theory. Any theory in social psychology or sociology that stresses the ability of people to take decisions in the light of their goals and their interaction with others. A vague term.

activated sleep. A synonym for REM SLEEP.

activation. The arousal of one organ by another, or of a part of the nervous sytem or of the whole organism.

activation pattern. The desynchronized EEG that occurs when a person is alert or has his eyes open.

activation theory of emotion. The principle that there is a continuum of degrees of arousal, and that emotions lie at the high end of this continuum.

active avoidance learning. Learning to do something in order to avoid punishment, e.g. a rat may learn to jump a hurdle every time a bell is rung in order to avoid shock. *Contrast* ESCAPE LEARNING and PASSIVE AVOIDANCE LEARNING.

active memory. A synonym for SHORT-TERM MEMORY.

active rehearsal. Thinking about the associations and meaning of material to be remembered, e.g. by forming connected images of the objects referred to by a pair of words; active rehearsal improves memory.

active sleep. A synonym for REM SLEEP.

active short-term memory. A synonym for WORKING MEMORY.

active therapy. Psychotherapy in which the therapist makes suggestions and injunctions. *Contrast* PASSIVE THERAPY.

active transport. The movement of ions across a cell membrane by an active mechanism that uses energy (i.e. not by diffusion). E.g. the sodium pump actively transports sodium ions to the outside of the nerve cell membrane, using energy from ATP. *Contrast* DIFFUSION.

active vocabulary. The number of words a person uses, which is lower than the number he understands. *Contrast* PASSIVE VOCABULARY.

active voice. A category applied to sentences, clauses, and verb forms in which the grammatical subject is the performer of the action, e.g. 'He threw the ball'.

activity cage. An apparatus for automatically recording how physically active an animal is over a period of time.

activity cycle. Regular variations in the output of energy by an animal, often but not necessarily circadian.

activity inventory. (Industrial psychology) A list of all the activities required to do a particular job. It can be used for selection or for reorganizing the activities to increase efficiency.

activity quotient. The ratio of verbs to adjectives used by a person; it is thought to be a measure of emotionality.

activity schema. A synonym for SCRIPT.

Activity Vector Analysis. A personality test in which cards describing traits are presented to the testee, who has to decide which best fit him, and which describe how others see him.

activity wheel. A drum that is free to revolve and is turned by an animal placed at the bottom. It is used to measure activity drive, endurance, etc.

actor. Anyone performing an action, in contrast to anyone observing it.

actor–observer difference. The phenomenon that people tend to attribute their own actions to situational factors and those of others to dispositional factors.

act psychology. The doctrine put forward by Brentano that psychology should study not merely the contents of consciousness (as did the structuralists), but the way in which mental acts refer to entities other than themselves.

actual conflict. (Psychoanalysis) The current conflict between conscious and unconscious forces that can lead to neurosis. *Compare* ROOT CONFLICT.

actualization. Short for SELF-ACTUALIZATION.

actualization theory. A theory of motivation espoused by Maslow and others that holds that motives are not all based on reducing tension, but that the most important motive is a striving to 'grow' and to enhance one's experience.

actual neurosis. (Psychoanalysis) A neurosis caused by current sexual frustrations (e.g. by abstinence or coitus interruptus) or by organic disorders, rather than by failure to cope with repressed wishes. Freud thought neurasthenia and anxiety neurosis were actual neuroses. *Contrast* PSYCHONEUROSIS.

actual self. Horney's term for all the attributes of a person at one moment, not to be confused with SELF-ACTUALIZATION.

actuarial prediction. A synonym for STATISTICAL PREDICTION.

acuaesthesia, acuesthesia. Synonyms for ACMAESTHESIA.

acuity. The capacity, in any of the senses, to detect fine detail. *See* TWO-POINT THRESHOLD and VISUAL ACUITY.

acuity grating. Black and white parallel stripes of equal width used to determine the MINIMUM SEPARABLE. *See also* SINE WAVE GRATING.

aculalia. Nonsensical speech occurring as a result of brain damage; it is usually associated with WERNICKE'S APHASIA.

acupuncture. The practice, originating in China, of attempting to relieve illness or to cause anaesthesia by implanting needles in specific places in the skin.

acute. Of illness, short-lasting. *Contrast* CHRONIC.

acute brain disorder. Any organic brain disorder that is temporary, and from which the patient makes a full recovery, e.g. a convulsive disorder or alcohol intoxication.

acute preparation. *See* PREPARATION.

acute schizophrenic episode. A condition lasting not more than a few months, in which schizophrenic symptoms (e.g. delusions, disorientation, and hallucinations) are experienced, usually as a result of emotional stress.

acute tolerance. Development of tolerance to a drug after only one or a few doses. *Contrast* CHRONIC TOLERANCE.

adaptation. 1. (Evolution) (i) The process by which through natural selection organisms change to maximize transmission of their genes. (ii) Any modification to an organism that is the result of this process. 2. (Psychology) In general, coming to fit in with the environment through learning or some other process. 3. (Perception) Adjustments to the sensitivity of a sensory system that tend to maximize the efficiency of discrimination under prevailing conditions, e.g. of light intensity. *See* e.g. DARK ADAPTATION and LIGHT ADAPTATION. 4. (Physiology) (i) The reduction in firing rates that usually occurs in sensory systems (except that for pain) if a stimulus is continuously presented. (ii) Changes in other organs that help an animal to survive under prevailing conditions (e.g. the development of more skin pigment in hot weather). (iii) Changes in the brain or other organs that increase TOLERANCE for an often-used drug such as alcohol.

adaptation level (AL). The quality or quantity of stimulation of a given kind to which someone has become accustomed, and which is taken as the norm. E.g. a moderately intense light looks bright to someone who has been in dim light, dim to someone who has been in bright light; British cars look small to Americans who are used to bigger ones. The expression can also be applied to the emotions, though with less obvious justification – people are said to adapt to a given level of happiness.

adaptation level theory. Helson's principle that how one perceives or thinks of anything depends on one's ADAPTATION LEVEL.

adaptation-produced potentiation. The strengthening of one taste after being exposed to another; e.g. after exposure to a very bitter taste, distilled water tastes sweet.

adaptation syndrome. Short for GENERAL ADAPTATION SYNDROME.

adaptation time. The length of time needed for a sensory system to adapt (*see* ADAPTATION 4(i)) completely to a stimulus and revert to the rate of firing occurring before the stimulus was presented.

adaptive value. The extent to which a characteristic increases the frequency in a species of the genes underlying it.

Adaptive Behaviour Scale. A test of the ability of mental retardates to cope with their environment; it is based on observers' reports on ten different functions.

addiction. Dependence on the use of a drug such as alcohol, heroin, or cocaine. The criteria for addiction are disputed; e.g. whether addiction can be entirely psychological, or can only exist if there have been physical changes in the body that make the drug necessary for normal functioning. Among other criteria are feeling miserable or having unpleasant physical symptoms (e.g. vomiting) if the drug is withdrawn, having a craving for the drug, and having a compulsive inability to resist taking the drug despite the knowledge that it is harmful.

Addison's disease. A degenerative illness caused by deficiency of adrenocortical hormone; it is characterized by weakness, vomiting, anorexia, hypertension, irritability, and other symptoms.

addition. A RORSCHACH TEST scoring term used when someone reports separate details of the inkblots but eventually combines them into a whole response.

additive colour mixing. See COLOUR MIXING.

additive-factors method. A method, invented by Saul Sternberg, of evaluating whether successive and independent processes underlie a task. E.g. a subject told to remember a set of items is asked to decide whether a probe is part of the set. This task can be broken down into encoding the probe, matching it to a member of the set and deciding 'Yes' or 'No'. If the time taken by each process can be independently influenced, it can be assumed that the processes are discrete.

additive genetic variation. The variation in a phenotypic trait produced when the effects of two different alleles combined (HETEROZYGOSITY) is the sum of the effects of the two homozygous combinations of each allele.

additive scale. A synonym for INTERVAL SCALE.

address. (Computing) A register where a given symbol string is stored, or the symbol string specifying the location of that register. See also ABSOLUTE ADDRESS and VIRTUAL ADDRESS.

adduction. Horizontal rotation of the eye in the direction of the nose, or the movement of a body part toward the medial plane. Compare ABDUCTION (1).

adductor. A muscle that when contracted causes ADDUCTION.

adenine. One of the four nucleotide bases in DNA and RNA.

adenohypophysis. See PITUITARY.

adenosine. See PURINES.

adenosine diphosphate (ADP). The precursor of ADENOSINE TRIPHOSPHATE, which is formed by the addition of an extra phosphate group. It may act as a neuromodulator or neurotransmitter, particularly in the autonomic system.

adenosine monophosphate (AMP). A phosphorylated compound of adenosine that is important in cell metabolism, and is thought to be an inhibitory neurotransmitter in the autonomic system. Cyclic AMP acts as a SECOND MESSENGER in synaptic transmission, and may act as a neuromodulator or neurotransmitter, particularly in the autonomic system.

adenosine triphosphate (ATP). The main intermediate energy-carrying compound in all the cells of all organisms. It carries the chemical energy obtained from the oxygenation of food. When it is converted to ADENOSINE DIPHOSPHATE and then ADENOSINE MONOPHOSPHATE, the reaction releases energy that is used in the cell's metabolism, e.g. to energize growth, muscular contraction, or the sodium pump. It may also act as a neurotransmitter or neuromodulator, particularly in the autonomic system.

adenyl cyclase. An enzyme that causes ATP to convert to AMP, and hence probably plays a role in the SECOND MESSENGER system.

adequate stimulus. 1. A stimulus that is the normal type of stimulus for a given sensory system, and is above threshold. Contrast INADEQUATE STIMULUS (1). 2. Any stimulation of the nervous system that causes a particular neuron to fire.

Ad fibres. A synonym for AIII fibres. See NERVE FIBRE.

ADH. An abbreviation for ANTIDIURETIC HORMONE.

ADHD. An abbreviation for ATTENTION DEPENDENT HYPERACTIVITY DISORDER.

ad hoc. Unprincipled, particularly of explanations constructed POST HOC to explain data.

adiadochokinesis. Impaired ability to perform repetitive movements, like tapping; it is a symptom of cerebellar damage.

adience. Approach behaviour.

adipocytes, adipose cells. The cells that store body fat; dieting appears to reduce the amount of fat stored in each, but not the number of such cells.

adipsia. An abnormally low drive to drink, which can be caused by lesions to the VENTROMEDIAL NUCLEUS OF THE HYPOTHALAMUS.

adjective. A part of speech used to describe the attributes of the referent of a noun (e.g. 'big', 'happy').

adjective checklist. A list of adjectives shown to a testee who is asked to tick those that apply to himself, to another person, or to a product, depending on what is being investigated.

adjunct. (Linguistics) A synonym for MODIFIER.

adjunctive behaviour. A synonym for SCHEDULE-INDUCED BEHAVIOUR.

adjusting schedule. Any schedule of reinforcement that changes in a way that is dependent on the subject's behaviour. E.g. in a CONSTANT INTERVAL SCHEDULE, the interval might be increased whenever the subject's first response occurs not more than 5 sec after the end of the current constant interval.

adjustment. Modifications in behaviour or thought processes that enable the organism to deal adaptively with changes in its environment or in its own capacities.

adjustment, method of. 1. (Psychophysics) A method for determining a threshold in which the subject adjusts a stimulus to the weakest value that is just perceptible (absolute threshold) or until it appears to be the same as a comparison stimulus (difference threshold).

The difference threshold is calculated from the deviation of the settings of the comparison stimulus from those of the standard. *See* AVERAGE ERROR, METHOD OF. 2. A synonym for PRODUCTION, METHOD OF.

adjustment disorder. Temporarily impaired and maladaptive functioning, with emotional distress, occurring soon after a stressful event, e.g. divorce or a new job.

adjustment method. A synonym for ADJUSTMENT, METHOD OF.

adolor. The inability to feel grief, a condition that many psychiatrists believe to be prevalent in the Western world.

adoption studies. Investigations that attempt to estimate the heritability of a characteristic by comparing its incidence in adopted children and children brought up by their natural parents.

ADP. An abbreviation for ADENOSINE DIPHOSPHATE.

adrenal cortex. The outer part of the ADRENAL GLAND, which secretes **adrenocortical hormones**, including the sex hormones (ANDROGENS, OESTROGENS, and PROGESTERONE), the GLUCOCORTICOIDS (e.g. cortisol), and the MINERALOCORTICOIDS (e.g. aldosterone).

adrenal glands. Two small bodies lying one above each kidney, each divided into the ADRENAL CORTEX and the ADRENAL MEDULLA.

adrenal hyperplasia. A congenital abnormality causing excess secretion of androgens and hence leading to masculine characteristics in females.

adrenaline. A synonym (mainly in the UK) for EPINEPHRINE.

adrenal medulla. The core of the ADRENAL GLAND; it secretes EPINEPHRINE and NOREPINEPHRINE, which play an important role in the SYMPATHETIC SYSTEM.

adrenergic. Pertaining to neurotransmission based on EPINEPHRINE and NOREPINEPHRINE.

adrenergic blocking agent (aba). A substance that blocks activity at adrenergic synapses. There are two kinds – ALPHA BLOCKERS and BETA BLOCKERS, which block respectively alpha and beta ADRENERGIC RECEPTORS.

adrenergic drugs. Substances, such as amphetamine, that increase activity at adrenergic synapses.

adrenergic receptor. The site on the post-synaptic cell activated by an adrenergic substance. There are two types, defined by their relative sensitivity to three substances. Their sensitivities are (from most to least): **alpha-adrenergic receptors**: epinephrine > norepinephrine > isoproterenol. **beta-adrenergic receptors**: isoproterenol > epinephrine > norepinephrine. Moreover, one synthetic compound (**phentolamine**) is an antagonist only at alpha receptors, whereas another (**propranolol**) is an antagonist only at beta receptors. Beta receptors themselves are of at least two types; stimulation of β_1 receptors increases heart rate and blood pressure, whereas stimulation of β_2 receptors relaxes the trachea.

adrenocortical homones. *See* ADRENAL CORTEX.

adrenocorticotropin, adrenocorticotrophic hormone (ACTH). A peptide hormone secreted by the anterior pituitary, often in response to stress, that activates the ADRENAL CORTEX and is probably also a neuromodulator in the central nervous system; some believe it is implicated in the formation of memories. *See also* HYPOTHALAMIC-RELEASING FACTORS.

adrenogenital syndrome. The syndrome in females caused by ADRENAL HYPERPLASIA.

adultomorphism. The interpretation of children's behaviour in ways appropriate only for that of adults.

adventitious deafness. Hearing loss caused by injury or disease.

adventitious reinforcement. A reinforcement occurring by accident after a response and not caused by it. *Compare* SUPERSTITIOUS BEHAVIOUR.

adverb. A part of speech mainly used to describe the way in which the action referred to by the verb is executed (e.g. 'He sang *raucously*').

adynamia. A synonym for NEURASTHENIA.

AEP. An abbreviation for AVERAGE EVOKED POTENTIAL.

AER. An abbreviation for AVERAGE EVOKED RESPONSE.

aerial perspective. A cue to depth perception, based on the fact that very distant objects appear blurred (because light is scattered by the atmosphere) and bluish (because short-wavelength light is added to the rays from the object since it is scattered by the atmosphere more than long wavelengths).

aeroacrophobia. A morbid fear of flying or of being in other high and open places.

aerobic. Pertaining to an organism that requires free oxygen, or to the uptake of oxygen by an organism.

aerophagia. Swallowing air, a common neurotic habit that can produce discomfort and belching.

aerophobia. A morbid fear of wind or draught.

aesthesiometer. A device for measuring skin sensitivity, usually by determining the TWO-POINT THRESHOLD.

aesthetics. The philosophical or psychological study of the nature of beauty.

aetiology. 1. The cause or causes of an illness. 2. The study of the causes of illness.

affect. Emotional tone.

affect-block. Inability to express emotion, occurring for example in some schizophrenics and obsessive-compulsives.

affective disorder. Any mental disorder in which the main abnormality is a very depressed or elevated mood.

affective fixation. A synonym for FIXATION (2).

affective psychosis. An increasingly used synonym for MANIC-DEPRESSIVE PSYCHOSIS.

affective ratio. In the RORSCHACH TEST, the ratio of the total number of responses to colour cards to the total number to achromatic cards.

afferent. Pertaining to any neural pathway or part thereof in which information is being conveyed inwards towards the cortex. *Contrast* EFFERENT.

afferent stimulus interaction. Hull's postulate that stimuli interact non-linearly to produce behaviour that is not merely determined by the sum of their separate effects. Here Hull seems to have suffered a touch of the *Gestalts*.

affiliation. The formation of a close (usually dependent) relationship with another person. *See also* ATTACHMENT.

affinity. (Neurochemistry) The strength of the tendency for a substance to bind to a RECEPTOR (2).

affirmative. Pertaining to a sentence in which there is no negation of the main verb.

affirming the consequent. Making the false argument that, because the consequent of a conditional proposition is true, the antecedent must also be true; for example, inferring from 'If this theory is true, X is true; and X is true', that 'this theory is true.'

affix. Any morpheme that is attached to the beginning (*un*pleasant) or end (tak*ing*) of another morpheme, and that cannot be used as a word on its own.

affordance. J.J. Gibson's term for the aspect of a stimulus that signals to the observer that the opportunity to perform a particular act is present; e.g. the opportunity to sit or mate are signalled respectively by the stimuli from a chair and a member of the opposite sex.

affricate. (Phonetics) A consonant composed of a PLOSIVE followed by a brief FRICATIVE, e.g. the 'ch' in 'chip'.

A fibre. *See* NERVE FIBRE.

afterbrain. A synonym for METENCEPHALON.

afterdischarge. Electrical activity in a neuron continuing for a brief time after the stimulus has stopped.

aftereffect. Any direct effect of a stimulus on perception that operates (usually briefly) after the stimulus has been removed. *See also* AFTERIMAGE, FIGURAL AFTEREFFECT, MCCOLLOUGH EFFECT, MOTION AFTEREFFECT, and TILT AFTEREFFECT.

afterexpulsion. A synonym for PRIMARY REPRESSION.

afterimage. An image of a visual stimulus persisting for a few seconds after part of the retina has been exposed to a high-contrast stimulus. The image is localized on that part of the retina on which the stimulus fell, and is therefore seen to move with the eyes. **Positive afterimages** preserve the brightness and hue relationships between stimulus and surround; in **negative afterimages** the relationships are reversed. When seen in the dark, seven successive afterimages have been detected, alternating between positive and negative. *See* HERING IMAGE, PURKINJE IMAGE, and HESS IMAGE.

afterimpulsion. A synonym for SECONDARY REPRESSION.

aftersensation. Any sensation remaining after the stimulus ceases, regardless of the sensory modality.

A-gamma fibre. A synonym for GAMMA MOTOR NEURON.

age-equivalent scale. A measure of the extent to which a given skill has been developed in a person, expressed as the age at which the average person reaches that level of development.

age-grade scale. Any standardized educational scale measured by tests that are appropriate for children of a given age and grade.

agenesis. 1. Congenital lack of some part of the body. 2. Inability to reproduce.

age norm. The average age at which children obtain a given score on a test.

agent. 1. (Linguistics) In a sentence, the person or thing who does the action. 2. (Parapsychology) The person who tries to transmit a signal in an ESP test. 3. *See* CATALYTIC AGENT.

agentive. *See* CASE GRAMMAR.

agerasia. The quality of being well-preserved in old age.

age regression. The reliving under hypnosis of forgotten experiences that took place at a younger age; a questionable phenomenon.

age scale. Short for AGE-EQUIVALENT SCALE.

age score. A score on a test expressed in terms of the age at which the average child performs at the level of the testee.

ageusia. Impairment or loss of the sense of taste.

agglutination. 1. (Physiology) The sticking together of biological substances, e.g. blood corpuscles. 2. (Linguistics) The formation of new words by combining existing words, e.g. 'aftereffect'.

agglutination language. A language in which the words typically contain several morphemes.

aggregate inhibitory potential ($_S\dot{I}_R$). In Hull's theory, the sum of REACTIVE INHIBITION and CONDITIONED INHIBITION, which must be deducted from GENERALIZED REACTION POTENTIAL to obtain NET REACTION POTENTIAL. *See* HULLIAN THEORY.

aggression. The deliberate attempt to overcome or harm others (and, in psychoanalysis, the self). This drive is thought to be in part innate; it can be a reaction to frustration. *See also* ANTICIPATORY AGGRESSION and DISPLACED AGGRESSION.

aggressive mimicry. The mimicking, developed in evolution, by a predator of the appearance of a harmless species in order to attack its prey under false pretences. *See also* MIMICRY.

aggressive oral phase. *See* ORAL STAGE.

aggressive socialized conduct disorder. A personality disorder in which a person persistently commits crimes against others, or ignores their rights (e.g. by stealing), but can form friendships or show concern for others on occasion.

agitated depression. A severe form of depression in which the patient is very restless and writhes about in an anguished way.

agitolalia, agitophasia. Abnormally rapid speech, usually containing distortion and slurring of words.

aglossia. Lack of comprehensible speech caused by damage to the vocal tract.

agnosia. Inability to recognize objects or other aspects of the visual world. It can be confined to a specific feature of the world, e.g. colours, faces, forms. It is usually caused by brain damage, but can be due to hysteria or schizophrenia. *See also* INTEGRATIVE AGNOSIA and TOPOGRAPHIC AGNOSIA.

agnosic alexia. Inability to read, with writing, speech, and speech understanding more or less unimpaired. The condition is associated with damage to those parts of the corpus callosum that serve the occipital cortex.

agonic. Pertaining to a group whose social cohesion depends on the dominance of one member, usually a male, as in baboons or chimpanzees.

agonist. 1. A compound that binds to a neuron's receptors and has the same effect (excitatory or inhibitory) on the postsynaptic cell as the neurotransmitter that would normally bind there. 2. A muscle whose contractual action operates in the same direction as that of another.

agoraphobia. A common phobia characterized by a morbid fear of public spaces: sufferers may confine themselves to their homes.

agrammatism, agrammaphasia. A form of APHASIA in which individual words may be correctly used, but sentences are ungrammatical, incoherent, and often lacking function words.

agranular cortex. Cerebral cortex lacking the granular layers (which are layers II and IV). Such cortex occurs in the posterior part of the frontal lobe in the motor areas. The rest of the neocortex contains layers II and IV, and is **granular cortex.**

agraphia. A form of APHASIA in which the person is unable to write meaningfully, a syndrome affecting many psychologists.

agyiophobia. A morbid fear of streets.

aha experience. The feeling that occurs on suddenly seeing the solution to a problem (or thinking one does).

ahistorical. Concentrating on the present, rather than thinking of what led to it; behaviour therapists, unlike psychoanalysts, are ahistorical.

AI. An abbreviation for ARTIFICIAL INTELLIGENCE. *See also* STRONG AI.

aichmophobia. A morbid fear of anything pointed.

aided recall. Recall obtained by prompting rather than by merely asking open-ended questions. The technique is widely used in police interrogations, and can easily lead to the recall of things that never happened.

ailurophobia. A morbid fear of cats, common in mice.

aim. (Psychoanalysis) The **external aim** is the activity a person wishes to pursue with an INSTINCTUAL OBJECT. The **internal aim** is the inner satisfaction the person wishes to gain through the activity.

aim-inhibition. (Psychoanalysis) The suppression of an underlying wish or the unconscious transfer of that wish to some other goal, e.g. by sublimation.

air bone gap. The difference in auditory sensitivity to sounds transmitted through the eardrum, and through the bone.

air encephalography. A synonym for PNEUMOENCEPHALOGRAPHY.

Airy's disc. The central part of the diffraction pattern of a point source passed through a circular aperture; it is a circle bordered by the contour at which the light first drops to zero, and has concentric rings of light around it. It contains about 90 per cent of the light. On the retina, its diameter is about $1'$ of arc, with a 4 mm diameter pupil.

akatamathaesia. An alternative spelling of ACATAMATHAESIA.

akataphasia. An alternative spelling of ACATAPHASIA.

akathisia, akatizia. Agitation so extreme that the person cannot even sit down; it can be a side effect of NEUROLEPTICS.

akinaesthesia, akinesthesia. Impairment to, or loss of, KINAESTHESIS.

akinesia. Loss of or impairment of motor control.

akinetic. Not moving or unable to move, as e.g. in catatonia.

akinetic apraxia. A form of APRAXIA in which voluntary movements cannot be executed.

akinetic mutism. (Neuropsychology) A state in which the person has his eyes open, but cannot move his skeletal muscles. It is caused by bilateral lesions of the brain stem.

akoasm. Any simple auditory hallucination, like whistles or buzzes; it does not include hearing voices.

AL. An abbreviation for ADAPTATION LEVEL.

alallia. Inability to speak.

alarm call. A call given by a member of a species – especially one governed by innate mechanisms – when danger threatens; the call is recognized by other members of the species as a signal to take cover.

alarm reaction. *See* GENERAL ADAPTATION SYNDROME.

alaterality. Equal (or nearly equal) dominance of the two cerebral hemispheres.

albedo. A synonym for REFLECTANCE.

alcohol abuse. A psychiatric expression for drinking too much. See ALCOHOL DEPENDENCE.

alcohol dependence. (DSM-III) A psychiatric term, similar in meaning to ALCOHOLISM, but stressing two facts: (i) with chronic heavy drinking, people develop tolerance to alcohol and require a larger dose to obtain the same effect; (ii) chronic drinkers may develop withdrawal symptoms (e.g. nausea or the shakes) if deprived of alcohol. See also ALCOHOLISM, CHRONIC ALCOHOLISM, and DIPSOMANIA.

alcoholic dementia. A synonym for KORSAKOFF'S PSYCHOSIS.

alcoholic idiosyncratic intoxication. The tendency to become drunk after imbibing an amount of alcohol so small that it would scarcely affect most people; a rare disorder.

Alcoholics Anonymous. An international organization, started in the US in 1935, for helping people to stop drinking and for rehabilitating them. Its branches function through meetings of members at which their problems are aired and discussed. It has a strong religious orientation, and is given to the production of catchy mottoes. Some spouses would rather see their partners drinking than attending Alcoholics Anonymous, but it appears to have considerable success, though firm evidence is lacking.

alcoholism. The condition of being chronically dependent on alcohol or of harming oneself or others by a chronic alcoholic intake. There are no clear criteria for alcoholism, but people are usually considered to be alcoholics if their drinking impairs their health, their work, or their relations with others, particularly their immediate family. Some alcoholics do not drink every day, but indulge in sustained bouts from time to time. The **gamma alcoholic** loses self control (in addition to having increased tolerance and withdrawal symptoms on quitting), whereas the **delta alcoholic** does not lose control but has the other symptoms. See also ALCOHOL DEPENDENCE.

alcohol withdrawal. An acute mental disorder caused by withdrawal from alcohol, and marked by tremor, nausea, sweating, anxiety, irritability, and depressed mood.

aldosterone. A steroid hormone secreted by the ADRENAL CORTEX that plays a part in regulating body fluid, and sodium and potassium levels.

aleatory theory. The belief that changes in society over time are largely due to chance.

alethia. Inability to forget.

Alexander technique. A therapy purporting to help mental disorders and other problems, partly by teaching people how to carry themselves correctly.

alexia. Inability to read, sometimes caused by temporal lobe damage. Compare DYSLEXIA.

alexithymia. An inability to describe one's feelings or mood. It is found especially in somatoform patients, usually combined with flattened emotions.

algedonic. Pertaining to a mixture of pleasure and pain, or to the pleasure pain dimension.

algesia, algaesthesia, algaesthesis. 1. The pain sense. 2. Sensitivity to pain, sometimes used to mean hyper-sensitivity.

algesimeter. An instrument, containing a calibrated needle, used to determine people's sensitivity to pain.

algesis, algesthesia, algesthesis. Synonyms for ALGESIA.

algolagnia, algophilia. The tendency to become sexually aroused through pain whether received (**masochism**) or administered (**sadism**).

algophobia. A morbid fear of pain.

algorithm. A finite sequence of operations which when carried out are certain to yield the solution to a problem. E.g. a procedure for finding the square root of a number. *Contrast* HEURISTIC.

alienation. 1. (Psychiatry) Mental illness (an old-fashioned term, though still sometimes used in forensic psychiatry). 2. (Psychiatry) The dissociation between a person's thoughts and his feelings; it can occur in obsessive-compulsives and some schizophrenics. 3. Marx's term for a feeling of powerlessness in workers in capitalist society caused by their being exploited and having no involvement in their work. 4. (Existentialism) Estrangement or separation of a person's feelings and thoughts from his hypothesized true inner self. 5. (Generally) A feeling that life is meaningless, a feeling of being dissociated from friends, estranged from the values of society, etc. (as depicted in, e.g. Camus, *The Stranger*).

alien hand. A hand that moves without the person willing it, sometimes in such a way as to cancel out the intentional behaviour of the other hand, e.g. by closing a drawer while the other hand is opening it; the phenomenon can occur in SPLIT-BRAIN patients.

alienist. The legal term in the USA for a doctor (usually a psychiatrist) giving evidence on mental health before a court of law; also an obsolete term for a psychiatrist in a mental institution.

alignment acuity. A synonym for VERNIER ACUITY.

alignment approach. A theory of object recognition holding that a PROTOTYPE is stored in memory and the representation of a new object is transformed in any or all of three ways – by rotation, translation and changes in size of the image. It may thus come to correspond almost exactly to the stored prototype, so that at this point recognition can be achieved by TEMPLATE MATCHING.

aliment. Piaget's term for any new concept that the child incorporates into his existing schemata.

alkali. A chemical compound that combines with acid in water to form a salt, hence neutralizing the acid. *See* pH.

alkaloid. Any of a group of nitrogenous substances found in plants, many of which, including nicotine, cocaine, and morphine, have pharmacological effects on the nervous system.

allaesthesia, allachaesthesia. Mislocation of a skin sensation, including feeling a sensation in the opposite limb to that touched.

Allais paradox. (Decision theory) A demonstration that people choose a 'certain' gain rather than an option with higher expected utility when there is a clear difference in the probability of the outcome of each option, but tend to choose the more risky option when there is no option with a certain gain. The gambles are rigged in such a way that the decisions taken break the INDEPENDENCE AXIOM.

allele, allelomorph. One of two or more different genes that can occupy the same site on a chromosome.

allesthesia. An alternative spelling of ALLAESTHESIA.

alley problem. The paradox that parallel lines appear to converge even though the observer may realize that they are parallel.

alloaesthesia, alloesthesia. Alternative spellings of ALLAESTHESIA.

allocation policy. When someone is conducting two or more tasks at once, each of which makes demands on his limited resources, the way in which he allocates these resources between the tasks. There is a trade-off between how well he performs each of them.

allocator. Someone in a position to reward or punish other members of his group.

allocentric. External to the self.

allochaesthesia. A synonym for ALLAESTHESIA.

allocheiria. An alternative spelling of ALLOCHIRIA.

allochesthesia. A synonym for ALLAESTHESIA.

allochiria. The transfer of the apparent location of a tactile stimulus to the same point on the opposite side of the body.

allochthonous. Pertaining to anything originating from outside a person or outside his body.

allocortex. The PALAEOCORTEX and ARCHICORTEX.

alloeroticism, alloerotism. Sexual interest or excitement generated by another person. *Contrast* AUTOEROTICISM.

alloesthesia. An alternative spelling of ALLAESTHESIA.

allograph. Any variant form of a letter, e.g. 'A' and 'a'.

allokinesis. A movement of a part of the body on the opposite side to that willed.

allolalia. Any speech defect.

allomone. A chemical signal that communicates between different species, e.g. between a predator and prey.

allomorph. Any variant of the same morpheme, e.g. the *s* in hat*s* and the *es* in bus*es* are variants of the morpheme signifying a plural.

allopatric speciation. The appearance of a new species that results from a community of the original species being isolated from the remainder, a condition favouring the survival of mutations.

allopatric species. A species having a different habitat from another.

allophone. (Phonetics) Any of the ways in which the same PHONEME can be sounded, e.g. in the word 'pit' the 'p' is aspirated, but in the word 'spit' it is not: the aspirated and non-aspirated sounds are thus allophones of the phoneme /p/.

alloplasty. 1. Adaptation achieved by altering the external environment to suit an organism's needs. *Contrast* AUTOPLASTY. 2. (Psychoanalysis). The expression of the libido through the external world rather than through the self.

allopreening. (Ethology) The preening of one individual by another of the same species, sometimes as part of courtship.

allopsychic. Pertaining to mental events that refer to the external world, or that transfer inner problems to the external world, as in projection. *Contrast* AUTOPSYCHIC.

all-or-none law. (Neurophysiology) The principle that, for a given segment of a nerve cell, the nerve impulse is always of the same strength.

all-or-none learning theory. (Psychology) The theory that the learning of a given stimulus response connection is either made at full strength within a single trial or is not made at all.

allotriogeusia, allotriogeustia. An abnormal sense of taste.

allotriophagy. The consumption of unusual food. *Compare* PICA.

allotropy. (Philosophy) The concept that the mind is something that endures throughout life despite changes in beliefs, emotions, etc. *Compare* EGO THEORY.

all-*trans*-retinal. *See* RETINAL.

alogia. Inability to speak, whether due to confusion, retardation, or brain lesions.

alpha (α). The probability of making a TYPE I ERROR. *Contrast* BETA.

alpha adrenergic receptor. *See* ADRENERGIC RECEPTOR.

alpha beta pruning. (AI) A method of cutting down search space, used particularly in a two-person game. The tracing of the possible consequences of a given move is terminated if any path from that move leads to an outcome that cannot be prevented and that is worse than the worst outcome from another move already considered.

alpha blocker. Any ANTAGONIST (3) that blocks the ALPHA ADRENERGIC RECEPTOR.

alpha blocking. The replacement in the electroencephalogram of alpha waves by faster beta waves that occurs when a person becomes alert.

alpha blocking agent. A synonym for ALPHA BLOCKER.

alpha conditioning. Conditioning (probably through sensitization) of a response initially elicited by the CS, which increases in amplitude but does not change its temporal position. In **beta conditioning** the response is not initially elicited by the CS, but is given to the US; in the course of training its onset moves backwards in time towards the CS.

alpha-fetoprotein. A protein produced by the fetal liver that binds to oestrogen in the blood and prevents it crossing the blood-brain barrier.

alpha level. (Statistics) The probability that the outcome of a statistical test will reject a hypothesis when it is in fact true. *Compare* SIGNIFICANCE LEVEL.

alpha male. (Ethology) The dominant male in a group of animals.

alpha motion. A form of apparent motion in which a line or figure is seen to expand or contract when stimuli of different sizes are presented stroboscopically. This motion is seen when the two different versions of the MÜLLER–LYER ILLUSION are presented.

alpha motor neuron. A large motor neuron that innervates EXTRAFUSAL FIBRES thus causing skeletal muscles to contract. *See* NERVE FIBRE.

alpha response. A low latency but weak response, like the eye-blink response, that may be particularly prone to SENSITIZATION. A **beta response** is the response elicited in genuine classical conditioning.

alpha rhythm. An electrical rhythm of 8–12 Hz that can be recorded from the skull by external electrodes. It appears most strongly when the subject has his eyes closed, is in a relaxed mood, and is not concentrating on anything. *See* ELECTROENCEPHALOGRAPH.

alpha wave. The EEG waves of 8–12 Hz that produce the ALPHA RHYTHM.

alteration defect. A defect of colour vision caused by an abnormality in the absorption spectra of the cones, e.g. PROTANOMALY and DEUTERANOMALY.

altered state of consciousness (ASC). Any abnormal state of consciousness, such as a fugue, twilight sleep, delirium, derealization, mystical experiences, or states of consciousness induced by psychedelic drugs.

alter. Any of the subsidiary personalities in someone with MULTIPLE PERSONALITY DISORDER.

alter ego. An intimate friend with whom a person can share all his experiences.

alter egoism. An altruistic feeling for someone in the same situation as oneself.

alternate form. A version of a test having two or more versions.

alternating personality. A synonym for MULTIPLE PERSONALITY.

alternating psychosis. A synonym for BIPOLAR MANIC-DEPRESSIVE DISORDER.

alternation. *See* SPONTANEOUS ALTERNATION.

alternation learning. Learning to alternate two different responses, usually from one trial to the next, where the organism must remember which response it last made, since there is no external signal to tell it which to make. *See also* DOUBLE ALTERNATION.

alternative hypothesis. *See* NULL HYPOTHESIS.

alternative psychology. Any psychological dogma that is not respectable enough even to be published in the standard learned journals, e.g. GESTALT THERAPY or astrology.

alternative reinforcement schedule. A compound reinforcement schedule with two or more simple components, where the animal is rewarded as soon as it fulfils either of the components, and the schedule is then reset. E.g. in an FI3, FR30 schedule the animal will receive reward for the first response after 3 minutes, or for the 30th response, whichever comes first.

altricial. Pertaining to an organism that needs parental care when young rather than being able to fend for itself.

altruism. 1. (Sociobiology) Any behaviour of an organism made to help a conspecific with a loss (or at least no gain) to itself. 2. More generally, any unselfish behaviour.

altruistic suicide. Durkheim's expression for a suicide undertaken in order to help others. *Compare* ANOMIC SUICIDE and EGOISTIC SUICIDE.

alveolar. (Phonetics) Pertaining to a consonant (e.g. [t], [d], [s], [z], [n] [l], and [r]) produced with the tongue against the alveolar ridge.

alveolar ridge. The ridge of the upper gum behind and covering the roots of the teeth.

Alzheimer's disease. A form of PRESENILE DEMENTIA caused by atrophy of brain cells, usually starting at about 55, and producing severe intellectual, sensory, and motor deterioration, and ultimately death.

amacrine cells. Small cells spreading horizontally across the retina, which are in contact with the terminals of bipolar cells and the dendrites of ganglion cells.

amathophobia. A morbid fear of dust.

amaurosis. Partial or complete loss of sight with no apparent damage to the eye itself; it can be congenital or can be caused by some diseases like diabetes, or by damage to the optic nerve.

amaxophobia. A morbid fear of vehicles.

ambidextrous. Being able to use both hands equally well.

ambient optic array. A synonym for OPTIC ARRAY.

ambiguity. The existence of more than one possible interpretation of a sensory input, particularly a language input. *See* LEXICAL AMBIGUITY and STRUCTURAL AMBIGUITY.

ambiguous figure. Any figure that can be seen in more than one way, e.g. the NECKER CUBE (reverses in depth) and RUBIN'S FIGURE (changes figure ground relationship). When continuously viewed, the appearance of such figures tends to alternate over periods of very approximately a minute. Ambiguous figures are sometimes mistakenly called illusions.

ambiguous mediation. (Social psychology) In social perception, uncertainty about the meaning of or reasons for an action because it could have been performed for several different reasons.

ambisexual. Pertaining to traits that are common to both sexes, e.g. pubic hair, jeans.

ambisexuality. Ferenczi's term to describe aspects of the libido (particularly in the young) that are neither masculine nor feminine. It is often used as a synonym for BISEXUALITY.

ambiversion. A balanced mixture of extraversion and introversion in the same individual.

amblyacousia. Any defect in hearing.

amblyaphia. Any defect in the sense of touch.

amblygeusia. Any defect in the sense of taste.

amblyopia. Poor visual acuity where the defect arises from no known physical cause, such as can occur in a squinting eye.

amblyoscope. An early form of HAPLOSCOPE.

ambulatory schizophrenia. A schizophrenic condition in which the patient stays out of hospital, but may present low-grade symptoms and be badly adjusted, eccentric, and liable to commit acts (e.g. of aggression) of a full-blown schizophrenic kind.

amentia. An obsolete term for severe congenital MENTAL RETARDATION.

American College Testing Program (ACT). An achievement test measuring academic ability and used in selection for admission to universities in the USA. It is a rival of the SCHOLASTIC APTITUDE TEST.

American Sign Language (ASL). A system of communication for the deaf based on hand and arm signals; it has a full-blown syntax.

Ames room. A room distorted by having one corner pulled back in such a way that when viewed monocularly from one particular position, every point in the room projects to the eye in exactly the same position as would a genuinely rectangular room. This false perspective deceives the observer into seeing a rectangular room. Because he makes mistakes about the true depth of objects in the room, he makes corresponding mistakes about their sizes (*see* SIZE–DISTANCE INVARIANCE HYPOTHESIS).

Ames window, Ames trapezoid. A window cut in a trapezoidal shape. When viewed while rotating about its vertical axis, it is seen to oscillate rather than rotating continuously. The false perspective of the window means that when it passes through the frontal parallel plane it is seen at an angle to it; hence the foreshortening that occurs at that point is interpreted by the observer as a change in the direction of rotation.

ametropia. Any refractive error in the eyes (e.g. MYOPIA).

amimia. Impaired ability to express oneself through gestures.

amines. Organic derivatives of ammonia in which one (primary), two (secondary), or three (tertiary) hydrogen atoms are replaced by organic radicals. *See also* BIOGENIC AMINES.

amino acids. The 20 nitrogen-containing organic acids of which PROTEINS are constructed.

amino-phosphonovaleric acid (APV). *See* APV.

amitriptyline. A commonly used TRICYCLIC ANTIDEPRESSANT.

amnesia. Impairment or loss of memory. It can be caused by physical insult to the brain (e.g. concussion or excessive use of drugs), or by a disturbed psychological state (e.g. hysteria). *See also* ANTEROGRADE AMNESIA, EPISODIC AMNESIA, INFANTILE AMNESIA, RETROGRADE AMNESIA, and TRANSIENT GLOBAL AMNESIA.

amnesic. Pertaining to amnesia.

amnesic aphasia. A synonym for NOMINAL APHASIA.

amnesic apraxia. Inability to carry out a sequence of movements on request, caused by an inability to remember the request.

amnesic syndrome. Inability to remember recent events, including those that occurred only a minute or two ago, but with consciousness otherwise intact. Most authorities use the expression to describe this kind of ANTEROGRADE AMNESIA, but DSM-III includes RETROGRADE AMNESIA as part of the syndrome.

amnestic. A synonym for AMNESIC.

amobarbital. A short-acting BARBITURATE.

amok. A mental disorder peculiar to South-East Asia, in which the person afflicted shows agitated mania and makes violent physical attacks on others.

AMP. An abbreviation for ADENOSINE MONOPHOSPHATE.

ampere (A). *See* OHM'S LAW.

amphetamine. A group of stimulant drugs related to the CATECHOLAMINES, and having a similar effect on the nervous system. They produce alertness, suppress the appetite, increase heart-rate, and can cause euphoria. They are used clinically to alleviate narcolepsy and, paradoxically, MINIMAL BRAIN DYSFUNCTION.

amphetamine psychosis. A psychosis with similar symptoms to schizophrenia that can be produced by the prolonged use of amphetamine.

amphigenous inversion. A synonym for BISEXUALITY.

amplifier. A device that takes an electronic signal as input and outputs a larger signal (i.e. one having a larger current or voltage) of the same waveform. It is used, e.g. in neurophysiology to make it possible to record small electric signals.

amplitude. 1. The physical intensity of a stimulus. 2. The size of the displacement of a wave. It is measured in three ways: (i) **peak amplitude** is the maximum positive displacement in a period; (ii) **peak-to-peak amplitude** is the difference between the maximum positive and negative displacement; (iii) **root mean square amplitude** is the square root of the average of the squared displacements of the wave at each point. The intensities of auditory stimuli are often measured in this way. For a sine wave, root mean square amplitude is 0.707 of the peak amplitude.

amplitude spectrum. A plot against frequency of the amplitude of each sine wave making up a complex tone.

ampulla. The bulbous ending of each of the three SEMICIRCULAR CANALS. Each ampulla contains a CRISTA to which vestibular receptors (HAIR CELLS) are attached. They respond to acceleration and deceleration of the head.

amusia. Inability to recognize or reproduce melodies.

amygdala. A cluster of cells shaped like an almond located in the rhinencephalon; it is heavily implicated in the emotions, including aggression, rage, sex drive, and arousal. *See* Appendix 5.

amygdalectomy. Removal of whole or part of the amygdala; it has been undertaken in humans in an attempt to reduce hallucinations and aggression. There is no evidence for its efficacy.

amygdaloid body, amygdaloid complex. Synonyms for AMYGDALA.

amygdaloidectomy. A synonym for AMYGDALECTOMY.

anabolism. The conversion of food into materials that form part of the body. *Compare* CATABOLISM. *See also* METABOLISM.

anaclisis. (Pschyoanalysis) Extreme dependence on another person for emotional, moral, or physical support.

anaclitic depression. Depression in a young child caused by separation from the mother.

anaclitic therapy. A psychotherapeutic procedure in which the patient is encouraged to regress to his infantile dependence on his mother by promoting extreme dependence on the therapist, thus making him relive his early experiences.

anacusis, anacousia, anacusia. Complete deafness.

anaerobic. Living in the absence of free oxygen.

anaesthesia. Absence of sensation.

anaglyph. A picture presenting two views of the same scene or pattern in different colours (usually red and green). When viewed through spectacles with the appropriate colour filters, one view is received by the left eye, the other by the right; the two views are fused and stereopsis occurs.

anagogic symbolism. Jung's expression for the representation by concrete objects of ideals or moral concepts, particularly in dreams.

anal aggressive character, anal aggressive personality. *See* ANAL CHARACTER.

anal character. (Pschyoanalysis) A person fixated at the ANAL STAGE, and hence exhibiting traits developed then. The **anal expulsive character** is thought to be generous, careless, and pliant; the **anal aggressive character** is cruel and destructive. Both these characters represent fixation at the anal expulsive stage. The **anal retentive character** is stingy, meticulous, and obstinate, and arises at the anal retentive stage.

There is no evidence that the traits ascribed do in fact originate in the anal stage.

analeptic. Any stimulant drug (e.g. caffeine or amphetamine), excluding the specific antidepressant drugs. *Compare* PSYCHO-ANALEPTIC.

anal eroticism. (Pschoanalysis) The release of the libido by taking pleasure in activities concerning faeces (e.g. their excretion or retention) and urine; this is hypothesized to be normal at the ANAL STAGE.

anal expulsive character, anal expulsive personality. *See* ANAL CHARACTER.

anal expulsive phase, anal expulsive stage. *See* ANAL STAGE.

analgesia. Insensitivity to painful stimuli.

analog. An alternative spelling of ANALOGUE.

analogical reasoning. Reasoning by using analogies. *See* the example under ANALOGIES TEST.

analogies test. A test in which two terms are given. The testee has to induce the relationship between them, and on presentation of a third term apply that relationship to it to yield a fourth term. E.g. he might be asked 'Boy is to girl, as husband is to what?'

analogue. 1. (Generally) Something similar to something else. 2. (Psychology) A term used in contrast to PROPOSITIONAL to mean a representation whose parts are related in the same way as those of the thing represented, and in which for any dimension of the thing represented there exists a corresponding dimension in the representation. Analogue representations have continuously varying dimensions, propositional ones have discrete states. Visual images are thought by some to be analogue representations of the world. *Contrast* DIGITAL.

analogue computer. A computer in which information is represented by a continuously variable physical quantity like voltage rather than by elements having discrete states. *Contrast* DIGITAL COMPUTER.

analogue study. The evaluation of a method of treatment by trying it out on normal subjects who have problems similar to those of disturbed people. E.g. different treatments for phobias may be tested on normal people who are afraid of taking examinations or of public speaking.

analogy. (Biology) Similarity of anatomical structure in an organ or organs of different species, caused not by sharing a common ancestor, but by convergent evolution. *Contrast* HOMOLOGY.

anal personality. *See* ANAL CHARACTER.

anal phase. A synonym for ANAL STAGE.

anal retentive character, anal retentive personality. *See* ANAL CHARACTER.

anal retentive phase, anal retentive stage. *See* ANAL STAGE.

anal sadistic phase, anal sadistic stage. *See* ANAL STAGE.

anal stage. (Psychoanalysis) The second of Freud's LIBIDINAL STAGES in which, so he believed, the infant of 18 months to three years of age derives pleasure from its urine and faeces. This stage is subdivided into an **anal expulsive stage** in which the child takes pleasure in expelling faeces and a later **anal retentive stage** in which it takes pleasure in retaining faeces. The aggressive elements present in the latter stage are emphasized in the expression **anal sadistic stage.**

anal triad. (Psychoanalysis) The three components of the anal retentive character – stinginess, meticulousness, and obstinacy.

analysable stimulus dimension. A synonym for INTEGRAL STIMULUS DIMENSION.

analysand. Anyone being psychoanalysed.

analyser. A Pavlovian term for any mechanism that discriminates different stimuli within a modality; there are many analysers in each modality, e.g. in vision one for different colours, another for different lengths, etc.

analysis. Short for PSYCHOANALYSIS.

analysis by synthesis. A method of recognition or parsing in which hypotheses about how to interpret the input are generated and compared with the input until a match is found. To use only analysis by synthesis would be extremely wasteful; it is, however, likely that some high-level hypotheses are often generated but that they are constrained by the input, and in turn help to constrain the interpretation of the input.

analysis of covariance. An ANALYSIS OF VARIANCE in which the variance caused by extraneous variables is calculated and subtracted out, thus increasing the sensitivity of significance tests between means. (It is also possible to compute mean values that are adjusted for the variation caused by extraneous variables.) E.g. if differences in subjects' ages or IQs are correlated with the dependent variable, their variances could be taken into account before assessing the significance of the independent variable.

analysis of variance (ANOVA). A statistical procedure for testing hypotheses about population means in which the overall variability in samples of data is split into additive components associated with the independent variables. These may reflect differences at different levels of a factor, interactions between factors or the effects of predictors in multiple regression. The statistical significance of the different components is assessed by F TESTS.

analytic. (Logic) A synonym for A PRIORI.

analytic language. (Linguistics) A language in which syntax is expressed by auxiliary words and by word order rather than by inflection. *Contrast* SYNTHETIC LANGUAGE.

analytic psychology. The doctrines developed by Jung after he parted from Freud. He placed less emphasis on the sex drive and more on achieving a balance between conflicting wishes; he also introduced elements of mysticism into his theories. *See also* ARCHETYPE and COLLECTIVE UNCONSCIOUS.

anamnesis. 1. Recall. 2. (Medicine) A patient's own account of his illness and its antecedents. *Contrast* CATAMNESIS.

anamorphy. A synonym for ANISEIKONIA.

anancasm. Any repetitive, stereotyped, or compulsive behaviour that a person performs in order to keep anxiety at bay, e.g. an obsessive compulsion.

anancastia. Any state in which the person feels compelled to act against his own will, as, e.g. in obsessions, compulsions, or phobias.

anandria. Absence of male characteristics.

anankastia. An alternative spelling of ANANCASTIA.

anaphia. Absence or impairment of the sense of touch.

anaphora. (Linguistics) The use of a word or expression to refer to the meaning of a word or expression that has already occurred in the discourse; e.g. 'John hurt *himself*. The word referred to is the **antecedent**. *Compare* CATAPHORA and EXOPHORA.

anaphylaxis. (Psychiatry) The reactivation of earlier symptoms caused by an upsetting experience similar to that which originally produced them.

anarithmia. A synonym for ACALCULIA.

anarthria. Inability to speak, caused by damage to the nervous system or vocal tract.

anchoring effect. The phenomenon that if a person is asked to estimate the value of a quantity, his estimate will be biased towards any value he has previously been given (even when he knows that the latter value was randomly determined). E.g. people claim to brush their teeth more often if asked how often they brush per day than if asked how often they brush per week.

anchor point. A reference point on a subjective scale in comparison to which the subject makes his judgements. Thus, the subject might be presented with two extreme stimuli on the scale with given values (e.g. 1 and 100) and then assign values to other stimuli in relation to the two anchor stimuli; a NORM (3) can also function as an anchor point, e.g. the tilt of a line may be judged by its deviation from vertical (the anchor point).

ancient mariner syndrome. *See* PASSING STRANGER EFFECT.

and (∧). A logical operation in the propositional calculus. Where p and q are propositions, 'p and q' is true if and only if p is true and q is true.

and gate. An electronic unit that has two inputs, and that gives an output only if both input signals are on.

androgen insensitivity syndrome. The characteristics of a chromosomal male (XY) in whom androgen has been underactive in the foetus: he has male sex organs but a female sexual identity, being attracted to men and sometimes becoming a transvestite.

androgenization. The transformation of any bodily structure or part of the brain into those typical of a male rather than of a female.

androgens. The hormones that cause male sexual characteristics to develop. They include TESTOSTERONE and ANDROSTERONE.

androgyny. The existence in a single individual of the characteristics either physical or psychological of both sexes. *Compare* BISEXUALITY and HERMAPHRODITE.

andromania. A synonym for NYMPHOMANIA.

androphilia. A liking for men.

androphobia. A morbid fear of men.

androstenedione. A precursor of both ANDROGEN and OESTROGEN; it is a breakdown product of TESTOSTERONE, produced by the adrenal cortex and the gonads.

androsterone. A breakdown product of TESTOSTERONE, which acts as an ANDROGEN.

anechoic room. A room (used in experiments on hearing) that is specially constructed to eliminate the reflection of sound from its surfaces and the entry of external sounds.

anemophobia. A morbid fear of wind or draughts.

anemotropism. Orienting the body with reference to air currents, a TROPISM.

anencephaly. The congenital absence of a brain.

anergasia. Loss of function; the term is usually used of psychiatric conditions with known organic causes.

anergia. Lack of energy.

anesthesia. An alternative spelling of ANAESTHESIA.

aneurysm, aneurism. A sac formed by dilation of the weakened walls of a blood vessel; it may cause neurological symptoms.

angel dust. *See* PCP.

anginophobia. A morbid fear of choking or suffocating.

angiography. *See* CEREBRAL ANGIOGRAPHY.

angioscotoma. A scotoma caused by the shadows of the retinal blood-vessels. *See* PURKINJE FIGURE.

angiotensin. A POLYPEPTIDE produced in the blood under the control of RENIN. Angiotensin I increases blood pressure and thirst, and stimulates the adrenal cortex. Its variant, angiotensin II, may be a CNS neuromodulator or neurotransmitter.

angle of incidence. The angle at which light strikes a surface. It is measured as the angular difference between the axis of the light and the axis perpendicular to the surface at the point where the light strikes it; hence the more obliquely the light strikes the surface, the higher the angle of incidence.

Angst. Used by the existentialists to mean an extreme terror about existence, which they mistakenly thought was felt by everyone.

ångström (Å). Ten-thousandth-millionth (10^{-10}) of a metre.

angular gyrus. Brodmann's area 39, which lies in the middle of the INFERIOR PARIETAL LOBULE. *See* Appendix 3.

anhedonia. An inability to feel pleasure.

anhypnia, anhypnosis. Insomnia.

aniconia. Absence of mental imagery.

anima. Jung's term, which has two meanings. 1. A person's inner or true self, which can communicate with the unconscious. *Contrast* PERSONA. 2. An ARCHETYPE present in everyone and representing their feminine side. *Compare* ANIMUS.

animal magnetism. An obsolete term for HYPNOTISM.

animal psychology. The study of animal behaviour through laboratory experiments. *Contrast* ETHOLOGY.

animal system. Hess's expression for those parts of the nervous system regulating relations with the external environment, as opposed to the VEGETATIVE SYSTEM.

animatism. The belief in a supernatural quality pervading the universe.

animism. 1. The ascription of mental processes to inanimate matter (such as clouds), common in primitive people and young children. 2. The philosophical doctrine that the soul has a causal influence on the body.

animus. In Jungian psychology, an ARCHETYPE present in everyone that represents the male side of their character. *Compare* ANIMA (2).

anion. A negatively charged ion. *See also* ANODE.

aniseikonia. A difference in the size (or shape) of the images projected on each retina, caused naturally by a defect in the lens, or artificially by wearing special spectacles; the size difference may occur equally along all axes or may be confined to one. A form of aniseikonia can also be caused by an object being closer to one eye than to the other. Magnification along the horizontal axis in one eye has systematic and predictable effects on STEREOPSIS.

anisocoria. Unequal sizes of the pupils in each eye.

anisometropia. Unequal refractive power in the two eyes.

anisopia. Any difference in vision between the two eyes.

anisotropy, anisotropia. 1. (Optics) The property of a lens or optical system that has different refractive power along different axes. 2. (Psychology) By extrapolation, the difference in the clarity of lines at different tilts caused not by the eye's optics but by the nervous system. Oblique stripes are less readily resolved by the nervous system than are horizontal and vertical, even when there is no anisotropy (1) in the retinal image. 3. (Psychology) The difference in the apparent length of a line when felt or viewed in different orientations. *See* HORIZONTAL–VERTICAL ILLUSION.

Anlage. 1. (Genetics) A genetic factor that gives rise to a particular trait or traits. 2. (Genetics) The complete hereditary disposition of an individual. 3. (Psychology) Any factor underlying the development of a trait or skill.

Anna O. A woman treated for hysteria by Joseph Breuer who rightly or wrongly attributed her recovery to his 'talking cure'; she thus became the first (and possibly the last) success of psychoanalysis.

annealing. (AI) In parallel distributed processing, the settling down of a system of connected units to a point where no further changes in connectivity or firing rates occur, because each unit is acting as consistently as is possible in conformity with the information it receives from its neighbours; the process involves randomly changing the states of units periodically. It is as though the system is searching through a hilly terrain for the lowest point in the terrain. If it simply moves downhill, it may get trapped in a local depression. Randomly changing the states of units helps to ensure that this does not happen, though the procedure cannot guarantee that the system will settle in the optimum (lowest in terms of the analogy) state. *Compare* RELAXATION TECHNIQUE.

anniversary reaction. The revival (sometimes unconscious) of a previous state of mind or of symptoms on the anniversary of a significant event, e.g. the recurrence of depression a year after the death of a spouse.

annoyer. Thorndike's term for a noxious stimulus, that is, one that an animal will learn to escape or avoid.

annulospiral ending. A sense organ in muscles that responds to stretch. *See* MUSCLE SPINDLE.

annulus. The area between two concentric circles.

anode. An ELECTRODE that is positively charged relative to another with a current flowing between the two; it attracts ANIONS. *See also* ELECTROLYSIS. *Contrast* CATHODE.

anoesia, anoesis, anoia. Obsolete terms for mental deficiency.

anomaloscope. An apparatus for measuring ANOMALOUS COLOUR VISION, usually in the red-green part of the spectrum, by determining the proportion of red and green needed by a person to match a given yellow. *See* RAYLEIGH EQUATION.

anomalous colour vision. A deficiency of colour vision. Although all three cone pigments may function (**anomalous trichromatism**), one or more has an abnormal spectral absorption curve, thus causing abnormalities in METAMERIC MATCHING, and unusually poor discrimination in one or more regions of the spectrum. Anomalous colour vision can also occur in dichromats; *see* ANOMALOUS DICHROMATISM. *See also* PROTANOMALY, DEUTERANOMALY, and TRITANOMALY.

anomalous contour. A synonym for SUBJECTIVE CONTOUR.

anomalous dichromatism, anomalous dichromacy. A rare form of dichromacy in which one of the two functioning pigments has the peak of its spectral sensitivity shifted from the normal; such dichromats, therefore, require different mixtures of two primaries to match a given hue from those needed by other dichromats of the same type.

anomalous stimulus. A stimulus that gives rise to sensation but is not the normal stimulus for the sense modality. E.g. pressure on the eye may lead to visual sensations.

anomalous trichromatism. *See* ANOMALOUS COLOUR VISION.

anomaly. (Medicine) Any deviation from normality that is not pathological.

anomia, anomic aphasia. Synonyms for NOMINAL APHASIA.

anomic suicide. Durkheim's expression for suicide undertaken because life seems pointless. *Compare* ALTRUISTIC SUICIDE and EGOISTIC SUICIDE.

anomie. A state of disintegration and despair, caused by a lack of clear group values; the term can be used to describe either the state of the society or the state of the individual within it.

anomie scale. A measure of social deviance, based on a questionnaire about attitudes to sex, cheating, bribery, etc.

anomy. An alternative spelling of ANOMIE.

anopia, anopsia. Defective vision.

anorexia. Loss of appetite for food.

anorexia nervosa. Pathological and chronic fasting, occurring most frequently in adolescent girls; it is usually accompanied by amenorrhoea, sickness, weakness, severe weight loss, and the feeling that the sufferer is much grosser than he or she is.

anorgasmia. Inability to have orgasms.

anorthopia. A visual impairment in which the shape of edges and lines is distorted.

anorthoscope. A device consisting of a slit behind which a drawing on a piece of paper is rapidly pulled at right angles to the slit's direction; although the details of the drawing appear successively in the same place (i.e. in the slit), the whole drawing can often be perceived by the observer.

anosmia. Inability to smell.

anosognosia. Failure to recognize an illness in oneself, common in organic brain disease and after some other forms of brain damage.

anosphresia. A synonym for ANOSMIA.

A-not-B error. A synonym for AB̄ ERROR.

ANOVA. An abbreviation for ANALYSIS OF VARIANCE.

anoxemia. A shortage of oxygen in the blood.

anoxia. A shortage of oxygen in the tissues.

ANS. An abbreviation for AUTONOMIC NERVOUS SYSTEM.

Antabuse. The trade name for a drug (DISULFIRAM) that interferes with the metabolism of alcohol. When alcohol is taken with the drug present in the body, unpleasant symptoms, like vomiting, nausea, and breathing difficulties, are experienced. It is used successfully in the treatment of alcoholism (but only so long as the patient continues to take it).

antagonist. 1. (Generally) Anything that opposes something else. 2. (Physiology) A muscle that pulls in the opposite direction to another; *compare* EXTENSOR and FLEXOR. 3. (Physiology) Any compound that blocks the action of another, e.g. a substance that blocks or reduces the action of a neurotransmitter. In **biochemical antagonism**, the antagonism is indirect, e.g. the antagonist may cause faster excretion of the substance whose action it inhibits. In **chemical antagonism**, the antagonist combines with the substance to form an inactive compound. In **pharmacological antagonism**, the antagonist prevents the substance from occupying its receptor sites, usually by occupying them itself. In **physiological antagonism**, the antagonist occupies different receptor sites from those occupied by the substance but has the opposite effect to it.

antagonistic colour. A synonym for COMPLEMENTARY COLOUR.

antecedent. 1. *See* CONDITIONAL. 2. *See* ANAPHORA.

antedating response. A response in a sequence of responses that occurs earlier than it did initially. *See also* FRACTIONAL ANTEDATING GOAL RESPONSE.

anterior. (Anatomy) Toward the front of the body or brain. It is synonymous with VENTRAL when used of the body but not when used of the brain. *Contrast* POSTERIOR.

anterior chamber. The part of the eye lying between the cornea and the lens.

anterior commissure. A bundle of myelinated nerve fibres connecting the anterior parts of the two hemispheres, particularly the two halves of the rhinencephelon, some others parts of the temporal lobe and some parts of the frontal lobes. *See* Appendix 2.

anterior corticospinal tract. *See* CORTICOSPINAL TRACT.

anterior horn. Grey matter at the front of the spinal cord from which large motor axons run.

anterior hypothalamic area. An area of the hypothalamus, stimulation of which tends to arouse the PARASYMPATHETIC SYSTEM, and damage to which causes insomnia.

anterior pituitary. *See* PITUITARY.

anterior ramus. A branch of the lateral sulcus at its frontal end. *See* Appendix 1.

anterior root. A synonym for VENTRAL ROOT.

anterior spinothalamic tract. *See* SPINOTHALAMIC TRACTS.

anterior thalamic nucleus. A thalamic nucleus receiving fibres from the mammillothalamic tract and projecting to the limbic system; it is involved in emotion.

anterior white commissure. A commissure towards the front of the spinal cord that connects the two lateral halves.

anterograde amnesia. Memory loss for experiences *following* the event that precipitated the amnesia. *Contrast* RETROGRADE AMNESIA.

anterograde degeneration. The degeneration of the part of an axon that has been severed from the cell body.

anterograde transportation. Transportation of substances from a neuron's cell body through the axon towards the axonal terminals.

anterolateral system. A synonym for CORTICOSPINAL TRACT.

anteroventral periventricular nucleus. A nucleus in the anterior hypothalamus involved in regulating the oestrus cycle.

anthophobia. Pathological fear of flowers.

anthropoid apes. The Pongidae family of apes, i.e. the gibbon, orang-utan, chimpanzee, and gorilla. They are the primates most nearly related to man. They all inhabit the Old World.

anthropology. The study of man, but in practice either CULTURAL ANTHROPOLOGY or PHYSICAL ANTHROPOLOGY.

anthropomorphism. The unnecessary attribution of human characteristics to lower organisms or to inanimate objects.

anthropophobia. A morbid fear of people in general, or of a particular person.

anthropos. Jung's ARCHETYPE of primal man.

antibody. A cell produced by the immune system that destroys antigens.

anticathexis. A synonym for COUNTER-CATHEXIS.

anticholinergic. Pertaining to the blocking of CHOLINERGIC activity.

anticipation method. A verbal learning technique, in which the subject is given one stimulus and is required to provide the next in a list, or the second member of a pair in

PAIRED ASSOCIATE LEARNING. After each response, he is shown the correct word.

anticipatory aggression. Aggression undertaken to ward off harm, e.g. against a predator, or in defence of territory.

anticipatory drinking. Drinking when there is no deficit of water, but when there is a conscious or unconscious expectation of a deficit. For example, drinking with a meal anticipates the water loss caused by eating. *Compare* ANTICIPATORY FEEDING.

anticipatory error. A response, particularly in a serial learning situation, that occurs earlier than it should. *Contrast* PERSEVERATIVE ERROR (1).

anticipatory feeding. Feeding when there is no deficit of food, but when there is a conscious or unconscious expectation of a deficit. *Compare* ANTICIPATORY DRINKING. .

anticipatory response. A synonym for ANTICIPATORY ERROR.

anticonformity. A tendency to sabotage the aims or mores of the group to which a person belongs.

antidepressants. Drugs that when administered over several weeks tend to elevate the mood of clinically depressed patients. They include the TRICYCLICS, MONOAMINE OXIDASE INHIBITORS and SSRIs; they may work by potentiating catecholaminergic activity. *See* CATECHOLAMINE HYPOTHESIS.

antidiuretic hormone (ADH). A peptide hormone (vasopressin) manufactured in the hypothalamus and released from the posterior pituitary that inhibits urine production, and causes smooth muscles (including those of the blood-vessels) to contract. The hormone is released in response to stimulation of both OSMORECEPTORS and BARORECEPTORS.

antidromic conduction. The conduction of a nerve impulse in the opposite direction from normal (i.e. away from the axonal terminals towards the cell body), a result of artificially exciting the axon at a point near its terminals. *Contrast* FORWARD CONDUCTION.

antidromic impulse. A nerve impulse undergoing ANTIDROMIC CONDUCTION.

antigen. Any foreign substance or microbe in the body that can stimulate the immune system to destroy it.

anti-intraception. A personality trait consisting of rejection of anything subjective, e.g. emotions or imagination; it was thought by some to characterize the AUTHORITARIAN PERSONALITY.

antimetropia. A condition in which the two eyes have a marked difference in refractive power.

antinociceptive. Reducing or abolishing painful stimuli, usually used of drugs.

antinode. *See* STANDING WAVE.

antinomy. A statement or statements that contain a logical contradiction, e.g. 'All swans are white; all swans are not white'.

antiophobia. A morbid fear of floods.

antipsychiatry movement. A movement criticizing psychiatrists for putting self-fulfilling labels (e.g. 'schizophrenic') on people, failing to treat the mentally ill as people, and cowing them with drugs or incarceration in a mental hospital, etc.

antisocial personality disorder. (DSM-III) Extreme antisocial behaviour (e.g. frequent cheating, lying, or stealing) that began before the age of 15, has continued with little break into adulthood, and is manifested in at least four areas of life. It is marked by a disregard of sanctions or punishment. Until recently it was called, more succinctly, PSYCHOPATHY or SOCIO-PATHY.

Anton's syndrome. A condition in which a person is blind, but denies that he cannot see: it can be caused by damage to the cortex.

antonym. A word that has a meaning opposite to that of another word, e.g. 'good' and 'bad'.

anulospiral endings. An alternative spelling of ANNULOSPIRAL ENDINGS.

anvil. A synonym for INCUS.

anxiety. A feeling of fear or dread; when severe it is accompanied by symptoms like sweating, shaking, and rapid heart-beat caused by arousal of the sympathetic system. There is a tendency among psychiatrists and psychologists to use this term when there is no obvious external cause for fear, and to use the word 'fear' when there is (*compare* FREE-FLOATING ANXIETY). Learning theorists, on the other hand, use the term to mean a drive that can be aroused by punishment, and can be classically conditioned to the stimuli preceding punishment; diminution of the anxiety drive can reinforce the instrumental responses of avoidance and escape. *See also* STATE ANXIETY and TRAIT ANXIETY.

anxiety disorders. A group of disorders marked by extreme anxiety; it includes PHOBIAS, ANXIETY NEUROSIS, OBSESSIVE-COMPULSIVE DISORDER, PANIC DISORDER, and POST-TRAUMATIC STRESS DISORDER.

anxiety hierarchy. A synonym for HIERARCHY (3).

anxiety hysteria. A synonym for PHOBIA.

anxiety neurosis. A neurosis in which chronic anxiety is the predominant symptom.

anxiety object. (Psychoanalysis) Anything to which anxiety that arises from other, usually unconscious, causes has been redirected.

anxiety relief response. (Behaviour therapy) A response to which a feeling of calmness or relief has been conditioned, and that can therefore in theory be used to reduce anxiety.

anxiolytics. A synonym for MINOR TRANQUIL-LIZERS.

AOC. An abbreviation for ATTENTION OPERATING CHARACTERISTIC.

aorist. A PAST TENSE used in some languages (though not in English) that does not indicate whether the action or event referred to was continuous or instantaneous. *Contrast* IMPERFECT TENSE and PERFECT TENSE.

A-over-A constraint. (Linguistics) The principle that a transformation cannot move a constituent that is embedded in another constituent of the same syntactic category out of the latter constituent. Thus, 'Bill noted the fact that the boy had seen the man' is grammatical, 'Which man did Bill note the fact that the boy had seen?' is not.

apareunia. Inability to copulate.

APB. An abbreviation for 4-amino-phosphonobutyric acid, a substance that selectively blocks one type of glutamate synapse. It can be used to eliminate the output from the on-centre part of a bipolar cell, allowing the surround output to be separately assessed.

apeirophobia. A morbid fear of infinity, usually of infinite time.

aperiodic reinforcement schedule. Any reinforcement schedule other than continuous reinforcement.

aperture colour. A synonym for FILM COLOUR when produced by viewing a coloured surface through a pin hole.

aperture effect. 1. The effect obtained in an ANORTHOSCOPE. 2. *See* APERTURE PROBLEM.

aperture problem. The problem of how the visual system detects the direction in which a line is moving when its ends are obscured. It is insoluble if the line is straight. In fact, straight lines filling an aperture always seem to move at right angles to their orientation, a phenomenon known as the **aperture effect**.

apex. The part of the COCHLEA furthest away from the OVAL WINDOW, where the BASILAR MEMBRANE ends and where there is an opening between the SCALA VESTIBULI and the SCALA TYMPANI.

aphagia. Inability to eat; it occurs e.g. in ANOREXIA NERVOSA or through damage to the lateral hypothalamus.

aphakia. The lack of a lens in an eye.

aphasia. Loss or impairment of the ability to understand or produce either spoken or written language or both when caused by brain damage. It has many forms. *See also* AGRAPHIA, AGRAMMATISM, ALEXIA, AUDIOVERBAL APHASIA, AUDITORY APHASIA, BROCA'S APHASIA, CONDUCTION APHASIA, ECHOLALIA, EXPRESSIVE APHASIA, GLOBAL APHASIA, NOMINAL APHASIA, RECEPTIVE APHASIA, SYNTACTICAL APHASIA, and WERNICKE'S APHASIA.

aphemia. An obsolete term for inability to speak.

aphephobia. A morbid fear of being touched.

aphonia. Loss of speech; the term is usually restricted to loss not caused by brain damage.

aphoria. A synonym for ASTHENIA.

aphrasia. Inability to speak or understand phrases while retaining some understanding of individual words.

aphrenia. An obsolete term for DEMENTIA.

apical dendrite. A pyramidal cell's dendrite. It has a long process ascending towards the surface of the cortex and ending in a bushy top.

Aplysia. The sea hare, a mollusc with a simple nervous system. It is used in neurophysiological research, particularly in connection with the neural basis of habituation.

apnea. Difficulty or irregularity in breathing.

apoclesis. Lack of desire for food, or aversion to it.

apodosis. A synonym for CONSEQUENT.

Apollonian. Rational and controlled. *Contrast* DIONYSIAN.

apomorphine. A drug that is a dopamine agonist.

apoplexy. A synonym for STROKE.

a posteriori. Of ideas, reasoning, propositions, etc. that are empirically based (i.e.

their truth depends on observation). 'All swans are white' is a (false) *a posteriori* proposition. *Contrast* A PRIORI.

a posteriori **probability.** The probability of an event when both the A PRIORI PROBABILITY and some additional information relevant to its probability are known.

a posteriori **tests.** Statistical tests which were not planned before inspection of the data, e.g. tests of whether, after inspecting the results of an experiment, the largest mean is significantly different from the smallest. *A posteriori* tests overcome the problem that when many comparisons are possible, some of them are likely to yield high significance levels merely through chance. The NEWMAN–KEULS TEST and the TUKEY TEST are examples.

apostilb. An obsolete measure of LUMINANCE that is equivalent to 0.3183 candela per square metre.

apparent. (Perception) Pertaining to subjective sensory experience.

apparent motion. Any illusion of motion occurring when the stimulus does not move. There are many different kinds. *See* ALPHA MOTION, GAMMA MOTION, DELTA MOTION, INDUCED MOTION, MOTION AFTEREFFECT, OPTIMAL APPARENT MOTION, and PHI PHENOMENON. *Contrast* REAL MOTION.

appeasement behaviour. (Ethology) A ritualized act signifying submission to a conspecific.

apperception. An old-fashioned term for the process of making a conscious experience clear.

appersonation. The delusion that one is someone else, usually accompanied by adopting the characteristics of the other person; it occurs in e.g. schizophrenia.

appetite. The urge to consummate a drive, usually used of innate drives like hunger, thirst, and sex.

appetitive behaviour. (Ethology) Any behaviour (e.g. animal courtship) directed at the satisfaction of a drive (usually an innate drive). *Compare* CONSUMMATORY RESPONSE.

appetitive phase. *See* SEXUAL RESPONSE CYCLE.

applied psychology. The attempt to solve practical problems (e.g. in advertising, industry, personnel selection, etc.) by applying psychological knowledge. Although strictly speaking clinical and educational psychology are branches of applied psychology, the term is usually used in such a way as to exclude them.

apport. The alleged movement of an object by psychic means.

apprehension span. A synonym for SPAN OF APPREHENSION.

approach–approach conflict. The difficulty of choosing between two equally attractive goals, a problem faced by Buridan's Ass when placed before equally tempting bundles of hay.

approach–avoidance conflict. The conflict that develops when an organism has a desire for a particular reward (e.g. food) but has learned that it will be punished (e.g. by shock) if it tries to get it. *See* APPROACH GRADIENT.

approach gradient. The increase in strength of an organism's tendency to approach a goal as its distance from it decreases. Thus a rat in a harness pulls more strongly the nearer it is to its goal. The approach gradient appears to be less steep than the avoidance gradient since animals in an APPROACH–AVOIDANCE CONFLICT will approach part of the way to the goal. *Compare* AVOIDANCE GRADIENT.

approach learning. Learning to go to a goal for positive reinforcement, rather than learning to move away from something to escape or avoid a punishment.

approximation, method of. A synonym for SHAPING.

approximation conditioning, approximation method. Synonyms for SHAPING.

appurtenance. A Gestalt term meaning 'belonging together', and used of parts of the perceptual field; e.g. the brightness constancy of a surface is determined by the luminance of surfaces lying close to it in 3-D space. These surfaces 'appertain' to it, while surfaces at a different distance or in a different direction do not.

apraxia. Inability to carry out intentional movements properly; it is caused by brain damage. *See* AKINETIC APRAXIA, AMNESIC APRAXIA, CONSTRUCTIONAL APRAXIA, IDEATIONAL APRAXIA, IDEOKINETIC APRAXIA, IDEOMOTOR APRAXIA, and MOTOR APRAXIA.

a priori. Pertaining to propositions or arguments whose truth does not depend on empirical evidence, but on their internal structure. 'Green is a colour' and '2 + 2 = 4' are true *a priori. Contrast* A POSTERIORI.

a priori **probability.** A synonym for PRIOR PROBABILITY.

a priorism. The hypothesis that the mind contains innate ideas.

a priori **test.** A synonym for PLANNED COMPARISON TEST.

a priori **validity.** The ability of a mental test to measure what it purports to measure as determined by intuition or common sense rather than by systematic investigation.

aprosexia. Inability to concentrate, caused by a functional or organic disorder.

aprosodia. A form of APHASIA in which there are deficits in the intonation; it is thought to be caused by lesions in the non-dominant hemisphere.

apsychognosia. Lack of awareness, particularly of the effects of one's own behaviour on other people.

aptitude. The capacity to learn a skill. Someone who has as yet acquired no mathematical ability may have an aptitude for mathematics. *Contrast* ABILITY.

Aptitude Research Project Tests (ARP Tests). Tests developed by Guilford, intended to measure creativity and ability to think divergently.

aptitude test. Any test to measure aptitude for or proficiency at a particular skill or skills; strictly speaking the expression should be restricted to tests whose results predict future performance (after training) in a particular job or at a particular skill, rather than current ABILITY.

APV. An abbreviation for AMINO-PHOSPHONOVALERIC ACID, which selectively blocks NMDA receptors.

aquaphobia. A morbid fear of water, bathing, or swimming.

aqueduct of Sylvius. A synonym for CEREBRAL AQUEDUCT.

aqueous humour. The transparent fluid lying between the cornea and lens.

arachneophobia. An alternative spelling of ARACHNOPHOBIA.

arachnoid layer. The middle of the three layers of tissue that enclose the central nervous system. *See* MENINGES.

arachnophobia. A morbid fear of spiders.

ARAS. An abbreviation for ASCENDING RETICULAR ACTIVATING SYSTEM.

arbitrary inference. Reaching a gloomy conclusion by false reasoning. The term is used of depressives by cognitive therapists.

arborization. The branching of nerve cells.

archaic brain. In the TRIUNE BRAIN theory, the part of the brain developed in primitive mammals, i.e. the limbic system.

archaic residue. Jung's expression for the primitive ways of thinking and feeling in the racial unconscious.

archetype. In Jungian psychology, one of the unlearnt concepts (e.g. religion) or sets of dispositions (e.g. ANIMUS) acquired in an unspecified way, held in the COLLECTIVE UNCONSCIOUS and possessed by everyone.

archicerebellum. The most posterior part of the cerebellum, and phylogenetically the oldest.

archicortex. The hippocampal formation, which evolved after the piriform lobe (the palaeocortex) and before the neocortex. It contains only between three to five cortical layers.

Archimedes spiral. A synonym for PLATEAU SPIRAL.

archipallium. A synonym for ARCHICORTEX.

architectonics. The division of the cerebral cortex into regions based on examining stained sections under an optical microscope. *See* BRODMANN AREAS.

architecture. The components of an information processing system and of their relationships to one another. In the case of the brain, it can be studied at many different levels ranging from neuronal connections to concepts like WORKING MEMORY. Similar considerations apply to the architecture of computer programs.

archival method. The use of records set up for some other purpose to test hypotheses in social, clinical, educational, or industrial psychology.

arc–sine transformation. A transformation often applied to data expressed as proportions; it reduces the differences between extreme proportions (those near 0 and 1) and increases the differences between those in the centre (around 0.5). It is used to increase the homogeneity of sample variances. The formula is: $2 \times \text{arc}-\text{sine} \sqrt{P}$, where P is a proportion.

arcuate fasciculus. A fibre bundle connecting Wernicke's area and Broca's area, damage to which can cause CONDUCTION APHASIA.

arcuate nucleus. The medial part of the ventral posterior thalamic nucleus, which contains a somatotopic map of the face.

a-reaction time. A synonym for SIMPLE REACTION TIME.

area centralis. A circular area of the retina in which the ganglion cells are so densely packed that they have several tiers. It includes the fovea and the immediately surrounding area in primates. It is about 17° across, and is roughly coterminous with the MACULA.

area postcentralis. The area immediately posterior to the CENTRAL GYRUS; it contains the SOMATOSENSORY CORTEX.

area sampling. The selection of samples according to geographic regions.

area striata. A synonym for STRIATE CORTEX.

argument. 1. (Mathematics, Logic, and Computing) *See* FUNCTION (2) and FUNCTION (3). 2. (Linguistics) Any noun phrase appearing as subject or object in a sentence: e.g. 'the boy' is an argument in 'the boy fled'.

argument constraints. The constraints on the nature of an ARGUMENT (2) imposed within a sentence by the other words; e.g. the verb 'buys' requires as subject an argument that is human.

aristocracy theory of rank acquisition. (Ethology) The hypothesis that in some species, an animal's social rank is partly determined by that of its parents, particularly the mother, who is more likely to aid her young in fights if she is of high social rank.

Aristotle's illusion. The illusion that a single object is two objects, obtained when the object is rubbed between two crossed fingers.

arithmetic mean ($\bar{X}$ or M). A measure of CENTRAL TENDENCY, obtained by dividing the sum of a set of numbers by the number in the set. *Contrast* GEOMETRIC MEAN, MEDIAN (1) and MODE (1).

arithmetic progression, arithmetic series. *See* PROGRESSION.

arithmomania. A compulsive urge to count things.

armchair psychology. A synonym for philosophy of mind.

Armed Forces Classification Test. A series of performance tests used to screen potential recruits in the USA; it replaced the Army Alpha and Beta Tests.

Army Alpha Test, Army Beta Test. Sets of tests for potential recruits developed by the US army in World War I. The Alpha test contained many verbal items, while the Beta, which was developed for illiterates and non-native speakers, contained few.

aromatase. An enzyme that transforms androgens into oestrogens.

arousal. 1. The state of being very alert or undergoing strong emotion like excitement or fear. 2. (Physiology) The state of having desynchronized EEG produced by activation from the reticular formation, and associated with behavioural arousal.

ARP Tests. An abbreviation for APTITUDE RESEARCH PROJECT TESTS.

array. (Computing) An ordered pattern of symbol strings having one or more dimensions.

artefact. An alternative spelling of ARTIFACT.

arteriography. *See* CEREBRAL ARTERIOGRAPHY.

article. (Linguistics) A DETERMINER that indicates the specificity of a noun phrase. The **definite article** ('the') indicates that the following noun has a specific reference, whereas an **indefinite article** ('a', 'an') indicates that it does not.

articulation. The production of speech sounds by movement of parts of the vocal tract; since no movement is produced when a vowel is uttered, only consonants and diphthongs are articulated. *See also* PLACE OF ARTICULATION.

articulatory coding. Remembering a verbal input by coding the words in terms of the articulatory mechanism needed to produce them, rather than e.g. in terms of their sound or their sense. *Contrast* ACOUSTIC CODING.

articulatory loop, articulatory rehearsal loop, articulatory store. The process thought to underlie immediate memory span for lists of words, in which the word string is repeatedly rehearsed in the system that controls articulation.

articulatory suppression. Disruption of the ARTICULATORY LOOP, thus preventing rehearsal of words there, and hence reducing immediate memory-span for words; it is usually induced by having the subject repeat aloud an extraneous word or words.

artifact. (Research) A misleading or spurious finding that is an accidental outcome of the way an experiment is conducted or an observation made.

artificial intelligence (AI). The study of how to make computers perform intelligently, which may be undertaken either to throw light on human intelligence or to advance computer technology.

artificialism. Piaget's term for young children's belief that natural phenomena are caused by a living agency.

artificial pupil. A synonym for REDUCTION SCREEN.

art therapy. Engaging the mentally ill in artistic activities like painting, in the belief that it ameliorates their illness or at least reduces boredom.

asapholalia. Indistinct or mumbled speech.

ASC. An abbreviation for ALTERED STATE OF CONSCIOUSNESS.

ascender. The part of a lower-case letter rising above the minimum height to which all such letters rise; e.g. 'b' and 'h' have ascenders, 'e' does not.

ascending ramus. A branch of the lateral sulcus at its frontal end. *See* Appendix 1.

ascending reticular activating system (ARAS). The ascending parts of the reticular formation. They consist of a diffuse network starting in the core of the brainstem and projecting diffusely to the thalamus and thence to the cortex. It has an input from the senses and can serve an alerting or arousing function.

ascending series. *See* LIMITS, METHOD OF.

Asch situation. An experimental situation devised by Asch, in which subjects in a group are asked to judge aspects of stimuli (e.g. which of several lines is longest) after hearing consistently incorrect judgements made by other members of the group who are stooges instructed by the experimenter; most subjects are influenced by the stooges and make errors.

ascribed status. Status based on the parents' position. *Contrast* ACHIEVED STATUS.

asemia, asemasia. Loss or impairment of the ability to understand or use communicative symbols, including e.g. gestures and traffic lights as well as language.

asexual. (Biology) Pertaining to reproduction achieved by division of a single cell rather than by the union of a male and female cell.

as if. 1. (Philosophy) The doctrine that in science it is necessary to assume the truth of some unproven hypotheses. 2. (Philosophy) The doctrine that it is impossible to know for certain that anything is true, but one must act as if some things were true. 3. (Adler) The tendency for a person to act as though he were genuinely superior to others when he is not.

asitia. A synonym for ANOREXIA.

ASL. An abbreviation for AMERICAN SIGN LANGUAGE.

asomatagnosia. Impairment or loss of somatosensory sensations.

asonia. An abnormal inability to discriminate different pitches.

asoticomania. Wild extravagance.

aspartic acid. An AMINO ACID thought to be an excitatory neurotransmitter.

aspect. (Linguistics) The duration or type of temporal activity implied by a verb and conveyed by its form, e.g. the distinction between continuous action ('I am writing') and non-continuous ('I write').

Asperger's syndrome. A form of EARLY INFANTILE AUTISM similar to Kanner's syndrome, but marked by poorer motor coordination, better social functioning and a higher IQ. As in Kanner's syndrome, there is flattening of affect, impaired language, repetitive activities, etc.

aspiration. (Phonetics) The puff of air that sometimes follows the pronunciation of a STOP CONSONANT.

aspiration level. The level of achievement at which a person aims. The level set affects his opinion of himself, depending on whether or not he achieves it.

aspiration rule. The principle that, in English, voiceless stops ([k], [p], [t]) are aspirated when in initial position but not elsewhere.

A-S scale. A scale for measuring anti-Semitism.

assertion therapy. Training people, preferably shy ones, to be more assertive, usually through behaviour therapy.

assertive. A synonym for CONSTATIVE.

assets–liabilities technique. A method used in therapy (mainly in cognitive and behaviour therapy) to decide what goals therapy should pursue; e.g. the client may be asked to list his good and bad traits; a decision is then taken about which to promote and which to reduce.

assignment. (Computing) An operation that places a VALUE in the memory location of a variable. *See* FUNCTION (3).

assimilation. 1. Piaget's term for the incorporation of new information into existing conceptual structures, used mainly of children. *Contrast* ACCOMMODATION (2). 2. Jung's term for the process of altering new material to make it fit a person's needs or preconceptions. 3. (Linguistics) The tendency for neighbouring phonemes to become similar or identical, e.g. 'ten mice' tends to be pronounced 'tem mais'. 4. (Physiology) The conversion of food to protoplasm. 5. (Learning) *See* ASSIMILATION, LAW OF. 6. (Perception) Assimilating one feature of a figure to another, a possible explanation of some illusions. E.g. one explanation of the MÜLLER–LYER ILLUSION is that the length of the central line is assimilated to the distance between the tips of the arrow heads. *Compare* CONTRAST (1). 7. (Social psychology) Thinking that attitudes close to one's own are even closer than they really are. *Contrast* CONTRAST (3). 8. (Memory) The tendency for memories to change in the direction of familiar events or objects. *Compare* LEVELLING and SHARPENING.

assimilation, law of. The principle that organisms respond to new stimuli in the way they have learned to respond to similar stimuli, nowadays called GENERALIZATION (2).

assimilation contrast change. A theory of social influence on attitude. It postulates that attitude change depends on the difference between a person's beliefs and those put forward by someone else, together with how much faith he has in the other person.

association. A connection (usually learned) between two or more mental elements such as ideas, thoughts, images, or percepts; also the element that is evoked when an associated element is active. The term is sometimes used of the connection between a stimulus and a response. Associations were thought by the British Empiricists to underlie all learning. *See also* ASSOCIATION LAWS, BACKWARD ASSOCIATION, CONTROLLED ASSOCIATION, FORWARD ASSOCIATION, FREE ASSOCIATION, IMMEDIATE ASSOCIATION, and REMOTE ASSOCIATION.

association cortex, association areas. All cortex other than PRIMARY CORTEX. In the old days it was thought that there were only a small number of areas with a direct sensory or motor projection, and all other areas were called 'association cortex'. It is now known that there are several projection areas for each modality and for the motor system. These areas (and all areas receiving no direct projections) continue to be called 'association cortex'. The expression is therefore now a misnomer, since it was originally thought to refer to areas of the cortex in which ideas were associated, but it now includes areas that appear to be devoted to the analysis of sensory data or to motor output.

association fibres. Neurons connnecting different parts of the same hemisphere.

associationism. The theory that all learning and thinking, however complex, can be explained by the association of ideas.

association laws. The laws thought to govern the association of ideas; in particular, Aristotle thought ideas tend to be associated when they are similar (SIMILARITY, LAW OF), when they occur close together in space or time (CONTIGUITY, LAW OF), and when they contrast with one another (CONTRAST, LAW OF). Other factors that have been thought to aid association are summarized in FREQUENCY, LAW OF and VIVIDNESS, LAW OF.

association priming. PRIMING of a word by first presenting a different word that is associated with it (e.g. priming 'doctor' by 'nurse').

association reflex. Bekhterev's expression for CONDITIONED RESPONSE.

association time. The time taken to produce an association to a stimulus. More generally, the time taken to respond to a stimulus, i.e. REACTION TIME.

association value. The extent to which a nonsense syllable has meaning, measured e.g. by the percentage of people who can assign a meaning to it.

associative illusion. Any illusion in which one perceptual element is distorted through the presence of another (e.g. the MULLER–LYER ILLUSION).

associative inhibition, associative interference. The interference of one learnt item with another. *See* PROACTIVE INHIBITION and RETROACTIVE INHIBITION.

associative meaning. Everything called to

mind by a word. The associative meaning of a word is considerably broader than its CONNOTATION (1).

associative memory. Any link formed between items through experience, e.g. stimulus–response bonds, or links between ideas.

associative net. A specific example of an associative network in which every input line connects with every output line. When a given input line fires at the same time as a given output line, the connection between them is strengthened. It exemplifies learning by the use of the Hebb synapse.

associative network. Any network of elements connected together that can influence one another's states. Usually such networks can take an input; they give as output some function of the input (or can learn to do so). There are many different kinds of associative network. *See* PARALLEL DISTRIBUTED PROCESSING and SEMANTIC NETWORK.

associative shifting. Thorndike's expression for the principle that a response learned to one stimulus may come to be given to a second if the first is gradually transformed over trials into the second.

associative storage. A synonym for CONTENT-ADDRESSABLE MEMORY.

associative strength. The strength of the association between one associated element and another or the strength of a stimulus–response bond.

assonance. The repetition in a word, or in consecutive words, of the same vowel sound.

assortative mating. The tendency in a population for similar individuals to mate with one another. *Contrast* NEGATIVE ASSORTATIVE MATING and PANMIXIA.

assumed similarity. The tendency to see one's own traits in others. *See also* PROJECTION (1).

astasia. Inability to stand for functional reasons, e.g. hysteria.

astasia-abasia. Inability to stand or walk for functional reasons when the person can make the appropriate leg movements while sitting or lying down.

astereognosis. Impairment of the ability to recognize objects by touch, sometimes caused by damage to the parietal lobes.

asthenia. 1. (Psychology) Severe weakness and fatigue, often associated with depression, though it can be of organic origin. 2. (Neurology) Muscular weakness, usually caused by cerebellar lesions.

asthenic type. A bodily type in KRETSCHMER'S CONSTITUTIONAL THEORY, characterized by being thin and long-limbed, and thought by him to have a SCHIZOTHYMIC PERSONALITY.

asthenophobia. A morbid fear of weakness.

asthenopia. Poor vision, used mainly of impairment caused by fatigue of the eye muscles.

astigmatism. The refractive error produced by a CORNEA that is more convex in some directions than others, so that lines and edges in different orientations cannot simultaneously be brought into focus on the retina.

astraphobia. A morbid fear of thunder and lightning.

astrocyte, astroglia. A glial cell in the central nervous system involved in the transport of material and formation of scar tissue; it is also implicated in guiding the growth cone of the developing axon to its correct destination. *See* NEUROGLIA.

asymbolia. A form of ASEMIA marked by the inability to understand or use a particular set of symbols, e.g. mathematical symbols or a music score.

asymmetric contingency. (Social psychology) A social interaction in which one person acts according to his own goals, while the responses of a second person are determined by those of the first, as when a powerful person interacts with a weak one.

asymptote. 1. (Statistics) The line approached by a decelerating or accelerating curve as it extends to infinity. 2. (Learning) The highest level of performance an organism can reach during training; once it has reached this level its performance will not be improved by further training.

asyndesis. Disconnected and largely unintelligible speech, in which different ideas are thrown together apparently at random; it occurs in e.g. schizophrenics.

asynergia, asynergy. Loss of coordination between different muscle groups that may make it impossible to perform a complex action, like standing up. It is a form of ATAXIA.

ataractics. Drugs producing calmness.

ataraxia, ataraxy. A psychiatric term for calmness.

atavism. (Biology) The reappearance of an inherited trait that has not been manifested for several generations.

ataxia. Impairment of muscular coordination, caused by damage to the central nervous system, e.g. by drugs, disease, or lesions.

ataxic aphasia. A synonym for MOTOR APHASIA.

ataxic speech. A synonym for CEREBELLAR SPEECH.

ataxophemia. Psychiatrese for incoherence.

atelesis. Lack of integration, particularly in schizophrenics, both with the outside world and between the parts of the self.

atelia, ateliosis. Incomplete development, the manifestation in adulthood of childhood physical or mental traits.

atephobia. A morbid fear of ruin.

athetosis. A disorder of the motor system, marked by slow twisting movements of the hands and feet, and an unstable posture; it is caused by damage to the PUTAMEN.

athletic type. A bodily type in KRETSCHMER'S CONSTITUTIONAL THEORY, characterized by being muscular and broad-shouldered, and thought by him to have a BARYKINETIC personality.

athymia. Obsolete term for melancholia.

atmosphere effect. The tendency to be influenced by one aspect of a person or situation in judging other aspects, e.g. handsome people tend to be rated as more intelligent than less handsome ones.

atmosphere hypothesis. A hypothesis to account for errors in drawing conclusions from syllogisms, to the effect that people tend to draw conclusions containing the same logical terms ('all', 'some', 'not', or 'no') as the premises. E.g. from 'Some As are Bs' and 'Some Bs are Cs' people often incorrectly conclude 'Some As are Cs'.

atmosphere perspective. A synonym for AERIAL PERSPECTIVE.

ATN. An abbreviation for AUGMENTED TRANSITION NETWORK.

atomism. The doctrine that perception and other aspects of consciousness are made up of separate mental elements joined together.

atonia, atonicity, atony. Lack of normal muscle tone.

ATP. An abbreviation for ADENOSINE TRIPHOSPHATE.

atrophy. Wasting away of the body or part of it.

atropine. An anticholinergic alkaloid, present in belladonna, that depresses the sympathetic system, relaxes smooth muscles, and is used locally to dilate the pupil in eye examinations.

attachment. Any emotional bond between two people, but usually used to refer to the infant's emotional dependence on its mother or on whoever is fostering him. Many believe that infants who are prevented from forming an attachment to a mother figure suffer permanent psychological damage.

attensity. Titchener's term for the change in a sensation (particularly the increase in clarity) produced by directing attention to it.

attention. Concentration on a particular stimulus, sensation, idea, or thought. *See also* SELECTIVE ATTENTION.

attention-deficit disorder, attention hyperactivity disorder. (DSM–III) A disorder, mainly of childhood, in which the child cannot concentrate and acts impulsively; it is usually, but not always, accompanied by hyperactivity. *Compare* MINIMAL BRAIN DYSFUNCTION.

attention operating characteristic (AOC). A plot of how good performance is on each of two tasks performed simultaneously where the attention given to each is systematically varied; one coordinate represents level of performance on one task, the other on the other task.

attention reflex. The increase in pupil size that occurs when attention is directed to something.

attention span. A synonym for SPAN OF APPREHENSION.

attenuation. Reduction in size or amplitude, used of waveforms and, in statistics, of the reduction in the size of an effect caused by experimental errors.

attenuation theory. The hypothesis that in selective attention the input from unattended stimulus channels is weakened but not eliminated.

attitude. The way a person consistently thinks or feels about something, or is disposed to react to it; often used with reference to how a person values something, i.e. how far he is for or against it.

attitude scales. Scales, often based on questionnaires, purporting to measure the strength and direction (for or against) of attitudes to specific objects, policies, groups of people, etc.

attraction, law of. The principle that a person will be attracted to another person (or to an object) in proportion to the rewards he receives from him (or it).

attractor. The state to which a system converges, regardless of its starting point.

attributional criteria. (Social psychology) The criteria for believing that a feeling or action is caused by an event. The probability of making such an attribution is thought to increase with: (i) the distinctiveness of the event; (ii) the extent to which that type of event has previously been followed by that action; (iii) the extent to which others respond in the same way to the event. *See* COVARIATION THEORY.

attribution error. Any error in assigning causes, particularly in deciding whether an action was caused by the situation or by the actor's individual traits and dispositions. *See* FUNDAMENTAL ATTRIBUTION ERROR.

attribution theory. (Social psychology) The study of how people assign causes, particularly causes for their own actions and those of others. *See also* ATTRIBUTIONAL CRITERIA, ATTRIBUTION ERROR, CORRESPONDENT INFERENCE THEORY, COVARIATION THEORY and FUNDAMENTAL ATTRIBUTION ERROR.

A-type personality. *See* TYPE A PERSONALITY.

atypical. (Psychiatry) Pertaining to a disorder in which the symptoms exhibited are not entirely typical, but where there is no better diagnosis, e.g. 'atypical anxiety disorder' or 'atypical psychosis'.

atypical depression. Depression in which the patient eats and sleeps too much.

Aubert effect. The phenomenon that, if a person's head is tilted to one side through a large angle (about 30° or more) a vertical bar in an otherwise dark room appears to be tilted in the opposite direction to the head. *Contrast* MULLER EFFECT.

Aubert–Fleischl paradox. The phenomenon that a moving stimulus seems to move more slowly when fixated and tracked with a smooth eye-movement than when the background is fixated.

Aubert–Forster phenomenon. The phenomenon that acuity is better for near objects than far objects, even if they subtend the same visual angle.

audible thought. A hallucination in which a person hears his own thoughts spoken aloud.

audile. Someone who relies more on auditory imagery than on visual.

audiogenic seizure. Convulsions induced by high frequency sounds, to which laboratory rats are particularly prone.

audiogram. A plot of the least intensity needed for a person to perceive a sound over the range of audible frequencies.

audiogravic illusion. Misperception of the localization of a sound source, caused by the subject misperceiving the tilt of his body.

audiogyral illusion. Misperception of the localization of a sound source, caused by the subject being rotated in the dark.

audiokinetic response. An eye movement controlled by the ear, which occurs when the position of the body relative to a steady sound source is altered, and which has the effect of keeping the eyes fixated on their target.

audiometric zero. The intensity threshold for a given frequency of sound that is considered normal for the human ear.

audiometer. A device to measure and record AUDIOGRAMS.

audiometry. The measurement of the sensitivity of the ear.

audio-oculogyric reflex. Reflex turning of the head and eyes towards the source of a sudden sound.

audioverbal aphasia. A condition in which the patient can repeat some individual words but cannot repeat a series of words.

auditory adaptation. See AUDITORY FATIGUE.

auditory aphasia. A form of APHASIA in which the main deficit is the inability to understand spoken words.

Auditory Apperception Test. A projection test for the blind.

auditory association area. Brodmann's area 22; see Appendix 3. It is implicated in speech.

auditory attribute. A synonym for TONAL ATTRIBUTE.

auditory canal. The tube between the external ear and the EARDRUM.

auditory cortex. The cortical areas receiving a projection from the COCHLEA; at present four such areas are known in the temporal lobe, together with one in the cortex of the insular and one in the somatosensory cortex. All or most of these areas contain a topographic map of the cochlea; some also receive inputs from other senses. *See also* PRIMARY AUDITORY CORTEX and SECONDARY AUDITORY CORTEX.

auditory dimension. A synonym for TONAL ATTRIBUTE.

auditory egocentre. *See* EGOCENTRE.

auditory fatigue. A temporary loss of auditory sensitivity caused by exposure to a strong tone; sensitivity is lost in the frequency range from that of the fatiguing tone to about half an octave above it. It is distinguished from AUDITORY ADAPTATION, in that the latter can be caused by a weaker stimulus.

auditory flutter. The sensation produced by interrupting a continuous sound at long enough periods.

auditory fusion. Hearing two sounds as one, whether they are presented to separate ears (**binaural fusion**) or to one. *See* PRECEDENCE EFFECT.

auditory lateralization. Detecting the direction of a sound in the horizontal plane.

auditory localization. The process of detecting the direction and distance of a sound source. Directional localization for the horizontal plane is based on differences in the intensity (for high frequencies) or in the phase (for low frequencies) of the sound at each ear; directional localization for the vertical plane is based on echoes from the pinna, which vary with the height of the sound.

auditory masking. The masking of one tone caused by the presence of another (or others). It is manifested by a rise in the threshold for hearing the masked tone or by a reduction in its loudness if it is above threshold. *See* CRITICAL BAND.

auditory meatus. A synonym for AUDITORY CANAL.

auditory nerve. The branch of the VESTIBULOACOUSTIC NERVE that serves the cochlea, and contains the axons of the ganglion cells. It ends at the ventral and dorsal cochlear nuclei.

auditory radiation. The fibres that spread from the medial geniculate to the auditory cortex.

auditory receptors. HAIR CELLS in the ORGAN OF CORTI which have their tips embedded in the TECTORIAL MEMBRANE. They are set in motion by movements of the BASILAR MEMBRANE. They are divided into two groups, the **outer hair cells** (or **external hair cells**) and the **inner hair cells** (or **internal hair cells**), the latter being located nearer to the auditory nerve.

auditory space perception. A synonym for AUDITORY LOCALIZATION.

auditory spectrum. The range of sound frequencies that can be heard by a member of a species with normal hearing (from about 20 Hz to 20,000 Hz in man).

auditory system. The ear and those parts of the nervous system devoted to hearing.

auditory tube. A synonym for EUSTACHIAN TUBE.

Aufgabe. The Wurzburg school's name for MENTAL SET, or determining tendency or aim; how a person thinks about a given piece of information is determined by his *Aufgabe*.

augmentation principle. The perceived increase in the role of a given cause of behaviour if other inhibitory causes are operating. E.g. A student from a poor background who does well at school may be seen as having more ability and motivation than one from a middle-class background who does as well.

augmented transition network (ATN). A TRANSITION NETWORK which is augmented by memory registers. E.g. on encountering the word 'whom', the information is stored that this word fits the slot for the object of a verb to be encountered later. Almost all augmented transition networks that have been implemented are **recursive augmented transition networks**, i.e. networks in which a routine can call itself, e.g. in order to analyse a subordinate clause within the main clause.

aulophobia. A morbid fear of flutes or similarly shaped wind instruments.

aura. A strange sensation or feeling, like an unusual taste, numbness, feelings of *déjà vu* or derealization that may precede an attack of epilepsy or migraine.

aural harmonic. A harmonic that is heard, but that is not present in the sound wave reaching the ear; it must, therefore, be produced within the auditory system.

aural microphonic. A synonym for COCHLEAR MICROPHONIC.

auricle. 1. A synonym for PINNA. 2. Either of the two anterior chambers of the heart that lead into the VENTRICLES (2).

Aussage **test.** A method of demonstrating the unreliability of witnesses invented by Stern. It is based on confronting people with a surprising event, and subsequently measuring their recall of the details.

authoritarian personality, authoritarian character. The characteristics of people who believe that human behaviour should be controlled by commands from those in authority, which are alleged to include adherence to conventional values and hostility to out-groups.

autism. 1. A pathological preoccupation with one's own thoughts, to the exclusion of attending to the outside world. It can occur in schizophrenia. 2. Short for EARLY INFANTILE AUTISM.

autistic child. A child displaying autism, often also showing stereotyped movements, e.g. constant rocking or banging the head, indifference to other people, and severely impaired language.

autobiographical cueing. A method of testing long-term memory by presenting a word to which the person must respond by describing an event in his life associated with the word and by dating the event.

autochthonous. Originating from within a person.

autocorrelation. The correlation between one part of a series (usually a time series) and a part that is shifted from it; it is a measure of the extent to which the series repeats itself.

autoecholalia. Stereotyped repetition of the same word or words; it can occur in e.g. CATATONIC SCHIZOPHRENIA.

autoechopraxia. Stereotyped repetition of the same action; it can occur in e.g. CATATONIC SCHIZOPHRENIA.

autoencoding. A three-layer connectionist system in which the output layer receives back-propagation that is identical to the input; the HIDDEN UNITS tend to extract critical features of the input, thus providing a compact description of it.

autoeroticism. Sexual arousal produced without a partner. *Contrast* ALLOEROTICISM.

autogenic. Self-produced.

autogenic training. A relaxation therapy based on graded exercises that the client can practice on his own, and on the use of auto-suggestion.

autohypnosis. Self-hypnosis. *Contrast* HETEROHYPNOSIS.

auto-inhibition. Short for NEURAL AUTO-INHIBITION.

autokinesis. Voluntary movement of the body.

autokinetic effect. The illusion that a stationary point of light viewed on its own in the dark is moving around.

autoleucotomy. A favourable change in personality following an aneurysm.

automatic speech. Involuntary speech not under conscious control.

automatic writing. A paranormal phenomenon, in which it is alleged that someone may unconsciously write in the style of another person, conveying that person's ideas and experiences, of which he has no conscious knowledge. A genuine form of automatic writing may occur in hypnosis: the person may record facts about himself of which he is unconscious at the time. E.g. when subjected to painful stimuli after being told by the hypnotist that he will not feel pain, he may write that he is in pain while otherwise seeming not to be in pain.

automatism. The mechanical performance, without conscious control, of a task usually under conscious control (e.g. sleepwalking, automatic writing); it can occur in a fugue or in psychomotor epilepsy.

automatization. The process by which, after much practice, it becomes possible to execute a complex task (e.g. driving a car) without conscious control.

automaton. A machine that can execute tasks in an intelligent manner.

automorphic perception. The tendency to perceive others as being more like oneself than they are.

autonomasia. A synonym for NOMINAL APHASIA.

autonomic balance. The balance between the activity of the parasympathetic system and that of the sympathetic system.

autonomic nervous system (ANS), autonomic system. The part of the PERIPHERAL NERVOUS SYSTEM that controls the internal organs, blood supply, digestion, excretion, etc. The expression usually refers only to the efferent fibres serving these systems, but some authorities include afferents. Its operation is mainly involuntary, in contrast to the SOMATIC NERVOUS SYSTEM, which is usually under voluntary control. It is divided into the PARASYMPATHETIC SYSTEM and SYMPA-

THETIC SYSTEM. The following table shows the effects of the outputs from each division.

Organ	Sympathetic stimulation	Parasympathetic stimulation
pupil	dilation	constriction
ciliary muscle	relaxation	contraction
nasal gland	vasoconstriction	secretion
lachrymal glands	vasoconstriction	secretion
sweat glands	sweating	none
heart	increased rate	slowed rate
bronchi	dilation	constriction
liver	glucose release	glycogen synthesis
kidney	decreased output	none
bladder	closed sphincter	micturition
penis	ejaculation	erection
blood-vessels to:		
abdomen	constriction	none
muscles	constriction and dilation	none
skin	constriction	none

autonomous stage. The second of Piaget's developmental stages of morality, in which the child comes to rely on his own judgements rather than on parental or other authority. *Compare* HETERONOMOUS STAGE.

autophagy. Eating oneself.

autophilia. Narcissism.

autophobia. A morbid fear of oneself or of being alone.

autoplasty. Adaptation achieved by changing oneself, rather than by changing the environment. *Contrast* ALLOPLASTY, which is a much easier task for most people.

autopsychic. Pertaining to mental events that arise from within a person, e.g. delusions or hallucinations. *Contrast* ALLOPSYCHIC.

autopsychic psychosis. A paranoid disorder in which the patient has distorted ideas about himself, e.g. thinking he is Christ.

autoradiography. A technique for discovering the location in tissue of a substance that has been given a radioactive tag and administered to an organism. If the substance is taken up by active neurons, its distribution signifies the sites at which there is most neural activity at a given time. Alternatively a substance that will not pass the blood–brain barrier can be used, and damage to blood-vessels can be detected from the sites at which it has leaked out. *See* DEOXY-GLUCOSE AUTORADIOGRAPHY and TRANSPORT AUTORADIOGRAPHY.

autoreceptor. A receptor on the endings of a presynaptic neuron to which the transmitter released by that neuron can bind, thus reducing the amount remaining in the synaptic cleft. *See* REUPTAKE.

autosexuality. A synonym for AUTO-EROTICISM.

autoshaping. A recently discovered learning phenomenon in which an animal given a stimulus (e.g. a pigeon presented with a suddenly illuminated key) will come to respond to the stimulus (e.g. by pecking it) if the reinforcer (e.g. food) appropriate to that response is given in the situation but at times not correlated with the occurrence of the response. It is regarded as a form of classical conditioning, since the response made to the stimulus is the same as that made to the reinforcer. Autoshaping can occur even if reinforcement is never given immediately after the response is made.

autosome. Any chromosome that is not a sex chromosome. *Contrast* HETEROSOME.

autostereotype. *See* STEREOTYPE.

autosuggestion. Suggesting to oneself that one will become what one wants to be, in the hope that it helps.

autotelic. Pertaining to behaviour or traits that are central to a person's major goals, like self-preservation.

autotopagnosia. Inability to recognize or locate parts of one's own body; it is caused by brain damage, particularly by lesions in the pathways between the thalamus and the parietal lobe.

auxiliary. (Linguistics) A word that does not refer to anything or describe anything, but which only has meaning when used with other words, e.g. conjunctions, prepositions, or auxiliary verbs.

auxiliary ego. In psychodrama, a person (usually trained) who plays the part of some significant figure (e.g. the mother) in a client's life.

auxiliary inversion. The placement of an auxiliary verb before the subject to form a question, e.g. '*Did* he go?'.

auxiliary verb. A verb, having no lexical content, which when used with another verb modifies its tense, aspect, mood, or voice, e.g. 'has', 'should', 'is'.

availability heuristic. The influence on a person's reasoning of the accessibility of the items needed for that reasoning. E.g. most people falsely conclude that there are more words beginning with the letter 'r' than having 'r' in third position, because they can access words beginning with 'r' more readily.

avalanche. (Neurophysiology) The spreading of neural excitation through a group of neurons, as in an epileptic seizure.

average. The arithmetic mean, but sometimes misleadingly used for other measures of central tendency such as the median or mode. When used by governments, 'average' means 'We have computed central tendency in the way that puts the best face on highly discreditable data'. *Compare* MEAN, MEDIAN, and MODE.

average deviation. A synonym for MEAN DEVIATION.

average error, method of. The method of adjustment as used to determine difference threshold. *See* ADJUSTMENT, METHOD OF (1).

average evoked response (AER), average evoked potential (AEP). The change in the amplitude of an EVOKED RESPONSE over time, based on averaging a large number of evoked potentials, hence reducing the noise present in the individual responses.

aversion therapy. A method, sometimes used in BEHAVIOUR THERAPY, of eliminating unwanted behaviour, by administering punishment when it occurs (e.g. inducing nausea after drinking, giving electric shock when a cigarette is lit, etc.).

aversive conditioning. Punishing an organism whenever it makes a particular response.

aversive stimulus. A noxious stimulus that an organism will avoid.

avoidance–avoidance conflict. Conflict engendered when an organism is compelled to choose between two or more equally undesirable alternatives.

avoidance gradient. The increasing strength of the tendency to withdraw, as an animal gets closer in time or space to a situation in which it has been punished, or of which it is afraid. *Compare* APPROACH GRADIENT.

avoidance learning. Learning to make an instrumental response that prevents the occurrence of a noxious stimulus. It is usually assumed that anxiety provoked by the noxious stimulus is conditioned to the preceding stimuli, and that the reinforcement for the instrumental response is the reduction in the conditioned anxiety that will occur if the noxious response does not occur. *Contrast* ESCAPE LEARNING. *See also* ACTIVE AVOIDANCE LEARNING and PASSIVE AVOIDANCE LEARNING.

avoidance ritual. Goffman's term for any method of avoiding intimate contact with others.

avoidant disorder of childhood or adolescence. (DSM-III) Extreme shyness with, and withdrawal from, strangers in childhood or adolescence.

avoidant personality disorder. (DSM-III) A personality disorder marked by extreme sensitivity to criticism or rejection, social withdrawal, and low self-esteem.

AVPV. An abbreviation for ANTEROVENTRAL PERIVENTRICULAR NUCLEUS.

A wave. *See* B WAVE.

axial command. A command to carry out actions involving the body axis, e.g. 'Turn round', 'Bow'. It is sometimes the only form of speech to which GLOBAL APHASICS can respond.

axiom. (Logic) An unproven statement assumed to be true; from a set of axioms and rules of inference, a body of theorems may be proved. *See* AXIOMATIC SYSTEM.

axiomatic system. A formal deductive system in logic or mathematics in which there are initial sets of definitions, of statements declared to be true (axioms or postulates), and of rules of inference which can be used to derive further true statements (theorems) from the initial ones.

axoaxonic synapse. A synapse between two axons, usually near their terminals, which normally produces presynaptic inhibition.

axodendritic synapse. A synapse of an axon on a dendrite.

axon. The long fibre of a neuron down which impulses are transmitted, usually from the cell body to the axonal terminals.

axonal terminals. The fine fibres at the end of an axon that terminate on the dendrites or cell body of the postsynaptic cell.

axonal transport. A synonym for AXOPLASMIC TRANSPORT.

axon hillock. The thickened projection arising from a cell body that gradually thins into the axon.

axoplasmic transport. Transport of materials from the cell body to the axonal terminals or vice versa.

axosomatic synapse. The synapse of an axon on a cell body.

azimuth. Direction in the horizontal plane.

B

Babinski reflex. The reflex curling upwards of the toes when the sole of the foot is stroked. It occurs in infants before they walk; later in life it can be a sign of damage to the motor system.

Babinski sign. The appearance of the Babinski reflex at an age when it should have disappeared, a sympton of neurological damage.

BAC. An abbreviation for BLOOD ALCOHOL CONCENTRATION.

back formation. Forming a word by eliminating a prefix or suffix from an existing word (e.g. 'edit' is derived from 'editor', and not the other way round as in 'act' and 'actor').

back phoneme. A phoneme uttered with the tongue at the back of the mouth.

back-propagation algorithm. In a parallel distributed processing network of several layers, a method of making the output for a given input conform to a desired state. For each input, the system is informed what the output ought to be; the current output is compared to this, and the weights of the connections to the output units are changed to reduce the difference. The difference between the weights of the connections from the next lower level and those needed to produce the correct activity at the first level down is then measured and the weights at the second level down are changed accordingly. The process is repeated down to the lowest level. The changes made are usually small on any one trial. By this method the system gradually learns to give the desired output. *See also* DELTA RULE.

backtracking. In a search task, having chosen a false alternative at one decision point, returning to that point and choosing another alternative.

backward association. An association linking a stimulus to a stimulus or response occurring before it in time. *Contrast* FORWARD ASSOCIATION.

backward chaining. *See* FORWARD CHAINING.

backward conditioning. The process whereby a conditioned response comes to be produced when the conditioned stimulus is given *after* the unconditioned stimulus; it is thought to depend on SENSITIZATION (1) rather than on association learning. *Contrast* FORWARD CONDITIONING.

backward masking. Reducing the visibility of a visual stimulus by presenting another stimulus soon after its offset. The expression is also sometimes used in a similar sense of other modalities, particularly touch. *See* BRIGHTNESS MASKING and METACONTRAST.

backwards propagation of error. A synonym for BACK PROPAGATION.

bad faith. In existentialism, an act of self-deception in which a person refuses to take responsibility for his actions, attributing them to unalterable aspects of his character or to social roles he is forced to play.

Bahnsen columns. Adjacent vertical black and white ragged columns in which every other column has horizontal symmetry. The symmetrical columns tend to be seen as figure, the non-symmetrical as ground.

bait shyness. A synonym for LEARNED TASTE AVERSION.

balanced replication. A replication of a

Bahnsen columns

previous experiment in which additional conditions are run to control or expose artifacts.

balanced scale. Any scale obtained by balancing out factors that are potential sources of bias, e.g. by equating the number of judgements to which 'greater than' and 'less than' are the likely responses.

balance theory. A cognitive consistency theory of attitudes and posits that when someone is associated with a person or object by a relationship that is normally favourable, e.g. kinship or ownership (UNIT FORMATION), he will tend to like that person or object or at least reduce any disliking he already has. Similarly he will come to dislike the person or object if the relationship is normally unfavourable.

Baldwin effect. The reciprocal influence of the development of mental processes and evolutionary selection.

Balint's syndrome. (Neuropsychology) A neurological syndrome characterized by impaired reaching for objects in space, inability to change fixation, and SIMULTAGNOSIA; it is caused by damage to the occipital or frontal lobes or the connections between them.

ball and field test. A question in the Stanford–Binet test, in which a child has to make a drawing showing how he would find a ball from a field.

ballistic movement. A movement that is

preset and, once set in motion, cannot be regulated by FEEDBACK (e.g. a SACCADE). *Contrast* SERVOMECHANISM.

ballistophobia. A morbid fear of missiles.

band-pass filter. A filter that passes only waves that are above one frequency and below another.

bandwagon effect. The tendency for a member of a group to adopt the attitudes of the other members, which increases with the proportion of members holding those attitudes.

bandwidth. The range of frequencies received or transmitted by a system (e.g. the auditory system). The bandwidth of a filter is the range of frequencies it passes.

baraesthesia, baraesthesis. The pressure sense.

baragnosis. An inability to judge weight, which may be caused by parietal lobe lesions.

Bárány nystagmus. A synonym for CALORIC NYSTAGMUS.

Bárány test. A test to discover whether the three semicircular canals are functioning properly; the subject is rotated in the direction to which each canal is sensitive and the effects of the rotation on eye movement are recorded. *See also* VESTIBULAR NYSTAGMUS.

barber's pole effect. The phenomenon that if diagonal stripes are rotated behind a vertical slit they appear to move vertically; similarly, if a horizontal slit is used, they appear to move horizontally. The stripes themselves move in the same direction in both cases, but their ends move vertically in one case and horizontally in the other. *Compare* APERTURE PROBLEM.

barbiturates. A group of CNS depressants derived from barbituric acid, until recently used as sedatives or soporifics, but now, because of their addictive properties, largely replaced by BENZODIAZEPINES.

bar chart. A diagram representing the frequencies or magnitudes of each category in a nominal dimension by bars of different lengths; since the dimension is not continuous the bars are separated by spaces. *Compare* HISTOGRAM.

Bard–Cannon theory. *See* CANNON–BARD THEORY.

bar detector. A cell in the visual area that responds maximally to a bar in a particular orientation and position on the retina; some cells respond to black bars, some to white, some to both. *See* FEATURE DETECTOR and *compare* EDGE DETECTOR.

baresthesia, baresthesis. Alternative spellings for BARAESTHESIA.

bar graph. A synonym for BAR CHART.

Barnum effect. The tendency for people to believe that a vague description or prediction (offered by e.g. a fortune teller) applies specifically to themselves.

barognosis. Sensitivity to weight, usually through lifting objects by hand.

barophobia. A morbid fear of gravity.

baroreceptor. Receptors sensitive to changes in blood pressure, found in blood-vessels and heart. They signal to the hypothalamus decreases in blood plasma pressure caused by extracellular fluid loss, thus producing thirst.

barotaxis. An orienting response determined by pressure.

barrel distortion. A distortion of the retinal image caused by aniseikonia in which the sides of the image of a square are bowed outward. *Compare* PINCUSHION DISTORTION.

barrier. 1. (Psychology) Lewin's term for psychological or physical obstacles that make it difficult or impossible to achieve a particular goal. 2. (Physiology) *See* BLOOD–BRAIN BARRIER.

barrier response. A synonym for PENETRATION RESPONSE.

baryglossia. An obsolete term for indistinct speech, such as might be produced by a malfunction of the tongue.

barykinetic personality. A personality type in KRETSCHMER'S CONSTITUTIONAL THEORY, having robust and well balanced characteristics and associated with the ATHLETIC TYPE.

barylalia. Slurred, indistinct speech, usually resulting from brain damage.

baryphony. The condition of having a heavy, deep, hoarse voice.

barythymia. Emotional flatness.

basal age. In a test, the standardized age for passing those items (rank ordered in terms of difficulty) that are all passed by an individual testee. Since he may pass some of the tests standardized for higher ages it represents his lowest possible age score.

basal ganglia. A mass of grey matter, lying below the central area of the cerebral cortex and comprising mainly the CAUDATE NUCLEUS, PUTAMEN, GLOBUS PALLIDUS, and CLAUSTRUM. It is part of the pyramidal system and is implicated in the control of posture and movement.

basal metabolism. The minimum expenditure of energy by the body as measured in the resting state.

base. 1. (Mathematics) In a logarithm, the number in terms of whose exponent another number is expressed. Thus, the logarithm to the base 10 ($\log_{10}$) of 1,000 is 3, because the base (10) has to be raised to the power of 3 to equal that number. 2. (Linguistics) The part of a grammar containing only phrase-structure rules, i.e. the part before transformation rules are applied. 3. (Linguistics) The background concept denoted by a word, in contrast to its **profile**, which is the set of features that differentiate it from other examples of that concept. E.g. the base of the term 'mother' is woman, while its profile is having at least one child. 4. (Molecular biology) Any of the four substances in a NUCLEOTIDE of DNA (or RNA), pairs of which bond together to make the double helix (adenine binds to thymine and guanine to uracil).

baseline performance. A measure of performance before learning starts or in the absence of any other experimental manipulation.

basement effect. A synonym for FLOOR EFFECT.

base of cochlea. The part of the cochlea next to the middle ear, where sound impulses are conveyed through the oval window.

base rate. A synonym for PRIOR PROBABILITY.

base rate fallacy. The failure to take sufficient account of the PRIOR PROBABILITY when estimating a CONDITIONAL PROBABILITY. E.g. in one experiment the judgement of whether a person described is more likely to be an engineer or a lawyer was unaffected by the knowledge that he had been sampled from a group of 70 engineers and 30 lawyers or 30 engineers and 70 lawyers.

basic act. An act performed directly (such as turning a steering wheel), as opposed to a more complicated act (such as driving a car) to which basic acts contribute.

basic antinomy. The conflict between wishful thinking and reality.

basic anxiety. Horney's term for neurotic anxiety or insecurity, originating from the child's being made to feel isolated or alienated from the parents.

basic colour. The hue and brightness that is the best example (PROTOTYPE) for a given colour name; there is a large measure of agreement across cultures on which colours are basic.

basic conflict. Horney's expression for the conflicts caused by a clash between different neurotic needs.

basic level category. The level of categorization most used where a hierarchy of levels exists; e.g. it is common to categorize a chair as a chair rather than using a subordinate category (like kitchen chair) or a superordinate (like furniture). The basic level category probably represents the category that is most useful to most people most of the time.

basic need. 1. A synonym for PHYSIOLOGICAL NEED. 2. As used by Maslow, physiological needs together with what he regarded as low-level psychological ones, such as the needs for self-esteem, for love, and for security.

basic orthographic syllabic structure. *See* BOSS.

basic research. Research that is of no use, i.e. research on fundamental scientific problems rather than on applied problems.

basic rest activity cycle (BRAC). A postulated cycle with a periodicity of 90 minutes, in which people alternate between feeling active and sleepy. The cycle is known to exist at night (when REM sleep is the active part) and may exist in infants in the day time. It is doubtful whether adults exhibit it by day.

basilar membrane. A membrane in the COCHLEA which is set in motion by sound waves and which supports the ORGAN OF CORTI where the movements are detected by hair cells. *See also* TRAVELLING WAVE.

basiphobia. A morbid fear of walking.

basket cell. A type of STELLATE CELL with a short vertical axon that divides into a large number of processes running horizontally. It is found in the cerebral cortex and in the molecular layer of the cerebellar cortex, where it is activated by the parallel fibres, and itself has an inhibitory action on the Purkinje fibres.

basket ending. A skin receptor, probably sensitive to pressure, near the base of a hair.

basophobia. An alternative spelling for BASIPHOBIA.

BAT. An abbreviation for BODY ADJUSTMENT TEST.

Batesian mimicry. The tendency of a palatable or inoffensive organism to mimic through evolution the appearance of an unpalatable or offensive one in order to reduce attacks by predators. *Compare* MULLERIAN MIMICRY.

bathophobia. A morbid fear of depths, particularly of looking down from a height. *Compare* ACROPHOBIA.

bathyaesthesia. The sensitivity of the receptors underneath the skin or in the internal bodily organs.

bathyphobia. A synonym for BATHOPHOBIA.

batrachophobia. A morbid fear of frogs.

baud rate. A measure of transmission rate in bytes per second (eight BITS per second).

Bayes theorem. The theorem that the probability of a hypothesis (H) being true conditional on some other proposition (D) being true is

$$p(H/D) = \frac{p(D/H) \cdot p(H)}{p(D)}$$

$$= \frac{p(D/H) \cdot p(H)}{p(D/H) \cdot p(H) + p(D/\bar{H}) \cdot p(\bar{H})}$$

Bayley Scales of Infant Development. A scale of infant development, comprising three sub-scales: (i) a mental scale (memory, perception, etc.); (ii) a motor scale; (iii) an infant behaviour scale (social behaviour, persistence, etc.).

beamsplitter. An optical system that separates a beam of light into two beams, e.g. a half-silvered mirror.

beats. Periodic increases and decreases in loudness produced by presenting two or more tones of different frequency and occurring when the wave peaks of the tones coincide or cancel one another out. *See also* COMBINATION TONE and DIFFERENCE TONE.

Beck Depression Inventory. Perhaps the most commonly used method for assessing the existence and severity of depression; it is based on a questionnaire.

behavioural contagion. The spreading of an action (e.g. weeping, yawning) through the members of a group.

behavioural contingency. The amount, frequency, and timing of reinforcement in rela-tion to a given response. *See also* REINFORCEMENT SCHEDULE.

behavioural contract. An explicit contract agreed between a behaviour therapist and a patient, in which the aims of therapy are stated, and the therapist undertakes to stick to particular lines of treatment and the patient to respond in particular ways. *See also* MICROSOCIAL ENGINEERING.

behavioural contrast. A synonym for BEHAVIOUR CONTRAST.

behavioural-directive therapy. A synonym for BEHAVIOUR THERAPY.

behavioural engineering. Skinner's obnoxious expression for the use of psychological methods and findings to 'engineer' people to behave in ways desirable to the engineer. It is not too difficult to guess whom Skinner had in mind as the engineer.

behavioural equivalence. A synonym for RESPONSE GENERALIZATION.

behavioural excitation. A synonym for EXCITATION (2).

behavioural genetics. A synonym for BEHAVIOUR GENETICS.

behavioural inhibition. A synonym for INHIBITION (2).

behavioural intention. (Social psychology) A disposition to act in particular ways towards an object about which an attitude is held.

behavioural medicine. The application of behaviour therapy techniques (e.g. BIOFEEDBACK) to the prevention or treatment of physical disorders.

behavioural oscillation ($_S O_R$). Hull's term for momentary fluctuations in an animal's readiness to make a learned response. *See also* HULLIAN THEORY and MOMENTARY REACTION POTENTIAL.

behavioural sciences. Those disciplines which purport to study people or animals scientifically, including psychology, anthropology, and sociology; since most aspects of these and similar disciplines are far from scientific, the expression appears to have been coined in an effort to increase their status.

behavioural sink. A locality (e.g. a small pen for animals, a tenement building) in which animals or people live crowded together under poor conditions.

behavioural specificity. The hypothesis that people act differently in different situations rather than exhibiting the same general traits in all situations.

behaviour constraint theory. The hypothesis that if an organism fails to gain control over punishing events it develops LEARNED HELPLESSNESS.

behaviour contrast. 1. The phenomenon that if a small reward is first given for an instrumental act and then a large one, the response rate will increase to a level higher than it would have been had the large one been given from the outset. Similarly, but less well established, if a large reward is succeeded by a small one, the response rate will be lower than it would have been had the small reward been given from the outset. The effect can also be produced by a switch from a less favourable reinforcement schedule to a more favourable one and by simultaneous exposure to two stimuli, one of which signals a much smaller reward than the other. 2. A rare synonym for INDUCTION (2).

behaviour control. A Skinnerian slogan emphasizing the hypothesis that behaviour is under the control of reinforcement.

behaviour disorder. Any maladaptive habit not caused by organic damage or directly related to a psychosis or neurosis, especially in children or young people, e.g. nail biting, truancy, drug abuse, stealing.

behaviour genetics. The study of genetic influences on behaviour and of the nature of the relevant genetic processes.

behaviourism. The idea, first put forward by Watson in 1913, that psychology should restrict itself to the study and explanation of stimuli and responses, and should ignore mental events. *See* HULLIAN BEHAVIOURISM, MEDIATION THEORY, PURPOSIVE BEHAVIOURISM, and RADICAL BEHAVIOURISM.

behaviour modification. The use of the principles of learning theory to change behaviour, e.g. in order to improve discipline or learning skills in a class. The expression is usually restricted to the application of these principles to the behaviour of normal individuals. *Compare* BEHAVIOUR THERAPY.

behaviour sampling. Recording an organism's behaviour over selected periods of time.

behaviour setting. The social circumstances in which an activity is performed.

behaviour system. All the actions that can be performed to achieve the same goal; e.g. if the goal is communication then speaking, writing, typing, gesturing, etc. form a behaviour system.

behaviour therapy. A form of therapy in which the principles of learning theory are used to devise methods of teaching patients to overcome maladaptive habits. It is based on the belief that most if not all neurotic (and some psychotic) symptoms have been learned in the first place, and that the substitution of more adaptive patterns of behaviour will of itself improve the emotional state of mentally disordered patients. Behaviour therapy has tended to place much emphasis on rewards and punishments and to follow a stimulus–response paradigm. These trends are fading and most behaviour therapists now also use COGNITIVE THERAPY. *See also* ASSERTION TRAINING, AVERSION THERAPY, COUNTERCONDITIONING, DESENSITIZATION, and FLOODING.

Behn test. A variant of the RORSCHACH TEST sometimes used with people who are already familiar with the Rorschach ink blots.

being. The state of being authentic, genuine, real. (A vague term coined by Maslow.)

being-in-the-world. An existentialist expression referring to the individual's authentic experience of himself, others, and the world, to which he must remain true in order to actualize himself; it is not yet known how to discriminate between what is authentic and what is not.

bel. A measure of the physical intensity of sound based on the logarithm to the base ten of the ratio between the intensities of two sounds; bel $= \log(I_1/I_2)$, where I is intensity. Thus if one sound is 100 times as intense as another the difference between them is $\log_{10}100$ bels $= 2$ bels. To become a ratio scale, an intensity must be chosen to represent 0.0 bel (the STANDARD REFERENCE PRESSURE LEVEL). *See also* DECIBEL.

belief congruence theory. The hypothesis (probably mistaken) that one's liking for another person depends mainly on whether he shares one's beliefs rather than on such factors as his appearance or race.

belief-driven learning. Learning in which beliefs and previous experiences influence what is learned. *Contrast* DATA-DRIVEN LEARNING.

belief premise. *See* SYLLOGISTIC MODEL OF ATTITUDE ORGANIZATION.

belladonna. *See* ATROPINE.

belle indifférence. See LA BELLE INDIFFER-ENCE.

Bellevue–Wechsler scales. A series of IQ scales for testing adults; each is composed of both verbal and performance items.

Bell–Magendie law. The principle that the afferent and efferent fibres of peripheral nerves are separated and connect with the spinal cord respectively at the dorsal and ventral roots.

bell-shaped curve. Any symmetrical curve shaped like the silhouette of a bell such as is produced by a NORMAL DISTRIBUTION.

belonephobia. A morbid fear of needles.

belongingess. 1. (Learning) The ease with which a specific response can be learned to a specific stimulus with a specific reinforcer, e.g. animals learn to reject food having a certain taste more readily if they are made sick after consuming it than if they are given an electric shock. 2. (Perception) The extent to which the parts of a perceptual array cohere together. E.g. if a series of high notes is played simultaneously with one of low notes, the listener either hears all the high notes distinctly (belonging together), while the low notes are heard indistinctly as background, or vice versa. 3. (Perception) A synonym for APPURTENANCE. 4. *See* BE-LONGINGNESS, LAW OF.

belongingness, law of. Thorndike's law that certain associations belong together more readily than others, and can therefore be learned more easily. *See also* BELONGING-NESS.

Bem Sex Role Inventory. A scale measuring the preponderance of masculine or feminine traits in a person.

Benary effect. The most commonly used variant of this effect is shown in the illustration below. Although the two grey triangles have the same length of contour adjacent to white, the lower triangle is seen as darker than the upper. It is difficult to explain this effect in terms of brightness contrast. The most likely explanation is that the observer sees the upper triangle as belonging to the black cross and the lower one as belonging to the white background.

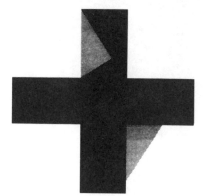

Benary effect

Bender-Gestalt test. A test in which the subject copies geometrical figures in each of which the components are grouped according to Gestalt LAWS OF GROUPING. The tests are thought to measure personality characteristics as well as visuo-motor ones; they have been used to assess both functional and organic disorders.

beneceptor. An obsolete term for a receptor for pleasant or beneficial stimuli.

Benham's top. A disc that is half black and half white, with black concentric arcs of different radii drawn on the white half. When the disc is rotated in white light the arcs produce different periods of alternating black and white on the eye, and for unknown reasons the observer sees different hues in the different rings.

Bennett Mechanical Comprehension Test. A test of mechanical and engineering aptitude.

Benton Visual Retention Test. A test in which people are asked to copy geometric figures after being shown them for a brief time: it is sometimes used to assess brain damage.

Benussi ring. The phenomenon that a continuous grey annulus or ring, half of which lies on a black background and half on a white, shows no effect of contrast and appears to be the same shade of grey throughout.

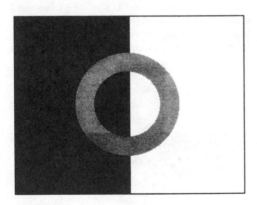

Benussi ring

Benzedrine. A trade name for D-AMPHETAMINE.

benzodiazepines. A group of minor tranquillizers and sedative drugs that are dopamine antagonists. They are in widespread use, and include those having the trade-names Librium, Mogadon, and Valium.

Berger rhythms. A synonym for BRAIN WAVES.

Bernoulli distribution. A synonym for BINOMIAL DISTRIBUTION.

Bernreuter Personality Inventory. A personality questionnaire containing 125 items; the responses yield scores on six scales (e.g. self-sufficiency, sociability).

beta (β). 1. (Statistics) The probability of making a TYPE II ERROR. *Contrast* ALPHA. 2. (Signal detection theory) *See* RESPONSE CRITERION.

beta adrenergic receptor. *See* ADRENERGIC RECEPTOR.

beta-alanine. An amino acid thought to be an inhibitory neurotransmitter.

beta alcoholism. *See* ALCOHOLISM.

beta blocker, beta blocking agent. Any ANTAGONIST (3) that blocks the beta ADRENERGIC RECEPTOR.

beta conditioning. *See* ALPHA CONDITIONING.

beta motion. A synonym for OPTIMAL APPARENT MOTION.

beta motor neuron. A comparatively rare motor neuron that innervates muscles giving a slow twitch.

beta response. *See* ALPHA RESPONSE.

beta waves. The high frequency (about 20 Hz), low amplitude brain waves occurring in an alert state.

between-brain. A synonym for DIENCEPHALON.

between-group variance. The variance due to differences between the scores of different groups. *Contrast* WITHIN-GROUP VARIANCE.

between-subjects design. An experimental design in which different subjects are run under different conditions. *Contrast* WITHIN-SUBJECTS DESIGN.

Betz cells. Giant pyramidal cells whose cell bodies are in the fifth layer of the motor cortex and which synapse with motor neurons in the spinal cord.

Bezold–Brücke effect. The phenomenon that when the distribution of wavelengths in a visual stimulus stays fixed but the luminance changes, small alterations occur in the perceived hue; with increasing intensity, red and green tend to shift towards blue and yellow.

B fibres. *See* NERVE FIBRE.

bibliophobia. A morbid fear of books or reading, common among university students.

biconditional. (Logic) A connective in the propositional calculus expressing 'if and only if . . . '. 'If and only if p, then q' is only true when p and q are both true or when they are both false.

bidirectional activation models. Theories of pattern recognition that postulate both TOP-DOWN and BOTTOM-UP processing.

Bidwell effect. The phenomenon that when a black colour wheel with a coloured sector is rotated, the observer sees the complementary colour.

Bidwell's ghost. A synonym for PURKINJE IMAGE.

Big Five System. The hypothesis that five main factors contribute to personality – namely extraversion (or surgency), agreeableness, conscientiousness, neuroticism (or emotional stability) and openness to experience.

bilabial. (Phonetics) Pertaining to a speech sound (e.g. [p], [b], [m]) articulated with the lips initially closed. *See also* ARTICULATION.

bilateral. Having to do with both sides of the body.

bilateral transfer. The transfer of training (or of other psychological effects, like adaptation or an aftereffect) from one side of the body to another or from one hemisphere to the other; e.g. practice on a task with one hand usually transfers to the other, and some aftereffects produced by stimulation of one eye may be observed with the other.

bilingual. Speaking two languages fluently, both of which were learned early in life.

bimodal distribution. (Statistics) A frequency distribution which shows two peaks, indicating that the scores tend to cluster around two separate values.

binary. Having two and only two exclusive states.

binary arithmetic. A form of arithmetic in which only two digits (0 and 1) are used. The numbers 0, 1, 2, 3, 4, 5 in decimal notation become 0, 1, 10, 11, 100, 101 in binary notation. Because digital computers use binary elements, numbers are represented in binary form in computer hardware.

binary digit. Either of the two digits 0 or 1, used in BINARY ARITHMETIC.

binary hue. Any hue that is not a UNIQUE HUE, i.e. any hue that can be regarded as a mixture of two other hues; e.g. orange looks like a mixture of red and yellow.

binaural. Pertaining to both ears. In psychology it is used of a stimulus that is presented to both ears rather than just to one, and when both ears function together. *Compare* DICHOTIC and *contrast* MONAURAL.

binaural beat. The periodic increase in apparent loudness that occurs when two low-frequency tones are presented one to each ear; it occurs when the peaks of the two sound waves are in synchrony.

binaural fusion. *See* AUDITORY FUSION.

binaural masking level difference (PMLD, MLD). The difference in amplitude threshold (in dB) between the case where a signal and a mask have the same phase and amplitude on both ears and the case where the phase and/or amplitude of the signal and mask are different on the two ears.

binaural ratio. The ratio between the intensities of the sounds reaching each ear.

binaural shift. Periodic changes in the apparent localization of sound, occurring when two low frequency sounds close together in frequency are presented one to each ear; it is caused by variation in the phase of the wave peaks of the sounds.

binaural summation. The increase in loudness of a sound when sent to two ears rather than just to one. The loudness threshold is about 3 dB lower for binaural than for monaural presentation.

binding. 1. (Neurophysiology) The attachment of a neurotransmitter molecule to a RECEPTOR (2). 2. (Linguistics) *See* GOVERNMENT AND BINDING PRINCIPLE.

binding affinity. The degree to which a neurotransmitter (or chemically similar substance) has the capacity to attach to a post-synaptic RECEPTOR (2).

binding problem. (Vision) The difficulty of discovering the method by which separately detected features (e.g. edge orientation, colour, motion, depth) of an object or part of a scene are put together to form a complete representation. The same problem occurs in other modalities, but the term has so far been limited to vision.

Binet scale, Binet–Simon scale. The first (1903) intelligence test for children.

binge eating. The periodic consumption of huge meals; it occurs in BULIMIA.

binocular. Pertaining to both eyes, especially to vision when both eyes are functioning together. *Compare* DICHOPTIC and INTEROCULAR.

binocular column. Any slab of cells in the visual cortex that receives an input mainly from one eye; alternate slabs receive an input from alternate eyes. *Compare* HYPERCOLUMN.

binocular disparity. The difference in the positions to which a point in space projects on each eye. In general all points farther away or nearer than the fixation point are horizontally displaced on one eye relative to the other; it is this cue that yields stereoscopic vision. Points nearer than the fixation point yield **crossed disparity**, i.e. in the visual field they are displaced relatively to the right when seen by the left eye and to

the left when seen by the right eye. Points more distant than the fixation point yield **uncrossed disparity**, i.e. in the visual field they are displaced relatively to the left for the left eye and to the right for the right eye.

binocular fusion. Combining retinal images that fall on disparate points on the eyes into a single percept, rather than seeing a double image or suppressing one image.

binocular rivalry. The restriction of perception to the image falling on one eye when very different images (not images merely containing binocular disparity) are presented to the whole or parts of each eye; when the images are different over the whole eye, some parts are usually visible with one eye and others with the other, and the parts seen with each eye keep changing. *Contrast* BINOCULAR FUSION.

binocular summation. The effect of stimulating the same area of each retina with light of the same or different BRIGHTNESS. Above threshold, the apparent brightness is very approximately an average of the brightness on each eye. *See* FECHNER'S PARADOX.

binocular suppression. Failure to perceive part or all of an image on one eye caused by there being a different image on the other eye. *See* BINOCULAR RIVALRY.

binomial distribution. (Statistics) The probability of a given event occurring x times when there are N independent occasions on which it might occur with x taking values from 0 to N, with the probability of the event occurring remaining the same on all trials. Thus if a dice was tossed 100 times, the binomial distribution would give the probability of a six occurring a given number of times (from 0 to 100). With large samples the distribution approximates to the normal distribution.

bioacoustics. The study of auditory communication in animals other than man.

bioamines. A synonym for BIOGENIC AMINES.

biochemical antagonism. *See* ANTAGONIST (3).

biochemistry. The study of the chemical structure and chemical interactions of living matter and of their function.

bioenergetics. 1. (Biology) The study of how living things, particularly cells, capture and store energy and use it to do work. 2. A form of psychotherapy derived from Reich and developed by Lowen which stresses freedom of movement and expression and which uses bodily exercises.

bioengineering. The study of the interface between people and their artifacts undertaken with a view to improving the efficiency with which the artifacts are used, e.g. by redesigning them.

biofeedback. The attempt to teach people to control their internal activities (such as heart rate) by feeding back to them information about the current state of the activity in question; although used in therapy, the value of the technique is disputed and it is not known how far people can learn to regulate their internal activities in this way.

biofunctional therapy. Any form of psychotherapy in which treatment is primarily aimed at putting right bodily functioning (e.g. BIOENERGETICS).

biogenetics. The study of heredity and the mechanisms through which new species evolve.

biogenic. 1. Pertaining to the replication of living things. 2. Pertaining to behaviour produced by biological rather than psychological factors.

biogenic amines. Any AMINE produced by living matter. Three groups of biogenic amines are neurotransmitters – CATECHOL-AMINES, INDOLEAMINES, and IMIDAZOLE-AMINES (all are MONOAMINES).

biological clock. Any internal mechanism controlling the frequency of a biological rhythm.

biological drive. A synonym for PHYSIO-LOGICAL DRIVE.

biological intelligence. *See* INTELLIGENCE.

biological noise. A synonym for INTRINSIC NOISE.

biological rhythm. Any recurrent change in the physiology or behaviour of an organism that occurs with a regular period, e.g. the menstrual cycle or circadian rhythm.

biomedical engineering. The development of prostheses and other devices to help handicapped or otherwise impaired people.

biometry, biometrics. 1. The use of statistical techniques to study biological (or psychological) phenomena, particularly the similarities and differences between different forms of life. 2. The study of factors that may affect the duration of life.

bionics. The study of physiological or behavioural mechanisms in organisms in order to use similar mechanisms in machines, particularly in computers.

bionomics. The study of the relationship between organisms and their environment.

biophysics. The application of the principles of physics to the study of the function of a cell or organ, e.g. nerve impulse transmission.

biopsychology. The study of the effects of the internal environment (e.g. hormones) on behaviour.

biorhythm. A synonym for BIOLOGICAL RHYTHM.

biosocial. Pertaining to the interaction of biological and social processes in determining behaviour (e.g. feeding behaviour).

biosphere. That part of the earth (including oceans and atmosphere) in which there are living organisms.

biotope. An area providing a particular kind of environment (e.g. rain forest), which may contain different ecological niches.

biotransport. (Physiology) A synonym for TRANSPORT.

biotype. A class of people having the same or a similar genetic make-up.

biotypology. The systematic study and classification of the physical and psychological characteristics of people. Biotypology is based on the PHENOTYPE not the GENOTYPE. *Contrast* BIOTYPE.

bipolar. Having two opposite poles, used e.g. of opposing personality traits or of electrodes.

bipolar affective disorder. *See* MANIC-DEPRESSIVE DISORDER.

bipolar cell. A neuron with two processes extending in opposite directions from the cell body, found as second-order neurons in the retina. They have only a graded potential and do not produce spikes. Other nerve cells are sometimes called bipolar cells since they also have two processes, but they all produce spikes.

bipolar manic-depressive disorder. *See* MANIC-DEPRESSIVE DISORDER.

birth trauma. (Psychoanalysis) The putative shock caused by being born; it is thought by some (e.g. Rank) to be the origin of all neurotic anxiety.

bisection, method of. A psychophysical scaling method in which the subject selects (or adjusts) a stimulus to appear half-way between two other stimuli, thus producing an INTERVAL SCALE.

biserial correlation. (Statistics) Often used as short for POINT-BISERIAL CORRELATION. There is also a **continuous biserial correlation** in which it is assumed that both variables are continuous, but one has been reduced to two categories. The correlation assumes that the dichotomized variable is normally distributed.

bisexuality. 1. The quality of being sexually attracted to members of both sexes. 2. The possession of the physical or psychological characteristics of both sexes. *Compare* ANDROGYNY and HERMAPHRODITE.

bistable. Any device with two, and only two, stable states; its states can be used to represent the binary digits 0 and 1.

bit (H). A term for INFORMATION THEORY that is short for BINARY DIGIT. The bit is the unit used to measure information. One bit represents a choice between two equally probable alternatives; two bits can therefore specify one of four alternatives A, B, C, D since it takes one bit to choose between AB and CD and another to choose a letter within the pair selected.

bite bar. A hollow mould of a subject's teeth on which he may be requested to bite in order to keep his head completely still during an experiment.

bivariate. Having two variables.

blackboard models. Models of cognitive processes, particularly ones cast as computer programs, in which the decisions made are based on the evidence supplied to a 'blackboard' by a number of specialist processes, whose activities are directed by a supervisory program in the light of the current state of the evidence. It is a method for putting together evidence from several different sources. *See also* HEARSAY.

black box. An imaginary object whose outputs are determined by its inputs and whose internal mechanisms cannot be directly examined. To attempt to discover the logical circuitry of the brain by studying stimuli and behaviour is to treat the organism as a black box.

Blacky pictures. A projective test in which pictures of dogs playing human roles are shown to children, who are asked to make up a story about each picture.

blanchophobia. Pathological fear of snow.

blank trial. 1. A trial in an experiment whose results will not be scored; it is usually introduced to ensure that the subject is paying attention. 2. A trial in which the subject is given no knowledge of results interspersed among trials where knowledge of results is given.

blastocyst. The mammalian embryo early in development (up to about two weeks in humans), when it is merely a mass of cells with a yolk sac.

bleaching. The loss of hue in a photopigment caused by the absorption of photons.

blending. 1. (Reading) The process of teaching a child to read by putting together the phonemes represented by individual letters; e.g. D-O-G is pronounced 'dog'. 2. (Linguistics) The co-occurrence of linguistic elements or their parts which cannot occur together according to the rules of a language. E.g. 'brunch' (from 'lunch' plus 'breakfast').

blind alley. An arm of a maze that leads only to a dead end.

blind judgements. Judgements carried out by an experimenter or co-worker without knowing to what conditions the items to be judged belong; e.g. in a clinical trial of the efficacy of different treatments, the patients' mental state might be evaluated by someone who did not know what treatment each had received. *See also* DOUBLE-BLIND PROCEDURE.

blind-matching technique. A technique by which the experimenter or others match parts of the data without knowing the crucial circumstances under which they were obtained. For example, an aphasic might be asked to repeat a list of words and might give words, which though not the words presented, appeared to be related to them. To decide whether there was a genuine relation, independent judges might be presented with the stimulus and response lists, each in scrambled order, and asked to form the pairs that seemed most similar in meaning: if there is a positive correlation between the judges' matches and the subject's responses to each word, then he is not responding randomly.

blindsight. The capacity to discriminate and respond to stimuli projected to a SCOTOMA without there being any conscious visual experience.

blind spot. A synonym for OPTIC DISC.

Bliss symbols. A logographic system that uses pictorial symbols. It can be taught to some non-verbal children who can then communicate in it.

Bloch's law. The law that the threshold for a small, brief (less than about 0.1 sec) flash of light is determined by its brightness multiplied by its duration. *Compare* BUNSEN–ROSCOE LAW.

block. In an experimental design a series of trials that are treated as a unit, either because a longer time gap occurs between blocks than between trials within a block, or because the experimental conditions are the same within a block but differ between blocks.

block design. 1. An experimental design in which subjects are divided into blocks, each of which contains the same number of subjects of each of a number of types. E.g. subjects might be equally divided into blocks according to sex and age and a different experimental condition would be run on each block. 2. An experimental design in which all conditions are given to all subjects, but over a block of trials a single condition is given to an individual subject. This design means that the subject knows what to expect on each trial within each block; in a **mixed-list design**, different conditions are given randomly to subjects from trial to trial.

block-design test. An intelligence test in which the testee is presented with an array of blocks which he has to copy using other blocks; it is used, e.g., as a subtest in the WAIS.

block diagram. A synonym for BAR CHART or HISTOGRAM, and sometimes used for FLOW CHART.

blocking. 1. (Conditioning) The reduced conditioning that occurs to a conditioned stimulus (CS_1) when it is presented simultaneously with a second conditioned stimulus (CS_2), to which conditioning has already taken place, as compared to the greater conditioning that occurs to CS_1 if it is presented with CS_2 from the outset of training. *Compare* OVERSHADOWING. 2. An inability to continue speaking that causes the speaker to stop suddenly. 3. An inability to recall a word that one is familiar with.

block sampling. Sampling in which the population is divided into separate categories (e.g. by social class), and a percentage of members of each category is sampled according to its frequency in the population as a whole.

blood alcohol concentration (BAC). The concentration in millilitres of alcohol per litre of blood.

blood–brain barrier. A membrane between blood-vessels and the central nervous system that is permeable by certain molecules but not by others.

blood sugar level. The proportion of glucose in the blood, normally about 80–100 milligrams per 100 millilitres.

Bloom's taxonomy. A classification of the mind into cognitive, affective, and psychomotor domains.

blue. *See* SPECTRAL HUE.

blue cone. *See* CONE.

blue–green. *See* SPECTRAL HUE.

blue–yellow blindness. A synonym for TRITANOPIA.

blunting. Dealing with a stressful situation by trying to distract oneself from it, e.g. by doing mental arithmetic during dental treatment. *Contrast* MONITORING, which is an inferior strategy.

body adjustment test (BAT). A small room is tilted clockwise or counterclockwise around the subject. The experimenter tilts his chair: the test is for the subject to reset it to the gravitational upright. It is used as a test of FIELD DEPENDENCE. Field-dependent people tend to set the chair away from the gravitational upright in the direction of the tilt of the room.

body build index. A measure introduced by Eysenck of body build, based on the ratio of height to chest circumference. *See also* EURYMORPHY, LEPTOMORPHY, and MESOMORPHY.

body-centred judgement, bodycentric judgement. *See* EGOCENTRIC JUDGEMENT.

body-centred therapy. Any psychotherapy that attempts to alter a person's personality or self-esteem by bodily training, e.g. BIOENERGETICS, ROLFING.

body image. A person's conscious image of his own body, his attitudes towards it, and his beliefs about how others see it. *Contrast* BODY SCHEMA.

body language. The information about a person's attitudes and emotions that he expresses, usually unconsciously, through his bodily posture and movements.

body schema. The stored information, mainly unconscious, that a person has about his bodily postures, which enables him to interpret incoming somatic information and to execute coordinated muscular movements. All motor skills must be based on the body schema, but little is yet known about it. *Contrast* BODY IMAGE.

body type. A category to which someone may be assigned in a scheme that classifies physique (e.g. ENDOMORPHY or PYKNIC TYPE). *Compare* CONSTITUTIONAL TYPE.

Bogardus social distance scale. *See* SOCIAL DISTANCE SCALE.

bogus pipeline. A bogus device intended to make subjects believe their attitudes are being accurately monitored.

boiler-makers' deafness. Loss of sensitivity to high-frequency tones caused by prolonged and intense exposure to them.

bolstering. The phenomenon that, after someone has chosen something, he tends to value it more highly than before the choice was made.

Boltzmann method. A synonym for ANNEALING.

bond. 1. (Learning theory) The putative link between a stimulus and response which results in a given response being made to a given stimulus. 2. (Social psychology) Any emotional attachment between people. Often used in a restricted sense to mean the forming of a close attachment between the mother and her newborn child.

bonding. Strong attachment to or dependence on another person, used particularly of a child's attachment to its mother.

bone conduction. The transmission of sound waves to the inner ear through the bones of the skull, which can mediate some hearing in people with damaged eardrums.

bony labyrinth. *See* LABYRINTH.

boomerang effect. A change in attitude in the opposite direction to that intended by someone attempting to persuade; it can result from crude or dogmatic attempts at persuasion.

bootstrapping. Constructing a programming routine or a set of ideas that is then used to develop more powerful routines or more elaborate thoughts; the whole of mathematics may be thought of as a bootstrapping operation, as too may language learning by children.

borderline. (Psychiatry) A term used by psychiatrists when they want to hedge their bets about whether the patient has a specific mental disorder.

borderline deficiency. *See* MENTAL DEFICIENCY.

borderline intelligence. The intelligence level at which a person is just able to function independently, sometimes defined as an IQ of between 70 and 84.

borderline personality disorder. (DSM-III) A very broad category in which are placed unstable people who cannot be allocated with certainty to any of the other personality disorders. According to DSM, it is a distinct clinical category in which should be placed people with prolonged mood swings, inability to form good relationships, inability to persevere, etc.

borderline schizophrenia. A condition in which a person, although liable to develop schizophrenia, is still in touch with reality, even though he may show some schizophrenic symptoms, particularly when under stress.

BOSS. Abbreviation for BASIC ORTHOGRAPHIC SYLLABIC STRUCTURE. It is the first part of a word that can be pronounced as a single syllable e.g. 'struct' in 'structure'.

Boston Diagnostic Aphasia Examination. A commonly used test to assess type and severity of aphasia.

bottom-up processing. (AI) Processing in which incoming information is analysed and transformed at successively higher levels, and where processing at one level is not affected by information supplied from higher levels. E.g. in vision, if lines and edges are extracted using only the information in the visual image, the processing would be bottom-up, but if a hypothesis of the object being viewed was used to help to recover lines and edges TOP-DOWN PROCESSING would be involved.

boulimia. An alternative spelling for BULIMIA.

boundary technique. (Psycholinguistics) A technique where a non-word or inappropriate word is placed at a given point in a text and is replaced by the appropriate word during the saccade the reader makes to that word; it is used to discover whether any information is gleaned about words falling on the parafovea.

bounded rationality. Knowingly taking a decision that is satisfactory but may not be optimal.

bound morpheme. A morpheme that cannot be used on its own but can make up a word when joined to another morpheme, e.g. '-ed' at the end of a verb. *Contrast* FREE MORPHEME.

bouton. Short for SYNAPTIC BOUTON.

bow-wow theory. The theory that language originated from emotional sounds.

boxology. The construction and ostentatious display of meaningless flow charts by psychologists as a substitute for thought.

BRAC. An abbreviation for BASIC REST-ACTIVITY CYCLE.

brachycephalic. Having a skull that is abnormally wide in relation to its length.

brachymetropia. A synonym for MYOPIA.

brachymorphy. A body type characterized by being short and broad.

bradyacusia. Poor hearing.

bradyarthria. Abnormally slow speech caused organically.

bradyglossia. Abnormally slow speech caused by a lesion of the tongue or mouth.

bradykinesia, bradykinesis. Making abnormally slow movements, a condition sometimes exhibited by schizophrenics.

bradylalia. Abnormally slow speech, whether of functional or organic origin, a condition that can occur in senile dementia, depression, etc.

bradylexia. Abnormally slow reading, when not caused by low intelligence.

bradylogia. Abnormally slow speech; the term is sometimes restricted to slowness that is organically caused, but it can also be used to include slowness caused functionally.

bradyphasia. A synonym for BRADYLALIA.

bradyphrenia. Abnormal slowness of thought.

bradypraxia. Abnormal slowness of action.

braidism. 1. An obsolete term for hypnosis. 2. Braid's theory of hypnosis.

brain. The mass of nervous tissue inside the skull, but excluding the peripheral nerves there. In mammals, it is split into three major divisions – FOREBRAIN, MIDBRAIN, and HINDBRAIN; these divisions are largely based on the way the brain develops in ontogeny from the NEURAL TUBE. The three major divisions are further divided into five: TEL-ENCEPHALON and DIENCEPHALON (making up the forebrain); MESENCEPHALON (the mid-brain); and METENCEPHALON and MYELENCEP-HALON (making up the hindbrain). *See* Appendices 1–5 for diagrams of brain structure.

brain localization. A synonym for LOCALIZA-TION OF FUNCTION.

brain potential. A synonym for BRAIN WAVES.

brain process theory. A synonym for IDEN-TITY THEORY OF MIND.

brain scan. Any non-invasive technique used to study brain function *in situ*, e.g. AUTO-RADIOGRAPHY.

brainstem. The MEDULLA (2), PONS, and MID-BRAIN, i.e. all the structures of the hindbrain and midbrain excluding the cerebellum.

brain stimulation. The excitation of a part of the brain by electrical stimulation.

brainstorming. The attempt, often uns-uccessful, to generate useful new ideas by encouraging a group to talk in an excited way and to express free associations and novel ideas, however disconnected from one another or from the main theme of the dis-cussion.

brainwashing. The attempt to make a prisoner change his views or confess by using a variety of techniques intended to break his confidence in himself, e.g. solitude, dark-ness, derision, and sometimes an alternation between cruel and kind inquisitors.

brain waves. The variation in the electrical activity of the brain, recorded through ex-ternal electrodes applied to the scalp. *See also* ELECTROENCEPHALOGRAPHY.

branching program. A form of programmed instruction in which the part of the program to which the student is directed after a given question depends on his answer to it (and sometimes to previous ones).

brand image. The way in which a product or brand is seen by potential users, including all the associations it evokes; marketing psy-chologists strive to give products an image that will appeal to potential customers.

brand loyalty. The extent to which someone using one or more products of a particular brand is reluctant to change to other brands.

b-reaction time. A COMPLEX REACTION TIME where one response is made to one stimulus, a different response to another. *Contrast* C-REACTION TIME.

breadth-first search. (AI) A search in which all nodes at one depth from the initial node are examined before proceeding to nodes at the next level down. *Contrast* DEPTH-FIRST SEARCH.

breadth of learning. The number of different stimuli or aspects of a situation that an organism learns about.

breakdown. Short for NERVOUS BREAKDOWN.

bridged junction. A synonym for GAP JUNCTION.

bridge principle. Principles used in the reduction of one theory to another; e.g. a definition that states that a given set of entities in one theory correspond to a given set of entities in another.

brief reactive psychosis. A syndrome lasting less than two weeks involving at least one psychotic symptom (e.g. delusions, incoherence), and triggered by a stressful event.

brief-stimuli technique. A form of ELECTRO-CONVULSIVE THERAPY in which each shock is very brief.

brightness. The apparent intensity of a visual stimulus. Except under special conditions brightness does not correlate in a simple way with the physical intensity of light. Thus a well-lit black surface may send more light to the eye than a badly lit white one, yet the latter may still be judged brighter. Moreover, the eye is differentially sensitive to light of different wavelengths. There is a tendency to use the term technically to mean the apparent intensity of light after the various wavelengths have been equated directly by HETEROCHROMATIC BRIGHTNESS MATCHING. *Compare* LUMINOSITY; *see also* LUMINANCE.

brightness constancy. The tendency to see a surface as the same shade of black, grey, or white, regardless of the intensity of the incident light and the orientation of the surface to the incident light; the term is misleading since it is not brightness that stays constant but apparent REFLECTANCE. It is sometimes called, more accurately, **whiteness constancy**.

brightness contrast. The tendency for a dark stimulus to look even darker than it is, or a bright stimulus to look even brighter when either is surrounded by, or adjacent to, the other.

brightness masking. The reduction in the visibility of a briefly presented visual stimulus caused by flashing a bright light, usually presented immediately (within 0.5 sec) after the target stimulus. Brightness masking does not show interocular transfer.

bril. A unit used in a subjective ratio scale of brightness; 100 bril corresponds to one millilambert.

Briquet's syndrome. A synonym for SOMATIZATION DISORDER.

Broca's aphasia. An EXPRESSIVE APHASIA in which a person has difficulty in speaking and writing, but may still have some understanding of language; it is caused mainly by lesions to BROCA'S AREA.

Broca's area. Brodmann's area 45 and parts of 44, 47, and 48; *see* Appendix 2. A region implicated in expressive language, lying in the lateral part of the FRONTAL LOBE just anterior to the PRECENTRAL GYRUS. *See also* BROCA'S APHASIA.

Broca–Sulzer effect. The phenomenon that the apparent brightness of a flash of a given luminance depends on its duration. For flashes in the photopic range, the brightness is maximal with a duration of about 40 msec.

Brodmann's areas. The areas (numbered 1–47) into which Brodmann divided the cerebral cortex on the basis of differences in the microscopic structure of the tissue in different areas.

bromide. A CNS depressant used to produce prolonged sedation and in treating epilepsy.

brontophobia. A morbid fear of thunder.

Brown–Peterson paradigm. An experimental technique in which on each trial the subject is given a few (e.g. three) items to remember, is then distracted for a period (usually by counting backwards), and finally has to recall the items. The technique is used to investigate proactive interference, since the items appearing on previous trials interfere with the recall of those appearing on subsequent trials.

Bruce effect. The blocking of pregnancy in a female mouse that is exposed to the odour of a male within two days of having copulated with a different male.

Brucke–Bartley effect. The phenomenon that a light flashing at about 10 Hz looks brighter than a steady light of the same luminance.

Brunswik faces. Schematic faces made up of lines representing the outline, eyes, lips, etc.; each part can differ in shape. They are used mainly in discrimination studies.

Brunswik ratio. A measure of constancy using the fomula $(A - R)/(S - R)$, where S is the standard to be matched, A is its appearance, i.e. the comparison stimulus picked as a match, and R is the match that would occur if the standard were judged solely in terms of its retinal characteristics. Thus suppose that in a size constancy experiment the standard is at 20 feet and is 2 feet high, the comparison is at 5 feet and a 1.5 foot high comparison is chosen, then the retinal size of the standard (R) at 2 feet is 0.5 (i.e. $2 \times 5/20$), and hence constancy is $(1.5 - 0.5)/(2 - 0.5) = 0.67$. A ratio of 0 represents no constancy, and a ratio of 1.0 complete constancy.

brute force. (AI) A technique for solving a problem in which all possible paths are explored and the successful one (or if more than one is successful, the shortest) is chosen; the alternative is to use HEURISTICS to guide the search for a solution. Computer chess programs tend to use more brute force than do people.

bruxism. Continual grinding of the teeth, usually during sleep.

B-type personality. *See* TYPE B PERSONALITY.

buccal. Pertaining to the cheek and mouth.

budget constraint. (Animal learning) The idea that for any schedule an animal will select a rate of responding that system-atically trades off the reward gained against freedom from responding (leisure).

buffer item. A synonym for FILLER MATERIAL.

buffer store. A store to hold data that are shortly to be sent elsewhere. It is needed if the locus to which they are being sent cannot receive them at the rate at which they are being input; in psychology, the term is often used to mean a temporary store.

buffoonery psychosis. A psychosis in which the patient acts the fool, often appearing to simulate mental derangement, although he is not in fact malingering.

bug. (Computing) An error in a program that stops it working.

bulbar. (Neuroanatomy) Pertaining to the MEDULLA OBLONGATA.

bulimia. A disorder in which a person repeatedly consumes vast quantities of food and drink ('binge eating'), which are often vomited up. Such binges may be followed by depression. Bulimia can be combined with anorexia.

bundle theory. The theory that a person is nothing more than the series of experiences he has in his life; these experiences are unified only by their causal connections, such as the connection between experiencing something and remembering the experience later. *Contrast* EGO THEORY.

Bunsen–Roscoe law. A law of photochemistry, stating that over a short period the number of pigment molecules bleached by incident light will be the same for a given number of quanta regardless of how they are distributed in time. *Compare* BLOCH'S LAW.

burnout. Emotional exhaustion, sometimes accompanied by depression, caused by attempting to help mentally disordered people or others under severe stress.

burnt. (Smell) Reminiscent of the smell of burning. 1. One of the six so-called primary odours in Henning's classification. *See* ODOUR PRISM. 2. One of the four basic odours of the CROCKER–HENDERSON SYSTEM.

bus. A pathway connecting the components of a computer.

bushy cell. A synonym for STELLATE CELL.

button. Short for SYNAPTIC BUTTON.

butyrophenone. A class of NEUROLEPTIC drugs, distinct from the phenothiazines; it includes haloperidol. It is a dopamine antagonist.

B wave. In the ELECTRORETINOGRAM a large positive wave that follows the brief negative **A wave** when a brief light is presented to the retina.

bystander effect. The phenomenon that the more people are around when someone needs help, the less likely a given person is to provide the help; each places the responsibility on the others.

byte. A specific number of bits (usually eight) stored in one location in a computer and treated as a single entity.

C

C. An abbreviation for 1. CONTROL CONDITION; 2. CONTINGENCY COEFFICIENT.

CA. An abbreviation for 1. CHRONOLOGICAL AGE; 2. CATECHOLAMINE.

cachexia, cachexis. Emaciation and weakness caused by malnutrition.

cachinnation. Inappropriate laughter: it can occur in e.g. HEBEPHRENIC SCHIZOPHRENIA.

cacodaemonomania, cacodemonomania. The delusion of being possessed by the devil or some other evil spirit.

cacogeusia. The illusion or hallucination of a nasty taste; it can occur in e.g. IDIOPATHIC EPILEPSY.

cacophoria. A feeling of unhappiness. *Contrast* EUPHORIA.

cafeteria feeding. A technique in which organisms are allowed to choose among a number of different foods. It is used to discover whether they will select a balanced diet or a diet that will correct an existing deficiency.

caffeine. An alkaloid that is a mild CNS stimulant; it is found in tea and coffee.

CAI. An abbreviation for COMPUTER ASSISTED INSTRUCTION.

CAL. An abbreviation for COMPUTER ASSISTED LEARNING.

calcarine cortex. The cortex surrounding the CALCARINE FISSURE, i.e. the STRIATE CORTEX.

calcarine fissure, calcarine sulcus. The fissure running roughly horizontally along the medial surface of the occipital lobe, in and around which the striate cortex is located. *See* Appendix 2.

calcium. A metal whose ions (positively charged) are admitted to the interior of a nerve cell when the CALCIUM CHANNELS are opened. Calcium is thought to be implicated in LONG-TERM POTENTIATION and the synaptic changes underlying learning.

California F scale. *See* F SCALE.

callosal gyrus. A synonym for CINGULATE GYRUS.

callosal sulcus. A fissure between the corpus callosum and the cingulate gyrus. *See* Appendix 2.

callosum. Short for CORPUS CALLOSUM.

caloric nystagmus. Nystagmus caused by placing hot or cold water in an ear, which stimulates vestibular receptors thus causing a VESTIBULO-OCULAR REFLEX.

calorie. A measurement of heat; one calorie is the amount of heat required to raise one gram of water at 18 °C by 1 °C; it is not part of the SI system. *Contrast* JOULE.

calpain. A hypothetical enzyme thought by some to erode the membrane of the postsynaptic cell, thus exposing more receptors and mediating the changes underlying learning.

cAMP. An abbreviation for CYCLIC ADENOSINE MONOPHOSPHATE.

campimetry. The measurement of the

extent of a person's visual field, usually by using a perimeter.

canalization. 1. Directing a drive (particularly the libido) toward a particular goal that is more specific than the range of possible goals for the drive. 2. More generally, confining a variable behaviour pattern to a less varied one.

cancellation method. (Hearing) The measurement of the loudness of a combination tone by delivering a real tone of the same frequency but 180° out of phase (a **cancellation tone**), and adjusting its intensity to the point where the combination tone is no longer heard.

cancellation test. A test in which someone is required to cancel certain symbols, e.g. the letter 'e' whenever it appears in a text.

cancellation theories. Theories to explain why no movement of the world is seen when the eyes are moved by a SACCADE. **Outflow theory** holds that the movement is cancelled by a corollary signal to the brain from the efferent output to the eye muscle. This theory is more likely to be correct than **inflow theory**, which holds that cancellation is effected by feedback from the eye muscles.

cancellation tone. *See* CANCELLATION METHOD.

candela (cd). The basic unit of LUMINOUS INTENSITY. It is equivalent to 1/683 watts per steradian at a wavelength of 540 nm. *See* PHOTOMETRY.

candela per square metre. The standard unit of LUMINANCE, being the amount of light reflected from one square metre of a perfectly diffusing and reflecting surface, illuminated by light of one candela per square metre (or equivalently by the light from an INTERNATIONAL CANDLE at a distance of one metre). *See* PHOTOMETRY.

candle. Short for INTERNATIONAL CANDLE.

candlepower. A synonym for LUMINOUS INTENSITY.

cannabis. The hemp plant, *Cannabis sativa*, from which HASHISH and MARIJUANA are derived.

Cannon–Bard theory, Cannon's theory. The hypothesis that the type of emotion felt depends on the pattern of stimulation sent from thalamus to cortex, while the bodily expression of emotion is governed by the efferent output from the thalamus. *Compare* JAMES–LANGE THEORY.

cannula. A hollow tube that can be of very small diameter, used to apply drugs selectively to small regions of the brain or body; it can also be used to remove fluids for analysis.

capillary. A very small blood-vessel.

caprylic. *See* CROCKER–HENDERSON SYSTEM.

carbachol. A compound having similar effects on the nervous system to ACETYLCHOLINE.

cardinal traits. Allport's term for those traits in an individual that are strongest, i.e. that affect the broadest range of his behaviour. *Compare* CENTRAL TRAITS AND SECONDARY TRAITS.

cardiophobia. A morbid fear of cardiac problems.

card sorting test. A test in which a pack of cards has to be sorted into separate piles according to the symbols each card bears.

CARE. An acronym standing for the three qualities thought to be required in a client-centred therapist, namely, *C*ommunicated *A*uthenticity, *R*egard, *E*mpathy (or genuineness, warmth, and understanding).

carotid arteries. The two large arteries conveying blood to the brain, head, and neck.

Cartesian. Pertaining to Descartes's theories, particularly to his advocacy of DUALISM.

Cartesian coordinates. A system for specifying where a point is located in an *n*-dimensional space by specifying its location in terms of the coordinates of its position on *n* axes at right angles to one another (in two-dimensional graphs they are conventionally called the x-axis and y-axis). *Contrast* POLAR COORDINATES.

case. (Linguistics) A grammatical category applying to nouns and pronouns (and adjectives when agreement is marked by inflection). The case of a word is determined by whether it is subject (e.g. 'he'), object ('him'), vocative ('you'), indirect object ('him'), genitive ('his') and by the preposition governing it.

case grammar. A grammar in which the elements are categorized according to their semantic role, which in the case of noun phrases is given by their semantic relationship to the verb. Some suggested case categories are **agentive case** (the person or thing who did the action), **instrumental case** (the thing with which the action was done), **locative case** (the place at which the action was done), and **objective case** (the person or thing to whom the action was done). E.g. in the sentence 'The *man* hit the *nail* with a *hammer*', the three nouns are respectively agentive, objective, and instrumental. Both in 'The door opened' and in 'The door was opened', the door is objective. Case grammars are unlikely to provide an adequate description of any natural language, but since they help to make semantics transparent they have been used in some AI programs designed to take a natural language input.

case study. The detailed study of an individual case, whether of a patient or of management within a firm, etc.

castration complex. (Psychoanalysis) A neurotic fear of castration, supposed to be caused in men by anxiety about losing something they have, and in women by anxiety about having already lost it.

CAT. An abbreviation for 1. COMPUTERIZED AXIAL TOMOGRAPHY; 2. COMPUTER OF AVERAGED TRANSIENTS; 3. CHILDREN'S APPERCEPTION TEST.

catabolism. The breakdown of the body's tissue and the expenditure of its stored energy. *Compare* ANABOLISM. *See also* METABOLISM.

catagelophobia. A morbid fear of ridicule.

catalepsy. A state in which the muscles are partly rigid, and in which the person maintains any pose in which he is placed, occurring e.g. in CATATONIC SCHIZOPHRENIA, under hypnosis, or through brain damage.

catalexia. A form of DYSLEXIA in which the same words or phrases are read repeatedly.

catalogia. Prolonged repetition of meaningless words; it can occur in schizophrenia.

catalyst. (Chemistry) A substance that increases the rate of a chemical reaction while not being permanently changed itself.

catalytic agent. In group psychotherapy, a member who promotes CATHARSIS in the others.

catamnesis. (Medicine) The history of a patient *after* recovering from an illness. *Contrast* ANAMNESIS (2).

cataphasia. A synonym for CATALOGIA.

cataphora. The use of a word or expression to refer to the meaning of a word or expression that will occur later in the discourse; 'As *he* breakfasted, John read the paper'.

cataplexy. Sudden loss of muscle tone, resulting in collapse, caused e.g. by violent anger or strong anxiety.

cataract. An illness in which the lens of the eye becomes opaque, resulting eventually in blindness. Cataract is common in old age, but it can also be congenital.

catarrhines. Old World anthropoids including the anthropoid apes, Old World monkeys, and hominids; they have nostrils set close together and opening to the front of the face. *Compare* PLATYRRHINES.

catastrophe theory. A recently developed branch of mathematics designed to analyse sudden changes of state; e.g. the surface of a three-dimensional graph may contain sudden drops so that the x coordinate-value changes abruptly as the y and z coordinate-values change continuously. Unsuccessful attempts have been made to apply the theory to psychological phenomena such as anorexia.

catastrophic reaction. Goldstein's term for an outbreak of panic in the brain-injured on realizing their own incapacity. The patient often becomes unresponsive, and will refuse to undertake tasks and tests even when he has the necessary capacity for them.

catathymic amnesia. A synonym for EPISODIC AMNESIA.

catatonia. A severe disturbance of muscular tonus that may involve muscular rigidity, catalepsy, or overactivity; it is functionally caused.

catatonic schizophrenia. Schizophrenia accompanied by CATATONIA; the patient may hold any position in which he is placed for hours or days, and be mute and wholly withdrawn from the environment.

catchment area. The region served by a hospital or other such institution.

catch trial. A trial included in some psychophysical methods for determining the absolute threshold in which no stimulus is presented. The results from such trials can be used to estimate the subject's bias towards making positive response.

catch-up saccade. See SACCADE.

catecholamine hypothesis. The theory that depression is caused by abnormally low levels of CATECHOLAMINES, such as norepinephrine, in the brain.

catecholaminergic. Pertaining to conduction across a synapse mediated by catecholamine transmitters or related substances.

catecholamines . (CAs). A group of monoamines that act as NEUROTRANSMITTERS in parts of the central nervous system and autonomic system; they have a six-carbon ring with hydroxyl groups attached. They are implicated in the regulation of mood.

They include DOPAMINE, EPINEPHRINE, and NOREPINEPHRINE. See also BIOGENIC AMINES.

catechol-o-methyl-transferase (COMT). An enzyme that degrades extracellular catecholamines. Compare MONOAMINE OXIDASE.

categorical differentiation. The exaggeration of the differences between the members of two categories.

categorical grammar. A grammar restricted to defining categories (e.g. noun phrase, sentence, relative clause) and to specifying rules for how these categories can be put together grammatically.

categorical memory. A synonym for SEMANTIC MEMORY.

categorical perception. Perceiving stimuli in categories rather than as a continuum. E.g. hues are seen as distinct categories, although the underlying physical dimension (wavelength) is a continuum; again with continuous variations in VOICE-ONSET TIME either a /b/ or /p/ may be heard but not something in between. In general, discrimination tends to be better at the boundary between two categories than it is in the middle of a category.

categorical scale. A synonym for NOMINAL SCALE.

categorical syllogism. See SYLLOGISM.

categorical variable. A variable that does not have continuous values, but is based on division into classes, e.g. being a man or a woman, or belonging to social class A, B, C, D, or E.

category. 1. A confusing term. In general, it stands for the class of subclasses into each of which items are classified. E.g. voice is a category of verbs, with subclasses active and passive; sex is a category with subclasses male and female. Unfortunately in everyday life and also in much science, the term is also used to stand for the subclass to which an item belongs, e.g. the category of active voice or that of male. 2. See NATURAL CATEGORY.

category method. A method of psychophysical scaling in which the subject is asked to place each of many stimuli into one of several classes which he is to regard as equally spaced along a sensory continuum.

category scaling. Dividing stimuli or responses into categories to yield either a NOMINAL SCALE or an ORDINAL SCALE.

catharsis. The discharge of strong emotions, leaving a sense of peace; in psychoanalysis it is thought to be brought about by the recovery of repressed material, or by sudden insight into the self.

cathexis. (Psychoanalysis) Concentration of the libido on something, e.g. on the conscious self (EGO CATHEXIS), on a wish or fantasy, or on an external person, situation or thing (OBJECT CATHEXIS).

cathode. An ELECTRODE that is negatively charged relative to another with current flow between the two; it attracts CATIONS. *See also* ELECTROLYSIS. *Contrast* ANODE.

cathode ray tube. The screen where information is displayed in an OSCILLOSCOPE.

cation. A positively charged ion. *See also* CATHODE.

catotrophobia. A morbid fear of mirrors, especially of breaking one.

caudal, caudad. (Anatomy) Pertaining to the tail (or posterior) end of the body or nearer to that end than some other structure. When used of the brain in an upright species, it means toward the base. *Contrast* ROSTRAL.

caudate nucleus. A curved mass of grey matter that ends at the AMYGDALA and is part of the BASAL GANGLIA.

causalgia. Intense burning pain caused by injury to a peripheral nerve.

cautious shift. A decision made by a group that is more cautious than the decision that would have been made by the group members acting on their own. It is probably rarer than a RISKY SHIFT.

CBF. An abbreviation for CEREBRAL BLOOD FLOW TECHNIQUE.

CCC. An abbreviation for CONSONANT TRIGRAM.

CCK. An abbreviation for CHOLECYSTOKININ.

cd. An abbreviation for CANDELA.

CE. An abbreviation for CONSTANT ERROR.

ceiling effect. Failure to find a difference between the scores of different individuals or groups, when caused by the measurement scale used being insensitive to differences between very high scores; in the limiting case, all scores might be the maximum possible. *Contrast* FLOOR EFFECT.

cell. 1. (Biology) The smallest organized unit of the body that can survive *in vitro*, comprising an enclosing membrane, PROTOPLASM, and a NUCLEUS (1). In the context of the nervous system the term is often used to mean neuron. 2. (Mathematics) A compartment in an array or matrix.

cell assembly. A hypothetical collection of cells in the brain, containing re-entrant pathways through which neural impulses tend to reverberate after initial excitation of some of the cells. The concept was proposed by Hebb, who thought that learning occurred because the more often one cell fired another, the stronger the connection became: hence new cell assemblies are constructed. According to Hebb they are the basis of all mental activity. *See* PHASE SEQUENCE and REVERBERATORY CIRCUIT.

cell body. The part of a cell containing the NUCLEUS (1). Most neurons have a cell body that is anatomically clearly distinct from the rest of the cell. *See also* AXON and DENDRITE.

cell division. The splitting of a cell into two daughter cells.

cell membrane. A semi-permeable structure that surrounds the cell's PROTOPLASM and holds it in place; it is made up of layers of LIPIDS and PROTEINS.

cell nucleus. *See* NUCLEUS (1).

cellular differentiation. The process by which, in ONTOGENY, successive generations of cells become more and more specialized, e.g. in order to become liver cells, nerve cells, or nerve cells of a particular kind.

cenaesthesia, cenesthesia. Alternative spelling for COENAESTHESIA.

cenophobia. An alternative spelling for KAINOPHOBIA.

cenotophobia. An alternative spelling for KENOTOPHOBIA.

cenotrope, coenotrope. Any behaviour, whether innate or learned, that appears in all members of a species.

censor. (Psychoanalysis) The mechanism that shields the conscious EGO from access to anxiety-provoking material in the unconscious (i.e. in the ID or SUPEREGO).

centring. 1. Goldstein's term for a mental state in which the individual is in complete rapport with his environment. 2. A synonym for CENTRATION.

centile. A synonym for PERCENTILE (2), but sometimes used to mean PERCENTILE (1).

central aphasia. A synonym for SYNTACTICAL APHASIA.

central canal. The channel running through the middle of the SPINAL CORD that contains CEREBROSPINAL FLUID.

central conflict. (Psychoanalysis) Horney's term for the conflict between a person's TRUE SELF and the IDEALIZED SELF to which he aspires.

central deafness. Deafness caused by damage to the inner ear or higher structures in the auditory system.

central executive. A synonym for CENTRAL PROCESSOR (2).

central executive system. A hypothetical system which is part of working memory and which controls and coordinates the ARTICULATORY LOOP and the VISUOSPATIAL SCRATCHPAD. Note the overlap with CENTRAL EXECUTIVE and CENTRAL PROCESSOR (2). Almost all psychologists want to invent their

own terms, thus adding to the general confusion.

central fissure. The deep vertical groove in the cerebral cortex, separating the frontal and parietal lobes. *See* Appendix 1.

central grey. The unmyelinated grey nerve fibres in the central part of the spinal cord.

central inhibition. The active reduction of activity in any part of the central nervous system.

centralism. The doctrine that behaviour is determined endogenously by the central nervous system rather than by incoming stimulation.

central limit theorem. (Statistics) The theorem that for any population, regardless of how it is distributed, the means of samples of independent observations will increasingly tend to be normally distributed as the sample size increases.

central motivational state. The totality at any one time of the hypothetical driving forces generated endogenously within the organism, and not produced by sensory stimulation.

central nervous system (CNS). The part of the nervous systems that lies inside the brain and spinal cord. *Contrast* PERIPHERAL NERVOUS SYSTEM.

central nystagmus. Nystagmus caused by damage to the vestibular nerve or vestibular nuclei.

central processing unit (CPU). The unit in a computer that carries out operations on data in accordance with the program. It is usually taken to include closely associated units like the program counter, which keep track of the point reached in the program.

central processor. 1. Short for CENTRAL PROCESSING UNIT. 2. By analogy, the postulated unit in the brain that takes conscious decisions; it receives information from mechanisms below the level of consciousness, may control their functioning to some extent, and controls voluntary behaviour. Like the central processing unit of a computer it can only handle a small number of items simultaneously.

central state identity theory, central state materialism. The doctrine that psychological states are identical with brain states, and that psychological descriptions of a person are just another way of referring to his brain states. *See* IDENTITY THEORY OF MIND.

central sulcus. A synonym for CENTRAL FISSURE.

central tegmental nucleus. A synonym for RAPHE NUCLEUS.

central tegmental tract. A synonym for VENTRAL NORADRENERGIC BUNDLE.

central tendency. 1. (Statistics) The tendency for scores (or other numerical data) to cluster around a central value. There are different ways of specifying this value, each normally yielding a different result. *See* MEAN, MEDIAN, and MODE. 2. (Psychometrics) The tendency for people filling up rating scales to use the middle ratings rather than the extreme ones. 3. (Psychophysics) The tendency for people judging a stimulus to move their judgement towards the mean of the preceding series of stimuli.

central traits. 1. Allport's term for traits that affect a moderate range of a person's behaviour, but not as broad a range as CARDINAL TRAITS. *Compare* SECONDARY TRAITS. 2. Traits that make a strong impression on others, e.g. ebullience.

central vision. Vision using the FOVEA.

centration. (Piaget) 1. A vague term meaning concentration of attention on one part or aspect of a percept. Piaget thought it was responsible for perceptual distortions (e.g. visual illusions). 2. The egocentric standpoint of the young child, who sees everything only in relation to its own needs. *Contrast* DECENTERING.

centrencephalic epilepsy. Epilepsy with *grand mal* seizures and generalized features that cannot be attributed to a localized focus. It is thought to derive from a focus deep in the brain.

centrifugal. Pertaining to the conveyance of information from higher to lower points of the central nervous system, e.g. from cortex to thalamus or from midbrain to spinal cord. *Contrast* CENTRIPETAL.

centrifuge. A rotating device in which cells (or other materials) are fragmented and the pieces separated by their weight – the lighter the piece, the nearer the top it is thrown.

centripetal. Pertaining to the conveyance of information from lower to higher parts of the central nervous system. *Compare* CENTRIFUGAL.

centroid method. (Statistics) A method of factor analysis in which the vector representing a factor is made to pass through the centroid (or centre of gravity) of the test vectors.

centromedial thalamic nucleus. A thalamic nucleus receiving fibres from other areas of the thalamus and the cerebellum, projecting to the basal ganglia and midbrain, and involved in posture and equilibrium.

cephalad. A synonym for CEPHALIC.

cephalalgia. Headache.

cephalic. (Anatomy) Pertaining to the head, or head end, or toward the head.

cephalic index. A measure of head shape, obtained from the ratio of length to breadth.

cephalic phase reflexes. The reflex reactions to the ingestion and digestion of food, including salivation, insulin secretion, and vomiting.

cephalization. A synonym for ENCEPHALIZATION.

cephalocaudad development, cephalocaudal development. The early stages in the development of the embryo, which proceed from the head through the rest of the body. *Compare* PROXIMODISTAD DEVELOPMENT.

CER. An abbreviation for CONDITIONED EMOTIONAL RESPONSE.

cerebellar ataxia. A lack of coordination in voluntary movements caused by damage to the cerebellum.

cerebellar cortex. The outer part of the CERE-BELLUM, which contains three layers distinguished by differences in the cell structures found in each.

cerebellar peduncle. Any of three tracts connecting the CEREBELLUM and the BRAINSTEM.

cerebellar speech. Speech that is jerky, irregular, slurred, and often explosive; it is caused by cerebellar disorder, and is common in multiple sclerosis.

cerebellum. A large midbrain structure, located behind the brainstem and involved in the control of movement. It is bounded by a cortex made up of three layers – from out to in, the molecular layer, the Purkinje layer, and the granular layer. *See* Appendix 5.

cerebral angiography. X-raying the brain after injecting a dye opaque to X-rays; CEREB-RAL ARTERIOGRAPHY is an example of this technique.

cerebral aqueduct. The canal connecting the third and fourth ventricles.

cerebral arteriography. X-raying the brain after injecting a dye opaque to X-rays into the carotid artery, a technique that shows up the position of the blood-vessels and any distortions caused by damage or abnormalities.

cerebral blood flow technique (CBF). A technique for measuring blood flow at each point of the brain, by injecting a radioactive tracer into the blood and measuring its concentration in different regions. Since blood flow increases in areas where there is neuronal activity, it is possible to monitor which areas are active when the subject undertakes different tasks..

cerebral cortex. The outer greyish layer of the CEREBRUM, consisting of unmyelinated, densely packed neurons, which are arranged in CORTICAL LAYERS, and which communicate with one another mainly vertically. The cortex is classified in several ways: into four lobes (FRONTAL LOBE, OCCIPITAL LOBE, PARIETAL LOBE, TEMPORAL LOBE); by its evolutionary origins (ARCHICORTEX, NEOCORTEX, PALAEOCORTEX); or by its function (ASSOCIATION CORTEX, MOTOR CORTEX, PRIMARY CORTEX, SENSORY CORTEX).

cerebral dominance. The tendency for one hemisphere to be more involved in certain functions (particularly language) than the other; in most people the left hemisphere is dominant. It has, however, been discovered that what is conventionally called the dominant hemisphere (that controlling language and the hand used for preference) can be the non-dominant one for some other functions (e.g. certain spatial tasks).

cerebral hemisphere. Either of the two lobes of the TELENCEPHALON.

cerebral peduncle. A band of fibres on the ventral surface of the midbrain; it includes the CORTICOSPINAL TRACT.

cerebrospinal fluid (CSF). The fluid in the spinal canal, brain ventricles, and the subarachnoid space that carries nutrients, etc. to the central nervous system. It also acts as a cushion against impacts that might damage the brain.

cerebrotonia. A personality type (cerebral, sensitive, restrained) in Sheldon's constitutional theory, said to be associated with ECTOMORPHY.

cerebrum. The dorsal part of the brain, also known as the TELENCEPHALON, comprising the cerebral cortex, the underlying white matter, and the basal ganglia.

certainty effect. (Decision theory) *See* PROSPECT THEORY.

certify. (Psychiatry) To arrange a committal to a mental hospital.

cerveau isolée. A preparation produced by sectioning the cerebral hemispheres from the remainder of the brain in order to study the function of the midbrain and hindbrain.

cervical nerves. *See* SPINAL NERVES.

cervico-ocular response. Involuntary eye movements occurring when the head moves, and caused by stimulation of joint receptors in the neck. They tend to preserve eye fixation on its target.

C factor. One of the factors into which some think intelligence can be decomposed, namely, rapidity of thought.

CFF. An abbreviation for CRITICAL FUSION FREQUENCY.

C fibres. 1. Small unmyelinated afferent axons in the spinal cord that can give rise to dull long-lasting pain when stimulated. 2. Small slow-conducting afferent neurons innervating PACINIAN CORPUSCLES and involved in KINAESTHESIS. 3. Unmyelinated postganglionic axons of the autonomic nervous system. *See also* NERVE FIBRE.

chained schedule. A REINFORCEMENT SCHEDULE in which the organism has to complete two or more SIMPLE SCHEDULES (e.g. FR10, VI30) in succession before reward becomes available, and in which a signal is given to indicate which schedule is operating. *Compare* TANDEM REINFORCEMENT SCHEDULE.

chaining. 1. A synonym for CHAIN REFLEX. 2. *See* BACKWARD CHAINING and FORWARD CHAINING.

chain reflex. A series of responses in which the stimulus fed back from each response elicits the next. At one time it was mistakenly thought by some behaviourists to underlie the mechanisms of thought.

chance error. A synonym for VARIABLE ERROR.

chance-half correlation. A synonym for SPLIT-HALF CORRELATION.

chance level. (Statistics) A probability level obtained by a test statistic that is too high to reject the NULL HYPOTHESIS. Conventionally and arbitrarily a probability of below 0.05 is usually taken to indicate that a result is not due to chance.

chandelier cell. A type of neuron in the cerebral cortex that has multiple inhibitory synapses on the initial segments of pyramidal cells.

change over delay schedule (COD schedule). A REINFORCEMENT SCHEDULE with more than one operant, in which the availability of reinforcement is delayed for a period after the animal has switched from one operant to another.

channel. 1. In information theory, a physical system that transmits information from a transmitter to a receiver; the nervous system and its discrete parts are often also regarded as channels. 2. *See* ION CHANNEL.

channel capacity. The maximum number of BITS per unit of time that can be transmitted through a given information channel.

character analysis. (Psychoanalysis) The attempt, using analysis, to break through the CHARACTER ARMOUR to the inner self.

character armour. (Psychoanalysis) Reich's term for the defensive front that a person presents (often unconsciously) in order to conceal his inner self and protect his self-esteem; Reich thought one of the main tasks of psychoanalysis was to break through the character armour.

character disorder. The condition of having an abnormal and usually maladaptive personality, characterized e.g. by over-impulsiveness, insecurity, immaturity, compulsive gambling, or other features of which the therapist disapproves.

character neurosis. Another term for CHARACTER DISORDER, but perhaps carrying the implication of a more severe abnormality, although still less severe than a neurosis.

characterology. An obsolete term for the study of personality.

Charpentier's bands. The illusion of seeing black spokes on a white background when watching the rotation of a wheel containing a white sector on a black background.

Charpentier's illusion. A synonym for the SIZE–WEIGHT ILLUSION.

chemical antagonism. *See* ANTAGONIST (3).

chemical senses. Any sense served by CHEMORECEPTORS.

chemical synapse. A synapse in which the influence of the presynaptic cell on the post-synaptic cell is mediated by the discharge of a neurotransmitter, which passes across the synaptic cleft and attaches briefly to a receptor on the membrane of the postsynaptic cell, changing its membrane potential.

chemoreceptor. A receptor that transduces chemical stimuli into nerve impulses, as in taste and smell.

chemoreceptor trigger zone. Nerve cells of the MEDULLA OBLONGATA that are sensitive to toxic chemicals, and can cause vomiting.

chemotaxis. A synonym for CHEMOTROPISM.

chemotherapy. The attempt to alleviate illness, including mental illness, by administering drugs.

chemotropism. The control of an organism's orientation or motion by a chemical gradient in the environment.

chiaroscuro. The balance, particularly when dramatic or artistically subtle, of light and dark masses in a painting.

chiasm. *See* OPTIC CHIASM.

chief ray. The ray of light that goes along the PRIMARY LINE OF SIGHT.

child abuse. Sexual or other maltreatment of children. Its PREVALENCE is unknown since it is impossible to determine the veracity of its alleged victims.

childhood autism, childhood-onset pervasive development disorder. (DSM-III) Synonyms for EARLY INFANTILE AUTISM.

childhood schizophrenia. Schizophrenia occurring before the age of 11.

Children's Apperception Test (CAT). A projective test for children based on the THEMATIC APPERCEPTION TEST.

child with special needs. A synonym for SPECIAL CHILD that piles euphemism on euphemism.

chimaeric face, chimeric face. A picture of a complete face, made by putting together the left half of one face and the right half of another; if a split-brain subject fixates the middle of the picture, he sees one half face with one hemisphere and the other with the other.

chi square test (χ^2). A test mainly applied to contingency tables that has many uses, including the following: (i) assessing how well an observed frequency distribution fits a hypothetical distribution (the chi square goodness of fit test); (ii) assessing whether two observed frequency distributions differ significantly from one another (the chi square test of independence); (iii) comparing an observed sample variance with a hypothetical variance, in samples drawn from a normal population; (iv) combining the probabilities from a number of independent significance tests. Of all statistical tests, it is perhaps the most misused, e.g. by applying it to percentages instead of observed frequencies.

chlorolabe. A quaint name for the medium wavelength pigment, which is not yet chemically identified. *See* VISUAL PHOTOPIGMENT.

chlorpromazine. A neuroleptic drug belonging to the PHENOTHIAZINES, used as a major tranquillizer and for schizophrenia.

choice, method of. Any psychophysical method based on rank ordering items, e.g. the method of paired comparisons or the method of ranking (*see* PAIRED COMPARISONS, METHOD OF and RANKING, METHOD OF).

choice point. Any point in a maze at which the organism is confronted with two or more paths, or more generally any point at which a decision must be taken.

choice reaction time. A synonym for COMPLEX REACTION TIME.

choice shift. (Social psychology) A decision made by a group after discussion that differs from the decision that would have been made by most of the individual members. *Compare* CAUTIOUS SHIFT and RISKY SHIFT.

choice stimuli. Two or more stimuli between which an organism has to choose in performing a task (usually a learning task).

cholecystokinin (CCK). A peptide which appears to have many functions. It is produced by the gut to aid digestion and may cause satiety; in the brain it may be implicated in reinforcement and locomotion.

choleric. *See* HUMOUR (2).

cholinergic. Pertaining to transmission across a synapse mediated by ACETYLCHOLINE or related substances.

cholinergic drugs. Drugs that mimic the action of ACETYLCHOLINE.

cholinergic receptor. The site on the post-synaptic cell activated by a CHOLINERGIC substance. There are two kinds – MUSCARINIC RECEPTORS and NICOTINIC RECEPTORS.

cholinesterase. An enzyme that breaks down ACETYLCHOLINE.

cholinomimetic. Any substance that has similar effects to those of ACETYLCHOLINE.

chorda tympani. The part of the VESTIBULOACOUSTIC NERVE that carries taste fibres from the anterior two-thirds of the tongue.

chorea. A disorder characterized by jerky movements; it is usually caused by damage to the basal ganglia. *See also* HUNTINGTON'S CHOREA.

choroid, choroid coat. A membrane covering all the eyeball except the CORNEA, and lying between the SCLERA and the RETINA; it contains a dark pigment to prevent light being reflected back onto the retina.

choroid plexus. A structure running through the brain ventricles that produces spinal fluid from blood.

chroma. The SATURATION (1) and HUE of a colour.

chromaesthesia. The association of a colour with something non-visual, such as a day of the week or a passage of music.

chromatic. Pertaining to HUE.

chromatic aberration. Any distortion in an optical system caused by the fact that light of different wavelengths is refracted through different angles; since the human lens refracts light of low wavelength more than light of high wavelength, it is impossible to bring white light into perfect focus on the retina.

chromatic adaptation. Adaptation to a HUE caused by light producing that hue falling on the same part of the retina for some time; the hue loses saturation and a negative aftereffect occurs if achromatic light is subsequently projected to that part of the retina.

chromatic audition. A form of SYNAESTHESIA in which sounds evoke colours.

chromatic colour. Any colour having HUE, i.e. any colour except black, white, or grey.

chromatic dimming. A decrease in apparent saturation when the light intensity is reduced.

chromatic induction. The process that produces INDUCED COLOUR.

chromaticity. The apparent HUE and SATURATION (1) of a visual stimulus, as determined by the ratios of the intensities of its component wavelengths (but not by its overall intensity, though *see* CHROMATIC DIMMING).

chromatic response. A synonym for CHROMATIC VALENCE.

chromatic scale. (Music) A scale consisting entirely of semitones: thus it has twelve different notes to the octave.

chromatic valence. A method for determining the strength of a HUE produced by a given wavelength, by measuring the intensity of a complementary wavelength that must be added for the hue no longer to appear. E.g. to measure the amount of yellow in a test stimulus, short-wavelength light would be added until the yellow component disappears (e.g. until a yellow stimulus looks achromatic, or until an orange stimulus looks a whitish red).

chromatography. (Chemistry) A technique for separating the different molecules in a mixture of compounds; it depends on their differential tendency to dissolve in, or be absorbed by, a given substance.

chromatophore. A cell in the skin that carries a pigment that can be exposed or withdrawn, thus enabling animals such as frogs or octopuses to change their coloration.

chromatopsia. A visual abnormality in which achromatic objects appear to have hue.

chromatotropism. The tendency of an organism to orientate towards or away from a particular colour.

chromesthesia. A synonym for CHROMAESTHESIA.

chromophobia. A morbid fear of colour.

chromophore. The part of a photopigment molecule that absorbs light quanta. The term is sometimes used to mean RETINENE, but this is not strictly correct in that the retinene and OPSIN are chemically linked to form the whole photopigment molecule. The chromophore (derived from the Greek for 'colour bearing') appears coloured; since the colour depends on reflected light, the absorption spectrum is completely different.

chromopsia. A synonym for CHROMATOPSIA.

chromosomes. Strands in the cell nucleus, each comprising two molecules of DNA, that carry the genes; in humans there are 23 pairs, the two members of each pair being derived one from each parent. *See also* X CHROMOSOME and Y CHROMOSOME.

chronaxie. 1. The time taken by a nerve cell to fire when stimulated by a current of twice the threshold intensity. 2. The length of time to produce a sensation (hot, cold, pressure, or pain) by stimulating a small area of skin with a current of twice the threshold strength.

chronic. Long lasting (particularly of illness). *Contrast* ACUTE.

chronic alcoholism. A tautology – all alcoholism is chronic.

chronic fictitious disorder with physical symptoms. DSM-III's lengthy synonym for MUNCHAUSEN SYNDROME.

chronic preparation. *See* PREPARATION.

chronic tolerance. Tolerance for a drug that develops gradually with repeated usage. *Contrast* ACUTE TOLERANCE.

chronobiology. The study of BIOLOGICAL RHYTHM.

chronograph. Any instrument that automatically records events, and plots them against the time of their occurrence.

chronological age (CA). Age from birth.

chronometric analysis. The study of the time course of mental processes, often based on the dubious assumption that the processes occur in series, and that the time taken by one is independent of the other. *See also* ADDITIVE-FACTORS METHOD and SUBTRACTION METHOD.

chunk. George Miller's term for a collection of mental elements that a person has organized together; for someone who knows letters but not words 'CAT' is three chunks, but for someone who knows words it is only one. It is thought that short-term memory can hold about seven chunks.

CIE. An abbreviation for COMMISSION INTERNATIONALE D'ECLAIRAGE.

ciliary muscle. The muscle controlling the curvature of the lens, which becomes more convex when the muscle contracts and less convex when it relaxes.

cingulate gyrus. Part of the LIMBIC SYSTEM; it runs from posterior to anterior on the medial surface of the CEREBRAL CORTEX and arches over the CORPUS CALLOSUM. It comprises Brodmann's areas 23, 24, 26, 29, 31, and 33; *see* Appendices 2 and 4. It is implicated in emotion, particularly aggression. Damage to it can impair aversion learning.

cingulate sulcus. A sulcus bordering the cingulate gyrus and dorsal to it. *See* Appendix 2.

cingulectomy, cingulotomy. Deliberate destruction of part of the CINGULATE GYRUS, as e.g. undertaken by some surgeons in the hope of alleviating mental disorder.

cingulum. A synonym for CINGULATE GYRUS.

circadian rhythm. Changes in physical or mental function (e.g. sleep, temperature, or memory) occurring regularly at approximately 24-hour intervals.

circular behaviour. Behaviour that provokes the same behaviour in others (e.g. crying).

circular psychosis. An obsolete synonym for BIPOLAR MANIC-DEPRESSIVE DISORDER.

circular reaction. Piaget's expression for repetitious behaviour in young children. *See* PRIMARY CIRCULAR REACTION, SECONDARY CIRCULAR REACTION, and TERTIARY CIRCULAR REACTION.

11-*cis*-retinal. *See* RETINAL.

city-block metric. The metric applied to similarity judgements between items varying along two (or more) dimensions when their judged similarity is the sum of their similarities on each dimension. This metric is found with SEPARABLE STIMULUS DIMENSIONS. *Contrast* EUCLIDEAN METRIC.

CL. An abbreviation for COMPARISON LEVEL.

cladistics. (Biology) The hierarchical classification of organisms in terms of homologous traits; the classification is represented by a branching tree which does not necessarily correspond to an evolutionary tree. It is a harmless pastime that has provoked unnecessary criticism.

clairaudience. (Parapsychology) The alleged ability to hear physically a sound too distant to reach the ears.

clairvoyance. (Parapsychology) The alleged ability to perceive by psychic means; clairvoyance may be of events in the past, present, or future.

CLalt. An abbreviation for COMPARISON LEVEL FOR ALTERNATIVES.

clamping. (Connectionism) Maintaining the output layer in the same state of activity while exciting the input layer, which has the effect of changing the connectivity of other layers to be more consistent with the output layer.

clan. A group of people related by ancestry or marriage, particularly a group claiming to have the same ancestor.

clang association. Associating two words by virtue of their similarity of sound (e.g. 'pet' and 'net'); it can occur in word association tests and pathologically in psychosis.

class. (Biology) *See* TAXONOMY.

classical autism. A synonym for EARLY INFANTILE AUTISM, particularly for the form of autism occurring in KANNER'S SYNDROME.

classical computational architecture. A computer system containing discrete symbolic representations, in which the operations are rule governed. *Contrast* CONNECTIONISM.

classical conditioning. A learning procedure, much used by Pavlov, in which a neutral stimulus (the CONDITIONED STIMULUS) is always accompanied or followed by a stimulus (the UNCONDITIONED STIMULUS) that evokes a reaction, such as salivation or eye blink (the UNCONDITIONED RESPONSE). Under most circumstances, the unconditioned response comes to be given to the conditioned stimulus, when it becomes known as the CONDITIONED RESPONSE. The procedure differs from INSTRUMENTAL LEARNING in that the reinforcement (the unconditioned stimulus) is given regardless of whether or not the response to be learned occurs. In fact, more responses are learned to the conditioned stimulus (e.g. approach or attentional responses) than merely the conditioned response, and the distinction between classical and instrumental conditioning has been blurred by the discovery of AUTOSHAPING.

The learning of emotional responses to new stimuli is normally mediated by classical conditioning. To ensure that genuine conditioning has occurred, PSEUDOCONDITIONING and SENSITIZATION must be excluded.

classical psychoanalysis. PSYCHOANALYSIS as practised by the master himself – Sigmund Freud.

class interval. (Statistics) A range within which values are grouped in a frequency distribution.

clause. A unit in a sentence that contains a subject and predicate; the **main clause** contains the main verb of the sentence, other clauses are **subordinate clauses**. Thus in 'Be ready, when I come', 'Be ready' is the main clause, 'when I come' the subordinate.

claustrophobia. A morbid fear of being confined in a small or enclosed space.

claustrum. A layer of grey matter in the BASAL GANGLIA, thought to be implicated in the sense of taste.

Clever Hans effect. The tendency for an organism to learn to perform by responding to cues unintentionally given by the experimenter or by others present; the name comes from a German horse who was thought to have been taught arithmetic, but was responding to minimal cues unintentionally provided by his trainer or the bystanders.

client. A euphemism for a patient receiving psychotherapy.

client-centred therapy. A non-directive psychotherapy devised by Rogers: the therapist avoids making suggestions or interpretations, but tries to help the client clarify his mind, and thus solve his own problems. *See* CARE.

climbing fibre. An input cell to the cerebellum that ends on PURKINJE CELLS.

clinical depression. Any episode of depression severe enough to require the intervention of psychiatrist or psychotherapist. The intervention is of course often not forthcoming, and may in any case be unhelpful.

clinical method. In psychology, particularly developmental psychology, collecting data in a natural situation in which subjects are free to act as they wish, rather than in the formal setting of a laboratory.

clinical prediction. The making of a prediction or diagnosis by intuitive means rather than by using a rigorous system to assess the evidence, such as obtaining the probability of a given illness being present by mathematically combining the probability that it is present yielded by each of the symptoms that occur. In clinical prediction the criteria on which a judgement is based are often vague or not explicit. *Contrast* STATISTICAL PREDICTION.

clinical psychology. The branch of psychology that studies mental disorder, and that applies psychological knowledge to the diagnosis and treatment of the mentally disordered.

clinical study, clinical trial. The systematic testing of the effectiveness of a particular form or forms of treatment for an illness or disorder.

clonic convulsion. *See* CONVULSION.

clonic phase. The phase of an epileptic seizure in which the muscles alternately contract and relax; it usually follows the TONIC PHASE.

clonus. Rapid and involuntary alternation of muscular contraction and relaxation, as in hiccups.

closed-class word. A synonym for FUNCTION WORD.

closed curve, closed contour. A continuous line that re-enters itself, thus enclosing a region.

closed economic system. A system in which a commodity can only be obtained at a cost; in an OPEN ECONOMIC SYSTEM it may be obtained at no cost. The concepts have been applied to the effects of reward on schedule performance: if food is the reward and the organism receives sufficient food outside the experimental situation to maintain its body weight (open system), responding on long FI and VI schedules decreases.

closed head injury. Damage to the brain caused by a blow to the head with no penetration of the skull.

closed instinct. (Ethology) An INSTINCT (1) in which the behaviour cannot be modified through experience, as occurs, e.g. in much insect behaviour.

closed loop. (Cybernetics) A system in which the effects of the output are fed back to alter further output; e.g. thirst produces drinking as an output which in turn stops thirst and hence alters the output. *See also* FEEDBACK. *Contrast* OPEN LOOP.

closed node. *See* NODE (2).

closed system. A system uninfluenced by anything external to it. *Contrast* OPEN SYSTEM.

close-ended question. A question, usually in a questionnaire, to which a person can only respond by selecting an answer from a fixed set provided. *Contrast* OPEN-ENDED QUESTION.

closure. The process by which, according to the Gestalt psychologists, any pieces missing from an otherwise regular contour or figure tend to be supplied both in perception and in memory.

closure, law of. The Gestalt principle that the components of a line forming a closed curve are seen as belonging together, and more generally that there is a tendency to close up gaps in any regular figure.

closure picture. An unnecessary synonym for STREET FIGURES.

cloze procedure. An experimental paradigm in which the subject is asked to fill in words that have been deleted from a text; the method is also used in teaching reading.

cluster analysis. (Statistics) Any technique for splitting a set of items into groups of similar items according to some measure of the similarity between items.

clustering. The phenomenon that in FREE RECALL similar terms tend to be recalled consecutively, regardless of their order during learning (e.g. if a random list of birds and other animals is given, the birds will tend to be recalled in a group).

cluttering. Rapid incoherent speech.

CM. An abbreviation for COCHLEAR MICROPHONIC.

CNS. An abbreviation for CENTRAL NERVOUS SYSTEM.

CNV. An abbreviation for CONTINGENT NEGATIVE VARIATION.

Co. An abbreviation for COMPARISON STIMULUS.

coacting group. A group working on the same kind of task, who do not communicate with one another directly about the task, though they may provide one another with some SOCIAL FACILITATION, e.g. a line of people fishing.

coadapted complex. A group of inherited characteristics such that a change in one would affect the value of the others.

coarse coding. Coding in which the same unit within a system may be activated in the representation of many different concepts. In such coding, what is represented depends on the ensemble of active units, not on any one of them. This kind of coding occurs in PARALLEL DISTRIBUTED PROCESSING.

coarticulation. The modification of the pronunciation of a phoneme as a result of the transition from or to neighbouring phonemes.

cocaine. An alkaloid that acts as a local anaesthetic. When taken centrally, it blocks the reuptake of norepinephrine, and hence is a central nervous system stimulant.

coccygeal nerves. *See* SPINAL NERVES.

cochlea. A snail-shaped organ in the inner ear containing the AUDITORY RECEPTORS. It is separated from the middle ear by the OVAL WINDOW, through which sound vibrations are conducted, and by the ROUND WINDOW. It contains three canals running along its length separated from one another by the BASILAR MEMBRANE and by REISSNER'S MEMBRANE.

cochlea duct. The duct whose cavity is the SCALA MEDIA.

cochlear microphonic (CM). The electric potentials that can be recorded from the COCHLEA. They have the same waveform as the sound producing them and are believed to be the sum of the responses of the hair cells.

cochlear nerve. A synonym for AUDITORY NERVE.

cochlear nucleus. A nucleus in the medulla, where axons from the AUDITORY NERVE terminate.

cochleogram. A synonym for COCHLEAR MICROPHONIC.

cochleotopic map. A synonym for TONOTOPIC MAP.

Cochran Q test. (Statistics) A nonparametric test for evaluating the significance of differences between three or more proportions in matched samples. It is a generalization of MCNEMAR'S TEST.

cocktail party phenomenon. The ability to follow one voice and ignore others when several people are talking at once. More generally, the ability to listen to a sound from one source among a medley of other sounds.

co-consciousness. 1. Mental events on or just beyond the fringe of consciousness. 2. The split forms of consciousness occurring in multiple personalities (or in split-brain patients).

code. Any method of representing information in symbols.

code test. Any intelligence test in which the testee has to encode material in a different form according to a rule.

codominance. 1. (Ethology) The equal sharing of dominance over a group by two or more members. 2. (Genetics) The determination of a trait by both members of a pair of alleles. *Compare* DOMINANCE and RECESSIVE.

codon. A triplet of DNA or RNA NUCLEOTIDES, of which 61 code for amino acids and three are instructions to stop coding.

COD schedule. An abbreviation for CHANGE OVER DELAY SCHEDULE.

coefficient. 1. (Mathematics) A constant value by which an expression is to be multiplied. 2. (Statistics) An index of measurement. *See also* the following terms.

coefficient of alienation. A measure of the amount of unexplained variance in a set of data, i.e. of the extent of random variation.

coefficient of concordance. Short for KENDALL'S COEFFICIENT OF CONCORDANCE.

coefficient of determination. The proportion of the total variance in a set of data attributable to the correlation betwen two variables; where r is the correlation coefficient, the coefficient of determination is r^2.

coefficient of dispersion. A measure of relative variability used when attempting to make allowance for unequal averages. It is obtained by dividing the STANDARD DEVIATION by the arithmetic mean, and multiplying by 100.

coefficient of reproducibility. A measure of the proportion of inconsistent responses made by someone taking a set of ordered test items (e.g. arithmetic problems of increasing difficulty or the items used in GUTTMAN SCALING) to which he might be expected to respond in the same way up to a particular item, and in a different way beyond that.

coefficient of stability (W). A synonym for TEST–RETEST COEFFICIENT.

coefficient of total determination. The square of the multiple correlation coefficient, which represents the proportion of the total variance of the dependent variable accounted for by the independent variables included in the multiple correlation.

coefficient of validity. The correlation between test scores and the criterion scores that are assumed to reflect what the test purports to measure.

coefficient of variability, coefficient of variation. Synonyms for COEFFICIENT OF DISPERSION.

coenaesthesia, coenesthesia. Awareness of one's own bodily condition, particularly of having a sense of well-being or malaise.

coenotrope. *See* CENOTROPE.

co-enzyme. An organic compound that is not a protein but that must be present for a protein enzyme to function.

cognition. The mental processes concerned with the acquisition and manipulation of knowledge, including perception and thinking.

cognitive appraisal theory. The theory that emotions result from a person's evaluation of the situation he is in. Thus a person will feel different emotions if he sees a smile as an attempt at seduction from those felt if he sees it merely as a sardonic gesture.

cognitive behaviour modification. The attempt to change behaviour by systematically modifying the way a person thinks, formerly known as persuasion. *See* COGNITIVE THERAPY.

cognitive behaviour therapy. The use in combination of the techniques of COGNITIVE THERAPY and BEHAVIOUR THERAPY; some behaviour therapy has in fact always been cognitive (e.g. the use of imaginal desensitization). The expression was originally used more narrowly to mean that the therapist takes into account what rewards or punishments the client *expects* to receive, not merely the effects of those he has received. It has also been used to mean the application of social learning theory as a technique in addition to behaviour therapy techniques.

cognitive complexity. The number of different dimensions (possibly multiplied by the number of points on each dimension) that a person uses in classifying social behaviour and in appraising people. The concept is associated with that of the REPERTORY GRID TEST.

cognitive consistency theory. Any model of attitudes based on the assumption that people strive to maintain consistency between their beliefs; it includes BALANCE THEORY, CONGRUITY THEORY, and COGNITIVE DISSONANCE.

cognitive contour. A synonym for SUBJECTIVE CONTOUR.

cognitive control. The extent to which a person uses narrow well-defined concepts and categories, rather than broad ill-defined ones.

cognitive development. The growth of the ability to act intelligently in children.

cognitive dissonance. Festinger's term for the mental conflict that occurs when a person encounters anything discordant with his beliefs; the conflict can be resolved by changing the belief or – only too often – by reinterpreting the discordant material to make it consistent with the belief.

cognitive evaluation theory. 1. (Social psychology) The doctrine that on experiencing high arousal a person decides cognitively in the light of his immediate circumstances what has caused it, and, according to the cause assigned, experiences it as either pleasurable or disagreeable. 2. The hypothesis that if rewards are seen as giving a person knowledge about how well he is performing, they will increase his intrinsic motivation, but if they are seen as an attempt to control him, they will reduce it.

cognitive labelling theory. The hypothesis that emotions emanate from physiological arousal, and are then labelled in the light of the context, e.g. as fear, joy, anger.

cognitive learning theory. Any learning theory that posits the occurrence in learning of any process, other than the learning of associations between stimuli and responses; the term is broadly used, e.g. the postulation of learned associations between one stimulus and another is sometimes taken to be an instance of cognitive learning theory.

cognitive map. Tolman's term for the mental representation of a task, situation, or spatial lay-out; he shocked his contemporaries by attempting to show that even rats had cognitive maps.

cognitive need. The drive to explore, understand, and master the environment.

cognitive penetrability, cognitive penetrance. Pylyshyn's expression for the extent to which a task is unconsciously affected by learnt expectations; e.g. he has argued that the reason why the time taken for mental rotation increases in proportion to the angle through which the image is rotated is because the subject expects objects in the real world to rotate smoothly through intermediate positions, rather than because of an innate analogue process.

cognitive psychology. A *soi disant* new approach that attempts to create theories (preferably rigorous, but in practice often not) adequate to explain cognitive processes (including perception), usually making use of experimental data. The approach is a complete break with behaviourism, since the theories often make unashamed use of mental terms; it has been influenced by developments in AI and formal linguistics. The expression is vague, and anyone who can draw a series of boxes on a piece of paper can call himself a cognitive psychologist. *See also* COGNITIVE SCIENCE and BOXOLOGY.

cognitive rehearsal. A BEHAVIOUR MODIFICATION technique in which a person goes over in his imagination a situation with which he finds it difficult to cope (e.g. in the case of an alcoholic, refusing a double gin), while calling to mind strategies that will enable him to cope with the situation.

cognitive restructuring. Any psychotherapeutic technique that attempts to get the patient to think about his problems more constructively and rationally, e.g. RATIONAL-EMOTIVE THERAPY.

cognitive science. In theory, any discipline that studies cognition scientifically; in practice, any discipline that purports to do so, including sociology, social anthropology, linguistics, psychology, and aspects of philosophy and AI: the expression has come into being mainly in order to allow workers who are not scientists to claim that they are. Cognitive scientists rarely pay much attention to the nervous system. *Contrast* NEUROSCIENCE – the two are almost mutually exclusive in that cognitive science deals with the brain's software, neuroscience with its hardware.

cognitive therapy. A new form of therapy that attempts to persuade someone suffering from a mental disorder to see the world and himself in a more sensible and adaptive way, and which is based on the belief that maladaptive emotions are caused by maladaptive thought processes. Clinical psychologists tend to follow the fashions of experimental psychology with a lag of about 20 years, hence the recent switch from behaviour therapy to cognitive therapy. In practice, it is often unclear how the approach of the cognitive therapist differs from that of most laymen confronted with mental disorder in others.

cognitive triad. In the cognitive theory of depression, the three kinds of pessimistic or negative thoughts held to be causative. They are negative thoughts about the self, about present experience, and about the future.

cohesion, law of. 1. A law of learning to the effect that acts occurring close together in time tend to become joined into a single higher order act. 2. A Gestalt law to the effect that stimuli are perceived as more regular, symmetrical, and coherent than they really are.

cohesive force. A synonym for INTERNAL FORCE OF ORGANIZATION.

cohort. A group of individuals selected for study because of a common characteristic, particularly in a longitudinal survey where the term refers to all individuals in the same age bracket.

cohort effect. *See* CROSS-SECTIONAL STUDY.

cohort model. (Psycholinguistics) The theory that, as a word is heard, the hearer activates the representations of all or most of the words that are possible given the number of syllables processed so far. As successive syllables follow, the mind eliminates words, leaving only the correct one when it has been fully heard or is no longer ambiguous.

co-indexing. The syntactic process by which different CONSTITUENTS – or a constituent and a TRACE (2) – of a sentence are marked to show they refer to the same entity. E.g. in 'The cat stayed where I put it', 'the cat' and 'it' would be so marked.

coisogenic. (Genetics) Pertaining to a member of an inbred strain whose genotype differs from other members at a single locus as a result of mutation.

cold spot. A small area of skin that is especially sensitive to stimulation by cold, and that presumably contains one or more cold receptors. *Compare* WARM SPOT.

collateral, collateral fibre. A branch of an axon that stems from the main axonal trunk, usually occurring at the end of the axon distal to the cell body. A **recurrent collateral** returns to the area of the cell body where it produces RECURRENT INHIBITION.

collateral sulcus. A fissure running approximately horizontally along the medial surface of the cortex from the occipital pole to the temporal pole. *See* Appendix 2.

collective consciousness. A synonym for GROUP MIND.

collective hysteria. A synonym for MASS HYSTERIA.

collective noun. A noun referring to a group of entities, e.g. 'gaggle', 'set', 'committee'.

collective unconscious. Jung's expression for that part of the unconscious mind that serves as a repository for ARCHETYPES. *Contrast* PERSONAL UNCONSCIOUS.

colliculi. Two pairs of protuberances in the roof of the midbrain; the anterior pair are the SUPERIOR COLLICULI and the posterior pair the INFERIOR COLLICULI; both pairs are thought to process information about spatial topography, the former being concerned with visual information, the latter with auditory.

colliculus. Singular of COLLICULI.

collusion. (Psychotherapy) Permitting another person to be nasty to oneself, a term much misused by psychotherapists in order to reduce the guilt of the nasty person by mistakenly indicating that the wronged person is just as much to blame.

color. *See* COLOUR.

colorimeter. Any device for measuring colour, usually in terms of three PRIMARIES (1).

colorimetry. The measurement of colour, usually based on the ratios of three PRIMARIES (1) needed to make a metameric match.

colour. The sensory quality of light that is determined largely by the mixture of wavelengths reaching the eye (though in the case of light reflected from a surface, the reflectance of the surface is important – *see* COLOUR CONSTANCY and BRIGHTNESS CONSTANCY). Achromatic colours (black, grey, white) have no HUE whereas chromatic ones do; the term is often used to refer only to chromatic colours.

colour adaptation. A synonym for CHROMATIC ADAPTATION.

colour assimilation. The tendency for one colour to appear tinged with the hue of a second colour next to it in space. The phenomenon occurs particularly with narrow stripes of one hue exposed against a background of a different hue.

colour blindness. Any defect in colour vision. It is thought to be caused by the absence of one or more of the three cone pigments, or by abnormal functioning of one of the three cone systems. It is marked by an impairment in the ability to distinguish certain hues. Although complete inability to distinguish hues is rare, 8 per cent of men exhibit some form of colour blindness, almost invariably in the red–green end of the spectrum. It is much less common in women because the gene or genes producing it are on the X chromosome, and for most types of colour blindness a woman would have to receive two of the aberrant alleles. *See also*

MONOCHROMATISM,   DICHROMATISM,   PRO-
TANOPIA, DEUTERANOPIA, TRITANOPIA, PRO-
TANOMALY,   DEUTERANOMALY,   and
TRITANOMALY.

colour circle. An arrangement of saturated
hues round a circle, with similar hues adjacent to one another. The hues are so arranged that complementary hues lie at opposite ends of a diagonal. The centre of the
circle represents white light, the direction of
a radius represents hue, and increases in
distance from the centre of the circle represent increased saturation. Apart from the
spectral hues, part of the circle is occupied
by the non-spectral hues, which yield violet
and purple, thus completing the gap between spectral blue and spectral red. *See
also* COLOUR TRIANGLE and COLOUR SOLID.

colour constancy. The tendency for the apparent HUE of a surface to remain approximately the same despite variations in the
wavelength of the incident light.

colour contrast. An alteration in the appearance of a colour, caused by viewing another
colour. In SIMULTANEOUS CONTRAST one
colour surrounds another, and the latter
tends to shift towards the COMPLEMENTARY
COLOUR of the surround; in SUCCESSIVE CON-
TRAST a colour is viewed for some time, and
any colour looked at immediately afterwards
is seen shifted in the direction of the complementary colour of the one first viewed.

coloured audition. A synonym for CHROMATIC
AUDITION.

coloured hearing. The synaesthetic sensation
of seeing colours when certain sounds are
heard.

coloured noise. In principle, any NOISE (2)
other than WHITE NOISE. It is generally
produced by passing white noise or PINK
NOISE through a frequency filter.

colour equation. The specification of the
ratios of PRIMARIES (1) needed by a subject to
obtain a metameric match to a light with a
particular distribution of wavelengths. *See
also* RGB SYSTEM and XYZ SYSTEM.

colour induction. *See* INDUCED COLOUR.

colour mixing. Producing light by mixing two
or more wavelengths in given proportions.
In **additive colour mixing** (which is used in
experiments) each colour mixed adds light of
its wavelength or wavelengths to the others.
Subtractive colour mixing is produced by
mixing paints or other absorptive substances; since they absorb light, the light
reflected by such materials can be determined by subtracting the sum of the light
absorbed by each material from the incident
light. *See also* GRASSMAN'S LAWS.

colour purity. The extent to which a colour is
saturated.

colour pyramid. *See* COLOUR SOLID.

colour solid. A three-dimensional representation of the similarities between colours, in
which the vertical dimension represents
brightness. The cross-section represents HUE
(direction from centre) and SATURATION (1)
(distance out from centre) as in the COLOUR
CIRCLE. The colour solid ends in a point at
the top (representing a very bright white)
with the bottom representing black. In
cross-section it can either be a circle (like the
colour circle), when it appears like two
cones meeting at their widest points, or it
can be in the form of two pyramids joined at
their bases (the **colour pyramid**).

colour surface. Any two-dimensional representation of the similarities between colours
in which they are arranged by hue and saturation. *See* COLOUR CIRCLE and COLOUR
TRIANGLE.

colour temperature. The temperature that a
substance would have to be at to emit radiation of the same wavelength as a given
source. The temperature is the same for all
substances.

colour triangle. A variant on the COLOUR
CIRCLE in which similar hues are arranged
next to one another around a triangle. A
point inside the triangle represents white,
and the colours are so arranged that any two
points on the triangle joined by a line passing through this point represent complementary colours. Hue and saturation are
represented respectively by direction and distance from the centre. The colour triangle

can give a more faithful representation of saturation than the colour circle.

colour weakness. Deficient colour vision, i.e. any form of colour blindness except monochromatism in which no hues can be discriminated.

colour wheel. A wheel containing segments of different hues or brightnesses; when rapidly rotated, it produces additive mixing of the colours in the segments. *See* COLOUR MIXING.

colour zones. Regions of the retina partitioned by their sensitivity to HUE. All hues can be discriminated in the fovea, further out reds and greens appear to be yellow and blue, and in the extreme periphery no hues can be discriminated.

column. *See* CORTICAL COLUMN.

columnar organization of the cortex. *See* CORTICAL COLUMN.

coma. Total lack of consciousness and somatic reflexes, caused by damage to the brain by injury, poison, or drugs, and sometimes occurring in CATATONIC SCHIZOPHRENIA.

combat neurosis. A state of anxiety or weakness caused by the stress of battle, which may be accompanied by other neurotic symptoms, and usually, but not always, short lasting.

combination tone. (Hearing) A subjective tone not present in the input to the ear and which is not a harmonic; it arises when two or more tones fairly close together in frequency are presented. It is caused either by distortion in the response of the BASILAR MEMBRANE or by non-linearity in the mechanisms analysing the movements of the HAIR CELLS. The most conspicuous combination tones are the DIFFERENCE TONE and the SUMMATION TONE.

combinative euchromatopsia. The phenomenon that the threshold for detecting a violet light against a blue adapting field falls if yellow is added to the adapting field, even though the adapting field becomes brighter, or the same phenomenon at the long-wavelength end of the spectrum.

combinatorial explosion. (AI) A positively accelerated increase in the number of operations needed to complete a search as the depth of the search increases. E.g. in chess positions there are often up to 50 legal moves; an exhaustive search five moves ahead would therefore necessitate examining 50^{10} possible continuations (taking into account the opponent's possible replies).

combinatorial productivity. The combination of units of language to yield a string that conveys a new meaning not contained in the individual units, e.g. through word order or inflection.

combined transcortical aphasia. APHASIA resulting from lesions that tend to isolate both the anterior and posterior language areas from the rest of the cortex. It may be manifested by ECHOLALIA, in addition to impairment in both expressive and receptive language functions. *See also* TRANSCORTICAL MOTOR APHASIA and TRANSCORTICAL SENSORY APHASIA.

commensalism. The sharing of the same home (e.g. burrow or shell) by two species that are not symbiotic.

comment. (Linguistics) The part of a sentence that says something about the person or thing that forms the TOPIC.

Commission Internationale d'Eclairage (CIE). An international committee established to agree conventions on the description of light as perceived, e.g. photometric measurements and the measurement of colour in terms of the XYZ SYSTEM.

commissive. A SPEECH ACT in which the speaker commits himself to doing something, e.g. 'I promise . . . ', 'with this ring I thee wed'.

commissure. Any bundle of fibres connecting opposite sides of the brain or spinal cord. *See also* ANTERIOR COMMISSURE and CORPUS CALLOSUM.

commissure of inferior colliculus. A commissure connecting the two INFERIOR COLLICULI.

commissure of Probst. A commissure connecting fibres from the LATERAL LEMNISCUS to the contralateral inferior colliculus, that is the colliculus that is ipsilateral to the ear from which the information originated.

commissurotomy. The surgical section of a commissure, particularly of the CORPUS CALLOSUM, which is sometimes cut in an attempt to prevent epilepsy spreading from one hemisphere to another; cutting it produces the SPLIT BRAIN preparation.

committal, commitment. (Psychiatry) Subjecting a person by legal means to involunntary confinement in a mental hospital.

common fate, law of. A Gestalt law of grouping, which states that parts of the visual field exhibiting the same motion are grouped together.

communality. (Statistics) In FACTOR ANALYSIS, that part of the variance of a test or item attributable to the factor or factors which it has in common with other tests or items, the remainder being due to specific factors or error terms.

communication channel. A CHANNEL over which information is passed.

communication deviance. Parental communication with a child that is frequently unclear, thought by some to be one of the causes of schizophrenia.

communication network. The directions in which communication flows between the members of a group.

community mental-health centre. A centre providing mental health facilities, usually of a broader range than those available in a mental hospital.

community psychology. A branch of applied psychology that attempts to help a community by working with its members, e.g. by organizing and advising lay counsellors.

commutative. (Mathematics and Formal logic) Pertaining to an operator that yields the same result, irrespective of the order of the arguments. Addition and multiplication are commutative operators, division is not.

comparable groups. Two or more groups selected by the same criteria from the same population.

comparative judgement. In psychophysics, a subject's decision on the direction in which two stimuli differ in intensity or quality, e.g. a subject may have to decide which of two pitches is higher. More generally, any judgement involving the comparison of two or more items. *See also* COMPARATIVE JUDGEMENT, LAW OF. *Compare* DIFFERENCE THRESHOLD and *contrast* ABSOLUTE JUDGEMENT.

comparative judgement, law of. The principle that in any perceptual discrimination between two items, the subjective difference between them corresponds to the frequency with which the difference is observed.

comparative psychology. Strictly, the study of differences in the behaviour of different species, undertaken in order to throw light on the mechanisms governing behaviour or on their evolution in the individual species; the expression is, however, often used for all animal psychology, even if there is little or no intention of making comparisons between species.

comparator. A unit in an information processing system that compares the size of two variables, and issues an instruction that depends on the difference (e.g. a unit within a thermostat that turns a boiler on if the ambient temperature is less than the point to which the thermostat is set); *see also* REAFFERENCE.

comparison function. (Social psychology) The function of a reference group when it is used to show what behaviour should be like; or if the reference group is disliked, what it should not be like.

comparison level (CL). (Social psychology) In EXCHANGE THEORY, a standard against which to evaluate the benefits of a current social relationship. It is the average value of the benefits of all other relationships, taking into account their relevance to the current one.

comparison level for alternatives (CLalt). (Social psychology) In EXCHANGE THEORY, a standard against which to judge the benefits from a current relationship, based on the benefits to be derived from the best available alternative.

comparison stimulus (Co). (Psychophysics) The stimulus with which a stimulus to be judged (the STANDARD STIMULUS) is compared. E.g. the subject may be asked to select from several comparison stimuli the one that appears the same as the standard, or to adjust a variable comparison stimulus until it looks the same as the standard, or to select which of the standard or the comparison is the greater, with different comparison stimuli being used on different trials.

compartmentalization. The isolation in the mind of conflicting thoughts and feelings so that the individual can conceal from himself the fact that he is behaving inconsistently, e.g. by separating off attitudes to family from attitudes to colleagues.

compassion. Pity. In current psychiatric circles compassion is good, pity is bad, but the main difference between the two terms appears to lie in the number of letters. Perhaps compassion conveys the idea of wishing to help more than does pity.

compensating error. An error that cancels the effects of a previous error.

compensation. The development by a person of strength in one area to offset weakness in another, occurring consciously or unconsciously. In the latter case it is, according to Freud, a DEFENCE MECHANISM.

compensation neurosis. 1. Neurotic striving for prestige arising from feelings of inferiority. See INFERIORITY COMPLEX. 2. The perpetuation of a neurosis arising from an injury in order to obtain financial recompense.

compensatory eye movement. A SMOOTH EYE MOVEMENT, occurring when the head moves, that keeps fixation on the same point in space.

compensatory model. The hypothesis that people with mental disorders or under stress are helped by being taught how to cope with

their problems and are harmed by being blamed for their inability to cope.

compensatory movement. An involuntary movement that restores the body's balance or orientation.

compensatory recovery. The alleged tendency of organisms, after being shocked for making a learned response, to make as many (or almost as many) responses to EXTINCTION as they would have made had no shock been given.

compensatory reflex. A synonym for COMPENSATORY MOVEMENT.

compensatory tracking. A tracking task in which the subject has to minimize an error signal showing the mismatch between the position controlled by his responses and the position of the target. This kind of tracking is harder than PURSUIT TRACKING, since it is more difficult to use knowledge of the current error than of the target position.

competence. (Linguistics) The idealized mastery of the formal rules of syntax, semantics, phonology, and the lexicon that a person could exhibit in PERFORMANCE (1) were it not for such *ad hoc* factors as limitations on immediate memory, and errors made for a variety of other reasons; a GENERATIVE GRAMMAR attempts to specify the competence of native speakers.

competence knowledge. (Social psychology) A person's evaluation of his own talents and skills, on which his self-esteem may be partially based. *Compare* LEGITIMACY KNOWLEDGE.

compiler. (Computing) A program that translates a program in a high-level language into MACHINE CODE, while checking and reporting errors of syntax.

complement. A phrase supplementing a verb in a verb phrase. E.g. 'He hid *under the bed*', 'He liked *her*'.

complementarity. In a social relationship, the existence of traits and skills in each member that are different from those of the other, but balance them.

complementarity principle. The hypothesis that close relationships tend to be based on complementary personalities.

complementary colour. A colour that when mixed additively with another produces an achromatic colour (e.g. yellow is complementary to blue). *See* COLOUR MIXING.

complementary distribution. (Phonetics) The obligatory appearance of one ALLOPHONE in one context and of another in another; e.g. after initial 's' the phoneme /l/ is unvoiced as in 'slim', but at the start of a word it is voiced as in 'limb'. *Contrast* CONTRASTIVE DISTRIBUTION.

complete learning method. Working through the same material repeatedly until it can be done without any errors.

completion. *See* VISUAL COMPLETION.

completion test. Any test in which a person is shown a number of items forming a series or pattern and has to select or supply an extra item missing from the original.

complexity factor. In psychological aesthetics, the judged complexity of a work of art.

complex. A group of related attitudes and desires existing over a long period of time, and having great emotional significance for a person. The term is usually used of repressed and maladaptive patterns of wishes. *See also* OEDIPUS COMPLEX.

complex cell. A cell in the visual cortex whose receptive field cannot be mapped by presenting a spot of light, but which responds maximally to bars or straight edges or both; although each cell responds maximally to only one orientation, the position of the stimulus is less critical than for a SIMPLE CELL and responses occur over a range of positions perpendicular to the long axis of the stimulus. Some complex cells respond to both black and white bars, or to edges with the brighter region lying to either side. *See also* HYPERCOMPLEX CELL.

complex indicator. In a free-association test, a response such as a long pause or an unusual association that indicates an underlying complex.

complex noun phrase constraint. The constraint that no element in a clause dominated by a head noun can be moved out of that noun phrase by a transformation. E.g. the sentence 'The book that I believed the information that George had written' is ungrammatical. It was once believed to be a LINGUISTIC UNIVERSAL constraint on all languages, but in fact is not.

complex reaction time. The REACTION TIME in an experiment containing two or more stimuli to which the subject has to react differently. *Contrast* SIMPLE REACTION TIME.

complex tone. Any tone made up of sound waves of more than one frequency, or any subjective tone having more than one pitch.

compliance. 1. (Physics) The ease with which a spring-like substance stretches, often used of the ease with which the OSSICLES move. 2. (Social psychology) A change in behaviour caused by exposure to the opinions of others.

complication experiment. Any experiment to demonstrate the LAW OF PRIOR ENTRY.

component instinct. (Psychoanalysis) Any pre-adult libidinal instinct, e.g. the oral instinct. Such instincts are normally subsequently integrated with the adult genital drive, but neurosis or maladaptive behaviour may occur if the person becomes fixated at the instinctual level of a component instinct.

composite score. The overall score on a test, often obtained by weighting the scores on individual items and then summing them.

compositional semantics. The attempt to characterize how the meaning of a string of words is determined by the meanings and order of the individual words in the string. *Compare* LEXICAL SEMANTICS.

compound conditioning. Conditioning with more than one stimulus as the conditioned stimulus.

compound eye. An eye, found in insects, in which an image is formed by tubes, each of which collects light from a particular direction in space, and guides it to photoreceptors at the far end of the tube. *See also* OM-MATIDIUM.

compounding. Combining two or more operators to make a MACRO-OPERATOR.

compound reaction time. A synonym for COMPLEX REACTION TIME.

compound schedule, compound reinforcement schedule. Any schedule in which two or more SIMPLE SCHEDULES are combined, e.g. a TANDEM REINFORCEMENT SCHEDULE or a CHAINED SCHEDULE.

compound stimulus. A conditioned stimulus consisting of more than one stimulus, e.g. a light and a tone. *See also* BLOCKING (1) and OVERSHADOWING.

compound tone. A synonym for COMPLEX TONE.

compromise formation. (Psychoanalysis) The release of a repressed wish in disguised form (e.g. hoarding money as a substitute for hoarding faeces); it is a DEFENCE MECHANISM. All neurotic symptoms are according to Freud a form of compromise formation.

compulsion. An irresistible urge to do something against one's better judgement (such as drinking, gambling, rape or more idiosyncratic actions). *See also* OBSESSIVE-COMPULSIVE DISORDER.

compulsive conduct disorder. Any disorder marked by the presence of COMPULSIONS.

compulsive personality. The personality of someone who sets himself very high standards, and who is rigid, meticulous, obsessive, and afraid of making mistakes.

compulsive personality disorder. The condition of having a COMPULSIVE PERSONALITY so extreme as to be considered abnormal by psychiatrists.

computer. A device, usually electronic, for processing information; it can receive coded instructions on what operations to execute (a PROGRAM) and the information (DATA) on which to execute the instructions. *See also* ANALOGUE COMPUTER and DIGITAL COMPUTER.

computer-assisted instruction (CAI), computer-assisted learning (CAL). The use of special purpose computer programs with which a student interacts in order to assist teaching.

computerized axial tomography (CAT), computerized tomography (CT). A method of producing three-dimensional X-ray pictures of the brain by moving an X-ray camera and an X-ray source around the head 180° out of phase. The results are fed to a computer, which computes a 3-D map of the structures revealed by the X-rays. The resolution is about 1 mm.

computer language. A synonym for PROGRAMMING LANGUAGE.

computer model. A synonym for COMPUTER SIMULATION (2).

computer of averaged transients. An instrument into which many examples of a waveform emanating from some part of the nervous system are fed and which yields the average waveform, thus eliminating noise. *See also* AVERAGE EVOKED RESPONSE.

computer simulation. 1. The construction of a computer program that models a psychological theory, usually undertaken in order to ensure that the theory is rigorous and will account for the task it purports to explain. 2. The model instantiated in the program.

computer vision. The study of how to program computers to process visual stimuli, e.g. in order to recognize objects, or to calculate distance or motion.

COMT. An abbreviation for CATECHOL-*O*-METHYL-TRANSFERASE.

concealed antisocial activity. Antisocial behaviour that is condoned by society (e.g. minor acts of smuggling).

concentration. (Chemistry) The ratio of solute to solvent in a solution.

concentration gradient. The variation in the CONCENTRATION of a substance between neighbouring areas, usually from one side of a membrane to the other.

concept. The mental representation of anything; arguably a concept has to be conscious – young children do not have a concept of 'adjective' and 'noun' although their linguistic behaviour shows that they discriminate between them. Many concepts are based on the sharing of common properties by items in a class (e.g. the concept of 'robin' or 'bird'). *See also* CONCEPT FORMATION, BASIC LEVEL CATEGORY, NATURAL CATEGORY, and PROTOTYPE.

concept formation, concept attainment, concept learning. The induction of concepts that divide items into classes (including highly abstract classes like 'true') according to their shared properties. Until recently most psychological experiments on concept formation were very artificial, since subjects were often told in advance what the relevant properties were, and the concepts could include disjunctive ones (e.g. possessing either property A or property B) or other complex combinations of properties that rarely define concepts in the real world. For a more realistic approach to concept formation *see* BASIC LEVEL CATEGORY and PROTOTYPE.

conceptual dependency. Schank's theory of how meaning is represented: the meaning of a proposition is reduced to a small number of semantic primitives, e.g. different kinds of actions, agents, and objects. Propositions are supposed to be interpreted in the light of knowledge held as SCRIPTS. E.g. the goal of acquiring a physical object is associated with such plans as buying or borrowing. The theory has the problem that the selection of semantic primitives is arbitrary, and that it fails to make contact with the external world.

conceptually driven process. A perceptual or parsing process that is guided by higher-level hypotheses. *Compare* TOP-DOWN PROCESSING.

conceptual nervous system. Any abstract model of the nervous system that attempts to explain behaviour by postulating the flow of information and the operations applied to it.

concinnity. Harmony in the arrangement of the parts of a work of art.

concord. (Linguistics) A synonym for AGREEMENT.

concordance. 1. The percentage of cases in which identical co-twins share the same specified trait. 2. (Statistics) *See* KENDALL'S COEFFICIENT OF CONCORDANCE.

concrete intelligence. Skill at handling non-abstract problems.

concrete operational stage. The third of PIAGET'S STAGES of intellectual development (lasting from about 7 to 11 years of age), in which the child develops logical thought processes, including e.g. REVERSIBLE OPERATIONS (which result in CONSERVATION). At this stage the operations can only be applied to concrete events, and the child still lacks the capacity for abstract thought and symbolic manipulation.

concrete operations. The operations developed in the CONCRETE OPERATIONAL STAGE.

concrete thinking, concretism. Thinking in which a person is preoccupied with his immediate situation and with the specific objects around him, and is unable to make general judgements or plan for the future. It can occur e.g. in children or in schizophrenics, or after frontal lobe damage.

concurrent schedule. Any REINFORCEMENT SCHEDULE in which two or more schedules are operating independently and simultaneously.

concurrent validity. VALIDITY (1) established by the degree of correspondence between two different measures, e.g. that between the results of two different tests purporting to measure the same thing.

condensation. (Psychoanalysis) The use of the same symbol to express more than one repressed wish or idea, particularly in dreams. E.g. dreaming of flying could represent both the desire to have intercourse with one's father (the aeroplane) and the danger attached to it, or again it could represent the comfort of the womb and the desire to penetrate one's mother, or anything else you care to dream (*sic*) up.

condensation click. A transient caused by a sudden rise in air pressure at the ear.

condition. One of two or more ways of treating subjects in an experiment in which the experimenter is testing whether different methods of treatment (i.e. different conditions) will yield differences in outcome. The treatment within a condition should vary as little as possible, and the only difference between conditions should be in the variable being examined. *See* CONTROL CONDITION and EXPERIMENTAL CONDITION.

conditionability. The ease with which an organism can be conditioned; *see* EXTROVERSION and INTROVERSION.

condition-action rules. The rules instantiated in a PRODUCTION SYSTEM.

conditional. A proposition made up of two elementary propositions – the **antecedent** (*p*) and the **consequent** (*q*). A conditional proposition is true only if *p* and *q* are true, or if *p* and *q* are false, or if *p* is false and *q* is true. The most common logical notation for the conditional is $p \supset q$. In natural English, the antecedent is usually preceded by 'if', e.g. 'If it rains, we will get wet', and there is usually a necessary connection between the truth of the antecedent and the truth of the consequent. No such connection is needed in logic, in which a sentence like 'If twice two is five, all the seas are dry' is a true sentence because the antecedent is false.

conditional discriminative stimulus. A stimulus that informs an organism how to react to another stimulus. E.g. an animal could be trained on a red–green discrimination to select red when a tone was on, and green when no tone was present.

conditional jump. (Computing) An instruction in a program to go to another specified instruction if a certain condition is fulfilled. *See also* JUMP.

conditional positive regard. Esteem for a person that is made dependent on how he behaves, a process frowned upon by Rogers. *Contrast* UNCONDITIONAL POSITIVE REGARD.

conditional probability. The probability of an event occurring, or of a hypothesis (A) being true given the occurrence of some other event (B), usually expressed as p(A/B).

conditional proposition. A synonym for CONDITIONAL.

conditional reflex, conditional response. Synonyms for CONDITIONED RESPONSE. Although the latter expression is in more common use, the word 'conditional' is a more accurate translation of Pavlov's original term.

conditional stimulus. A synonym for CONDITIONED STIMULUS. *See* CONDITIONAL RESPONSE.

conditioned. Learnt. Originally and best used of a response learnt through CLASSICAL CONDITIONING (or of the stimulus to which that response has become attached), the term is now often applied to any form of response learning (except when it forms part of a technical expression such as 'conditioned stimulus'). It retains overtones of involuntary behaviour, as in the frequently heard defence of bad behaviour. 'He can't help it – he was conditioned to act like that'. Psychologists have helped to foul things up by using such expressions as 'instrumental conditioning' instead of 'instrumental learning'.

conditioned avoidance response. An instrumental response which averts punishment altogether (rather than merely allowing the organism to escape from it). *Contrast* CONDITIONED ESCAPE RESPONSE.

conditioned emotional response (CER). An emotional response (e.g. fear or frustration) classically conditioned to a neutral stimulus, used particularly of the emotional response that causes CONDITIONED SUPPRESSION.

conditioned enhancement. An increase in the strength of a learned reaction as a result of an increase in the strength of the relevant drive, caused by presenting a stimulus to which that drive has been conditioned. E.g. if an animal has been trained to jump a hurdle to avoid shock, and has at another time been presented with a tone followed by shock, the presentation of the tone in the avoidance situation increases the strength of the jumping response. *Contrast* CONDITIONED SUPPRESSION.

conditioned escape response. An instrumental response that allows the organism to terminate punishment but not to avoid it altogether. *Contrast* CONDITIONED AVOIDANCE RESPONSE.

conditioned inhibition ($_sI_R$). In Hull's theory, inhibition accumulated as a result of learning, which causes EXTINCTION if reinforcement is withdrawn. According to Hull some conditioned inhibition accumulates even in the presence of reinforcement, since reactive inhibition is always generated to whatever stimuli are present, thus producing conditioned inhibition. *See* HULLIAN THEORY.

conditioned reflex. A synonym for CONDITIONED RESPONSE.

conditioned reinforcement, conditioned reinforcer. Synonyms for SECONDARY REINFORCEMENT.

conditioned response (CR). In CLASSICAL CONDITIONING, the response that is learned, i.e. the one that comes to be given to the conditioned stimulus.

conditioned stimulus (CS). In CLASSICAL CONDITIONING, the neutral stimulus (e.g. a light) that is followed by the unconditioned stimulus (e.g. food), and that with repeated presentations comes itself to elicit the same response as the unconditioned stimulus (e.g. salivation).

conditioned suppression. The reduction in the frequency of a learned response (e.g. bar pressing for food) that occurs if a neutral stimulus (e.g. a light) is first paired with punishment and is then presented on its own.

conditioned taste aversion. A synonym for LEARNED TASTE AVERSION.

conditioning. Strictly speaking CLASSICAL CONDITIONING, but the term is often used to indicate any form of learning about contingencies in the environment, including contingencies between stimuli, as well as stimulus response contingencies. *See also* INSTRUMENTAL CONDITIONING.

conduct disorder. (DSM-III) A disorder in which the person violates social norms (e.g. by stealing or taking drugs) to such an extent that psychiatrists consider him disordered.

Four categories are recognized, based on how far a person possesses social skills, and how directly aggressive he is to others: **undersocialized-aggressive conduct disorder, socialized-aggressive conduct disorder, undersocialized-nonaggressive conduct disorder**, and **socialized-nonaggressive conduct disorder**.

conduction. The movement of a nerve impulse along the AXON.

conduction aphasia. A form of APHASIA in which there is an impairment in repeating speech sounds just heard, but little impairment of spontaneous speech or understanding. It is thought to be caused by lesions that sever the connections between BROCA'S AREA and WERNICKE'S AREA.

conduction deafness. Impairment of hearing caused by damage to the middle ear, which impairs conduction between the eardrum and oval window.

cone. 1. One of the two kinds of retinal receptors. They are concentrated in the FOVEA, and become much fewer towards the periphery; in contrast to RODS, cones are used in daylight, yield high acuity, and subserve colour vision. In man, there are three different types of cone, each having a different photopigment, with peak absorption wavelengths of about 420, 530 and 570 nm. They are often called respectively **blue cones, green cones**, and **red cones**, but since the latter two do not peak in the green or red regions of the spectrum, this is a misnomer, and they are better called **short-wavelength cones, medium-wavelength cones**, and **long-wavelength cones**. Cones have a diameter of about 2 μm and subtend about 20″ of arc. 2. *See* GROWTH CONE.

cone monochromatism. *See* MONOCHROMATISM.

confabulation. The invention of material or episodes to fill in missing memories, whether undertaken consciously or, as is common in amnesics, unconsciously.

confederate. A synonym for STOOGE.

confidence interval. An interval calculated from sample statistics (e.g. the mean and standard deviation) for which there is a certain probability that it includes the value of a population parameter (e.g. the mean). The probability values are conventionally set at 0.95 or 0.99.

confidence limits. The lower and upper levels of the CONFIDENCE INTERVAL.

configuration, law of. The Gestalt principle that any pattern will be organized in vision into its most regular and symmetrical components.

configurational learning. Learning to respond to a pattern of stimuli rather than to one part. E.g. an animal might be trained to go to one oblique rectangle (/) while presented simultaneously with the opposite oblique rectangle (\) beside it. Instead of learning to go to /, it might learn 'Go left if ∧ and go right if ∨'.

confirmation bias. Maintaining a belief by ignoring or distorting evidence against it, and by seeking only confirmatory evidence.

conflict. The existence of drives or wishes, whether conscious or unconscious, that cannot be reconciled with one another. *See also* APPROACH–APPROACH CONFLICT, APPROACH–AVOIDANCE CONFLICT, and AVOIDANCE–AVOIDANCE CONFLICT.

conflict specificity theory. The doctrine that a given psychosomatic disorder is the specific outcome of underlying psychological conflicts.

confluxion. A synonym for ASSIMILATION (6) when used to explain the geometric illusions.

confluence model. A theory that attempts to explain the average difference in intelligence found with the birth order of siblings in terms of the effects on the child of the mean intelligence of other siblings.

confound. To fail to separate two variables in an experiment or study. E.g. in tests of psychotherapy it is not enough to show that the psychotherapy works better than no treatment, since the psychotherapy is confounded with the attention the patient receives.

confrontation. Making a person face his weaknesses, a technique of doubtful morality and efficacy sometimes employed in encounter groups.

confusion matrix. A matrix showing the frequency with which subjects confuse each member of a set of stimuli with each of the other stimuli in the set. The matrix can be used to extract the factors underlying the confusions (i.e. the dimensions of similarity) or to test hypotheses about these factors. E.g. the confusions made between consonants roughly support the DISTINCTIVE FEATURES hypothesis about speech, since pairs having the most distinctive features in common tend to be the most readily confused.

congenital. Pertaining to a characteristic or illness present at birth, whether hereditary or caused by the environment in the womb.

congruent points. Any two points, one on each retina, which are stimulated by light from the same point in space. If the point in space is on the HOROPTER, the congruent points will be CORRESPONDING POINTS, if it is not, they will be DISPARATE POINTS.

congruent validity. VALIDITY (1) established by comparing a new test's results with those of one already shown to be valid.

congruity theory. The hypothesis that attitudes tend to change in a direction that reduces inconsistency.

conjoint measurement. (Statistics) Measurement of the effects of two or more variables on a variable influenced by all of them; their effects need not be additive.

conjoint therapy. Therapy in which a married couple (or unmarried partners) together meet a therapist or therapists to discuss their problems.

conjugate eye movement. A synonym for CONJUNCTIVE EYE MOVEMENT.

conjugate schedule. A REINFORCEMENT SCHEDULE in which the intensity or speed of movement of a stimulus varies in proportion to the rate of responding.

conjunction. 1. (Linguistics) A part of speech used to connect linguistic constituents like words or sentences, e.g. 'and', 'but', 'however'. 2. A logical connective usually written '.' or '∧' and meaning (approximately) 'and'. If *p* and *q* are propositions, then $p \land q$ is true if and only if both *p* and *q* are true. *Compare* DISJUNCTION.

conjunction fallacy. The fallacy of judging that a combination of two qualities is more probable than the occurrence of one on its own. E.g. If 'Linda is a feminist' is much more probable than Linda being a 'bank teller', people often think it is more probable that Linda is a 'feminist bank teller' than that she is just a 'bank teller'.

conjunctive concept. A concept based on the presence of two or more attributes (e.g. red balls).

conjunctive eye movement. An eye movement in which the eyes turn in the same direction. *Contrast* DISJUNCTIVE EYE MOVEMENT.

conjunctive schedule. A REINFORCEMENT SCHEDULE in which two or more SIMPLE SCHEDULES are operating simultaneously, with all responses contributing to both schedules, and in which reward is given only when both schedules are completed. *Compare* CONCURRENT SCHEDULE, in which reinforcement is given as soon as one of the two schedules is completed.

conjunct simplification. (Logic) A rule of inference that allows one validly to infer the truth of either of two conjuncts. E.g. from 'Sam was young and slender', it can be inferred that 'Sam was slender'.

connectionism. Nowadays a synonym for PARALLEL DISTRIBUTED PROCESSING, and rapidly becoming preferred to that expression. The term goes back to Thorndike, who used it to describe the connections formed between stimuli and responses.

connective. Any word, e.g. 'and', 'or', or 'not', that indicates the connections between propositions or expressions. *See* LOGICAL CONNECTIVE.

connector neuron. A synonym for INTERNUNCIAL CELL.

connotation. 1. (Logic) The meaning of an expression, i.e. the properties that it signifies as opposed to the individual objects or events to which it may be correctly applied. *Contrast* DENOTATION and *see* SENSE. 2. (Generally) The set of ideas, associations, and emotions conjured up by a word.

conscious. (Psychoanalysis) The part of the mind in which awareness occurs, in contrast to the PRECONSCIOUS and the UNCONSCIOUS (2).

consciousness. The having of perceptions, thoughts, and feelings; awareness. The term is impossible to define except in terms that are unintelligible without a grasp of what consciousness means. Many fall into the trap of equating consciousness with self-consciousness – to be conscious it is only necessary to be aware of the external world. Consciousness is a fascinating but elusive phenomenon: it is impossible to specify what it is, what it does, or why it evolved. Nothing worth reading has been written on it.

consensual eye reflex. The contraction or expansion of the pupil of one eye in response to changes in the light falling on the other.

consensual validity. The VALIDITY (1) of a test or principle as determined by the proportion of people who agree that it is valid, i.e. by a head count.

consensus. (Social psychology) *See* COVARIATION THEORY.

consequent. *See* CONDITIONAL.

conservation. Piaget's term for the application of the knowledge that if nothing is added, or taken away, physical quantities remain constant despite changes in appearance. E.g. according to Piaget, when water is poured from a broad jug into a tall thin one, young children think, because of its higher level, that there is more water in the second container than there was in the first. For reasons that are obscure, the child develops conservation in the CONCRETE OPERATIONAL STAGE.

conservation of effect, law of. A synonym for the USE, LAW OF.

consistency. (Social psychology) *See* COVARIATION THEORY.

consistency paradox. The discrepancy between the belief that people have personality traits that operate in all situations and the fact that they often act 'out of character'.

consolidation. The hypothetical process by which, in learning, material becomes fixed in long-term memory; it is usually thought to continue for some time after exposure to the material.

consonance. A pleasant auditory sensation caused by a complex tone in which the different tones appear to blend together well.

consonant. (Phonetics) Any speech sound made by closing or narrowing the vocal tract so that the airflow is either completely blocked (as in [b]) or produces audible friction (as in [s]).

consonant trigram (CCC). A string of three consonants used in some experiments instead of nonsense syllables.

conspecific. An organism of the same species as another.

constancy. 1. (Experimental psychology) The tendency for the properties of objects to be correctly perceived despite changes in the conditions of observation. *See* e.g. BRIGHTNESS CONSTANCY, COLOUR CONSTANCY, MOTION CONSTANCY, SHAPE CONSTANCY, and SIZE CONSTANCY. 2. (Social psychology) Agreement between a person's beliefs or attitudes. 3. *See* CONSTANCY, LAW OF.

constancy, law of. 1. (Psychoanalysis) Freud's principle that mental processes move toward a state of equilibrium. 2. (Perception) A synonym for CONSTANCY HYPOTHESIS.

constancy hypothesis. The assumption that the way the properties of objects are perceived varies directly with the proximal stimulus. The assumption is incorrect, since an object five feet away does not look ten times the size it appears at fifty feet, although it is ten times as large on the retina. The expression means almost the reverse of CONSTANCY.

constant. 1. A term in a mathematical expression whose value is fixed (often represented by $\mathbf{K}$, e.g. $\Delta I/I = \mathbf{K}$). 2. An aspect of an experiment that remains the same under different conditions.

constant effects procedure. A learning procedure under which subjects are practised until they reach the same criterion; the measure of performance is the time or number of trials to learn. *Contrast* CONSTANT TREATMENT PROCEDURE.

constant error (CE). A systematic error in judgement. The term is primarily applied to psychophysical results; e.g. a subject asked to judge a set of weights may consistently underestimate the heavy ones and overestimate the light ones. *Contrast* VARIABLE ERROR.

constant interval schedule. A REINFORCEMENT SCHEDULE in which reward becomes available after a fixed and unvarying interval.

constant stimuli, method of. A psychophysical method for determining a threshold, in which different stimuli are presented in random order, and the subject has to say for each whether he can perceive it (absolute threshold) or whether it differs from a standard stimulus (difference threshold).

constant treatment procedure. A learning procedure under which subjects are given the same amount of practice; performance is measured (usually after learning) by their skill at the task. *Contrast* CONSTANT EFFECTS PROCEDURE.

constative. A speech act that describes a state of affairs: such statements are either true or false. *Contrast* PERFORMATIVE.

constituent. (Linguistics) Any linguistic unit that forms part of a larger unit, e.g. a clause, a noun phrase, a word, or a morpheme.

constitutional type. A category of body build. The expression refers mainly to the categories used by people who believed that body type was largely innate, and that it is correlated with innate personality types. For the two main proponents of this view, *see* KRETSCHMER'S CONSTITUTIONAL THEORY and SHELDON'S CONSTITUTIONAL THEORY. *Compare* BODY TYPE.

constrained association. A synonym for CONTROLLED ASSOCIATION.

constraint. 1. (Perception) A feature of the world that restricts the way in which the stimulus can be interpreted and hence can be used to facilitate a correct interpretation. E.g. most bodies are rigid, and this constraint can be used to derive a 3-D representation of a body from motion parallax. 2. (Linguistics) In generative grammar, a condition that restricts the occasions when a rule can be used. E.g. the consonant cluster 'trp' cannot occur in English, although 'tr' or 'rp' can occur on their own.

construct. 1. Any concept or integrated set of concepts of which one is conscious. 2. Any concept derived from Kelley's REPERTORY GRID TECHNIQUE.

constructional apraxia. Impaired ability to assemble a complete pattern or object from its parts; it can be caused by damage to the occipital or parietal cortex.

constructionism. A synonym for CONSTRUCTIVISM.

construction memory. *See* MEMORY RECONSTRUCTION.

constructive alternatism. In Kelley's theory, the recategorization of individuals or events to facilitate the solution to a problem – usually a social problem.

constructivism. The doctrine, held among others by Piaget, that complex mental structures are neither innate nor passively derived from experience, but are actively constructed by the mind. Piaget thought such mental structures were constructed by children largely through observing the effects of their own actions on the world. The mind may be capable of BOOTSTRAPPING in this way, but just how it does it is rarely made clear.

construct validity. An estimation of the extent to which a test (or other score) measures the factors it purports to measure, based on analysing the factors into their components (constructs) and analysing how far the test is *prima facie* likely to measure each of these components.

consumer-jury technique. Getting members of the public to make comparative evaluations of different advertisements of a product or service, as a test of the advertisements' efficacy, or discovering in a controlled situation whether advertisements influence the choice of comparable products.

consumer psychology. The psychological study of marketing and purchasing, including the effects of advertising, display, and packaging on potential buyers, and the motives that induce people to buy.

consummatory response. (Ethology) Any action, like eating or drinking, that is normally directly followed by the reduction of an instinctive drive. *Compare* APPETITIVE BEHAVIOUR.

contact comfort. The comfort acquired by making contact with the bodies of conspecifics or with similar surfaces (e.g. surfaces that are soft, warm, furry, etc.).

contact desensitization. A form of desensitization in which the therapist tries to reduce the patient's anxiety by making physical contact with him.

contact hypothesis. The doctrine that if contact between members of hostile groups is increased, the hostility will decrease.

contact lens. A lens fitted over the CORNEA and separated from it only by a thin layer of fluid, so that it moves with the eye.

contagion. (Psychology) The spread of ideas, attitudes, feelings, and, some think, neuroses through a community or group by suggestion, gossip, imitation, etc. *See also* BEHAVIOURAL CONTAGION.

contamination. The distortion of experimental or other results brought about by bias or stupidity, or both, on the part of the experimenter.

content-addressable memory. (Computing) Computer memory that can be accessed by specifying the type of information held there, rather than by an arbitrary address; software converts the instruction to find an address given by content into the code for the correct hardware address. All connectionist systems are automatically content-addressable, and so presumably is the brain.

content analysis. The systematic counting of the occurrence of ideas, themes, etc. in any body of verbal material; it is not a completely objective technique, since it usually depends on the judgement of the person carrying out the analysis.

content validity. The extent to which the questions in a test both cover everything the test purports to measure and do not require other skills. E.g. a test of arithmetic ability should not be based merely on ability to add, and the questions must be worded in such a way that the testees' knowledge of English does not affect their scores.

content word. A word (such as an adjective, verb or noun) that describes something in the world (or in a possible world) as opposed to a FUNCTION WORD (such as a conjunction) that does not.

context discrimination. Recalling under what circumstances a given happening occurred. E.g. at what party a given friend was present or which of several lists presented in an experiment contained a particular word.

context-free grammar. A GENERATIVE GRAMMAR in which symbols are rewritten according to rules that apply to a symbol or set of symbols, regardless of the context. Thus rules of the form 'Rewrite A as A+B' are allowable, rules of the form 'Rewrite A as A+B if C' are not; grammars in which the legitimate application of a rule depends on the context are known as **context-sensitive grammars**.

context, law of. The principle that less is remembered if a person attempts to remember something that was learned in a different context than if he is in the same context (e.g. if he is shifted from one room to another).

context-sensitive grammar. *See* CONTEXT FREE GRAMMAR.

context specific rules. Rules of reasoning that are specific to a given topic, e.g. 'If x is a cat, x is an animal'.

contextual information. Information about the context in which a statement is uttered that enables the child to learn a language, e.g. the utterance of the word 'cat' in the presence of a cat, or that enables the listener to understand the meaning of an (otherwise ambiguous) sentence.

contiguity, law of. A law of association to the effect that objects or events occurring to the mind in temporal or spatial contiguity tend to become associated.

contiguity theory. Guthrie's theory of learning, which states that an organism always gives the same response to a set of stimuli that it last gave to them. The role of reinforcement is to remove the organism from the situation; it will then give the response immediately preceding reinforcement on next entering the situation. The reason why the response last made in a situation is not always given on re-entering it is that the stimuli present (including internal stimuli) vary from trial to trial within the situation. The theory has largely been discarded.

contingency. The dependence of one event on the occurrence of another. In psychology the term is mainly applied to the way in which a reinforcement depends on one or more responses being emitted. *See* REINFORCEMENT SCHEDULE.

contingency coefficient (C). (Statistics) A coefficient measuring the strength of an association between two CATEGORICAL VARIABLES on the basis of a contingency table. It is a simple function of the CHI SQUARE statistic as used for testing the independence of two variables. Unlike the PHI COEFFICIENT it can be used with variables containing more than two values.

contingency contrast. A synonym for BEHAVIOUR CONTRAST.

contingency management. The attempt to eradicate maladaptive habits by systematically punishing them or systematically reinforcing other behaviour, as in BEHAVIOUR THERAPY.

contingency model of leadership. A theory postulating that the success of a leader depends on his personality and the nature of the leadership situation; his control is said to depend on how reliable his group is, on how well structured the task and goal are, and on how far he can legitimately reward or punish members of the group.

contingency table. (Statistics) A table of cells made from the intersection of two or more sets of independent categories, giving, within each cell, the frequency of occurrence of the combination. E.g. people could be divided into those with an IQ greater or less than 120, and those who did or did not go to university. The number of people in each of the four categories thus engendered could be shown as a two-by-two contingency table.

contingent aftereffect. A visual aftereffect produced by adapting a subject simultaneously on two different dimensions, using two different values on each dimension with each value paired with a different value on the other dimension (e.g. broad green stripes and narrow red stripes). When the subject is tested with one of the original values on one dimension paired with a neutral value of the second dimension, he sees the neutral stimulus shifted away from the value it originally had when paired with the value of the first dimension presented at test. E.g. after adaptation to broad green stripes and narrow red ones, on being presented with broad grey stripes the subject sees a reddish tinge on the stripes, while if he is presented with narrow grey stripes he sees a greenish tinge. The contingent aftereffect can last for several days and can occur with many pairs of dimensions. *Compare* MCCOLLOGH EFFECT.

contingent negative variation (CNV). A long and large negative wave in the EVOKED POTENTIAL that occurs when a stimulus is given as a warning signal for a second stimulus to which the person must respond. It is thought to signify that the subject is attending.

continuant. Any speech sound in which the vocal tract does not completely close, i.e. all vowels and fricatives.

continuation. *See* GOOD CONTINUATION, LAW OF.

continuity, law of. A law of association stating that in anything continuous, neighbouring portions tend to become associated in the mind; it is similar to CONTIGUITY, LAW OF.

continuity constraint. The assumption that in a scene sudden changes in depth are rare: it is used to solve the CORRESPONDENCE PROBLEM in stereopsis.

continuity theory. The hypothesis (espoused by Hull and Spence) that organisms learn a little about all stimuli present on every trial; hence learning is gradual or continuous. *Contrast* DISCONTINUITY THEORY and NON-CONTINUITY THEORY.

continuous biserial correlation. *See* BISERIAL CORRELATION.

continuous recognition memory test. A test of memory in which successive items are presented, some of which have occurred before in the sequence: the testee has to discriminate repeated from non-repeated items.

continuous reinforcement (crf), continuous reward. The provision of reinforcement on every trial on which the organism makes the instrumental response. *Contrast* PARTIAL REINFORCEMENT.

continuous tense. A tense, whether past, present, or future, signifying that the action is continuous over a period of time, e.g. 'I *was eating*', 'I *am eating*' 'I *will be eating*'.

contour. A visual line or edge, which may be determined directly by differences in luminosity, or less directly, e.g. by a change from one texture to another. *See also* SUBJECTIVE CONTOUR.

contract. *See* BEHAVIOURAL CONTRACT and MICROSOCIAL ENGINEERING.

contractibility. The capacity of living tissue to change shape, particularly in response to a stimulus.

contraction bias. The tendency for people using a dimensional rating scale (e.g. the numbers 1–7) to employ mainly the middle points on the scale and to avoid extreme points.

contradiction. (Logic) A proposition that is logically false (e.g. 'The book is big and small') or the relation between two propositions that can neither both be true nor both false (e.g. 'John is big' and 'John is not big'). *Compare* CONTRARY.

contralateral. On the other side of the body (e.g. stimulation from a limb is received in the contralateral cortex).

contrary. (Logic) A proposition that is related to another proposition in such a way that they cannot both be true, but may both be false (e.g. 'It is a lion' and 'It is a tiger'). *Compare* CONTRADICTION and SUBCONTRARY.

contrast. 1. (Perception) The displacement of the apparent quality of a stimulus away from that of a different stimulus that is next to it in space, or precedes it in time. *See* e.g. BRIGHTNESS CONTRAST and COLOUR CONTRAST. Contrast is often used as an explanation of the geometric illusions. *Contrast* ASSIMILATION (6). 2. (Vision) The difference in luminosity of two adjacent fields, usually measured as $(L_{max} - L_{min})/(L_{max} + L_{min})$ where L_{max} is the luminosity of the brighter field and L_{min} that of the darker. *See* CONTRAST SENSITIVITY FUNCTION. 3. (Learning theory) Short for BEHAVIOURAL CONTRAST. 4. (Generally) Any shift in judgement produced by the effect of one experience on a related experience. E.g. after viewing a British football crowd, a British pub may seem a haven of peace, whereas it may seem like hell let loose after reading Jane Austen by the fireside. 5. *See* CONTRAST, LAW OF. 6. (Social psychology) Thinking that attitudes different from one's own are even more different than they are.

contrast, law of. One of Aristotle's laws of association, to the effect that thinking of something tends to conjure up its opposite in the mind.

contrast effect. A synonym for BEHAVIOURAL CONTRAST.

contrastive analysis. (Linguistics) The analysis of the similarities and differences in the structure of two languages. It is postulated that the more similar the two languages are, the easier it will be for someone who has learned one to learn the other as a second language.

contrastive distribution. The ways in which the members of a given type of linguistic unit (e.g. phonemes or morphemes) may legitimately substitute for one another in a given context, when the substitution results in a difference in meaning. E.g. 'he', 'she', and 'it' form a contrastive set. *Contrast* COMPLEMENTARY DISTRIBUTION.

contrastive stress. (Linguistics) STRESS (2) used to emphasize the importance of a particular item in a sentence, e.g. 'The *small* boy cried' or 'The small boy *cried*'.

contrast sensitivity function (CSF). A plot of the threshold CONTRAST (2) for detecting the lines in a sinusoidal SPATIAL FREQUENCY GRATING as a function of the grating's frequency. The curve is usually shown as the reciprocal of contrast; in people the lowest threshold is found at about 3–5 cycles per degree.

contrast set. (Linguistics) A set of terms having the same BASE but different PROFILES. E.g. 'bat', 'club', 'racquet' are all instruments for hitting balls but function in different ways.

control. *See* ILLUSION OF CONTROL and LOCUS OF CONTROL.

control condition. A condition in an experiment that serves as a baseline against which to compare the effects of the EXPERIMENTAL CONDITION. E.g. in testing the efficacy of a treatment for depression, it is necessary to compare patients receiving the treatment, with a matched group who have not received the treatment, but who have otherwise been treated as nearly as possible in the same way as the treatment group. One experiment may need several different control conditions, either because each experimental group needs its own control, or because each different aspect of the treatment of one experimental group requires a different control group.

control experiment. An experiment run to ensure that the results of a previous experiment were not brought about by some factor other than that hypothesized. Control experiments are only needed if the first experimenter did not have the wit to run the necessary CONTROL CONDITIONS.

control group. A group of subjects who undergo the CONTROL CONDITION.

controlled association. A verbal response to a stimulus (usually a word) in which the subject is told what class of association to choose (e.g. 'Give a word that rhymes with the stimulus').

controlled-exposure technique. A method of testing the effectiveness of advertisements by showing them to a captive audience watching a show (e.g. a film) while measuring their responses, e.g. by photographing them, taking galvanic skin responses, or questioning them afterwards.

controlled sampling. A sampling technique in which an effort is made to minimize chance errors by selecting the same proportion of people belonging to each of several (usually overlapping) categories.

controlled variable, control variable. Synonyms for INDEPENDENT VARIABLE.

conventional level. The second of Kohlberg's three levels of moral development, which like the others is itself divided into two stages. In stage 3, the emphasis is on helping others in a conventional way; in stage 4, the child begins to grasp the notions of duty, obligation, and obedience to the law.

conventional sign. Anything which signifies something as a result of social agreement, e.g. the position of the hands on a clock, a barber's pole.

convergence. An inward and coordinated smooth movement of the two eyes, made to bring the image of the point fixated to the centre of each fovea; convergent movements are needed when fixation changes from a more distant to a nearer point. *Contrast* DIVERGENCE.

convergent evolution. The tendency for unrelated animals having the same environmental constraints to acquire similar structures; these evolve from structures that may originally have been very different (e.g. the eye of an octopus and of a mammal).

convergent operations. Different studies that confirm the truth of a hypothesis each in a different way. E.g. the existence of separate short-term and long-term memories could in principle be confirmed both by behavioural experiments showing differences between the two kinds of memory, and by studies of neurological patients showing that each type of memory could be eliminated by brain damage while the other was left intact.

convergent thinking. Thinking in the controlled, analytic way needed for problems that can be solved algorithmically; such thinking is also needed in other problems to test whether the solutions provided by DIVERGENT THINKING actually work.

convergent validity. The extent to which scores on a test correlate with the several different factors with which they should correlate if the test is measuring what it purports to measure. *Compare* DISCRIMINANT VALIDITY.

conversational implicature. Any valid inference drawn from another's conversation, based on the assumption that he is obeying the conversational maxims (being relevant, honest, etc.). E.g. if one asks someone the time and he says he does not know, it is normally safe to infer that he is not carrying a watch. *See* CONVERSATIONAL MAXIMS on the observance of which conversational implicature is based.

conversational maxims. Four maxims, formulated by Grice for the successful conduct of a conversation, given here in shortened form. **Maxim of quantity**: Be as informative as necessary but no more informative. **Maxim of quality**: Do not lie or affirm anything you do not know. **Maxim of relation**: Be relevant. **Maxim of manner**: Be clear, brief and orderly.

converse. (Logic) Any proposition that can be validly derived from another after exchanging the subject and object. Thus the converse of 'No S is P' is 'No P is S', but the converse of 'All S is P' is 'Some P is S'.

conversion disorder. A synonym for CONVERSION HYSTERIA.

conversion hypothesis. A hypothesis to explain errors in drawing conclusions from syllogisms, stating that people convert the premise to one seemingly the same but actually different. E.g. 'All As are Bs' may be taken to mean 'A is the same as B', which could lead to the false inference that 'All Bs are As'.

conversion hysteria. A neurosis in which the patient suffers physical symptoms (e.g. deafness, paralysis, loss of sensation in part of the body) that have no organic cause.

conversion of affect. (Psychoanalysis) The symbolic representation of a repressed wish or of a conflict as a physical symptom. *See* CONVERSION HYSTERIA.

convexity, law of. A Gestalt law stating that regions whose boundaries contain convexities are more likely to be taken as figure than as ground.

convolution. 1. (Neuroanatomy) A synonym for GYRUS. 2. (Mathematics and Image processing) The application of the same logical or mathematical operation to every region in an image. The operation applied is called a MASK, and when masks are convoluted with a GREY-LEVEL IMAGE (which may be thought of as containing numbers at each point representing light intensity), a new number will be output by each mask. In a convolution the numbers from masks that overlap at points in the image are summed.

convulsion. An involuntary and intense contraction of all the muscles, which may be a **clonic convulsion** (contractions may alternate with relaxation) or a **tonic convulsion** (continuous contraction).

convulsion therapy. Any physical treatment for mental illness whose aim is to induce a convulsion, e.g. ELECTROCONVULSIVE THERAPY and INSULIN THERAPY.

Coolidge effect. Shortening of the sexual refractory period caused by the introduction of a new partner.

cooperative algorithm. A synonym for RELAXATION TECHNIQUE.

cooperative play. The final stage in the development of play, when the child plays interactively with other children. *Compare* PARALLEL PLAY.

cooperative principle. The principle that people do what is needed to further the purpose of their conversation.

coordinates. Values on axes specifying the position of points in an n-dimension space. *See also* CARTESIAN COORDINATES and POLAR COORDINATES.

coordination of secondary schemata. The putting together of previously learned sequences of behaviour to achieve some new end, occurring, according to Piaget, at about one year of age, i.e. at the end of the sensorimotor stage.

coping behaviour. Any behaviour, whether deliberate or not, that reduces stress or enables a person to deal with a situation without excessive stress; it is a vogue expression in psychotherapeutic circles.

coping skills training. A form of cognitive therapy in which the subject is asked to imagine situations that make him anxious, proceeding from those that make him least anxious to those that make him most anxious, while he imagines the coping behaviour he would use for each. Relaxation techniques are used to keep him relaxed throughout.

coprolagnia. The derivation of sexual excitement from faeces.

coprolalia. Repeated utterance of obscenities.

coprophagia, coprophagy. The consumption of faeces.

coprophilia. A liking for faeces, sometimes combined with obtaining sexual excitement from them.

coprophobia. A morbid fear of faeces.

copula. The verb 'to be' when used to link a subject and a predicate, e.g. 'He is happy'.

core. The fundamental properties that distinguish a category. E.g. a bird must be the offspring of a bird and have the genes of a bird. PROTOTYPE qualities (e.g. 'flying', 'having feathers') are easier to detect but less reliable.

corepresentation. An association between two representations that is governed by rules. E.g. 'cat' is associated with 'chat' by the rule 'French translation of'.

core store. (Computing) The store that forms an integral part of a computer; it can be directly accessed very quickly by the central processor. *Contrast* PERIPHERAL STORE.

corium. The layer of skin below the epidermis, containing the hair follicles and sweat glands.

cornea. The transparent outer layer of the eyeball, lying over the PUPIL and the IRIS, and continuous with the SCLERA. At this junction there is a small furrow, since the curvature of the cornea is greater than that of the sclera. It is the part of the eye mainly responsible for focusing the image, having a refractive power of about 42 diopters. It measures about 12 mm horizontally and 11 mm vertically.

corneal reflection technique. A method of observing or recording eye movements by automatically tracking the direction in which one or more lights are reflected from the cornea.

Cornell technique. A synonym for GUTTMAN SCALING.

Cornsweet–O'Brien effect. The phenomenon that, if in the retinal image one region is surrounded by another of equal intensity, and if between them there is a band across which there is a gradual decline in light intensity and then a sudden increase ending at a plateau, the region on the side of the gradual decline looks darker than that on the other side. In determining apparent brightness, the visual system is not affected by gradual changes in intensity, but sudden changes produce contrast.

corollary. A subsidiary proposition that follows from a theory, and requires little or no additional proof.

corollary discharge. A signal taken from the

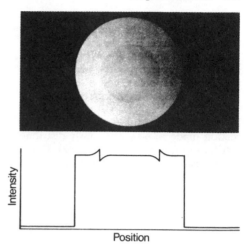

Cornsweet–O'Brien effect.

motor output, and sent to perceptual centres in the brain, where it can be used to modify the interpretation of changes in sensory input caused by the motor movement. In particular, it can cause them to be attributed to the observer's own movement, not to movement in the external world. The cancellation of the movement of the retinal image produced by a saccade is brought about in this way. *See also* REAFFERENCE.

coronal. (Phonetics) Pertaining to speech sounds uttered with the tongue raised, e.g. [t].

coronal section. (Anatomy) A TRANSVERSE SECTION made towards the back of an organ.

corpora quadrigemina. A synonym for the nuclei of the SUPERIOR COLLICULUS and the INFERIOR COLLICULUS.

corpus callosum. A large commissure linking corresponding points of the two hemispheres; *see* Appendix 2. *See also* SPLIT BRAIN.

corpus luteum. A temporary endocrine gland in the ovary, which secretes oestrogen and progesterone during the LUTEAL PHASE, and which is stimulated by luteinizing hormones from the pituitary.

corpus striatum. The part of the BASAL GANGLIA that comprises the CAUDATE NUCLEUS, PUTAMEN, and GLOBUS PALLIDUS.

correction for chance. The adjustment of scores to allow for the number that could be correct by chance. E.g. the following formula is sometimes applied, $R-W/(n-1)$, where R and W are respectively the number of right and wrong responses, and n the number of alternative responses to each question.

correction for continuity. (Statistics) A correction made to discontinuously distributed statistics in order that they will more closely approximate the tabled continuous distributions to which they are usually referred. Compare YATES CORRECTION.

correction for guessing. A synonym for CORRECTION FOR CHANCE.

correction method. A method of training in which, if the organism makes a mistake, it is allowed to correct it within the trial. E.g. a rat going to the wrong arm of a T-MAZE would be allowed to retrace its steps and go down the other arm to find reinforcement. In the non-correction method, the organism is removed from the situation on making an error and moves on to the next trial.

corrective emotional experience. The revival and discussion of an experience stressful to the patient in order to provide insight, a technique used by Franz Alexander.

correlated schedule. A REINFORCEMENT SCHEDULE in which the length of time for which the reinforcement (usually food or water) is exposed varies in proportion to the rate of responding in the period between one reinforcement and the next.

correlation cluster. A group of variables that correlate more highly with one another than with other variables, and are therefore all likely to be expressions of the same common factor.

correlation coefficient. A statistical measure of the extent to which two variables covary; its value lies between $+1$ and -1, with 0 representing absence of correlation. Increasing positive correlation coefficients indicate increasing covariance in the same direction between the variables, and decreasing negative correlation coefficients (from 0 to -1) indicate increasing covariance in opposite directions. See R and TAU.

correspondence problem. The task (solved unconsciously by the human visual system) of matching up the parts of the two retinal images that are stimulated by the same points in space. The problem must be solved in stereoscopic vision, since BINOCULAR DISPARITY can only be detected after the corresponding parts of the images on each eye have been matched. A similar problem arises in stroboscopic motion – each part of the first image must be matched with part of the second. Note that what corresponds in CORRESPONDING POINTS is completely different. See also FALSE CORRESPONDENCE PROBLEM.

correspondent inference. The inference that a person's behaviour reflects some underlying disposition.

correspondent inference theory. The hypothesis that people infer the disposition of an ACTOR from the most likely outcome of the action, taking into account the NON-COMMON EFFECTS PRINCIPLE.

corresponding points, corresponding retinal points. A pair of points, one on each retina, that, when independently stimulated, results in the stimulus being seen in the same spatial direction with each eye. Corresponding points depend solely on retinal position, whereas the corresponding parts of an image are those that come from the same part of space, and they do not necessarily or even usually fall on corresponding retinal points (see CORRESPONDENCE PROBLEM). See also BINOCULAR DISPARITY.

corridor illusion. The phenomenon that in a two-dimensional drawing of a corridor, objects of the same size in the drawing look larger the further away they appear. It is an instance of size constancy.

cortex. The outer layers of an anatomical structure, often used to mean CEREBRAL CORTEX. See also ADRENAL CORTEX and CEREBELLAR CORTEX.

Corti. See ORGAN OF CORTI.

cortical area. A region of the cerebral cortex defined either anatomically (e.g. BRODMANN'S AREAS) or functionally (e.g. PRIMARY MOTOR CORTEX).

cortical column. A column of tissue running through the six layers of the cerebral cortex in a direction perpendicular to its surface. The expression is confusing: (i) columns have been recognized histologically by examining vertical cell connections: such anatomically defined columns have a diameter of about 0.03 mm; (ii) physiological recording has shown slabs of vertically organized cortical tissue within each of which the cells seem to have a common function. These slabs have been misnamed 'columns'. As examples, Mountcastle found alternating slabs in the somaesthetic cortex responding respectively to deep pressure and kinaesthesia. These slabs are about 0.4 mm wide. Hubel and Wiesel have found slabs in the visual cortex, within which all cells respond to a visual stimulus in one orientation (*see* ORIENTATION COLUMN). The width of these columns is probably of the order of 0.05 mm. They also found HYPERCOLUMNS having a width of about 1–2 mm, and containing one cycle of OCULAR DOMINANCE COLUMNS and two cycles of orientation columns.

cortical dominance. *See* CEREBRAL DOMINANCE.

cortical evoked response. A synonym for EVOKED RESPONSE.

cortical grey. The grey seen in complete darkness. The expression implies that this grey is produced by cortical events. *Compare* RETINAL GREY.

corticalization. The phylogenetic tendency for the cortex to become increasingly important in regulating behaviour.

cortical layers. The layers of cells parallel to the surface of the cerebral or cerebellar cortex. The neocortex has six layers, which are identified by differences in cell structure. From the surface inwards they are: PLEXIFORM LAYER (1) (layer 1), EXTERNAL GRANULAR LAYER (layer 2), MEDIUM PYRAMIDAL LAYER (layer 3), INTERNAL GRANULAR LAYER (layer 4), LARGE PYRAMIDAL LAYER (layer 5), FUSIFORM LAYER (layer 6). The ARCHICORTEX, PALAEOCORTEX, and CEREBELLAR CORTEX, which are phylogenetically earlier, have fewer layers. Layer 1 consists mainly of the apical dendrites of pyramidal cell bodies. Layers 2 and 3 have many pyramidal cells, which project only to other parts of the cortex or to layer 4. Layer 4 has many stellate cells connecting with cells in other layers in the same region of the cortex. Layer 5 has many pyramidal cells and projects both to other parts of the cortex and outside it. Layer 6 projects to the thalamus and claustrum.

corticobulbar tract. A tract carrying axons originating in the motor cortex and other cortical areas through the thalamus and basal ganglia to the brainstem nuclei of the CRANIAL NERVES.

corticofugal. Descending from the cortex (of axons or nerves).

corticoid. An old-fashioned synonym for CORTICOSTEROID.

corticopetal. Ascending towards the cortex (of axons or nerves).

corticospinal tract. The part of the pyramidal system projecting to the spinal cord. Most of its fibres decussate at the medulla and descend the spinal cord in the **lateral corticospinal tract**; most of the uncrossed fibres descend through the **anterior corticospinal tract**.

corticosteroids. Steroid hormones produced by the adrenal cortex. They play an essential role in the control of metabolism and sexual function, and include MINERALOCORTICOIDS, GLUCOCORTICOIDS, ANDROGENS, OESTROGENS, and PROGESTERONES.

corticosterone. A glucocorticoid hormone secreted by the adrenal cortex and implicated in the metabolism of carbohydrates, proteins, and fats, and in the regulation of salt and potassium.

corticotrophic hormone. Short for ADRENOCORTICOTROPHIC HORMONE.

corticotrophic-releasing factor (CRF). A peptide secreted by the hypothalamus in response to stress that causes the pituitary to release ADRENOCORTICOTROPHIC HORMONE.

corticotrophin, corticotropin. Synonyms for ADRENOCORTICOTROPHIC HORMONE.

Corti's membrane. A synonym for TECTORIAL MEMBRANE.

cortisol, cortisone. A steroid hormone secreted by the adrenal cortex and implicated in the regulation of fats and carbohydrates. The level in the blood rises under stress.

cosine law. The law that the illuminance of a surface is proportional to the cosine of the angle of incidence of the light.

cost–benefit analysis. A method of taking decisions by translating each possible OUTCOME of each option into its monetary value, multiplying each value by the probability of the outcome occurring, summing the results for each option and choosing the option that yields the highest resulting figure.

cost reward analysis. (Social psychology) The attempt to explain altruistic behaviour by analysing its costs and benefits to the person exhibiting it.

Cottard's delusion. The delusion that one is dead, when one is not.

Couéism. A synonym for AUTOSUGGESTION.

counselling. The discussion of a person's problems and the provision of advice by a comparative stranger, whether professionally trained or not. Counsellors with a great deal of training are known as clinical psychologists, those with rather less as psychiatrists, but there are many other varieties. Nowadays counselling may be obtained on almost every aspect of one's life from grooming to gardening, and from coping with one's career to coping with one's leisure time.

counter. In operant conditioning, a stimulus that changes its value (usually increasing in intensity) after every operant response, thus indicating to the subject the number of responses made.

counterattitudinal advocacy. A person's advocacy of beliefs that are counter to his own beliefs at the behest of another person – usually an experimenter; the person's attitudes tend to change in the direction of the beliefs he is made to advocate.

counterattitudinal behaviour. Behaviour that does not conform to one's own attitudes, e.g. doing something unpleasant as a result of having been talked into it. As a result of COGNITIVE DISSONANCE such behaviour is often seen in retrospect as more worth while than it actually was.

countercathexis. (Psychoanalysis) 1. The expenditure of energy by the ego to prevent repressed libidinal urges from expressing themselves. 2. A change in the affective tone of urges entering the ego from the id, e.g. a change from love to hate.

countercompulsion. A compulsion adopted in place of another compulsion, often because external circumstances prevent the person executing the original compulsion.

counterconditioning. The weakening of a conditioned response by conditioning the organism to make a different response that is incompatible with the original one. It is used as a technique in behaviour therapy to eliminate undesirable responses, particularly emotional ones. E.g. since relaxation is incompatible with anxiety, a phobia may be treated by attempting to condition relaxation to the object of the phobia.

counterego. (Psychoanalysis) That part of the unconscious that is opposed to the wishes of the ego.

counterfactual. (Philosophy) A CONDITIONAL proposition that assumes that the antecedent is not true. E.g. 'If I had tried harder, I would have won'. All causal statements imply counterfactuals.

counterinvestment. (Psychoanalysis) A defence mechanism in which a repressed feeling is unconsciously concealed by displaying the opposite feeling, e.g. by showing love to someone unconsciously hated or vice versa.

countershock phase. See GENERAL ADAPTATION SYNDROME.

countertransference. (Psychoanalysis) The projection of the analyst's unconscious wishes on to the patient or the use of the patient by the analyst to satisfy his own wishes; making a virtue of necessity, analysts claim that analysing the countertransference helps the analyst to understand the patient (as well as himself).

courtship behaviour. (Ethology) The behavioural signals passing between opposite-sexed members of a species preparatory to mating.

covariance. (Statistics) The variance between a set of pairs of data points, X and Y, calculated as: $\Sigma XY/(N-\bar{X}\bar{Y})$, where X and Y represent the values of each member of the pairs and $\bar{X}$ and $\bar{Y}$ the means of all X and all Y. It serves as the numerator in the PEARSON PRODUCT-MOMENT CORRELATION COEFFICIENT.

covariation principle. The principle in ATTRIBUTION THEORY that people tend to pick as the cause of an effect something that is present when, and only when, the effect is present.

covariation theory. A form of attribution theory postulating that in deciding whether an action was caused by the actor's internal disposition or by the situation, three factors are taken into account: (i) the extent to which the action is restricted to that situation (DISTINCTIVENESS); (ii) the proportion of people who perform that act in that situation (CONSENSUS); (iii) the frequency with which the actor performs that action in other situations (CONSISTENCY).

cover memory. A synonym for SCREEN MEMORY.

cover story. A plausible but false explanation of an experiment given to subjects before it starts, usually in order to reduce DEMAND CHARACTERISTICS.

covert conditioning. Conditioning in which the unconditioned stimulus is imagined; such conditioning is employed in behaviour therapy.

covert extinction. A behaviour therapy technique in which an attempt is made to get the patient to stop behaving in a certain way, simply by having him imagine that the behaviour will no longer be reinforced.

covert modelling therapy. A form of cognitive therapy in which the client rehearses in his mind how he should behave, particularly in situations that cause him anxiety or stress.

covert reinforcement. A behaviour therapy technique in which the patient is asked to imagine the positive reinforcement he would receive for behaving in a desirable way, or the negative reinforcement he would receive for behaving badly, in the hope that this will make him behave better.

cps. An abbreviation for CYCLES PER SECOND.

CPU. An abbreviation for CENTRAL PROCESSING UNIT.

CR. An abbreviation for CONDITIONED RESPONSE.

Craik–Cornsweet–O'Brien effect. A synonym for CORNSWEET–O'BRIEN EFFECT.

cranial division. The upper division of the parasympathetic division of the autonomic nervous system, so-called because it is controlled by cranial nerves.

cranial index. A synonym for CEPHALIC INDEX.

cranial nerves. The 12 (numbered) pairs of peripheral nerves that emanate from the brain above the spinal cord, which are: I, OLFACTORY NERVE; II, OPTIC NERVE; III, OCULOMOTOR NERVE; IV, TROCHLEAR NERVE; V, TRIGEMINAL NERVE; VI, ABDUCENS NERVE; VII, FACIAL NERVE; VIII, VESTIBULOACOUSTIC NERVE; IX, GLOSSOPHARYNGEAL NERVE; X, VAGUS NERVE; XI, ACCESSORY NERVE; XII, HYPOGLOSSAL NERVE. *Compare* SPINAL NERVES.

craniometry. Measurement of the shape of the skull.

craniosacral division. The parasympathetic division of the autonomic nervous system, so called because it emanates from the brain (cranial division), and from the lower part of the spinal cord (sacral division).

c-reaction time. A COMPLEX REACTION TIME where one response is made to one stimulus, a different response to another.

creationism. The doctrine that God created life, usually held in opposition to any form of evolution.

creativity tests. Tests of creative thinking, most of which require as much creativity to interpret as to perform.

Creole. Any language derived from PIDGIN (and usually much more complex than pidgin) that has become the native language of a community.

Crespi effect. A synonym for BEHAVOUR CONTRAST (1) when caused by an increase in the size of reinforcement.

cresyl violet. A histological stain that colours only the cell body.

cretinism. Congenital motor and intellectual retardation caused by thyroid underactivity.

crf. An abbreviation for CONTINUOUS REINFORCEMENT.

CRF. An abbreviation for CORTICOTROPHIC RELEASING FACTOR.

crisis intervention. Short-term therapeutic help given to someone who has experienced a severe crisis (e.g. rape, marital break-up, or burglary) in order to help him cope with the problem.

crista. The structure located in each AMPULLA, from which the receptors (HAIR CELLS) of the SEMICIRCULAR CANALS emanate.

criterion. 1. (Mental testing) A well-defined measure, or test against which something else can be evaluated. 2. (Learning) The level of performance, arbitrarily determined by the experimenter, that subjects have to attain. 3. Short for RESPONSE CRITERION.

criterion group. A group (often of experts) against whose performance on an ability test the performance of others is judged.

criterion problem. (Social psychology) The difficulty of judging the strength of a personality trait (e.g. self-esteem, extraversion) in another person caused by variations in his behaviour under different circumstances and different moods.

criterion validity, criterion-related validity. The extent to which scores on a test correlate with an independent criterion of whatever it is the test is intended to measure.

critical band. A band of frequencies to either side of a tone, within which NOISE (2) can mask the tone; noise outside this band has no effect on the audibility of the tone. Within the critical band the loudness of two or more frequencies is determined by the addition of their waveforms, while if the frequencies are separated by more than the critical band, the loudness is approximately the sum of the loudness of the component tones. *Compare* CRITICAL RATIO.

critical duration. The duration over which Bloch's law holds.

critical fusion frequency (CFF), critical flicker frequency, critical flicker fusion frequency. The maximum frequency at which the flicker in a flickering light can be seen; above this frequency the light appears to be of constant brightness.

critical incident technique. (Human factors). The collection, analysis, and classification of many observed examples of incidents in which a worker has performed exceptionally well or badly, with information about the full context; the results are used in an attempt to improve efficiency.

critical period. (Ethology) An innately determined period in development within which the organism is specially adept at acquiring a given task, and outside which it may not be able to acquire it at all. Thus, it is thought that imprinting can only occur at a very young age, and that acquiring a natural language becomes much more difficult after about seven.

critical ratio. (Hearing) An estimate of the CRITICAL BAND, based on the assumption that a tone will be masked when the noise power over the critical band is equal to the power of the tone to be masked; if this were true, the critical band could be estimated by using wide-band noise and adjusting its power until the tone was masked. More direct methods of measuring the critical band, e.g. by varying the bandwidth of the masking noise, have shown the assumption to be false.

critical region. The set of all values of a test statistic for which the null hypothesis must be rejected.

Crocker–Henderson system. A system for classifying odours based on four basic ones – fragrant, acid, burnt, and caprylic (smelling of goat or putrid). It is an alternative to the ODOUR PRISM.

cross adaptation. Adaptation to one stimulus caused by exposure to another, e.g. exposure to one taste may diminish the strength of a different taste.

cross conditioning. Conditioning to a stimulus that is present by accident at the same time as the conditioned stimulus to which conditioning is intended to occur. *Compare* SUPERSTITIOUS BEHAVIOUR.

cross-correspondence. (Parapsychology) The alleged conveyance of messages from the dead by two or more mediums that become meaningful to the living only when combined.

cross cuing. In split-brain patients, the transmission of information from one hemisphere to the other by means of a peripheral response made by one hemisphere, and detected by the other through the senses.

cross-cultural psychology. The psychological study of differences between cultures (e.g. in rearing habits), usually undertaken in the hope that by correlating one set of differences with others (e.g. adult emotionality) causal mechanisms will be revealed.

cross-dressing. A synonym for TRANSVESTISM.

crossed disparity. *See* BINOCULAR DISPARITY.

crossed reflex. A reflex response on the opposite side of the body to that stimulated. *Contrast* DIRECT REFLEX.

crossing over. The mutual exchange of genes between two homologous chromosomes.

cross-modality matching. (Psychophysics) Matching the apparent strength of a stimulus in one modality to that of a stimulus in another modality.

cross-modality matching, method of. A psychophysical scaling method in which the subject has to match stimuli differing along a dimension in one modality with stimuli from another modality; the method is used mainly as a check on the validity of scales obtained by other methods.

cross-modal transfer. The influence of information acquired through one sense on performance using another, e.g. monkeys can identify visually an object they have palpated.

crossover design. An experimental design in which two treatments (one of which may be a control treatment) are administered in succession to the same subject (but in a different order to half of the subjects).

crossover effect. The crossing over of two curves representing two different parameters when plotted against the same values on the x-axis. In other words, for some value on the x-axis, the value of parameter A is higher than that of parameter B, and vice versa at some other value of x.

cross-sectional study. An investigation of age differences, performed by studying people of different ages at the same point in time. It has the disadvantage that many of the differences found may be due to differences in upbringing and other experiences – the **cohort effect**. *Contrast* LONGITUDINAL STUDY.

cross tolerance. Tolerance for one drug produced by exposure to a related one, e.g. tolerance to alcohol causes tolerance to benzodiazepines.

cross validation. A method of evaluating the validity of a test by administering it to a second sample drawn from the same population as the original sample.

Crovitz technique. A synonym for AUTOBIOGRAPHICAL CUEING.

crowd psychology. The study of the behaviour of crowds and of their individual members.

CRT. An abbreviation for CATHODE RAY TUBE.

crude score. A synonym for RAW SCORE.

cryophobia. A morbid fear of cold.

cryptaesthesia, cryptesthesia. (Parapsychology) A hidden (and non-existent) sense responsible for telepathy, precognition, etc.

cryptarithmetic. Given the information that each letter represents a number and a mathematical operation (such as addition) set out in letters, the task of inferring what number each letter represents.

cryptomnesia. A memory that a person takes to be a new experience or idea.

cryptophasia. A language used between two or more people that is unintelligible to others. It is sometimes developed by twins or siblings.

crystalline lens. The lens of the vertebrate eye. *See* LENS.

crystallized intelligence. A person's performance level on skills (like mathematics) that have been learned. *Contrast* FLUID INTELLIGENCE.

CS. An abbreviation for CONDITIONED STIMULUS.

CSF. An abbreviation for 1. CEREBROSPINAL FLUID; 2. CONTRAST SENSITIVITY FUNCTION.

CT. An abbreviation for COMPUTERIZED TOMOGRAPHY.

cubic difference tone. A subjective tone heard when two tones are presented to the ear, differing in frequency by not more than 20 per cent. Its pitch is $2f_1 - f_2$, where f_1 is the lower frequency tone, and f_2 the higher. It is caused by a non-linearity in the response of the BASILAR MEMBRANE.

cue. 1. In general, any stimulus that can guide an organism's behaviour, or that allows it to construct an accurate representation of the world. In perception, the term often refers to stimuli that can provide information about depth (*see* DEPTH CUES). In memory studies, it refers to any stimulus that can suggest to the subject an item he is trying to recall (*see* CUED RECALL). 2. *See also* VANISHING CUES.

cue-arousal theory. The theory, of doubtful validity, that frustration only leads to aggression if either there are stimuli present to which aggression has been classically conditioned or aggression is appropriate in the situation.

cued recall. Recalling items from memory, with a hint about each provided by the experimenter, e.g. the first few letters of a word to be recalled might be given.

cue-specificity. The extent to which a given cue assists CUED RECALL.

cultural absolute. A value or standard held by the members of a society that is valid (or is believed to be valid) in all societies.

cultural anthropology. The study of the mores and habits of a society, their functions, and the ways in which they relate to one another.

cultural blindness. A synonym for ETHNOCENTRISM.

cultural deprivation. Lack of opportunity to participate in the customs of one's society, brought about e.g. by being poor, being a member of a minority group, or even (according to some) being a member of a majority group like women.

cultural determinism. The hypothesis that people's personality and ways of thought are produced by their culture.

cultural diffusion. The spread of cultural traits to other societies.

cultural drift. The gradual change over time in the mores and norms of a society, particularly when brought about by random factors.

cultural item. An item in an intelligence test that is more likely to be answered correctly by a particular group (or groups) of people taking it than by others, because of differences in their cultural experiences. *Compare* CULTURE-FAIR TEST.

cultural parallelism. (Anthropology) The independent development of similar customs by different societies.

cultural relativism. The hypothesis that a culture can only be evaluated on its own terms, which can lead, if carried to extremes, to such absurdities as holding that primitive beliefs about medicine are as 'true' or 'scientific' as those of the Western world.

cultural residue. Customs surviving in a culture after they have ceased to have any practical use.

culture. The beliefs, customs, and artifacts that the members of a society tend to have in common, and that they pass on to one another.

culture bias hypothesis. The hypothesis that social and racial differences on intelligence tests are caused by differences in upbringing, and by the contents of the tests being unsuitable for those who do badly at them.

culture-bound disorder. A mental disorder peculiar to a particular ethnic group.

culture conflict. Conflict within the individual (or between groups) engendered by exposure to different cultural mores existing either within a society or in different societies.

culture-fair test, culture-free test. Mental tests whose outcome is supposed not to depend on a person's experience. Many think it impossible to devise such tests.

culture-loaded fallacy. The belief that because an intelligence test contains questions that require culturally-specific knowledge, it is *necessarily* biased against groups that do badly on it.

culturgen. Any element in a culture – an ugly and unnecessary neologism.

cumulative distribution, cumulative frequency curve. The frequency with which a variable is less than or equal to a particular value. A graph of cumulative frequency plots on the y-axis the *total* number of events up to a given point on the x-axis instead of plotting separately the number of events occurring at each point on the x-axis. *Compare* CUMULATIVE RECORDER.

cumulative recorder. A device invented by Skinner in which a pen is driven horizontally across a sheet of paper and increases its vertical height by a small amount with every occurrence of the event to be recorded, thus forming a CUMULATIVE DISTRIBUTION. The rate of responding therefore appears as the *slope* of the line (not its height). Ingeniously, Skinner kept one on his office desk; the pen moved upwards whenever his office light was on; hence the slope of the recording reinforced him for working (except when it was flat, which it rarely was).

cumulative scaling method. A synonym for GUTTMAN SCALING.

cuneate nucleus, cuneus. A nucleus in the MEDULLA on which end the axons carrying information from the upper trunk and arms; it is part of the LEMNISCAL SYSTEM.

cunnilingus, cunnilinctio, cunnilinction, cunnilinguam. Stimulation of the female genitalia with the mouth or tongue.

cupula. A gelatinous structure in each SEMICIRCULAR CANAL that fits on to the CRISTA, and into which the hair cells from the crista embed themselves.

curare. A toxic plant extract containing *d*-tubocurarine that causes paralysis by occupying the cholinergic receptor sites of the skeletal muscles. It can cause death by stopping respiration. It has been used to demonstrate that learning (and thinking) can occur in the absence of motor move-ments.

curiosity drive. The drive, strong in higher animals, to investigate and master the environment.

current control phase. The deceleration phase of a bodily movement during which corrections may be made to bring it on target. *Contrast* INITIAL IMPULSE.

curvature. *See* PRINCIPAL CURVATURE.

curve fitting. Fitting a curve to a set of points.

curvilinear. Pertaining to a line that is not straight.

curvilinear regression. (Statistics) Fitting data points by regression on to a curved line or surface, usually by using a non-linear mathematical function of the independent variables.

Cushing's disease. A disorder, usually of women, caused by chronic hypersecretion of CORTISOL. The patient suffers sodium and water retention, and hence becomes puffy; hallucinations, delusions, and hypomania may also result.

cutaneous receptors. The skin receptors. As well as temperature receptors, there are about a dozen types of mechanoreceptors. Most adapt quickly, but **T1 receptors** (Merkel cell complexes) and **T2 receptors** (Ruffini endings) adapt slowly.

cutaneous senses. The skin senses, including pressure, temperature, and pain; the expression is sometimes also used to include taste and smell.

cut-off (Ethology). A posture or movement that takes one organism out of sensory contact with another with which it had been interacting.

CVC, CVC trigram. A trigram consisting of (in order) a consonant, a vowel, and a consonant. *Compare* NONSENSE SYLLABLE.

cyanolabe. A quaint name for the visual pigment of the short wavelength cone, which is not yet identified chemically.

cyanopsin. A photopigment with peak absorption at 620 nm first synthesized by Wald from photopsin and retinene, and found in the chicken eye. It is based on 3-dehydroretinal. The term should be dropped: *see* VISUAL PHOTOPIGMENT.

cybernetics. The scientific study especially the mathematical description of control systems particularly those involving NEGATIVE FEEDBACK.

cycles per second (cps). The number of times a waveform or other period stimulus repeats every second. Now obsolete and replaced by HERTZ.

cyclic. (Chemistry) Pertaining to a molecule containing a chain of components forming a closed loop; it is normally used only when a molecule can have more than one structural configuration, of which one is cyclic.

cyclic adenosine monophosphate, cyclic AMP. *See* ADENOSINE MONOPHOSPHATE.

cyclic disorder. A synonym for CYCLOTHYMIA.

cyclofusional eye movement. A rotation of the eyes about the antero-posterior axis to bring them both into the same angle of rotation.

cycloid. A person having CYCLOTHYMIA.

Cyclopean vision. Helmholtz's term for the phenomenon that under normal circumstances the two retinal images are fused in the visual system to yield a single percept.

cyclophoria. A form of HETEROPHORIA in which the misalignment of the eyes is caused by one eye being incorrectly rotated about the axis, usually because of a weakness in the oblique extraocular muscle.

cycloplegia. (Vision) Inability to ACCOMMODATE (1), due to paralysis of the CILIARY MUSCLE, usually accompanied by pupillary dilation. It can be caused by disease or by muscle-blocking drugs like ATROPINE.

cyclothymia, cyclothymic disorder. A personality type in KRETSCHMER'S CONSTITUTIONAL THEORY, characterized by wild swings of mood from elation to dejection; he thought it was associated with a PYKNIC physique.

cyclotorsion. An eye movement in which the eye is rotated about the antero-posterior axis.

cyclotropia. Strabismus caused by the eyes having different rotations about the antero-posterior axis.

cynophobia. A morbid fear of dogs (common in postmen).

cypridophobia. A morbid fear of sex or venereal disease.

cysteic acid. An amino acid thought to be an excitatory neurotransmitter.

cytoarchitectural fields. Divisions of the cortex made by neuroanatomical criteria. Usually a synonym for BRODMANN'S AREAS.

cytoarchitecture. The structural arrangement of cells in an organ, used especially of cells in the cerebral cortex.

cytogenic syndrome. Any disorder caused by abnormalities in the structure or arrangement of the chromosomes, e.g. KLINEFELTER'S SYNDROME.

cytology. The scientific study of living cells.

cytoplasm. The protoplasm inside a cell membrane, excluding that in the nucleus. *Contrast* NUCLEOPLASM.

D

D. An abbreviation in Hull's system for 1. DRIVE; 2. DRIVE STRENGTH.

2-D. Two-dimensional.

3-D. Three-dimensional.

d. Hull's symbol for the difference between the stimuli present in training and those on the current trial, which is used to calculate generalization decrement.

d′ (d-prime). *See* SIGNAL DETECTION THEORY.

DA. An abbreviation for DOPAMINE. *See also* D2 RECEPTOR.

dactylaplasia. (Neurology) Inability to distinguish which finger is being touched.

dactylology. Communication through finger signs.

DAF. An abbreviation for DELAYED AUDITORY FEEDBACK.

Dale's principle. The rule that all synaptic junctions made by one neuron use the same neurotransmitter, to which there are now known to be exceptions.

Dallenbach stimulator. A device for presenting temperature stimulation by altering the heat of water flowing inside a metal jacket which is applied to the skin.

Daltonism. An obsolete synonym for PROTANOPIA.

dampening. (Neural networks) Preventing the FAN EFFECT from activating too many nodes by weakening spreading activation the further it spreads.

damping. Reduction in the amplitude of a waveform or oscillation.

DAP. An abbreviation for DRAW-A-PERSON TEST.

dark adaptation. The process of adjusting the visual system to ensure good vision when the illumination is markedly reduced and SCOTOPIC VISION is being used. Full dark adaptation takes about 30 minites; it is achieved by expansion of the pupil, switch from cone to rod vision, regeneration of rod pigment, and more central changes in the visual system. *Compare* LIGHT ADAPTATION.

dark light. The subjective impression of a faint grey light occurring in complete darkness. It is thought to be caused by spontaneous activity in the photoreceptors.

dart and dome. A synonym for SPIKE-AND-DOME DISCHARGE.

Dasein. A term used by Heidegger, which is usually translated as BEING-IN-THE-WORLD.

DAT. An abbreviation for DIFFERENTIAL APTITIUDE TEST.

data. Results (the pural of 'datum'). The term is often used by psychologists to increase the credibility of their results by making them sound more scientific than they are.

data-driven learning. Learning that is unaffected by prior beliefs or expectations. *Contrast* BELIEF-DRIVEN LEARNING.

data-driven process. Any process using BOTTOM-UP PROCESSING.

dative. A case taken by a noun (or pronoun)

signifying that it is an indirect object; in English it can be the case of nouns preceded by 'to'.

Davis Ellis Test of General Intelligence. A test for children aged 5–12 that purports to be culturally fair. The testee looks at a cartoon picture and has to choose which of three descriptions read by the tester is most apt.

day blindness. A synonym for HEMERALOPIA.

day residue. Freud's expression for those aspects of the manifest content of dreams that are derived from the events of the previous day.

dB, db. Abbreviations for DECIBEL.

deadline procedure. An experimental procedure in which the subject is given a time within which he must respond; by varying the time, SPEED–ACCURACY TRADE-OFF can be measured.

deafferentation. Cutting the sensory nerves in the spinal cord of a living animal.

death instinct, death wish. A synonym for THANATOS.

debriefing. (Psychology) Informing subjects after an experiment is over of its purpose and rationale, allaying any worries they may have about it, and revealing any deceptions that were practised.

debug. To remove a fault in a computer program; hence, by analogy, to correct any form of fault.

décalage. Piaget's term for the attainment of different but related concepts of operations at different times. There are three kinds: **horizontal** *décalage*, the appearance of one aspect of a concept after another aspect has been developed within the same developmental stage (e.g. the ability to conserve volume appears after the ability to conserve weight); **vertical** *décalage*, the changes in a concept that occur as the child moves from one stage of cognitive development to another; **oblique** *décalage*, the refinement of concepts at one stage that prepares the way for the changes in them that appear at a subsequent stage.

decay theory. The hypothesis that forgetting is caused by the passive decay of memory traces.

decentering, decentration. 1. Piaget's term for the process by which the young child changes from seeing things only in relation to itself and its own wishes, to perceiving the world more objectively. *Contrast* CENTRATION. 2. Piaget's term for the change from being influenced only by one immediate and salient property of a stimulus to assessing it cognitively in terms of many of its properties, e.g. taking into account the width as well as the height of liquid in a cylinder in the development of conservation at the concrete operations stage. 3. The ability to take others' feelings and attitudes into account, whether in the developing child or in the adult.

decerebrate. Having no TELENCEPHALON.

decerebrate rigidity. Extreme muscular tonus in mammals, caused by a section through the midbrain.

de Cherambault delusion. A delusion, occurring mainly in women, in which the person believes a comparative stranger is her (or his) lover or spouse.

decibel (dB, db). One tenth of a BEL, a measure of the physical intensity of sounds. Since the difference between two intensities I_1 and I_2, measured in bels, is $\log_{10}I_1/I_2$ the difference in decibels is $10.\log_{10}I_1/I_2$. Although the difference between two intensities can be measured in decibels, the absolute value in decibels of an intensity is only fixed if a specified intensity is chosen for the beginning of the scale. This is usually taken to be 0.0002 dyne per square centimetre of sound pressure, which is the normal human threshold for a tone of 1,000 Hz. On this scale, the sound of normal speech is about 55 dB, of a full orchestra about 100 dB, and of a rock band 140 dB, which is approximately the threshold for pain.

decile. 1. One of the nine points that divide a set of scores into ten parts, each containing an equal number of scores. 2. One part of a partitioning of a set of scores into ten parts: the scores are divided according to rank into ten sets with an equal number in each set. The first decile contains the highest 10 per cent. Some authorities maintain that only usage (1) is correct, but the term is nowadays used just as frequently in usage (2).

decision criterion. A synonym for RESPONSE CRITERION.

decision theory. Any theory of how decisions are made, including decisions based on unconscious mechanisms (like choice reaction times or discriminating a stimulus at threshold); the term is usually used of theories that are mathematical, e.g. theories that involve stochastic processes, or random walks. Empirical decision theories must be distinguished from normative decision theories: the latter (e.g. GAME THEORY, UTILITY THEORY) specify how decisions should be taken in order to obtain optimal results.

decision tree. A TREE DIAGRAM in which the nodes represent decision points and the lines between nodes represent alternative decisions or outcomes.

declaration. A SPEECH ACT that brings about a new situation in the world, e.g. 'I christen thee Mary-Jane'.

declarative. A sentence or its verb form that makes a statement, as opposed to e.g. a command or a question.

declarative knowledge, declarative memory. The knowledge that something is the case, as opposed to the knowledge of how to do something (PROCEDURAL KNOWLEDGE).

decoding. Translating a coded message into an uncoded one or into one that is more readily interpretable, e.g. a loudspeaker decodes electrical signals back into sounds.

decompensation. (Psychoanalysis) A breakdown in the individual's defences for dealing with libidinal drives; it may produce neurosis or psychosis.

deconditioning. The removal of a maladaptive habit through extinction, desensitization, etc., as attempted in behaviour therapy.

decorticate. Lacking a CEREBRAL CORTEX.

decremental conduction. (Neurophysiology) The conduction down a branch of the neuron of a subthreshold change in the polarization of its membrane; the size of the change decreases with distance from the point at which it was initiated.

decussation. The crossing over of ascending or descending fibres in the nervous system so that fibres are connected from each side of the body to the opposite side of the brain, as occurs for half the fibres in the OPTIC CHIASM.

deduction. Drawing a conclusion that is logically implied by its premises. Also the conclusion drawn. *Contrast* INDUCTION (1)

deep dyslexia. A form of ACQUIRED DYSLEXIA, in which there is an inability to read nonsense words like 'BAST', a tendency to make visual errors (e.g. reading 'rate' as 'rat'), a gross impairment in reading function words, and a tendency to substitute words of a similar category to those being read (e.g. 'table' for 'chair').

deep structure. (Linguistics) The underlying structure of a sentence which in a phrase structure grammar may be represented as a tree. Everything above the dotted line in the example given belongs to the deep structure, and lexical rules produce from it the SURFACE STRUCTURE, shown below the dotted line. In a transformational grammar, transformational rules operate to modify the output from the deep structure (e.g. to convert an active verb to a passive one, or a statement to a question) to produce the SURFACE STRUCTURE.

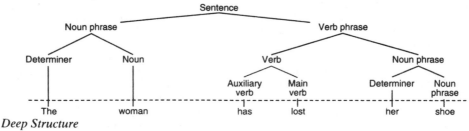

Deep Structure

default assignment. (AI) In the absence of contradictory information, the inference that any object, event, or situation has the features it normally has, which in AI programs are stored in FRAMES. An example is the inference that if a kitchen is mentioned, it will contain an oven, pots, and pans, etc.

default value. Any VALUE assigned by a DEFAULT ASSIGNMENT.

defect theory. The hypothesis that the thinking of the mentally retarded is different in kind from that of normal people.

defence mechanism. (Psychoanalysis) Any process by which the EGO protects itself from recognizing the demands of the ID; defence mechanisms include PROJECTION (1), REACTION FORMATION, REPRESSION, AND SUBLIMATION.

defence reaction. (Psychoanalysis) The behavioural manifestation of a DEFENCE MECHANISM.

defence reflex. Any involuntary reflex that tends to preserve the organism from injury, e.g. an eye-blink triggered by an object approaching the eye.

defence response. An attack, often involving biting and threatening, normally made to a threat. The response can be elicited by stimulation of the medial hypothalamus. *Compare* QUIET BITING.

defensive attribution. The refusal to take responsibility for something bad, usually by attributing it to external rather than internal factors.

defensiveness. Excessive sensitivity to criticism, whether real or imagined. It is a vogue term among psychotherapists who counter clients' attacks by saying 'You're being very defensive'.

defensive reflex. A synonym for DEFENCE REFLEX.

deficiency love. Maslow's expression for a possessive and dependent love, in which there is too little concern for the other partner.

deficiency motive. Any motive based on the need to restore the genuine lack of something. *Contrast* ABUNDANCY MOTIVE.

definite. (Linguistics) Pertaining to an article ('the') or pronoun (e.g. 'this', 'that'), which identifies the referent. *Contrast* INDEFINITE.

definite article. *See* ARTICLE.

definite description. A noun phrase that specifies an individual entity.

definitional validity. The validity of a test, based on the fact that the items comprising it by definition measure what the test is intended to measure. In practice it is hard to think of any examples.

degeneration. (Neurophysiology) The decay and death of neural tissue, usually due to the neuron having been cut or damaged at some point. *See* ANTEROGRADE DEGENERATION, RETROGRADE DEGENERATION, and TRANS-SYNAPTIC DEGENERATION.

degradation. (Neurophysiology) The breaking up of a neurotransmitter in the synaptic cleft by enzymes.

degraded stimulus. A stimulus that is difficult to perceive because it has been distorted, e.g. by having noise added to it.

degrees of freedom (df). The number of individual values that can be arbitrarily assigned within the specification of a system. E.g. if the mean of a set of scores is fixed, then the degrees of freedom of the scores is one less than the total number since, if the mean is to remain the same, the value of any one score is determined by the sum of the rest.

3-dehydroretinal. *See* RETINAL.

deictic. Pertaining to DEIXIS.

deindividuation. A condition in which a person feels he has lost his identity and is an anonymous member of a group. It is thought to cause a loss of the sense of responsibility and hence to account for mob violence, panic etc.

Deiters' cells. Cells that support the outer hair cells in the COCHLEA.

Deiters' nucleus. The lateral nucleus of the VESTIBULAR NUCLEI which sends excitatory impulses to motor neurons.

deixis. The use of a word or expression whose referent can only be understood by taking into account the non-linguistic context in which the word is used (e.g. 'here' or 'there'). *Compare* ANAPHORA.

déjà vu. A feeling, usually eerie, of familiarity, when in fact the experience is new and has never previously occurred.

de Jong's law. The principle that the time taken to perform a task is an exponential function of the time spent practising it.

delayed alternation learning. Learning to alternate between two responses with a delay between them and with no signal to indicate which response to choose, e.g. learning to alternate between arms in a T-maze with a delay between trials. Successful performance on such tasks poses problems for stimulus–response theorists since the responses are not under the control of an external stimulus.

delayed auditory feedback (DAF). Repeating someone's voice back to him over earphones after a short (about 250 msec) delay, a procedure that can cause stuttering and inability to speak.

delayed conditioning. Classical conditioning in which the conditioned stimulus is present for a considerable time before the unconditioned stimulus is given; the organism learns to withhold the conditioned response until shortly before the unconditioned stimulus is due to start. *Contrast* TRACE CONDITIONING.

delayed matching to sample. *See* MATCHING TO SAMPLE.

delayed reaction. A synonym for DELAYED RESPONSE.

delayed reinforcement. Reinforcement given only after a time interval has elapsed after the instrumental response has occurred.

delayed response. A procedure in which a subject is given a discriminative stimulus, and has to wait for an interval after the stimulus has ended before making a response; e.g. a monkey might be shown one of two food cups being baited and have to pick the correct one after an interval of a minute.

delay of gratification. Putting off an immediate reward because by so doing a larger reward can be obtained later, e.g. giving up smoking in order to live longer.

delay reduction theory. The hypothesis that the strength of conditioning reduces as the interval between the conditioned and unconditioned stimulus increases.

Delboeuf illusion. The geometrical illusion that when two concentric circles are presented the size of the outer one is underestimated and that of the inner one is overestimated. It is now known that when there is a large difference in the diameters of the circles (about 5:1) these subjective effects reverse – the outer circle is now seen as too large and the inner one as too small.

deletion. (Genetics) The loss of a segment of a chromosome and the genes it contains.

Delilah syndrome. (Psychoanalysis) Female promiscuity intended to weaken the men seduced; it is said to be caused by the woman taking over the behaviour of a father who had exploited her when young.

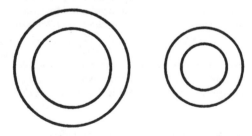

Delboeuf illusion. The left inner circle is the same real size as the right outer one.

delirium. A severe disruption of conscious thought which may be accompanied by hallucinations and sensory illusions; it can be caused by psychosis, senile dementia, drugs, alcoholism, etc.

delirium tremens. Delirium caused by the withdrawal of alcohol from an alcoholic, and characterized by incoherent thought and speech, hallucinations, delusions, sweating, rapid heart beat, etc.

delta ($\triangle$). The difference between two quantities, e.g. $\triangle I$ is a change in intensity.

delta motion. The illusion that the second of two successively presented stimuli moves to the first; it occurs when the stimuli are only slightly displaced from one another in space, and when the second is brighter than the first.

delta rule. (Connectionism) A rule governing BACK PROPAGATION, in which the strength of the connection between input and output units is changed as a function of the difference between the actual output and the target value as determined by a TEACHING UNIT.

delta waves. The high-amplitude, slow (0.5–4 Hz) electroencephalogram waves recorded in the deepest stage of sleep. *See* SLOW-WAVE SLEEP.

delusion. A false belief that would not be held by any normal person. Such beliefs are common in schizophrenia. *See* the following entries and *contrast* HALLUCINATION and ILLUSION.

delusional speech. Speech exhibiting a person's delusions.

delusions of control. A synonym for DELUSIONS OF INFLUENCE.

delusions of grandeur. A mistaken and pathological belief in one's own importance, as held by many professors, most pop stars, and all politicians.

delusions of influence. The mistaken and pathological belief that one's thoughts or actions are being controlled by an external agency.

delusions of persecution. The mistaken and pathological belief that one is being persecuted by others, or that they are plotting or conspiring against one.

delusions of reference. The mistaken and pathological belief that others are constantly talking or writing about one, or are plotting against one. *Compare* PARANOIA.

demand character. A Gestalt expression for a feature of a situation that tends to evoke a particular desire or response (e.g. a sunny beach may evoke the desire to swim). *Compare* Gibson's more modern term AFFORDANCE: many psychologists confuse inventing new terms for old ideas with inventing new concepts.

demand characteristics. 1. The features of an experiment that, without the experimenter realizing it, may prompt the subject to behave in a particular way. 2. A synonym for DEMAND CHARACTER.

demand feeding. Short for SELF-DEMAND FEEDING.

dementia. An impairment or loss of mental ability, particularly of the capacity to remember, but also including impaired thought, speech, judgement, and personality. It occurs in SENILE DEMENTIA, and in conditions involving widespread damage to the brain (such as KORSAKOFF'S PSYCHOSIS) or narrowing of the blood-vessels.

dementia praecox. An obsolete synonym for SCHIZOPHRENIA.

demography. The statistical study of the growth and geographical distribution of populations, and also of such other distributional factors as marriage, class, and income.

demon. (AI) A routine that draws inferences from data, taking into account existing knowledge; a particular demon is brought into play only when the requisite conditions for its use are satisfied.

demonomania. The delusion of being possessed by an evil spirit.

demonstrative pronoun. *See* PRONOUN.

demophobia. A morbid fear of crowds.

dendrite. The thin fibres of a neuron that transmits information in the form of a change in MEMBRANE POTENTIAL towards its CELL BODY; the axonal terminals of the presynaptic cell normally synapse on the dendrites (and cell body) of the postsynaptic cell.

dendritic spine. A thorn-like extension of a DENDRITE on which excitatory presynaptic fibres synapse.

dendrodendritic synapse. A synapse between the DENDRITES of two neurons.

denervation. The abolition of nerve conduction to or from an organ, e.g. by severing a nerve connected to it.

denial. 1. (Psychoanalysis) A DEFENCE MECHANISM in which the EGO refuses to acknowledge unconscious material in the ID, which if acknowledged would cause a painful reaction, like anxiety or guilt. Freud thought denial occurred mainly in children because they were poor at reality testing. 2. (Neuropsychology) The delusory belief, caused by brain damage, that some part of the body (e.g. a limb) or of the perceived world does not exist. 3. (Neuropsychology) A synonym for ANOSAGNOSIA.

denominator. The divisor of a fraction, e.g. 4 in 3/4.

denotation. The REFERENT of a word or expression as opposed to its meaning. The denotation of 'dogs' is all individual dogs, but its CONNOTATION is an animal that barks, is man's best friend, etc.

densitometry. Short for RETINAL DENSITOMETRY.

density. (Hearing) An auditory dimension that is difficult to specify, but that corresponds approximately to whether a sound sensation is thin or full, or compact or dense. Density increases with both frequency and intensity.

dental. Pertaining to a consonant produced with the tongue against the back of the teeth, e.g. the 'th' in 'think'.

dentate gyrus. A gyrus of the PALAEOCORTEX that surrounds the curved tip of the hippocampus, and is tucked away in the middle portion of the temporal lobe.

dentate nucleus. A nucleus in the CEREBELLUM to which most of the cerebellar cortex projects. Lesions to it produce staggering gait and intention tremor.

denying the antecedent. The fallacy of deducing that because the antecedent of a conditional proposition is false its consequent must be false; e.g. deducing from 'If he's late, I'll be cross; he's not late' the conclusion 'I'm not cross'.

deoxyglucose autoradiography. A form of AUTORADIOGRAPHY using 2-deoxyglucose, a substance similar to glucose, which is taken up by cells but which stays in the cell because it cannot be properly metabolized. Radioactive deoxyglucose can be injected into the nervous system and will later show up which cells or areas have been most active.

deoxyribonucleic acid (DNA). The molecule carrying the genetic code. The code is expressed as the sequence in the DNA molecule of four nucleotide bases (adenine, guanine, cytosine, and thymine); each of the 20 amino acids is specified by one or more sequences of three bases, but some triplets act as stops.

dependence. 1. (Psychiatry) Habitual reliance on a drug whose withdrawal will lead to craving, disruption of behaviour, and possibly organic withdrawal symptoms. 2. (Social psychology) Habitual reliance on another person, whether emotional, financial, etc. 3. (Statistics) Changes in one variable occurring systematically with changes in another.

dependent personality disorder. A personality disorder in which the person is excessively passive and reliant on others.

dependent variable. A variable measured or observed in an experiment (e.g. mental health or reaction time) whose value may be influenced by the INDEPENDENT VARIABLE. See also INTERVENING VARIABLE.

depersonalization. 1. (Psychiatry) An abnormal state of mind in which the person feels his thoughts and feelings are unreal, and that he is not part of the world around him; it can occur in depression, schizophrenia, after withdrawal from a drug, etc. Contrast DEREALIZATION. 2. More generally, the feeling of having no real self, of not existing as an individual person.

depolarization. (Neurophysiology) A reduction in the resting potential across the membrane of a neuron, which if sufficiently large, triggers a nerve impulse. *See* ACTION POTENTIAL and *contrast* HYPERPOLARIZATION.

depotentiation. The reduction or reversal of the potential difference across a nerve cell's membrane caused e.g. by PRESYNAPTIC INHIBITION.

depressant. Any substance that tends to calm people, like the barbiturates or benzodiazepines.

depression. A state of extreme dejection, usually characterized by sleeplessness, inability to concentrate, lack of interest in the world, feelings of guilt and helplessness, and the beliefs that nothing can be done to ameliorate the condition and that it will last for ever; it is also often accompanied by lassitude and slowness of movement, though some depressives are extremely agitated (*see* AGITATED DEPRESSION) and anxious. The word is loosely used by the layman to mean 'misery', but it is unclear whether depression is on a continuum with ordinary human unhappiness. Nowadays depression requiring professional intervention is often called CLINICAL DEPRESSION in order to distinguish it from misery. *See* also ENDOGENOUS DEPRESSION and REACTIVE DEPRESSION.

depression with melancholia. (DSM-III) A synonym for ENDOGENOUS DEPRESSION.

depression without melancholia. (DSM-III) A synonym for REACTIVE DEPRESSION.

depressor nerve. Any nerve that reduces motor or glandular activity. More specifically a branch of the VAGUS NERVE that lowers blood pressure.

depth. 1. When followed by words like 'psychology' or 'therapy', synonymous for 'dynamic' as in DYNAMIC PSYCHOLOGY. 2. (Vision) Distance from an observer.

depth cue. Any kind of information used by the organism to estimate distance or the 3-D shape of an object, including INTERPOSITION, LINEAR PERSPECTIVE, MOTION PARALLAX, STEREOPSIS, and TEXTURE GRADIENTS.

depth-first search. (AI) A technique for searching a network in which each path is searched to its end (or to a depth specified by the programmer) before the next path is searched. *Contrast* BREADTH-FIRST SEARCH.

depth from motion. The perception of the depth or three-dimensional shape of a body from its movement relative to the observer, whether it is the body that moves or the observer. *See* MOTION PARALLAX.

depth from shading. The use of the amount of light reflected from a surface to determine its slant or curvature, an important DEPTH CUE.

depth interview. An interview that attempts to uncover aspects of the interviewee's wishes and attitudes to which he would not normally admit, or of which he is unconscious; this may involve e.g. persuading him to give free associations to material presented to him.

depth of field, depth of focus. The range of depth over which objects are in reasonably good focus for a given degree of accommodation.

depth of processing. The cognitive level to which a stimulus is processed. E.g. the visual stimulus 'CAT' may be seen as a collection of curved and straight lines, or as letters, or it may be translated into the corresponding speech sounds, or the word 'cat' may be retrieved from the mental lexicon, or a visual image of a cat may be generated, and so on. Many think that the greater the depth to which a stimulus is processed, the more likely it is to be remembered.

depth perception. Seeing the world in three dimensions, both by seeing the distance away of objects and by seeing their 3-D shape.

depth therapy. Any psychotherapy that attempts to uncover unconscious motives or dynamic forces.

derealization. The abnormal feeling that the world around one, including the people in it, is unreal; it can occur in schizophrenia. *Contrast* DEPERSONALIZATION.

dereflection. A psychotherapeutic technique in which the patient's attention is drawn away from his symptoms, and he is shown what a good time he could have if he were not so preoccupied with his troubles.

dereistic thinking. Illogical thought processes that are not based on reality, of the sort that may occur in a daydream or in schizophrenia.

derivational morphology. The rules for creating new words out of existing morphemes. E.g. 'eat' + 'able' = 'eatable'.

derivative. (Mathematics) A coefficient representing the rate of change of one quantity with respect to another. In the case of movement, the first derivative is distance traversed per unit time (**velocity**), the second is the change in velocity per unit time (**acceleration**), and the third is the change in acceleration per unit time. An increase in rate is called **positive acceleration**, a decrease is **negative acceleration**.

derived need. A synonym for ACQUIRED DRIVE.

derived score. A score derived by mathematical operations from a raw score, e.g. a percentage or a score expressed in units of standard deviation.

dermal. Pertaining to the skin.

dermatome. The band of skin innervated by one spinal nerve.

dermis. A layer of connective tissue lying below the epidermis, and containing most of the skin's receptor cells.

dermo-optical perception. (Parapsychology) The alleged ability to see with the skin, e.g. by detecting colours with the fingers.

desaturated. *See* SATURATION.

descender. That part of a lower-case letter that falls below the line, e.g. 'j' and 'y' have descenders, 's' does not.

descending fibres. Axons proceeding from a higher to a lower centre in the nervous system.

descending series. *See* LIMITS, METHOD OF.

descriptive statistics. The study and application of mathematical methods of summarizing or describing data, e.g. means, medians, variances, ranges, correlations. *Contrast* INFERENTIAL STATISTICS.

desensitization. In psychotherapy, reducing the power of thoughts, events, or situations to disturb the patient, by exposing him to them. *See* SYSTEMATIC DESENSITIZATION.

destrudo. (Psychoanalysis) The expression of the THANATOS instinct.

desynchronization. In general the loss of periodicity in a waveform; as applied to ELECTROENCEPHALOGRAPHY, the disappearance of the alpha rhythm that occurs when a subject concentrates on something.

DET. An abbreviation for DETERMINER.

detached effect. (Psychoanalysis) An emotion that becomes separated from its original source, and attaches itself to something else. Freud thought obsessions and phobias could be explained in this way.

detachment. 1. The adoption of an objective, unfeeling attitude to others, thought by some psychoanalysts to be a neurotic DEFENCE MECHANISM. 2. In ontogeny, the reduction in a child's dependence on its mother (beginning at about two years of age).

detail perspective. The reduction in the retinal size of objects of the same real size with increases in their distance from the observer; it can be a DEPTH CUE. *Compare* TEXTURE GRADIENT.

detail response. In the RORSCHACH TEST any response which is made to a part of the figure rather than to the whole.

detection task. A task in which the subect has to perceive that something is there without necessarily being able to tell what it is. E.g. when shown sinusoidal gratings the subject may be able to detect that some pattern is present at a contrast too low for him to see the width and orientation of the gratings. *Contrast* IDENTIFICATION TASK.

detection theory. Short for SIGNAL DETECTION THEORY.

detection threshold. A synonym for ABSOLUTE THRESHOLD.

detector. *See* FEATURE DETECTOR.

deterioration index. A measure of the adverse effects of ageing on performance.

determiner (DET). A part of speech that qualifies a noun by indicating its number, whether it is definite or indefinite, etc., e.g. 'a', 'the', 'each', 'every', 'any'.

determining set. A disposition to behave or respond in a particular way.

determining tendency. A synonym for AUFGABE.

determinism. The philosophical doctrine that every event has a cause and hence that all future states of the universe are determined by previous ones.

detour problem. Any problem in which to reach a goal the organism has first to move away from it because there is an obstacle blocking the direct route.

deutan. Being either a DEUTERANOPE or DEUTERANOMOLOUS.

deuteranomaly. A mild form of colour blindness in which an abnormally high proportion of green light is needed when matching a spectral yellow with a mixture of red and green lights. Although deuteranomalous people are trichromatic, they have a reduced sensitivity to green.

deuteranope. A person with DEUTERANOPIA.

deuteranopia. The commonest form of DICHROMATISM, in which the medium wavelength (green) cones appear to be non-functional; it is characterized by poor hue discrimination in the red–green region of the spectrum.

developmental age. A measure of an ability in which the child's score is converted to the average number of years of age at which its score is made by other children.

developmental aphasia. A synonym for DEVELOPMENTAL LANGUAGE DISORDER.

developmental dyslexia. Impaired ability to read or to learn to read, occurring in childhood and not caused by low IQ or manifest brain damage. *Contrast* ACQUIRED DYSLEXIA.

developmental language disorder. Any disorder in the development of language not due to known organic causes.

developmental psychology. The study of the mental changes, both emotional and cognitive, that take place in people at different ages, and of how these changes are brought about.

developmental quotient. DEVELOPMENTAL AGE divided by CHRONOLOGICAL AGE.

developmental task. Any skill that is normally acquired by a particular age (e.g. walking or talking).

deviance. The breaking by an individual of his society's customs or precepts.

deviation. (Statistics) The degree to which a score or scores differ from the mean. *See* STANDARD DEVIATION.

deviation score. The extent to which a given value departs from the mean of a set of values.

devil effect. *See* HALO EFFECT.

Devil's pitchfork. The IMPOSSIBLE FIGURE illustrated below. The line XY appears convex at the top and concave at the bottom because of contradictory local DEPTH CUES. It therefore cannot be construed as a 3-D shape.

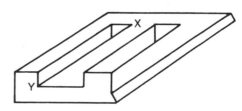

Devil's pitchfork

de Vries–Rose law. The principle that the brightness difference threshold rises as the square root of the background intensity.

Dexedrine. The trade name for an isomer (*d*-form) of amphetamine.

dextral. Pertaining to or towards the right.

dextrality. A preference for using the right hand.

dextrosinistral. Pertaining to a person who at first preferred to use his left hand, but who has learnt to use his right.

df. An abbreviation for DEGREES OF FREEDOM.

diachronic. Pertaining to the changes in, or development of, a system over time, used particularly of the historical development of language. *Contrast* SYNCHRONIC.

diacritical marking system (DMS). A way of teaching children to read by giving them text with additional markings showing how syllables are to be pronounced. *Compare* INITIAL TEACHING ALPHABET.

diadochokinesis. The ability to make alternating movements of flexion and extension.

diagnosis. (Psychiatry) Assigning a patient's mental disorder to a category of mental disorders (which are revised every few years). *See* DIAGNOSTIC AND STATISTICAL MANUAL OF MENTAL DISORDERS and LOTTERY.

Diagnostic and Statistical Manual of Mental Disorders (DSM). A manual published by the American Psychiatric Association, now in its fourth revised edition (DSM-IV), published in 1994, that defines categories of mental illness. It seeks, sometimes at the cost of being euphemistic, to be progressive. It has, for example, replaced the word 'neurosis' with 'disorder'. No attempt is made here to repeat all the diagnostic expressions it uses since many of them are self-explanatory.

diagnostic problem-solving. The politically correct synonym for FAULT FINDING.

diagnostic test. Any test used to clarify the nature or aetiology of a disorder.

dialectic. The attempt to arrive at truth by disputation, particularly by using argument and counterargument to lead to a synthesis.

dialectical psychology. Any psychological approach based on the thesis that cognitive and emotional conflicts, and the resolution of such conflicts, play a key role in the operation of the human mind.

diallel cross. (Genetics) Assessing the effects of a strain's genotype by mating members of that strain with those of other strains and observing the effects on the F^1 generation.

Diana complex. (Psychoanalysis) A woman's repressed wish to be a man.

dianetics. An unvalidated form of psychotherapy put forward by Ron Hubbard that uses a mishmash of concepts drawn from psychoanalysis, cybernetics, and other disciplines. It was the forerunner of scientology.

diaschisis. The production of a deficit after brain injury caused not directly by the lesion, but by its secondary effects, e.g. by increased cranial pressure or by an effect of the damaged centre on another centre in the brain.

diathesis. A hereditary or acquired predisposition to develop a particular illness.

diazepam. A minor tranquillizer used to reduce anxiety; it is one of the most commonly used BENZODIAZEPINES (trade name Valium).

dichoptic. Pertaining to the presentation of different stimuli to the two eyes simultaneously or in very close succession. E.g. in dichoptic masking a target stimulus is sent to one eye and the masking stimulus to the other. *Compare* BINOCULAR and INTEROCULAR. *Contrast* MONOPTIC.

dichotic. Pertaining to the stimulation of the two ears simultaneously but with different sounds; this technique has been much used in the study of attention. *Compare* BINAURAL. *Contrast* MONAURAL.

dichromatism, dichromacy, dichromasy, dichromatopsia, dichromia, dichromopsia. Colour blindness in which any hue can be metamerically matched by a mixture of only two PRIMARIES (1); it is thought to be due to a functional lack of one of the three cone pigments. *See also* DEUTERANOPIA, PROTANOPIA, and TRITANOPIA.

didactic analysis. (Psychoanalysis) An analysis given to a trainee analyst as part of his training.

diencephalon. The part of the FOREBRAIN lying below the cerebral hemispheres including the HYPOTHALAMUS, PITUITARY, and THALAMUS.

difference limen (DL). A synonym for DIFFERENCE THRESHOLD.

difference of Gaussians (DOG). (Neurophysiology) An arrangement whereby a central unit (e.g. a ganglion cell) receives from the retina a steep GAUSSIAN DISTRIBUTION of excitation in the middle of its receptive field, and a shallower Gaussian distribution of inhibition extending beyond the excitatory region. This arrangement explains the observed properties of on-centre cells, and transposing inhibition and excitation would explain those of off-centre cells. Marr argued that cells wired in this way would be particularly efficient at detecting local brightness changes. *See also* ZERO CROSSING.

difference threshold. The smallest difference between two stimuli that can just be detected, usually arbitrarily taken to be the difference that can be correctly detected on 75 per cent of trials. *Compare* ABSOLUTE THRESHOLD.

difference tone. A COMBINATION TONE heard when two tones not too far apart in pitch are presented. It has the frequency of the BEATS made when the peaks of the waveform of the two tones coincide; its frequency is therefore the difference in frequency of the two tones presented.

Differential Aptitude Test (DAT). A test battery measuring eight different aptitudes, e.g. verbal reasoning and spatial ability.

differential-association theory. The hypothesis that a person's beliefs and actions (e.g. whether or not he becomes a criminal) are determined by conformity to the group to which he belongs.

differential conditioning. Conditioning in which the organism is reinforced for responding to one stimulus but not for responding to another.

differential extinction. Extinguishing responses to one stimulus by not reinforcing them, while maintaining responses to another by continuing to reinforce them.

differential inhibition. The process that narrows the generalization gradient to the positive (reinforced) stimulus when a negative (non-reinforced) stimulus is presented.

differential psychology. A synonym for the PSYCHOLOGY OF INDIVIDUAL DIFFERENCES.

differential rate reinforcement. A reinforcement schedule in which the availability of the reinforcer depends on the rate at which the organism responds. In differential reinforcement of high response rates (DRH), the organism is reinforced only if it responds within a set period after its previous response. In differential reinforcement of low response rates (DRL), the organism is reinforced if it responds only after the lapse of a set interval following its previous response.

differential reinforcement. Reinforcement that is contingent on which of more than one responses the animal makes, e.g. a pigeon may be reinforced for pecking a red key but not for pecking a green one.

differential reinforcement of high response rate (DRH). *See* DIFFERENTIAL RATE REINFORCEMENT.

differential reinforcement of low response rate (DRL). *See* DIFFERENTIAL RATE REINFORCEMENT.

differential reinforcement of other behaviour (DRO). A simple reinforcement schedule in which an organism is reinforced only when it fails to make a specific response for a set period of time; any other responses that happen to occur immediately before the reinforcer will therefore be reinforced.

differential reinforcement of paced responding (DRP). A reinforcement schedule in which an organism is reinforced only if its rate of responding stays within specified limits, i.e. neither too fast nor too slow.

differential response. A synonym for DISCRIMINATIVE RESPONSE.

differential stimulus. A synonym for DIS-CRIMINATIVE STIMULUS.

differential validity. The VALIDITY (1) of a test judged by the extent to which it predicts differential performance on two or more other tasks.

differentiation. 1. (Perception) Short for STIMULUS DIFFERENTIATION. 2. (Cognition) The process of becoming aware of differences betweeen different thoughts, feelings, emotions, etc. 3. The calculation of a coefficient (a DERIVATIVE) that represents the rate of change of one quantity with respect to another. 4. (Biology) Short for CELLULAR DIFFERENTIATION.

diffraction. A deviation in the direction of a light wave (or other electromagnetic wave) on striking the edge of an obstacle. Diffraction caused by the edges of the pupil, particularly when contracted, results in some blur on the retina. *See* AIRY'S DISC.

diffusion. (Chemistry) Movement of molecules of a given kind from a region where they are highly concentrated to one where their concentration is low. E.g. if sodium is more concentrated on one side of a cell membrane than on the other, there will be a tendency for it to cross the cell membrane to equalize the concentration. *Contrast* ACTIVE TRANSPORT.

diffusionism. (Anthropology) The doctrine that aspects of one society's culture spread to neighbouring societies.

diffusion of responsibility. The reduction in individual responsibility felt by members of a group. It can cause the BYSTANDER EFFECT.

digital. Pertaining to an information processing device whose components have discrete states (e.g. ones in which information is represented by on–off switches) rather than by continuously varying quantities. *Contrast* ANALOGUE.

digital computer. A computer in which information is represented by elements having discrete states, in practice invariably binary ones. *Contrast* ANALOGUE COMPUTER.

digit-span. The number of digits that a person can report in the correct sequence shortly after having been presented with them.

digraph. Any two letters that represent one PHONEME (e.g. 'th').

dihydroxyphenylalanine. A substance usually (and with good reason) referred to by its abbreviation, DOPA.

dilution effect. The weakening of a belief by providing irrelevant neutral information. E.g. a subject told that a person has sadomasochistic fantasies is less likely to believe he is a child abuser if told in addition that he repairs cars in his spare time.

dimension. Any way in which something can vary continuously (and in some uses, non-continuously). For example, the position of a point in space relative to an observer can be specified along three dimensions – vertical, horizontal, and depth. Colour, a subjective quality, has three dimensions – hue, saturation, and brightness.

dimetric projection. A form of ORTHO-GRAPHIC PROJECTION in which two faces of an object are symmetrically projected.

dimorphism. (Biology) Any characteristic of a species that has two forms (e.g. male and female).

ding-dong theory. A sarcastic synonym for the NATURAL RESPONSE THEORY OF LANGUAGE.

Dionysian. Thinking and behaving in a riotous, uncontrolled, and highly spontaneous way. *Contrast* APOLLONIAN.

diopter. The reciprocal of the FOCAL LENGTH of a lens measured in metres.

dioptre. A variant spelling of DIOPTER.

dioptrics. The study of the curvature of the cornea and lens and of their refractory indices.

diotic. Pertaining to a stimulus that is the same on each ear.

diphthong. A speech sound produced by gliding from one vowel to another as in 'beer'.

diplacusis. Hearing a tone of the same frequency as having a different pitch when it is presented successively to each ear.

diplegia. Paralysis of the same muscles on both sides of the body.

diploid. Pertaining to a cell having the full complement of chromosomes arranged in pairs (one member of each pair from each parent). *See* HAPLOID and MEIOSIS.

diplopia. Seeing double. *Compare* POLYOPIA.

dipsomania. A form of alcoholism in which a person periodically indulges in excessive bouts of drinking.

directed forgetting. A synonym for INTENTIONAL FORGETTING.

directed graph. A model or description in the form of a set of labelled nodes connected by unidirectional arrows, which are usually labelled to indicate the relationship between connected nodes. The nodes usually represent entities or attributes.

directed thinking. Thinking intended to solve a problem or achieve a goal, as opposed e.g. to daydreaming.

directional test. A synonym for ONE-TAILED TEST.

directive. A SPEECH ACT whose purpose is to persuade the listener to do something, e.g. a command. It is often expressed indirectly, e.g. 'The window's open' can mean 'Close the window.'

directive therapy. A synonym for ACTIVE THERAPY.

direct object. The main object of a transitive verb. In contrast to an **indirect object**, it cannot be omitted from a sentence. Thus in 'He gave his son a pound', 'pound' is the direct object and 'son' the indirect. 'He gave a pound' is a grammatical sentence, but 'He gave his son' (meaning 'to his son') is not.

direct perception. J.J. Gibson's curious theory of perception, postulating that what is seen is uniquely given by the patterns of light on the retina, i.e. the sample of the OPTIC ARRAY taken over time (and *pari passu* for the other senses). He believed that perception does not involve cognitive operations, inferences, computation, or the construction of representations. Perception would be a dull subject if he were right.

direct priming. A synonym for REPETITION PRIMING.

direct realism. Gibson's doctrine of perception. *See* DIRECT PERCEPTION.

direct reflex. A reflex in which the stimulus and the response are on the same side of the body. *Contrast* CROSSED REFLEX.

direct scaling. *See* PSYCHOPHYSICAL SCALING METHODS.

disaster syndrome. The reaction of people, particularly civilians, to a catastrophe, thought to consist first of dazed shock and anxiety, then dependence on others who give orders, and finally gradual recovery marked by tenseness, some anxiety, and a desire to talk about the experience.

discharge. The production of a nerve impulse in a nerve cell.

disconnection syndrome. Any neurological syndrome produced by the destruction of the pathways between one part of the brain and another, rather than by the loss of tissue devoted to a particular function. e.g. CONDUCTION APHASIA.

discontinuity theory. Lashley's hypothesis that animals do not learn gradually about all stimuli with which they are confronted, but that they form hypotheses (e.g. 'always go left'), and learn on a given trial only about events relevant to their current hypothesis; he thought one hypothesis could be suddenly replaced by another. *Contrast* CONTINUITY THEORY.

discordance. A difference in a trait between two blood relatives, most often used of twins.

discounting principle. (Attribution theory) The principle that people are less likely to attribute a given cause to a given effect if other plausible causes are present.

discourse analysis. The study of how meaning is conveyed and extracted from spoken or written language ranging from a single sentence to a novel. At one end such topics as the interpretation of EXOPHORA are considered, while for lengthy material such questions as how it should be segmented, the relation between segments and the form in which arguments are expressed have been considered. Progress has been made with single sentences, but the complexity and variability of lengthier material has produced more NOISE than LIGHT (2).

discrete trials experiment. An experiment in which the start of each trial is determined by the experimenter, and in which the subjects' behaviour between trials is irrelevant to the outcome of the trial; maze learning is a typical example. *Contrast* FREE OPERANT EXPERIMENT.

discriminability. The ease with which two or more stimuli can be distinguished from one another. In SIGNAL DETECTION THEORY, the term refers to d' – the distance in standard deviations between the peak of the noise curve and that of the curve of signal plus noise.

discriminanda. Any stimuli between which the subject must learn to discriminate in order to make the correct response.

discriminant function. The function of a set of variables, each measured on a sample of items, whose value can be used to allocate correctly items to one of two populations. A **multiple discriminant function** allocates items to one of more than two populations. Most discriminant functions are linear.

discriminant validity. The difference in the extent to which a test correlates with the trait it purports to measure and with other traits. A test of numerical aptitude that did not predict performance on arithmetic any better than it predicted verbal peformance would be a poor test. *Compare* CONVERGENT VALIDITY.

discriminated operant. Skinner's expression for a response emitted under the control of a specified stimulus.

discriminating range. The minimum difference in scores on a test that will reliably predict a difference between testees on some other criterion (e.g. educational success).

discrimination. 1. (Experimental psychology) The perception of a difference between two or more stimuli. 2. (Social psychology) Unequal treatment of individuals, groups, or races based on prejudice.

discrimination function. The DIFFERENCE THRESHOLD plotted along a continuum such as wavelength.

discrimination hypothesis. An explanation of the PARTIAL REINFORCEMENT EFFECT, postulating that it occurs because it is more difficult for the organism to distinguish between partial reinforcement and extinction than between continuous reinforcement and extinction.

discrimination learning. Learning in which the organism must discriminate between two or more stimuli in order to make the right response; some but not all experiments of this kind are run to test the animal's discriminative capacities.

discriminative response. A response made to one of two or more stimuli between which the organism has to discriminate in order to obtain reward.

discriminative stimulus. In operant learning, a stimulus that signifies the availability of reward contingent upon a particular response being made (or that signifies a specific schedule of reinforcement). *Compare* NEGATIVE STIMULUS and POSITIVE STIMULUS.

dishabituation. The process underlying the reappearance of a response to which the organism has become habituated; e.g. dishabituation can occur if a very strong stimulus is presented at the same time as a stimulus to which habituation has taken place.

disidentification. (Social psychology) Distancing oneself from the group to which one belongs; it is often a reaction to being in a low status or despised group.

disillusioning process. Horney's term for the process by which the patient learns in the early stages of therapy to stop seeing himself in either an idealized or an over-critical way.

disinhibition. In conditioning, the process whereby a conditioned response that has been inhibited suddenly reappears as a result of the presentation of a novel or very strong stimulus.

disjoint sets. Sets having no members in common.

disjunction. A logical connective approximately equivalent to the inclusive use of 'or' and usually written 'V'. In an **inclusive disjunction**, if *p* and *q* are propositions, then *p* V *q* is true if and only if either *p* is true or *q* is true or both are true. In an **exclusive disjunction**, *p* V *q* is true if and only if *p* is true or *q* is true but not both are true. *Compare* CONJUNCTION.

disjunctive eye movement. An eye movement in which the eyes turn in opposite directions. *See also* VERGENCE. *Contrast* CONJUNCTIVE EYE MOVEMENT.

disjunctive fallacy. Failure to take an action, when either of two events is sufficient cause for it, and one event is known to have occurred but the other cannot be known to have occurred until some time in the future.

dismantling treatment strategy. In behaviour therapy, the attempt to decide which components of therapy are effective, by systematically comparing groups that receive all components with groups that receive only some components.

disorder. (Psychiatry) A mental malady. It is a fashionable term that is both useful and euphemistic: useful because by employing it the psychiatrist no longer has to distinguish neurosis from psychosis, which may be no bad thing; and euphemistic because it avoids the use of pejorative terms like 'neurosis' or 'illness', which may be no bad thing either.

disorganized schizophrenia. (DSM-III) A synonym for HEBEPHRENIC SCHIZOPHRENIA.

disorientation. A condition in which a person is confused about time, place, or people; it can be caused by brain damage, psychosis, or extreme fright.

disparate points, disparate retinal points. Any two points, one on each retina, which when stimulated do not yield an impression of the same direction in space, i.e. the points are not CORRESPONDING POINTS. When a pair of such points is stimulated by the same distal stimulus, BINOCULAR DISPARITY occurs.

disparity. Short for BINOCULAR DISPARITY.

dispersion. (Statistics) The extent to which numerical data are spread about their mean, usually measured by the STANDARD DEVIATION.

displaced aggression. Aggression directed at an organism (or object) other than the one that provoked anger; in other words, 'kicking the cat'.

displaced speech. Bloomfield's term for speech that refers to items or events outside the immediate environment, e.g. to the future or to other places, Young children gradually develop the capacity for such speech.

displacement activity. (Ethology) The activation of components of one drive when another is frustrated, e.g. a stickleback thwarted in mating may execute some of the components of nest building. *Contrast* REDIRECTED ACTIVITY and VACUUM ACTIVITY.

displacement of affect. (Psychoanalysis) A defence mechanism which allows a repressed drive to be released by changing its object, e.g. the anal drive may be released by hoarding money instead of faeces. Displacement is also said to occur in dreams, e.g. when a neutral figure is substituted for someone of importance in the dreamer's life.

display behaviour. (Ethology) Ritualized patterns of movement or posture occurring in courtship or in confrontation with conspecifics and used to communicate.

display rules. The rules that govern within a society the ways in which emotions may be expressed in a socially acceptable manner.

dispositional attribution. Ascribing one's own or another's behaviour to internal rather than external factors.

dispositional inertia, dispositional rigidity. *See* INERTIA, LAW OF.

disruptive selection. (Evolution) The splitting of one population into two as a result of different traits being developed.

dissociated learning. A synonym for STATE DEPENDENT LEARNING.

dissociation. 1. (Neuropsychology) The retention of one capacity when another is lost after brain injury. *See also* DOUBLE DISSOCIATION. 2. (Vision) Elimination of the stimulus for fusion, e.g. by occluding one eye. 3. (Personality) The splitting or loss of different parts of consciousness, as in DISSOCIATIVE DISORDERS and possibly in hypnotism.

dissociative amnesia. A sudden inability to remember who one is (and sometimes one's past life), though other skills are preserved.

dissociative disorders. Disorders in which parts of behaviour or consciousness seem to become separated from the rest, e.g. FUGUES, PSYCHOGENIC AMNESIA, and MULTIPLE PERSONALITY.

dissociative hysteria. Hysteria in which dissociative symptoms are the most prominent. *See* DISSOCIATIVE DISORDERS.

dissociative identity disorder. DSM-IV's synonym for MULTIPLE PERSONALITY.

dissonance. An unpleasant or harsh auditory sensation caused by a complex tone in which the different tones do not blend together.

dissonance theory. The doctrine that holding dissonant attitudes or beliefs is aversive, and that the person tries to change such attitudes or beliefs to make them more consistent. *Compare* COGNITIVE DISSONANCE.

distal. (Anatomy) Towards the periphery of the body, or towards the periphery of a part of the body; e.g. the thumb is distal to the elbow. *Contrast* PROXIMAL.

distal response. The effects of a response in regions removed from the PROXIMAL RESPONSE; e.g. in driving a car the proximal response is turning the wheel, the distal response is making the car turn.

distal stimulus. The object in the environment that causes the pattern of stimulation (the PROXIMAL STIMULUS) on the receptors.

distance paradox. (Vision) 1. The phenomenon that in a figural aftereffect (and other spatial aftereffects like the tilt aftereffect) the size of the effect at first increases with increases in the distance apart (relative tilts) of the inspection and test figures, reaches a maximum, and then decreases with further increases in their distance apart (relative tilts). 2. Duncker's expression for the phenomenon that when a rectangle (frame) enclosing a fixed dot is moved, the rectangle and the dot may be seen to move through distances that when summed are greater than the actual movement of the frame. *See* INDUCED MOTION.

distance receptors. Sensory receptors that enable a person to detect objects at a distance (e.g. in hearing, smell, vision)

distance vision. Vision for points more than 20 feet away.

distance zones. The area of physical distance surrounding a person within which another person normally does not approach; the size of the area depends on the intimacy between people and the social situation (e.g. in a bar or at work). *See also* INTERPERSONAL DISTANCE.

distinctive features. (Phonetics) A set of contrasting features (usually binary) in terms of which it is claimed phonemes can be distinguished; e.g. presence of voicing versus absence of voicing, plosive versus non-plosive, nasal versus non-nasal, etc.

distinctiveness. (Social psychology) *See* COVARIATION THEORY.

distorted room. A synonym for AMES ROOM.

distortion. (Psychoanalysis) A defence mechanism, used particularly in dreams, in which repressed wishes or their objects are represented in disguised form.

distortion tone. A synonym for COMBINATION TONE.

distractible speech. Speech that moves incoherently from one topic to another, as e.g. in mania.

distractor. 1. In a recognition task, a new item not previously presented to the subject to which he should make a negative response. 2. More generally, any stimulus that reduces the attention a subject can give to a task.

distress relief quotient. The ratio of expressions of distress to those of relief, sometimes used to measure recovery in psychotherapy.

distributed knowledge, distributed representation. A representation of knowledge in which many units contribute to the storage of a given piece of knowledge and each contributes to the storage of other knowledge, as in a CONNECTIONIST system.

distributed practice. Practice that is spread out in time, by leaving intervals either between successive trials or between successive blocks of trials. *Contrast* MASSED PRACTICE.

distributed term. (Logic) Any term in a syllogism governed by the universal quantifier (i.e. 'all').

distributed trials. A series of trials between each of which there is a long interval. *Contrast* MASSED TRIALS.

distribution. (Statistics) The frequencies with which scores or other numerical data fall at each of a set of values, or in each of a set of categories.

distribution-free statistics. A synonym for NON–PARAMETRIC STATISTICS.

distributive justice. The principle that what a person gets out of a situation should be proportional to what he puts in. It is sometimes used in determining the appropriate wages for different jobs in the same firm taking into account the quality of skill, amount of effort, etc. needed by each job. *Contrast* ABSOLUTE JUSTICE.

disulfiram. A drug better known by its trade name ANTABUSE.

disuse, law of. Thorndike's principle that a stimulus–response association will become weaker if not used.

disuse principle. The hypothesis that forgetting occurs because the material to be remembered has not been rehearsed, or because a learned skill has not been used.

disutility. Negative utility, i.e. states of affairs that, to varying degrees, a person wishes to avoid; the term is used particularly in game theory.

disynaptic arc. A reflex arc containing two synapses, made up from three nerve cells – a receptor, an interneuron, and a motor nerve cell.

diurnal rhythm. Rhythmic changes in bodily or psychological processes occurring on an approximately 24-hour cycle. *See also* BIOLOGICAL CLOCK.

divagation. Confused or rambling speech.

divergence. The turning outward of the two eyes that occurs when fixation shifts to a point further away; it is needed to ensure that the fixation point falls at the centre of each fovea. *Contrast* CONVERGENCE.

divergent thinking. Thinking in unusual, imaginative, non-logical ways, thought by some to be necessary in order to provide possible solutions to problems that cannot be solved algorithmically. *Contrast* CONVERGENT THINKING.

divided line illusion. The illusion that a line bisected in the middle is shorter than it really is. *Contrast* OPPEL–KUNDT ILLUSION.

dizygotic twins (DZ twins). Non-identical twins produced by the fertilization of two eggs.

DL. An abbreviation for DIFFERENCE LIMEN.

DMS. An abbreviation for DIACRITICAL MARKING SYSTEM.

DNA. An abbreviation for DEOXYRIBONUCLEIC ACID.

DOG. An abbreviation for DIFFERENCE OF GAUSSIANS.

doing gender. The study of how a person's sex influences the responses made by others.

dolichocephalic. Pertaining to a long narrow head, whose CEPHALIC INDEX is under 0.75.

dolorology. The study of the nature, origins, and treatment of pain.

domain. In psychology and in AI, a particular stage or type of information processing. In vision the extraction of lines and edges is usually regarded as one domain, and the construction of a 3-D model of the scene as another.

domains of processing theory. The hypothesis that the more thoroughly and elaborately information is processed at a given level of processing, and the higher the levels at which it is processed, the better it will be remembered.

domal sampling. Selecting a sample to interview (e.g. in a poll) on the basis of where people live (e.g. sampling every 100th house).

dominance. 1. The extent to which, when two different ALLELES are present, one determines the phenotype more than the other. When the phenotype is completely controlled by one allele, it is called the **dominant** gene. *Compare* CODOMINANCE and RECESSIVE. 2. *See* CEREBRAL DOMINANCE, DOMINANCE HIERARCHY, DOMINANT, EYE DOMINANCE, and OCULAR DOMINANCE.

dominance hierarchy. (Ethology) The arrangement of members of an animal community in terms of their superordination over others, with the most successfully aggressive member at the top. It occurs in many animal communities, e.g. domestic chickens peck other chickens lower down the hierarchy but not those above them. The term is also used in the same sense in social psychology of groups of people.

dominant. (Genetics) Pertaining to an ALLELE that when present on a chromosome determines the phenotype even if the other member of the pair is a different allele; or

pertaining to a trait produced by such a gene. *Compare* CODOMINANCE and RECESSIVE.

dominant hemisphere. The hemisphere (usually the left) in which language functions are primarily located; at one time it was thought that where there was a difference in the extent to which the two hemispheres controlled behaviour, the dominant hemisphere was always the more important. Since it is now known that the other hemisphere is dominant for some other functions, the term has become a misnomer. *See also* CEREBRAL DOMINANCE.

dominant wavelength. The monochromatic wavelength that yields the same HUE as a standard stimulus made up of light of one or more wavelengths.

dominator. Granit's term for a hypothetical retinal ganglion cell that respond – though usually not equally – to all parts of the visible spectrum. *Contrast* MODULATOR.

Donders' law. The principle, to which there are exceptions, that when a point is fixated, the eyes always have the same angle of torsion that is specific to the direction of fixation.

Donders' method. A synonym for SUBTRACTION METHOD.

door-in-the-face technique. The phenomenon that if an impossibly difficult request is made of a person, he is more likely subsequently to accede to a milder one.

DOPA. An abbreviation for dihydroxyphenylalanine, a precursor of DOPAMINE.

dopamine (DA). A catecholamine neurotransmitter, an excess of which may be associated with schizophrenia, and a deficit of which may cause Parkinsonian symptoms. It is a precursor of EPINEPHRINE and NOREPINEPHRINE.

dopamine hypothesis. The hypothesis that excessive dopaminergic activity in the limbic system is implicated in schizophrenia.

dopaminergic. Pertaining to transmission by DOPAMINE, or substances that mimic its action.

Doppelgänger. A fantasized double of a person, who looks and acts in the same way as the person himself.

Doppler effect. The rise (or fall) in the frequency of a sound wave caused by the source approaching (or receding from) the observer.

dorsal, dorsad. (Anatomy) On or toward the back of the body; when used of the brain in upright species, it means toward the top. *Contrast* VENTRAL.

dorsal columns. Large bundles of sensory nerve fibres at the back of the spinal cord, next to the midline, comprising the FASCICULUS CUNEATUS and FASCICULUS GRACILIS, and forming part of the LEMNISCAL SYSTEM.

dorsal ramus. *See* RAMUS.

dorsal root. *See* SPINAL ROOT.

dorsal root ganglion. A ganglion in the dorsal root that contains the cell bodies of the afferent fibres that enter the spinal cord.

dorsal tegmental bundle. A noradrenergic pathway projecting from the locus coeruleus to the hippocampus, thalamus, and cerebral cortex.

dorsolateral nucleus. A synonym for LATERAL DORSAL NUCLEUS.

dorsomedial nucleus. 1. A thalamic nucleus receiving fibres from other thalamic nuclei, projecting to the frontal association cortex, and involved in emotion. 2. A nucleus of the HYPOTHALAMUS.

dose–response effects. (Medicine) The effects (physical or behavioural) of different levels of a drug.

Dostoevsky syndrome. A synonym for INTER-ICTAL SYNDROME, from which Dostoevsky may have suffered.

double alternation. 1. A task in which the animal must make two responses of one kind, then two of another (and may be required to continue this cycle) in order to obtain reward; no signal is given to indicate which response was made last time. E.g. the animal might be placed in a maze where, whichever way it turns, the path leads it back to the start, and it might have to learn to run left, left, right, right, at the choice point in order to obtain reward. 2. A reward schedule in which reinforcement is given for two trials, non-reinforcement for two, etc.

double-aspect theory. (Philosophy) The hypothesis that mental terms refer to the functioning of the brain, and that mental and physical terms are simply alternative ways of describing it.

double bind. Bateson's term for putting a person in a conflict situation by giving him contradictory messages (e.g. of love and hate); Bateson hypothesized that schizo-phrenia was caused by parents placing the child in a double bind.

double-blind procedure. A procedure in which neither the experimenter nor the subject knows which experimental condition the subject is in, thus ensuring freedom from bias in the experimenter's observations. E.g. in testing the effectiveness of psychotherapy, there might be an experimental and a placebo group, and the experimenter evaluating out-come would not know to which group a subject had been assigned. *Contrast* OPEN STUDY and SINGLE-BLIND PROCEDURE.

double depression. A combination of episodes of MAJOR DEPRESSION with chronic DYSPHORIA.

double dissociation. The finding that in sub-jects with one or other of two different brain lesions, those with one brain lesion are im-paired on one task but not a second, whereas those with the other are impaired on the second task but not the first. As first pointed out by Charcot and Piètre, such a finding is proof that each lesion damages an area of the brain that is implicated in a specific function.

double-opponent cell. A type of cell found in some visual areas of the cortex. It has a receptive field in which the centre contains an opposite input from two colour-opponent processes; the surround contains the same opposition, but with the excitatory and in-hibitory processes reversed. E.g. the centre might respond to R+,G− and the surround R−,G+.

double-sided test. A synonym for TWO-TAILED TEST.

double vision. A synonym for DIPLOPIA.

dove strategy. *See* EVOLUTIONARY STRATEGY.

Down's syndrome. A disorder caused by having three instead of two chromosomes at the 21st or 22nd chromosome, and characterized by mental retardation and mongoloid features.

d-prime. The spoken version of the symbol d'.

DQ. An abbreviation for DEVELOPMENTAL QUOTIENT.

drama therapy. A synonym for PYSCHO-DRAMA.

dramatization. (Psychoanalysis) A defence mechanism in which repressed wishes or repressed thoughts are expressed in symbolic form, e.g. in dreams.

Draw-a-Person Test (DAP). A clinical test in which someone is asked to draw a person. It was believed that paranoid people emphasize the eyes, dependent people the mouth, etc., but since no such correlations exist the test is useless.

dream content. *See* LATENT CONTENT and MANIFEST CONTENT.

dream ego. Jung's term for the part of the ego that is conscious in dreams.

dream instigator. A synonym for DAY RESIDUE.

dream interpretation. Any attempt to uncover the meaning of a dream, particularly that made by psychoanalysts who believe dreams represent repressed wishes and thoughts in disguised form. It is a highly speculative enterprise.

dreams. The succession of images (both visual and from other senses) occurring in sleep (particularly REM SLEEP). They usually portray events in a distorted way. The function of dreams is unknown: Freud thought they released repressed wishes in disguised form, others think they help to retain the previous day's events, and yet others (e.g. Crick) believe they help the dreamer to forget them.

dream work. (Psychoanalysis) The conversion of repressed wishes and thoughts into the disguised form in which they appear in a dream, using the mechanisms of CONDENSATION, DISPLACEMENT OF AFFECT, DRAMATIZATION, SECONDARY ELABORATION, and SYMBOLIZATION.

D2 receptor. A dopamine receptor that is blocked by neuroleptics.

DRH. An abbreviation for differential reinforcement of high response rates. *See* DIFFERENTIAL RATE REINFORCEMENT.

drift. 1. (Vision) A slow smooth movement of the eye occurring in PHYSIOLOGICAL NYSTAGMUS. 2. *See* EVOLUTIONARY DRIFT.

drive (D). Any internal force that motivates an organism to pursue a goal; drives are often divided into primary or physiological drives (e.g. hunger, thirst, sex), which have a strong innate basis, and secondary or non-physiological drives, which do not (e.g. avarice). It is unclear in which division drives like competitiveness and curiosity should be placed.

drive displacement. *See* DISPLACEMENT ACTIVITY.

drive-reduction theory. The hypothesis, adopted particularly by Hull, that learning only occurs when a response is followed by the drive reduction that takes place when the goal of the drive is reached.

drive stimuli (S_D). The afferent impulses produced by different drives, postulated by Hull in order to make the mechanism by which drives direct behaviour the same as that by which stimuli direct it.

drive strength (D). The current intensity of one or more drives. It is used as a technical term by Hull, and enters into his equation for GENERALIZED REACTION POTENTIAL when multiplied by GENERALIZED HABIT STRENGTH and other factors. *See* HULLIAN THEORY.

DRL. An abbreviation for differential reinforcement of low response rates. *See* DIFFERENTIAL RATE REINFORCEMENT.

DRO. An abbreviation for DIFFERENTIAL REINFORCEMENT OF OTHER BEHAVIOUR.

DRP. An abbreviation for DIFFERENTIAL REINFORCEMENT OF PACED RESPONDING.

drug-dispositional tolerance. A synonym for PHARMACOKINETIC TOLERANCE.

drug-induced psychosis. An organic psychosis caused by a drug.

2 1/2-D sketch. *See* TWO-AND-A-HALF-D SKETCH.

D-sleep. Any period of sleep in which dreams occur, but often used as synonymous with REM SLEEP.

DSM. An abbreviation for DIAGNOSTIC AND STATISTICAL MANUAL, which is revised every few years. The roman numeral following refers to the revision. The latest version (DSM-IV) was published in 1994.

DSM-III-R. A minor revision of DSM-III adopted in 1987.

d-structure. An abbreviation for DEEP STRUCTURE.

dual ambivalence. The conflicting emotions of parents and adolescents, produced by the need of the adolescents for both independence and support.

dual-coding theory. The hypothesis that regardless of how it is presented, material tends to be stored in memory in both verbal and visual form.

dualism. (Philosophy) The hypothesis that mind and body are separate entities. Some dualists believe they interact, and others that they operate in parallel.

dual personality. A condition in which a person exhibits contrasting personalities and in which when in one state he seems to have no knowledge of what he did in the other. *See* MULTIPLE PERSONALITY.

dual process theories. 1. (Social psychology) Theories postulating that the changes in attitude produced by a message are dependent on many factors other than its semantic content, e.g. the status of the person delivering the message, the need for the recipient to preserve his self-esteem, etc. 2. *See also* TWO-PROCESS THEORY.

dual threshold. The phenomenon that in some sensory modalities there are two thresholds for changes in the intensity of the same stimulus, one for perceiving its existence and the other for perceiving its quality. E.g. a light may be detected at a very low intensity, but it requires a much higher intensity to detect its hue.

duck-rabbit. A REVERSIBLE FIGURE, invented by Jastrow, which can be seen either as a duck or a rabbit.

ductless gland. A synonym for ENDOCRINE GLAND.

dull normal. An obsolete expression for a person with low normal intelligence, i.e. with an IQ of between 80 and 89.

Duncan test. (Statistics) An A POSTERIORI TEST for comparing the significance of the difference between several means. It is a modification of the NEWMAN–KEULS TEST, and redistributes the probabilities of error among the components of the multiple comparison procedure.

Dunnett test. (Statistics) A PLANNED COMPARISON test that can be applied if several conditions are each to be compared to a single condition to decide whether the results of any of these conditions are significantly different from those of that one.

duo. A word pair uttered by an infant (e.g. 'my ball').

duplexity theory. A synonym for DUPLICITY THEORY.

duplication. (Genetics) The duplication of a segment of a chromosome, a form of MUTATION.

duplicity theory. The hypothesis, now confirmed, that vision is based on two separate systems, one for bright light (cones) and one for dim light (rods). *Compare* PHOTOPIC VISION and SCOTOPIC VISION.

dura mater. The outermost of the three membranes covering the brain and spinal cord. *See* MENINGES.

Dwarfism. Very short stature; it can be hereditary, congenital, or caused by disease or dietary deficiency.

dwell time. The length of time for which an object is fixated.

dyad. Two people who interact, usually closely, e.g. husband and wife.

dyadic effect. The phenomenon that in a conversation the more one person discloses about himself, the more the other is likely to disclose about himself.

dynamic equilibrium. Any state in which different forces exactly balance one another.

dynamic memory span. When a continuous sequence of items is presented to a subject to be memorized, the number of items back from the most recent that he can recall perfectly when the sequence unexpectedly stops. Usually only about three items will be remembered, as opposed to the seven or eight that can be perfectly recalled when the sequence is only that long.

dynamic psychology. Any form of psychology that stresses internal interacting processes, particularly unconscious drives. All forms of psychoanalysis are dynamic. When interactive forces are postulated at a perceptual or cognitive level the approach is often known as FIELD THEORY, which sounds more scientific.

dynamic range. The range of inputs over which a system will register different responses. E.g. rods and cones differ in their dynamic ranges to light intensity, while a household weighing machine cannot differentiate between 1 ton and 10 tons.

dynamic system. A system in which a change in one part alters many other parts.

dynamic system theory. Any approach to individual or group behaviour that stresses the interaction of different forces.

dynamism. Sullivan's term for DEFENCE MECHANISM; he used it because he believed the defence mechanisms were active processes.

dynamometer. A device for measuring muscular strength.

dyne. A unit of force defined as the force needed to accelerate one gram by one centimetre per second per second; one dyne is equal to 0.000001 newton. The pressure of sound waves is usually measured in dynes per square centimetre.

dynorphine. A class of OPIOID PEPTIDES containing 17 amino acids.

dysacousia. 1. Extreme discomfort caused by loud noise. 2. Difficulty in hearing.

dysaesthesia. Impairment or distortion of the sense of touch.

dysarthria. Impaired ability to speak caused by an inability to control the muscles of the vocal tract.

dysautonomia. Dysfunction of the autonomic system; it can be caused by brain damage.

dysbasia. Difficulty in walking.

dysbulia. 1. Difficulty in thinking coherently. 2. Lack of will-power.

dyscalculia. Difficulty in doing arithmetic.

dyschiria. Difficulty in telling which side of one's body has been touched.

dyschromatopsia, dyschromia, dyschromopsia, dyschromacy. Any impairment of colour vision.

dyschronaxis. A disturbance to the sense of time, which can be caused e.g. by flying through several time zones.

dyscontrol syndrome. Abnormal social behaviour marked by outbursts of extreme aggression, sexual offences, etc.; it can be caused by damage to the limbic system or temporal lobe.

dysdiadochokinesia, dysdiadochokinesis. Difficulty in performing fast alternating movements, e.g. of the fingers.

dyseidetic dyslexia. DYSLEXIA caused primarily by difficulty in the visual recognition of letters and words.

dysergasia. Any syndrome produced by a TOXIC PSYCHOSIS, e.g. delirium.

dysesthesia. An alternative spelling of DYSAESTHESIA.

dysgenic. Pertaining to any genetic factor that tends to lower the quality of a stock. *Contrast* EUGENICS.

dysgeusia. Impairment of the taste sense.

dysgnosia. An obsolete term for intellectual impairment.

dysgraphia. Impairment of the ability to write; it can be caused by brain damage occurring near the boundary between the temporal and occipital lobes.

dysinergia. Lack of coordination between related muscle groups, causing the patient to under- or over-shoot the target. It can be caused by damage to the cerebellum.

dyskinesia. Impairment of voluntary movements or the presence of involuntary tics or spasms.

dyslalia. Impaired speech, usually reserved for impairment not due to brain damage. *Contrast* APHASIA.

dyslexia. Impaired ability to read or to learn to read. DEVELOPMENTAL DYSLEXIA occurs in children for unknown causes, whereas ACQUIRED DYSLEXIA is caused by brain damage. When the term 'dyslexia' is used without qualification it normally means developmental dyslexia. *Compare* ALEXIA.

dyslexia with dysorthographia. A synonym for LEGASTHENIA.

dyslogia. Incoherence of speech.

dysmentia. Poor performance on psychological tests that is not caused by low IQ but by other factors like unwillingness to co-operate.

dysmetria. Impaired ability to control the direction, force, and length of bodily movements.

dysmnesia. Impairment of memory; it may be caused by brain damage.

dysmorphophobia. A morbid fear or morbid conviction that one is deformed or otherwise abnormal.

dysorexia. Any disturbance of appetite.

dysosmia. Impairment or distortion of the sense of smell.

dyspareunia. 1. Painful sexual intercourse. 2. An impaired capacity for obtaining sexual pleasure.

dysphagia. Any disturbance of eating, e.g. ANOREXIA or BULIMIA.

dysphasia. A rare synonym for APHASIA.

dysphemia. A defect in speech functionally caused, e.g. stuttering.

dysphonetic dyslexia. DYSLEXIA caused primarily by difficulty in mapping written symbols onto the corresponding phonemes.

dysphonia. Impaired voice quality.

dysphoria. An unpleasant mood, marked by discontent, anxiety, mild depression, etc.

dysphrenia. An obsolete term for mental disorder.

dysplasia. Abnormal development of body tissue as occurring, for example, in dwarfism or gigantism.

dyspraxia. A defect in the ability to perform skilled movements. *See also* APRAXIA.

dyssocial behaviour. Antisocial behaviour, e.g. delinquent or criminal behaviour.

dysstasia. Difficulty in standing upright.

dyssymbiosis. A pathological relationship between mother and child in which the child uses neurotic or psychotic mechanisms to control the mother.

dystaxia. Mild ATAXIA.

dysthymia. 1. Prolonged depressed mood, not sufficiently severe to be classified as a manic-depressive disorder. 2. Eysenck's term for the characteristics of people high on his NEUROTICISM DIMENSION and at the introvert end of his EXTRAVERSION–INTROVERSION DIMENSION.

dystonia. Abnormal muscle tonus.

dystrophy. Muscular atrophy.

E

E. An abbreviation for 1. experimenter; 2. EXPERIMENTAL GROUP; 3. ENERGY; 4. E DIMENSION.

E. An abbreviation for ILLUMINANCE.

$_sE_R$. Hull's abbreviation for REACTION POTENTIAL.

$_s\bar{E}_R$. Hull's abbreviation for GENERALIZED REACTION POTENTIAL.

$_s\bar{E}_R$. Hull's abbreviation for NET REACTION POTENTIAL.

$_s\dot{E}_R$. Hull's abbreviation for MOMENTARY REACTION POTENTIAL.

eardrum. The membrane separating the outer and middle ear, which transmits sound waves to the ossicles.

early infantile autism. A severe form of AUTISM beginning at birth or shortly afterwards. The term is misleading, for the syndrome usually persists into adulthood. It is characterized by extreme withdrawal from others, difficulties with language, motor tics and repetitious movements. About 10 per cent of sufferers exhibit abnormal talents in some sphere such as music, painting, or calculating. See also ASPERGER'S SYNDROME and KANNER'S SYNDROME.

early selection. In attention, the idea that unwanted messages are filtered out at an early stage of processing.

Easterbrook hypothesis. The (correct) hypothesis that arousal narrows the range of attention.

Ebbinghaus curve. A curve plotting the amount of learned material retained against time, i.e. a curve of forgetting.

EBS. An abbreviation for ELECTRICAL BRAIN STIMULATION.

eccentric fixation. Fixation in which the image of the object fixated falls outside the foveola.

eccentricity. (Vision) The distance of a point on the retina from the centre of the fovea, usually measured as the visual angle out from the fovea.

eccentric projection. Locating a sensation in the outside world rather than in the sense organ stimulated, as in perception of objects.

echoencephalograph. A device for mapping the structure of the brain using ultrasonic waves.

echoic memory, echoic store. An auditory short-term memory in which all aspects of a heard sound are preserved; it takes a few seconds to decay. Compare ICONIC MEMORY and PRECATEGORICAL ACOUSTIC MEMORY.

echokinesis. A synonym for ECHOPRAXIA.

echolalia. Meaningless repetition of others' words or phrases, occurring in catatonic schizophrenia and sometimes through brain damage or deterioration.

echolocation. The ability to detect the direction, distance, and shape of objects by transmitting high-frequency sound, and monitoring its echo. This ability is possessed e.g. by bats and dolphins: it can be used to some extent by blind people, who listen to the echoes of their footsteps.

139

echopathy. Pathological imitation of others' movements and speech.

echophrasia. A synonym for ECHOLALIA.

echopraxia. Pathological imitation of others' movements and postures.

ecmnesia. A rare synonym for RETROGRADE AMNESIA.

ecological niche. The role occupied by a species within an ecosystem, including all the means by which it survives (e.g. its eating habits, home, etc.).

ecological perception. Perception in a natural rather than laboratory environment. Brunswik believed that perception should be studied in a natural environment, and more recently Gibson held that ecologically important properties of the natural environment are 'picked up' directly from the optic array.

ecological validity. 1. The extent to which a result (or theory) applies not merely to a limited experimental situation or situations but to ordinary life. 2. As used by Brunswik and Gibson, the extent to which aspects of the proximal stimulus are directly correlated with the distal stimulus, and hence can be used to perceive it correctly.

ecology. (Biology) The study of the relationship between organisms and the environment they inhabit.

ecomania. Acting badly towards, or being morbidly preoccupied with, members of one's family.

economics. (Psychoanalysis) The ways in which a person preserves his PSYCHIC ENERGY.

ecosystem. A community of interacting species, and the environment they inhabit.

écouteur. A person who derives sexual pleasure from overhearing sexual activities in others or listening to accounts of such activities.

ecphoria. An obsolete term for establishing or recalling a memory.

ECS. An abbreviation for ELECTROCONVULSIVE SHOCK.

Ecstasy. *See* MDMA.

ECT. An abbreviation for ELECTROCONVULSIVE THERAPY.

ectoderm. The outer layer of cells of an embryo, from which skin, hair, glands, the nervous system, etc. are developed.

ectogenous. Outside the body.

ectomorphy. A body type (tall and skinny) in SHELDON'S CONSTITUTIONAL THEORY, said to be derived from the embryonic ectoderm and to be associated with CEREBROTONIA.

ectopic. Congenital displacement of a part of the body. *See also* HOMEOTIC MUTANT.

ectoplasm. 1. (Physiology) The outer layer of a cell. 2. (Parapsychology) A synonym for muslin, i.e. the substance exuded from the body of a medium, which may take on the shape of the dead.

ectosylvian gyrus. A gyrus of the temporal lobe that exists in carnivores (it has become part of the INSULA in primates). It is part of the auditory cortex and also contains visual association areas.

edema. An excess of fluid in any part of the body's tissue; edema in the brain occurring after a lesion may produce pressure which impairs the functioning of non-lesioned tissue.

edge detector. A cell in the visual cortex that responds maximally to a straight edge (dark on one side, light on the other) in a particular orientation and position on the retina. *See* FEATURE DETECTOR and *compare* BAR DETECTOR.

edge effect. The phenomenon that when a subject has to learn to identify each of a range of stimuli differing along a dimension, he performs better with stimuli towards the ends of the range than on those in the middle.

E dimension. A synonym for the EXTRAVERSION–INTROVERSION DIMENSION.

EDR. An abbreviation for ELECTRODERMAL RESPONSE.

educable mentally retarded (EMR). A mildly retarded person who is able to receive some formal education; the expression is usually applied to those with IQs between 55 and 69. *Compare* TRAINABLE MENTALLY RETARDED.

educational age. A measurement of the level of a child's educational attainment, expressed as the average age at which children reach the standard he has attained.

educationally subnormal (ESN). Unable to benefit from attendance at an ordinary school.

educational pyschology. The systematic study of methods of teaching and learning, and of disorders that arise in schoolchildren (such as delinquency and truancy), and the application of such knowledge to improving methods of teaching and learning, and ameliorating disorders. This branch of psychology has few secure principles.

educational quotient (EQ). The ratio of educational age to chronological age.

education stage. Jung's expression for the stage at which the patient seems to be getting better.

eduction. The discovery by thought of new relationships or new concepts. *Compare* DEDUCTION and INDUCTION (1).

Edwards' Personal Preference Schedule. A personality inventory measuring the strength of a person's needs, e.g. those for achievement or affiliation.

EEG. An abbreviation for ELECTRO-ENCEPHALOGRAPHY.

effect, law of. Thorndike's principle that a response is strengthened when it is followed by something pleasant and weakened when followed by something unpleasant. *See also* EMPIRICAL LAW OF EFFECT and STRONG LAW OF EFFECT.

effective habit strength ($_s\bar{H}_R$). A synonym for GENERALIZED HABIT STRENGTH.

effective motive. The desire to gain control over the environment.

effective reaction potential ($_s E_R$). A synonym for GENERALIZED REACTION POTENTIAL.

effective stimulus. The stimulus that controls a response in a given situation.

effector. A muscle or gland.

effector nerve. A synonym for MOTOR NEURON.

effector organ. A synonym for EFFECTOR.

efference copy. A copy of the motor output sent to a perceptual centre of the brain. It is transmitted by the COROLLARY DISCHARGE, and is used to null reafferent sensations caused by the motor movement.

efferent. Pertaining to any neural pathway or part thereof in which information is being conveyed outwards from any part of the nervous system towards the muscles or glands. *Contrast* AFFERENT.

efficacy. *See* SELF-EFFICACY.

effort. *See* LEAST EFFORT PRINCIPLE.

effort after meaning. The attempt to give meaning to material both in perception and memory (even when, as in the case of nonsense syllables, it has little meaning). Bartlett thought that it always occurs.

effort sydrome. A neurotic overreaction to exertion, accompanied by e.g. breathlessness, palpitations, and anxiety.

E–F scale. A subscale of the Minnesota Multiphasic Personality Inventory designed to measure social prejudice and authoritarian attitudes.

ego. (Psychoanalysis) The part of the mind that is in touch with reality and that mediates between the libidinous urges of the ID and the puritanical disapproval of the SUPEREGO; it represses direct knowledge of the naughty wishes of the id, while cleverly releasing them in the form of dreams, slips of the tongue, and works of art. *See* DEFENCE MECHANISM.

ego-alter theory. The innocuous hypothesis that a person's reactions to others are determined by how he sees himself in relation to them.

ego anlaysis. Analysis in which the focus is on discovering why some wishes are repressed and cannot be tolerated by the EGO; less attention is paid to conflicts in the ID than in ordinary psychoanalysis.

ego anxiety. (Psychoanalysis) Anxiety arising from a threat to the EGO.

ego boundary. A vague term signifying the boundary between a person's self and other people.

ego cathexis. A state in which most psychic energy is in the EGO and in which it controls the forces of the ID and SUPEREGO satisfactorily by channelling them to objects that will not arouse anxiety (e.g. by SUBLIMATION). *Compare* OBJECT CATHEXIS.

egocentre. The point on the body toward which all stimuli from a given modality are perceived to converge, i.e. the point to which their direction is referred. The **visual egocentre** is (according to different authorities) either the point midway between the eyes or the point of convergence of lines in visual space having the same subjective direction on each eye (which corresponds roughly to the centre of rotation of the head). The **auditory egocentre** is the centre of the head. It is disputed whether there are one or more **tactual egocentres**: there may be different ones for the different parts of the body.

egocentric bias. The tendency for people to think they have contributed more than they have to a joint task, e.g. a committee meeting etc.

egocentric judgement. A judgement of the tilt of an object relative to part of the body. **Oculocentric judgements** are made with respect to the eye (e.g. by setting a line parallel to the eye's vertical meridian), **headcentric judgements** with respect to the head (e.g. by facing an object), and **bodycentric judgements** with respect to the body (e.g. by setting a line parallel to the long axis of the body).

egocentric localization. The apparent direction and distance of objects in space with respect to the observer.

egocentric speech. Speech in which there is no intention to communicate with another person.

egocentrism. Piaget's expression for a phenomenon he thought he had observed, namely, that until about 7 years of age children talk and think entirely in terms of their own needs and viewpoints without taking other people into account.

ego control. Ability to control one's impulses, e.g. to delay gratification, inhibit aggression, give up smoking, and finish writing a dictionary on time. Probably not a unitary trait.

ego defence. (Psychoanalysis) The defence of the EGO against any threats, particularly inner ones from the SUPEREGO or ID. *Compare* DEFENCE MECHANISM.

ego development. (Psychoanalysis) The gradual formation of the EGO occurring through contact with the external world and the learning of self-control and independence.

ego dystonic. (Psychoanalysis) Pertaining to anything unacceptable or threatening to the EGO (e.g. repressed wishes in the ID). *Compare* EGO SYNTONIC.

ego-dystonic homosexuality. (DSM-III) Homosexuality in which the homosexual does not accept his proclivities but longs to become heterosexual. It is classified as a mental disorder by DSM-III.

ego eroticism. A synonym for NARCISSISM.

ego ideal. (Psychoanalysis) The standards someone consciously wishes to meet, which are according to Freud usually introjected from the parents. It is hard to separate the ego ideal from the SUPEREGO, but the standards embodied in the ego ideal are more modifiable and are chosen more consciously.

ego instincts. (Psychoanalysis) The nonsexual instincts, particularly those having to do with self-preservation.

egoistic suicide. Durkheim's expression for suicide undertaken through feelings of self-reproach, e.g. for being a failure in life. *Compare* ALTRUISTIC SUICIDE and ANOMIC SUICIDE.

ego libido. (Psychoanalysis) The wish to gratify one's own ego in an entirely self-centred way, as in the young child. *Contrast* OBJECT LIBIDO.

egomorphism. A synonym for PROJECTION.

ego neurosis. (Psychoanalysis) A neurosis in which the EGO is seriously disturbed, as in hysteria, fugue states, disorientation, and delirium.

egopathy. Aggressive behaviour towards others caused by a pathologically exaggerated sense of one's own importance.

ego psychology. (Psychoanalysis) Concentration, in therapy or theory, on the EGO and its role in controlling impulses and mastering the environment. Ego psychologists, e.g. Sullivan, emphasize that the ego can at least in part develop independently of the ID, and have also stressed the role of social relationships in its development.

ego resiliency. The ability to vary impulsiveness to meet the demands of the situation. Someone with too much EGO CONTROL tends to be inhibited and to lack spontaneity.

ego resistance. The tendency of the EGO to refuse to acknowledge repressed drives because of the anxiety they provoke, or to refuse to overcome neurosis because of its secondary gains.

ego strength. (Psychoanalysis) The extent to which the EGO can handle without disruption the demands of the ID and SUPEREGO and can reconcile them with the environment. An individual with a strong ego is strong-willed, patient, and can withstand frustration. According to many psychoanalysts he is also the most suitable case for treatment: he may not need it, but at least it won't upset him.

ego syntonic. Pertaining to ideas or wishes that are acceptable to the ego. *Contrast* EGO DYSTONIC.

ego-syntonic homosexuality. Homosexuality in which the homosexual accepts his proclivities.

ego theory. The philosophical theory that a person is an entity (a mind, soul, or spirit) that has experiences. The continuity of the person depends on the continuity of this entity. *Contrast* BUNDLE THEORY.

E group. An abbreviation for EXPERIMENTAL GROUP.

Ehrenstein illusion. 1. *See* the illustration below. Subjective bright circles appear at the ends of the lines, presumably caused by brightness contrast or, more likely, a KANIZSA CONTOUR. *Compare* HERMANN GRID. 2. The two geometric illusions invented by Ehrenstein that are variants on ORBISON FIGURES.

Ehrenstein illusion

eiconic memory. An alternative spelling for ICONIC MEMORY.

eidetic image. A vivid and detailed visual image of a scene corresponding exactly to the original perception; at one time it was thought to be common in children but many now doubt its existence. The expression is sometimes also used of vivid auditory images of the same type.

eidetiker. A person who has eidetic imagery.

Eigenwelt. (Existentialism) A person's attitude towards himself. *Contrast* MITWELT and UMWELT (2).

eighth cranial nerve. A synonym for VESTIBULOACOUSTIC NERVE.

eikon. An alternative spelling of ICON.

eikonometer. A set of vertical strings in a plane, used to detect the effect of aniseikonic lenses on depth vision.

Einstellung. An obsolete term for attitude or set, used particularly of expectations about the stimuli a person is about to receive.

eisotropophobia. A morbid fear of mirrors.

ejaculatio praecox. A synonym for PREMATURE EJACULATION.

ejaculatio retardata. Very delayed ejaculation caused by old age, anxiety, drugs, etc.

EKG. An abbreviation for ELECTROCARDIOGRAM.

elaborated code. Bernstein's expression for the way people from completely different backgrounds talk to one another – slowly, carefully, and taking nothing for granted. *Contrast* RESTRICTED CODE.

elaboration. 1. *See* SECONDARY ELABORATION. 2. Within DOMAINS OF PROCESSING THEORY, the extent to which information is processed in a given domain. 3. (Social psychology) The extent to which a person processes the arguments in a message and connects them with his existing knowledge.

elaboration–likelihood model. A model of persuasion postulating that when a message intended to sway a person's opinion is received, the amount of attitude change in either direction depends on how much ELABORATION (3) the person performs.

elaboration–likelihood model of persuasion. A theory postulating that the effectiveness of a persuasive message increases the more the receiver thinks about (elaborates) its contents.

elaborative rehearsal. Keeping an item in short-term memory while carrying out deeper processes on it, for example, examining its meaning or associating it with other terms, a procedure thought to facilitate its strength in long-term memory. *Contrast* MAINTENANCE REHEARSAL.

élan vital. The 'life force' which Bergson thought drove all living things.

elation effect. (Animal learning) The enhancement of responding when large rewards are substituted for small ones in BEHAVIOUR CONTRAST.

elective mutism. A childhood disorder in which the child refuses to speak although it could if it would.

Electra complex. (Psychoanalysis) The postulated desire of a daughter to sleep with her father, accompanied by jealousy and hatred of the mother for removing the daughter's penis. *Compare* OEDIPUS COMPLEX.

electrical brain stimulation (EBS). Any weak and localized electrical stimulation of part of the brain. It may be undertaken to investigate its behavioural or mental consequences or to discover what other brain sites are affected by the stimulation.

electrical self-stimulation of the brain (ESSB). The performance of a response by an animal because it is rewarded by a small shock to a part of the brain. *See also* PLEASURE CENTRE.

electrical stimulation of the brain (ESB). A synonym for ELECTRICAL BRAIN STIMULATION.

electrical synapse. A SYNAPSE operating by the conduction of an electrical charge. *See* GAP JUNCTION and TIGHT JUNCTION.

electrocardiogram. A record of the electrical activity of the heart, sometimes used as a component of a lie detector.

electroconvulsive shock (ECS). A train of brief shocks given to the head that are sufficient to induce a convulsion and loss of consciousness. The technique is used experimentally to investigate retrograde amnesia in animals, and therapeutically in people as ELECTROCONVULSIVE THERAPY.

electroconvulsive therapy (ECT). The treatment of mental illness by applying a train of brief shocks to the head, thus producing convulsions; several such treatments are usually given over a period of about ten days. The treatment is nowadays given under a general anaesthetic and a muscle relaxant to minimize the convulsions. The efficacy of the treatment for some cases of severe depression is reasonably well proven.

electroculograph (EOG). An alternative spelling for ELECTRO-OCULOGRAPH.

electroculography (EOG). Measuring eye movements by recording their electrical activity.

electrode. An electrical conductor through which current enters or leaves an electrolyte; electrodes are used both to produce and to record current flow in parts of the nervous system.

electrodermal response. A synonym for GALVANIC SKIN RESPONSE.

electroencephalography (EEG). Recording the gross electrical activity of the brain through electrodes attached to the skull. *See* ALPHA WAVES, BETA WAVES, DELTA WAVES and THETA WAVES.

electrolysis. The conduction of electricity through a solution, producing a chemical reaction.

electrolyte. 1. A liquid or gel containing free ions that can therefore conduct electricity. 2. Molecules, such as sodium chloride, that produce free ions when dissolved.

electrolytic lesion. The destruction of specific neural tissue by passing an electric current between two inserted electrodes.

electromagnetic senses. The senses that respond to electrical or magnetic fields. E.g. sharks can detect prey by changes in the electrical field, and pigeons can navigate by their sensitivity to the earth's magnetic field.

electromagnetic spectrum. The range of wavelengths of electromagnetic waves, running from very short to very long wavelengths; it includes cosmic rays, X-rays, ultraviolet rays, light, infrared, and radio waves.

electromyography (EMG). Recording the electrical activity of muscles.

electronarcosis. Electroconvulsive therapy in which the strength and duration of shock are adjusted so that they cause the initial tonic (rigid) but not the clonic (spastic) phase of the convulsion; loss of consciousness results.

electron microscope. A device in which a beam of electrons is focused on an object to yield very high magnifications; it can resolve detail down to a few ångström units.

electro-oculograph. A device for recording eye movements by monitoring the electrical potential of the eye muscles.

electrophobia. A morbid fear of electricity.

electrophoresis. A method of separating molecules of different kinds from one another, by placing them in solution on a medium (e.g. blotting paper) while applying an electric current.

electrophysiology. The study of the role of electricity in animal tissue, particularly in the nervous system.

electroretinogram (ERG). A recording of the gross electrical activity of the retina.

electroshock therapy. A synonym for ELECTROCONVULSIVE THERAPY.

electrotonus. 1. The passive spread of a graded potential over the membrane of a dendrite or of a cell body, particularly when stimulated electrically. 2. Köhler's term for the hypothetical spread of electrical excitation in the brain as in a volume conductor, a notion to which no-one now subscribes. He used it to explain figural aftereffects. *See* SATIATION.

elementarism. A synonym for ATOMISM.

element movement. *See* TERNUS PHENOMENON.

elevated maze. A maze whose paths are raised off the ground and have no sides.

elevator illusion. A form of OCULOGRAVIC ILLUSION in which the subject is centrifugally rotated at an increasing velocity, thus producing a Coriolis force; his head is kept normal to the resultant of gravitational force and the Coriolis force. Instead of experiencing his body as tilted, he feels it rising, and hence sees a stationary point of light in darkness as rising.

eleventh cranial nerve. A synonym for AC-CESSORY NERVE.

elexethymia. Impairment in the use of emotional terms, caused by brain damage.

El Greco fallacy. The fallacy (which can be generalized) that the reason why El Greco exaggerated the ratio of height to width in his paintings of people was that he was aniseikonic. It is a fallacy because even had he been aniseikonic he would have seen a normal portrait of a person in the same way as he saw real people; therefore aniseikonia cannot account for the distortion in his paintings.

elimination by aspects. (Decision theory) A model in which the different aspects of possible outcomes are ranked in importance; all choices leading to outcomes not having the most important aspect are eliminated. If more than one option remains, the second most important aspect is examined in the same way, and so on until only one option remains.

ellipsis. (Linguistics) The omission of a phrase, e.g. 'Yes, you can' (what it is that you can do is implied by the context).

elucidation. (Psychoanalysis) The second stage of Jung's therapy, in which the analyst concentrates on interpreting the patient's unconscious.

emancipatory knowledge. (Sociology) Knowledge of the distortions to one's attitudes and beliefs that can occur through relationships, particularly those in which one person is dominant; such knowledge is supposed to free the person from the alleged distortions.

embedded figure. A pattern forming part of a more complex figure that may be hard to find; embedded figures are used in experiments on perception and in testing visual abilities. They are also used as a test of FIELD DEPENDENCE: field-dependent people have more difficulty finding the figure than field-independent ones.

embedding. (Linguistics) In generative grammar, placing in the surface structure one sentence within another, e.g. 'John, who was very strong, overcame James'. In early transformational grammar the surface sentence derives from two sentences at deep structure level ('John overcame James' and 'John was very strong').

embolalia. A speech disorder in which meaningless material is inserted in sentences.

embolism. The blockage of blood flow by an obstruction in a blood vessel.

embryo. The organism in its first phase (in man the first eight weeks after conception), after which the embryo becomes a fetus.

embryogenesis. The development of the embryo.

emergency theory. The hypothesis that emotions prepare the organism for sudden effort.

emergenesis. A phenotype, especially an unusual one, caused by the non-additive effects of a rare combination of genes.

emergent property. A property possessed by a system that is not possessed by its parts. It need not be a mystical notion, if one can understand how the new property arises. Thus although it is unhelpful to describe the mind as an emergent property of the brain, physiological drives are emergent properties of complex neural mechanisms of which we have a basic understanding.

emetophobia. A morbid fear of vomiting.

EMG. An abbreviation for ELECTROMYOGRAPH.

emic. Pertaining to concepts or beliefs not found in all cultures. *Contrast* ETIC.

emitted behaviour. Responses occurring spontaneously, governed more by internal factors than by external stimuli and not occurring as the result of reinforcement. *See also* OPERANT CONDITIONING.

Emmert's law. The law that an afterimage increases in apparent size in direct proportion to the distance from the observer of the surface on which it is projected. In fact the perceived size is proportional to the *apparent* distance of the surface.

emmetropia. Normal vision with no refractive errors. More technically, the condition in which, when the lens is completely relaxed, the eye's focus is at infinity.

emotion. Characteristically, any feeling accompanied by autonomic arousal, and by a predisposition to behave in a certain way (but is 'serenity' not an emotion?). It is a term that is impossible to define and about which no two psychologists agree.

emotional deprivation. The condition of being brought up without receiving emotional responses (particularly favourable ones like love) from others; it is used particularly of a child brought up without parental affection.

emotional inoculation. The process whereby a person forewarned of a future stressful event prepares himself for it, e.g. by rehearsing how to cope or by self-desensitization, thus improving his ability to deal with it.

emotional release. A synonym for CATHARSIS.

emotion-focused coping. Reducing stress without directly dealing with the stressful situation, e.g. by the use of DEFENCE MECHANISMS. *Contrast* PROBLEM-FOCUSED COPING.

emotion specificity hypothesis. The hypothesis that in psychosomatic disorders a given emotion always causes the same physical disorder.

empathy. The capacity to participate in another's feelings and experiences and to understand them. Showing empathy is thought by most psychotherapists to be a good thing; showing sympathy is a bad thing.

empathy theory. (Vision) Lipp's explanation of the geometrical illusions which postulates that the observer empathizes with the figure. E.g. since it takes more effort to move vertically upward than horizontally, a vertical line of the same length as a horizontal one is seen as longer.

empirical. Based directly on facts or observations rather than on inferences, theories or intuitions.

empirical equation. An equation derived *ad hoc* to fit a given body of data, as opposed to an equation derived from a theory. *Contrast* RATIONAL EQUATION.

empirical horopter. The HOROPTER as determined by empirical methods (*see* e.g. NONIUS METHOD). It is much flatter than the VIETH–MULLER CIRCLE; it passes through (or near) the fixation point, but does not pass through the nodal points of the lenses. At near distances it is slightly convex; with increases in fixation distance it tends to become a straight line or even a line concave to the observer. Its shape suggests that CORRESPONDING POINTS are more widely spaced in the nasal hemisphere than in the temporal.

empirical law of effect. The tautological law proposed by Thorndike that when a response is followed by a satisfying state of affairs, it is more likely to occur again. Unlike the STRONG LAW OF EFFECT, this law does not state that learning occurs only if reinforcement is given.

empirical rational strategy. (Social psychology) The attempt to make people change their habits or attitudes by providing evidence and appealing to their reason.

empirical validity. The extent to which a test can be empirically shown to measure what it purports to measure.

empiricism. 1. The philosophical hypothesis (put forward by Locke) that there are no innate ideas and that the contents of the mind are acquired entirely from information supplied through the senses. *Contrast* NATIVISM. 2. The doctrine that science (and some other studies like history) should be based on the systematic collection of data.

empty-chair technique. A GESTALT THERAPY technique in which the client talks to a person (e.g. his wife) imagined to be in an empty chair, and then sits in the chair himself pretending to be the other person.

empty word. A word without meaning that is introduced to make a sentence grammatical, e.g. the 'it' in 'It's snowing'.

EMR. An abbreviation for EDUCABLE MENTALLY RETARDED.

enactive. Pertaining to the infant's attempt to gain control of its environment.

enantiodromia. Jung's term for the opposition between different tendencies or aspects of a person (e.g. having both introversive and extraversive tendencies).

enantiomorph. The mirror-image version of a 3-D shape; the left and right hands are enantiomorphs.

encapsulated nerve ending. The receptive part of a receptor in skin or muscle (e.g. a Pacinian corpuscle) that is sheathed by a membrane. *Contrast* FREE NERVE ENDING.

encéphale isolé. A preparation in which the brain is transected just above its junction with the spinal cord.

encephalin. An alternative spelling of ENKEPHALIN.

encephalitis. Inflammation of the brain, caused e.g. by a virus.

encephalization. The progressive taking over by the brain in the course of evolution of functions previously carried out by ganglia below the brain.

encephalography. The study and practice of recording the location and shape of structures in the brain without opening up the skull. *See* ELECTROENCEPHALOGRAPHY, PNEUMOENCEPHALOGRAPHY, and RADIOISOTOPIC ENCEPHALOGRAPHY.

encephalon. The anatomical name for the brain.

encoding. The transduction of a message into another form. E.g. a word may be encoded acoustically or by an image of whatever it represents.

encoding specificity hypothesis. The principle that retrieval depends on the same or similar stimuli being present as those that were present and encoded during learning.

encounter group. A group in which people (usually strangers) meet to air their frustrations and problems. Emotional confrontations, sometimes violent, are produced. Some think encounter groups promote sensitivity and personal growth; others think they merely increase selfishness.

enculturation. A synonym for ACCULTURATION.

end brain. A synonym for TELENCEPHALON.

end brush. A cluster of very small ramifying branches at the end of an axon.

end bulb of Krause. *See* KRAUSE END BULB.

end button, end foot. Synonyms for SYNAPTIC BUTTON.

end inhibition. A feature of the receptive fields of HYPERCOMPLEX CELLS and some complex cells, namely that if the optimal stimulus (a bar or an edge in a certain orientation) continues beyond a certain point in the receptive field, the firing rate is reduced.

endocathexis, endocathection. Withdrawal from the outer world and concentration exclusively on one's own thoughts.

endocochlear potential. The resting potential between the endolymph of the scala media and the perilymph of the scala tympani (+80 millivolts) or scala vestibuli (+75 millivolts) with the perilymph being positive.

endocrine gland. Any gland whose products are secreted directly into the bloodstream, rather than (as with an EXOCRINE GLAND) passing down a duct. The secretions of the endocrine glands (HORMONES) play a major role in regulating the activity of the body and nervous system. Some examples are the ADRENAL GLANDS, the PITUITARY, and the THYROID.

endocrinology. The study of hormones and other internal secretions, and of their effects.

endoderm. The innermost of the three layers of cells in the embryo; it gives rise to the inner organs of the body (lungs, liver, etc.).

endogamy. (Anthropology) The practice of always marrying within one's own social group. *Contrast* EXOGAMY.

endogenous. Arising wholly from within an organism.

endogenous depression. A depression occurring without sufficient external cause. The distinction between endogenous depression and REACTIVE DEPRESSION is disputed.

endolymph. The fluid in the semicircular canals and cochlea.

endolymphatic potential. A synonym for ENDOCOCHLEAR POTENTIAL.

endomorphy. A body type (rounded, fleshy) in SHELDON'S CONSTITUTIONAL THEORY thought to be derived from the embryonic endoderm; it is said to be associated with VISCEROTONIA.

endophasia. Inner speech.

endophora. The use of a word or expression to refer to another word or expression in the discourse, i.e. ANAPHORA or CATAPHORA. *Contrast* EXOPHORA.

endoplasmic reticulum. A network of membranes found in nerve cells and many other cells, to which (in the case of rough endoplasmic reticulum) ribosomes are attached, and on which proteins and peptides are synthesized.

endopsychic. Pertaining to the contents of the mind.

end organ. The terminal part of a somaesthetic receptor (e.g. the ending of a skin receptor).

endorphins. A class of OPIOID PEPTIDES containing many amino acids. β-endorphin contains 31 amino acids; other endorphins (e.g. α-endorphin, γ-endorphin, and neoendorphin) are composed of large or small fragments of β-endorphin.

end plate. The flattened end of a motor neuron, which is the part that is in contact with the muscle.

end plate potential (EPP). The depolarization of a muscle membrane caused by release of acetylcholine from the motor nerve end plate.

end pleasure. (Psychoanalysis) The pleasure achieved when a drive is reduced, used particularly of an orgasm.

end spurt. Improved performance occurring as the end of a task draws near.

end-stopped receptive fields. A visual RECEPTIVE FIELD that responds to the presence of a bar or edge in a certain orientation but which reduces or stops firing if the stimulus is extended beyond a certain point in the receptive field.

end test. A synonym for POST-TEST.

enelicomorphism. The ascription of adult characteristics to children. *Contrast* PAEDOMORPHISM.

energetics. An old-fashioned term for the study of the physiological mechanisms of arousal, including their psychological correlates.

energostatic control. The internal control of eating by monitoring the number of calories consumed.

energy (E). The capacity of a body or any other system (e.g. electromagnetic waves) to perform work. It is measured in JOULES, DYNES, or ERGS.

engram. The physical change in the brain that underlies memory.

enkephalin. A class of OPIOID PEPTIDES that contains five amino acids; it includes **met-enkephalin** and **leu-enkephalin**.

enlarged semantic halo. A form of semantic dissociation in which the meaning of words is overgeneralized, thus making language vague and ambiguous, but still coherent.

enlightenment effects. Providing a subject with an account stated in general terms of the sort of error he may make in taking a decision. He is then asked to take the decision (but usually remains unenlightened).

enosophobia. A morbid fear of sin.

entailment (→). Strictly a synonym for LOGICAL IMPLICATION, but often used more broadly as a synonym for IMPLICATION in general.

entelechy. (Philosophy) 1. Anything actualized. 2. The soul. 3. A synonym for VITAL-ISM.

enteric nervous system. A proposed third division of the AUTONOMIC NERVOUS SYSTEM (in addition to the sympathetic and parasympathetic systems). It serves the gut and differs from the other two divisions in several ways, e.g. its morphology is more like that of the central nervous system.

enteroception. An alternative spelling of INTEROCEPTION.

enthymeme. Any argument (including syllogistic deduction) in which a premise is unstated because it is obvious.

entomophobia. A morbid fear of insects.

entoptic. Pertaining to perceptual images arising from within the eye e.g. MUSCAE VOLITANTES or sensations like DARK LIGHT.

entorhinal cortex. Brodmann's area 28 (*see* Appendix 4), which lies proximal to the RHINAL SULCUS and next to the HIPPOCAMPUS. It is palaeocortex and is implicated in the control of aggression.

entrainment. The adjustment of an internal rhythm (e.g. circadian rhythm) to synchronize with an external cycle (e.g. light and dark).

entrance pupil. The virtual image of the pupil formed by the cornea; it determines the number of rays entering the eye from a given point and is 13 per cent larger than the EXIT PUPIL.

entrapment. Becoming increasingly involved in an activity to justify previous involvement. *Compare* SUNK COSTS.

entropy. 1. (Information theory, in which the abbreviation H is used). The average amount of information conveyed by the occurrence of any one of a set of independent events; it is calculated by summing the information conveyed by each event $(\log_2 \frac{1}{p})$ multiplied by the probability of that event, i.e.

$$H = \overset{i}{\Sigma} pi \log_2 \frac{1}{p_i},$$

where Pi is the probability of the ith signal occurring. A more complex formula is needed to deal with the case where there are sequential dependencies between events (as in written or spoken English). 2. (Psychoanalysis) Loss of the ability to switch mental energy from one object or goal to another, i.e. set habits. 3. (Social psychology) The mental energy that is invested in set patterns and hence cannot be used to change the state of a society, thus potentially leading to the society's decline.

enucleation. The removal of a bodily organ from the tissue surrounding it.

enuresis. Involuntary urination.

envelope. The curve obtained by connecting all the peaks and all the troughs of a waveform or oscillating time series.

envelope delay. A difference in the time of arrival at the two ears of the abrupt onset of a sound, or of an abrupt change in its envelope. It is a cue for AUDITORY LOCALIZATION.

environmental assessment. The evaluation of the effects of the environment on a mentally disordered person, e.g. how far it disturbs or supports him; it is undertaken to discover whether the environment, and hence the mental disorder, could be improved.

environmental demand. A synonym for DEMAND CHARACTERISTICS.

environmentalism. A synonym for EMPIRICISM (1).

environmental psychology. The study of the interaction between people and their environment, usually undertaken with a view to improving it.

enzymes. Protein molecules that act as catalysts by promoting chemical reactions without being changed themselves.

EOG. An abbreviation for ELECTROCULO-GRAPH and ELECTROCULOGRAPHY.

eonism. The adoption of the female role by a male.

esophobia. A morbid fear of dawn and sunrise.

EP. An abbreviation for EVOKED POTENTIAL.

ependyma. The membrane lining the ventricles of the brain and the central canal in the spinal cord.

ephapse. An ELECTRICAL SYNAPSE consisting of the juxtaposition of the pre- and postsynaptic cells' membranes with a very small gap (e.g. 20 nm) between them. This synapse is common on the smaller branches of dendrites and axons.

EPI. An abbreviation for EPINEPHRINE.

epicritic. Pertaining to the ability of some skin receptors to respond to fine differences in pressures or temperature, a term first used in this way by Head. *Contrast* PROTOPATHIC.

epidemiology. The study of the distribution of diseases in a population, and of the factors that predispose to them (e.g. nutrition, age, or sex).

epidermis. The outer layer of the skin. On the surface it contains dead cells that are progressively sloughed off, with layers of live cells underneath.

epigenesis. 1. (Biology) The ontogenetic development of a new structure, brought about by an interaction between the genes and the environment. 2. Piaget's term for the development of new structures of thought in the developing child.

epilepsy. A sudden and brief clouding or loss of consciousness, often accompanied by tonic and clonic seizures, which can be caused by heavy synchronous discharges of neurons in a part of the brain. *See also* GRAND MAL and PETIT MAL.

epileptic equivalent. A synonym for MASKED EPILEPSY.

epileptogenic focus. The area in an epileptic's brain in which the neurons sometimes discharge abnormally, thus causing epilepsy.

epinephrine (EPI). A CATECHOLAMINE hormone secreted by the adrenal medulla, particularly when the organism is under stress. It stimulates the sympathetic system and is also a CNS neurotransmitter or neuromodulator. The adjective is ADRENERGIC.

epinosis. The gaining of indirect advantage from illness (e.g. absence from work, not having to face responsibility), thought to be a factor in prolonging mental illness.

epiphenomenalism. The hypothesis that consciousness is a by-product of the brain and has no causal effect on behaviour.

epiphysis. A synonym for PINEAL GLAND.

epipolar constraint. The fact that from information about the position and rotation of each eye it is possible to infer for a line imaged on one eye its CORRESPONDING POINTS on the other eye. This constraint is needed for the solution of the CORRESPONDENCE PROBLEM.

episcotister. A rotating disc with a wedge cut out. It was used to reduce light intensity when rotated fast and to measure flicker fusion frequency when rotated at slower rates.

episodic amnesia. Inability to remember certain episodes (often significant ones), but with the rest of the memory intact.

episodic memory. The hypothetical part of the memory that stores personal experiences (as opposed to the part storing general information that is remembered independently of the circumstances under which it was learned). *Contrast* PROCEDURAL MEMORY and SEMANTIC MEMORY.

epistasis. (Genetics) Any non-linear change in the effect of a gene on the phenotype caused by the presence of a particular gene at another locus.

epistemic response. Exploration occurring entirely within the mind by manipulating its contents.

epistemology. (Philosophy) The study of the nature of knowledge.

epithalamus. A small area of the brain above the thalamus that contains the pineal gland.

epithelium. A thin tissue that continuously coats internal and external surfaces of an organism, including skin and the linings of the respiratory and alimentary tracts.

EPP. An abbreviation for END PLATE POTENTIAL,

EPQ. An abbreviation for the EYSENCK PERSONALITY QUESTIONNAIRE.

EPSP. An abbreviation for EXCITATORY POST-SYNAPTIC POTENTIAL.

EQ. An abbreviaiton for EDUCATIONAL QUOTIENT.

equal and unequal cases, method of. An example of the method of constant stimuli in which a difference threshold is determined by presenting on each trial two stimuli which the subject has to judge as equal or not equal. See CONSTANT STIMULI, METHOD OF.

equal-appearing intervals method. 1. Any psychophysical scaling method in which subjects have to adjust the intervals between stimuli until they all appear equal (or to pick stimuli that appear to be separated by equal intervals), thus obtaining an INTERVAL SCALE, e.g. METHOD OF BISECTION. 2. A synonym for THURSTON SCALE.

equal interval scale. A synonym for INTERVAL SCALE.

equality, law of. The Gestalt principle that perceptual elements that are the same as one another tend to be grouped together.

equal loudness contour. A synonym for ISOPHONIC CONTOUR.

equally noticeable difference. A synonym for JUST NOTICEABLE DIFFERENCE.

equal sense differences method. A synonym for EQUAL-APPEARING INTERVALS METHOD.

equated scores. Scores from different tests that have been converted so that they can legitimately be compared, e.g. by expressing them as units of standard deviations from the mean.

equation, method of. A synonym for AVERAGE ERROR, METHOD OF.

equifinality. The end-point of the movements of a limb when it can be reached by several different trajectories.

equilibration. Piaget's term for the process whereby a child achieves a balance between taking in new information and modifying existing concepts to accommodate it. See also ACCOMMODATION and ASSIMILATION.

equilibratory sense. A synonym for VESTIBULAR SENSE.

equilibrium hypothesis. The hypothesis that when two people are together there is an optimal physical distance between them that will depend on their situation or relationship, and that if this distance is too big (or too small) they will compensate by increasing (or decreasing) eye contact.

equilibrium potential. The voltage across the nerve cell membrane at which no net transfer of ions occurs, i.e. the RESTING POTENTIAL.

equilibrium sense. A synonym for VESTIBULAR SENSE.

equinophobia. A morbid fear of horses.

equipotentiality. Lashley's term for the capacity of one part of the brain to take over the function of another that has been lesioned, a capacity that he greatly exaggerated.

equity theory. (Social psychology) 1. The hypothesis that people will be satisfied, particularly in their place of work, if they see their own treatment as fair in relation to that received by others, taking into account such factors as pay, hours of work, qualifications needed, intrinsic interest of job, etc. 2. The theory that people expect to get gains out of a relationship that are proportional to what they put into it (e.g. effort, intelligence, etc.).

equivalence. *See* RESPONSE EQUIVALENCE and STIMULUS EQUIVALENCE.

equivalence coefficient. The correlation between two equivalent forms of the same test, which if high suggests the test is reliable.

equivalence test. A synonym for TRANSFER TEST.

equivalent background brightness. The intensity of a background light that produces a rise in the brightness threshold at the fovea that is the same as that produced by a glowing light (e.g. a car light). It is a way of quantifying glare.

equivalent forms. Different forms of the same test designed so that the same individual will have the same score on each.

equivalent processing assumption. The assumption that where an array of stimuli are briefly presented the subject will process information at the same rate and in the same way per unit time (e.g. during the first and last 50 msec of a 250 msec presentation). The assumption is only likely to be fulfilled if the subject does not know in advance on any trial the length of the presentation.

equivalent rectangular bandwidth (ERB). A measure of the sharpness of an auditory filter, being the frequency range of a rectangular filter that has the same peak value as the original filter and that passes the same total power of white noise.

equivalent stimulus. A stimulus to which exactly the same response is made as to another stimulus to which the response has already been learned.

ERB. An abbreviation for EQUIVALENT RECTANGULAR BANDWIDTH.

erectile dysfunction. DSM-III's euphemism for IMPOTENCE.

eremophobia, eremiophobia. A morbid fear of oneself or of being alone.

erenthrophobia. A morbid fear of blushing.

erethism. An obsolete term for abnormally high sensitivity or irritability in any part of the body.

ERG. An abbreviation for ELECTRORETINO-GRAM.

erg. A measure of energy or work; one erg equals 10^{-7} joule.

ergasia. Meyer's term for all the mental and physical activities taking place in a person.

ergasiophobia. 1. A morbid fear of moving, often with the illusion that one's movements will have disastrous effects on the world. 2. A morbid fear of working, common among students.

ergodic. Pertaining to a stochastic process in which any sequence has the same statistical properties as any other.

ergograph. Any device for measuring the amount of work done by a muscle.

ergonomics. The study of the factors that affect efficiency at work, and the application of this knowledge to improving efficiency and satisfaction at work. Factors studied include the design of machines and other artifacts (e.g. chairs), room size and colour, temperature, diurnal rhythms, etc. Ergonomics now includes the study of environmental effects on human efficiency and satisfaction outside the place of work, e.g. in the home, in aircraft, etc.

ergot. A fungus which produces several psychotropic drugs, including LSD and ADRENERGIC BLOCKING AGENTS.

ergotrophic process. Hess's outmoded expression for the neural processes underlying anabolic activity, e.g. sleep or rest. *Contrast* TROPHOTROPHIC PROCESS.

Erhard Seminar Training. *See* EST (3).

Erikson's psychosocial development stages. These are set out in the following table.

erogenous zone. Any part of the body that can give rise to sexual pleasure when stimulated.

Stage	Approx. age	Psychosocial crisis	Optimal outcome
I Oral-sensory	1	Trust vs Mistrust	Trust and optimism
II Muscular anal	2	Autonomy vs Shame, Doubt	Sense of control over oneself and the environment
III Locomotor-Genital	3–5	Initiative vs Guilt	Goal-directedness and purpose
IV Latency	5–12	Industry vs Inferiority	Competence
V Puberty and adolescence	13–18	Identity vs Role confusion	Reintegration of past with present and future goals, fidelity
VI Early adulthood	19–22	Intimacy vs Isolation	Commitment, sharing, closeness and love
VII Young and middle age	23–45	Generativity vs Self-absorption	Productivity and concern about larger issues
VIII Mature adult	46–	Integrity vs Despair	Wisdom, satisfaction with one's past life

Eros. Freud's term for the instinct for life both of the individual and of the species; it combats THANATOS. In Freud's thinking it replaced LIBIDO, to which it is similar.

erotic type. In Freudian theory a personality type in which the libido expresses itself mainly in the ID and the person is interested in loving and being loved; it is said to be associated with hysteria. See LIBIDINAL TYPE.

erotogenic zone. A synonym for EROGENOUS ZONE.

erotomania. 1. Abnormally strong hetero-sexual lust. 2. A person's belief (usually false) that many others are violently sexually attracted to him or her.

ERP. An abbreviation for EVENT-RELATED POTENTIAL.

error of estimate. 1. The error that occurs in regression analysis when estimating the value of the dependent variable from given values of the independent variables. 2. The margin of error to be expected in predicting performance on a criterion task from a test score due to imperfect validity of the test.

error of refraction. See REFRACTIVE ERROR.

error variance, error term. The variance in the dependent variable due to uncontrolled factors in an experiment, such as individual differences between subjects. Virtually every statistic in analysis of variance is computed as the ratio of the variance due to the experimental manipulation to that due to the error variance. It is also called **residual variance**, as it is variance that cannot be accounted for in terms of systematic or controlled factors.

erythrolabe. A quaint name for the visual pigment of the long wavelength cone, not yet identified chemically.

erythrophobia. A morbid fear of redness, particularly of blood; or of activities associated with redness, such as blushing.

erythropsia. Vision in which everything appears to have a reddish tinge; it can be induced by prolonged exposure to very bright light.

Esalen. A place in California where people could stay to take part in encounter groups or in the personal growth movement; many well-known psychotherapists and even some experimental psychologists have attended.

ESB. An abbreviation for electrical stimulation of the brain. See ELECTRICAL BRAIN STIMULATION.

E scale. An attitude scale used to measure ETHNOCENTRISM.

escape learning. Learning to make a response that reduces the duration of an aversive stimulus; in escape learning the organism receives the aversive stimulus on every trial, whereas in AVOIDANCE LEARNING it can avoid it altogether.

escape mechanism. Any device (e.g. hysteria, amnesia, denial) used to avoid confronting a threatening situation. Compare DEFENCE MECHANISM.

ESN. An abbreviation for EDUCATIONALLY SUBNORMAL.

esophoria. A PHORIA marked by the occluded eye pointing too far inward.

esotropia. A form of STRABISMUS in which one eye (the squinting eye) consistently points more inward than the other.

ESP. An abbreviation for EXTRASENSORY PERCEPTION.

ESSB. An abbreviation for ELECTRICAL SELF-STIMULATION OF THE BRAIN.

essential. (Medicine) Pertaining to an abnormal condition of whose causes doctors are ignorant.

essential amino acid. An AMINO ACID not synthesized within the body, which must therefore be contained in the diet.

EST. 1. (Psychology) An abbreviation for ELECTROSHOCK THERAPY. 2. (Linguistics) An abbreviation for EXTENDED STANDARD THEORY. 3. (Psychotherapy) An acronym for ERHARD SEMINAR TRAINING, which is a form of personal growth or sensitivity training in which several hundred people gather for several hours to be harangued, abused, and deprived (of food, water, toilet facilities, etc.): its outcome is uncertain.

esthesiometer. An alternative spelling for AESTHESIOMETER.

estrus. An alternative spelling for OESTRUS.

etherial odour. One of the six so-called primary odours of the ODOUR PRISM, reminiscent of the smell of ether or fruit. It is also one of the four odours of the ODOUR SQUARE.

ethics. The philosophical study of moral concepts.

ethnic. Pertaining to a comparatively large group of people, who tend to have the same laws, customs, and language, and to be of the same race.

ethnocentrism. The belief that one's own ethnic group is superior to others, usually accompanied by prejudice towards members of other groups.

ethnogenics. The attempt by sociologists to understand the belief systems that underlie the interaction between people. In short, ETHNOMETHODOLOGY by another name.

ethnography. The branch of anthropology that studies primarily a single community, usually by the investigator becoming a member of that community for several years.

ethnolinguistics. The study of natural languages in so far as they relate to the customs and behaviour of the society of the native speakers.

ethnology. The branch of anthropology that studies the culture of peoples, races, or ethnic groups from a comparative viewpoint.

ethnomethodology. (Sociology) Garfinkel's term for the study of how everyday conclusions and decisions are reached. The investigator listens to, and often records, the conversations of the group under study. The only discernible methodology is the use of a tape recorder and occasionally some common sense in interpreting what is going on. Ethnomethodologists commonly spend years in an institution, but their conclusions are rarely surprising.

ethnopsychology. The study of the comparative psychology of different ethnic groups.

ethnoscience. The systematic attempt to specify the rules operating in a society (most of which are below the level of conscious awareness) and to understand the functioning of the society in terms of these rules.

ethogram. (Ethology) A record of the behaviour of an animal in the wild over a period of time, with the behaviour classified by its type (e.g. preening, aggressive display, etc.).

ethology. The study of animal behaviour, particularly innate behaviour, laying emphasis on animals' interaction with the natural environment and on the evolutionary processes that have led to the behaviour. Traditionally ethologists have tended to explain behaviour by its function, psychologists by the mechanisms underlying it, but this distinction has long been eroded. Moreover ethologists may nowadays try to confirm their hypotheses by laboratory experiments. *Contrast* ANIMAL PSYCHOLOGY.

etic. Pertaining to concepts or beliefs found in all cultures. *Contrast* EMIC.

etiology. An alternative spelling of AETIOLOGY.

EU. An abbreviation for EXPECTED UTILITY.

euchromatopsia. Good colour vision. *See also* COMBINATIVE EUCHROMATOPSIA.

Euclidean metric. (Psychology) The distance metric that applies to similarity judgements between items varying along two (or more) dimensions which conforms (for two dimensions) to the equation $\sqrt{(A^2 + B^2)}$ where A and B represent the differences between the items on each dimension. The result is found with INTEGRAL STIMULUS DIMENSIONS. *Contrast* CITY-BLOCK METRIC.

eugenics. The attempt to improve the characteristics of a population (particularly a human one) by systematically controlled breeding. *Contrast* DYSGENIC.

Euler circle. A method of expressing the class inclusion relationship between different sets, in which each set is represented by a circle. 'All A are B' would be represented by having a circle A entirely contained in B. 'Some A are B' would be represented by having circle A overlapping with circle B. With sufficient care Euler circles can be used to assist in the validation of syllogisms.

eumorphy. The bodily type of someone of normal build.

euphoria. A feeling of well-being or happiness. *Contrast* CACOPHORIA.

eurymorphy. In Eysenck's body-build typology, a heavy, stocky build.

eupareunia. Coitus with a satisfactory orgasm.

euryplasty. The body build of someone with a short, thickset body.

eusociability. The characteristic of a society or species in which the organisms work harmoniously together for the good of the society (e.g. a hive of honeybees).

Eustachian tube. A tube running between the middle ear and the throat, whose function is to equalize pressure on either side of the eardrum.

eustress. Stress that is beneficial to the organism.

euthenics. The attempt to promote human welfare and happiness by improving the environment.

euthymia. A pleasant and contented state of mind.

evaluation apprehension. The stress that a person may undergo if he is observed performing a task by others. Depending on the circumstances, the stress may either improve or impair his performance.

evaluation function. A synonym for EXPECTED VALUE.

evaluation research. Any research that systematically examines the effects of a system (e.g. of a business management) or of any procedure in business, education, medicine, etc., usually in the hope of making improvements.

evaluative premise. *See* SYLLOGISTIC MODEL OF ATTITUDE ORGANIZATION.

event-processing theories. (Animal learning) A set of disparate theories constructed to explain why the contiguity of the US and CS can under certain circumstances fail to result in conditioning. *Compare* BLOCKING (1) and OVERSHADOWING.

event-related potential (ERP). A synonym for EVOKED POTENTIAL.

event sampling. Recording how often one type of behaviour is followed by another where the types of behaviour to be recorded have been chosen in advance.

eviration. A man's pathological belief that he has been turned into a woman.

evocative interaction. The phenomenon that different people evoke different responses from others and that these different responses may in turn shape their own personalities. *Compare* PROACTIVE INTERACTION and REACTIVE INTERACTION.

evoked potential (EP), evoked response. The series of brain waves that follows the presentation of a brief stimulus, such as a light or a tone, and that can be recorded by the ELECTROENCEPHALOGRAPH.

evolutionarily stable strategy (ESS). An expression introduced by Maynard Smith for any EVOLUTIONARY STRATEGY that remains invariant because a departure from it by an individual would reduce its evolutionary fitness. Such strategies can be of three kinds. **Pure strategies** are those adopted by all members of the species. In **mixed strategies** each member of the species adopts two or more strategies (e.g. fight on 50 per cent of confrontations with another member of the species, flee on 50 per cent). In **polymorphous strategies**, different members of the species adopt different pure strategies but the overall strategy is stable if the proportion adopting each optimizes the fitness of the individuals adopting each. Thus there may be an optimum ratio of animals who fight to those who flee. Clearly if all but one fled, the aggressor would have a great advantage. But if all but one fought, the one who did not fight might have an advantage since he would not be damaged in fights. Depending on the payoffs for winning and losing fights, the stable proportion of fighters and fleers will lie somewhere in between.

evolutionary drift. A gradual change in the genes of a species caused not by adaptation to the environment but by random mutations that happen to be propagated.

evolutionary strategy. Any behaviour pattern or physical trait that appears in an individual member of a species and that is genetically determined as a result of its survival value, particularly where alternative behaviour patterns or traits can be envisaged. Different members of a species may adopt different strategies, e.g. some males may flee on encountering another male (**dove strategy**), others may fight (**hawk strategy**). Again, some male ruffs have the strategy of defending a territory and competing for females, others have no territory but sneak on to another bird's territory to copulate with the female while the owner is otherwise engaged. For a classification of strategies, *see* EVOLUTIONARILY STABLE STRATEGY.

exafference. A change in stimulation resulting from a change in the environment rather than from a movement of the organism. *Contrast* REAFFERENCE.

exchange theory. A theory of interpersonal interaction that maintains it is based on the exchange of rewards between the participants and that each is trying to maximize his gains and minimize his losses. *Compare* RELATIVE DEPRIVATION.

excitation. 1. (Neurophysiology) The firing of a nerve cell or group of cells or the depolarization of the postsynaptic membrane which increases the likelihood of the cell firing. 2. (Experimental psychology) The process that underlies the tendency to produce a response; it is opposed by INHIBITION (1).

excitation transfer. The transfer of autonomic arousal from one situation (e.g. running) to another (e.g. sex).

excitation transfer theory. The principle that aggression may be increased by other causes of arousal, e.g. by humid and hot weather.

excitatory postsynaptic potential (EPSP). The reduced potential difference across the membrane of the postsynaptic cell, caused at excitatory synapses by the firing of the presynaptic cell; if the depolarization is sufficiently great, the postsynaptic cell will fire.

excitatory potential ($_sE_R$). A term from Hull's first theory. It is roughly equivalent to GENERALIZED REACTION POTENTIAL in his later theory. *See* HULLIAN THEORY.

excitatory synapse. A synapse transmission across which increases the likelihood of the postsynaptic cell firing.

excitement phase. *See* SEXUAL RESPONSE CYCLE.

exclusion anxiety. Anxiety caused by the possibility of being rejected by a group to which one belongs.

exclusive disjunction. *See* DISJUNCTION.

executive. (Computing) The part of a computer that executes instructions, determining to which instruction to proceed, etc. In psychology the term is used by analogy to refer to that part of working memory that operates on the data temporarily stored there. *See* CENTRAL EXECUTIVE SYSTEM.

exemplar theory. The hypothesis that classes are represented in the mind by typical examples or prototypes rather than by a formal list of properties defining the class.

exercise, law of. Thorndike's principle that 'other things being equal' repetition of a response increases the probability that it will be made in future.

exhaustion stage. *See* GENERAL ADAPTATION SYNDROME.

exhaustive search. A search through memory (particularly immediate memory) in which all possible items are examined: the search continues even after the item sought has been found. *Contrast* SELF-TERMINATING SEARCH.

exhibitionism. 1. The public exposure of a person's genitals in front of someone else, usually a member of the opposite sex, an act which is often compulsive. Exhibitionism is much more frequent in men than in women. 2. A tendency to show-off (usually frowned upon by therapists).

existential anxiety. (Existentialism) General anxiety caused by realizing that one cannot escape responsibility for one's actions through BAD FAITH or by the inability to find a meaning to life.

existentialism. A philosophical movement in which Kierkegaard and Sartre were prominent. Existentialists believe that we make ourselves what we are by our own choices and actions. They think that man can be free only if he finds his authentic inner self and acts on its dictates. They are, however, unclear both about how to find the inner self and what to do about it when it is discovered.

existential neurosis. A neurosis in which the person can see no meaning in life.

existential psychology. A movement started by Titchener in which people's inner thoughts were examined; the expression is now largely synonymous with HUMANISTIC PSYCHOLOGY.

existential psychotherapy. The attempt to help patients by exploring their current emotions, values, and feelings, and attempting to help them to discover the meaning of their lives. The therapist encourages clients to seek novelty rather than sticking to their previous ways, in the hope that this will encourage growth rather than stagnation. Unlike psychoanalysts, existential therapists take seriously what the patient says rather than explaining it away in terms of disguised wish-fulfilment.

existential quantifier. *See* QUANTIFIER.

exit pupil. The image of the pupil formed by the lens. *Compare* ENTRANCE PUPIL.

exocathexis. The tendency to be concerned with external rather than internal matters.

exocentric motion. The perception of motion based on seeing one thing move relative to another rather than relative to the observer.

exocrine gland. Any gland which, unlike an ENDOCRINE GLAND, secretes its products through a duct, e.g. sweat glands.

exocytosis. The emptying of the contents of a synaptic vessel into the synaptic cleft.

exogamy. (Anthropology) The practice of marrying outside one's own group, e.g. marrying a member of another tribe.

exogenous depression. A synonym for REACTIVE DEPRESSION.

exophora. (Linguistics) Any expression that refers directly (deictically) to something in the external world (e.g. 'there', 'that', 'my'). *Contrast* ENDOPHORA.

exophoria. A PHORIA marked by the occluded eye pointing too far outwards.

exotropia. A form of STRABISMUS, in which one eye (the squinting eye) points consistently further out than the other, thus preventing BINOCULAR FUSION. The condition often arises in childhood and unless treated may produce AMBLYOPIA in one eye.

expansion. *See* NODE EXPANSION.

expansive delusions. A synonym for DELUSIONS OF GRANDEUR.

expectancy theory. Any theory of learning (such as Tolman's) that holds that animals pursue goals by having expectancies about the consequences of a given act in the presence of a given stimulus, as opposed to theories containing only stimulus–response links.

expectancy value models. (Social psychology) Theories that assume that a person's decisions depend on taking into account both the value and the probability of each outcome for each course of action.

expectancy wave. A synonym for CONTINGENT NEGATIVE VARIATION.

expected payoff. (Game theory) The mean gain or loss that will be made over a period of time if a consistent strategy is pursued.

expected utility (EU). The desirability of a given option given the UTILITY (u) and the probability (p) of occurrence of the outcome: it is $p.u.$ *Compare* EXPECTED VALUE.

expected value. 1. (Statistics) The mean value of a random variable in repeated sampling. It is not necessarily the most frequently occurring value nor even a possible value. If a variable takes the values 0 and 1 with equal probability, the expected value is 0.5. 2. The benefit (or cost) of a probabilistic OUTCOME of a decision expressed as its value multiplied by the probability of it occurring. When the value is expressed as a UTILITY, the expression EXPECTED UTILITY is usually used.

experiential group. An ENCOUNTER GROUP with the emphasis on the participants sharing one another's feelings.

experimental analysis of behaviour. The use (usually in animal learning) of the techniques and principles advocated by Skinner, e.g. concentrating on response rate as a dependent variable, abjuring statistics, studying operant rather than classical conditioning, etc.: the expression has acquired a surprisingly narrow connotation.

experimental condition. A condition in which some treatment is administered to subjects in order to discover whether it alters their behaviour as compared with that of a CONTROL GROUP; e.g. to discover whether PARTIAL REINFORCEMENT affects rats' running speed, some subjects might be run under partial reinforcement (experimental condition), and others under continuous reinforcement (control condition). There may be more than one experimental condition in an experiment.

experimental control. A synonym for CONTROL GROUP.

experimental extinction. A synonym for EXTINCTION (1).

experimental group. The group run or tested under the EXPERIMENTAL CONDITION. The expression is sometimes used to mean any group in an experiment including the CONTROL GROUP.

experimental neurosis. A state of disturbance in animals, usually induced either by making a discrimination problem too hard for them to master, or by giving uncontrollable shocks.

experimental psychology. Originally, any approach to psychology that was based on the results of experiments, but the meaning is now somewhat different. Although many experimental psychologists still employ experiments, experimental psychology now tends to mean the study of those psychological processes in the individual that are or appear to be amenable to rigorous (scientific) explanation. Such processes include perception, language, learning, memory, cognition, and motor skills, and it is these topics that will be found in the many current journals of experimental psychology.

experimental realism. The attempt to design experiments, particularly in social psychology, in which the subjects' interactions, emotions, and responses will be natural and not influenced by the artificial situation created in most experiments.

experimental scenario. (Social psychology) The setting in which an experiment is conducted and the COVER STORY offered, both usually designed to make the subject believe that he is in a realistic situation.

experimental variable. A synonym for INDE-PENDENT VARIABLE.

experimenter bias. Distortion of the results of an experiment, caused by the experimenter (consciously or not) making mistakes in recording or analysing the data because of his own attitudes.

experimenter-expectancy effect. Distortion of the results of an experiment caused by the experimenter (consciously or not) inducing expectations in the subjects about the right way to respond, e.g. by looking pleased when they do one thing and annoyed when they do another.

expert system. (AI) Any program to solve an applied problem normally solved only by human experts (e.g. medical diagnosis). Such programs are based on systematically incorporating the experts' knowledge, usually in the form of decision rules, which are often probabilistic.

expiatory punishment. The concept of punishment held, according to Piaget, by children under 8 years old. They feel the severity of punishment should depend only on the severity of the effects of the crime and should not take into account e.g. the motive of the wrong-doer.

explicit learning, explicit memory. Learning in which what is learned can be consciously recalled. *Contrast* IMPLICIT LEARNING.

explicit naming, principle of. Marr's principle that as entities (e.g. lines, edges) are recovered from a sensory input they should be labelled so that they can subsequently be correctly accessed.

exploratory drive. The drive that leads all higher animals to explore and to learn to manipulate their environment even in the absence of other drives, and indeed often in their presence at the expense of fulfilling them.

explosive disorder. Any disorder in which a person indulges in serious and gratuitous violence against other persons or property.

exponent. The power to which another number (the BASE) is to be raised. If positive it is the number of times the base is to be multiplied by itself; if negative it is the reciprocal of that number. When the exponent is a fraction it denotes a root of the base, e.g. $16^{\frac{1}{2}} = 4$.

exponential curve, exponential function. A curve that can be fitted by the formula $x = a.b^y$ where a and b are constants and x and y are variables. It shows an accelerated rate of increase as the variable y increases. When x is positive, it rises more steeply than a POWER FUNCTION.

exposure deafness. Impairment of hearing, either temporary or permanent, caused by loud sounds.

exposure therapy. A behaviour therapy technique in which obsessive-compulsive patients are exposed to the stimuli that trigger compulsions, for a period sufficiently long for their anxiety to begin to decrease.

expressed emotion. (Psychiatry) An expression used particularly of the families or households of schizophrenics; it is hypothesized that schizophrenics are less likely to suffer schizophrenic episodes if they live in a family where emotions (both good and bad ones) are not strongly expressed than in one in which they are (**high expressed emotion**).

expression. (Genetics) Short for GENE EXPRESSION.

expressionism factor. The aspects of a work of art that reflect the artist's emotions.

expressive. A SPEECH ACT in which the speaker expresses his feelings (e.g. by apologizing, reproving, or welcoming).

expressive aphasia. Aphasia in which the ability to speak or write is more severely damaged than the ability to comprehend. *Compare* BROCA'S APHASIA, with which expressive aphasia is virtually synonymous.

expressive therapy. Psychotherapy that encourages the patient freely to give vent to his thoughts and feelings, e.g. through psychodrama.

extended family. A family that includes members other than just the parents and children (e.g. grandparents, cousins, etc.). *Contrast* NUCLEAR FAMILY.

extended source. Any source of illumination not small enough to be treated as a POINT SOURCE.

extended standard theory (EST). A type of generative grammar developed in the 1970s. It is based on Chomsky's STANDARD THEORY, but allows some aspects of the surface structure such as stress and intonation direct access to the semantic rules.

extension. A synonym for DENOTATION.

extensor. A muscle whose contractions straighten a joint. *Contrast* FLEXOR.

external aim. *See* AIM.

external auditory canal, external auditory meatus. Synonyms for AUDITORY CANAL.

external capsule. A layer of white fibres in the basal ganglia that separates the claustrum from the putamen.

external force of organization. A force postulated by the Gestaltists, deriving from the external stimulus, which limits the extent to which the INTERNAL FORCE OF COHESION can form a stable and cohesive percept.

external granular layer. *See* GRANULAR LAYER.

external hair cells. *See* AUDITORY RECEPTORS.

external hunger hypothesis. The hypothesis that obese people do not govern eating by internal signals of hunger but through external stimuli associated with food.

external inhibition. Pavlov's expression for the process underlying the reduction in the strength of a conditioned response when a strong stimulus is presented together with the conditioned stimulus. *Contrast* INTERNAL INHIBITION.

externalization. 1. (Developmental psychology) The formation of a distinction between the self and the external world in childhood. 2. (Attribution theory) The attribution of the cause of an action to an external factor rather than to something within the person. 3. (Drive) The process by which a drive comes to be conditioned to external stimuli. 4. (Psychoanalysis) A synonym for PROJECTION (1).

externalizing disorder. A disorder, like delinquency, that is manifested to others.

external pyramidal layer. *See* PYRAMIDAL LAYER.

external rectus. An EXTRAOCULAR MUSCLE that rotates the eye outwards.

externals. *See* LOCUS OF CONTROL.

external validity. A synonym for CRITERION VALIDITY.

exteroception. Any sensory system that responds to stimuli emanating from outside the body (e.g. auditory hair cells or skin receptors). *Contrast* INTEROCEPTION.

extinction. 1. The reduction in the strength of a response that occurs when the stimulus controlling it is repeatedly presented without a reinforcer being given, or the process that gives rise to this reduction. *Contrast* HABITUATION. 2. A synonym for SENSORY SUPPRESSION.

extinction, law of. Pavlov's law that if a conditioned reflex is elicited by a conditioned stimulus without reinforcement, the conditioned reflex is weakened.

extinction stage. *See* GENERAL ADAPTATION SYNDROME.

extinction to simultaneous stimulation. (Neuropsychology) The failure to perceive a visual or tactile stimulus projected to a damaged hemisphere when a stimulus is presented contralaterally, if the stimulus to the damaged hemisphere would have been perceived when presented on its own. It is one form of UNILATERAL NEGLECT.

extirpation. The surgical removal of a bodily structure.

extorsion. A rotation of the eye in which the top of the cornea rotates outwards towards the temples. *Compare* INTORSION.

extracellular fluid. Any fluid in the body outside the cells, e.g. the fluid in the spinal column. It is formed from plasma with the larger molecules filtered out. In discussions of thirst, the term is used to mean the extracellular fluid in which cells are bathed. The fluid has the same tonicity as blood, and if it is hypertonic, water passes into it from the cells. *See* OSMORECEPTORS.

extracellular thirst. A synonym for VOLU-METRIC THIRST.

extraception. The tendency to be governed by objective or external events. *Contrast* INTROCEPTION.

extra cost error. The mistake of not proceeding with a beneficial course of action that has a cost, because some cost has already been wasted. E.g. someone who has lost his theatre ticket may refuse to buy another one because he thinks he is paying twice, but the fact that he has already lost a ticket is irrelevant.

extradimensional shift. The change in reinforcement contingency that occurs when an organism is first trained to discriminate along one dimension (e.g. colour), with a second dimension either irrelevant or not present, and is then trained to discriminate along the second dimension (e.g. shape). *Contrast* INTRADIMENSIONAL SHIFT.

extrafusal fibres. The contractile fibres contained in muscle, consisting of longitudinally arranged filaments some made up of MYOSIN, some of ACTIN. When an extrafusal fibre is stimulated (always by a single motor neuron), the actin filaments slide and increase their overlap with the parallel myosin filaments, thus causing the muscle to contract. The muscle is striated since it contains light bands (**I bands**) where there is only myosin, and dark bands (**A bands**) where myosin and actin overlap. The I bands contain a third dark band (**Z band**) where myosin fibres connect with one another. *Compare* INTRAFUSAL FIBRES.

extrajection. A synonym for PROJECTION.

extraocular muscles. The muscles lying outside the eyeball that change the direction of gaze. There are three pairs, with the members of each pair working in opposition to one another. The pairs are: SUPERIOR RECTUS and INFERIOR RECTUS; SUPERIOR OBLIQUE and INFERIOR OBLIQUE; LATERAL RECTUS and MEDIAL RECTUS. *See also* ABDUCTION, ADDUCTION, and TORSION. *Compare* INTRINSIC EYE MUSCLES.

extraocular nerves. The third (oculomotor), fourth (trochlear), and sixth (abducens) CRANIAL NERVES. They act together to control the extraocular muscles.

extrapolation. Inferring a value or values for points on a dimension from the obtained values of points on a limited range of the dimension. *Compare* INTERPOLATION.

extrapunitive. An alternative spelling of EXTROPUNITIVE.

extrapyramidal motor system. The basal ganglia and associated nuclei and their projections to e.g. the spinal cord and parts of the reticular system. Together with the PYRAMIDAL SYSTEM and CEREBELLUM it plays a major part in motor control. Damage to the system can cause PARKINSON'S DISEASE, CHOREA, ATHETOSIS, and HEMIBALLISMUS.

extrapyramidal syndrome. A neurological syndrome caused by damage to the EXTRAPYRAMIDAL MOTOR SYSTEM; the symptoms may include tremor, rigidity, restlessness, and difficulty in making voluntary movements.

extrasensory perception (ESP). (Parapsychology) The alleged acquisition of knowledge about the world without the use of the senses.

extraspectral hue. A hue such as purple, produced by a mixture of blue and red light; such mixtures produce highly saturated colours which complete the gap in the colour circle between the spectral hues violet and red.

extrastriate cortex. Visual areas excluding, but near to, the STRIATE CORTEX, particularly Brodmann's areas 18 and 19 in the occipital lobe, and areas 20 and 21 in the temporal lobe; *see* Appendix 3.

extraversion, extroversion. A constellation of personality traits, proposed by Jung and sponsored by Eysenck, marked mainly by interest in the outside world, but including confidence, sociability, etc. Eysenck believes that extraverts are slow to condition and therefore need a high level of stimulation. *Contrast* INTROVERSION.

extraversion–introversion dimension. A personality dimension based on factor analyses of personality tests, particularly as assessed by the MAUDSLEY PERSONALITY INVENTORY and the EYSENCK PERSONALITY QUESTIONNAIRE. On this dimension the extravert is sociable, assertive, sensation-seeking, and dominant; the introvert is the opposite.

extrinsic eye muscles. A synonym for EXTRAOCULAR MUSCLES.

extrinsic motivation. Movitation that depends on pursuing an external goal (e.g. money, food, avoidance of shock) rather than on doing something (e.g. studying) for its own sake. *Contrast* INTRINSIC MOTIVATION.

extrinsic noise. NOISE (1) arising from outside a system or organism, e.g. quantum fluctuations on the retina.

extrinsic surface property. (Computer vision) Any property of a surface, such as luminance, slant or motion relative to an observer, that changes with viewing or lighting conditions. *Contrast* INTRINSIC SURFACE PROPERTY.

extropunitive. Directing aggression outwards rather than blaming oneself, e.g. after being frustrated. *Contrast* IMPUNITIVE and INTROPUNITIVE.

extroversion. An incorrect but commonly used spelling of EXTRAVERSION.

eye contact. Looking another person in the eye, usually measured as the total duration of such contact over a period of time.

eye dominance. The tendency for one eye (usually the right) to be used rather than the other. The dominant eye often has greater acuity than the non-dominant one. Where BINOCULAR DISPARITY occurs, the object tends to be seen in the direction yielded by the dominant eye. In BINOCULAR RIVALRY, the pattern projected to the non-dominant eye is more likely to be suppressed than that projected to the dominant eye.

eye–head system. A system operating after the IMAGE–RETINAL SYSTEM that computes the motion of a stimulus, taking into account the motion of the eyes relative to the head.

eye movement. Any movement of the eyeball, including OPTOKINETIC NYSTAGMUS, PHYSIOLOGICAL NYSTAGMUS, SACCADES, SMOOTH FOLLOWING MOVEMENTS, TORSION and VERGENCE.

eye muscles. *See* CILIARY MUSCLE and EXTRAOCULAR MUSCLES.

eye span. A synonym for READING SPAN.

eye–voice span. The mean number of letters or words between the word being fixated and the word being spoken when reading aloud.

Eysenck Personality Questionnaire (EPQ). A questionnaire designed to measure three main factors – extraversion–introversion, neuroticism, and psychoticism.

F

F. An abbreviation for 1. F RATIO; 2. FORCE.

F. An abbreviation for LUMINOUS FLUX.

f. An abbreviation for 1. FREQUENCY; 2. function in logical or mathematical expressions such as $x = f(y)$.

F₁. 1. (Genetics) The offspring of any two parents. *Compare* F₂. 2. (Statistics) *See* F RATIO.

F₂. 1. (Genetics) The offspring of two F₁ parents (i.e.the third generation). 2. (Statistics) *See* F RATIO.

F'. *See* F RATIO.

face–hand test. A test for brain damage, in which the patient's hand and face are simultaneously touched; it is thought that with diffuse brain damage he cannot perceive both sensations simultaneously.

face validity. The extent to which a test intuitively seems to measure what it is designed to measure. *See also* EMPIRICAL VALIDITY.

facial nerve. The seventh CRANIAL NERVE, which is both motor and sensory; it controls facial expression and conveys sensory information from the anterior part of the tongue.

facial vision. The ability to sense the presence of an object or obstacle without using vision, possibly through air currents; it is sometimes found in the blind.

facilitation. Short for NEURAL FACILITATION.

facilitation, law of. The principle that a reflex response to one stimulus can be increased by the application of a second stimulus that does not itself elicit the response.

facilitator. Anyone whose task it is to promote interaction in a therapy group.

factitious disorder. A disorder in which a person produces psychiatric symptoms (**factitious disorder with psychological symptoms**) or physical symptoms (**factitious disorder with physical symptoms**) when he knows he is being observed. The disorder is not a case of malingering, since the patient does not necessarily stand to gain by the symptoms, and since the physical symptoms may be produced by his deliberately abusing his body (e.g. by taking anticoagulant drugs to produce bleeding). *Compare* PSYCHOSOMATIC DISORDER.

factor. 1. (General) Anything having a causal influence on something, usually where there are several different causal influences. 2. (Statistics) A discrete variable used to classify data (e.g. an independent variable) *Compare* LEVEL. 3. (Statistics) Any of the intervening variables discovered through FACTOR ANALYSIS that accounts for a significant proportion of the variance of the data. 4. (Mathematics) A number that divides into another number without remainder.

factor analysis. A generic term for techniques whose objective is to discover whether the correlations or covariances between a set of observed variables can be accounted for in terms of their relationships to a small number of unobservable or intervening variables (the factors). Essentially factor analysis postulates a linear relation between the observed variables and the underlying factors, which may be estimated by a variety of methods. At its simplest, factor analysis is a method for data reduction, reducing a large number of intercorrelated variables to a smaller number of intervening variables which account for as much of the variance as possible. Factor analysis has mainly been employed on the results of mental and personality tests. It can usually be manipulated to produce different solutions, i.e. different sets of factors, each set corresponding to different constraints, e.g. that of SIMPLE STRUCTURE.

factor axes. (Statistics) In FACTOR ANALYSIS the axes representing the relations of the factors to one another; they may be orthogonal or oblique.

factorial design. An experimental design in which each value (level) of each independent variable (factor) is combined with each value (level) of every other independent variable (factor); e.g. if there are two factors (A and B) each with two levels (1 and 2) the following combinations would be used: A1B1, A1B2, A2B1, A2B2.

factorial validity. (Statistics) The extent to which scores on different tests purporting to measure the same thing are correlated.

factorization problem. (Linguistics) The difficulty of deciding whether the meaning of a word is contingent on the (arbitrary) way in which that word is used in a given language or on the external reality to which it refers.

factor loading. (Statistics) In FACTOR ANALYSIS the correlation between a test item and a factor: i.e. the extent to which the score on an item is determined by a factor.

factor matrix. (Statistics) A table showing the FACTOR LOADING of each test item with each factor.

factual knowledge. A synonym for DECLARATIVE KNOWLEDGE.

faculty psychology. The hypothesis that the mind has separate abilities (e.g. language and mathematics) and that the capacity for performance on one is not highly correlated with the capacity for performance on others. The idea that different mechanisms underlie different abilities is again becoming fashionable.

fading. The gradual reduction, after a discrimination has been learned, of the difference between the discriminative stimuli. The procedure can result in the organism discriminating successfully between stimuli too similar for it to discriminate if trained on them from the outset.

FAE. An abbreviation for FIGURAL AFTER-EFFECT.

fall. In PITCH CONTOURS, a drop in pitch in an accented syllable that can occur within a word that the speaker wishes to emphasize.

fallopian tube. A tube down which the egg moves to the uterus after being discharged from the ovary.

fall-rise. In PITCH CONTOURS, a drop in pitch in an accented syllable followed by a rise which can be used to indicate e.g. GIVEN INFORMATION in a word or phrase that contrasts with another.

false alarm. (Psychophysics) In an experiment in which the subject has to detect the presence of a stimulus, the error of responding that it was present when it was not. *See* SIGNAL DETECTION THEORY.

false consensus bias, false consensus belief. The tendency to see one's own actions, attitudes, feelings and beliefs as more typical than they are.

false correspondence problem. The difficulty in deciding which points on each eye are stimulated by light from the same point in space. Usually a given point on one eye can correspond with several different points on the other and the visual system has to infer which points in the images of each eye emanate from the same point in space. *See* CORRESPONDENCE PROBLEM.

false negative. 1. Excluding something from a category in which it should have been placed, e.g. failure to diagnose schizophrenia when the person is schizophrenic, or failure to admit to university a student who would have done well. 2. A synonym for MISS.

false positive. 1. Placing something in a category in which it should not have been placed, e.g. admitting to university a student who fails. 2. (Psychophysics) A synonym for FALSE ALARM.

falsificationism. (Philosophy) Popper's thesis that scientific theories cannot be proved true, though they may be accepted until they are falsified.

familiarity effect. The phenomenon that in general the more often a stimulus is presented, the better it is liked.

familiar size. The remembered size of an object which, particularly in the absence of other cues, can serve as a depth cue.

family. (Biology) *See* TAXONOMY.

family-centred therapy. Therapy in which the family are seen as a group and an effort is made to improve their understanding of themselves and one another, and of the interaction between them.

fan effect. An effect predicted by ACT, namely, that the more associations a given node (concept) has the longer it will take to activate (retrieve) any one of them.

FAP. An abbreviation for FIXED ACTION PATTERN.

far point, far point of accommodation. The point in space that is in focus on the retina when accommodation is fully relaxed: it lies at the furthest distance for which a person can accommodate correctly (infinity in a normal eye).

far point of vergence. The furthest point that can be correctly fixated by both eyes simultaneously; for normal eyes, it is at infinity.

far-sightedness. A synonym for HYPEROPIA.

fascicle, fasciculus. A slender bundle of nerve fibres.

fasciculus cuneatus. A bundle of nerve fibres in the dorsal spinal cord carrying somaesthetic information from the upper limbs and trunk to the medulla.

fasciculus gracilis. A bundle of nerve fibres in the dorsal spinal cord carrying information from the lower limbs and trunk to the medulla.

fashioning effect. The phenomenon that the social role adopted by a person influences how he behaves and how he sees himself.

FAS test. A test of word fluency, in which the testee is given a category and asked to produce exemplars belonging to it.

fate neurosis. Failure, particularly in a person's career, through an unconscious desire to fail.

father complex. A synonym for ELECTRA COMPLEX.

father figure. A man to whom a person looks up and whom he treats like a father.

fatigue. (Neurophysiology) The reduction (which can last several seconds) in the tendency of a nerve cell to fire that follows a period of continuous firing. *See also* AUDITORY FATIGUE.

fault finding. Any task in which a person has to find a fault in an artifact (e.g. a car or computer). People mistakenly check the most probable faults first without taking sufficient account of the relative time it takes to check different faults.

faxen psychosis. A synonym for BUFFOONERY PSYCHOSIS.

F distribution. (Statistics) The theoretical distribution of the F RATIO. It is the distribution of the ratio of the variances of two independent samples drawn from normal populations. It is used when testing the hypothesis that the samples yielding the F ratio have been drawn from the same population. It plays a part in numerous tests including ANALYSIS OF VARIANCE and regression analysis.

fear. The desire to avoid or escape from something, accompanied when intense by arousal of the sympathetic system. *See also* ANXIETY and TWO-FACTOR LEARNING THEORY.

feature. 1. Any aspect or property of a sensory input or its source. A **local feature** is confined to a part of the stimulus (e.g. in vision, an indentation in a shape). A **global feature** is a property of the whole stimulus (e.g. symmetry). 2. *See* DISTINCTIVE FEATURES. 3. *See* SEMANTIC FEATURE.

feature comparison models. Any theory positing that to decide whether something (e.g. an owl) belongs to a given class (e.g. birds) the features of the instance (e.g. wings) are systematically compared to those of the class.

feature detector. A nerve cell that responds predominantly to one feature of the input, e.g. a cell in the visual cortex that responds maximally to a white vertical bar on a dark background. In fact single cells do not really detect features, since each can be fired by many different stimuli, but features can be detected by taking into account the relative strength of firing of a large number of cells, each of which responds maximally to different features. *See also* BAR DETECTOR, EDGE DETECTOR, SIMPLE CELL, COMPLEX CELL, HYPERCOMPLEX CELL.

feature integration theory. A. Treisman's theory, based on her experimental findings, that the features of an object such as colour and line tilt are separately detected and later integrated into the perception of the whole object. It is not a theory of recognition unlike FEATURE THEORY. *See also* BINDING PROBLEM.

feature list theory. The hypothesis that categories are formed by listing the features of their exemplars. *Contrast* PROTOTYPE THEORY.

feature positive learning. (Animal learning) Classical conditioning in which reinforcement is given when the US is Stimulus A + Stimulus B, but no reinforcement is given when A is presented alone. In **feature negative learning** reinforcement is given when Stimulus B is presented only on its own, but not when A+B is presented.

feature theory. Any theory postulating that recognition is achieved by recognizing the individual features present in the stimulus and matching them to a stored list of similar features. The model fails because it does not take into account the relationship between features, thus the letters T and L both have as features a horizontal and vertical line, but they are differently arranged.

febriphobia. A morbid fear of fever.

Fechner scale. A psychophysical scale based on the assumption that all JUST NOTICEABLE DIFFERENCES represent subjectively equal intervals.

Fechner's colours. Illusory hues perceived when a wheel containing black and white sectors is rotated rapidly. *Compare* BENHAM'S TOP and CHARPENTIER'S BANDS.

Fechner's law. The law that the apparent strength (A) of a stimulus is a logarithmic function of its intensity (I), which usually holds good to a first approximation except at very low and very high physical intensities. Fechner formulated the law as $A = k.\log(I/I_t)$, where I_t is the threshold intensity. *Compare* WEBER'S LAW, on which Fechner's law is in part based.

Fechner's paradox. The phenomenon that the world looks brighter when viewed with one eye than when viewed with two eyes with the light coming to the second eye attenuated by an achromatic filter. *See* BINOCULAR SUMMATION.

feeble-mindedness. An obsolete term for mental retardation or mental deficiency.

feedback. The influencing of the behaviour of a system by signals received about the effects of its output. In **negative feedback** (the most common kind) the activity of the system is reduced by feedback (a thermostat turns off the boiler when the external temperature has risen enough). Most drives involve negative feedback. In **positive feedback** the signals fed back increase the activity of the system, producing a runaway process. *See also* CYBERNETICS and HUNTING.

feedback loop. The channel through which the output of a system is fed back to it. *See* FEEDBACK.

feedforward. The use of a signal to correct error where the signal is propagated before the error occurs. E.g. the signal that cancels the impression of motion when the image moves across the eye in a saccade is the efferent output to the eye muscles rather than sensory feedback from them.

feeding centre. An expression sometimes used to refer to the LATERAL HYPOTHALAMUS, which when stimulated may produce feeding.

feeling type. *See* FUNCTION TYPES.

felicity conditions. (Linguistics) The conditions that must be met for a SPEECH ACT to be valid. E.g. if a speaker makes a promise, he must intend to carry it out and it must be to do something the hearer wants him to do (otherwise it might be a threat).

fellatio. Stimulation of the penis with the mouth or tongue.

feminism. 1. The appearance of female secondary characteristics (e.g. large breasts) in a man. 2. The doctrines and attitudes of the women's liberation movement.

fenestra ovalis. A synonym for OVAL WINDOW.

fenestra rotunda. A synonym for ROUND WINDOW.

feral child. Any child reputedly brought up by animals in the wild. *See* WILD BOY OF AVEYRON.

Feré method. A method of measuring the GALVANIC SKIN RESPONSE by passing a weak current through the skin and measuring changes in the skin's resistance to it. *Compare* TARCHANOFF METHOD.

Ferry–Porter law. The hypothesis that critical fusion frequency increases in proportion to the logarithm of light intensity.

FERS odour square. *See* ODOUR SQUARE.

fetal stage. The stage of prenatal existence that follows the embryonic stage; it lasts from about the eighth week after conception until birth.

fetishism. 1. (Anthropology) The worshipping of an inanimate object believed to have magical powers. 2. The derivation of sexual pleasure from objects (e.g. stockings) or parts of the body (e.g. the foot) not directly connected with sex.

fetus. The developing organism at the FETAL STAGE.

FI. An abbreviation for FIXED INTERVAL SCHEDULE.

fibre. Any long thread-like structure in the body, often used of AXONS, and sometimes of DENDRITES. *See* NERVE FIBRES for a classification.

fibril. Short for NEUROFIBRIL.

fibrillation. Rapid alternation of contraction and relaxation in muscles.

fiction. Adler's term for a person's lifestyle and attitudes when developed in order to conceal feelings of inferiority.

fidgetometer. A special chair fitted with sensors to detect how much a subject sitting in it moves about.

fiducial interval. The interval within which a given population parameter (e.g. the population mean) lies with a certain probability (e.g. greater than 0.95), based on sample observations.

fiducial limits. The end points of the FIDUCIAL INTERVAL.

field. Any bounded area. *See also* FIELD THEORY and VISUAL FIELD.

field defect. Blindness or some other abnormality occurring in only a part of the visual field, and therefore caused by a discrete lesion in part of the visual system.

field dependence. The tendency, on which people are thought to differ, to respond without thought to environmental cues. One test of field dependence is to make a subject set a rod to vertical while it is surrounded by a tilted frame: field-dependent people tilt the rod more towards the orientation of the frame than do non-field-dependent. Another test is the ability, possessed by field-independent people, to find embedded figures. Although some think field dependence is a major dimension of personality, it is doubtful whether it is a unitary trait.

field independence. The capacity to make correct judgements, despite misleading environmental cues. *See* FIELD DEPENDENCE.

field research. A synonym for FIELD WORK.

field theory. Any theory that postulates inter-active forces, on the analogy of field theories in physics, as an explanation of behaviour or mental processes. The Gestaltists proposed such a theory of visual perception and other aspects of the mind (*see* e.g. PRÄGNANZ, LAW OF), and Lewin proposed such a theory of motivation. Both mistakenly thought that they could quantify the forces. Theories postulating forces with no intent to quantify their interaction belong to DYNAMIC PSYCHOL-OGY, though the similarities are often more obvious than the differences.

field work. The study of organisms in their natural surroundings; e.g. the study of animals in the wild as undertaken by ethologists or the study of crowd behaviour as undertaken by social psychologists.

fifth cranial nerve. A synonym for TRI-GEMINAL NERVE.

fight–flight reaction. Cannon's expression for the reaction of the autonomic system to an emergency, which prepares the organism either to fight or flee.

figural aftereffect (FAE). An aftereffect in which after a contour has fallen on the same part of the subject's retina for 30 sec or more, a second contour placed near the position of the original one is seen as displaced in a direction away from the locus of the first contour. More generally, the expression is applied to any distortion of a figure caused by the presence of a previous figure (e.g. the successive tilt effect) and to certain similar haptic illusions, e.g. if a person repeatedly rubs his fingers over a bent surface and then rubs them over a flat one, it will feel bent in the opposite direction to the original surface.

figural flexibility test. A test in which subjects are required to generate a variety of different solutions to problems involving figural material.

figural goodness. A synonym for GOODNESS OF FIGURE.

figurative knowledge. Piaget's term for know-ledge acquired more or less by rote, e.g. knowledge of words, position of countries,

etc., upon which he frowned in contrast to OPERATIONAL KNOWLEDGE,

figure. 1. (Logic) *See* SYLLOGISM. 2. (Percep-tion) *See* AMBIGUOUS FIGURE. 3. (Perception) *See* EMBEDDED FIGURE.

figure–ground. The phenomenon that ob-jects or shapes appear to stand out against a background, that the contours seem to belong to them not to the background, and that they are seen more clearly than the background. There are ambiguous cases where the same region in space can be seen either as figure or background; in such cases there is a tendency to take a 'good figure' as the figure. *See* e.g. RUBIN'S VASE and *compare* GOODNESS OF FIGURE.

file drawer problem. The distortion of the literature that occurs because positive results are more likely to be published than negative ones.

Filehene illusion. The phenomenon that when the eye tracks a moving object, sta-tionary objects appear to move in the oppos-ite direction.

filial regression. The principle that if a parent is extreme on some trait (e.g. IQ, height) his or her children are likely to revert towards the population norm. It is an example of REGRESSION TOWARD THE MEAN.

filial regression, law of. *See* FILIAL REGRES-SION.

filiform papillae. A synonym for LINGUAL PAPILLAE.

filled and unfilled extent illusion. The illusion that a filled space is larger than an unfilled space that is physically identical in other respects. *Compare* OPPEL–KUNDT ILLUSION and HELMHOLTZ'S SQUARE.

filled pause. A gap in speech that is filled with meaningless conventional sounds like 'um', 'well', 'er'.

filled space illusion. A synonym for the OPPEL–KUNDT ILLUSION and its variants, in which a filled space looks larger than an empty space.

filler material. Items inserted in a test that will not be scored and have no relevance to whatever is being tested, but are placed there usually to prevent the testee guessing what the test is about.

fillers. In a SCHEMA or SCRIPT the items used to fill the SLOTS on a given occasion.

film colour. The appearance of a colour when no detail is visible in it; it appears filmy or like a mist and at no fixed distance. *Contrast* SURFACE COLOUR.

filter. 1. (Psychology) Any device, whether within or outside the nervous system, that systematically restricts the stimuli that will reach the senses or that will be processed at a higher level. *See* e.g. BAND-PASS FILTER. 2. A synonym for MASK.

filtering algorithm. (AI) A synonym for RELAXATION TECHNIQUE.

filter theory. The hypothesis that in selective attention the input from unattended stimuli is blocked, and that the physical characteristics of the stimuli determine which are blocked. The hypothesis has been largely discarded and replaced by ATTENUATION THEORY.

fimbria. The fibres leaving the HIPPOCAMPUS which come together to form the FORNIX.

final common path. Sherrington's term for the motor neurons, through which all excitation must be channelled if behaviour is to occur.

finalism. The attempt to explain mental processes, life, etc. in terms of a purpose.

finger agnosia. Impairment in the ability to discriminate which finger or part of a finger has been touched, particularly when more than one stimulus is applied simultaneously.

finite state automaton. An automaton that can only be in a limited number of states. Since such an automaton would have a finite memory, it could not handle recursion beyond a fixed depth and hence could not handle multiple embeddings in a sentence beyond a fixed depth. Although it is fashionable to decry finite state automata, the brain itself must be one.

firing. The initiation of a nerve impulse.

first cranial nerve. A synonym for OLFACTORY NERVE.

first-in first-out store. A temporary store in a computer from which items are withdrawn in the same order as they were input.

first moment. *See* MOMENT.

first-order factor. A factor that emerges directly from the intercorrelation of the scores on which a factor analysis is performed.

first-rank symptom. A set of symptoms believed by Schneider to be peculiarly diagnostic of schizophrenia. The symptoms fall into five groups: auditory hallucinations; the feeling that the patient's thoughts are not his own or are being broadcast to others; delusions; the attribution of bodily sensations to outside agencies; and feelings of having actions or thoughts controlled by outside agencies.

first signal system. Pavlov's expression for the system that responds to, and acquires knowledge from, the immediate environment through the senses, as opposed to the SECOND SIGNAL SYSTEM which deals with symbols like language or abstract concepts.

Fisher's exact probability test. (Statistics) A test of independence in two-by-two contingency tables giving exact probability levels for all sample sizes.

Fisher's z-test. (Statistics) A test to determine the significance of a correlation coefficient employing FISHER'S Z-TRANSFORMATION.

Fisher's z-transformation. A transformation of the product–moment correlation which yields an approximately normal distribution. It is useful in constructing tests of the significance of correlations and their differences.

fissure. A groove in a surface, particularly a comparatively large groove in the surface of the cortex. SULCUS is used of smaller grooves in the cortex, but in practice the terms are often interchangeable.

fissure of Rolando. A synonym for CENTRAL FISSURE.

fissure of Sylvius. A synonym for LATERAL SULCUS.

fistula. An opening either into the interior of the body or in an internal organ, such as can be produced by a wound, or by surgery (e.g. a tube implanted through the wall of the stomach). The term is used both for the opening in the tissue and for any tube that is passed through it.

fitness. See INCLUSIVE FITNESS.

Fitts' law. The hypothesis that in moving between two similar targets, each of which must be touched in turn, movement time decreases with the size of the target and increases with the amplitude of the movement. More specifically, with two vertical rectangles varying in width (W) and distance apart (D), movement time from one to the other is equal to $a+b\log_2(2D/W)$. *Compare* HICK'S LAW.

fixation. 1. (Vision) The directing of the eye so that a given point in space falls at the centre of the fovea and the subsequent stationary position of the eye that ensures the point continues to fall on the centre of the fovea. Although people normally accommodate on the object they are fixating, the two mechanisms are quite different and should not be confused. 2. (Psychoanalysis) The arrest of the libido at an earlier stage of development (e.g. anal or oral) and more generally concentration on any inappropriate sexual object. 3. (Anatomy) Preserving the shape of newly excised tissue (e.g. brain tissue) by impregnating it with a chemical (e.g. formaldehyde) that prevents subsequent change due to metabolism or decay; this is the first step in preparing tissue for slicing and examination under a microscope. 4. See FIXATION, LAW OF.

fixation, law of. The principle that with repeated practice learned material becomes more or less permanently fixed in the mind.

fixation disparity. A synonym for VERGENCE DISPARITY.

fixation hysteria. A form of CONVERSION HYSTERIA in which the hysterical symptom is based on a part of the body that is or has been subject to disease or injury.

fixation pause. A pause between SACCADES, during which the eye is approximately stationary. Little if any visual information can be taken in during a saccade; it is absorbed in the fixation pause.

fixation point. The point in space that is being fixated.

fixed action pattern (FAP). (Ethology) A stereotyped response normally given to a RELEASER. It is more complicated than a reflex in that it may depend on the animal's drive state, but it still depends largely or wholly on innate connections in the nervous system.

fixed alternative. A synonym for FORCED CHOICE.

fixed alternative question. A synonym for CLOSE-ENDED QUESTION.

fixed delay schedule. A REINFORCEMENT SCHEDULE in which reinforcement is delivered after the response with a constant delay.

fixed effect factor. A synonym for FIXED FACTOR.

fixed effects fallacy. The fallacy of generalizing over the whole range of a variable when only one or a few values have actually been tested. E.g. findings obtained from college students may or may not apply to other groups of people.

fixed factor. An independent variable that has or is assumed to have only a limited number of values, e.g. sex has two. *Compare* LEVEL.

fixed image. A synonym for STABILIZED IMAGE.

fixed interval method. (Decision theory) A method of obtaining probability estimates of a quantity by dividing its possible values into ranges (e.g. 100 to 90, 90 to 80, etc.) and asking the subject to estimate the probability of the true quantity lying within each range.

fixed interval schedule (FI). A SIMPLE SCHEDULE in which the organism is reinforced for the first response it makes after a set interval; the duration in seconds of the interval used is given after FI, thus FI30. *Compare* FIXED RATIO SCHEDULE and VARIABLE INTERVAL SCHEDULE.

fixed level. (Statistics) *See* LEVEL.

fixed ratio schedule (FR). A SIMPLE SCHEDULE in which the organism is reinforced after every *n*th response made; the number of responses required is given by the expression FR*n*, e.g. FR10. *Compare* FIXED INTERVAL SCHEDULE and VARIABLE RATIO SCHEDULE.

fixed role therapy. A therapy invented by Kelley in which the patient pretends in real life to be a person who differs from himself on at least one personal construct. The therapist meets the client frequently to support and evaluate his role playing. Kelley believed this technique would facilitate the development of more adaptive personal constructs.

flashback. A recurrence of a hallucination caused by a hallucinogenic drug that occurs when the drug is no longer present.

flashbulb memory. The vivid and detailed memory for the situation in which an important event occurred. E.g. many Americans think they can remember exactly what they were doing when they first heard of John Kennedy's death. Such memories are often incorrect.

flattening of affect. The showing, inappropriately, of little or no emotion.

flavour aversion learning. A synonym for TASTE AVERSION LEARNING.

Flesch formula. A formula for assessing how easy it is to read a given passage of prose; it is based on the average length of the words and sentences. It predicts that Plato's *Republic* will be easier to read than *The Legend of Sleepy Hollow*. Needless to say psychologists continue to use it.

flexibilitas cerea. A catatonic condition in which a person will remain for long periods in any bodily position in which he is placed.

flexion reflex. A spinal reflex in which a limb is withdrawn when it receives a painful stimulus.

flexor. A muscle that makes a limb bend or that draws it towards the body. *Contrast* EXTENSOR.

flicker fusion. The sensation of a continuous light, occurring when the light is in fact flickering rapidly. *See* CRITICAL FUSION FREQUENCY.

flicker fusion frequency, flicker fusion point. Synonyms for CRITICAL FUSION FREQUENCY.

flicker photometer. *See* PHOTOMETER.

flight from reality. Avoiding confronting the harshness of the external world by taking refuge in fantasies, day-dreams, alcohol, drugs, and, some would add, psychoanalysis.

flight into health. (Psychoanalysis) The disappearance of symptoms because the patient is unconsciously afraid to continue self-exploration through analysis; to the outsider, the concept might appear to have been invented to persuade the patient to stay in analysis.

flight into illness. (Psychoanalysis) Magnifying phsycial symptoms as a defence against neurotic symptoms.

flight into reality. (Psychoanalysis) A defence mechanism in which attention is concentrated on work or other activity to avoid facing up to unpleasant feelings.

flight of colours. The series of afterimages of many different hues that occur after prolonged exposure to a strong light while maintaining fixation.

flight of ideas. Rapid and incoherent thinking with leaps from one theme to another; it can occur in mania and schizophrenia.

flocculonodular lobe. A lobe of the medial cerebellum, with connections to the vestibular system.

flooding. A behaviour therapy technique for extinguishing anxiety, in which the patient is exposed to the situation of which he is most anxious and kept in it until the anxiety reduces. It is used to alleviate phobias. The term 'flooding' is best kept for exposure to the real object, 'implosion' for exposure to a mental image of the object, though the terms are sometimes used interchangeably.

floor effect. Failure to find a difference between different sets of scores caused by the measuring scale being insensitive to small differences between low scores. *Contrast* CEILING EFFECT.

flow chart. A series of boxes linked with arrows, in which each box represents a process and the arrows indicate how the output from one process is fed into another; a box can also represent the taking of a decision or the answering of a question, in which case two or more possible outputs will be shown (each representing a possible result of the decision or answer to the question). Used with care and with precise specification of the operation carried out in each box, flow charts can be a good way to represent how information is processed by a system. Unfortunately, when psychologists use flow charts, they are often too vague about the processes, e.g. it is unhelpful to have three boxes labelled 'input to memory', 'memory', and 'retrieval from memory'. *See* BOXOLOGY.

flow field. Movement of part or all of the retinal image.

flower-spray ending. An ending, having many small branches, of a stretch receptor in a muscle spindle.

flowery odour. A synonym for FRAGRANT ODOUR.

fluent aphasia. A synonym for WERNICKE'S APHASIA.

fluid intelligence. That part of the capacity to learn or to reason that is based not on experience but on heredity, health, age, etc. *Contrast* CRYSTALLIZED INTELLIGENCE.

fluoxetine. *See* SSRI.

fluroxamine. *See* SSRI.

flutter. *See* AUDITORY FLUTTER.

focal attention. Titchener's term for the highest degree of attention; the expression is today mainly used to mean the direction or domain in which attention is strongest.

focal colour. A colour that is prototypical of its kind (e.g. a particular shade of green, red or blue) and that is therefore easily remembered.

focal epilepsy. A form of epilepsy in which seizures initially affect only one part of the body, but then spread to other parts, after which consciousness is often lost.

focal length. The distance behind the nodal point of a lens at which parallel rays of light are brought into focus.

focal member. A synonym for PROTOTYPE.

focal plane. A plane perpendicular to the OPTICAL AXIS of a lens and passing through the focal point.

focal point. The point on the OPTICAL AXIS of a lens at which parallel rays converge.

focal psychotherapy. Therapy aimed at removing a specific conflict symptom without treating the patient in depth.

focal stress. The point in a sentence receiving the strongest vocal stress. It can indicate the word that is providing new and important information.

focus. 1. (Optics) The point or plane at which light rays (or other electromagnetic rays) converge after passing through an optical system. An image on this plane is said to be 'in focus' and will have the minimum amount of blur. 2. (Optics) A synonym for FOCAL LENGTH. 3. (Linguistics) The new information provided in a sentence as opposed to anything presupposed; e.g., in 'It was James who wrote that letter', the fact that the letter was written is taken for granted and the emphasis is on providing the writer's name. 4. (Neurology) Short for EPILEPTOGENIC FOCUS.

focusing. 1. (Optics) Adjusting a lens or optical system so that light rays from points at a given distance converge to form an image in a particular plane. *See also* ACCOMMODATION (1). 2. (Cognition) A strategy for deducing a concept from successive exemplars of it by forming a hypothesis and changing the hypothesis to accommodate any new exemplar that does not fit it. *Contrast* SCANNING.

foetal. A variant spelling of FETAL.

foetus. A variant spelling of FETUS.

foil. A synonym for DISTRACTOR (1).

foliate papillae. A synonym for LINGUAL PAPILLAE.

folie à deux. The sharing of a delusion or mental disorder by two people, often husband and wife.

folk psychology. The way in which the man in the street thinks about mental processes, as opposed to the way psychologists think he ought to think.

folk taxonomies. (Anthropology) The class inclusion relationships formed in a given society, e.g. a car is a vehicle.

follicle. Any small sac in a bodily organ whose function is excretion, secretion, or protection, e.g. HAIR FOLLICLE, OVARIAN FOLLICLE.

follicle-stimulating hormone (FSH). An anterior PITUITARY hormone, which stimulates development of the OVARIAN FOLLICLE, maturation of the ovum in females, and sperm production in males. *See also* HYPOTHALAMIC-RELEASING FACTORS.

follicular phase. The phase of the OESTROUS CYCLE in which the ovum matures; in women, roughly the first 14 days of the cycle.

following behaviour. (Ethology) The following of a parent by the young caused either by innate mechanisms or by IMPRINTING: in the latter case the young will follow members of other species if they are imprinted on them.

following movement. (Vision) *See* SMOOTH FOLLOWING MOVEMENT.

fontanelle. The hole covered by a membrane in the infant's skull where the bones are not yet fully closed.

food aversion. *See* LEARNED TASTE AVERSION.

footcandle. An obsolete unit of ILLUMINANCE, being the amount of light falling on a surface of one square foot, one foot away from an international candle. See PHOTOMETRY.

foot-in-the-door technique. A method of gaining compliance in which a person first asks someone to do something trivial and gradually increases the demands he makes.

footlambert. An obsolete unit of LUMINANCE, being the light reflected from a perfectly diffusing and reflecting surface of one square foot, one foot from a standard candle; it is equivalent to 3.426 candela per square metre.

foramen magnum. The hole in the base of the skull through which the spinal cord passes to the brain.

force. The agency that alters the motion of a body, whether it is resting or already in motion; it is equal to the body's mass multiplied by its acceleration. The SI unit of force is the NEWTON.

forced choice. Pertaining to a test (or experiment) in which the subject has to select one of two or more alternatives presented. E.g. in response to the question 'Do you ever lie?', the subject might have to select one of three alternatives – 'Never', 'Sometimes', 'Often'. (*Compare* YES–NO TEST).

forced compliance. As a result of pressure placed on a person by an experimenter, the making of a statement in which the person disbelieves, or the carrying out of an action that he thinks is wrong.

forced compliance effect. Overrating an action undertaken under FORCED COMPLIANCE (in order unconsciously to convince oneself that it was worth doing after all).

forebrain. Phylogenetically the most recent of the three main divisions of the brain. It lies immediately under the skull and is divided into the TELENCEPHALON and DIENCEPHALON. *See* BRAIN and NEURAL TUBE.

foreconscious. A synonym for PRECONSCIOUS.

forensic psychology. A branch of applied psychology that studies and makes practical suggestions about the working of the law.

foreperiod. In reaction time experiments, the period between the warning signal and the stimulus to which the subject must respond.

foreplay. Sexual activity (e.g. kissing, stroking) occurring before sexual intercourse.

forepleasure. Sexual pleasure obtained from FOREPLAY.

forgetting, law of. The principle that forgetting increases linearly with the logarithm of the time since learning occurred.

formal discipline. A subject that should be studied not so much for its own sake as because it helps to develop the mind in general: it is debatable whether there are any such subjects.

formal grammar. A synonym for GENERATIVE GRAMMAR.

formal logic. The study of the correctness of deduction independently of any semantics. *Compare* SYLLOGISM and SYMBOLIC LOGIC.

formal operational stage. The fourth of PIAGET'S STAGES of child development, lasting from about 11 to 15 years of age, in which the child learns to use fully integrated mental operations, to reason abstractly, and to understand mathematical and scientific thinking.

formal procedure. Any procedure that constitutes an ALGORITHM for the performance of a task.

formal universal. *See* LINGUISTIC UNIVERSAL.

formant. Any one of five frequency bands in the speech spectrum at which energy may be present when a vowel is spoken; the ratios of the frequencies and their relative intensities determine which vowel is heard. The lowest three formants are much the most important for the recognition of vowel sounds.

formant transition. The change from one set of FORMANT frequencies to another.

formboard test. A test in which the subject fits blocks into slots in a board.

form constancy. A synonym for SHAPE CONSTANCY.

form discrimination. The discrimination of two-dimensional shapes by vision or touch (or in some species by echo location).

formes frustes. Comparatively mild symptoms that may precede the onset of a mental disorder.

formication. The hallucination that insects (or other beasts) are crawling over or under one's skin.

form quality. The Gestalt psychologists' expression for any aspect of a pattern that emerges from the whole and is not produced by one of its components.

form response. A response to a Rorschach blot that is triggered by its shape.

form word. A synonym for FUNCTION WORD.

fornix. A long arched tract of fibres linking the HYPOTHALAMUS and HIPPOCAMPUS. *See* Appendices 2 and 5.

forward association. An ASSOCIATION linking a stimulus to a stimulus or response occurring later in time. *Contrast* BACKWARD ASSOCIATION.

forward chaining. 1. (Social psychology) Inferring from a person's actions (including his speech) their intended effects. **Backward chaining** is inferring the actions a person is likely to take from a knowledge of his goals. 2. A form of BEHAVIOUR MODIFICATION in which a person is taught how to perform a task involving successive steps by training him thoroughly on the first process then the second and so on. **Backward chaining** starts with the last process and works back to the first.

forward conditioning. Classical conditioning using the normal procedure in which the conditioned stimulus precedes the unconditioned stimulus. *Contrast* BACKWARD CONDITIONING.

forward conduction. The propagation of a nerve impulse away from the dendrites and cell body and towards the axonal terminals, which is what normally happens. *Contrast* ANTIDROMIC CONDUCTION.

forward masking. Reducing the visibility of a brief stimulus by presenting another stimulus shortly before its onset. The expression is sometimes used in a similar way of other modalities, particularly touch. *See also* BRIGHTNESS MASKING, METACONTRAST, and PATTERN MASKING.

four-card problem. *See* WASON SELECTION TASK.

fourfold-point correlation. A synonym for PHI COEFFICIENT.

Fourier analysis. The decomposition of a waveform into its constituent sine and cosine waves (a **Fourier series**) made possible by Fourier's proof that all waveforms could be so decomposed.

Fourier series. *See* FOURIER ANALYSIS.

fourth cranial nerve. A synonym for TROCH-LEAR NERVE.

fourth moment. *See* MOMENT.

fovea, fovea centralis. A circular depression in the centre of the retina containing almost entirely cones; it is found in primates and in some other vertebrates. It subtends about 5° of visual angle in man and is the area of maximal visual acuity. The term is often wrongly used to mean FOVEOLA (1).

foveola. 1. The base of the fovea, a circular area in which there are no blood-vessels and which is very thin in comparison with the rest of the retina. Its diameter in man is about 1°20′. It contains no short-wavelength cones, but the other cones are most densely packed here and it has the highest acuity. 2. The depression in the part of the embryo's head where the eye will develop.

FR. An abbreviation for FIXED RATIO SCHEDULE.

fractile method. (Decision theory) A method of obtaining probability estimates of a quantity. The subject is given a number of probabilities, e.g. 0.05, 0.25, 0.50, 0.75, 0.95, and for each is asked to specify a value for the quantity that occurs with a probability less than the specified probability.

fractional antedating goal response. A minimal response associated with reaching a goal (e.g. salivation if the goal is food). According to Hull, through conditioning such responses occur earlier and earlier in a chain of instrumental responses; hence they become part of the stimulus for these responses and can, for example, explain why an animal can learn to do one thing when hungry, and another when thirsty with the same external stimuli.

fractional antedating goal stimulus (s_G). A stimulus caused by a FRACTIONAL ANTEDATING GOAL RESPONSE.

fractional method. (Psychophysics) A scaling method in which the subject is presented with a stimulus and asked to select another stimulus that is perceived to have a given ratio (usually 1/2) to the first.

fractionation, method of. A synonym for PRODUCTION, METHOD OF.

fragrant odour. One of the six so-called primary odours of the ODOUR PRISM, and one of the four odours of the ODOUR SQUARE.

frame. 1. (Programmed instruction) A question or set of questions to be answered; the frame that is next presented to the student may depend on what answers he has given to the previous one. 2. (AI) Minsky's word for SCHEMA, i.e. a body of organized knowledge that can be used to interpret and supplement incoming information. *Compare* DEFAULT ASSIGNMENT. 3. (Social psychology) The way in which a person perceives his social situation, including his role and the social conventions that govern his actions. 4. *See* FRAMING EFFECT.

frame analysis. The analysis of social behaviour in terms of FRAMES (3).

frame of reference. 1. (Vision) The background of a visual scene; it is normally taken to be stationary. Where the only background is a rectangle and the only other object present is a dot, the dot is seen to move if the

Fraser's spiral

rectangle (the background) moves. (*See* IN-DUCED MOTION.) 2. More generally, any standard or context used by someone in evaluating a stimulus or situation.

framing effect. The effect of irrelevant aspects of the context on reaching a conclusion or making a decision. E.g. someone who has seen a car accident will estimate the car's speed as higher if asked 'How fast was it going when it crashed into the other car?' than if asked 'How fast was it going when it hit the other car?'

Fraser's spiral. A visual illusion consisting of a set of concentric circles that look like a spiral; *see* the illustration below. The apparent curvature of the circles at any one point is influenced by the tilt of the black and white

segments composing them. There are several variants of this illusion; *compare* TWISTED CORD ILLUSION.

fraternal twins. A synonym for DIZYGOTIC TWINS.

F ratio. (Statistics) The ratio of the VARIANCES of two independent samples from normal populations. It is used in analysis of variance. In testing data from psychological experiments by analysis of variance, F_1 stands for any effect in which subjects are the source of error variance, F_2 for any effect in which experimental materials are the source of error variance, and F' for any effect in which two or more sources contribute to the error variance. *See* F DISTRIBUTION.

free association. A technique, used in psychoanalysis, to overcome defence mechanisms, in which the patient gives vent to his thoughts without any attempt to suppress them or make them logical; patients or experimental subjects may also be presented with words and asked to respond as fast as they can with the first word they think of.

free field. (Audition) Any system of sound waves that is unaffected by boundaries, i.e. is free from echoes.

free-floating anxiety. Chronic anxiety or severe uneasiness that has no apparent cause; it occurs in anxiety neurosis and in many other kinds of mental disorder.

free morpheme. A morpheme that is used as a word without modification by another morpheme (e.g. 'blue'). *Contrast* BOUND MORPHEME.

free nerve ending. A receptor widely distributed in the skin, mucous membranes, and linings of internal organs; it has no obvious receptor apparatus but ends in branches of small filaments. These receptors were once thought to be sensitive primarily to pain, but it is likely that some respond to touch and temperature. *Contrast* ENCAPSULATED NERVE ENDING.

free operant. A response that is freely emitted in a situation (e.g. a bar press, turning the head to the left). Such responses are not directly under stimulus control, but they can be brought under stimulus control through OPERANT CONDITIONING.

free operant experiment. An experiment in which the subject makes a given FREE OPERANT, and has to learn to make it consistently to a given stimulus. The expression is normally reserved for experiments in which an animal is kept in the same situation (usually a Skinner box) throughout each experimental session and is free to make the operant response at any time. *Contrast* DISCRETE TRIALS EXPERIMENT.

free recall. The task of recovering a set of items from memory without specifying their serial order.

free responding. A synonym for FREE OPERANT behaviour.

free rider effect. The failure of a member of a task-orientated group to contribute to the task.

free sound field. A homogeneous medium without boundaries in which sound is conducted evenly and without reflections.

freezing. A state in which the animal's muscles are contracted so that it remains motionless; it is usually induced by fear.

frequency. 1. The rate at which something, particularly a wave, repeats. *See also* WAVELENGTH. 2. (Statistics) The number of times a given phenomenon occurs. *Compare* FREQUENCY DISTRIBUTION. 3. *See* FREQUENCY, LAW OF.

frequency, law of. The principle, of doubtful validity, that the more often a response is repeated the higher will be its response strength and the better it will be remembered.

frequency, method of. A synonym for CONSTANT STIMULI, METHOD OF.

frequency curve. A curve in which the frequency of occurrence of each of a set of consecutive values (or of values grouped in intervals) is plotted on the vertical axis and the values on the horizontal axis.

frequency distribution. The frequency with which the members of a sample or of a population take one of a set of consecutive values (or values grouped in intervals) or with which they are distributed among different categories.

frequency domain. (Hearing) The description of a waveform in terms of its constituent sine waves. *Contrast* TIME DOMAIN.

frequency method. *See* CONSTANT STIMULI, METHOD OF.

frequency polygon. (Statistics) A graphical representation of a frequency distribution in which frequencies are represented by the ordinate, and variable values by the abscissa, with successsive ordinate values joined by lines.

frequency range. A synonym for BANDWIDTH.

frequency spectrum. A graph plotting the Fourier components of a wave (particularly a sound wave) over time and showing the amplitude of each frequency component by the density of the line representing it. *See* FOURIER ANALYSIS.

frequency theory. (Hearing) The theory that sound frequency is coded by the frequency of firing in the auditory nerve and that this frequency is decoded by central mechanisms; the theory is now thought to apply only to low frequencies of sound. *Contrast* PLACE THEORY and VOLLEY THEORY.

Freudian slip. A synonym for PARAPRAXIS.

fricative. (Phonetics) A speech sound made by expelling air through a small opening in the vocal tract, thus causing friction, e.g. between teeth and lips (the 'f' in 'fish') or between tongue and roof of mouth (the 's' in 'soup').

Friedman test. (Statistics) A non–parametric test applicable to data in which there are more than two MATCHED SAMPLES (2). It is based on ranking the scores within each sample. *Compare* WILCOXON TEST.

frontal. (Anatomy) Towards the front of the body or of an organ.

frontal eye field. A cortical area in the frontal lobe comprising Brodmann's area 8 and parts of 6 and 9. It is implicated in eye movements. *See* Appendix 4.

frontal leucotomy. Surgical separation of the prefrontal lobe from the rest of the brain by severing the white matter. In FRONTAL LOBOTOMY, the intention is to cut deeper into the lobe, but in practice there is little difference between the two. The operation was mistakenly undertaken in an attempt to cure mental illness.

frontal lobe. One of the four main divisions of the cerebral cortex, being that part lying in front of the CENTRAL FISSURE. It includes the MOTOR CORTEX and the PREFRONTAL LOBE. It comprises Brodmann's areas 4, 6, 8, 11, and 44, 47; *see* Appendices 3 and 4.

frontal lobectomy. The surgical excision of tissue from the prefrontal lobes, undertaken to relieve psychosis. It is doubtful whether any patients benefitted from the operation, though many surgeons did. *Compare* FRONTAL LOBOTOMY.

frontal lobe syndrome. A disorder caused by lesions of the prefrontal lobe, marked by such symptoms as impulsiveness, inability to plan or sustain a course of action, apathy, etc.

frontal lobotomy. The surgical sectioning of the nerve fibres connecting the prefrontal lobes to the rest of the brain, a less drastic procedure than FRONTAL LOBECTOMY and one that was formerly widely used in an attempt to cure psychoses and other mental disorders. There is no evidence that it helped, but it did produce the FRONTAL LOBE SYNDROME.

frontal-parallel plane. Any vertical plane parallel to the line between a person's eyes. The expression is usually used in connection with vision and the plane would therefore by sited in front of the observer.

frontal section. (Anatomy) A TRANSVERSE SECTION made towards the front of an organ.

front phoneme. A phoneme uttered with the tongue towards the front of the mouth.

frottage. Rubbing against people, usually in a crowd, in order to gain sexual pleasure.

frozen noise. A section of WHITE NOISE that is repeated again and again.

fruity odour. A synonym for ETHERIAL ODOUR.

frustration. The emotional state that is aroused in men and animals if an attempt to achieve a goal is blocked or prevented. It can lead to aggression and possibly to REGRESSION (1).

frustration–aggression hypothesis. The hypothesis, advanced by N.E. Miller and Dollard, that frustration causes aggression.

frustration effect. (Animal learning) The phenomenon that frustration energizes subsequent behaviour (presumably by creating arousal).

frustration non-reward hypothesis. The hypothesis that the withholding of an expected reinforcer acts like a punishment.

frustration theory. The theory that organisms extinguish because the frustration experienced through non-reward is aversive. The theory is also a possible explanation of the partial reinforcement effect since during partial reinforcement some frustration is conditioned to responding, hence in extinction the organism will continue to respond for more trials than one that has been continuously reinforced.

frustration tolerance. The ability to withstand frustration without behaving aggressively or irrationally.

F scale. A scale designed to measure the extent to which someone has an AUTHORITARIAN PERSONALITY.

FSH. An abbreviation for FOLLICLE-STIMULATING HORMONE.

F test. (Statistics) A statistical test based on the F RATIO and F DISTRIBUTION. It is used in ANOVA and in testing whether two variances are equal.

fugue. A state, which may last for many days, in which a person is unconscious of his previous life; in this condition he may leave home and begin a completely new life.

Fullerton–Cattell law. The law that the error of a perceptual judgement measured in physical terms increases with the square root of the stimulus intensity. It is a possible substitute for WEBER'S LAW.

full primal sketch. *See* PRIMAL SKETCH.

function. 1. (General) The natural use to which anything can be put, its role or purpose. 2. (Mathematics and Logic) A systematic mapping from one set of variables (the **arguments**) onto another (the **values**). E.g. in the expression $6 - 4 = 2$, the function is 'subtract', the arguments are 6 and 4, and the value is 2. 3. (Computing) Any operation performed by a program, a use similar to the term's mathematical meaning, since normally an operation will be performed on certain **arguments** (data) and will return a value. E.g. 'find head list (x)' will return as a value the item in the first position of list (x).

functional. 1. (Psychiatry and Psychology) Caused by psychological factors rather than physiological ones. *Contrast* ORGANIC. 2. (General) Pertaining to function.

functional analysis of behaviour. The application of the principles of learning theory or (more usually) of Skinnerian analysis to the stimuli and reinforcement schedules that determine behaviour. The method is used in behaviour therapy to determine the variables that control symptoms.

functional antagonism. A synonym for PHYSIOLOGICAL ANTAGONISM.

functional attitude theory. Any theory postulating that people hold attitudes because they serve a function, e.g. to help them adjust to their background or to protect themselves from criticism.

functional autonomy. The tendency for a drive or habit to become independent of the goal that originally motivated it. E.g. a person may set out to try to make money in order to have a more comfortable life, but wind up pursuing riches for their own sake.

functional deafness. Deafness with no organic cause, such as can occur in CONVERSION HYSTERIA.

functional disorder. A disorder that cannot be directly traced to an organic cause, e.g. a neurosis.

functional fixedness. The tendency when solving a problem to see objects only in terms of their usual function and to fail to see that they can be used in other ways that would help to solve the problem. E.g. the inside of a matchbox when glued to the wall could serve as a candlestick holder.

functionalism. 1. (Psychology) A school of psychology developed in Chicago in the early 20th century, and associated with Angell and Carr. It emphasized the function and causes of mental processes and behaviour, in contrast to STRUCTURALISM (1), which emphasized the static contents of consciousness. 2. (Philosophy) The theory that what is important about mental states is their relationship to one another and to the external world. Today functionalists identify consciousness with higher-order states of the brain that are causally related to a person's interactions with the external world. 3. (Anthropology) The hypothesis that the different institutions and customs of a society sustain both one another and the survival of the culture in general.

functional knowledge. A synonym for PROCEDURAL KNOWLEDGE.

functional mental disorder. A mental disorder for which there is no known organic cause, e.g. manic-depressive disorder or schizophrenia. Since it is now suspected that these disorders do have biochemical causes, the expression is a misnomer.

functional psychology. A synonym for FUNCTIONALISM (1).

functional psychosis. Effectively a synonym for FUNCTIONAL MENTAL DISORDER, which is nowadays the preferred expression.

functional stimulus. The aspect of a stimulus that predominantly exerts control over behaviour.

function engram. Jung's term for an inherited neural structure that preserves an ARCHETYPE or other racial memory.

function types. Jung's term for any of his four personality types. He divided people into **rational type** and **irrational type**; the former he subdivided into **feeling type** and **thinking type**, and the latter into **sensing type** and **intuitive type**. The meaning of the terms should be obvious.

function word. A word, like a preposition, conjunction, or particle, that does not refer to a state of affairs, but is needed to specify the grammar of a sentence and contributes to its meaning in the context of the words around it. *Contrast* CONTENT WORD.

functor. A synonym for FUNCTION WORD.

fundamental. 1. The lowest frequency tone in a set of tones (HARMONICS) whose frequencies are integer multiples of it. *See also* MISSING

FUNDAMENTAL. 2. The FUNDAMENTAL (1) frequency at which the vocal cords vibrate; they produce harmonics in the rest of the VOCAL TRACT.

fundamental attribution error. The common mistake of explaining actions in terms of factors intrinsic to the person rather than in terms of his external situation. The mistake is thought to arise because superficially there is a closer link between actor and action than between situation and action.

fundamental colour. A synonym for PRIMARY (1) or PRIMARY (2).

fundamental frequency. A synonym for FUNDAMENTAL.

fundamental need. Maslow's term for PHYSIOLOGICAL NEED.

fundamental symptoms. Bleuler's term for the basic or primary symptoms of schizophrenia (e.g. disturbed associations), which he thought gave rise to the **secondary symptoms (accessory symptoms)** like delusions and hallucinations.

fundamental tone. A synonym for FUNDAMENTAL.

fundus. The base of an organ or the part furthest away from its opening; in the case of the eye, the retina.

fungiform papillae. A synonym for LINGUAL PAPILLAE.

funnel technique. The technique of starting a questionnaire with broad questions and gradually making them more specific.

fusiform cell. A type of STELLATE CELL in the cortex that has two short vertical projections which divide into many long processes running upwards or downwards from the cell body.

fusiform layer. The innermost (sixth) layer of nerve cells in the cerebral cortex, containing mostly FUSIFORM CELLS. *See also* CORTICAL LAYERS.

fusion. 1. (Perception) *See* AUDITORY FUSION, BINOCULAR FUSION, or CRITICAL FUSION FRE-

QUENCY. 2. (Psychoanalysis) The coordination of the life and death instincts.

fusion field. (Vision) An area surrounding and including the fovea, within which fusional responses are initiated, i.e. if retinal disparity occurs within this area, vergence movements are made to eliminate it. The area is longer horizontally than vertically.

fusional movement. Vergence when triggered by retinal disparity.

future perfect tense. *See* PERFECT TENSE.

future tense. Any TENSE used of an action or event occurring after the time of utterance.

fuzzy set theory. The mathematical theory of sets that do not have sharp boundaries. Since most concepts are fuzzy in this sense (e.g. bald, bad), some believe the mathematical theory could throw light on cognition, but it has not so far done so.

G

G. An abbreviation for 1. GENERAL ABILITY; 2. GOAL.

GABA. An abbreviation for **gamma-aminobutyric acid**, an amino acid that is an inhibitory NEUROTRANSMITTER; it is found in the cortex, basal ganglia, and elsewhere in the central nervous system.

GAD. An abbreviation for GENERALIZED ANXIETY DISORDER.

GAI. An abbreviation for GUIDED AFFECTIVE IMAGERY.

gain. (Cybernetics) The degree to which a signal is amplified (positive gain) or reduced (negative gain) when it passes through a system or from one system to another.

gain loss theory of attraction. The hypothesis that a person who increases (or decreases) his liking for someone else has a bigger impact on the other person, i.e. makes the second person like him more (or less), than if he had maintained from the outset the degree of liking to which he shifted.

galeophobia. A morbid fear of cats.

Galton bar. A rod used in experiments to establish the just noticeable difference in visual judgements of distance.

Galton whistle. A high-pitched whistle used to determine the maximum frequency that can be heard.

galvanic. Pertaining to direct current, as opposed to alternating current.

galvanic skin response (GSR). A decrease in the electrical resistance of the skin, occur-ring in a state of arousal, whether pleasant or unpleasant; it is produced by activity of the sweat glands. The resistance change is often measured in order to detect arousal. *See also* LIE DETECTOR, FERE METHOD, and TARCHANOFF METHOD.

galvanometer. A device for measuring small electric currents.

galvanotaxis, galvanotropism. (Ethology) Orienting the body with respect to an external electric current.

gambler's fallacy. The fallacy that, in a series of independent chance events, future events can be predicted from past ones. E.g. the belief that if a coin has come down heads many times in succession it has an increased probability of coming down tails on the next throw.

games. (Psychotherapy) 1. The deliberate adopting by a patient of a role in a situation in order to reveal his attitudes and feelings about it. 2. A term used pejoratively by many psychotherapists of manipulative interactions in which 'true feelings' are not displayed, e.g. interactions in which one person is trying to get the better of another.

gamete. A reproductive cell (i.e. a sperm or ovum) which contains only half the parental genes; when fertilization takes place the full complement of genes is acquired.

game theory. The mathematical study of formal games (usually between two persons), where the probability of each outcome depends on what the players do and where different outcomes have different payoffs or costs for the players: the theory is normative (i.e. it prescribes optimal strategies) and it is largely based on the MINIMAX

PRINCIPLE. It is widely used in sociobiology and psychological studies of decision making.

gamma alcoholism. *See* ALCOHOLISM.

gamma-aminobutyric acid. *See* GABA.

gammacism. (Phonetics) The replacement in speech of velar consonants (e.g. the 'g' in 'get') by dental ones (e.g. the 'd' in debt'), characteristic of infants.

gamma motion. The illusion that a light expands for a brief time after coming on and contracts briefly when it is extinguished.

gamma motor neuron. A small motor neuron that stimulates the INTRAFUSAL FIBRES, thus keeping them taut. *See* NERVE FIBRES.

gamma oscillation. The oscillation (at 35–75 Hz) of bursts of firing in the cat's visual cortex: Crick believes it may provide the solution to the BINDING PROBLEM.

gamma waves. EEG waves with the high frequency of 40–50 Hz; they are thought to occur during thinking.

gamophobia. A morbid fear of marriage, a syndrome that is becoming endemic.

ganglion. A cluster of the bodies of nerve cells, usually lying outside the central nervous system. *Compare* NUCLEUS (2).

ganglion blocking agents. Any drug that is an ANTAGONIST to drugs that excite the autonomic ganglia.

ganglion cell. A cell with a large roughly spherical body. They are found, e.g. as the third-order retinal cells (whose axons enter the optic nerve) and as the first order auditory cells, as well as in other sensory systems.

Ganser syndrome. A pathological tendency to give vague answers to questions and not to keep to the point.

Ganzfeld. A completely homogeneous evenly illuminated field, containing no visible detail and covering the whole retina; it looks like a mist.

gap junction. (Neurophysiology) A synapse at which the gap between the presynaptic and postsynaptic cells is very small (about 2 nm) and is bridged by channels of membranous particles. Ions and other small molecules can pass through it from one cell to the other. Gap junctions are the basis of the electrical synapse.

Garcia effect. A synonym for LEARNED TASTE AVERSION.

garden path sentence. A sentence whose early part is normally misinterpreted, with the result that subsequently it is necessary to change the interpretation in order for the sentence to make sense. E.g. 'The horse raced past the barn fell'.

gap threshold. (Audition) The minimum pause in an otherwise continuous and unvarying sound that can just be detected. In white noise it is about 2–3 msec.

gargalaesthesia, gargalesthesia. Sensitivity to tickling.

gargoylism. Severe disfigurement of the bones of the head and face, caused by a genetic disorder.

GAS. An abbreviation for GENERAL ADAPTATION SYNDROME.

gate. Any element whose output depends systematically on a combination of two or more inputs. *See* e.g. AND GATE.

gate control theory. Wall's theory of pain, which in essence postulates that as a result of the firing of large sensory nerve fibres, pain messages in small fibres may be blocked at the level of the spinal cord so that they do not reach the brain.

gating. The prevention of one set of stimuli reaching central attention, while another set is being attended to.

gatophobia. A morbid fear of cats.

Gaussian curvature. The product of the two PRINCIPAL CURVATURES of a surface. It is positive if both have the same sign as on a sphere, and negative if they differ in sign as on a saddle point.

Gaussian curve, Gaussian distribution. Synonyms for NORMAL DISTRIBUTION. *See also* DIFFERENCE OF GAUSSIANS.

Gaussian filter. A method of smoothing temporal or spatial variations (e.g. in an image) by averaging sets of neighbouring values while weighting their contribution to the computed value of each set by a Gaussian function. Gaussian filters can be used as the masks in a CONVOLUTION.

Gedanken **experiment.** A process of thought in which the thinker tries to work out in his head what would happen under one or more sets of circumstances.

Gelb effect. The phenomenon that a spinning black wheel illuminated by a circle of light in a dark room looks white. It looks blacker if a white piece of paper is inserted into the light immediately in front of it. The effect suggests that brightness constancy is at least in part determined by the gradients of luminance between neighbouring surfaces. *Compare* KARDOS EFFECT.

Gellermann series. Sequences of random Rs and Ls with the constraints that no more than three of either letter occur in succession and that in each successive block of ten letters there are five Ls and five Rs. The series has been widely used to generate trial sequences in two choice discrimination learning.

Geller–Seifert test. A test for the effectiveness of an anxiolytic drug. A thirsty rat is given shocks whenever it drinks: the effectiveness of the drug is measured by the amount it drinks or the number of shocks it is prepared to take.

gemellology. The study of twins, usually to determine heritability.

gender. A grammatical category describing such contrast between nouns (and words agreeing with a noun) as masculine, feminine, and neuter.

gender identity disorder. Any disorder in which there is a conflict between the actual sex of a person and the sex with which he or she identifies.

gender role. The ways of behaving thought to be typical of the sex to which a person belongs.

gene. The basic unit of heredity, made up of a sequence of DNA forming part of a chromosome. *See* MUTATION.

gene expressivity, gene expression. The extent to which a particular gene's effects are realized in the PHENOTYPE.

gene mutation. *See* MUTATION

gene pool. The total number of ALLELES in an interbreeding population.

general ability (G). The hypothetical and much debated factor postulated by Spearman and others that contributes positively to performance on all intelligence tests. Whether or not it appears in a factor analysis of a set of tests usually depends on how the analysis is carried out. Now you see it, now you don't. *Contrast* SPECIAL FACTOR.

general adaptation syndrome (GAS). The hypothesized reaction to prolonged stress as postulated by Selye. It has three stages. (i) The **alarm reaction** comprises two phases: (a) The **shock phase**, in which there is a drop in temperature, blood pressure, and muscle tone; (b) the **countershock phase**, in which the sympathetic system is aroused with release of pituitary and adrenocortical hormones that defend the organism against the stress. (ii) The **resistance stage**: the adrenal cortex secretes corticosteroids to continue the protection against stress and the sympathetic system returns to normal levels of excitation. (iii) The **extinction stage**: if the stress is too prolonged, the protective mechanisms break down and the organism may contract various physical or mental ailments.

General Aptitude Test. A test battery in common use in the USA, measuring intelligence, verbal, numerical, spatial, and motor skills, etc.

general factor. 1. (Generally) Any factor that has a positive loading on all the items in a factor analysis. 2. (Specifically) A synonym for GENERAL ABILITY.

generalization. 1. (Generally) The inference that what is known to be true of all known members of a class is true of all members including those not yet known, or the process of making such an inference. 2. (Experimental psychology) The phenomenon that an organism that has learned to make a response to a stimulus will make the same response to a similar stimulus (**stimulus generalization**). 3. (Experimental psychology) More rarely, the tendency for organisms that have learned to make one response to a stimulus to make a different response that is similar in its effects, particularly if they are not allowed to make the original response. E.g. if a rat has learned to run down a maze it will swim through the correct path if the maze is flooded (**response generalization**).

generalization decrement. In Hull's theory, the reduction in response strength caused by any difference between the stimuli present on the current trial and those that were present on previous reinforced trials.

generalization gradient. The shape of the curve of response strength plotted against stimuli increasingly dissimilar to the stimulus to which the response was learned.

generalized anxiety disorder (GAD). A modern euphemism for ANXIETY NEUROSIS.

generalized conditioned inhibition. A synonym for GENERALIZED INHIBITORY POTENTIAL

generalized cone. The surface created by moving a cross-section of constant shape but varying size (but with no sudden jumps in size) along an axis. Marr proposed it as the basic building block in the representation of 3-D objects.

generalized habit strength ($_s\bar{H}_R$). Hull's term for the strength of a habit after taking GENERALIZATION DECREMENT into account: it enters into the equation determining REACTION POTENTIAL. *See* HULLIAN THEORY.

generalized inhibitory potential ($_s\bar{I}_R$). Hull's term for the total amount of conditioned inhibition to be subtracted from reaction potential to yield the net reaction potential

after making allowance for any generalization decrement in inhibition caused by variations in the stimulus. *See* HULLIAN THEORY.

generalized matching to sample. *See* MATCHING TO SAMPLE.

generalized oddity problem. *See* ODDITY PROBLEM.

generalized phrase structure grammar. The attempt to show that natural languages can be generated without the use of TRANSFORMATIONS, and using only phrase structure rules.

generalized reaction potential ($_s\bar{E}_R$). In Hull's theory the strength of reaction potential after allowing for GENERALIZATION DECREMENT, formed from GENERALIZED HABIT STRENGTH, DRIVE STRENGTH, and several other variables. *See* HULLIAN THEORY.

generalizing assimilation. Piaget's expression for the formation of new concepts, particularly by children, through a process of GENERALIZATION (1); e.g. the formation of new classes or categories.

general paresis. The final stage of syphilitic infection, which is accompanied by deterioration of mental powers, irritability, and many physical symptoms.

General Problem Solver (GPS). A program written by Newell and Simon which solves problems by working back from the goal to find subgoals and applying tests to discover which subgoals are nearest to the current state. Despite the program's name, problems have to be put into a standard form before it can solve them.

general process theory. A misguided form of behaviourism holding that the underlying processes of learning are the same in all species, that they apply equally to all stimuli and responses and that all learning can be explained by S–R connections.

general psychology. 1. Effectively, all psychology. 2. The study of the principles that apply to all people. *Contrast* PSYCHOLOGY OF INDIVIDUAL DIFFERENCES. (Rare in either sense).

general semantics. The broad study of how people interpret language and gestures, and of how they communicate with or influence one another.

general systems theory. Whether applied to man or to the universe as a whole, the attempt to see a system as made up of a hierarchy of subsystems and to specify the flow of information or forces that keeps the whole in balance.

generation. The average time period in a species (particularly man) between being born and starting to reproduce.

generative grammar. An explicit and rigorous set of rules from which it is possible to derive as theorems all and only all the grammatically well-formed sentences of a language. *See also* DEEP STRUCTURE, and *compare* PHRASE STRUCTURE GRAMMAR and TRANSFORMATIONAL GRAMMAR.

generative semantics. (Linguistics) The hypothesis that the input to the transformational component of a grammar is the semantic representation of the sentence.

generator potential. A graded change in voltage across the membrane of a receptor, caused by the appropriate stimulus. In some receptors, e.g., the rods and cones, stimulation produces hyperpolarization, which inhibits the postsynaptic cell; in others it produces depolarization, which excites it.

generic memory. A synonym for SEMANTIC MEMORY (1).

genetic code. A code which consists of three nucleotide bases occurring in a DNA or RNA molecule. It determines which amino acid is incorporated into a protein at a given point in the sequence.

genetic drift. A change, occurring randomly and not through evolutionary pressure, in the frequency of particular genes in a population.

genetic epistemology. Piaget's expression for the way in which he thought cognitive development occurred. He believed it moved through stages at each of which the child was constructing more complex cognitive operations and organizing knowledge adaptively

through such processes as ASSIMILATION (1) and ACCOMMODATION (2). He emphasized the active part played by the mind rather than innate factors.

geneticism. A synonym for NATIVISM.

genetic marker. A gene whose position on a chromosome and whose alleles are known. *See* LINKAGE ANALYSIS.

genetic memory. Inheritance in so far as it reflects evolutionary adaptations made by a person's distant ancestors. The expression is unhelpful and unnecessary.

genetics. (Biology) The study of inheritance.

geniculate bodies. *See* LATERAL GENICULATE NUCLEUS and MEDIAL GENICULATE NUCLEUS.

genital character. (Psychoanalysis) The personality of someone who has reached the GENITAL STAGE and has successfully integrated the other stages of sexual development along the way.

genital stage. (Psychoanalysis) The final (fifth) stage of libidinal development normally reached at puberty, in which the libido is directed to genital sex with a partner. *See also* LIBIDINAL STAGES,

genitive. A CASE of a noun or pronoun, used to denote possession or close association as in '*John's* hat', 'The end *of the book*'.

genome. The total DNA sequences belonging to a given species or to a particular member of that species. *See also* GENOTYPE.

genotype. The genetic make-up of an organism or that part of that make-up that produces a particular trait in the PHENOTYPE.

genus. *See* TAXONOMY.

geometric axis of eye. A synonym for PRIMARY LINE OF SIGHT.

geometric illusion. Any visual illusion in which the shape, size, length, or orientation of part of a figure is misperceived because of the simultaneous presence of the other parts of the figure. Similar misperceptions (e.g. of orientation) can occur as AFTEREFFECTS, but they are not then normally called geometric illusions. AMBIGUOUS FIGURES are not illusions, though they are sometimes mistakenly so called.

geometric mean. (Statistics) A measure of central tendency, arrived at by taking the *n*th root of the product of all scores, where *n* is the number of scores. *Contrast* ARITHMETIC MEAN.

geometric progression, geometric series. *See* PROGRESSION.

geons. Hypothetical 3-D entities into which an object can be divided for the purpose of recognition, e.g. a sphere, a cube, a cylindrical shape etc. *Compare* GENERALIZED CONE.

geotaxis, geotropism. A movement that helps to maintain an organism's balance or its orientation with respect to the ground.

germ cell. A synonym for GAMETE.

germinal stage, germinal period. The first stage of embryonic development, during which there is little cellular differentiation; it lasts about two weeks in the human embryo.

gerontology. The study of ageing.

Gerstmann's syndrome. A neurological disorder marked by dysgraphia, finger agnosia, right left disorientation, acalculia, and agraphia, and often accompanied by other symptoms; it is caused by lesions of the parietal cortex usually near the angular gyrus; it is probably not a very useful classification since the symptoms do not necessarily all occur together.

gerund. A noun formed from a verb by adding '-ing', e.g. 'his excessive *drinking*'.

gerundive. An adjective formed from a verb by adding '-ing'; it is used in English to express the continuous tense, e.g. 'he is drinking'.

Geschwind syndrome. A synonym for INTERICTAL SYNDROME.

Gesell Developmental Scales. A set of tests, largely observational, for assessing the development of language in preschool children, and their motor and social performance.

Gestalt. A total configuration, a whole emerging from its parts. The term was used by the Gestalt psychologists to stress the importance of the whole stimulus, which is more than the sum of its parts. In German the word means 'essence' or 'form', but there is no simple translation into English.

Gestalt psychology. A school of psychology founded early in this century by Wertheimer that rejected ATOMISM, and emphasized that in perception and other mental processes the whole is often more than the sum of its parts. The Gestaltists thought the mind was always trying to create good wholes, e.g. trying to see shapes as regular and symmetrical. They postulated dynamic forces (*see* INTERNAL FORCE OF ORGANIZATION and EXTERNAL FORCE OF ORGANIZATION) at work in the brain and believed that mental experience was ISOMORPHIC with activity in the brain. This led to their adopting an incorrect view of the brain, namely, that it worked by the interplay of dynamic forces rather than through activity in local units. The Gestaltists' theorizing was vague, but they discovered many important phenomena. *See also* PRAGNANZ, LAW OF.

Gestaltqualität. Any property (e.g. symmetry) that is possessed by a stimulus in virtue of its being a whole and that is not simply derivable from the sum of its parts.

Gestalt therapy. A type of psychotherapy originated by Frederick Perls. It has no direct connection with Gestalt psychology; it emphasizes the spontaneous expression of feelings, living in the here-and-now and personal growth. Whether given to individuals or to groups, the therapy can be aggressive. There is no evidence that it works.

gestation. The process of carrying the embryo and fetus from conception to birth.

geumaphobia. A morbid fear of tastes.

g factor. Short for GENERAL FACTOR.

GH. An abbeviation for GROWTH HORMONE.

ghosts. Pairs of image points, one on each eye, that can mistakenly be taken to be stimulated by the same points in space. *See* FALSE CORRESPONDENCE PROBLEM.

giant pyramidal cell. A synonym for BETZ CELL.

Gibsonian. Pertaining to J.J. Gibson's views on perception. He believed aspects of the stimulus remained invariant with aspects of the world. These INVARIANTS were directly 'picked up' by the nervous system to yield veridical perception. He believed, curiously, that no mental processes entered into perception and he abhorred the use of words like 'inference' or 'representation' in discussing perception. He did for perception what Skinner did for animal learning: he handicapped a generation of workers by his blinkered and oversimplified approach.

gifted. In technical usage, having an IQ of more than 140.

gigantism. The state of having abnormally large bones, caused by an excess of GROWTH HORMONE.

given information. (Linguistics) The part of a sentence recapping information already known to the listener. E.g. if in answer to 'When are you coming?' someone replies 'I'm coming in a minute', 'I'm coming' is given information and 'in a minute' is NEW INFORMATION. *Contrast* FOCUS (3).

glabrous. Hairless.

glands. Organs that secrete substances. EXOCRINE GLANDS secrete through a duct; ENDOCRINE GLANDS have no ducts, and control the body's internal environment by secreting (mostly) into the blood stream.

glia. Short for NEUROGLIA.

gliosis. The growth of NEUROGLIA to occupy the space left by dead nerve cells.

glissade. A slow monocular eye movement of uncertain origin, though muscular fatigue may be involved.

global amnesia. Total or very severe ANTEROGRADE AMNESIA, usually accompanied by some RETROGRADE AMNESIA. Perceptual and motor skills, and short-term memory are often unimpaired. The syndrome is caused by damage to the diencephalon or medial temporal lobe.

global aphasia. Severe impairment or loss of all language abilities, both receptive and expressive, usually caused by widespread lesions in the left hemisphere.

global feature. *See* FEATURE.

global focusing strategy. A possible strategy for use in a concept formation task, in which the person keeps all possible concepts in his mind, and, as he comes across negative instances of a concept, reduces the number of possible concepts until he is only left with one; the strategy imposes a severe load on memory.

global stereopsis. Stereopsis occurring with complex patterns on the two eyes (e.g. a JULESZ STEREOGRAM) where the corresponding parts could be selected locally in different ways but are in fact selected so as to yield a consistent unitary (global) image.

global syntactic parsing. Parsing that involves the construal of ANAPHORA, the use of TRACES, etc. It depends on semantics unlike LOCAL SYNTACTIC PARSING.

globus hystericus. A psychosomatic symptom in which the patient feels he has a lump in his throat.

globus pallidus. One of the BASAL GANGLIA, implicated in the control of eating and drinking.

glomerulus. One of many bundles of cells where olfactory receptors synapse and which make up the olfactory bulb.

glossalgia. A pain in the tongue occurring for no organic reason.

glossodynia. Any itching or burning feeling in the tongue or mouth.

glossolalia. The use of a series of neologisms that render speech incomprehensible; it occurs e.g. in some religious sects under ecstasy, and sometimes in schizophrenia.

glossopharyngeal nerve. The ninth CRANIAL NERVE, which carries sensations from the posterior part of the tongue, the palate, and the pharynx to the brain. It also has efferents to the throat.

glossosynthesis. The pathological invention of new and meaningless words.

glossy. Pertaining to a surface that reflects in one direction much of the light falling on it. The observer will see highlights whose position will alter with changes in his viewpoint. *Contrast* MATT.

glottal. (Phonetics) A speech sound made by closing or narrowing the glottis, e.g. [h].

glottal stop. The audible release of air after a complete closure of the glottis, occurring in English between two consecutive but separate vowel sounds, e.g. between the first two vowels in 'coordinate'.

glottis. A slit in the LARYNX, through which air from the lungs passes to reach the PHARYNX.

glove anaesthesia. A hysterical symptom in which sensation is lost in the area of the hand and forearm that would be covered by a glove. *Compare* STOCKING ANAESTHESIA.

glucagon. A pancreatic hormone that increases blood sugar level.

Glück prediction tables. Tables that purport to make predictions about how delinquent a person is, based on such factors as how much he was disciplined by his father.

glucocorticoids. Steroid hormones (e.g. CORTISOL) secreted by the adrenal cortex that promote the conversion of fats and proteins to glycogen and glucose. They also regulate the sensitivity of some nerve cells to neurotransmitters through intracellular receptors.

glucoreceptor. A hypothetical receptor sensitive to the level of glucose in the blood, thought to exist in the hypothalamus.

glucose. A simple sugar that is one of the body's main energy sources.

glucostatic theory. The theory that eating is regulated by the brain's monitoring of the rate at which glucose is removed from the blood (as measured by the difference in glucose levels between arteries and veins): the lower the rate the more the animal eats. Low use of glucose indicates that the blood levels are low and are being replaced by glucose derived from fats.

glutamate, glutamic acid. An amino acid that is the main excitatory neurotransmitter in the TELENCEPHALON and DIENCEPHALON.

glutamine. An AMINE derived from GLUTAMIC ACID.

glycaemia. The concentration of sugar in the blood.

glycine. An amino acid thought to be an inhibitory neurotransmitter.

glycogen. A polysaccharide stored in the liver, which when required can be broken down into glucose for release into the blood stream under the control of epinephrine.

gnosis. Knowledge or knowing.

gnostic function. The EPICRITIC sense.

goal. The aim or object of some behavioural or mental activity.

goal attainment model. In evaluation research, a model of a system used to assess how quickly or efficiently subgoals are reached, etc.

goal gradient. 1. Hull's expression for the phenomenon that the nearer an organism gets to its goal, the harder it strives to reach it. 2. The phenomenon that when an animal learns a chain of responses, those nearer the goal are normally learned first.

goal response. The consummatory act (e.g. eating) that an animal has been seeking. *See also* FRACTIONAL ANTEDATING GOAL RESPONSE.

goal stimulus. Proprioceptive or other stimuli derived from a consummatory response.

go-around. A group therapy technique in which each member is asked to perform some action in turn, e.g. talking to his neighbour.

Gödel's theorem. 1. The theorem that in any axiomatic system adequate to characterize arithmetic there exists at least one well-formed formula whose truth or falsity cannot be determined within the system but that can nevertheless be seen to be true. 2. The theorem that the consistency of a formal system adequate for arithmetic cannot be proved within the system itself. (This is sometimes known as **Gödel's second theorem.**)

golden section. The division of a line or area in such a way that the ratio of the small part to the large part is the same as that of the large part to the whole. It was once fallaciously thought to be aesthetically pleasing.

Goldstein–Scheerer tests. Tests of the ability to abstract or form concepts, used mainly in neurology.

gold-thioglucose. A substance that in some animals is selectively taken up by cells in the ventromedial hypothalamic nucleus, and that can therefore be systemically injected to cause specific damage to that nucleus.

Golgi aphasia. Aphasia in which the patient can read aloud text fluently but cannot extract the meaning.

Golgi apparatus. A network of membranes found in the cytoplasm of all neurons. It is implicated in the manufacture of membranes and chemicals, and in their packaging. The synaptic vesicles and their contents are manufactured in the Golgi apparatus.

Golgi cell. A large interneuron found in the cerebellum, which is an instance of a GOLGI TYPE II CELL. They are activated by mossy fibres, climbing fibres, and parallel fibres, and they inhibit the granule cells.

Golgi corpuscle. A synonym for GOLGI TENDON ORGAN.

Golgi–Mazzoni corpuscles. A type of encapsulated nerve endings in the skin that possibly plays a role in sensitivity to pressure.

Golgi stain. A histological staining technique used to make nerve cells visible under the microscope. It is a silver stain which percolates to all parts of a living nerve cell.

Golgi tendon organ. A proprioceptor at the junction of a muscle and a tendon that fires when the tendon is stretched.

Golgi type I cell. A nerve cell characterized by a long axon that connects different parts of the nervous system.

Golgi type II cell. A nerve cell characterized by a very short axon which ends in the region of the cell's own cell body and which is usually if not always inhibitory. Some of these neurons have no axon at all. The GOLGI CELLS in the cerebellum are type II.

gonadotrophic hormone, gonadotrophin. The ANTERIOR PITUITARY hormones that promote growth or activity of the gonads. *See* LUTEINIZING HORMONE and FOLLICLE-STIMULATING HORMONE.

gonads. The sex glands, i.e. testes and ovaries.

go no-go task. A SUCCESSIVE DISCRIMINATION TRAINING task in which the organism is rewarded both when it makes a response to one stimulus within a certain time, and when it refrains from responding to a different stimulus for more than that time.

good continuation, law of. The Gestalt principle that if a line or contour is straight, has a regular curvature, or regularly repeats a change in curvature, its components are seen as belonging together. In a drawing in which different segments of lines can be grouped in different ways to yield whole lines, the segments are grouped in such a way as to yield lines having good continuation.

goodness of figure. A Gestalt expression for the extent to which a figure exhibits a good Gestalt, i.e. is closed, regular, simple, symmetrical, etc.; there is a tendency to group together features in such a way as to yield good figures.

goodness of fit. (Statistics) The extent to which data points match theoretical expectations or match a REGRESSION EQUATION derived A POSTERIORI to fit them.

Gottschaldt figures. Simple figures, hidden in a more complicated drawing, which the subject has to find.

governing domain. *See* GOVERNMENT AND BINDING PRINCIPLES.

government and binding principles. (Linguistics) A set of principles introduced into generative grammar in the late 1970s to explain such phenomena as the assignment of case. E.g. in 'The man loved her' the case of 'her' is governed by the verb. Again, in traditional Latin grammar, to which binding principles bear a marked resemblance, the case of an adjective is governed by that of the noun it qualifies. **Binding** occurs when two or more constituents of a sentence have the same reference, e.g. in 'The man who laughed', 'who' and 'man' are bound. (*See also* COINDEXING.) The expression 'government and binding theory' is usually taken to include principles other than those of government or binding, some of which apply e.g. to the movement of a constituent of a sentence.

GPS. An abbreviation for GENERAL PROBLEM SOLVER.

Graafian follicle. A synonym for OVARIAN FOLLICLE.

graceful degradation, principle of. Marr's principle that in any information processing system, the effects of an error should be restricted and should not produce completely false results. The human mind appears to obey this principle, since few of the errors it makes are catastrophic.

gracile nucleus. A nucleus in the MEDULLA; it receives fibres from the fasciculus gracilis in the dorsal spinal cord, carrying somatic information from the lower trunk and legs; it is part of the lemniscal system.

gradation method. Any psychophysical technique in which the subect gradually zeroes in on his judgement, e.g. in the LIMITS, METHOD OF.

graded potential. Any depolarization (or hyperpolarization) of a nerve cell that does not cause firing. Some cells (e.g. rods and cones, and bipolar cells) produce only graded potentials (i.e. they have no nerve impulse). Graded potentials occur in other cells whenever there is excitatory or inhibitory transmission at a synaptic ending; only if the change in graded potential reaches a certain level through TEMPORAL SUMMATION and SPATIAL SUMMATION will they fire.

gradient. A term used by Gibson to express the fact that most cues to depth systematically change their values with changes in distance (e.g. amount of binocular disparity in stereopsis or rate of motion on the retina in motion parallax). *See also* TEXTURE GRADIENT.

gradient descent. The settling down of a PARALLEL DISTRIBUTED PROCESSING system by gradually changing the weights between units in such a way that each unit comes to act in accordance with the messages it receives from the units connected to it. *See also* ANNEALING.

gradient of effect. The diminishing effect of a reinforcement or punishment on responses occurring further and further away from it. *See also* SECONDARY REINFORCEMENT.

gradient of generalization. A synonym for GENERALIZATION GRADIENT.

gradient of reinforcement. The progressive reduction in the effects of reinforcement on the learning of a response the further away the response is in time from the reinforcement.

gradient of texture. A synonym for TEXTURE GRADIENT.

Graduate Record Examination (GRE). A test of verbal and mathematical abilities used in the USA to select candidates for graduate schools.

grammar. The abstract system of rules governing a language, particularly its SYNTAX, MORPHOLOGY (2), PHONOLOGY, and SEMANTICS. *See also* GENERATIVE GRAMMAR, PHRASE-STRUCTURE GRAMMAR, and TRANSFORMATIONAL GRAMMAR.

grammatical word. A synonym for FUNCTION WORD.

grand mal. A major epileptic seizure with both tonic and clonic convulsions and loss of consciousness. *Contrast* PETIT MAL.

grandmother cell. A purely hypothetical cell in the visual system that responds to a complicated object, like a grandmother or motor car. The expression was invented to deride the idea that single cells could detect complex, individual objects, but there is now evidence for cells in monkeys that respond primarily to faces.

granular cortex. *See* AGRANULAR CORTEX.

granular layer. 1. Either of two layers of nerve cells in the cerebral cortex; numbered from the surface inwards, the **external granular layer** is the second layer and the **internal granular layer** is the fourth layer; the name derives from the large number of GOLGI TYPE II CELLS or GRANULE CELLS in these layers. *See also* CORTICAL LAYERS. 2. The innermost of the three layers of the CEREBELLUM, which contains granule cells and receives an input from the mossy fibres.

granule cell. A small stellate cell; the name 'granule' is used because these cells look granular under a microscope. The expression 'granule cell' is preferred to 'stellate cell' for the granule cells in the granular layers of the cortex and cerebellum.

grapheme. (Linguistics) The minimal unit of a written language, such that if one grapheme is substituted for another a change in meaning can result. In English the grapheme is the letter.

grapheme phoneme correspondence rules. (Linguistics) The rules by which graphemes are mapped onto phonemes. Reading could be performed by using these rules to infer the sound of a word, but many grapheme strings are ambiguous, e.g. 'ough' in 'rough' and 'though'.

graphic rating scale. Any rating scale in which the rater makes his judgement by indicating a point on a figure, e.g. he may be presented with a line marked 'like' at one end and 'dislike' at the other and asked to express his degree of liking by placing a mark at the appropriate point on the line.

graphodyne. A device for measuring the pressure of handwriting.

graphology. The study of handwriting, including the detection of forgeries and the (bogus) attempt to deduce a person's personality from his handwriting.

graphomania. An obsessive desire to write, a characteristic of overambitious psychologists.

graphometry. A projective technique in which someone is blindfolded and asked to draw a picture. He then describes the picture twice, once while still blindfolded and again while looking at it.

graphophobia. A morbid fear of writing, common in students.

graphorrhea. Writing long lists of meaningless words which can happen, e.g. in mania. *See also* BOXOLOGY.

grasping reflex. A reflex, normally present in infants for four months after birth, in which the fingers or toes make a grasping response when the hand or sole of the foot is touched; the appearance of this reflex in later life is normally a sign of damage to the motor cortex.

Grassman's laws. A set of laws governing additive colour mixing equations. If we adopt the convention that letters stand for an amount of a certain wavelength and the equals sign means 'look the same as', then if $A+B = C+D$ (i.e. there is a metameric match), it follows that: (i) $A+B+E = C+D+E$ (additive law); (ii) $k(A+B) = k(C+D)$ (multiplication law); and (iii) in any match in which $C+D$ occurs, a match will still obtain if it is replaced by $A+B$ (substitution law).

grating. A series of stripes alternating either in brightness or in colour (usually with all stripes of the same width). *See* SPATIAL FREQUENCY GRATING.

Graves' disease. A synonym for HYPERTHYROIDISM.

gray-level image. An alternative spelling for GREY-LEVEL IMAGE.

GRE. An abbreviation for GRADUATE RECORD EXAMINATION.

Great Vowel Shift. A change in the pronunciation of vowels that occurred in the 15th century: long vowels were shortened and pronounced with the tongue humped instead of flat.

Greco-Latin square. A LATIN SQUARE in which there are two conditions each with the same number of values, and in which each combination of values appears once in each row and once in each column.

green. *See* SPECTRAL HUES.

green cone. *See* CONE.

Greenspoon effect. An increase in the frequency with which a speaker uses a given word that may occur if the listener gives a sign of approval whenever it is used.

grey-level image. The point-by-point distribution of the intensities in an optical image, when they are represented discretely in an array of units distributed across the image (e.g. by the strength of responding of photocells or visual receptors).

grey matter. Any region of the central nervous system containing many cell bodies and their processes, and having unmyelinated axons (all parts of a cell look grey except for a myelinated axon). The expression usually refers to the layers of the cerebral cortex, but grey matter also exists in the cerebellar cortex and spinal cord.

grey ramus. The root through which the unmyelinated peripheral nerve fibres of the sympathetic system leave the sympathetic ganglion. *See* RAMUS COMMUNICANS.

grooming. The cleaning of one's own or a conspecific's body, which is practised instinctively by many animals.

ground. Short for 'background'. *See also* FIGURE–GROUND.

ground bundles. A synonym for INTERSEGMENTAL TRACTS.

group absolutism. The belief in a group that its customs and attitudes are the only correct ones.

group contagion. *See* CONTAGION.

group dynamics. The interactions within a group or the study of these interactions.

group factor. A factor extracted in a factor analysis that accounts for the correlations between several but not all of the tests.

group hysteria. A synonym for MASS HYSTERIA.

grouping. 1. (Perception) The perception of elements of a figure as a whole; those elements are grouped together that yield wholes having the most regular and simple structure. The principles of grouping include those of GOOD CONTINUATION, GOODNESS OF FIGURE, PROXIMITY, CLOSURE, and COMMON FATE. Grouping occurs in senses other than vision, e.g. if different high tones are alternated rapidly with different low tones, the listener will hear two separate sequences (high and low) with one in the foreground of consciousness the other in the background. 2. (Statistics) Assigning data to class intervals.

grouping error. Any statistical error introduced by the way in which data are grouped, e.g. by grouping in such a way that the distribution of scores within a group is not normal.

group interval. (Statistics) A synonym for CLASS INTERVAL.

group mind. A collective mind to which members of a society or group have access; the concept is distinctly mystical.

group movement. *See* TERNUS PHENOMENON.

group polarization. The tendency for a group's decisions and attitudes to be more extreme than those of the individual members when not acting as part of the group.

group selection. The false hypothesis that evolutionary selection acts on a group of animals of the same species rather than on its individual members.

group test. A test of individual ability, personality, etc. that is administered simultaneously to several people in the same room. *Contrast* INDIVIDUAL TEST.

group therapy. Psychotherapy conducted on two or more people at once, in the hope that their interaction and their expression of feelings to each other will help them; it may or may not, but at least it saves the therapist's time. *Contrast* INDIVIDUAL THERAPY.

groupthink. The tendency for the members of a group to move towards agreement with one another; it can result in biased and incorrect opinions, and vast overconfidence.

growth. (Psychotherpay) *See* PERSONAL GROWTH GROUP.

growth centre. A place that purports to facilitate personal growth.

growth cone. A small expansion at the tip of the terminal filaments of a growing AXON. it is motile, can change direction, and can be guided in its direction of growth by the substrate.

growth curve. A graph showing the growth of something plotted against time (or trials), e.g. a learning curve.

growth hormone. An anterior PITUITARY hormone promoting growth. *See also* HYPOTHALAMIC-RELEASING FACTORS.

GSR. An abbreviation for GALVANIC SKIN RESPONSE.

guanine. One of the four nucleotide bases in DNA and RNA.

guessing bias. Any systematic tendency to make a particular kind of guess if the correct response or answer is not known. E.g. in answering questionnaires, if the answer to several successive questions has been 'yes', many people tend to answer 'no' to the next one.

guidance. A synonym for COUNSELLING. Oddly the word is only used with some more specific prefatory word, e.g. vocational guidance.

guided affective imagery (GAI). Fantasies deliberately prompted by a therapist or group leader.

guiding fiction, guiding idea. Adler's expression for how a person sees himself, which may, particularly in neurotics, be very different from the way he is.

gust. A unit used in scales of taste; one gust is produced by a 1 per cent sucrose solution.

gustation. The sense of taste.

gustatory nerve. A synonym for LINGUAL NERVE.

gustometer. A device for measuring taste thresholds. It consists of a U-tube with a small hole at the bottom; the tube is placed upright on a particular part of the tongue, and a solution is poured through it: the tongue is thus exposed to a constant amount of solution.

Guttman scaling. A method for deriving an attitude scale, developed by Guttman; items are ranked so that it can be assumed that a positive response to any one entails that responses to all items of lower rank would also have been positive.

guttural. (Phonetics) Pronounced from the back of the mouth or from the throat as in VELAR and UVULAR consonants.

gynandromorph. A hermaphrodite.

gynophobia. A morbid fear of women.

gyrus. A raised fold or bulge in the surface of the cortex.

H

H. An abbreviation for ENTROPY.

$_sH_R$. Hull's abbreviation for HABIT STRENGTH.

$_s\bar{H}_R$. Hull's abbreviation for GENERALIZED HABIT STRENGTH.

h^2. An abbreviation for HERITABILITY RATIO.

habit. 1. A persistent pattern of learned behaviour. 2. Often used in psychology to mean any learned response or sequence of responses. *See* e.g. HABIT STRENGTH.

habit disorder. A bad habit that a person finds difficult to break, e.g. enuresis or smoking.

habit family hierarchy. Hull's term for different sequences of learned responses that can be evoked by a given situation. Each sequence has a different strength. By using this concept he tried unconvincingly to explain phenomena such as rats taking short cuts in mazes.

habit regression. Substituting for a current way of behaviour a different pattern learned earlier but since abandoned; such substitution is thought to occur under the influence of frustration.

habit strength ($_sH_R$). Hull's term for the basic strength of a learned stimulus–response bond. Habit strength represents the strength of learning; REACTION POTENTIAL derived from it and other variables, governs performance. *See* HULLIAN THEORY.

habituation. 1. (Learning theory) The weakening of an unlearned response through repeated exposure to the stimulus that evokes it. *Contrast* EXTINCTION, which is

the weakening of a learned response. 2. (Psychiatry) The physiological and psychological processes that with repeated exposure render a person less sensitive to the effects of a drug such as alcohol or heroin. 3. (General) Becoming accustomed to any situation.

habitus apoplecticus. One of Hippocrates' two constitutional types, characterized by physical strength and a predisposition to apoplexy.

habitus phthisicus. One of Hippocrates' two constitutional types, characterized by a thin, weak body and a predisposition to tuberculosis.

haematophobia. A morbid fear of blood.

hair. Strands of dead cells coated with keratin, which is secreted by the hair follicle. Distinguish from HAIR CELL.

hair aesthesiometer. A device consisting of a hair on the end of a spring for measuring skin sensitivity.

hair cell. A receptor cell found in the auditory and vestibular systems. Such cells have **stereocilia** (bunches of microvilli) at their tips. They emanate from the BASILAR MEMBRANE and from the CRISTA; their tips are embedded in the TECTORIAL MEMBRANE and the CUPULA. They transduce mechanical stretch into a graded potential which is passed down the receptor. Distinguish from HAIR and KINOCILIA.

hair follicle. The sac containing the root of a hair.

half height. *See* TUNING CURVE.

half life. Of a drug, the time elapsing for its level in the blood to drop to 50 per cent of its peak level.

half-silvered mirror. A mirror with a thin coat of silver that reflects some light but also transmits some. If a subject sits in bright light on one side of the mirror and the experimenter sits in dim light on the other, the subject sees an ordinary mirror, while the experimenter can observe the subject without the latter's knowledge.

hallucination. A vivid sensory impression in an awake person that is not caused by external stimuli, and is usually thought by the person to be produced by the external world. Hallucinations can occur, e.g., under LSD or in schizophrenia. *Contrast* DELUSION and ILLUSION.

hallucinogen. A drug, such as LSD or mescaline, that causes hallucinations.

hallucinosis. A mental disorder in which hallucinations occur chronically.

halo effect. The tendency of people on being impressed by one or more good qualities of someone else to overrate his other qualities, or contrariwise if they see predominantly bad qualities to underestimate the other qualities (sometimes called the **devil effect** or **reverse halo effect**); the expression is also sometimes used in the same way of someone's assessment of an object or situation rather than a person.

haloperidol. A BUTYROPHENONE neuroleptic, used in the treatment of schizophrenia and mania. It is a dopamine antagonist.

Halstead Impairment Index. A test battery designed to measure intelligence; it includes tests of the presumed biological correlates of intelligence (e.g. CRITICAL FUSION FREQUENCY).

Halstead–Reitan battery. A large number of tests for neurological patients that measure cognitive, sensory, and motor function; the results can be used to diagnose the site of brain lesions with considerable accuracy.

halving, method of. A PSYCHOPHYSICAL SCALING METHOD in which the subject has to set a stimulus to appear half as intense (e.g. half as bright or loud) as another. It yields an interval scale.

Hamilton rating scale. A systematic rating scale for the type and severity of a mental disorder carried out by a psychiatrist in an interview with the patient.

hammer. A synonym for MALLEUS.

Hampton Court Maze. A maze at Hampton Court, near London, made from hedges: some early mazes for rats were based on it.

handedness. The tendency to use one hand more than the other.

Hans. See CLEVER HANS EFFECT and LITTLE HANS.

haphalgesia. An abnormal tendency to feel pain when the skin is stimulated; it is usually caused psychogenically.

haphephobia. A morbid fear of being touched.

haplodiploid hypothesis. An explanation of why in some social insects (like ants) there are castes that never reproduce but look after their sisters and their sisters' offspring. Since the males are haploid and the females diploid, and provided the mother always mates with the same male, a female offspring will have 75 per cent of her genes in common with her sisters (50 per cent from the father and 25 per cent from the mother), instead of the usual 50 per cent. She may therefore promote the survival of her own genes by caring for her sisters.

haploid. Pertaining to a cell (a GAMETE) that has only one unpaired set of chromosomes (23 chromosomes in man). *Contrast* DIPLOID.

haplology. Very rapid speech in which syllables are omitted; it can occur in schizophrenia.

haploscope. A device for producing different images on the two eyes; it is similar to a stereoscope but it makes it possible to vary the real distance of the displays and their lateral position. Convergence, accommodation, and retinal disparity can thus be independently controlled.

haptephobia. A synonym for HAPHEPHOBIA.

haptic. Pertaining to the sense of touch, particularly when used actively to feel things.

haptometer. A device for measuring touch sensitivity.

hard colours. The colours that are most easily seen when they appear in an achromatic background of the same luminosity.

hard palate. *See* PALATE.

hard schizophrenic spectrum. *See* SCHIZO-PHRENIC SPECTRUM.

hardware. *See* SOFTWARE.

hard-wired. A circuit that is set to carry out a particular task and that cannot be changed by a program or in the case of the brain by learning.

harmonic. Any component of a complex tone (i.e. a tone containing more than one frequency) that is an integer multiple of the FUNDAMENTAL. The term is best used to include the fundamental (which becomes the first harmonic), but some authorities exclude the fundamental. *See also* OVERTONE and PARTIAL TONE whose usages are more consistent.

harmonic analysis. A synonym for FOURIER ANALYSIS.

harp theory. (Hearing) A synonym for PLACE THEORY.

Harvey's principle. The principle that, when a grating is viewed, the number of vertical stripes per unit of total breadth is overestimated, and is underestimated for horizontal stripes.

hashish. A purified resinous substance prepared from the flowers of the female hemp plant; it has hallucinogenic and narcotic effects, and is more potent than MARIJUANA.

hawk strategy. *See* EVOLUTIONARY STRATEGY.

Hawthorne effect. The phenomenon that if an attempt is made to improve workers' performance by introducing new methods, productivity tends to increase regardless of the value of the new methods; the workers may become more enthusiastic because they are receiving more attention or because they feel the management is trying. This phenomenon makes it hard to test the value of an innovation.

HBM. An abbreviation for HEALTH BELIEF MODEL.

head. 1. (Linguistics) The constituent in a larger constituent that is distributionally equivalent to the larger constituent and that determines aspects of the other words in the clause such as number, case, etc. The verb is taken to be the head of the sentence: in 'He bit her', it determines the case of the pronouns. *See* X-BAR GRAMMAR NOTATION. 2. (Linguistics) *See* TONE GROUP. 3. (Linguistics) The morpheme within a word that determines the word's syntactic category, e.g. 'lark' in 'skylark'. 4. (Computing) The first item in a list.

head-centred judgements, headcentric judgements. *See* EGOCENTRIC JUDGEMENTS.

Headstart Program. A large-scale attempt, started in the USA in 1965, to improve the background of disadvantaged children almost from birth and to provide them with enriched educational facilities in the early years of school.

Health Belief Model (HBM). The theory that whether people take steps to safeguard their health (e.g. indulge only in 'safe' sexual behaviour) depends on the seriousness of the consequences to their health and their beliefs about their own vulnerability. In addition they balance the disadvantages of the behaviour against its advantages.

hearing theories. *See* FREQUENCY THEORY, PLACE THEORY, and VOLLEY THEORY.

Hearsay. A program for speech understanding based on a BLACKBOARD MODEL and using mainly production rules. In disambiguating speech sounds it can use a variety of evidence including phonological, syntactic, and semantic constraints. Since the original program was written, its control structure has been used to implement a variety of EXPERT SYSTEMS.

Hebb synapse. An excitatory synapse that increases its tendency to fire the postsynaptic cell every time that cell fires immediately after the presynaptic cell has fired. Thus a given synaptic connection is strengthened if there is excitation at it at the same time as the postsynaptic cell fires, even if the firing is a result of other synaptic inputs.

hebephrenia. A synonym for HEBEPHRENIC SCHIZOPHRENIA.

hebephrenic schizophrenia. A form of schizophrenia in which the patient loses touch with reality, is incoherent and silly, has bizarre delusions, and often shows emotions completely inappropriate to the situation.

hebetic. Pertaining to adolescence or growth.

hebetude. A state of apathy and withdrawal, occurring in some schizophrenics.

heboid. A synonym for HEBETIC.

hedge. (Linguistics) A qualification in a sentence indicating that the sentence is not exact or that its truth is uncertain, e.g. 'a bit of' in 'He's a bit of an idiot' or phrases like 'loosely speaking'.

hedonic. Pertaining to the amount of pleasure or pain given or received.

hedonic relevance. The extent to which a person's action pleases or displeases another person.

hedonism. (Philosophy) The doctrine that the prime purpose of life is the pursuit of pleasure.

hedonistic relevance. A synonym for HEDONIC RELEVANCE.

height in the visual field. A perspective depth cue, based on the fact that if objects are resting on a surface their bases will be higher in the visual field the farther away they are from the observer.

Heilbronner's method. A technique that demonstrates some new learning in patients with anterograde amnesia. A fragment of a picture of an item is shown followed by progressively more complete fragments until the patient can see the item depicted. On subsequent presentations he is able to see the item at earlier points in the series.

helicotrema. An opening inside and at the apex of the cochlea where the scala tympani and the scala vestibuli meet.

heliophobia. A morbid fear of the sun or sunlight.

heliotropism. A synonym for PHOTOTAXIS.

Helmholtz square. A square made up of parallel vertical lines or parallel horizontal lines. Because of the FILLED AND UNFILLED EXTENT ILLUSION, the square looks shorter in the direction along which the parallel lines run than in the direction perpendicular to the lines.

Helmholtz square

helplessness. 1. The attribute of someone who blames his failings on lack of ability rather than lack of effort. *Contrast* MASTERY ORIENTATED. 2. *See* LEARNED HELPLESSNESS.

hematophobia. A variant spelling of HAEMATOPHOBIA.

hemeralopia, hemeralopsia. Poor vision in moderate or strong illumination (photopic vision), normally due to a deficiency in the cones. *Contrast* NYCTALOPIA.

hemiachromatism. ACHROMATISM occurring only in one half of the visual field.

hemiamblyopia. AMBLYOPIA occurring only in one half of the visual field.

hemianaesthesia, hemianesthesia. Loss of

sensation on one side of the body; it is caused by unilateral damage to the somaesthetic system.

hemianopia, hemianopsia. Loss of vision in the right or left half of the visual field of one or both eyes (sometimes with some vision spared in the fovea on the affected side); it is caused by unilateral damage to the visual cortex, optic radiations, or optic chiasm.

hemiballismus, hemiballism. Involuntary flailing of the limbs on one side of the body, probably caused by lesions to the extrapyramidal system.

hemidecortication. The surgical removal of the cerebral cortex of one hemisphere, an operation which has less serious effects than might be expected if performed on young children.

hemifield. *See* VISUAL FIELD.

hemiopia. An alternative spelling of HEMIANOPIA.

hemiparesis. Paralysis or partial paralysis occurring only on one side of the body.

hemiplegia. Paralysis of one side of the body; it is caused by unilateral damage to part of the motor system.

hemispatial neglect. A synonym for UNILATERAL NEGLECT.

hemisphere. The left or right half of the cerebrum or of the cerebellum.

hemispherectomy. A synonym for HEMIDECORTICATION.

hemispherical dominance. A synonym for CEREBRAL DOMINANCE.

hemispheric specialization. The extent to which one cerebral hemisphere is more implicated in a particular function than the other.

hemophobia. An alternative spelling of HEMATOPHOBIA.

hemp plant. *Cannabis sativa*, the plant from which hashish and marijuana are derived.

Henning's odour prism. A synonym for ODOUR SQUARE.

Henning's odour square. A synonym for ODOUR SQUARE.

Henning's tetrahedron. A tetrahedron with the four primary tastes (salty, sweet, sour, bitter) at the corners and other tastes represented elsewhere on the tetrahedron's surface.

here-and-now. A slogan of GESTALT THERAPY that emphasizes the desirability of living in the immediate present and coping with immediate feelings and relationships.

hereditability. A synonym for HERITABILITY.

hereditarianism. Any approach stressing the role of innate factors in determining physical and mental traits.

hereditary predisposition. An innate predisposition to develop a trait, illness, etc., which, depending on environmental factors, may or may not be actualized.

heredity. The process by which genes and therefore innate characteristics and predispositions are transmitted from parents to offspring. *See also* HERITABILITY and GENE.

Hering–Hermann illusion. A synonym for HERMANN GRID.

Hering–Hillebrand deviation. The difference between the empirically determined HOROPTER and the VEITH–MULLER CIRCLE.

Hering illusion. The geometrical illusion that two parallel straight lines are bowed away from one another when other lines intersect them at an angle and thus cause a SIMULTANEOUS TILT EFFECT.

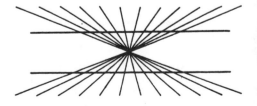

Hering illusion

Hering image. The first AFTERIMAGE to appear. It is positive and brief (about 0.05 seconds). It is thought to be caused by neural firing continuing after the stimulus has ceased.

Hering's colour vision theory. The hypothesis that there are three mechanisms involved in colour vision, each having two opposed processes, red versus green, blue versus yellow, and black versus white. Above the level of the receptors, the theory is now known to be basically correct. *See also* YOUNG–HELMHOLTZ THEORY.

Hering's law of equal innervation. The principle that the muscles of each eye always operate in synchrony because they receive the same innervation. The principle applies to the lens as well as to the extraocular muscles, and to both conjunctive and disjunctive eye movements, though in the latter case the muscles innervated together must be reversed.

heritability. The extent to which a given characteristic is determined by heredity, usually measured as the proportion of the variance of the characteristic in a given population that can be accounted for by hereditary factors. The heritability will depend both on the variance of the genes and on the variance of the environment; both factors may differ from one population to another within the same species.

heritability ratio (h^2). A measure of heritability, namely $h^2 = V_g/V_t$ where V_g is the variance in a trait accounted for by hereditary factors and V_t is its total variance.

Hermann grid. *See* the illustration below. Small dark patches appear at the intersections of the white lines, presumably caused by changes in brightness contrast. *Compare* EHRENSTEIN ILLUSION (1).

hermaphrodite. A person who has both the male and the female sex organs; someone with the female chromosomes (XX) may be partially masculinized in the womb if there are high levels of androgen present. *Compare* ANDROGYNY.

hermeneutics. Originally, interpretation of the scriptures, but the term has come to mean

Hermann grid

the art of interpreting any text and assigning an inner meaning to it that is not obvious on the surface. Today the word is normally used only to dignify foolish speculations.

heroin. A highly addictive opiate derived from morphine.

Herpes simplex encephalitis (HSE). Brain damage caused by herpes simplex mainly in the temporal, orbito-frontal and parietal lobe. It usually results in ANTEROGRADE AMNESIA and some RETROGRADE AMNESIA but leaves SHORT-TERM MEMORY intact. It can produce symptoms resembling the KLUVER–BUCY SYNDROME.

Hertz (Hz). The internationally agreed term for number of cycles per second; it is used e.g. of wave frequency.

Heschl's gyrus. A gyrus in the INSULA that is hidden behind the superior temporal lobe: it is the PRIMARY AUDITORY CORTEX. It is Brodmann's areas 41 and 42; *see* Appendix 3.

Hess image. A faint positive AFTERIMAGE sometimes appearing after the second negative afterimage (i.e. as the fifth in the series of afterimages).

heterarchy. (AI) The characteristic of a computer program that does not process data merely through successively higher levels, but can call many different routines to help in the processing of the data at each level, including routines from higher levels. SHRDLU is an example of such a program: in it semantic information is used, when necessary, to disambiguate alternative syntactic parsings.

heterochromatic brightness matching. Equating the brightness of differently coloured light. *See* PHOTOMETER.

heterochromatic flicker photometer. *See* PHOTOMETER.

heterochrony. A difference in the rate of timing of events.

heteroeroticism. Sexual arousal produced by another person. *Contrast* AUTOEROTICISM.

heterogeneous summation. (Ethology) The increase in the strength of SPECIES SPECIFIC BEHAVIOUR caused by the presence of more than one relevant RELEASER.

heterohypnosis. Hypnosis performed by one person on another. *Contrast* AUTOHYPNOSIS.

heterolalia. Consistently talking nonsense by using the wrong word.

heteronomous stage. Piaget's first stage of moral development, in which the child is entirely governed by his parents' edicts. *Compare* AUTONOMOUS STAGE.

heteronym. One of two or more words with the same spelling but different pronunciations, e.g. 'bow'.

heteronymous hemianopia. Blindness in opposite halves of the two eyes (left half in one, right half in the other); it can be caused by transecting the optic chiasm.

heterophemy. A synonym for HETEROLALIA.

heterophonic continuity. The phenomenon that if two tones are repeatedly alternated with one another and if one would mask the other if both were presented simultaneously, the tone that would be masked is heard all the time, presumably because there is no evidence that it is not still present when the masking tone is on. This phenomenon has been used to establish masking thresholds, since if the softer tone is below the level at

which it would be masked, it is no longer heard when the other tone is on. The amplitude at which it ceases to be heard is known as the **pulsation threshold**.

heterophoria. A misalignment of the two eyes with respect to one another, occurring when one eye is fixating a point and the other is occluded. The misalignment is usually corrected when both eyes are fixating the same point. There are five kinds: CYLCOPHORIA, ESOPHORIA, EXOPHORIA, HYPERPHORIA, and HYPOPHORIA. *Contrast* TROPIA.

heteroscedacity. *See* SCEDACITY.

heterosis. Increased vigour occurring in an organism because it is a hybrid.

heterosome. The X or Y chromosome, each of which, unlike the other chromosomes (the AUTOSOMES), can pair with a different chromosome.

heterostereotype. *See* STEREOTYPE.

heterotropia. A synonym for STRABISMUS. *See also* ESOTROPIA and EXOTROPIA.

heterozygote. An organism having two different ALLELES at the same locus on a pair of CHROMOSOMES. *Contrast* HOMOZYGOTE.

heuristic. A method of solving a problem that does not guarantee a solution, but that raises the chance of solving it or tends to decrease the time taken to solve it. *Contrast* ALGORITHM.

heuristic theory of persuasion. The hypothesis that, when a person cannot or does not evaluate arguments put to him to make a case, he judges the case by extraneous considerations such as the number of arguments or the expertise of the person putting them.

Heyman's law. The psychophysical principle that the threshold for detecting one stimulus increases with the intensity of a stronger stimulus simultaneously presented.

5-HIAA. An abbreviation for 5-hydroxy-indoleacetic acid, which is the main metabolite of SEROTONIN; there is evidence that its levels are low in the spinal fluid of bipolar manic-depressed patients when they are depressed, suggesting a low turnover of serotonin.

hibernation. A state in which there is a gross reduction of activity accompanied by a large decrease in metabolic rate and by drowsiness; many animals hibernate in winter when food is scarce.

Hick's law. The principle that in a choice reaction task, the reaction time increases as the amount of information transmitted increases. Thus, reaction time will increase with the number of choices, and decrease with increasing difference in the probability of the different choices and with the number of errors made. In the simple case with no errors and equiprobable alternatives, RT = k.log(n + 1), where n is the number of choices. *Compare* FITTS' LAW.

hidden figure. A synonym for EMBEDDED FIGURE.

hidden observer. The part of a person's mind that functions unconsciously in hypnosis and that may enable him after hypnosis to recall events of which he was unaware during hypnosis.

hidden unit. Any unit in a PARALLEL DISTRIBUTED PROCESSING system that is neither an input unit nor an output unit. *Compare* INTERNUNCIAL CELL.

hide-in-the-crowd effect. The reduction of responsibility caused by being a member of a crowd or in-group.

hierarchical control theory. The hypothesis that a skilled motor task is controlled by a hierarchy of control centres, with successive movements being governed by one high-level centre. *Contrast* LINEAR CHAINING THEORY.

hierarchy. 1. (Ethology) *See* DOMINANCE HIERARCHY. 2. (Animal learning) *See* HABIT FAMILY HIERARCHY. 3. (Behaviour therapy) The grading by a patient of stimuli that produce phobic responses or anxiety from most fearful to least. *See* SYSTEMATIC DESENSITIZATION.

hierophobia. A morbid fear of anything

religious. It is becoming endemic in archbishops.

higher brain centres. A vague expression meaning either the cerebral hemispheres or the areas of the brain devoted to HIGHER MENTAL PROCESSES.

higher mental processes. Conscious processes that require elaborate operations, e.g. memory, thinking, or using a language.

higher needs. Maslow's expression for needs that can only be satisfactorily pursued once the BASIC NEEDS (2) are satisfied. They include SELF-ACTUALIZATION, and aesthetic and cognitive needs, such as the need for knowledge.

higher-order conditioning. In classical conditioning, the conditioning of a response to a conditioned stimulus (CS2) by first conditioning it to another conditioned stimulus (CS1), and then presenting CS2 followed by CS1 without the unconditioned stimulus. The process can in theory extend further back, e.g. CS2 can be used to reinforce conditioning to CS3, etc. *Compare* SECONDARY REINFORCEMENT, which is the equivalent process in instrumental learning.

higher-order interaction. In analysis of variance (and similar statistical techniques), an interaction between more than two factors.

higher-order schedule, higher-order reinforcement schedule. Any COMPOUND SCHEDULE in which one component must be satisfied before the next component starts.

high expressed emotion. *See* EXPRESSED EMOTION.

high-level language. (Computing) Any programming language that allows the programmer to specify complex series of operations in one or a few instructions. The high-level program is translated into MACHINE CODE and the allocation of addresses is taken care of automatically.

high-pass filter. A filter that transmits from a waveform only the frequencies higher than a specified frequency.

high phoneme. A phoneme uttered with the tongue raised.

high rise. In PITCH CONTOURS, a large rise in pitch that starts from an already high pitch; it can be used to indicate that a question is being asked.

hill climbing. (AI) Searching for the best (highest) spot on a surface where the height of each position represents its desirability; the search is conducted by proceeding in the direction of steepest ascent. The technique has the problem that it is possible to get trapped on top of a local maximum (hill) when there are higher points (the tops of other hills) elsewhere. Various methods have been suggested to ameliorate this problem. *See* ANNEALING.

hillock. Short for AXON HILLOCK.

hindbrain. Phylogenetically the oldest of the three main divisions of the brain. It lies immediately above the spinal cord and is divided into the MYELENCEPHALON and METENCEPHALON (*see* Appendix 5). *See* BRAIN and NEURAL TUBE.

hindsight bias. The false but common belief that one could have predicted a past event more accurately than one would have done or that in a past situation one would have taken a decision with a better outcome than the one actually taken by someone else.

hippocampal gyrus. A synonym for PARA-HIPPOCAMPAL GYRUS.

hippocampus. Part of the palaeocortex and limbic system that is shaped like a sea horse. It is implicated in emotions and also possibly in memory, since bilateral removal in man produces severe and permanent anterograde deficits in memory. There is also evidence from animals that it plays a role in their capacity to identify their position in space. *See* Appendix 5.

hippophobia. A morbid fear of horses.

Hiskey Nebraska Test of Learning Aptitude. An intelligence test for deaf children based entirely on non-linguistic tasks.

histamine. A BIOGENIC AMINE that is a neurotransmitter in certain parts of the brain.

histogram. A chart containing adjacent parallel bars, usually vertical, whose lengths represent the frequency distibution on a continuous dimension. *Compare* BAR CHART.

histology. The study of the structure of tissue particularly at the microscopic level.

histrionic personality disorder. (DSM-III) The personality of someone who overdramatizes and is exceptionally self-centred and exhibitionistic.

hit. The detection of a signal when it is there. *Contrast* FALSE ALARM and *see* SIGNAL DETECTION THEORY.

hoarding. The storing for long periods of food (and sometimes other items) by animals.

hodological space. Lewin's term for the field through which he thought the mind moved, which is governed by both internal and external factors.

hodophobia. A morbid fear of travelling.

Höffding step. In Gestalt psychology, the matching of the representation of a stimulus to a stored representation, an operation that is necessary for recognition to occur.

holergasia. Any severe psychosis affecting the entire personality.

hole screen. A synonym for REDUCTION SCREEN.

holism. The doctrine that mental (or any other) processes cannot be understood merely in terms of the components into which they can be decomposed.

Holmgren test. An obsolete test of colour blindness based on matching coloured wool.

holography. A technique for recording and regenerating an image of a scene. The object is illuminated by a coherent light source, and a photographic plate records the interference pattern formed between light reflected from the object and light coming directly from the coherent source. If the coherent light is subsequently shone on the plate, the scene can be seen in three dimensions (i.e. not like a picture but like a real scene in which stereopsis, motion parallax, etc. can produce cues to depth). Some psychologists see holography as a model of how the brain works, because information about all parts of the scene is distributed over the whole plate and local damage to it has little effect; they believe there is an analogy here with brain damage and memory.

holophrasis. A single word utterance of the sort made by young children (e.g. 'Mummy', 'ball'); such utterances often convey ideas more complex than the meaning of the single word used. The term is sometimes used to include two-word utterances. Holophrastic speech begins at about 12 months and lasts until about 18 months when TELEGRAPHIC SPEECH begins.

homeostasis. The maintenance of balance within a system or the maintenance of certain factors in a system within set limits. All organisms contain numerous homeostatic mechanisms, e.g. for the regulation of salt, glucose, or oxygen in the blood; homeostatic mechanisms must also operate within a society if it is to endure. *See also* FEEDBACK.

homeostatic principle. In social psychology, the hypothesis that all members of a society seek a level of stimulation (including social stimulation) that is optimal for them.

homeotic mutant. A mutant that transforms a part of the body into a part normally belonging elsewhere. E.g. in drosophila one mutant transforms the distal part of the antenna into a leg which gives a proboscis-extension reflex when stimulated by sugar.

homing instinct. The drive, supported by the ability to return home, particularly after lengthy journeys; many animals have this capacity.

hominid. Any member of the family Hominidae, which includes man, his immediate ancestors, and other extinct species that produced man-like fossils, e.g. Neanderthal man.

Homo. Any member of that genus of Hominidae that most closely resembles man, in e.g. brain size, big toe not being opposable to other toes, etc. The only surviving species is man, which is curiously misnamed *Homo sapiens.*

Homo oeconomicus theory. The principle that people try to maximize their gains.

homoeroticism. A synonym for HOMOSEXUALITY.

homogamy. The tendency to marry someone who is similar to oneself.

homogeneity of variance. (Statistics) Similarity of variance, i.e. lack of a significant difference in variance. Most parametric tests are only valid if the samples being compared are from populations with the same variance.

homograph. A word that has the same spelling as another word of different meaning regardless of how the two words are pronounced; e.g. 'row' can mean a quarrel, a straight line, or 'to pull an oar'. *Compare* HOMOPHONE, HOMONYM, and HETERONYM.

homolateral. A synonym for IPSILATERAL.

homology. (Biology) Similarity of anatomical structure in the organs of different species that is not caused by the function of the organ, and therefore suggests a common evolutionary ancestor. Thus, the structure of a bird's wing is similar (homologous) to that of the forelimb of reptiles. *Contrast* ANALOGY.

homomorph. A mapping of one set of entities onto another in which many entities in the first set are mapped onto one in the second. In this sense mental models of the world are homomorphs of it, e.g. all robins may be mapped onto the single concept of a robin.

homonomy drive. The desire to fit in with a social group.

homonym. One of two (or more) words having different meanings but the same pronunciation and spelling, e.g. 'bank'. *Compare* HOMOGRAPH and HOMOPHONE, and *contrast* HETERONYM.

homonymous hemianopia. Blindness in the same half of each eye, i.e. either both left or both right halves; it is caused by a lesion of the visual system beyond the optic chiasm. *See also* HEMIANOPIA.

homonymous quadratic field defect. Blindness in the same quadrant of both eyes (e.g. top right); it can be caused by lesions to the visual cortex.

homophobia. 1. A morbid fear of homosexuality. 2. A morbid fear of mankind.

homophone. A word that has the same sound as another, regardless of whether they are spelled the same; e.g. 'one' and 'won' are homophones. *Compare* HOMONYM *and* HOMOGRAPH.

Homo sapiens. See HOMO.

homoscedacity. *See* SCEDACITY.

homosexuality. The derivation of sexual excitement from contact with members of one's own sex. *See* EGO-DYSTONIC HOMOSEXUALITY and EGO-SYNTONIC HOMOSEXUALITY.

homosynaptic depression. Reduction in the amount of neurotransmitter released by the presynaptic cell with repeated stimulation, a possible cause of habituation.

homozygote. An organism having two identical alleles at the same site on a pair of chromosomes.

homunculus. 1. (Psychology) A little man within the brain who examines data and takes decisions; most, but not all, psychological theories are incomplete, and are therefore said to require a homunculus to perform the mental processes that cannot be accounted for by the theory. 2. (Neurophysiology) A sketch of the body drawn on a diagram of the motor cortex (MOTOR HOMUNCULUS) or sensory cortex (SENSORY HOMUNCULUS) and representing the mapping of the body onto these areas; the sketches are distorted because the amount of cortex occupied by different parts of the body depends not just on their physical size, but on the sensitivity of the motor system or sensory system in that area. E.g. the lips and tongue are much enlarged in the sensory homunculus.

Honi effect. The phenomenon that the size and shape of a familiar person (especially the spouse of the observer) are more correctly perceived in the AMES ROOM than are those of an unfamiliar person.

hopelessness theory. The hypothesis (developed from LEARNED HELPLESSNESS) that depression is caused by pessimistic cognitions.

horizontal cells. Cells connected to cones and bipolar cells whose processes spread horizontally across the RETINA. They respond in opposite directions to opponent colours. They are found in mammals with colour vision.

horizontal cells of Cajal. Fusiform cells in the plexiform layer of the cortex whose dendrites spread horizontally in opposite directions.

horizontal décalage. *See* DÉCALAGE.

horizontal growth. The acquisition of the ability to perform more tasks at the same level of difficulty as one already mastered, e.g. learning to subtract, having already learned to add.

horizontal oblique projection. *See* OBLIQUE PROJECTION.

horizontal sampling. Sampling from within the same social class.

horizontal section. (Anatomy) A cut into an organ or into the body that is perpendicular to the dorsal–ventral axis.

horizontal–vertical illusion. The illusion that a vertical line looks longer than a horizontal line of the same real length.

hormic psychology. MacDougall's school of psychology, which emphasized drives, goals, planning, and other purposive activities.

hormone. A chemical released by an ENDOCRINE GLAND to regulate the activity of other organs.

Horner's law. The principle that red–green colour blindness is transmitted from male to male through the intermediary of a female, who normally does not exhibit it.

horopter. The locus of all points in space that for a given fixation point stimulate CORRESPONDING POINTS on the two eyes (i.e. points yielding no BINOCULAR DISPARITY). In practice only the horizontal horopter is usually measured, i.e. the part of the horopter lying on a horizontal plane passing through the nodal point of each lens and the fixation point. *Compare* EMPIRICAL HOROPTER and VIETH–MULLER CIRCLE.

horse race model. The hypothesis that in recognizing a written word both phonological properties and direct access from its visual appearance are used and whichever yields an answer first determines recognition.

horseradish peroxidase. An enzyme that is taken up by nerve cells and that flows in a retrograde direction from axon terminals to the cell body and dendrites; it leaves coloured traces that can be used to identify the location of cell bodies whose axonal terminals are elsewhere.

horses for courses. *See* SITUATIONAL APPROACH.

horseshoe crab. The common name for LIMULUS.

hospitalism. Physical or mental retardation of infants caused by being brought up in a hospital or other institution that fails to provide enough stimulation.

hot-seat technique. A Gestalt group therapy technique in which the patient sits in a special chair and the other members of the group take it in turns to tell him what they think of him.

Hough transform. Transforming an image by taking a dimension of it and computing the frequency of all values on that dimension. E.g. if the image is of a black pot against a white wall and the frequency of different intensities throughout the image is plotted, the plot would have two peaks (corresponding to black and white). By returning to the image and dividing all points in it into two classes on either side of the minimum of the frequency distribution, it would be possible to assign all points in the image to figure and background.

house–tree–person test. A projective test in which a person draws a house, a tree, and a person; the interpretation takes account of the amount of detail, the speed of execution, and anything said by the testee while drawing.

Howard–Dolman test. A synonym for TWO-ROD TEST.

HRAF. An abbreviation for HUMAN RELATIONS AREA FILES.

HSE. An abbreviation for HERPES SIMPLEX ENCEPHALITIS.

Hsu's test. (Statistics) An UNPLANNED COMPARISON TEST to assess whether the results of any one out of a set of conditions is significantly different from those of the others.

5-HT. An abbreviation for 5-hydroxy-tryptamine; *see* SEROTONIN.

HTRF. An abbreviation for HYPOTHALAMIC-RELEASING FACTORS.

hue. The component of colour that is determined mainly by the predominant wavelength or wavelengths present. The same hue can vary in SATURATION (1), e.g. red and pink have the same hue, but pink looks lighter because it contains more white light, i.e. it is DESATURATED. *See also* EXTRASPECTRAL HUE, PRIMARY HUE, SPECTRAL HUE, and UNIQUE HUE.

Hullian behaviourism. Hull's belief that only stimuli and responses can be studied and that behaviour, not the mind, is the only fit subject for psychology. He did believe in intervening variables, which he thought must be operationally defined in terms of stimuli and responses, and were not to be identified with mental processes. Since he was ambivalent about the existence of mental processes his was a METHODOLOGICAL BEHAVIOURISM, and not a RADICAL BEHAVIOURISM.

Hullian theory. The most elaborate theory of learning ever produced. It was based on the hypothetico-deductive method and contained about 50 intervening variables, each of which was supposed to be operationally defined in terms of independent variables:

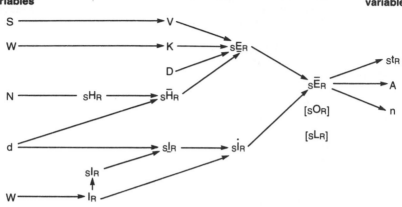

A	response amplitude	$_s\dot{I}_R$	aggregate inhibitory potential
D	drive strength	$_s\bar{I}_R$	generalized inhibitory potential
d	difference between the current stimuli and the stimuli used in learning	K	incentive motivation
		$_sL_R$	reaction threshold
$_sE_R$	reaction potential	N	number of reinforced trials
$_s\bar{E}_R$	generalized reaction potential	n	responses to extinction
$_s\bar{\underline{E}}_R$	net reaction potential	$_sO_R$	behavioural oscillation
$_s\dot{E}_R$	momentary reaction potential	$_st_R$	reaction latency
$_s\underline{H}_R$	habit strength	S	stimulus
$_s\bar{H}_R$	generalized habit strength	V	stimulus intensity dynamism
I_R	reactive inhibition	W	work involved in response
$_sI_R$	conditioned inhibition	w	weight of food incentive

unfortunately few of the definitions were quantitatively precise. It had two versions. In the first, learning was affected by number of reinforcements, drive strength, and size of reward. In the second, which is followed here, drive strength and size of reward bore only on performance. A much simplified version of the second theory is set out in the diagram. The text should be read in connection with it. The diagram reads from left to right and comprises independent variables, intervening variables and dependent variables. Learning is represented by habit strength ($_sH_R$), performance strength by reaction potential ($_sE_R$). The theory states that HABIT STRENGTH ($_sH_R$) is determined only by the number of reinforcements received (N). GENERALIZED HABIT STRENGTH

($_s\bar{H}_R$) is derived from $_sH_R$ by taking into account the difference between the training stimulus and the current stimulus (d). GENER-ALIZED REACTION POTENTIAL ($_sE_R$) is reached by multiplying together generalized habit strength, DRIVE STRENGTH (D), INCENTIVE MOTIVATION (K), which is determined by the size of the rewards recently provided, and STIMULUS INTENSITY DYNAMISM (V), which is a function of the strength of the stimulus both in training and currently. REACTIVE INHIBITION (I_R) is generated by the work done (W) in recent responses and decays rapidly; it is conditioned to the stimulus to form CONDI-TIONED INHIBITION ($_sI_R$). Taking the differ-ence between the current and previous stimuli into account, this becomes GENERAL-IZED INHIBITORY POTENTIAL ($_s\bar{I}_R$) which when added to reactive inhibition becomes AGGRE-GATE INHIBITORY POTENTIAL ($_s\bar{I}_R$). This potential is deducted from the generalized reaction potential to form NET REACTION POTENTIAL ($_s\bar{E}_R$), whose strength fluctuates through BEHAVIOURAL OSCILLATION ($_sO_R$). A response will only be made if its strength, MOMENTARY REACTION POTENTIAL ($_s\dot{E}_R$), is above threshold ($_sL_R$). The strength of the net reaction potential determines the AMPLITUDE (A) and LATENCY ($_st_R$) of the response; it also determines the number of trials to extinction (n).

human engineering. 1. A branch of applied psychology that studies how to improve performance and efficiency at work by improving the design of tools, the work flow, the environmental conditions, and the organization within a firm. 2. A synonym for BEHAVIOURAL ENGINEERING.

human factors. The study both of how to make man's environment more suitable for him (and sometimes of how to make him suit it, e.g. by training). It covers all aspects of human life, from the workplace, the home, and the car to the optimal design of a tennis racquet.

humanism. Respect for other people and their values and rights when it is not based on religion. Humanists tend to abhor cant, hence humanism should not be confused with HUMANISTIC PSYCHOLOGY.

humanistic psychology. The doctrine that psychologists should concentrate on conscious processes, particularly emotional ones, and should encourage others to be autonomous and to seek personal growth. Many humanistic psychologists hold the optimistic belief that all men are naturally good and only need the right environment to develop their potential. Humanistic psychology was fed by the cult of irrationalism prevalent in the USA in the 1960s. The cult is now receding and so is it.

human potential movement. The exponents of the view that people can, and should, be helped to grow. Oddly, this movement concentrates on PERSONAL GROWTH; few of its adherents seem to care about intellectual growth. The movement is not homogeneous. The means to personal growth (Zen Buddhism, encounter groups, acupuncture, etc.)

are of uncertain value, and the ends of personal growth are obscure and sometimes contradictory. They include becoming more selfish ('doing your own thing'), less selfish, more aggressive, less aggressive, etc.

human relations area files (HRAF). Files of ethnographic data on primitive tribes, coded so that the same topics can be accessed in all tribes.

humour. 1. Any fluid in the body. *See* AQUEOUS HUMOUR and VITREOUS HUMOUR. 2. (More specifically) The body fluids – blood, black bile, yellow bile, or phlegm – associated by ancient typologists with respectively **sanguine, melancholic, choleric**, and **phlegmatic** temperaments.

Humphrey's law. The principle that once performance of a task has become automatized, conscious thought about the task, while performing it, impairs performance. The principle clearly applies to motor skills (e.g. a golf stroke); some believe it also applies to more intellectual skills such as writing.

hunting. (Cybernetics) The oscillation of a negative feedback system caused by delay in the reception of information about the effects of the output. If the system is on, it will tend to overshoot; similarly, when it is off, if there is a delay in the arrival of information to turn it on, it will undershoot. Hence the oscillation.

Huntington's chorea. A hereditary disease of the nervous system that is progressive and degenerative, and produces involuntary movements and dementia.

Hunt Minnesota Test. A psychological test for brain damage.

hyalophagia. The ingestion of glass.

hyalophobia. A morbid fear of glass.

hybrid. The offspring of parents that are genetically unlike, particularly of parents of different species or of different varieties within a species.

hybrid vigour. A synonym for HETEROSIS.

hydraulic theory. Any behavioural model whose concepts are analogous to the pressure of fluid within a system. Almost all such models have to do with drives, e.g. the Tinbergen–Lorenz model of instinctive behaviour.

hydrocephalus. An excess of fluid in the brain cavity; the resulting pressure can cause permanent damage.

hydrophobia. 1. A morbid fear of water, as evinced by G.K. Chesterton. 2. A morbid fear of rabies.

5-hydroxyindoleacetic acid. *See* 5-HIAA.

6-hydroxydopamine (6-OH-DA). A toxic substance taken up by catecholaminergic neurons, which kills their nerve terminals.

3-hydroxyretinal. *See* RETINAL.

5-hydroxytryptamine. A synonym for SERO-TONIN.

5-hydroxytryptophan. A precursor of SERO-TONIN.

hygrophobia. A morbid fear of moisture.

hyoscine. A synonym for SCOPOLAMINE.

hypacusia. Impaired hearing.

hypaesthesia. 1. Unusually low sensitivity in any of the senses. 2. Unusually low sensitivity in the sense of touch.

hypalgesia, hypalgia. Unusually low sensitivity to pain.

hyperactive child syndrome. A synonym for ATTENTION-DEFICIT DISORDER or MINIMAL BRAIN DYSFUNCTION.

hyperactivity. A synonym for HYPERKINESIS.

hyperacuity. Very fine acuity of the sort that is found in normal subjects in such tasks as VERNIER ACUITY and STEREOSCOPIC ACUITY, but not e.g. in MINIMUM SEPARABLE.

hyperacusia, hyperacusis. Unusually keen hearing.

hyperaesthesia. 1. Extreme sensitivity to stimuli in any of the senses, such as can occur in hysteria. 2. Extreme sensitivity in the sense of touch.

hyperalgesia, hyperalgia. Unusually high sensitivity to painful stimuli.

hyperbulimia. A synonym for HYPERPHAGIA.

hypercolumn. A slab of cells in the visual cortex across which there is a complete cycle of changes in OCULAR DOMINANCE (1) of the cells' receptive fields, and probably two complete cycles of changes in their orientation preference.

hypercomplex cell. A cell in the visual system having a receptive field with the same properties as a COMPLEX CELL, except that the cell ceases to fire if the kind of line or edge to which it normally fires is extended beyond a certain point. Since this property has been found even in simple cells, the classification of cells as 'hypercomplex' is currently being abandoned.

hypercorrection. (Linguistics) An attempt to speak like a member of a high-status group, exaggerating any aspect of their speech, e.g. by assuming an exaggerated upper-class accent, or using too many sesquipedalian words.

hyperesthesia. An alternative spelling for HYPERAESTHESIA.

hypergasia. Frenetic activity of the sort that can occur in mania.

hypergeometric distribution. (Statistics) The theoretical distribution of a discrete variate obtained when sampling from a finite population without replacement.

hypergeusia. Unusually good sensitivity to taste.

hyperglycaemia. Excess of sugar in the blood; it occurs in diabetes.

hypergraphia. Writing too much, a condition that can be induced by a lesion of the temporal lobe (or by being called Anthony Burgess).

hyperkinaesthesia. Unusually good kinaesthetic sensitivity.

hyperkinesis, hyperkinesthesia. Overactivity or restlessness of the sort that can occur in mania or minimal brain damage.

hyperkinetic syndrome. A synonym for AT-TENTION-DEFICIT DISORDER.

hyperlexia. Learning to read at an unusually early age without much formal instruction.

hyperlogia. A synonym for LOGORRHEA.

hypermania. An extremely manic state, characterized by overoptimism, restlessness, and incoherence.

hypermetropia. A synonym for HYPEROPIA.

hypermnesia. An abnormally good memory, found e.g. in some infant prodigies and *idiots savants*, sometimes in hypomania and sometimes in otherwise normal people.

hyperopia. Far-sightedness, a condition in which the lens cannot be made sufficiently convex to bring nearby objects into focus at the retina unless vision is corrected by glasses. *Contrast* MYOPIA.

hyperorexia. A tendency to eat too much, usually restricted to cases where it is not caused by a brain lesion. *Compare* HYPER-PHAGIA.

hyperosmia. An abnormally acute sense of smell.

hyperparaesthesia, hyperparesthesia. An abnormally sensitive skin sense.

hyperphagia. The tendency to eat too much, particularly when caused in animals by lesions of the VENTROMEDIAL NUCLEUS or elsewhere.

hyperphasia. A synonym for LOGORRHEA.

hyperphoria. A form of HETEROPHORIA, in which an upwards deviation of one eye occurs when that eye is occluded and the other is fixating a point.

hyperphrasia. A synonym for LOGORRHEA.

hyperphrenia. Excessive mental acitivity.

hyperpolarization. An increase in the potential difference across a neuron's membrane relative to the resting potential. In most neurons hyperpolarization reduces the tendency to fire and can be caused by stimulation across an inhibitory synapse. Some neurons (e.g. the visual receptors and bipolar cells) have only graded potentials involving hyperpolarization. *Contrast* DEPOLARIZATION.

hyperprosexia, hyperprosessis. Compulsive and prolonged attention to a stimulus or thought.

hypersomnia. Sleeping too much.

hyperthemic. Someone who is optimistic, quick, decisive and energetic, but within normal limits. *See also* HYPOMANIA.

hyperthymia. Excessive emotionality.

hyperthyroidism. *See* THYROID.

hypertonic. Having a higher concentration of a solute, used of one solution with reference to another. If the solution of salt in cells is hypertonic with respect to its solution in the blood, water will tend to pass from the blood into the cells through OSMOSIS. *Compare* HYPOTONIC.

hypertrophy. Abnormally large growth of a bodily organ.

hypertropia. STRABISMUS in which one eye points too far upwards with respect to the other.

hypesthesia. An alternative spelling of HYPAESTHESIA.

hypnagogic imagery. Vivid imagery occurring just before a person falls asleep. *Compare* HYPNOPOMPIC IMAGERY.

hypnoanalysis. A psychoanalysis in which hypnosis is used to reveal the patient's repressed wishes and thoughts.

hypnogenic. Inducing sleep.

hypnogogic imagery. An alternative spelling of HYPNAGOGIC IMAGERY.

hypnograph. An instrument used to measure sleep and its depth.

hypnoid, hypnoidal. Pertaining to hypnosis.

hypnonarcosis. Sleep induced by hypnosis.

hypnopaedia. The largely disproven phenomenon that people can learn from instruction given while they are asleep.

hypnophobia. A morbid fear of sleep.

hypnopompic imagery. Vivid images that may occur while waking from sleep. *Compare* HYPNAGOGIC IMAGERY.

hypnosis. A state in which a person, as a result of suggestion and often of relaxation, comes to concentrate on and obey the suggestions of another, sometimes even to the point of tolerating painful stimuli that he would not normally tolerate, and denying that they feel painful; the interpretation of the phenomenon is controversial.

hypnosuggestion. Suggestions made to someone hypnotized, particularly those to be carried out after the hypnosis, e.g. that he will give up smoking, will stop beating his wife, etc.

hypnotherapy. The use of hypnosis in psychotherapy.

hypnotic. 1. (Noun) A drug that induces sleep. 2. (Adjective) Relating to or caused by hypnosis.

hypnotic regression. The alleged but questionable phenomenon that under hypnosis people can revert to a much earlier age, and act and talk in exactly the way they then did without using conscious memory.

hypnotism. The topic or practice of hypnosis.

hypoacusia. An alterntative spelling for HYPACUSIA.

hypoaesthesia. Abnormal insensitivity to somaesthetic stimuli.

hypobulia. A synonym for ABULIA.

hypochondria. Excessive concern and worry about one's own health, often involving the misinterpretation of bodily signs as symptoms of illness.

hypochondriasis. (Psychiatry) Pathological HYPOCHONDRIA.

hypoergasia. Abnormal underactivity such as may occur in depression.

hypoesthesia. An alternative spelling for HYPOAESTHESIA.

hypogeusia. Impaired taste sensitivity.

hypoglossal nerve. The 12th cranial nerve, whose primary function is to innervate the muscles of the tongue.

hypoglycaemia, hypoglycemia. Too low a level of blood sugar.

hypognathy. The condition of having a lower jaw that projects beyond the upper.

hypohedonia. A person with a low capacity for feeling pleasure, but not clinically depressed.

hypokinaesthesia. Loss of sensitivity to the positions or movements of the parts of the body.

hypokinesis. Pathological underactivity.

hypokinesthesia. An alternative spelling of HYPOKINAESTHESIA.

hypolexia. A rare synonym for DYSLEXIA.

hypologia. Severely impaired ability to speak when not caused by brain damage. *Contrast* APHASIA.

hypomania. A pathological condition in which the person is 'mildly' manic; he is too optimistic, too exuberant, too talkative, and too active. He may also spend money wildly and play pranks that seem funnier to him than to others. *See* BIPOLAR MANIC-DEPRESSIVE DISORDER.

hypometropia. A synonym for MYOPIA.

hypomnesia. Impaired ability to remember.

hypophagia. Eating abnormally little food.

hypophoria. A form of HETEROPHORIA in which an occluded eye is directed to a point below that being fixated by the other eye.

hypophrasia. A synonym for BRADYPHASIA.

hypophysis. A synonym for PITUITARY.

hypopolarization. A synonym for DEPOLARIZATION.

hypoprosexia, hypoprosessis. Impaired ability to attend.

hyposmia. Impaired sensitivity to smell.

hyposomnia. Reduced sleep.

hypothalamic–hypophyseal portal system. A system of blood-vessels connecting the hypothalamus with the anterior pituitary, through which hypothalamic hormones flow to the pituitary.

hypothalamic-releasing factors (HTRF). Hormones produced by nerve cells in the hypothalamus that selectively promote the release of the five pituitary hormones – adrenocorticotropin, luteinizing hormone, thyrotropin, follicle-stimulating hormone, and growth hormone.

hypothalamus. A body about the size of a pea, lying in the DIENCEPHALON below the thalamus; it is implicated in the control of the autonomic nervous system, the emotions, hunger, thirst, sex, and sleep. Hormones secreted by the hypothalamus are fed both to the posterior and anterior pituitary. *See also* ANTERIOR HYPOTHALAMIC AREA, LATERAL HYPOTHALAMIC SYNDROME, MEDIAL HYPOTHALAMIC AREA, PARAVENTRICULAR NUCLEUS, POSTERIOR HYPOTHALAMIC AREA, SUPRAOPTIC NUCLEUS, and VENTROMEDIAL NUCLEUS.

hypothermia. A body temperature well below normal.

hypothesis. (Animal learning) Krechevsky's term for the mechanisms underlying the tendency of animals (particularly that of rats in mazes) to make the same response for many trials (e.g. always going left) and then suddenly to switch to a new response; he thought the animals were testing hypotheses.

hypothetical construct. An unobserved entity or process in a system used to explain its behaviour. The id, working memory, the logogen and the $2\frac{1}{2}$D sketch are all hypothetical constructs. Hypothetical constructs differ from INTERVENING VARIABLES in that the latter are more abstract and must be quantifiable.

hypothetico-deductive reasoning. 1. Piaget's expression for the ability to use abstract ideas, make deductions, and test hypotheses; he thought such reasoning began in the formal operational stage. 2. A method of constructing scientific theories by putting forward and then testing hypotheses, naively thought by some philosophers to be the way scientists proceed.

hypothetico-deductive system. A scientific theory in which hypothesized INTERVENING VARIABLES are rigorously linked to INDEPENDENT VARIABLES and DEPENDENT VARIABLES. In this sort of theory (espoused particularly by Hull), output from the system can be unequivocally deduced from input; hence the theoretical model can be rigorously tested – at least in principle.

hypothymia. Dejection.

hypothyroidism. *See* THYROID.

hypotonic. 1. Having a lower concentration of a solute, used of one solution with reference to another. *Compare* HYPERTONIC. 2. Having a severe loss of muscle tone, usually the result of a cerebellar lesion.

hypotrophy. A synonym for ATROPHY.

hypotropia. STRABISMUS in which the affected eye points too far down.

hypovolaemia. A decrease in the volume of fluid in the extracellular spaces, which can be caused by lack of water or severe bleeding and which produces VOLUMETRIC THIRST.

hypoxemia. Deficiency of oxygen in the blood.

hysteresis. The lag in a system changing from one state to a second, particularly when had it not already been in the first state, the external input would have made it enter the second.

E.g. if rows and columns of dots are presented with a wider spacing between the rows than the columns, the observer will see rows of dots; if the spacing between rows is gradually decreased, he will usually continue to see rows for some time after the spacing between columns exceeds that between rows. Hysteresis is common in mental processes.

hysteria. 1. *See* CONVERSION HYSTERIA. 2. *See* DISSOCIATIVE HYSTERIA. 3. Apart from its use to refer to the above two fairly specific neurotic disorders, the term is used more loosely to refer to almost any form of neurosis (particularly ones in which the person seems to be seeking attention), with the possible exception of ANXIETY NEUROSIS, PHOBIAS, and OBSESSIVE–COMPULSIVE DISORDERS.

hysterical. Pertaining to a symptom having a functional rather than an organic origin, as in e.g. hysterical ataxia or hysterical amnesia.

hysterical contagion. *See* MASS HYSTERIA.

hysterical personality. The personality of someone having a HISTRIONIC PERSONALITY DISORDER.

hysteriform. Resembling HYSTERIA.

Hz. An abbreviation for HERTZ.

I

I. An abbreviation for INTENSITY, particularly LUMINOUS INTENSITY.

I_R. Hull's abbreviation for REACTIVE INHIBITION.

sI_R. Hull's abbreviation for CONDITIONED INHIBITION.

sĪ_R. Hull's abbreviation for GENERALIZED INHIBITORY POTENTIAL.

sİ_R. Hull's abbreviation for AGGREGATE INHIBITORY POTENTIAL.

iatrogenic. Caused by medical treatment or mistreatment.

I band. *See* EXTRAFUSAL FIBRES.

ICD. An abbreviation for IMPULSE CONTROL DISORDER and INTERNATIONAL CLASSIFICATION OF DISEASES.

iceberg principle. In consumer psychology, the principle that consumers' purchases are motivated by underlying wishes and thoughts, of which they can give no account.

ichthyophobia. A morbid fear of fishes.

icon. 1. The image preserved in ICONIC MEMORY. 2. (Semiotics) A sign that resembles its reference, e.g. the signs on the outer doors of public lavatories.

iconic gesture. A gesture that looks like the object or action represented, e.g. making the motion of drinking to indicate it is high time someone filled your glass.

iconic memory. Very short-term visual memory in which all aspects of the stimulus are preserved; it takes about 0.5 sec to decay completely. *Compare* ECHOIC MEMORY.

iconophobia. A morbid fear of images or the visual arts.

ICS. An abbreviation for INTRACRANIAL STIMULATION.

ICSH. An abbreviation for INTERSTITIAL CELL-STIMULATING HORMONE.

ICSS. An abbreviation for INTRACRANIAL SELF-STIMULATION.

ictal emotion. An emotional feeling (e.g. anxiety) that appears suddenly and without external cause and is due to a brain disorder, e.g. to SUBICTAL EPILEPSY.

ictus. 1. (Medical) An acute stroke or epileptic fit. 2. (Linguistics) The accentuation of a syllable.

id. The unconscious part of the mind from which, according to Freud, drives (particularly the LIBIDO) emanate, and which contains forbidden wishes and associated thoughts that have been repressed. *Compare* EGO and SUPEREGO.

ID. An abbreviation for INDIVIDUAL DIFFERENCE.

idealism. (Philosophy) The doctrine that only ideas are real and that the outer world consists entirely of ideas. *Contrast* MATERIALISM and REALISM (2).

idealization. (Psychoanalysis) A defence mechanism in which an ambivalent object is split conceptually into something wholly good (i.e. ideal) and something wholly bad.

idealized self, idealized image. (Psychoanalysis) A person's image of what he would like to be. According to Horney, people have a neurotic tendency to fail to distinguish what they are from what they would like to be, by taking too favourable a view of themselves.

ideal observer. (Pschyophysics) A hypothetical observer that can discriminate stimuli with the maximum of accuracy possible given the level of noise in the transmission to the receptors. *Compare* STANDARD OBSERVER.

ideas of influence. A synonym for DELUSIONS OF INFLUENCE.

ideas of reference. A synonym for DELUSIONS OF REFERENCE.

ideational agnosia. Impaired ability to recognize symbols.

ideational apraxia. A form of APRAXIA in which it would appear that the patient is unable to relate the function of an object (e.g. a glass) to the movements needed to fulfil that function (e.g. raising it to his mouth). The patient can often copy an action that he cannot otherwise carry out. It is thought to be caused by widespread cortical damage. *Compare* IDEOMOTOR APRAXIA.

ideational fluency. A cognitive ability, measured e.g. by how many instances of a given class a testee can write down in a given time.

idée fixe. An idea that preoccupies a person and that he is unwilling to give up despite contrary evidence; people can become pathologically obsessed with such ideas.

id-ego. (Psychoanalysis) The undivided composition of the mind at birth, from which the ID and EGO are later differentiated.

identical elements. Elements in two tasks that are identical. In his account of TRANSFER Thorndike proposed that only when tasks contained identical elements could there be positive transfer between them. Unfortunately the concept of an element is ill-defined.

identical twins. A synonym for MONOZYGOTIC TWINS.

identification. 1. (Social psychology) Seeing oneself as similar to someone else and adapting that person's values and attitudes. 2. (Psychoanalysis) A defence mechanism in which a person fulfills needs he is afraid to fulfill himself; this is achieved by identifying with someone who does fulfill those needs. In another manifestation of identification a person gains strength by identifying with someone of whom he is afraid; this is known as **identification with the aggressor**: it was common in Nazi concentration camps.

identification task. An experimental task in which the subject has to recognize a stimulus (as opposed merely to detecting its presence, which is a DETECTION TASK).

identification test. An intelligence test in which a person is asked to name objects or their parts.

identification with the aggressor. *See* IDENTIFICATION (2).

identity crisis. Uncertainty about what role to play in society and about one's goals, values, capacities, etc.; it is common in adolescence.

identity disorder. (DSM-III) A mental disorder arising from undergoing an identity crisis.

identity theory of mind. The philosophical theory that conscious phenomena are identical with processes occurring in the brain. *See also* TYPE IDENTITY THEORY and TOKEN IDENTITY THEORY.

ideogram. A symbol that directly represents a concept (as used in e.g. Chinese writing) rather than representing a speech sound (as letters do in English).

ideographic psychology. The attempt to investigate single cases and to understand and interpret them without forming general laws or making wide generalizations. *Contrast* NOMOTHETIC PSYCHOLOGY.

ideokinetic apraxia. A form of APRAXIA in which the person can carry out isolated movements but cannot execute the sequence of movements making up an action.

ideomotor apraxia. A form of APRAXIA in which the person seems to know what to do, but to be unable to translate this knowledge into a sequence of motor movements. He may be able to carry out habitual actions, such as brushing his teeth, spontaneously but not on command. It can be caused by damage to the left parietal cortex.

ideomotor centre. A hypothesized centre in the brain in which the 'image' of a motor act is generated and which triggers the motor pathways to perform the act.

ideophobia. A morbid fear of ideas, common among behaviourists and Gibsonians.

ideoplasty. The control of a person's thoughts by hypnotic suggestion.

idiocy. An obsolete term for the possession of an IQ less than 25, the severest category of mental retardation.

idiodynamics. The principle that each person's individual needs, goals, interests, etc. determine his behaviour.

idioglossia. A synonym for CRYPTOPHASIA.

idiographic psychology. An alternative spelling of IDEOGRAPHIC PSYCHOLOGY.

idiolalia. A synonym for CRYPTOPHASIA.

idiolect. (Linguistics) The dialect of an individual speaker.

idiopathic. Pertaining to a disease having no discernible external cause.

idioretinal light. The diffuse grey light seen in complete darkness, possibly caused by the spontaneous activity of retinal cells.

idiosyncrasy-credit model. The hypothesis that a leader can depart from his group's standards if he has first established his credentials by conforming to them.

idiot. *See* MENTAL DEFICIENCY.

idiotropic. Introspective.

idiot savant. A person of low IQ who has mastered some intellectual skill to a point few

normal people ever reach, e.g. by being able to calculate within seconds on what day of the week a particular date fell or will fall.

I/E ratio. Length of inspiration divided by length of expiration; a low value is thought to indicate emotionality. The measure has been used in some LIE DETECTORS.

IE scale. A scale of introversion–extraversion, based on the MINNESOTA MULTIPHASIC PERSONALITY INVENTORY.

I–E scale. A scale measuring the extent to which a person's motivation is governed by internal or external factors. *Compare* LOCUS OF CONTROL.

ikonic. An alternative spelling of ICONIC.

ill-formedness. (Linguistics and Logic) Failure to conform to the correct syntax in a sentence or in an expression in formal logic, mathematics or a computer program.

illocutionary force, illocutionary act. The intended function of an utterance, e.g. to inform, promise, question, or command; an utterance's illocutionary force may be different from its grammatical form, e.g. 'Will you pass the salt?' is a polite command, not a question.

illuminance (E). The amount of light falling per unit area on a surface as measured by PHOTOMETRY; the standard unit of measurement is the LUX.

illusion. An error in perception, triggered by the external stimulus. *Compare* GEOMETRIC ILLUSION and *contrast* DELUSION and HALLUCINATION.

illusion of control. The belief that one is controlling a series of events far more than one actually is.

illusory conjunction. Wrongly putting together in perception the attributes of two distinct entities, e.g. seeing a red X when a green X and red S are shown.

illusory contour. A synonym for KANIZSA CONTOUR.

illusory correlation. The mistaken belief that a correlation exists when it does not, usually caused by failure to observe contingencies and by being influenced by irrelevant presuppositions, e.g. the belief that red-headed people are fiery induced by the association of red with fire.

illuminometer. A device for measuring luminance by matching a comparison field of known brightness to the standard. *See also* MACBETH ILLUMINOMETER.

image. 1. A point-to-point projection of the light in a scene on to a surface, as achieved e.g. by a lens. *See also* RETINAL IMAGE. 2. A conscious representation of previous perceptions in any sense modality or of their rearranged components that is similar to a percept, but is less vivid and is not directly created through the senses (i.e. a **mental image**). (It is important to distinguish the two separate but related meanings.)

imageless thought. Thinking without using mental images, a form of thought that the WURZBURG SCHOOL believed to be possible.

image–retinal system. The system that computes whether an object is moving by taking account of changes in its position on the retina. *Compare* EYE–HEAD SYSTEM.

imagery. A synonym for MENTAL IMAGE.

imaginal flooding. FLOODING using mental images, not real situations (i.e. IMPLOSION THERAPY).

imaginary contour. Any perceived contour that is not determined in a simple way by a brightness difference in the retinal image (as are ordinary lines and edges). Some examples are contours that depend on grouping elements (e.g. a row of dots), on stereoscopic disparity in a JULESZ STEREOGRAM, or on a change from one texture to another. The term is sometimes reserved solely for the contours in KANIZSA FIGURES.

imaging. The formation of a MENTAL IMAGE.

imago. 1. (Psychoanalysis) The unconscious image of another person, e.g. of one's father (Freud) or of one of the archetypes (Jung). 2.

(Biology) An adult insect, used particularly of species that metamorphose.

imbecile. *See* MENTAL DEFICIENCY.

imidazoleamines. A class of BIOGENIC AMINES containing an imidazole ring, e.g. histamine.

imipramine. One of the TRICYCLICS.

imitation learning. Learning in animals and man that is based on copying the behaviour of a conspecific, especially learning by imitating parental behaviour.

immanent justice. Piaget's expression for the belief of children under eight that punishment should be proportional to the damage done by an action regardless of intent or motive.

immaturity. The condition of not having developed the adult qualities that people ought to develop; a perjorative term much used by psychotherapists to subdue recalcitrant patients.

immediacy behaviour. Any intimate action, e.g. touching another person.

immediate association. Any response to a word in a word association test that is both the first to be given and has a low latency.

immediate constituent. (Linguistics) Any constituent generated at a particular level by a generative grammar. Thus, in the sentence 'The man was laughing', 'the man' and 'was laughing' (the noun phrase and verb phrase) are the immediate constituents at one level; at a lower level 'the' and 'man' are the immediate constituents of the noun phrase. 'Man was' is not an immediate constituent of any higher-level constituent.

immediate memory. A synonym for SHORT-TERM MEMORY.

immunohistochemistry. The use of antibodies to locate the presence of a particular biochemical molecule. *See* IMMUNOHISTO-FLUORESCENCE as an example.

immunohistofluorescence technique. An ingenious method of locating the cell groups secreting a given catecholamine transmitter.

Cells known to contain the transmitter are injected into another animal, which develops antibodies to them. Some of these antibodies are removed from the bloodstream and a fluorescent dye is chemically attached to them. On being applied to other parts of the original animal's brain, the antibodies attach to the same neurotransmitter and reveal its presence by their fluorescence.

impact analysis. In evaluation research, the measurement (preferably quantitative) of the difference made to an organization or system by a new programme.

impedance. *See* ACOUSTIC IMPEDANCE.

imperative. 1. A speech act in which a command is made. 2. The verb form that expresses a command.

imperfect tense. A PAST TENSE used to indicate that an action or event was continuous or repeated, e.g. 'he was walking'.

implication ($\supset$). (Logic) A LOGICAL CONNECTION between two propositions, such that '$p \supset q$' is true except when p is true and q is not true. Note that '$p \supset q$' is true when both p and q are false. The term LOGICAL IMPLICATION is sometimes used when the implication is true *a priori* as in '$p \supset p$' and MATERIAL CONNECTION when the truth is empirical as in '$p \supset q$'.

implicature. *See* CONVERSATIONAL IMPLICATURE.

implicit learning, implicit memory. Memory without conscious knowledge of what was learned. E.g. knowing that a face is familiar without being able to recall anything else about it.

implicit personality theory. The way in which a person views personality, i.e. which traits he thinks are positively correlated, which negatively correlated, etc.

implicit speech. A synonym for SUBVOCALIZATION.

implosion. *See* IMPLOSION THERAPY.

implosion therapy. A behaviour therapy technique used in the treatment of phobias

(and of other forms of anxiety). The patient is asked to imagine those scenes that produce the most intense anxiety until the anxiety extinguishes. **Implosion** is sometimes used synonymously with **flooding**, but it is best used only of exposure to mental imagery, and not of exposure to a physical object or scene. *Contrast* SYSTEMATIC DESENSITIZATION.

impossible figure. Two-dimensional figures that can be partially interpreted as representing a 3-D object through local depth cues, but that contain a contradiction about the relative depths or slants of parts of the picture and hence cannot be consistently interpreted. For an illustrated example *see* DEVIL'S PITCHFORK. Impossible figures are sometimes wrongly referred to as illusions.

impotence. Inability of the male to achieve an adequate erection or to sustain one for sufficient time.

impression management. The methods used by a person to present himself to others in the way he wants to be seen.

impression management theory. The hypothesis that people try to appear consistent to others, sometimes at the expense of dissembling.

impress method. A technique for helping poor readers, in which child and teacher read aloud simultaneously with the teacher at first speaking slightly before the child but gradually dropping behind.

imprinting. (Ethology) Quickly and irreversibly learning to discriminate a visual or auditory stimulus to which an animal is exposed; a response, innately determined, such as following, is thereafter made to the stimulus. The initial learning may determine the animal's preference for a sexual partner later in life. Such unusually rapid learning occurs in a CRITICAL PERIOD, and the process is largely innately controlled. E.g. goslings learn to follow their parents through imprinting, but can be imprinted to a member of another species, in which case they make sexual responses to that species rather than their own in later life.

impulse. 1. (Psychoanalysis) Any sudden and strong desire, especially desires originating in the ID. 2. (Neurophysiology) The sudden change in the polarization of a nerve cell's membrane that propagates down the axon. *See* ACTION POTENTIAL.

impulse control disorder (ICD). (DSM-III) Any disorder in which a person typically acts on impulse (e.g. exhibitionism or pathological gambling).

impunitive. Responding to frustration not with anger but by rationalizing it or by denying its existence. *Contrast* EXTROPUNITIVE and INTROPUNITIVE.

inaccessibility. The state of being withdrawn and unresponsive; it can occur in autism and schizophrenia.

inadequate stimulus. 1. A stimulus that gives rise to perception, but is not the normal stimulus for the modality; e.g. pressure on the eyeball may cause visual sensations. *Contrast* ADEQUATE STIMULUS (1). 2. A synonym for INEFFECTIVE STIMULUS.

inappropriate affect. Emotional responses that are out of keeping with the situation; they are common in schizophrenia.

inborn. A synonym for CONGENITAL.

inbreeding. Reproducing by the mating of closely related individuals.

incentive. Any reward that may induce an organism to do something; although a reinforcer and an incentive are always one and the same thing, the words emphasize different roles. A reinforcer strengthens the behaviour preceding it, whereas an incentive motivates the organism. In animal learning the term 'incentive' is used when it is the short-term effects of the reward (particularly of its magnitude) that are at issue. *See also* INCENTIVE MOTIVATION.

incentive motivation (K). Hull's expression for the intervening variable that mediates the immediate effect of reinforcement strength on response strength. The effects of changing the strength of reinforcement on the strength of the response are too sudden to be accounted for in terms of underlying HABIT STRENGTH (*see* BEHAVIOUR CONTRAST). Moreover, Hull believed that reinforcement size had no influence on habit strength. The effects of reinforcement size on performance are mediated by incentive motivation, which fluctuates rapidly with the size of reinforcement on each trial. *See* HULLIAN THEORY.

incest fantasy. (Psychoanalysis) The wish to have a sexual relationship with a parent, usually of the opposite sex.

incest taboo. The social prohibition of sexual intercourse between close relatives, which appears to exist in all human societies.

incidence. 1. (Epidemiology) The rate of occurrence of new cases of a disorder over a given period of time, usually expressed as the number of new cases per 100,000 members of the population. *Contrast* PREVALENCE. 2. *See* ANGLE OF INCIDENCE.

incidental learning. Unintentional and unmotivated learning. The expression is usually used of people; LATENT LEARNING is used of animals. *Contrast* INTENTIONAL LEARNING.

incident sampling. The sampling over time of a specified type of behaviour, e.g. aggression.

inclusive disjunction. *See* DISJUNCTION.

inclusive fitness. The probability of the replication of an organism's genes based both on its PERSONAL FITNESS and on the extent to which it can promote the survival of the same genes in relatives (KIN SELECTION).

incomplete pictures test. A test in which the testee is shown a series of incomplete pictures, which become more and more complete as the series progresses. He has to identify the object depicted, and his skill at interpreting visual information is measured by the point in the series at which he does so.

incomplete sentence completion test. A projective test in which the testee has to complete sentences like 'What embarrasses me most is . . .'.

incorporation. (Psychoanalysis) The fantasy that someone else or some part of another (e.g. the mother's breast) has been taken into oneself. *Contrast* INTERNALIZATION and INTROJECTION.

incremental learning theory. The hypothesis that learning occurs gradually and continuously and not in sudden jumps. *Compare* CONTINUITY THEORY.

incremental validity. The extent to which a test, by becoming progressively more refined (e.g. by dropping items that yield results contradictory to most of the others), develops into a valid measure of what it purports to measure.

increment threshold. A synonym for DIFFERENCE THRESHOLD.

incubation. (Cognitive psychology) The period in creative thinking believed to occur after first grappling with a problem when ideas about it are being turned over (often unconsciously while not thinking about it) and which may be followed by INSIGHT into the problem.

incus. A small anvil-shaped bone in the middle ear, which is one of the OSSICLES; it transmits sound vibrations from the MALLEUS to the STAPES.

indefinite. (Linguistics) Pertaining to an article ('a' or 'an') or pronoun (e.g. 'one', 'some') that does not identify the referent. *Contrast* DEFINITE.

indefinite article. *See* ARTICLE.

indefinite pronoun. *See* PRONOUN.

independence principle. (Decision theory) The normative principle that when there is an option between accepting (two or more) gambles and there is a possible outcome with the same expected utility in each gamble, the nature of this outcome should not affect the decision.

independent assortment, law of. A synonym for MENDEL'S SECOND LAW.

independent samples. Samples in which the members of the different samples are not individually matched. *Contrast* MATCHED SAMPLE (1).

independent segregation, law of. A synonym for MENDEL'S FIRST LAW.

independent variable. Any factor deliberately varied by the experimenter whose effects he is investigating. *Contrast* DEPENDENT VARIABLE and INTERVENING VARIABLE.

index case. A synonym for PROBAND.

indexicality. The property of a word or expression whose referent depends on the context or the occasion of its use. Words like 'now', 'here', 'you', 'then' are indexical.

Index of Adjustment and Values. A personality test measuring a person's attitudes to himself.

index of variability. Any measure of dispersion, particularly the standard deviation.

indicative. The unmarked MOOD (2) of a verb, which is used in statements and questions.

indifference point. A synonym for the POINT OF SUBJECTIVE EQUALITY.

indirect. (Linguistics) Pertaining to a speech act expressed in a linguistic form that does not reflect its purpose. E.g. 'Would you pass the salt?' is a question in its linguistic form, but as a speech act it is a command.

indirect object. *See* DIRECT OBJECT.

indirect scaling. *See* PSYCHOPHYSICAL SCALING METHODS.

indirect vision. A synonym for PERIPHERAL VISION.

indissociation. Piaget's term for the failure of young children to distinguish themselves from the outer world or objects from one another.

individual differences. The differences people exhibit in their traits, abilities, etc. *See also* PSYCHOLOGY OF INDIVIDUAL DIFFERENCES.

individualism. 1. (Philosophy) The doctrine that beliefs can be identified with particular information processing operations in the mind. For two varieties of this doctrine *see* METHODOLOGICAL SOLIPSISM and NATURALISTIC INDIVIDUALISM. 2. (Moral and political philosophy) The doctrine that the rights and interests of the individual are primary and that the form of any social system can only be justified in these terms. 3. (Social psychology) *See* METHODOLOGICAL INDIVIDUALISM.

individualization. The process of becoming an individual with characteristics and attitudes that differ from those of other people.

individual psychology. 1. Adler's theory. He believed that people each seek their own goals, which are not (*pace* Freud) merely based on sex, and that most people have feelings of inferiority. In consequence they may seek power and attempt to conceal their weaknesses from others; this can lead to their acting out of character, thus producing neuroses. 2. A synonym for PSYCHOLOGY OF INDIVIDUAL DIFFERENCES.

individual symbol. (Psychoanalysis) A symbol whose meaning is peculiar to the individual person. *Compare* UNIVERSAL SYMBOL.

individual test. A test designed to be given to one person at a time. *Compare* GROUP TEST.

individual therapy. Psychotherapy given to one person at a time. *Contrast* GROUP THERAPY.

individuation. The development in ontogeny of independence and autonomy or (Jung) of an awareness of one's own individuality.

individuo-centred approach. A synonym for METHODOLOGICAL INDIVIDUALISM.

indoleamine hypothesis of depression. The hypothesis that depression is caused by a deficiency of SEROTONIN.

indoleamines. A class of BIOGENIC AMINES formed by the combination of indole with an amine group. They are neurotransmitters and include SEROTONIN.

induced aggression. Aggression deliberately provoked in an experimental situation by the experimenter. E.g. if a rat is repeatedly shocked, it may attack another rat in the apparatus.

induced colour. An illusory colour such as FECHNER'S COLOURS or a colour produced by COLOUR CONTRAST.

induced effect. 1. The tilting of the HOROPTER out of the frontal parallel plane when vertical magnification is introduced in the image of one eye; the horopter is tilted in the opposite direction to that produced by horizontal magnification in the same eye. 2. A synonym for INDUCED MOTION.

induced motion. The apparent movement of a stationary object caused by another object moving. E.g. if a luminous dot is presented inside a luminous rectangle in a dark room, and the rectangle is moved, then it is the dot that will normally be seen to move. Induced movement is often experienced when one's own or another train leaves a platform.

induced schizophrenia. The taking over of delusions or other schizophrenic symptoms from a schizophrenic by another member of his family.

induction. 1. (Logic) Drawing general principles or conclusions from evidence when they cannot be reached by DEDUCTION (i.e. by the application of logical or other formal rules). Although induction does not have the certainty of deduction, all generalization, all scientific theories, and most acts of everyday reasoning depend upon it. 2. (Conditioning) Pavlov's term for the process underlying his finding that presenting an inhibitory conditioned stimulus immediately before an excitatory one increases the strength of the response to the latter (**positive induction**), while presenting an excitatory one before an inhibitory one increases the inhibitory effect of the inhibitory stimulus (**negative induction**). He explained this phenomenon by postulating that inhibition at one point in the cortex was always succeeded by excitation (and vice versa). 3. *See* NEURAL INDUCTION. 4. (Developmental psychology) A method of child rearing in which the child is gently encouraged to behave and have a sense of responsibility.

inductive statistics. A synonym for INFERENTIAL STATISTICS.

industrial psychology. The psychological study of all aspects of work and of the working environment, and the application of psychological findings to improving efficiency and contentment at work, through e.g. better selection methods, improved design of machinery, improved training, or improved organizational and management strategies.

ineffective stimulus. A stimulus that does not produce a sensation (or that does not excite a neuron) because it is too weak or because it is outside the range of the receptor (e.g. a very high-pitched tone).

inertia, law of. Spearman's principle that people are slow to start a particular mental process and slow to finish. In mental testing, Cattell subsequently isolated two different aspects: (i) inertia in which the person cannot switch between two existing skills; (ii) **dispositional inertia** in which he cannot apply an old skill to a new situation.

infancy. In people, approximately the first year of life.

infantile amnesia. The inability to remember anything about the first year or so of one's life.

infantile autism. A synonym for KANNER'S SYNDROME.

infantile neurosis. A neurosis which develops inconspicuously in the infant and manifests itself in the adult.

infantile sexuality. The sexual drive (libido) of infants, as postulated by Freud. *See* ORAL STAGE and ANAL STAGE.

inference. Drawing a conclusion from empirical evidence (i.e. INDUCTION (1)) or from premises using a set of logical rules (i.e. DEDUCTION), or the conclusion so drawn.

inference engine. The part of an EXPERT SYSTEM that operates on the input data and the KNOWLEDGE BASE in order to make inferences or draw conclusions, by e.g. using the rules of the predicate calculus or using a production system.

inferential statistics. The branch of statistics that enables one to assess the validity of a conclusion drawn from the data, e.g., whether two means are significantly different from one another, or whether there is a significant correlation between two variables. *Contrast* DESCRIPTIVE STATISTICS.

inferior. (Anatomy) Towards the lower part of the body, the brain or any other organ. *Contrast* SUPERIOR.

inferior colliculus. A midbrain nucleus of the auditory pathway. *See* COLLICULI.

inferior frontal gyrus. *See* Appendix 1.

inferior frontal sulcus. *See* Appendix 1.

inferiority complex. Adler's expression for the set of feelings and thoughts that are generated by thinking one is inadequate, helpless, or unsuccessful; these feelings are usually successfully dealt with and supply people's drives, but they can also lead to neuroses.

inferior oblique. An EXTRAOCULAR MUSCLE that pulls the eye upwards and outwards.

inferior olive. A nucleus in the medulla, implicated in motor coordination.

inferior parietal lobule. The lower portion of the parietal lobe, which curls over the temporal lobe; *see* Appendix 1. It is thought to be implicated in putting togther cross-modality information from vision, hearing, and touch, and hence to play a role in reading and writing.

inferior rectus. An EXTRAOCULAR MUSCLE that pulls the eye downwards and slightly towards the nose.

inferotemporal cortex, inferior temporal gyrus. A gyrus at the base of the lateral surface of the temporal lobe; it is known to be implicated in visual pattern recognition. It is Brodmann's areas 20 and 21; *see* Appendix 2.

infinitive. A verb form that is not inflected for tense or person and that can be used without a subject; in English it consists of 'to' followed by the unmarked form of the verb (e.g. 'to go').

inflection. 1. (Morphology) The use of affixes or other modifications to express the grammatical form or function of a word, e.g. talk*ing*, talk*ed*. 2. (Phonology) Modulation of voice pitch.

inflow theory. *See* CANCELLATION THEORIES.

information. For the technical use of this term, *see* INFORMATION THEORY.

informational influence. The influence on a person of information about the world derived from others.

information overload. The state of having too much information to deal with, thought by some to cause stress, a breakdown of social relations, and even schizophrenia.

information theory. A mathematical theory that makes it possible to measure how much information is being conveyed down a channel, the maximum amount of information a given channel could convey if the coding system were perfect, the redundancy of a message, the limitations imposed on a channel by NOISE (1), and so on. The standard measure of the amount of information (H) is the BIT, i.e. the information needed to select one of two equiprobable alternatives. Less information is needed to select between alternatives that are not equiprobable, and the formula governing the amount of information takes this into account: $H = \Sigma p_i \log_2(1/p_i)$ or (equivalently) $H = -\Sigma p_i \log_2 p_i$, where p_i is the probability of the ith signal occurring. Information theory has brought home such facts as that language is highly redundant. It has also been used to investigate how far the coding of information by people is optimal in a variety of tasks; in general it is found that reaction time increases with information transmitted, but where events have unbalanced probabilities, the assumption that subjective probability is the same as objective probability is not necessarily fulfilled.

informed consent. Agreement to take part in an experiment or medical trial, or to receive a medical procedure, with sufficient knowledge of what is in store (including the risks) to reach a rational decision.

infradian rhythm. Any biological rhythm with cycles longer than a day, e.g. the menstrual cycle.

infrared. Electromagnetic radiation having a wavelength in the region from 740 nm (just above the visible spectrum) to about 1 mm. Some snakes have receptors for infrared radiation, and use it to detect the presence of warm-blooded prey.

infundibulum. 1. A stalk attaching the pituitary to the hypothalamus; through it pass the blood-vessels and nerves by which the hypothalamus controls the pituitary. 2. More generally, any funnel shaped passage in the body.

in-group. An exclusive group whose members tend to treat one another preferentially as compared to outsiders. *Contrast* OUT-GROUP.

inheritance. The acquisition of a characteristic through genetic factors or the characteristics so acquired.

inhibition. 1. (Experimental psychology) The process that weakens a response through HABITUATION (1) or EXTINCTION (1) and in some other circumstances. *See* EXTERNAL INHIBITION, INHIBITION OF DELAY, REACTIVE INHIBITION, and CONDITIONED INHIBITION. *See also* PROACTIVE INHIBITION, RETROACTIVE INHIBITION. *Contrast* EXCITATION. 2. (Social psychology) The deliberate restraining of an impulse or the failure to act spontaneously, usually through fear or shyness. 3. (Neurophysiology) A reduction in the tendency of a cell to fire, caused by hyperpolarization of the cell's membrane as a result of inhibitory transmission across a synapse from a presynaptic cell. 4. (Psychoanalysis) The damping of wishes in the id by the superego; if they are sufficiently damped, it is not necessary to repress them.

inhibition of delay. Pavlov's name for the process that prevents a response occurring until the unconditioned stimulus is due, under conditions where there is a lengthy delay between the conditioned and unconditioned stimuli. The organism is usually first trained with shorter delays.

inhibition of inhibition. A synonym for DISINHIBITION.

inhibitor. 1. (Psychology) A stimulus that prevents a response. Both the response and the inhibitor may be either learned or innate. 2. (Biochemistry) Any substance that prevents or slows down the synthesis of a specific biochemical substance.

inhibitory postsynaptic potential (IPSP). A brief hyperpolarization of a nerve cell's membrane, caused by inhibitory transmission at a synapse.

inhibitory potential (sIR). A synonym for CONDITIONED INHIBITION.

inhibitory synapse. A synapse at which the firing of the presynaptic cell reduces the tendency of the postsynaptic cell to fire by increasing its membrane potential.

initial impulse. The acceleration phase of a bodily movement occurring at its initiation. *Contrast* CURRENT CONTROL PHASE.

initial segment. (Neurophysiology) The first segment of the axon beyond the AXON HILLOCK where its diameter is still decreasing.

initial teaching alphabet (ITA). A writing system using an alphabet in which every word is spelled as it sounds, e.g. 'rough' becomes 'ruff'. Its use in teaching reading has not proved very successful. *Compare* DIACRITICAL MARKING SYSTEM.

initial values, law of. A synonym for RATE-DEPENDENCE EFFECT.

initiatory structure. (Social psychology) The ways in which a given leader leads his group, e.g. by allocating responsibilities to them, caring for them, bullying them, etc.

inkblot test. The RORSCHACH TEST and any other projective tests based on inkblots.

innate. Genetically caused; innate characteristics sometimes only appear quite late in life.

innate releasing mechanism (IRM). (Ethology) The innate process through which, when the appropriate drive is present, an animal 'releases' a specific response to a SIGN STIMULUS, e.g. the male three-spined stickleback's zigzag dance is released by the presence of a shape resembling a female with a swollen abdomen.

inner-directed. (Sociology) Pertaining to a person who is not moved by external pressures, but adheres to and acts on his own system of goals and values.

inner ear. A synonym for LABYRINTH.

inner hair cells. *See* AUDITORY RECEPTORS.

inner layers of retina. *See* RETINA.

inner limiting membrane. A membrane encasing the retina on the inside (the side towards the lens) of the eye.

inner nuclear layer. That layer of the retina that contains the cell bodies of the bipolar and horizontal cells.

inner plexiform layer. *See* PLEXIFORM LAYER (2).

inner segment. The part of a rod or cone extending from the pigment bearing segment to the OUTER LIMITING MEMBRANE where in the case of cones it joins the cell body.

innervation. The distribution of nerve fibres in the body, and more particularly their connections to a given organ.

innovation. (Social psychology) A synonym for MINORITY INFLUENCE.

inoculative hypothesis. (Social psychology) The hypothesis that the persistence of a specific belief held by a person can be increased by providing him with arguments against it that are weak enough for him to be able to refute.

input. Information or energy fed into a system.

input/output relations. The function that determines what output will occur for each input.

insectophobia. A morbid fear of insects.

insight. 1. A sudden flash of understanding, e.g. in seeing how a problem may be solved. 2. More generally, understanding. Psychoanalysts believe their patients achieve insights into themselves, but corroboration is lacking.

insight therapy. Therapy based on the belief that it is helpful to patients to have insights about themselves.

insistence. A synonym for SALIENCE, but usually used of the attention-compelling quality of a bright light.

inspection stimulus. A stimulus presented at the first stage of a visual experiment that is followed at the second stage by a TEST STIMULUS: such experiments measure the effects of the inspection stimulus on the appearance of the test stimulus. E.g. subjects might fixate a rotating spiral for 30 sec and then be asked to fixate a stationary one, which will be seen in motion.

inspiration/expiration ratio. See I/E RATIO.

instigation therapy. A form of behaviour therapy in which the therapist encourages the patient to behave in certain ways or to follow certain models.

instinct. 1. (Ethology) An innate drive or an innately organized body of behaviour centred on a goal. A given instinct (e.g. the sex drive) is associated with a wide range of responses, usually including many different innate releasing mechanisms. 2. (Psychoanalysis) Freud used the term initially to mean the libido and the self-preserving instincts (e.g. hunger); he later referred to THANATOS and EROS as instincts. In his usage, instincts innately motivate the person but they are not necessarily associated with specific behaviour patterns. 3. (Generally) Any drive, whether innate or learned.

instinctive drift. The tendency for learned behaviour to drift towards the species-specific behaviour produced by the instinct operating at the time. E.g. a pig trained to drop a wooden token into a container (a piggy bank) to obtain a food reward will repeatedly drop it on its way to the container and then root it up.

instinctual. 1. Pertaining to an instinct. 2. (Psychoanalysis) Pertaining to anything derived from the ID.

instinctual aim. A synonym for AIM.

instinctual anxiety. (Psychoanalysis) Anxiety provoked by fear of an instinct in the ID.

instinctual fusion. (Psychoanalysis) A well-balanced combination of EROS and THANATOS.

instinctual object. A synonym for OBJECT (2).

instinctual renunciation. (Psychoanalysis) A refusal by the EGO to satisfy the wishes of the ID.

institutionalization. 1. (Psychiatry) The deterioration of a person's personality and capacities caused by being kept for a long time within an institution. 2. (Generally) The process of developing formal structures in some aspect of society, e.g. the development of professional football.

instrumental act regression. A synonym for HABIT REGRESSION.

instrumental aggression. Aggression directed to some further purpose (e.g. obtaining money).

instrumental case. See CASE GRAMMAR.

instrumental conditioning. A synonym for INSTRUMENTAL LEARNING.

instrumentalism. 1. (Social psychology) The exploitation of others. 2. (Philosophy) The pragmatic doctrine that the value of an idea depends only on how far it can be successfully applied in the real world.

instrumental learning. Learning in which reinforcement is provided only if the animal makes the response to be learned, as opposed to CLASSICAL CONDITIONING. In practice it is synonymous with OPERANT CONDITIONING, though 'instrumental learning' tends to be used of DISCRETE TRIALS EXPERIMENTS (e.g. a maze) while 'operant conditioning' tends to be used of FREE OPERANT experiments (e.g. a Skinner box).

instrumental response. A response learned through INSTRUMENTAL LEARNING.

insula. An area of the human cerebral cortex that lies hidden inside the Sylvian fissure, and is distributed between the frontal, temporal and parietal lobes. It comprises Brodmann's areas 13–16; see Appendix 2. It receives afferent fibres from the viscera. Stimulating it in man produces visceral sensations, belching, and salivation.

insulin. A peptide hormone secreted in the

pancreas that facilitates the transfer of glucose through the cell walls and its conversion to glycogen. Insufficient insulin leads to an excess of glucose in the blood (HYPERGLYCAEMIA), and is the cause of diabetes.

insulin therapy. Putting mental patients into a coma by using insulin to reduce blood glucose levels, an unpleasant treatment for which there was no rationale and which has been largely abandoned.

integral membrane protein. A protein in a membrane, such as the visual pigments.

integral stimulus dimension. A dimension that cannot exist without the presence of a second integral dimension, e.g. hue and saturation. *Contrast* SEPARABLE STIMULUS DIMENSION.

integrative agnosia. An acquired inability to recognize an object (or a large part of a scene) with an ability to recognize its parts. E.g. one patient shown a face could recognize the nose, mouth and ears but could not see the face as a face.

intellectualization. (Psychoanalysis) Dealing dispassionately with emotional problems using the head rather than the heart, while ignoring feelings and emotions; it is considered to be a defence mechanism. The term is pejorative and has become a cant word among psychotherapists, who tend to use it when confronted with patients who are cleverer than they are.

intellectually gifted. An expression normally reserved for those with an IQ of 140 or more.

intelligence. In general, the aptitude for solving those problems that can be solved by thought. *See* GENERAL ABILITY. Intelligence is sometimes divided into **biological intelligence**, the structure of the brain; **social intelligence**, the application of intelligence in dealings with others; and **psychometric intelligence**, ability on intelligence tests.

intelligence quotient (IQ). A measure of intelligence originally calculated as MA/CA × 100 (MA is MENTAL AGE, CA is CHRONOLOGICAL AGE). It is now calculated in terms of standard deviations from the mean score for people of the same age; the scores are normalised to yield a population mean of 100 and a standard deviation of 15.

intelligence tests. Tests that purport to measure innate intelligence, e.g. by posing problems that require no specialized knowledge for their solution. Since in general women tend to do better on verbal tests and men on spatial tests, the test designers provide a judicious mixture of both types of question so that the sexes come out equal. *See* CULTURE-FAIR TESTS, SPATIAL ABILITY, and VERBAL ABILITY.

intelligent knowledge-based system. A tendentious synonym for EXPERT SYSTEM.

intension. A synonym for CONNOTATION (1).

intensional object. Anything that a belief or experience is about.

intensity. *See* LIGHT INTENSITY and SOUND INTENSITY.

intention. 1. (General) A conscious aim. 2. (Philosophy) *See* INTENTIONALITY.

intentional forgetting. 1. (Psychoanalysis) Failure to remember something because it has been repressed. 2. (Psychology) Deliberately erasing something from memory, a process that can be more readily executed on a computer than in the human mind.

intentionality. (Philosophy) A technical word meaning the property that many mental states have of referring to something or being about something; walking is not an intentional activity, but 'desiring', 'believing', and 'hating' are. It has been argued that no computer program, no matter how much it mimics human behaviour, could exhibit intentionality.

intentional learning. Learning something deliberately. *Contrast* INCIDENTAL LEARNING.

intention movement. (Ethology) A movement that prepares the animal for a given action and that may signal the action the animal is about to perform to its conspecifics. It often incorporates RITUALIZATION, e.g. many birds before taking off crouch, raise the tail, and tuck in the head.

intention tremor. A tremor occurring in voluntary but not in involuntary movements, usually the result of damage to the cerebellum.

interaction. (Statistics) The reciprocal dependence of the effects of one factor on the levels of one or more others. When the factors sum additively there is no interaction. The amount of the variance that can be accounted for by interactions can be measured e.g. by ANALYSIS OF VARIANCE. One example of interaction is that between drive and task difficulty – high drive facilitates performance on easy tasks, but low or medium drive is better for difficult tasks. An interaction can sometimes be removed by arithmetically converting the data, e.g. to a logarithmic scale.

interactional psychology. The doctrine that a person, through his traits and mental make-up, influences his environment and that the environment influences him. *Contrast* SITUATIONALISM.

interactionism. 1. A synonym for a form of DUALISM in which mind and body influence one another. 2. A synonym for INTERACTIONAL PSYCHOLOGY.

interaction process analysis (IPA). Bales's expression for a system for coding the interaction between the members of a small group in terms of 12 categories, e.g. agreement, antagonism, support.

interaction territory. The space around two or more people in conversation which others recognize they should not enter.

interaction variance. The proportion of the total variance caused by the interaction of the independent variables.

interaural differences. Differences in a sound's intensity or in its time of arrival at the two ears; these are two of the main cues to AUDITORY LOCALIZATION.

interaural transfer. TRANSFER from one ear to the other.

interbrain. A synonym for DIENCEPHALON.

intercept. The distance from the origin of a graph to the point at which a line (or plane) cuts one of the coordinates.

interdental. (Linguistics) Of a consonant articulated with the tongue between the teeth.

interdental sigmatism. (Phonetics) Pronouncing the sounds 's' and 'sh' (as in 'sin' and 'shin') with the tongue against the teeth, thus producing a 'th' (as in 'thin'), a form of lisping.

interdependence. The dependence of the outcome of an interaction between two or more people on what each does, as e.g. in the relationship between husband and wife but not in that between warder and prisoner.

interdependence payoff structure. The specification of the preferences (and the relationship between the preferences) for all possible outcomes in the members of an interacting group.

interest inventory. A list of a person's interests (sometimes including latent as well as active ones) usually derived from a questionnaire and used mainly for vocational guidance or personnel selection.

interface. The point at which two systems (or two parts of one system) interact, e.g. the junction between the central processor of a computer and its peripherals. *See also* MAN–MACHINE INTERFACE.

interference. 1. (Psychology) The deleterious effect of performing one task on the performance of another. *See* NEGATIVE TRANSFER, PROACTIVE INTERFERENCE, AND RETROACTIVE INTERFERENCE. 2. (Physics) A reduction in the amplitude of a waveform caused by the presence of another wave that is out of phase.

interference theory of forgetting. The doctrine that forgetting is caused mainly by interference from the learning of other material. *See* PROACTIVE INHIBITION and RETROACTIVE INHIBITION.

interhemispheric fissure. The large groove that runs between the front and back of the two cerebral hemispheres, and that separates them from one another.

interhemispheric transfer. The TRANSFER of learned material or of a sensory residue (e.g. an aftereffect) from one hemisphere to the other; e.g. a person may be able to recognize an object originally presented only to one hemisphere when it is presented to the other.

interictal syndrome. A psychiatric disorder characterized by obsessive productiveness, e.g. in writing or drawing, an intense concern with spiritual or mystical matters, and a remarkable memory for some facets of life. It can be associated with temporal lobe epilepsy.

interiorized imitation. Piaget's term for the child's capacity, starting in the SENSORY–MOTOR STAGE, to form and manipulate representations of the world.

interjectional theory. A theory of the origin of language that assumes it was developed from interjections like 'ugh', 'ow', etc.

interleukin-1. A peptide produced by glial cells that increases sleep and enhances the activity of the immune system.

interlocking schedule. Any REINFORCEMENT SCHEDULE in which the number of responses that have to be made to obtain reinforcement changes with the time that has elapsed since the last reinforcement. Hence the availability of reinforcement is determined both by time elapsed and number of responses made.

intermanual transfer. TRANSFER (usually positive) of performance on a task learned with one hand to the other hand.

intermediate gene. A gene whose effects can be modified by an allele so that the phenotype lies between the two pure characteristics; e.g. when the allele for a red flower is combined with that for a white flower, a pink flower might result.

intermediate horn. In the grey matter of the spinal cord, the location of the cell bodies of preganglionic neurons of the thoracic and lumbar parts of the sympathetic system and of the sacral part of the parasympathetic system.

intermediate pituitary. *See* PITUITARY.

intermediate size problem. Training to discriminate a stimulus lying on a dimension from two stimuli lying on either side of it. Such training produces a steep generalization curve, peaking at the middle stimulus.

intermittence tone. A synonym for INTERRUPTION TONE.

intermittent reinforcement. A synonym for PARTIAL REINFORCEMENT.

intermittent reinforcement schedule. Any schedule in which the organism does not get reinforced for every response.

intermodal transfer. TRANSFER from one modality to another, e.g. if a person learns to recognize something by touch, he may be able to recognize it visually.

internal aim. *See* AIM.

internal capsule. Part of the telencephalon lying between the thalamus and basal ganglia; it consists of axons running from the cerebral cortex to subcortical structures and the spinal cord, and includes axons of the pyramidal system.

internal consistency. The extent to which the measures provided by the different parts of a test agree with one another. *See* RELIABILITY.

internal ear. The middle and inner ear.

internal environment. The condition of the internal organs in so far as it affects the nervous system, e.g hormonal levels, blood sugar levels, internal temperature, etc.

internal–external scale. An inventory that measures how far a person sees his behaviour as controlled from within, and how far by external factors.

internal force of organization. A force postulated by the Gestaltists which tends to render a percept stable and cohesive despite any counter force from the EXTERNAL FORCE OF ORGANIZATION.

internal granular layer. *See* GRANULAR LAYER.

internal hair cells. *See* AUDITORY RECEPTORS.

internal inhibition. Pavlov's expression for the process that weakens a response through the generation of an internal inhibitory force (as in EXTINCTION or INHIBITION OF DELAY) rather than through an inhibitory force generated by an external stimulus. *Contrast* EXTERNAL INHIBITION.

internalizing disorder. A disorder, like anxiety, that may not be manifested to others.

internalization. (Psychoanalysis and Social psychology) The incorporation into the self of the attitudes and standards of others, particularly those of the parents, a process by which the SUPEREGO is formed.

internal nuclear layer. A synonym for INNER NUCLEAR LAYER.

internal plexiform layer. A synonym for INNER PLEXIFORM LAYER.

internal pyramidal layer. *See* PYRAMIDAL LAYER.

internals. *See* LOCUS OF CONTROL.

internal segment. A synonym for INNER SEGMENT.

internal validity. A synonym for A PRIORI VALIDITY.

international candle. At one time the source used as the basis of photometric measurements, namely, a candle whose dimensions, composition, etc., were specified. It has been replaced by the CANDELA, a unit approximately equal to one candle in the old system.

International Classification of Diseases (ICD). A classification, made by the World Health Organization, of diseases including mental disorders. It is frequently revised.

International Phonetic Alphabet. A notation in which individual speech sounds are represented. The notation distinguishes sounds that differ phonetically, that is it discriminates between sounds having any difference in articulation, not merely sounds that differ phonemically. *See also* PHONETIC ALPHABET.

internuncial cell, interneuron. Any neuron that can be excited or inhibited by another and can in turn excite or inhibit a further neuron, i.e. all neurons except receptors and motor neurons.

interoception. The sense that conveys information about organs within the interior of the body, including information about the viscera, blood-vessels, salt concentrations, etc., but excluding proprioception (information from muscles and from the vestibular system). *Compare* EXTEROCEPTION.

interoceptor. A receptor located in or on an internal organ.

interocular. From one eye to the other.

interocular distance. The distance between the two pupils when vergence is set at infinity.

interocular transfer. The TRANSFER of an effect (including learning and aftereffects) from one eye to the other. Some aftereffects show such transfer, e.g. the motion aftereffect; others do not, e.g. afterimages are restricted to the eye originally stimulated.

interpersonal continuum. A continuum applying to a member of a group: it ranges from actions performed entirely as a result of being a member, to activities that are completely uninfluenced by group membership.

interpersonal control. A person's regulation of his interaction with others.

interpersonal distance. The spatial distance that two people preserve between themselves; as intimacy increases, the distance tends to decrease.

interpersonal theory. Sullivan's expression for his psychoanalytic therapy, in which he examined the patient's interpersonal relations (including those with the therapist) and attempted to rectify distortions in them. Sullivan believed that a person's attitudes to himself and indeed his whole personality were a reaction to how others saw him.

interpolated reinforcement schedule. A schedule given, usually briefly, in the middle of a different schedule with no signal provided to indicate the change in schedule.

interpolation. Inferring a value or values for points on a dimension from the obtained value of points lying to each side. *Compare* EXTRAPOLATION.

interposition. The concealing of part of an object by another object placed between it and the observer; although interposition is a cue to depth it can only be used to infer that one object is behind another and yields no information about absolute depth. *Compare* T-JUNCTION.

interpretation. (Psychoanalysis) The attempt to reveal unconscious thoughts and wishes by examining those aspects of behaviour thought to reflect them, e.g dreams, free associations, and parapraxes.

interpreter. (Computing) A program that translates another program written in a high-level language into machine code and executes each instruction before translating the next. An interpreter is slower in execution than a COMPILER and the user's program must be translated afresh every time it is run.

interquartile range (IQR). In a frequency distribution, the difference between the upper and lower quartiles (*see* QUARTILE (1)); hence it contains the middle 50 per cent of cases.

interresponse time (IRT). The time between successive responses, often used as a dependent variable in operant conditioning.

interrogative. A speech act whose purpose is to elicit information.

interrogative pronoun. *See* PRONOUN.

interrupt. (Computing) A procedure whereby, on receiving a message with high priority, a computer halts the processing currently being executed, executes the instructions in the message, and then returns to its previous assignment.

interrupted time-series design. A design in which subjects are repeatedly exposed to two or more conditions over time, e.g. the ABA DESIGN.

interruption tone. A tone produced by periodically and rapidly interrupting a sound.

The tone is most clearly heard when noise is interrupted periodically with silence. The frequency of the tone is the same as the frequency of the interruption. *See also* HETEROPHONIC CONTINUITY.

intersegmental reflex. A spinal reflex in which the motor output is in a different segment of the spinal cord from that receiving the sensory input.

intersegmental tracts. Short tracts connecting different segments of the spinal cord.

intersensory transfer. A synonym for CROSS-MODAL TRANSFER.

intersexuality. The possession of characteristics of both sexes.

intersexual selection. Sexual selection within a sex based on the characteristics of that sex that are preferred for the purpose of mating by members of the opposite sex. *Contrast* INTRASEXUAL SELECTION.

interstimulus interval (ISI). Where two stimuli are given in succession within a trial, the time from the offset of the first to the onset of the second.

interstitial cells. Cells lying between parts of a tissue or in a space.

interstitial cell-stimulating hormone (ICSH). A male hormone (chemically identical to luteinizing hormone in the female) produced in the anterior pituitary; it stimulates the testes to produce androgen.

intertectal commissure. A synonym for POSTERIOR COMMISSURE.

intertone. A tone heard when two tones differing very little in frequency are presented. The listener hears only a single tone intermediate in pitch between the pitches of the tones presented.

intertrial interval (ITI). The interval between the end of one trial and the beginning of the next.

interval. (Statistics) *See* CLASS INTERVAL.

interval estimate. (Statistics) The interval

within which the value of a population statistic (e.g. the mean) is likely to lie with prescribed confidence. *Compare* CONFIDENCE INTERVAL and *contrast* POINT ESTIMATE.

interval of uncertainty. In psychophysical experiments on difference thresholds, the range over which the comparison stimulus is likely to be judged equal to the standard; e.g. in judging relative brightness, the range would extend from the threshold at which the comparison was judged less bright to that at which it was judged brighter.

interval reinforcement, interval schedule. Reinforcement delivered on a time schedule, e.g. to the first response made one minute after delivery of the last reinforcement. *See also* FIXED INTERVAL SCHEDULE and VARIABLE INTERVAL SCHEDULE.

interval scale. A scale having equal intervals, but no zero point (e.g. Celsius temperature scale). Multiplication and division cannot be carried out in such a scale, but it is meaningful to add and subtract. *Compare* BISECTION, METHOD OF and EQUAL APPEARING INTERVALS, METHOD OF.

intervening variable. A quantified variable in a theoretical model whose value is determined by the INDEPENDENT VARIABLES (or sometimes indirectly by the values of other intervening variables). The values of the intervening variables determine those of the DEPENDENT VARIABLES. Hull's system used such intervening variables as DRIVE STRENGTH and HABIT STRENGTH. *See also* HYPOTHETICAL CONSTRUCT.

intervention research. Research designed to measure the effects of a deliberate change to a system on that system's functioning.

interview effect. The influence of a particular interviewer's behaviour on the interviewee's answers and performance, particularly in so far as it distorts them.

intimate zone. An area close to a person, within which only very intimate friends or relatives intrude.

intolerance of ambiguity. *See* TOLERANCE OF AMBIGUITY.

intonation. (Linguistics) The variations in pitch, loudness, and timing made while speaking. Changes in intonation can change the meaning of a sentence; e.g. if 'He is going' ends with a rise in pitch, it becomes a question not a statement. Some authorities confine the use of the term to changes in pitch, using PROSODY for changes in stress and rhythm. *See also* ACCENT and STRESS (2).

intonation contour. The INTONATION with which the syllables of an utterance are spoken.

intorsion. A rotation of the eye in which the top of the cornea moves inwards towards the nose.

intracellular fluid. The fluid contained within the cell membrane.

intracellular recording. A recording of the potential across a nerve cell membrane with an electrode that has penetrated the cell membrane.

intraception. The tendency to be governed by subjective or internal factors. *Contrast* EXTRACEPTION.

intraconscious personality. In cases of multiple personality, a personality of whose thoughts a second personality is conscious.

intracranial stimulation. Any electrical stimulation applied within the skull to a part of the brain.

intracranial self-stimulation (ICSS). A synonym for ELECTRICAL SELF-STIMULATION OF THE BRAIN.

intractable problem. A problem that cannot be solved in a feasible time because of the COMBINATORIAL EXPLOSION.

intradimensional shift. The change in reinforcement contingency that occurs when an organism, after being rewarded for selecting a particular value of one dimension (e.g. colour), is then trained to select a different value within the same dimension (e.g. red instead of green). Such REVERSAL LEARNING is one kind of intradimensional shift, but there are others, e.g. two new values of the dimension present during the first stage of training may be introduced. *Contrast* EXTRADIMENSIONAL SHIFT.

intrafusal fibres. Fibres in striped muscle lying between, and running parallel to, the EXTRAFUSAL FIBRES. They do not contract, though they are kept taut by the gamma motor neurons that innervate them. They act as stretch receptors and signal the tautness of the muscle. If the muscle is bent by a force, the annulospiral endings in the intrafusal fibres fire and, through a feedback loop, initiate firing in the motor neurons, thus keeping the muscle in a steady position. The hypothesis that gamma motor neurons cause firing of extrafusal fibres by biasing the intrafusal fibres has been shown to be incorrect.

intralaminar nuclei. A group of thalamic nuclei receiving fibres from the reticular formation and projecting diffusely to the cortex.

intransitive. *See* TRANSITIVE.

intraocular modification. Any distortion of a visual stimulus on the retina caused by the eye's physical structure.

intrapsychic. Within the mind.

intrapsychic ataxia. A synonym for MENTAL ATAXIA.

intrasexual selection. Sexual selection within a sex based on the need to compete with other members of the same sex for the opportunity to mate with the opposite sex. *Contrast* INTERSEXUAL SELECTION.

intrinsic behaviour. An action that can be performed only by one organ or muscle group, e.g. an eyeblink.

intrinsic eye muscles. The muscles inside the eyeball, i.e. the IRIS and the CILIARY MUSCLE. *Compare* EXTRAOCULAR MUSCLES.

intrinsic image. (Computer vision) A mapping of the visual image that makes explicit an aspect of the surfaces being viewed. Different intrinsic images might carry information about depth, reflectance, colour, texture, and motion. In psychological terms, an in-

trinsic image carries information about the visual world after the operation of depth perception and the constancies.

intrinsic motivation. A drive to do something (e.g. solving a crossword) for its own sake, and not for some other end. *Contrast* EXTRINSIC MOTIVATION.

intrinsic noise. Noise arising due to internally caused fluctuations in the state of the nervous system. It has the effect of raising thresholds.

intrinsic surface property. (Computer vision) Any property of a surface that can be described in an INTRINSIC IMAGE.

intrinsic validity. A synonym for A PRIORI VALIDITY.

introjection. (Psychoanalysis) The adoption at a deep level of another's (e.g. a parent's) moral standards, outlook, beliefs, etc.; it forms the basis of the SUPEREGO.

introns. Segments of DNA that are 'rubbish' – i.e. they are not translated into amino acids.

intropunitive. Blaming oneself or feeling guilty in response to frustration or failure. *Contrast* IMPUNITIVE and EXTROPUNITIVE.

introspectionism. The doctrine that introspection is the best way of studying the mind, held, e.g., by Titchener.

introversion. A major personality trait characterized by a preoccupation with the self, lack of sociability, and passiveness. *Contrast* EXTRAVERSION.

introversion–extraversion dimension. *See* EXTRAVERSION–INTROVERSION DIMENSION.

intrusion error. An error of recall, in which an item other than those to be recalled is produced. *Compare* ANTICIPATORY ERROR and PERSEVERATIVE ERROR.

intuition. An insight arrived at without conscious knowledge of how it can be justified. In other words the faculty that assures you you are right, when you are wrong.

intuitive type. *See* FUNCTION TYPES.

invariable hue. Any hue that does not change hue with changes in brightness.

invariant. J.J. Gibson's term for any feature of the optic array that remains constant for a given property of the external world. E.g. for a given convergence a given retinal disparity signals a given distance. Again the rate of change of the size of the elements of a texture is invariant for a given surface slant relative to the observer.

inventory. Any questionnaire in which the testee is required to assent to one of a set of answers; personality inventories are the commonest.

inverse correlation. A synonym for NEGATIVE CORRELATION.

inverse derivation. A synonym for BACK FORMATION.

inverse factor analysis. (Statistics) A synonym for Q TECHNIQUE.

inverse nystagmus. A synonym for POST-ROTATIONAL NYSTAGMUS.

inverse probability. A CONDITIONAL PROBABILITY in which the probability and the conditional are reversed. E.g. the inverse probability of $p(X/Y)$ is $p(Y/X)$. Many people mistakenly think such probabilities must be equal.

inverse square law. The law that the intensity of a wave (e.g. light or acoustic waves) travelling in a homogenous medium decreases in proportion to the square of the distance from the source.

inversion. 1. A MUTATION consisting of the reversal of the order of the genes in part of a chromosome. 2. Homosexuality. 3. (Linguistics) Changing the position of the subject and the verb. E.g. 'Are you thirsty?'

inversion of affect. A synonym for REVERSAL (1).

invert. 1. A homosexual. 2. A person who adopts the role of the opposite sex.

inverted factor analysis. A synonym for Q TECHNIQUE.

inverted Oedipus complex. (Psychoanalysis) A person's desire, whether conscious or unconscious, to obtain sexual gratification from the parent of his or her own sex.

inverted perspective. *See* PERSPECTIVE.

inverted qualia. *See* QUALIA.

inverted-U curve. A curve that looks like a letter U upside-down, starting low, reaching a peak and then declining; when performance on a task is plotted against arousal level or drive strength such curves are frequently obtained.

investigatory response. A synonym for ORIENTING RESPONSE.

investment. (Psychoanalysis) A synonym for CATHEXIS.

in vitro. Pertaining to an experiment that is carried out on a part of the organism that has been removed from the body. *Contrast* IN VIVO.

in vivo. Pertaining to an experiment carried out on a part of the living body. *Contrast* IN VITRO.

involuntary muscle. A synonym for SMOOTH MUSCLE.

involution. Regression to an earlier stage of development of mental or physical capacities.

involutional melancholia, involutional depression. An obsolete term for prolonged depression with first onset in middle or late life.

involutional psychotic reaction. DSM-III's expression for INVOLUTIONAL MELANCHOLIA.

I/O. An abbrevation for INPUT/OUTPUT RELATIONS.

iodopsin. A cone photopigment with peak absorption at 560 nm, first extracted from the chicken eye. It is based on RETINAL, and was the first cone pigment to be extracted. It provided the first evidence that retinal was implicated in cone visual pigments as well as in those of rods. The term is confusing and should be dropped: *see* VISUAL PIGMENTS.

ion. A positively or negatively charged particle.

ion channel. A protein molecule in a cell membrane that allows specific ions to enter or leave the cell; some ion channels open or close in response to the reception of neurotransmitters or to a change in voltage across the cell membrane and thus regulate the firing of nerve impulses.

iontophoresis. The transport of ions by an electric current. During extracellular and intracellular recording a double-barrelled electrode may be used, in which one half deploys a particular ion on or in the cell, and the other half records changes in potential.

iophobia. A morbid fear of being poisoned.

IPA. An abbreviation for INTERACTION PROCESS ANALYSIS.

ipsative questionnaire. A questionnaire in which the respondent uses his own values and norms as the baseline for his judgements.

ipsative scale. A scale in which the respondent uses his own values and norms as the baseline for his judgements.

ipsilateral. On the same side of the body or brain.

IPSP. An abbreviation for INHIBITORY POST-SYNAPTIC POTENTIAL.

IQ. An abbreviation for INTELLIGENCE QUOTIENT.

IQR. An abbreviation for INTERQUARTILE RANGE.

iris. A pigmented disc of muscle that surrounds the pupil and changes its size as it relaxes or contracts.

IRM. An abbreviation for INNATE RELEASING MECHANISM.

irradiance. The power of light falling on an area of a surface. It is measured in watts per square metre.

irradiation. 1. Pavlov's term for the spread of excitation or inhibition outwards from a locus in the sensory areas of the brain, a concept introduced in order to account for generalization. Pavlov also used the term to mean GENERALIZATION (2), but this use is now obsolete. 2. (Perception) The phenomenon that a bright stimulus on a dark background looks larger than a dark stimulus on a bright background where both stimuli have the same shape and size; it may be caused by the spread of light on the retina. 3. (Physics) The spreading out of electromagnetic energy (e.g. light) from a source. 4. (Neurophysiology) The spread of excitation or inhibition in an afferent system.

irrational type. *See* FUNCTION TYPES.

irregular word. A word that is inflected in an unusual way. E.g. 'mouse' → 'mice' not 'mouses', 'bring' → 'brought' not 'bringed'.

irrelevant language. A language that can be understood only by the speaker; autistic children sometimes produce such a language.

irritability. (Biology) The capacity of living tissue, particularly nerve tissue, to react to stimuli.

IRT. An abbreviation for INTERRESPONSE TIME.

Isakower phenomenon. Strange hallucinations usually felt in the mouth, hands, or skin. They include the feelings of an object pulsating or approaching and receding: they occur mainly when falling asleep.

ischemia. An inadequate supply of blood to an organ or part of an organ, caused e.g. by an obstruction to the blood flow; in the brain it can cause strokes.

ischophonia, ischiophonia. Stuttering.

Ishihara plates. A set of plates made up of discs of different hues and brightnesses. A normal observer can see in each plate a numeral picked out by the colour of the discs comprising it. Colour-blind observers will fail to see some of these numerals but may see others delineated by brightness differences.

The plates on which the colour-blind observer fails reveal the nature of the colour deficiency. *Compare* PSEUDOISOCHROMATIC CHARTS.

ISI. An abbreviation for INTERSTIMULUS INTERVAL.

island of hearing. A synonym for TONAL ISLAND.

island of Reil. A synonym for INSULA.

islands of Langerhans. Clusters of pancreatic cells that secrete glucagon (alpha cells) and insulin (beta cells).

isochrony. 1. (General) The property of having the same time interval. 2. (Linguistics) The tendency for the intervals between stressed syllables to approximate to equality, or the tendency for the listener to hear these intervals as more nearly equal than they are.

isocoria. The state of having pupils of the same size, which is normal even when the eyes are differentially illuminated.

isocortex. A synonym for NEOCORTEX.

isolation. 1. (Psychoanalysis) A defence mechanism in which the person deals with painful material by experiencing it without emotion, thus isolating it from the attached affect. 2. (Ethology) The use of a locus for breeding that is separated from other members of the species.

isolation effect. 1. A synonym for VON RESTORFF EFFECT. 2. (DECISION THEORY) *See* PROSPECT THEORY.

isomerization. A change in the spatial configuration of a molecule with no change in its chemical composition.

isometric contraction. The activation of a muscle without its shortening, which happens if there is a force operating in the opposite direction. *Compare* ISOTONIC CONTRACTION.

isometric projection. A form of ORTHOGRAPHIC PROJECTION in which the visible surfaces of the object projected all have the same angle of slant to the picture plane (e.g. a cube viewed with one corner directly in front).

isomorphic. Being related by ISOMORPHISM.

isomorphism. In experimental psychology, particularly in Gestalt psychology, the doctrine that neurophysiological events have the same structure as the concurrent mental events. Thus the Gestalt psychologists believed that any continuous dimension of experience (e.g. depth, pitch, brightness) must be represented by some continuous neurophysiological dimension.

isophilia. Affection (not necessarily sexual) between members of the same sex.

isophonic contour. A plot of the sound pressure levels of different frequencies at which they all sound equally loud; thus a 200 Hz tone must be considerably more intense than a 1,000 Hz tone for the two to have the same loudness.

isoproterenol, isoprenaline. A synthetic adrenergic agonist. *See* ADRENERGIC RECEPTOR.

isotonic. Having equal concentrations of a solute, used of solutions. If two solutions (e.g. blood and the interior of a cell) are separated by a permeable membrane they will tend to become isotonic through osmosis.

isotonic contraction. A muscular contraction causing movement in which there is equal tension on the muscle throughout the movement. *Compare* ISOMETRIC CONTRACTION.

isotope. One of two or more atoms that have the same atomic number, but contain different numbers of neutrons. *See also* RADIOACTIVE TRACERS.

isotropy. The state of having the same physical properties in all directions.

IT. Short for INFEROTEMPORAL CORTEX.

ITA. An abbreviation for INITIAL TEACHING ALPHABET.

item analysis. An analysis of each item in a test to determine whether it is reliably measuring what it is intended to measure.

ITI. An abbreviation for INTERTRIAL INTERVAL.

J

Jacksonian epilepsy. A form of epilepsy that starts with local contractions, which usually increase in magnitude and spread to the whole body; it can result in loss of consciousness.

Jackson's law. The principle that when the brain deteriorates the higher functions or those most recently developed in evolution are the first to be impaired.

jactation. Extreme restlessness.

jamais vu. Failure to realize that something has been experienced before.

James–Lange theory. The theory that emotion is caused only by the sensations elicited by bodily activity, both those engendered by the autonomic system, and those from the somatic system. Different sensations are alleged to cause different emotions. As James said, 'We are sad because we weep.'

jargon aphasia. A type of aphasia in which speech is incoherent with garbled syntax and misuse of content words. It is often regarded as a form of WERNICKE'S APHASIA.

Jastrow's illusion. *See* the illustration below. The upper shape looks smaller than the lower, probably because there is a tendency to compare the two neighbouring contours of the shapes. Wundt invented a slightly different form of the illusion before Jastrow.

J coefficient. The correlation between the items of a vocational test battery and the successful performance of the different components of a job.

J curve, J distribution. A curve (or distribution) with low values at the left side of the abscissa and sharply ascending values at the other end.

jerk nystagmus. *See* NYSTAGMUS.

jet-lag. The symptoms caused by failure of the circadian rhythms to keep in step with the time of day (as determined by the sun) as a result of being transported through several time zones.

jnd. An abbreviation for JUST NOTICEABLE DIFFERENCE.

job-component method. A technique for analysing a job by its components, usually undertaken to evaluate the pay for the job by comparing it with the pay for jobs having similar components.

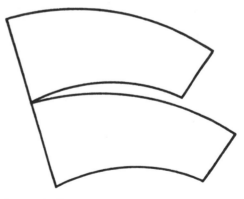

Jastrow's illusion

Jocasta complex. (Psychoanalysis) The abnormal love of a mother for her son, based on sexual desire.

Johari window. A concept from human relations training. It is an imaginary window with four panes which display respectively:

(i) the public behaviour of the self and others, (ii) behaviour known to others but not to the self, (iii) behaviour known to the self but not to others, (iv) behaviour known neither to the self nor to others.

joint probability. The probability that two or more events will occur together (e.g. the joint probability of throwing two sixes when casting two dice is 1/36).

Jonckheere test. (Statistics) A non–parametric *a priori* trend test of the hypothesis that the values of a variable of different samples are ordered in a specific sequence.

Jost's law. Two laws of learning. (i) If two associations are of equal strength but different ages, further study will increase the strength of the old one more than that of the more recent one. (ii) If two associations are of equal strength but different ages, the older one will decay more slowly over the further passage of time.

joule. An SI unit of energy, work, or heat; it is the work done when a force of one newton moves the point of application one metre in the direction of the force.

Julesz stereogram. A stereogram made from an array of random dots in which part of the array is horizontally shifted on one eye with respect to the other. Although no difference can be seen between the two members of the stereogram when they are each inspected with both eyes, they are seen in depth when projected one to each eye.

jump. 1. (Computing) In a computer program, an instruction (usually conditional) to move to a particular place in the sequence of instructions, instead of simply moving to the next in the sequence. 2. (Vision) A synonym for SACCADE.

jumping stand. Short for LASHLEY JUMPING STAND.

junction type. A synonym for VERTEX TYPE.

juncture. Any intonational feature signalling the end of one linguistic unit and the beginning of another (e.g. the end of a word, of a noun phrase, of a clause, etc.). One such feature is a pause, but changes in pitch, stress, and length are also used.

Jung's personality types. A synonym for FUNCTION TYPES.

just discernible differences, method of. *See* JUST NOTICEABLE DIFFERENCES, METHOD OF.

just noticeable difference (jnd). The smallest difference between two stimuli along a physical dimension (such as intensity or frequency) that can be reliably perceived, usually arbitrarily taken to be the difference that can be detected on 50 per cent of trials.

just noticeable differences, method of. A psychophysical method for determining a difference threshold by getting subjects to judge the smallest difference between stimuli that they can discern.

just not noticeable differences, method of. A psychophysical method for estimating a difference threshold by presenting the comparison and the standard stimulus initially with a large difference between them and successively reducing the difference until a subject reports that the difference in sensation is just not noticeable.

just-world hypothesis. The false hypothesis believed by most that the world is fair and that the bad are punished and the good rewarded.

K

K. The strength of INCENTIVE MOTIVATION in HULLIAN THEORY.

K'. In HULLIAN THEORY the physical size of the reinforcement, which gives rise to INCENTIVE MOTIVATION

31-K, 50-K. *See* PROHORMONE.

kainophobia, kainotophobia. A morbid fear of anything new.

Kaizer. (Organizational psychology) The belief that organizations should attempt to progress continuously at all levels rather than making drastic changes.

kakorrhaphiaphobia. A morbid fear of failure.

Kallmann's syndrome. A congenital condition characterized by delayed puberty and anosmia.

Kamin effect. The phenomenon that animals trained on an avoidance task, when tested at different times after training, show a U-shaped curve of performance. They perform well at first, and much worse after an hour or so; performance recovers after about two hours.

Kana. A Japanese system of writing which is a SYLLABARY containing 47 basic signs. *Contrast* KANJI.

Kanizsa contour. A contour not marked by a change in luminance, but produced by imposing a white (or black) patch over what would otherwise have been continuous black (or white) lines or shapes; the white (or black) patch is seen as an opaque figure in front of the background and its brightness (or darkness if dark) is perceived as greater than that of the background. *See* illustration.

Kanizsa contour and figure

Kanizsa figure. The figure bounded by a KANIZSA CONTOUR.

Kanji. A LOGOGRAPHIC Japanese script. *Contrast* KANA.

Kanner's syndrome. A form of autism that shows itself very early, often at birth; the infant is unresponsive, and its language is retarded, though it may show good motor skills and normal intelligence in some activities. *See* EARLY INFANTILE AUTISM.

kappa effect. The phenomenon that when three lights in different places are successively flashed at equal intervals with the distance between one pair greater than that between the other, the perceived interval between flashes is greater for the pair whose members are further apart. *Compare* TAU EFFECT.

239

kappa waves. Brain waves of about 10 Hz that are similar to ALPHA WAVES but of lower amplitude.

Kardos effect. The phenomenon, having to do with brightness constancy, that a white rotating disc exactly covered by a shadow, looks dark grey or black. *Compare* GELB EFFECT.

K complex. An isolated slow wave occurring in the electroencephalogram, usually during stage II sleep.

Kendall's coefficient of concordance (W). A measure of the extent to which two or more rank orderings agree with one another. Complete agreement between the rankings gives W = 1; lack of agreement gives W = 0 (or nearly 0). It is a function of the average SPEARMAN RANK ORDER CORRELATION between the rankings.

Kendall's tau (τ). (Statistics) A coefficient of rank correlation between two sets of scores based on the number of inversions of ranks in one ranking compared with the other. It is an alternative measure to the SPEARMAN RANK ORDER CORRELATION.

kenophobia. A morbid fear of empty spaces or the void.

Kent–Rosanoff test. A test of free association to 100 words for which the relative frequencies of different responses in the population have been established. Hence unusual responses by the testee can be singled out for discussion and interpretation.

keratometer. An instrument for measuring the radius of curvature of the cornea.

keratoscope. An instrument for examining the cornea that makes it possible to detect irregularities of curvature.

keraunophobia. A morbid fear of lightning.

kernel sentence. An active indicative sentence from which, so it has been proposed, passives, questions, commands, etc. are derived by transformations. *See* TRANSFORMATIONAL GRAMMAR.

kinaesthesis. The sense that monitors the movements and position of the parts of the body through receptors in the muscles, joints, and tendons; the vestibular sense is also usually included.

kinaesthetic method. 1. A method of teaching correct speech by making the pupil pay attention to the feel of the movements he makes. 2. A method of teaching reading by making the pupil outline letters with his fingers.

kindling. (Neurophysiology) A long-lasting increase in readiness to conduct in a particular region of the brain that is caused by repeated stimulation of the same point. It results in a greater spread of subsequent excitation and a tendency to epileptiform convulsions. *Compare* LONG-TERM POTENTIATION.

kinematogram. An array of dots randomly positioned on a visual display unit, which after a brief interval are succeeded by the same array shifted in position. If the shift is small (less than 15' arc of visual angle at the fovea), the observer sees the pattern moving as a whole to the new position.

kineme. A bodily movement having the same role in non-verbal communication as a phoneme does in speech.

kinemorph. A series of KINEMES; it is equivalent to a morpheme in speech.

kinesics. The study of communication (unintentional as well as intentional) through movements of parts of the body.

kinesis. A tropism in which an animal's speed or its number of changes of direction depend on the intensity of a stimulus. Thus flatworms congregate in dark places because they move fast and make many turns in bright light, but not in dim light.

kinesophobia. A morbid fear of motion.

kinesthesis. An alternative spelling of KINAESTHESIS.

kinetic aftereffect. An apparent motion of an object caused by its having been seen undergoing the same motion (e.g. approaching) for some time as a result of the KINETIC

DEPTH EFFECT. The aftereffect is in the opposite direction from that in which the original motion was perceived.

kinetic apraxia. Impairment of fine movements, such as those made when using a pen, on one or other side of the body, usually caused by damage to the prefrontal cortex on the opposite side to the affected limb.

kinetic depth effect, kinetic motion. Originally used to refer to the impression of depth obtained from watching on a flat screen the two dimensional image projected by a body rotating in depth. Nowadays often used to refer to any form of DEPTH FROM MOTION.

kingdom. (Biology) *See* TAXONOMY.

kinocilia. Cells containing cilia found in the vestibular system. They serve a purely mechanical purpose, and anchor the CRISTA to the CUPOLA. *Contrast* STEREOCILIA.

kin selection. (Sociobiology) The evolutionary selection of an organism's genes when based on the organism influencing their transmission through close kin, thus perpetuating or not those of its own genes that are also possessed by its kin.

kinship. An anthropological term for family relationships.

kleptolagnia. The obtainment of sexual excitement from stealing.

kleptomania. A compulsive desire to steal.

kleptophobia. A morbid fear of thieves or of becoming one.

Klinefelter's syndrome. A disorder, limited to males, caused by having an extra X chromosome (XXY); the male characteristics tend to be diminished, and there is a predisposition to mental illness and mental retardation.

K-lines. Minsky's term for connections that reactivate memories; in other words, the connections in an associative network. The term is short for 'knowledge lines'.

klinotaxis. (Ethology) A taxis in which

movement is directed through regular lateral swings of the head or body; the swings are made to assess the stimulus intensity in each direction. E.g. a maggot retreating from light may stop and turn its head from side to side and lunge toward the dimmer side. *Contrast* TELEOTAXIS.

Kluver–Bucy syndrome. Visual agnosia, accompanied by rage reactions, hypersexuality, loss of fear, and a tendency to feel objects and put them to the mouth. It was first observed by Kluver and Bucy in monkeys after temporal lobe lesions, but has since been seen in people with similar lesions. The amygdala is probably implicated.

knee. In free operant conditioning, a sudden increase in responding followed by a decrease in responding to below the previous rate, thus producing a bump (or 'knee') in the cumulative recording.

knee-jerk reflex. A synonym for PATELLAR REFLEX.

knowledge base. (AI) The part of an EXPERT SYSTEM in which the expert knowledge is stored. *Compare* INFERENCE ENGINE.

knowledge based system. (AI) A synonym for EXPERT SYSTEM.

knowledge by acquaintance. (Philosophy) Knowledge about aspects of the world that has been obtained directly through perception. *Contrast* DECLARATIVE KNOWLEDGE and PROCEDURAL KNOWLEDGE.

knowledge of results. The receipt of information by a person about how well he is performing a task, particularly when the information is given immediately. It may help him to improve his performance.

Koenig bars. Sets of bars having the same width and separation, used to measure visual acuity.

Koenig cylinders. Metal cylinders that give high pitched tones, once used to determine the upper frequency limit of hearing.

Koffka–Benussi ring. *See* BENUSSI RING.

Kohlberg's stages of moral judgement. *See*

PRECONVENTIONAL LEVEL, CONVENTIONAL LEVEL, and POSTCONVENTIONAL LEVEL. Each of these stages is divided into two, so altogether there are six stages. Kohlberg emphasized that there was considerable overlap between stages.

Kohs Block Design Test. A test of spatial ability in which a subject is shown a design made out of blocks and later told to reproduce it.

Kolmogorov–Smirnov test. (Statistics) A non–parametric significance test, with considerable power, for the difference between two sets of scores or the difference between a set of scores and a hypothetical population of scores.

koro. A Chinese mental disorder in which it is feared that the penis or labia will disappear into the body.

Korsakoff's psychosis. A disorder found mainly in chronic alcoholics, in which damage to brain tissue causes anterograde amnesia, with much confabulation, disorientation, and clouding of consciousness.

Korte's laws. The laws that purportedly govern the conditions under which OPTIMAL APPARENT MOTION between two stimuli will be seen. If T is the temporal interval between the stimuli, S their separation in space, and B their brightness, then once these parameters are set to obtain optimal motion any change in one necessitates a change in another. In particular, S varies with T; S varies with B; T varies with $1/B$. Variations in the length of time for which the stimuli stay on operate in the same way as variations in their brightness.

Krause end bulb. An encapsulated skin receptor probably sensitive to cold.

Krebs cycle. A chain of biochemical reactions in which compounds derived from the metabolism of carbohydrates, fatty acids, and amino acids are oxidized to yield water, carbon dioxide, and phosphate compounds, such as ATP.

Kretschmer's constitutional theory. A theory proposing a relationship between body type and a predisposition to develop a particular form of mental illness. The three body types proposed were ASTHENIC TYPE, PYKNIC TYPE, and ATHLETIC TYPE; the corresponding three dispositions were respectively to SCHIZOPHRENIA, MANIC-DEPRESSIVE DISORDER, and good mental health. In addition the three body types were thought to be associated respectively with the SCHIZOTHYMIC PERSONALITY, CYCLOTHYMIC PERSONALITY, and BARYKINETIC PERSONALITY.

Kruskal–Shepard scaling. A non-parametric MULTIDIMENSIONAL SCALING technique applied to subjects' judgements of the similarity or psychological distance between items in a set. The scaling is carried out in order to estimate the minimum number of dimensions required to represent the psychological distances between them.

Kruskal–Wallace test. A non–parametric rank test of the hypothesis that two or more independent samples have been drawn from the same population. *Compare* MANN–WHITNEY U TEST.

K strategy. (Genetics) An evolutionary strategy in which an animal gives birth only to a very small number of young at any one time, and invests much effort in rearing them. *Contrast* R STRATEGY.

Kuder Preference Record. A test of vocational interest.

Kundt's rules. The principles that (i) a distance divided in two looks greater than an undivided one, and (ii) when a person tries to bisect a line using only one eye, he tends to divide it at a point too close to the nasal side of the eye used.

kurtosis. A measure of the extent to which a frequency distribution is peaked, i.e. has short tails. *See* MOMENT.

kymograph. A rotating drum bearing paper, formerly used to record events and their temporal sequence through the deviations of one or more pens.

L

L. An abbreviation for 1. LAMBERT; 2. LIMEN.

L. An abbreviation for LUMINANCE.

$_sL_R$. An abbreviation for REACTION THRESHOLD.

la belle indifférence. Janet's expression for the lack of concern shown by hysterics about their purportedly physical symptoms.

labelling. Putting people in pigeon holes, a procedure much frowned upon by the culture of encounter groups and personal growth. The term is often used pejoratively of psychiatric diagnosis on the grounds that the diagnostic categories are uncertain and that applying them may make someone behave in the way expected of people so diagnosed. It should be borne in mind that any description involves labelling.

labial. (Phonetics) Pertaining to a speech sound articulated by the use of one or both lips, e.g. LABIODENTAL and BILABIAL consonants, and ROUNDED VOWELS.

labiodental. (Phonetics) Pertaining to a speech sound (e.g. [f], [v]) articulated with the bottom lip pressed against the front teeth.

labiovelar. (Phonetics) Pertaining to a speech sound articulated at the velum (*see* VELAR) with the lips simultaneously rounded (e.g. the 'w' in 'well').

labyrinth. A chamber also known as the **inner ear**. The outside of the chamber is bone (the **bony labyrinth**) and contains perilymph; it is separated by a membrane from the inner part (the **membranous labyrinth**) which consists of the COCHLEA, VESTIBULE, and SEMICIRCULAR CANALS, all of which contain endolymph.

labyrinthine nystagmus. Nystagmus caused by damage to the labyrinth.

labyrinthine sense. The sense of balance. *See* VESTIBULAR SYSTEM and SEMICIRCULAR CANALS.

lacunar amnesia. A synonym for EPISODIC AMNESIA.

LAD. An abbreviation for LANGUAGE ACQUISITION DEVICE.

Ladd–Franklin theory. A theory of the evolution of colour vision, based on the incorrect postulation of four cone photopigments.

lallation, lalling. 1. Speech, usually infantile, in which consonants tend to be omitted or fricatives changed (e.g. 'lue' for 'blue', 'ickle' for 'little'). 2. Infantile babbling.

lalopathy. Any speech disorder.

lalophobia. A morbid fear of speaking or of stammering, unfortunately unknown in politicians.

laloplegia. Inability to speak caused by paralysis of the muscles of the vocal tract.

lalorrhea. A synonym for LOGORRHEA.

Lamarckism. The discredited theory that characteristics acquired in life can be transmitted genetically to offspring.

lambda (λ). An abbreviation for WAVELENGTH.

lambert. (Photometry) An obsolete unit of LUMINANCE, being the amount of light reflected from a perfectly diffusing and reflecting surface of one square centimetre, one centimetre from a standard candle. It is equivalent to 3183 candela per square metre.

Lambert's law. The principle that the amount of light reflected from a perfectly diffusing surface varies with the cosine of its ANGLE OF INCIDENCE.

lamina. An anatomically discriminable layer in a part of the nervous system, e.g. in the cortex, lateral geniculate nucleus, etc. *See* CORTICAL LAYERS.

Land effect. A phenomenon, described by Land. An array of different colours is photographed twice, once through a red filter, once through a green; each photograph is printed on grey-level transparencies, and the subject is shown two superimposed pictures, each produced by light passing through one or other transparency. If the light illuminating the transparency originally produced with red light is red, and that passing through the other transparency is white, an almost complete range of hues is seen despite the fact that all points in the image contain only a mixture of red and white light. Land had several other demonstrations, some of which are also called the Land effect. *See* RETINEX THEORY.

Landolt circle, Landolt ring. An annulus containing a small gap. The size of the annulus and of the gap can be varied to test visual acuity by finding subjects' thresholds for detecting the presence of the gap.

Langerhans. *See* ISLANDS OF LANGERHANS.

Language Acquisition Device (LAD). The innate mechanisms that make it possible for the child to reconstruct the rules of his natural language from the examples he hears. They remain unspecified.

language centres. Those parts of the brain whose main function has to do with language, e.g. BROCA'S AREA and WERNICKE'S AREA.

language disability. Impairment, whether receptive or expressive, in any aspect of language use. The expression is mainly used of children with a language disorder.

Language Personality Sphere. 4,500 names of traits abstracted from the English language by Allport, who thought they could be used to describe all facets of personality.

language universal. A synonym for LINGUISTIC UNIVERSAL.

langue. (Linguistics) Saussure's term for the complete language system of a community of speakers. *Contrast* PAROLE.

Laplacian (∇^2). A mathematical function, which is the sum of the second differential in each of two orthogonal dimensions (usually vertical and horizontal). In COMPUTER VISION the function is applied to brightness changes around a point in order to extract edges. Retinal ganglion cells are thought to perform an approximately Laplacian function on their input.

lapsus linguae. A slip of the tongue.

large numbers, law of. The principle that the larger the sample taken from a population the more likely is the sample's mean to approximate to that of the whole population.

large pyramidal layer. A synonym for INTERNAL PYRAMIDAL LAYER.

larynx. A hollow space in the air passage from lungs to throat that contains the vocal cords.

Lashley jumping stand. An apparatus for training rats on visual discriminations. The rat is placed on a platform and has to jump to one of two vertical cards, each containing a visual stimulus. Normally the animal has to learn to jump to one of two stimuli regardless of whether it is on the left or right. If it jumps correctly, the card falls down and the rat lands in a chamber containing a food reward. If it jumps incorrectly it bumps against a fixed card and falls into a net. Because the rat has to jump, it hesitates and peers towards the stimuli before jumping and so is presumably likely to notice them.

latah. A culture-bound disorder in Malaya

and Indonesia, in which the person imitates the actions and words of others, shows total obedience, and is anxious.

latency. The time between the presentation of a signal and the response to it; the term is used mainly in studies of animal learning instead of REACTION TIME.

latency stage. 1. (Psychoanalysis) The fourth of Freud's LIBIDINAL STAGES, which occurs between the PHALLIC STAGE and the GENITAL STAGE. It lasts from about 5 to 11 years of age, and is marked by a lack of interest in sex. 2. See ERIKSON'S PSYCHOSOCIAL DEVELOPMENTAL STAGES.

latent content. Freud's expression for the unconscious wishes and thoughts of which according to him a dream is a disguised expression. *Contrast* MANIFEST CONTENT.

latent extinction. Extinction occurring without the subject having made the response to be extinguished, but having had the opportunity to discover that no reward will be forthcoming. E.g. if rats that have learned to run a maze for a food reward are placed several times in the goal box without food and with no opportunity to run, the response of running the maze undergoes considerable extinction.

latent homosexual. According to Freud, anyone who is not a practising homosexual.

latent inhibition. In classical conditioning, the phenomenon that presenting the conditioned stimulus several times without reinforcement before the start of training retards subsequent conditioning.

latent learning. Learning that takes place without obvious reward, e.g. a rat learns something about a maze if it is allowed to explore it without external reward. Latent learning is used mainly of animals. The corresponding expression for people is IN-CIDENTAL LEARNING.

latent schizophrenia. Any form of schizophrenia in which, despite the presence of symptoms, no psychotic episode or break with reality has occurred. *See also* AMBULATORY SCHIZOPHRENIA, BORDERLINE SCHIZOPHRENIA, PSEUDONEUROTIC SCHIZO-PHRENIA, and PSEUDOPSYCHOPATHIC SCHIZO-PHRENIA.

latent squint. The tendency of one eye not presented with a target stimulus to fixate incorrectly when the other eye is fixating the target. The condition is often accompanied by small vergence errors.

latent trait. Any trait that is not expressed in an organism's phenotype, but that can be passed on through its genes to descendants.

latent variable. A variable that cannot be observed, e.g. a FACTOR (3) or INTERVENING VARIABLE.

lateral. (Anatomy) Lying towards the side; away from the mid-line. *Contrast* MEDIAL.

lateral corticospinal tract. See CORTICOSPINAL TRACT.

lateral dominance. A synonym for CEREBRAL DOMINANCE.

lateral dorsal nucleus. A hypothalamic nucleus that projects to the cingulate gyrus.

lateral fissure. A synonym for LATERAL SULCUS.

lateral geniculate nucleus (LGN). A nucleus of the THALAMUS on which the OPTIC TRACT ends; it projects to the VISUAL CORTEX. It contains six layers of cells, alternate layers receiving an input from alternate eyes. *See also* MAGNOCELLULAR LAYERS and PARVOCEL-LULAR LAYERS.

lateral horn. Grey matter lying on either side of the spinal cord between the dorsal and ventral horns, and forming part of the autonomic system.

lateral hypothalamic syndrome. The deficits produced by lesions of the lateral hypothalamus, particularly ADIPSIA and APHAGIA, from which, with careful nursing, the subject may partially recover, though its body weight remains low. The symptoms may be caused less by a reduction in hunger *per se* than by damage to the sensory and motor pathways involved in feeding that run through the lateral hypothalamus.

lateral hypothalamus. A region of the hypothalmus implicated in hunger. *See* LATERAL HYPOTHALAMIC SYNDROME.

lateral inhibition. The horizontally propagated inhibition between neighbouring cells at the same level of a sensory system, where the cells represent different points along a dimension (e.g. frequency in the ear). It was first demonstrated physiologically in the LIMULUS eye, in which stimulation of one point on the retina inhibits the output from neighbouring points; but it is thought to exist for many other sensory dimensions (e.g. visual orientation of edges, skin position) and in all sensory systems.

laterality. Sidedness, especially the difference in the use of the two sides of the body or brain for the performance of a task, like writing, map-reading, speaking, or arithmetic.

lateralization. The extent to which a function is predominantly mediated by one cerebral hemisphere, or the ontogenetic or phylogenetic process by which it came to be so mediated.

lateral lemniscus. An auditory tract forming part of the LEMNISCAL SYSTEM and passing from the olivary body through the medulla and pons to the inferior colliculus.

lateral line organ. A structure on the side of a fish's body that is sensitive to vibration in the water.

lateral masking. The masking of a visual stimulus by two other stimuli lying on either side of it, a form of metacontrast.

lateral occipito-temporal gyrus. *See* Appendix 2.

lateral rectus. An EXTRAOCULAR MUSCLE that turns the eye outwards towards the temple.

lateral spinothalamic tract. *See* SPINO-THALAMIC TRACTS.

lateral sulcus. A sulcus of the lateral cerebral cortex that divides the anterior temporal lobe from the inferior frontal lobe. It runs vertically and then horizontally towards the rear of the brain; the horizontal section separates the temporal and parietal lobes. In addition it has two rami running into the inferior frontal lobes. *See* Appendix 1.

lateral thinking. A synonym for DIVERGENT THINKING.

late selection. In attention, the idea that unwanted messages are filtered out at a late stage of processing, i.e. after semantic categorization.

Latin square design. An experimental design whose aim is to remove experimental error due to variation arising from two sources. The design is identified with the rows and columns of a square. The number of conditions arising from each source and the number of treatments are the same, and each treatment occurs once in each column and row. E.g., where the sources are subjects and trials and the treatments are a, b, c, and d:

		Trials			
		1	2	3	4
	1	a	b	c	d
Subjects	2	b	c	d	a
	3	c	d	a	b
	4	d	a	b	c

The above example is intended to balance out the order in which different conditions are given across subjects and trials. The usual analysis of this design requires the independence of the 16 observations (which is rarely fulfilled) and the lack of interaction between trials and subjects (which is unlikely).

law. 1. In science, a generalization or theoretical postulate known to be true. In psychology, a generalization or theoretical postulate thought by at least one person to be true. 2. *See also* ASSOCIATION LAWS.

law-and-order orientation. A stage in Kohlberg's CONVENTIONAL LEVEL of moral reasoning, in which authority, duty, and rules of conduct are stressed.

law of X. *See under* X, LAW OF.

laws of association. *See* ASSOCIATION LAWS.

laws of grouping, laws of configuration. The

principles that govern the way in which the parts of a stimulus are grouped in perception. *See* GROUPING.

lax. (Phonetics) A distinctive feature of speech sounds caused by the vocal tract being in its resting position.

LD. An abbreviation for 1. LEARNING DISABILITIES; 2. LANGUAGE DISABILITY.

L-data. Data about a person's traits obtained from observations of his behaviour in real life or from peer ratings of him. *Compare* Q-DATA and T-DATA.

L-DOPA. Levorotatory dihydroxyphenylalanine, a synthetic precursor of DOPAMINE, used to alleviate the symptoms of Parkinson's disease. *See also* DOPA.

leaf room. A cubical room (with sides of about 2 metres) with artificial vines covering all surfaces and standing out from them in various orientations. It yields few cues to depth except stereopsis, and has been used to test the effects of manipulations of stereoscopic vision such as ANISEIKONIA.

learned helplessness. An inability to act, acquired by being placed in a situation where no action can help (e.g. one in which inescapable electric shocks are presented); it is thought by some to be the cause of depression.

learned taste aversion. Avoidance of a food with a particular taste that develops if an organism is made to feel ill after (even several hours after) eating the food, particularly if it has a novel taste.

learning curve. A graph recording the course of learning, with a performance measure plotted on the vertical axis and trials or time on the horizontal.

learning disabilities (LD). The unusually slow mastery of one or more skills, where the deficit is not caused by mental retardation. Examples are DEVELOPMENTAL DYSLEXIA and MINIMAL BRAIN DYSFUNCTION.

learning set. A set, usually learned, to learn to solve a particular kind of problem in a particular way. E.g. in a series of two-choice discrimination learning tasks, learning to obey the rule 'win stay, lose shift', i.e. if a stimulus chosen is rewarded, go on selecting it, if it is not rewarded, select the other stimulus.

learning strategy. Any technique adopted in order to learn something or to solve a problem, e.g. rehearsing material, paraphrasing text, elaborating material, or the 'win stay, lose shift' strategy.

learning to learn. The process that causes a decrease in the time or number of trials taken to solve a problem after repeated exposure to similar problems. *Compare* LEARNING SET.

least action, law of. A Gestalt law stating that the course of action chosen is that which subjectively requires the least expenditure of mental energy.

least commitment, principle of. Marr's principle that a task will be more efficiently executed if no decisions are taken that may subsequently have to be reversed; i.e. at each point in processing a decision should only be taken when there is enough evidence to warrant it. Operations proceeding along a wrong path are wasteful and have to be undone.

least effort principle. The hypothesis that, other things being equal, an organism will attain a goal by the means that requires least effort.

least mean square rule. A synonym for DELTA RULE.

least noticeable difference. A rare synonym for JUST NOTICEABLE DIFFERENCE.

least squares method. An estimation technique in which the sum of the squares of the deviations about a point, line, or surface is minimized. E.g. the selection of the regression line that minimizes the sum of the squared deviations from it of the observed points.

left-branching tree. A TREE in which the leftmost nodes branch more than the right. In generative grammar, 'My father's house's door' is a left-branching structure.

left-sided apraxia. Inability of a person with a dominant left hemisphere to carry out skilled movements with his left hand, thought to be caused by a lesion in the corpus callosum that reduces the transfer of motor information from the left to the right hemisphere.

legasthenia. Inability to compose letters into words, affecting both reading and writing; it is probably a congenital condition.

legitimacy knowledge. (Social psychology) The contribution to a person's estimate of himself made by his perception of how the group or groups to which he belongs see him. *Compare* COMPETENCE KNOWLEDGE.

leisure counselling. Advising people what to do when they have nothing better to do, the latest development in counselling. Not surprisingly it has been written, 'It as yet lacks a substantive theoretical base and solid research support for its concepts', but all is not lost for 'these are beginning to appear'.

Leitner International Performance Scale (LIPS). An IQ test purporting to be culturally fair in which the testee copies designs of blocks.

lemma. 1. (Linguistics) The representation of a word said to occur below the conceptual level (the idea the word represents) and above the phonological level (its sound or articulation). Different inflections of the same word, e.g. 'go', 'goes', 'gone', form the same lemma. 2. (Logic and mathematics) A proposition assumed to be valid that is used in the proof of another proposition.

lemniscal system. An afferent pathway that ascends to the thalamus through the pons and medulla. It has four different components: LATERAL LEMNISCUS, MEDIAL LEMNISCUS, SPINAL LEMNISCUS, and TRIGEMINAL LEMNISCUS.

lens. Any transparent substance with two opposite surfaces that refract light, most often used of a disc having a spherical curvature on one or both sides, which through refraction can be used to form an image, to magnify an image, etc. The mammalian eye contains a single lens with convex faces, lying behind the cornea. By changing its convexity, it brings the image of objects at different distances into correct focus on the retina; it should be remembered, though, that most of the refraction is done by the CORNEA. The refractive power of the human lens is about 20 diopters. *See* ACCOMMODATION (1).

lens model. Brunswik's model of vision, in which distal stimuli produce proximal stimuli, from which, by mental processes (the metaphor ical lens) the distal stimulus is reconstructed. The cues in the proximal stimulus are only probabilistic: the visual system learns which to rely upon in different contexts.

lenticular nucleus, lentiform nucleus. A nucleus in the basal ganglia comprising the PUTAMEN and GLOBUS PALLIDUS.

leptokurtic. (Statistics) Of a frequency distribution, having a sharper peak than a reference distribution such as the normal curve.

leptomorphy. In Eysenck's body build classification, a tall, thin build.

leptosomatic type. A synonym for ASTHENIC TYPE.

LES. An abbreviation for LOCAL EXCITATORY STATE.

lesion. A region of damage to an organ, whether produced deliberately or by pathology.

leucotomy. *See* FRONTAL LEUCOTOMY.

leu-enkephalin. *See* ENKEPHALIN.

level. (Statistics) A subclassification of a FACTOR, e.g. the factor 'sex' has two levels – male and female. The level of a factor corresponds to the value of an independent or intervening variable. A **fixed level** is any one level of a factor where all possible levels are investigated. A **random level** is a level chosen to be representative of the factor levels where only some levels are investigated. E.g. in investigating age as a factor, the levels 20 years old, 30 years old, and 40 years old might be investigated.

levelling. The tendency for memories to become simplified with the passage of time, and for irrelevant, inconspicuous, and insignificant details to drop out. Events tend to be remembered as more consistent than they were. *Contrast* SHARPENING and ASSIMILATION (8).

levelling effect. The tendency after many trials for scores to cluster closely around the mean.

level of aspiration. A synonym for ASPIRATION LEVEL.

levels of processing theory. The hypothesis that an item to be remembered can be processed to a greater or lesser extent in a number of domains (e.g. the word 'dog' could be processed at the acoustic, verbal, semantic, or imagery level), and that the higher the domain at which processing occurs, and the more processing there is in each domain, the better the item will be remembered.

levophobia. A morbid fear of anything to the left of the body.

lexeme. The minimal meaningful unit of a language. 'Sing' is a lexeme, so is '-ing', but 'singing' is not.

lexical ambiguity. Ambiguity that arises from a word having more than one meaning, e.g. the words 'bank' and 'row' are lexically ambiguous. *Contrast* STRUCTURAL AMBIGUITY.

lexical decision task. The task of deciding as fast as possible whether a string of letters is a word. It is used to investigate the nature of the lexicon and the processes that access it.

lexicalist grammar. A grammar that maps meaning directly onto syntactic structures without the interposition of a kernel sentence. E.g. active and passive versions of the same sentence would both be directly derived from the same underlying meaning.

lexical meaning. The meaning of a word in terms of the external world or of concepts extracted therefrom. Only CONTENT WORDS have lexical meaning.

lexical rules. (Linguistics) The hypothetical rules that take the output from the DEEP STRUCTURE component of a generative grammar, and supply the words that form the SURFACE STRUCTURE.

lexical semantics. The study of the meanings of individual words. *Compare* COMPOSITIONAL SEMANTICS.

lexical stress. The stress pattern in a spoken word or words. Stress can be used to differentiate a sequence of the same phonemes, e.g. 'black bird' versus 'blackbird'.

lexical word. A synonym for CONTENT WORD.

lexicographic rule, lexicographic method. (Decision theory) The principle, sometimes used, that in deciding between alternatives the alternative that ranks highest on the most important of several attributes should be chosen.

lexicon. 1. (General) Vocabulary (or dictionary). 2. (Psychology) Short for MENTAL LEXICON.

LGN. An abbreviation for LATERAL GENICULATE NUCLEUS.

LH. An abbreviation for 1. LUTEINIZING HORMONE; 2. LATERAL HYPOTHALAMUS.

LHRH. An abbreviation for LUTEINIZING HORMONE RELEASING HORMONE.

liar paradox. The paradox presented by such statements as 'This statement is false': if it is false it must be true, but if it is true it must be false. *See* METALANGUAGE.

libidinal stages. The development stages that, according to Freud, are based on changes in the object of the libido. They are (in sequence) the ORAL STAGE, the ANAL STAGE, the PHALLIC STAGE, the LATENCY STAGE, and the GENITAL STAGE.

libidinal type. A personality classification suggested by Freud; it depends on whether the libido finds expression in the id (EROTIC TYPE), the ego (NARCISSISTIC TYPE), or the superego (OBSESSIONAL TYPE).

libido. (Psychoanalysis) The energy of the sexual drive, broadly interpreted to include excretion and ingestion, which can be channelled (e.g. by SUBLIMATION) into other activities; the basic energy is in the ID. In his later writings, Freud used libido to refer to EROS, making the term even vaguer and equivalent to the 'life force' of Bergson or Shaw. *Compare* MORTIDO.

Librium. A trade name for a substance that is one of the BENZODIAZEPINES.

Liebmann effect. The appearance of a fuzzy overlap around the border of two adjacent colours of the same brightness.

lie detector. A device that detects one or more of the physiological concomitants of sudden arousal, such as the psychogalvanic skin response, or changes in heart rate, respiration, or intonation, and is used to detect the arousal presumed to occur when a lie is told; it is not very reliable and there are methods of defeating its purpose.

Life Career Rainbow. A way of representing the stages in a life span – pre-school child, school child, worker, spouse, parent, etc. Each colour of the rainbow represents a different stage; the width of the colour indicates the time spent in a stage, and its saturation the commitment to it.

life chance. (Social psychology) The possibilities in life open to someone as determined by their inherited traits, education and upbringing, parental wealth and station, etc.

life-change rating scale. A measure of the stress produced by different LIFE EVENTS, like being divorced, becoming unemployed, or having a serious illness.

life event. Any event that might be expected to upset someone gravely, e.g. death of a spouse, divorce, loss of a job. Not surprisingly, the occurrence of such life events predisposes to depression and also physical illness. Major events usually thought of as beneficial, e.g. inheriting a large sum of money, marrying, obtaining promotion, are sometimes also included as life events, since they too can have deleterious effects.

life instinct. A synonym for EROS.

life lie. (Psychoanalysis) The belief, when false, that one can never achieve one's goals, which, according to Adler, is a method of evading responsibility. More generally, any false belief that forms a basis for a person's life.

life space. Lewin's expression for a person's representation of himself and of his environment, and of all the possibilities open to him within it, each of which has a positive or negative VALENCE.

ligand. (Neurophysiology) Any compound that binds to a specific type of RECEPTOR (2).

light. Electromagnetic radiation that can be sensed by the eye. Its approximate range is 390 to 770 nm. The fundamental particle is the PHOTON.

light adaptation. The process whereby, when there is a marked increase in illumination, the visual system adjusts so that it can make fine discriminations between light of different intensities at the higher level of illumination. Light adaptation involves pupillary contraction, a switch from rod to cone vision, the bleaching of pigment, and more central processes. *Compare* DARK ADAPTATION.

light guide. A tube of transparent material that conducts light (which enters from one end at a low angle of incidence) along its length by reflecting the light from side to side. OMMATIDIA are light guides.

light intensity. The radiant energy emitted per unit time. The SI unit of measurement is the WATT. The subjective correlate is brightness. *Contrast* LUMINOUS INTENSITY.

lightness. (Experimental psychology) The subjective quality of a surface colour that corresponds to how black, grey, or white it looks. The term is confusing and is sometimes used to mean BRIGHTNESS.

lightness constancy. A synonym for BRIGHTNESS CONSTANCY, and in fact a less misleading term since it is LIGHTNESS that stays constant not BRIGHTNESS.

light reflex. A change in the diameter of the pupil caused by changes of illumination. The pupil decreases in size in bright light and increases in dark.

life-span approach. The relating of all stages of life to one another in the belief that earlier stages influence later ones, and that later ones in turn guide earlier ones through anticipation.

likelihood. 1. (Statistics) The probability that the value of a SAMPLE STATISTIC was obtained from a particular theoretical population or model. 2. (Psychology) Sometimes used to mean subjective probability, i.e. the probability someone assigns to an event.

likelihood principle. 1. (Statistics) Short for MAXIMUM LIKELIHOOD PRINCIPLE. 2. (Perception) The principle, originating with Helmholtz, that people interpret sensations in such a way as to perceive what is most likely to have given rise to those sensations. *Contrast* SIMPLICITY PRINCIPLE.

likelihood ratio. (Statistics) The ratio of the likelihood of obtaining an observed set of data under one hypothesis to the likelihood of obtaining the same data under another. It is widely used in significance tests and plays an essential role in SIGNAL DETECTION THEORY.

Likert scale. A scale for measuring attitudes, in which the subject indicates the strength of an attitude by picking one of a number of statements ordered along a dimension, e.g. 'I strongly dislike X', 'I dislike X', 'I feel neutral towards X', 'I like X', 'I like X very much'. A number (in this case 1–5) is assigned to each statement.

limbic lobe. An area of tissue on the medial side of the brain comprising the older cortex (the ARCHICORTEX and PALAEOCORTEX) and adjacent areas of the NEOCORTEX. It includes the CINGULATE GYRUS, the PARAHIPPOCAMPAL GYRUS, the UNCUS, and the HIPPOCAMPUS as well as the AMYGDALA, SEPTAL REGION, and MAMMILLARY BODIES (which are subcortical), *see* Appendix 2. *See also* LIMBIC SYSTEM.

limbic system. The LIMBIC LOBE together with associated structures including the HYPOTHALAMUS and parts of the THALAMUS. The system is not precisely defined; some authorities include the frontal association areas. It is heavily implicated in emotions in man.

limbus. The point of transition between the SCLERA and the CORNEA.

limen. A synonym for THRESHOLD.

liminal. Barely discriminable, or pertaining to threshold.

limited capacity. Of a channel or store, only able to transmit or hold a limited amount of information; all stores or channels have a limited capacity, hence the expression tends to be used where the capacity sets a severe constraint on the working of the system, as in short-term memory.

limits, method of. A psychophysical method for determining a threshold. Two kinds of trial are given usually in alternation. In one (**ascending series**), the intensity of a stimulus is gradually increased until a subject can just perceive it (absolute threshold), or until he can just detect a difference from a comparison stimulus (difference threshold). In the other kind of series (**descending series**) the stimulus intensity is reduced until it cannot be perceived, or until it is indistinguishable from the standard stimulus. The threshold is taken to be midway between the values determined by each type of series. *See* STAIRCASE METHOD, a variant that is now much more extensively used than the original method.

Limulus. The horseshoe crab, from whose eyes the first recordings from single units in the visual system were made.

linear. Pertaining to a straight line or plane. *See also* LINEAR SYSTEM and LINEAR FUNCTION.

linear chaining hypothesis. The hypothesis that in a skilled motor task each step is triggered by the successful completion of the previous one. *Contrast* HIERARCHICAL CONTROL THEORY.

linear correlation coefficient. *See* CORRELATION COEFFICIENT. The expression emphasizes the fact that both regression lines between two variables must be straight if the product moment correlation coefficient is to be meaningful. This assumption is easily, but rarely, examined. In fact correlation may be defined as the cosine of the angle between the regression lines.

linear discriminant function. A DISCRIMINANT FUNCTION that is linear.

linear function. 1. (Statistics) A sum of weighted variables; they can be graphically expressed as a line or plane. 2. (General) Any function describing the relationship of output to input in a LINEAR SYSTEM.

linearization problem. The problem of deciding the order in which to present ideas or concepts in speech.

linear perspective. See PERSPECTIVE.

linear programming. 1. (Computer-assisted instruction) A form of programmed learning in which progressively more advanced material is explained and tested; all students work through the same material without being switched to different materials if they make mistakes. 2. (Statistics) A procedure for maximizing or minimizing a linear function of several variables that are subject to inequalities.

linear regression. Fitting a straight line to the data points produced when one variable is plotted against another. See LEAST SQUARES METHOD.

linear syllogism. A SYLLOGISM whose PREMISES state transitive relations, one between items A and B, the other between B and C. E.g. from the premises 'A is bigger than B' and 'B is bigger than C', the conclusion 'A is bigger than C' may be drawn.

linear system. A system in which the output varies in direct proportion to the input, and in which, if there is more than one input, the response is proportional to the weighted sum of the inputs (with the possibility that some inputs may have negative weights).

linear transformation. (Statistics) A transformation of scores (e.g. test scores) that changes their mean and standard deviation, but retains other aspects of the original distribution. Compare NORMALIZATION.

line spread function. (Vision) The distribution on the retina of the light from a line that can be treated as infinitely thin.

linguadental. (Phonetics) A spoken consonant made by placing the tongue against the teeth (e.g. the 't' in 'talk').

lingual. (Phonetics) Pertaining to speech sounds made with the tongue (e.g. the 't' in 'tongue').

lingual nerve. A branch of the TRIGEMINAL NERVE supplying the anterior two-thirds of the tongue.

lingual papillae. See PAPILLAE.

linguistic constituent, linguistic unit. Synonyms for CONSTITUENT.

linguistic relativity, linguistic determination. The hypothesis that a person's native language has a considerable influence on how he categorizes and views his environment.

linguistics. The study of language, usually excluding the psychological mechanisms governing its use and its history (see PHILOLOGY) but including PHONETICS, PHONOLOGY, MORPHOLOGY, SYNTAX, and SEMANTICS.

linguistic universal. Any aspect of language that is common to all languages. They are of two kinds: (i) **substantive universals**, which are the components of languages, e.g. the phonemes or the parts of speech; (ii) **formal universals**, which are the general constraints on the generative rules that specify the syntax of all languages.

linguodental. A synonym for LINGUADENTAL.

linkage. (Genetics) The tendency for genes close to one another on the same chromosome to be passed on to the same zygote, which causes the traits to which they give rise to be correlated.

linkage analysis. The use of a GENETIC MARKER to determine whether the neighbouring genes come from the mother (ovum) or father (spermatazoon) as a result of LINKAGE.

link analysis. (Human factors) The analysis of the connections between all the elements in a work process, including those between operatives and machines. Such analyses are undertaken with a view to improving the system.

linonophobia. A morbid fear of string.

lipid. Any of several organic molecules that are attracted to water at one end and to fat at the other; it is an important part of the cell membrane.

lipostatic theory. The theory that long-term regulation of hunger is governed by monitoring the metabolites (free fatty acids) of fat. A high level of metabolites indicates the breakdown of fat, and is accordingly thought to increase hunger; low levels, on the other hand, are thought to reduce it.

LIPS. An abbreviation for LEITNER INTERNATIONAL PERFORMANCE SCALE.

liquid. (Linguistics) A consonant pronounced with almost no obstruction in the vocal passage (e.g. /h/).

LISP. A LIST PROCESSING LANGUAGE that facilitates the programming of non-numerical information. It can store terms in lists and has commands like 'Find head of list A'.

Lissajous figure. The curve traced by a point set in harmonic motion in two directions at right angles to one another; it was originally produced by shining a light on a mirror attached to tuning forks.

lissophobia. An alternative spelling of LYSSOPHOBIA.

listeme. An element of language that must be individually memorized because it does not conform to a rule. 'Sing' is a listeme but the '-ing' in 'singing' is not.

Listing's law. When the eye fixates a point other than the PRIMARY POSITION, its TORSION is given by assuming that it has rotated about an axis that is perpendicular to the initial direction of fixation and to the new direction of fixation at the intersection of the two directions. The law holds good regardless of how the eye reaches the final fixation point. It implies that there is always some eye torsion except in the primary position and SECONDARY POSITION.

list learning. The learning by rote of lists of items, e.g. nonsense syllables.

list processing language. (Computing) A programming language that provides facilities for the programmer to set up lists with complex structures (e.g. TREES). Such languages contain commands for processes like finding the first member of a given list, forming a sublist, etc. They have been particularly useful in AI simulations of the mind, since many mental activities can be represented as the formation and manipulation of lists.

literal alexia. A pathological inability to recognize letters and numbers or to confuse them.

literal dyslexia. A form of DEVELOPMENTAL DYSLEXIA, in which, while whole words can be read, the individual letters within them cannot.

literal paraphasia. A pathological tendency to substitute one phoneme for another in speaking.

lithium. A metal which, when given as a salt, partially replaces sodium in body tissues, thus affecting the permeability of membranes. It is used to reduce mania, and on a long-term basis, to alleviate bipolar manic-depressive illness. Some believe it may also help unipolar depression.

Little Albert. A young boy in whom Watson claimed to have induced a fear of white rats by shocking the poor lad in the presence of a rat. Watson also claimed to have subsequently extinguished the fear, thus making Albert the first beneficiary of behaviour therapy.

Little Hans. A boy with a fear of horses, treated by Freud at one remove through his father; the unfortunate child was browbeaten into a reluctant acceptance of a psychoanalytic interpretation of his disorder, which was probably caused by seeing a horse bolt.

Lloyd Morgan's canon. The principle that behaviour should always be explained in terms of the most elementary mental or physiological structures capable of explaining it, and that higher faculties should only be invoked when necessary.

lm. An abbreviation for LUMEN.

loading. Short for FACTOR LOADING.

lobe. Any round part of an organ, and particularly the four major divisions of the cortex (the frontal, occipital, parietal, and temporal lobes).

lobectomy. Short for FRONTAL LOBECTOMY.

lobotomy. Short for FRONTAL LOBOTOMY.

local circuit neuron. Any neuron whose processes are distributed over a small area rather than conveying information through an axon from one area to another. *See* GOLGI TYPE II CELLS.

local excitatory state (LES). The initial local change in the potential across the membrane of a nerve cell, with the outside becoming relatively less positive, produced by the arrival of an excitatory stimulus. It does not necessarily become large enough to generate an impulse. *See* POSTSYNAPTIC POTENTIAL.

local feature. *See* FEATURE.

localization. *See* AUDITORY LOCALIZATION.

localization of function. The ascription of a given function (e.g. language) to a given part of the brain.

localized amnesia. Memory loss for very restricted material or experiences.

local potential. A synonym for GRADED POTENTIAL.

local representation. Representing a concept by a single node or connection. *Contrast* DISTRIBUTED REPRESENTATION.

local sign. The information carried by the position of a receptor on the retina or skin; in vision this information signifies a direction in space, in somaesthesis a bodily location.

local syntactic parsing. Parsing that depends merely on interpreting the parts of speech of the input words and their order. *Contrast* GLOBAL SYNTACTIC PARSING.

location constancy. The tendency for an object to appear to have the same spatial relationship to its immediate environment, despite changes in the observer's position.

locative. A noun, pronoun, or phrase specifying the place at which an action occurs, e.g. 'there' or 'in the park'.

locative case. *See* CASE GRAMMAR.

loci, method of. A mnemonic, based on carefully memorizing a series of locations (e.g. by imagining oneself walking round one's house); when someone wishes to remember a list of items, he imagines each stored in series at one of these locations, and in retrieval he calls up each location in turn and recovers the item associated with it.

locomotor ataxia. Difficulty in walking, often caused by tabes dorsalis.

locomotor genital. *See* ERIKSON'S PSYCHOSOCIAL DEVELOPMENTAL STAGES.

locus. (Genetics) The site of a given gene and of its alleles.

locus coeruleus. Several nuclei in the brainstem at the base of the fourth ventricle that belong to the limbic system; they are rich in norepinephrine. Intracranial self-stimulation can be obtained from them; they affect sleep and mood.

locus of control. (Social psychology) A dimension of personality, being the extent to which people see the OUTCOME of a task as under their own control (EXTERNALS) or under the control of other factors such as luck (INTERNALS). Externals are likely to try harder than internals.

log. Short for LOGARITHM.

logagnosia. An impairment of reading in which a person can recognize written words but cannot assign meanings to them.

logamnesia. Impairment of the ability to recognize spoken or written words.

logarithm (log). The power to which another number (the BASE) must be raised to equal a given number. The base is indicated by a subscript to the abbreviation 'log'. Thus, $\log_2 8 = 3$.

logarithmic curve. A curve governed by an equation of the form $y = a.\log x$.

logic. 1. The branch of philosophy that analyses how conclusions can be validly drawn from premises. The term is sometimes extended to include the study of INDUCTION as well as of DEDUCTION. 2. Short for SYMBOLIC LOGIC.

logical connective. The formal connectives used in the PROPOSITIONAL CALCULUS, namely, NEGATION, CONJUNCTION, DISJUNCTION and IMPLICATION.

logical implication. See IMPLICATION.

logical operator. A sequential connective in the propositional calculus; e.g. 'and', 'or', 'not', and the quantifiers.

logical positivism. A philosophical theory which abjures metaphysics, and holds that the only propositions that have meaning are those whose truth values can in principle be ascertained.

LOGO. A list processing computer language. It is best known for its use to control the path of a 'turtle' on a screen, a device employed in the education of children; great claims for its educational value have been made, but they have yet to be substantiated.

logoclonia. The pathological repetition of parts of words, usually a symptom of SENILE DEMENTIA.

logogen. A hypothetical unit representing a particular word, regardless of whether it is activated by speech sounds, writing, or by the object the word represents. Connections from logogens activate semantic features of the word, its association with other words and so on. Logogens activated only by a specific modality (vision or hearing) have also been postulated.

logograph. A symbol in a system of writing derived from PICTOGRAPHY, but more abstract. E.g. the symbols for 'speech' and 'tongue' may be conjoined to mean 'story'.

logomania. A synonym for LOGORRHEA.

logopathy. Any speech disorder.

logorrhea. Pathologically fast and incoherent speech such as may occur in mania.

logospasm. Explosive speech or LOGORRHEA.

logotherapy. A psychotherapy, developed by Frankl, which attempts to help the patient to find a meaning in his life by examining his attitudes to work, love, suffering, etc. It makes use of PARADOXICAL INTENTION.

longitudinal fissure. A synonym for LONGITUDINAL SULCUS.

longitudinal horopter. The part of the HOROPTER that lies on a plane passing through the nodal points of the eyes and the fixation point.

longitudinal study. Any study of a group of people over a long period of time (usually years). It avoids the problems that arise in RETROSPECTIVE STUDIES and in CROSS-SECTIONAL STUDIES, but cannot take into account the effects of repeated testing.

longitudinal sulcus. The sulcus running from the front to the back of the cortex and separating the two cerebral hemispheres.

long-range motion system. A high-level system that can detect apparent motion over several degrees and with time intervals as long as 500 msec. Unlike the SHORT-RANGE MOTION SYSTEM it can detect motion when exposures are made to separate eyes.

long-term memory (LTM). Long-lasting (sometimes permanent) memory. *Compare* SHORT-TERM MEMORY.

long-term potentiation (LTP). An increase, lasting several weeks, in the excitability of nerve tissue, caused by a brief burst of high-frequency electrical stimulation; it is found particularly in the mammalian forebrain. *Compare* KINDLING.

long-term store (LTS). A synonym for LONG-TERM MEMORY.

long-wavelength cone. *See* CONE.

looking-glass self. One's self-image as based on how one thinks others see one.

look say method. A synonym for WHOLE WORD METHOD.

look-up table. A table in which something is looked up rather than calculated from scratch. E.g. some hypothesize that the limb trajectory to reach a target can be looked up rather than calculated.

looming. (Vision) The symmetrical expansion of the retinal image of a visual stimulus, normally caused by an object moving towards the head; looming produces an avoidance reaction in most animals and in children even when under two weeks old.

lordosis. A concave downward posture of the back adopted by many female mammals when sexually excited.

lose–shift strategy. *See* WIN–STAY, LOSE–SHIFT STRATEGY.

Lothe's law. The law that if k is the number of contributors to a given field, half the contributions will be made by $\sqrt{k}$.

lottery. A synonym for psychiatric diagnosis.

loudness. The apparent intensity of a sound. *See* SONE.

loudness contour. A graph showing the sound pressure for each frequency required to produce a given sensation of loudness for a typical subject.

love. A form of mental illness not yet recognized in any of the standard diagnostic manuals.

low-grade defective. An American term for a retardate with an IQ of less than 50 who has to be in an institution.

low-pass filter. A filter that transmits from a waveform only frequencies below a given frequency.

low phoneme. A phoneme uttered with the tongue lowered.

low-rise. In PITCH CONTOURS, a small rise in pitch that can be used to indicate that what is being said at that point is new or unexplained,

and requires a further contribution from the listener.

LSD. An abbreviation for lysergic acid diethylamide, a hallucinogenic drug that can produce quasi-psychotic states (including delusions) and dramatic mood swings.

LTH. An abbreviation for LUTEOTROPIC HORMONE.

LTM. An abbreviation for LONG-TERM MEMORY.

LTP. An abbreviation for LONG-TERM POTENTIATION.

LTS. An abbreviation for LONG-TERM STORE.

lucid dreams. Dreams in which the dreamer is consciously aware that he is dreaming; some people claim they can control their dreams to make them pleasanter when in this state.

ludic. Pertaining to play, including curiosity, playful fighting, etc.

lumbar. Pertaining to the lower back, a region that comes between the sacral and thoracic regions.

lumbar nerves. *See* SPINAL NERVES.

lumen (lm). A measure of LUMINOUS FLUX equal to 4π candela (since a steradian is $1/4\pi$ of the solid angle surrounding a point source, and a candela is flux per steradian).

luminance (L). The photometric intensity of the light emitted or reflected by a surface per unit area. The standard unit is candela per square metre (or nits), others are lamberts, millilamberts, and footlamberts. If the illuminance (in lux) and the reflectance (R) of a surface are known, its luminance is lux $\times$ R. *See* PHOTOMETRY.

luminosity. The apparent brightness of a surface or light source. It tends to be used to mean the apparent intensity of a light as derived from the LUMINOUS EFFICIENCY FUNCTION. *Compare* BRIGHTNESS.

luminosity coefficient. The coefficient that weights different wavelengths in the LUMINOUS EFFICIENCY FUNCTION.

luminosity curve. A curve showing the relative radiant power needed by light of different wavelengths in order for them to appear equally bright. Different curves are needed for bright light (which stimulates mainly cones – **photopic luminosity curve**), and for dim light (which stimulates mainly rods – **scotopic luminosity curve**). *Compare* LUMINOUS EFFICIENCY FUNCTION.

luminous efficiency function. A function that can be applied to light of any mixture of wavelengths to yield its apparent brightness or luminosity. It weights the intensity of each wavelength according to the sensitivity of a hypothetical standard observer to that wavelength, e.g. yellow light receives a higher weighting than blue. Different functions are used for scotopic, mesopic, and photopic conditions. The photometric functions are only an approximation to those of real observers. *Compare* LUMINOSITY CURVE.

luminous flux (F). The total amount of light per unit time emitted from a source, as measured by photometry; the standard unit of measurement is the LUMEN. *See* PHOTOMETRY.

luminous intensity (I). The luminous flux emitted per unit solid angle (steradian) by a light source; the standard unit of measurement is the candela. *See* PHOTOMETRY.

lunate sulcus. *See* Appendix 1.

lure. A synonym for DISTRACTOR (1).

lustre. The appearance of shininess on a surface caused by highlights striking different parts of each eye, and changing position with head movements.

luteal phase. The stage of the menstrual cycle that starts with ovulation and ends (unless fertilization occurs) with the onset of menstruation; during this stage PROGESTERONE is secreted by the CORPUS LUTEUM.

luteinizing hormone (LH). A gonadotrophic hormone secreted by the anterior pituitary that causes the follicle to grow until it ruptures and releases the ovum. It also promotes the secretion of testosterone from the gonads. It is chemically identical to the male INTERSTITIAL CELL-STIMULATING HORMONE. *See also* HYPOTHALAMIC RELEASING FACTORS.

luteinizing hormone releasing hormone (LHRH). A hormone secreted by the hypothalamus that causes the pituitary to secrete LUTEINIZING HORMONE.

luteotropic hormone (LTH). A synonym for PROLACTIN.

lux. The photometric unit in which illuminance is measured, being the incident light falling on one square metre from a point source having a luminous flux of one lumen and at a distance of one metre. *See* PHOTOMETRY.

lycanthropy. The delusion that one is an animal, especially a wolf.

lysergic acid diethylamide. *See* LSD.

M

M. An abbreviation for ARITHMETIC MEAN.

M1. Short for PRIMARY MOTOR CORTEX.

M2. Short for SUPPLEMENTARY MOTOR CORTEX.

M3. Short for SECONDARY MOTOR CORTEX.

MA. An abbreviation for MENTAL AGE.

Macbeth illuminometer. A device for measuring luminance; an observer views a surface through it and adjusts a light of known intensity to appear the same brightness as the light from the surface.

McCollough effect. The phenomenon that when an observer views horizontal and vertical stripes of different colours (e.g. red and green) for 30 sec or more and is then shown achromatic horizontal or vertical stripes, the horizontal stripes appear tinged with the complementary colour to that of the original horizontal ones and the vertical stripes appear tinged with the complementary colour to that of the original vertical ones. The phenomenon is an instance of a CONTINGENT AFTEREFFECT.

McGurk effect. The phenomenon that if one phoneme is presented to the ears (e.g. 'ba') and another formed by the lips ('ga'), a sound intermediate along the common phonemic dimension ('da') will be heard. The place of articulation of 'da' (the teeth) is between that of 'ga' (the palate) and 'ba' (the lips).

Mach bands. Illusory bands of light seen under certain conditions. When there is a steady increase in light (a ramp) from a dark plateau to a light plateau, a dark band is seen at the point where the light begins to increase and a light band at the point where

it stops increasing: the phenomenon is caused by lateral inhibition. In the illustration below, D indicates the position of the dark band, and B that of the light band.

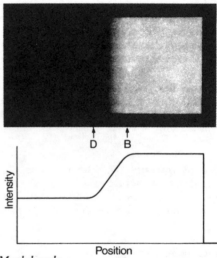

Mach bands

Mach–Dvorak phenomenon. Stereoscopic depth perceived as a result of delaying the presentation of a moving object to one eye as compared to the other. *Compare* PULFRICH PENDULUM.

Machiavellian scale. A scale that measures how far people condone deviousness and the manipulation of others.

machine code. The basic set of instructions for a computer, which are in binary code and can be directly implemented by the central processor. They are limited in both number and scope. These instructions are used to construct the more complex and versatile instructions of high-level languages, which must be translated back into machine code when a higher-level program is run.

machine intelligence. ARTIFICIAL INTELLIGENCE, with the emphasis on writing programs that show intelligent behaviour either for its own sake or for possible applications, rather than in an attempt to simulate the human mind.

machine language. A synonym for MACHINE CODE.

Mach scale. A synonym for MACHIAVELLIAN SCALE.

McNemar's test. (Statistics) A non–parametric test for the significance of the difference between two proportions in matched samples, usually used when the same set of subjects are tested at two different times. *Compare* COCHRAN Q TEST.

macro, macro operator. (Computing) A procedure or operator built from a sequence of other procedures or operators.

macrocephaly. A congenital disorder in which the head is swollen through excess cerebrospinal fluid and the person is mentally retarded.

macrocolumn. A synonym for HYPERCOLUMN.

macromania. A synonym for MEGALOMANIA.

macropsia. Seeing things as too large; it can be caused by retinal disease, by conversion hysteria, or by epilepsy.

macrosomatognosia. The perception of one's body or parts of it as abnormally large.

macula. Any of the surfaces in the VESTIBULAR SACS and SEMICIRCULAR CANALS from which the hair cells originate and to which the vestibular nerve is connected.

macula lutea. A region in the middle of the primate retina that includes the fovea centralis and is about 12° in diameter; it is defined by the presence of a yellow pigment through which light must pass to reach the receptors. The purpose of the pigment is probably to absorb blue light so that the rods in the area are not saturated in photopic vision. The area is rich in cones.

MAD. An abbreviation for MONOAMINE OXIDASE.

Maddox rod. A device for testing HETEROPHORIA.

MAE. An abbreviation for MOTION AFTEREFFECT.

MAF. An abbreviation for MINIMAL AUDIBLE FIELD.

magazine. A device for delivering reward automatically, e.g. food pellets in an animal learning experiment.

magenta. An EXTRASPECTRAL HUE produced by a mixture of high and low wavelengths; it is a purplish red in appearance.

magical number seven. George Miller's term for the phenomenon that performance in many tasks seems to be limited by man's incapacity to deal with more than about seven CHUNKS at once. E.g. only about seven items can be held in immediate memory, and only about seven categories can be successfully discriminated by absolute judgements along some sensory dimensions.

magical thinking. Thinking based on the belief that thought on its own can influence the world.

magic helper. Fromm's term for a person on whom someone else places too much reliance in the belief that he can solve all his problems.

magna mater. The primordial mother figure, one of Jung's archetypes.

magnetic apraxia. A form of apraxia in which the patient perseverates a gesture, e.g. by lifting a glass to his mouth and holding it there for several minutes without tilting it.

magnetic resonance imaging. A non-intrusive technique for localizing brain lesions and tumours, in which the brain is placed in a strong magnetic field for about 15 minutes. The resulting changes in the magnetic orientation of atomic nuclei are measured, particularly those of hydrogen which is abundant in normal tissue. The resolution is very fine – about 0.1 mm.

magnetotropism. The tendency for an animal to orientate itself in relation to magnetic fields.

magnification. (Psychotherapy) Exaggerating how catastrophic or unbearable an event is, a term used of depressives by cognitive therapists.

magnitude estimation. A psychophysical scaling method in which the apparent size of stimuli along a dimension is determined by having subjects give numerical values to the stimuli. It can produce a ratio scale.

magnitude estimation, method of. A psychophysical scaling method in which an arbitrary number is assigned to a comparison stimulus and subjects have to assign numbers to other stimuli in accordance with how much each appears proportionately to differ from the comparison, thus producing a ratio scale.

magnocellular layers. The two ventral layers of the lateral geniculate. They contain M cells. *Contrast* PARVOCELLULAR LAYERS.

magnocellular system (M system). A visual pathway containing large ganglion cells (**magnocellular cells**) in the retina and in the two ventral layers of the lateral geniculate. It has large fast conducting axons. *See also* Y CELLS, which are almost certainly identical to magnocellular cells.

maieusiophobia. A morbid fear of childbirth.

main clause. *See* CLAUSE.

main effect. In analysis of variance, the variance due to any one of the independent variables as opposed to the INTERACTION VARIANCE.

main score. In Rorschach tests, the score based on the subject's initial response, disregarding his subsequent free associations.

maintaining cause. Anything in someone's environment that tends to perpetuate a habit (usually a bad one).

maintaining stimulus. (Ethology) Any stimulus that elicits a particular behaviour pattern so long as it is present.

maintenance level. The level of growth at which further physical development ceases.

maintenance rehearsal. Keeping an item in short-term memory merely by regenerating it over and over again, a procedure that in itself probably does not increase the strength of the item in long-term memory. *Contrast* ELABORATIVE REHEARSAL.

major affective disorder. A severe disorder of mood, e.g. unipolar manic-depressive disorder.

major depressive disorder (MDD). Severe depression, as established by having the symptoms listed for it in the RESEARCH DIAGNOSTIC CRITERIA.

major depressive episode. (DSM-III) An affective disorder in which the patient has been depressed for at least two weeks and has experienced each day several of a list of symptoms, including insomnia, agitation, and feelings of guilt or worthlessness.

major hemisphere. A synonym for left hemisphere, or for the hemisphere in which language functions are mainly located.

majority influence. Attitudes or behaviour conforming to and caused by the opinions of the majority of one's group. *Contrast* MINORITY INFLUENCE.

major premise. *See* SYLLOGISM.

major solution. Horney's term for the repression of aspects of the self that conflict with the idealized self.

major term. *See* SYLLOGISM.

major tranquillizers. Drugs (e.g. the PHENOTHIAZINES) that calm agitated or psychotic patients but do not make them drowsy. In practice, these drugs may reduce many other symptoms of schizophrenia and the expression is somewhat misleading.

make-a-picture-story test (MAPS test). A projective test in which the subject arranges cardboard figures and makes up a story about them.

maladaptive. 1. (Psychology) Pertaining to behaviour or traits that are not in someone's best interests. 2. (Evolution) Pertaining to any inherited characteristic that reduces the chance of the individual's genes surviving.

maladjustment. Failure to cope with internal or external pressures.

malignant neurosis. A neurosis that becomes progressively worse until the patient is incapacitated.

malingering. Deliberately feigning illness to achieve some other purpose.

malleus. A small hammer-shaped bone in the middle ear, one of the OSSICLES. It is set in motion by the eardrum and transmits sound vibrations to the INCUS.

mammary gland. The gland in the female breast that secretes milk.

mammillary bodies. Two protrusions at the bottom of the posterior hypothalamus – the medial and lateral mammillary nuclei. They are implicated in emotion and the sexual drive.

mammillothalamic tract. A projection from the mammillary body to the anterior nucleus of the thalamus that forms part of PAPEZ CIRCUIT.

management of objective. The systematic development of a programme within an organization to improve efficiency; the programme may include the setting of targets, incentive schemes, etc.

managerial psychology. The study of relations within management, and between management and workers, undertaken with a view to increasing efficiency.

mand. Skinner's term for a speech utterance intended to make the listener do something the speaker wants him to do.

mandala. A Hindu or Buddhist symbol (usually circular) for the cosmos that is used in meditation. Jung thought of it as an archetypal symbol for man's striving to unify his inner conflicting forces.

mandibular nerve. *See* TRIGEMINAL NERVE.

mania. Pathological over-excitement, often involving extreme agitation, excessive optimism, restlessness, flights of idea, and incoherent speech; it can occur in the manic phase of bipolar manic-depressive disorder.

maniaphobia. A synonym for LYSSOPHOBIA.

manic-depressive disorder. A severe affective disorder in which the patient has episodes of depression or mania (or hypomania). It is called **unipolar manic-depressive disorder** if it is marked by episodes of either depression or mania but not both, and **bipolar manic-depressive disorder** if the patient oscillates between these two extremes of mood.

manic-depressive psychosis. A severe MANIC-DEPRESSIVE DISORDER.

manifest anxiety. (Psychoanalysis) The surface signs of anxiety, taken to indicate an unconscious conflict.

Manifest Anxiety Scale (MAS). A scale to measure the anxiety to which the testee admits: he is presented with a set of anxiety symptoms and selects those that apply to him.

manifest content. The elements of a dream that are consciously experienced in the dream. *Contrast* LATENT CONTENT.

manifest goals. In evaluation research, the declared objectives of an institution or programme.

manikin test. A performance test in which the subject has to assemble the parts of a wooden model of a person.

manipulandum. Any object (e.g. a bar or panel) that an organism is trained to manipulate in order to obtain reinforcement.

man–machine interface. The points at which information or energy is transferred in either direction between a man and a machine; research is undertaken to improve the man–machine interface by e.g. improving the training of the operator, or improving the machine to make it more compatible with the human operator.

Mann–Whitney U Test. A non–parametric test of whether two independent samples come from the same population. It is equivalent to Wilcoxon's test. The test compares each value in one sample with each value in the other but does not require ranking, as in Wilcoxon's algorithm. It is a non–parametric version of a t-test for independent samples. *Compare* KRUSKAL–WALLACE TEST.

manoptoscope. A device for measuring eye dominance.

mantra. A repeated word or expression used in transcendental meditation to assist concentration and relaxation.

manual method. Teaching the deaf to communicate by a sign language rather than by lip reading.

MAO. An abbreviation for MONOAMINE OXIDASE.

MAOI. An abbreviation for MONOAMINE OXIDASE INHIBITOR.

MAP. An abbreviation for MINIMAL AUDIBLE PRESSURE.

map. *See* COGNITIVE MAP and TOPOLOGICAL MAP.

mapping. A correspondence between two sets of elements. Where each element in one set corresponds to a single element in the other, it is a **one-to-one mapping**. There are numerous examples of mapping in the brain, e.g. the retinal image is mapped onto the VISUAL CORTEX. *See also* e.g. HOMUNCULUS (2).

MAPS test. An abbreviation for MAKE-A-PICTURE-STORY TEST.

marathon group. An encounter group extended for many hours or even days.

Marbe's law. The generalization that in word association tests the more frequently a response is made the lower will be its latency.

Marchi stain. A histological stain that makes myelinated nerve fibres visible.

marginal consciousness. The part of consciousness of which a person is only dimly aware since he is not attending to it.

marginal intelligence. A synonym for BORDERLINE INTELLIGENCE.

marginal utility. Any additional payoff in a system, created by a change to that system, and taking into account both the benefits and the costs associated with the change.

margin of attention, margin of consciousness. Synonyms for MARGINAL CONSCIOUSNESS.

marijuana, marihuana. A narcotic prepared from hemp. It has mildly hallucinogenic effects.

marital skew. A marital condition in which the subordinate partner accepts the pathological behaviour of the dominant one.

marital therapy. Psychotherapy intended to help a couple resolve their problems, sometimes by separating. Typically two therapists are involved, each starting by seeing one member of the couple on his or her own; in later sessions all four meet together.

markedness. (Linguistics) The phenomenon that where there is a pair of opposing words, one member is often marked by a linguistic feature, while the other is not. E.g. most plurals are marked with the suffix '-s' or '-es', while singulars are not marked; 'unhappy' is marked, while 'happy' is not. Markedness may also occur without there being any differentiating linguistic features; the unmarked word can appear in more contexts than the marked, e.g. it is more natural to ask how high (unmarked) something is than how low (marked) it is.

marker. (Linguistics) Any element of the speech sound that signifies the presence or absence of a linguistic feature. E.g. '-s' (plural), '-ed' (past), or voicing (marking the difference between a voiced and unvoiced consonant). *See also* SEMANTIC MARKER.

market research. The study of marketing and purchasing behaviour, usually undertaken in order to increase the sales of a given product. *See also* CONSUMER PSYCHOLOGY.

Markov chain. A stochastic model in which it is postulated that a system passes from an initial state through a series of discrete states, with alternative states at each step; the probabilities of selecting the alternatives from a given state depend solely on the transitional probabilities from that state to others, and not on any aspect of the path by which that state was reached. Markov chains have been used in theories of learning and decision processes. *See also* STATISTICAL LEARNING THEORY and STOCHASTIC PROCESS.

Markov process. The continuous version of a MARKOV CHAIN, in which states change continually rather than in discrete steps.

marriage counselling, marriage guidance, marriage therapy. Synonyms for MARITAL THERAPY.

Martinotti cells. Spindle-shaped cells with cell bodies in the internal granular layer of the cortex, and with axons extending to the cell bodies of the outer pyramidal layer. *See* CORTICAL LAYERS.

masculine protest. Adler's expression for the refusal to be submissive, and the attempt to dominate, which he believed stemmed from a neurotic compensation for inferiority feelings; it can occur in both men and women.

mask. A function computed over a set of values. For example, in vision, the connections to a single unit from its receptive field act as a mask. *See* CONVOLUTION (1) and MASKING.

masked audiogram. A graph of the amount of masking (in dB) produced by a given mask as a function of the frequency of the sound being masked.

masked epilepsy. A mild form of epilepsy with no convulsions, but with some disturbance of consciousness, such as an aura or fugue state.

masking. (Perception) The abolition or weakening of one sensation by another. *See* AUDITORY MASKING and VISUAL MASKING.

masking level difference (MLD). *See* BINAURAL MASKING LEVEL DIFFERENCE.

masking stimulus. Any stimulus that causes MASKING.

masochism. *See* ALGOLAGNIA.

mass action. Lashley's term for the hypothesis that behaviour depends on a general pattern of activity, set up in the brain or in a particular part of the brain, rather than on the state of individual neurons. Lashley pilfered the term from physics, but its scientific ring cannot conceal the vagueness of the concept.

massa intermedia. A bridge of tissue running across the third ventricle between the left and right halves of the thalamus.

mass behaviour, mass contagion. The tendency of a mass of people or of a whole society to act in the same kind of way at a given time, e.g. by adopting similar customs, moral principles, etc., or simply, in a crowd, by all running in the same direction.

massed practice. Learning in which the material to be learned is given in rapid succession. *Contrast* DISTRIBUTED PRACTICE.

massed trials. A series of trials between each of which there is only a brief interval. *Contrast* DISTRIBUTED TRIALS.

mass hysteria. Irrational, foolish, and excited behaviour occurring in a group of people, with the ingredients of the behaviour being communicated from one person to another.

Masson disc. A white (or black) rotatory disc bearing a radial band of the opposite brightness. It was used to measure the brightness difference threshold by varying the width of the band.

mass reflex. A reflex involving many different muscle groups, e.g. the STARTLE REFLEX.

mass spring model. The hypothesis that in a movement of part of the body a force is applied to antagonistic muscles that will bring the opposing muscles into equilibrium when the target of the movement is reached.

mass to specific development. The change from the gross movement of many muscles to the specific movement of particular muscle groups that occurs in development.

mastery orientated. Pertaining to people who see their failures as caused by lack of effort rather than lack of ability. *Contrast* HELP-LESSNESS (1).

mastery training. A synonym for ASSERTION THERAPY.

masticatory nerve. A synonym for MANDIBULAR NERVE.

mastigophobia. A morbid fear of flogging.

masturbatory orgasmic inadequacy. A disorder that in the topsy-turvy world of sex therapy, as practised by Masters and Johnson, afflicts women 'who regularly obtain orgasms through coitus but not through masturbation'.

matched dependent behaviour. A cumbersome synonym for 'imitation'.

matched groups. Groups assigned to different experimental conditions but not differing in other ways (e.g. in IQ or age) that might be relevant to the outcome of the experiment. The expression is sometimes used of the MATCHED PAIRS METHOD, which is a special case.

matched pairs method. Obtaining two MATCHED GROUPS by matching each member of one group against a member of the other group by reference to qualities other than those under investigation.

matched sample. 1. (Statistics) A sample chosen in such a way that each member of it is the same on some characteristic or characteristics (other than those being investigated) as a member of another sample to be compared with it. E.g. the same subjects may each be run under two conditions. In this case a PAIRED COMPARISON TEST can be run on the differences in the effects of the two conditions. *Contrast* INDEPENDENT SAMPLES. 2. (General) A sample chosen in such a way that its members are on average the same on some category as those of another sample (but are not necessarily matched pair by pair) This usage is confusing and not recommended.

matching. *See* PROBABILITY MATCHING.

matching law. The hypothesis that organisms exhibit PROBABILITY MATCHING; they rarely do.

matching test. A test based on MATCHING TO SAMPLE.

matching to sample. A task in which the organism has to learn that on each trial it is to pick the stimulus that is the same as a sample stimulus. The sample stimulus may be presented with the choice stimuli, or it may be presented some time before them (**delayed matching to sample**). In **generalized matching to sample** the organism must learn to pick the stimulus that matches the sample even when completely new stimuli are presented. A series of problems, each involving new stimuli are given, and initially each problem may take many trials to learn. The question is whether later problems will be learned more quickly as a result of SERIAL LEARNING .

material implication. *See* IMPLICATION.

materialism. (Philosophy) The doctrine that only matter exists or in some versions that mind is merely an epiphenomenon, completely dependent on matter. *Contrast* IDEALISM.

materialization. (Parapsychology) The alleged production of a body by psychic means.

maternal aggression. Aggression by a mother towards an organism that threatens her young.

maternal deprivation. Lack of adequate care and fostering from the mother or from another person substituting for the mother; it is thought by some to predispose towards mental illness and other problems.

maternal drive, maternal instinct. The mother's instinct to feed and care for her young.

mathematical learning theory. Any theory that describes the learning process in mathematical terms. Such theories have been applied mainly to animal learning and treat learning as a Markov process in which the state changes probabilistically from one trial to the next. *See also* STATISTICAL LEARNING THEORY AND STIMULUS-SAMPLING THEORY.

mathematical psychology. The application of mathematics in the explanation of psychological phenomena (e.g. SIGNAL DETECTION THEORY, STATISTICAL LEARNING THEORY, etc.).

mathematico-deductive method. The formulation of a theory in terms of rigorous equations from which testable predictions can be drawn. Hull was an exponent of this sort of theory; he created many equations, but little rigour.

matriarchy. A society in which power is predominantly exercised by women. No such society is known to have existed. Distinguish MATRILINEAL SOCIETY.

matrilineal society. A society in which inheritance and descent pass down the female line; few if any matrilineal societies are MATRIARCHIES.

matt. Pertaining to a surface that reflects light approximately equally in all directions. *Contrast* GLOSSY.

maturation. The development of an organism into an adult, whether effected by genetic or environmental factors; the term is used of mental and emotional development as well as physical. It is sometimes misleadingly used to exclude environmental factors, and to mean innate development; *see* MATURATION THEORY.

maturation crisis. A crisis caused by a person having difficulty adjusting to the transition from one stage of his life to another (e.g. on first going to school or on first having to deal with the sex drive).

maturation theory. The hypothesis that many innate behaviour patterns appear only when the organism has reached the right stage of physical maturity.

maturity. *See* IMMATURITY, which is more interesting.

Maudsley Personality Inventory. A questionnaire developed by Eysenck, which is intended to measure position on two scales (neuroticism and introversion–extraversion); it has been replaced by the EYSENCK PERSONALITY QUESTIONNAIRE.

maxillary nerve. *See* TRIGEMINAL NERVE.

maximal age. In a test, the standardized age at which children pass the items immediately below those that are all failed by an individual testee. Since the testee cannot pass any items standardized for higher ages, this represents his highest possible age score.

maximizing. 1. (Game theory) Any strategy that maximizes the expected payoff, computed by subtracting possible costs from possible gains, and weighting each by their probability of occurrence. The term is used in the same way in evolutionary theory in which organisms are said to maximize their inclusive fitness. 2. Where two or more alternatives yield unequal probabilities of reward, always picking the alternative with the highest probability of reward. *Contrast* PROBABILITY MATCHING.

maxims of manner, quality, quantity and relation. *See* CONVERSATIONAL MAXIMS.

maximum amplitude. A synonym for PEAK AMPLITUDE.

maximum likelihood principle. (Statistics) The principle that we should estimate the value of a population parameter as the value which maximizes the LIKELIHOOD of the obtained data.

Maxwell disc. A synonym for COLOUR WHEEL.

Maxwell spot. The perception, when viewing a homogeneous purple-blue field, of a dark or grey area in the shape of an ellipse of about 1–2° of visual angle in the centre of the field. The effect is probably caused by an increase in the density of macula pigment in the centre of the fovea. It is possible to use this phenomenon to estimate the degree of eccentric fixation by asking the subject to state whereabouts the fixation point appears in relation to the grey area.

Maxwellian view. The technique of using lenses to ensure that all light reaching the eye passes through a small area in the centre of the pupil; the amount of light reaching the retina can then be controlled regardless of variations in pupil size, and diffraction caused by the edges of the pupil is eliminated.

maze bright rats, maze dull rats. Strains of rats bred to be very good or very bad at learning to run a maze.

MBD. An abbreviation for MINIMAL BRAIN DYSFUNCTION.

M cell. An abbreviation for magnocellular cell. *See* MAGNOCELLULAR SYSTEM.

MD. An abbreviation for MUSCULAR DYSTROPHY.

MDD. An abbreviation for MAJOR DEPRESSIVE DISORDER – confusing since it could, but does not, stand for MINOR DEPRESSIVE DISORDER.

MDMA. A hallucinogenic drug related to amphetamine, commonly known as ECSTASY.

MDS. An abbreviation for MULTIDIMENSIONAL SCALING.

ME. An abbreviation for MYELINCEPHALIC ENCEPHALITIS.

mean. A term that is short for ARITHMETIC MEAN when used on its own; *see also* GEOMETRIC MEAN.

mean deviation. (Statistics) The arithmetic mean of the absolute deviations from the mean.

mean gradation method. A synonym for EQUAL-APPEARING INTERVALS, METHOD OF.

means–ends analysis. (AI) Analysing the nature of the difference between a starting state and a goal, and finding operators to reduce this distance; if in order to apply the operator a subgoal has to be achieved, the procedure is applied recursively. The GENERAL PROBLEM SOLVER depends on means–ends analysis.

means–ends readiness. Tolman's term for animals' ability to find the means to reach a goal by acquiring expectancies about the outcome of different actions in the situation they are in.

mean square. (Statistics) The arithmetic mean of the squared deviations from the mean, i.e. the VARIANCE.

meatus. A passage or canal in the body, such as the EXTERNAL AUDITORY MEATUS.

mechanism. 1. The structure of a machine (or part of a machine) in virtue of which it works. The term is often used to describe a well-specified theoretical model that might account for a given psychological function. It is also used to give cachet to other psychological theories that are vague or incoherent. 2. The philosophical doctrine that all phenomena can be explained mechanically, e.g. in terms of collisions between pieces of matter, the behaviour of levers, etc.

mechanistic theory. A theory that attempts to explain a psychological function in material terms (e.g. in terms of the nervous system, or by models based on computer simulation) and which does not introduce mental concepts.

mechanophobia. A morbid fear of machines.

mechanoreceptor. A receptor sensitive to a mechanical force, e.g. pressure receptors, hair cells, muscle receptors.

MED-50. The minimum dose of a drug that is effective in 50 per cent of cases.

Medea complex. (Psychoanalysis) A mother's wish to kill her children in order to spite their father.

medial. (Anatomy) Toward the mid-line of the body or of an organ. *Contrast* LATERAL.

medial dorsal nucleus. A synonym for DORSOMEDIAL NUCLEUS.

medial forebrain bundle (MFB). A tract of axons passing through the lateral hypothalamus and running in both directions between the forebrain and brainstem. It has many connections with the limbic system and self-stimulation can readily be obtained from it.

medial frontal gyrus. *See* Appendix 2.

medial geniculate nucleus. A nucleus in the thalamus relaying auditory information received from the inferior colliculus to the cortex.

medial hypothalamic area. A region of the hypothalamus, stimulation of which tends to arouse the PARASYMPATHETIC SYSTEM.

medial lemniscus. A nerve tract which is part of the lemniscus and which conveys somaesthetic information from the medulla to the thalamus.

medial plane. The vertical plane that divides the body into two symmetrical halves.

medial rectus. An EXTRAOCULAR MUSCLE that pulls the eye inward towards the nose.

median. 1. (Statistics) A measure of the central tendency of a set of values, obtained by picking the middle value, i.e. that above and below which the same number of values fall. 2. (Anatomy) Straddling the mid-line.

median eminence. A swelling at the base of the hypothalamus that releases hormones into the portal circulation of the anterior pituitary.

median test. (Statistics) A non–parametric test for the significance of the difference between two or more samples. The median for all samples combined is calculated; in each sample the number of values above and below the combined median is found and the results are evaluated by a CHI SQUARE TEST.

mediate association. An indirect association between two ideas produced by their both being associatively linked to another idea, or by each being linked to opposite ends of a chain of ideas.

mediated generalization. Stimulus generalization not brought about through perception, but mediated by some other process such as SEMANTIC GENERALIZATION. *Contrast* PRIMARY STIMULUS GENERALIZATION.

mediation theory. The hypothesis that internal responses (or fractional ones, *see* FRACTIONAL ANTEDATING GOAL RESPONSE) can be conditioned to stimuli and can themselves control (mediate) overt responding. The idea was current in the 1930s and 1940s in a forlorn attempt to save behaviourism and stimulus response theory. *Compare* SEMANTIC GENERALIZATION.

medical model. As applied to mental illness, the hypothesis that it is caused by physical factors, with the corollary that physical methods of treatment should be used, and that it is right to look for symptoms and to make diagnoses and prognoses.

medical psychology. The psychological study of the interaction between doctors and patients, and of patients' psychological reactions to illness.

meditation. A state of prolonged and tranquil cognition advocated by some psychotherapists and by adherents of Eastern religions. It is a possible alternative to PROGRESSIVE RELAXATION.

medium. (Parapsychology) A person purporting to convey messages from the dead.

medium pyramidal layer. A synonym for EXTERNAL PYRAMIDAL LAYER.

medium-wavelength cone. *See* CONE.

medulla. 1. The inner part of an organ. 2. A synonym for MEDULLA OBLONGATA.

medulla oblongata. The lower of the two divisions of the hindbrain; it is immediately above the spinal cord and below the pons. It contains many nerve tracts, and also the autonomic nuclei implicated in the control of breathing, heartbeat, etc. *See* MYELENCEPHALON.

medullary layer. The innermost of the three layers of the cerebellar cortex.

medullary sheath. A rare synonym for MYELIN.

megalomania. Extreme overestimation of one's own importance and worth, endemic in politicians.

megalophobia, megalopsia. A morbid fear of anything large.

meiosis. A special type of cell division in which GAMETES (ova or sperm cells) are formed each having only half the chromosomes (one from each pair) of the parent cell. When the gametes combine, the new cell has the normal number of chromosomes. *Contrast* MITOSIS.

Meissner's corpuscle. A skin receptor thought to be sensitive to pressure.

mel. A unit in a ratio scale of pitch; one mel is a tone of 1,000 Hz at a loudness level of one sone.

melancholic. *See* HUMOUR (2).

melanocyte. A pigmented cell in the skin, containing melanin.

melanocyte-stimulating hormone (MSH). A peptide hormone produced by the intermediate lobe of the pituitary that increases production of melanin.

melatonin. A substance found in the pineal gland that is implicated in circadian rhythms.

mellow. (Linguistics) Pertaining to a speech sound produced by a simple stricture of the vocal tract, and having relatively low frequency and intensity. *Contrast* STRIDENT.

membership group. A group to which a person belongs.

membrane. *See* CELL MEMBRANE.

membrane channels. *See* ION CHANNELS.

membrane potential. The voltage difference between the inside and outside of a cell membrane, particularly of a nerve membrane. *See* RESTING POTENTIAL.

membranous labyrinth. *See* LABYRINTH.

memory. The store of information acquired by an organism through experience; also used metaphorically of a computer store.

memory afterimage. An obsolete synonym for SENSORY INFORMATION STORE or for EIDETIC IMAGE.

memory buffer. Any system that holds incoming material for a short time while it is processed or while it is being added to a longer-term store; two examples are the ARTICULATORY LOOP and SHORT-TERM MEMORY.

memory colour. The remembered colour of an object, particularly when the memory changes the appearance of a perceived object, e.g. a leaf-like shape that is really grey may be seen as greener than it is.

memory drum. A rotating drum carrying a list of items, usually words, to be remembered; it presents the items one at a time for a constant duration and with a constant interval between them.

memory falsification. A synonym for CONFABULATION.

memory-operating characteristic curve. A RECEIVER-OPERATING CHARACTERISTIC CURVE obtained from data in recognition experiments. Items correctly recognized are counted as hits, and items incorrectly thought to have been perceived before as false alarms. *See* SIGNAL DETECTION THEORY.

memory reconstruction. The process by which in recall fragmented items in memory are put together to reconstruct (often with errors) the material originally learned.

memory scanning task. A task in which the subject has to remember several digits and is then shown a probe digit. He has to respond positively if it is one of the digits remembered, negatively if it is not. Reaction time increases with the number of digits to be remembered.

memory span. The number of items (e.g. letters or words) that a person can recall in correct order immediately after one presentation of the list.

memory trace. Any physical change in the state of the brain that underlies the preservation of a memory.

memory transfer. The alleged but much disputed transfer of a learned response from one organism to another as a result of transferring homogenized brain tissue from the first to the second organism.

menarche. A girl's first menstrual period.

Mendelism. The principles of genetics put forward by Mendel, who postulated the existence of genes, both dominant and recessive, and the rules governing their transmission. *See also* next three entries.

Mendel's first law. The principle that two alleles carried by an individual separate in the gametes without interaction, and are propagated independently through further generations (law of independent segregation).

Mendel's second law. The principle that there is no correlation between the distribution in the gametes of one pair of alleles and another; thus if there are two pairs of alleles, Aa, and Bb, in the first generation A is as likely to be paired with B as with b (independent assortment, law of). The principle is correct for genes on separate chromosomes but not for genes on the same chromosome (*see* LINKAGE).

Mendel's third law. Some alleles are DOMINANT over others.

meninges. The three layers of protective tissue that enclose the brain and spinal cord, which are, from outside to inside, the DURA MATER, ARACHNOID LAYER, and PIA MATER.

menotaxis. (Ethology) A TAXIS in which the animal's orientation or pathway is at an oblique angle to the controlling stimulus rather than towards or away from it; e.g. the path taken by an ant towards its nest, which is guided by the position of the sun.

menstrual age. The age of the fetus, starting from the beginning of the mother's last menstruation.

menstrual cycle. A cycle occurring in women and containing the following stages. (i) The growth of the OVARIAN FOLLICLE, stimulated by follicle-stimulating hormone. (ii) The rupturing of the follicle to release the ovum, caused by luteinizing hormone secreted by the pituitary under the influence of oestrogens produced by the follicle. (iii) The growth of a lining in the uterus to receive the embryo, caused by progesterone released by the corpus luteum, a body that develops from the follicle. (iv) If the ovum is not implanted, the lining of the uterus is sloughed off (menstruation).

menstruation. *See* MENSTRUAL CYCLE.

mental age (MA). A measure of a child's mental ability derived from tests: the child's score is expressed as the average age at which children on average perform as well as he does.

mental ataxia. A dissociation between a person's emotions and his thoughts or his situation, e.g. laughing when the death of a close friend is announced. The condition is common in schizophrenia.

mental chronometrics. The measurement of the time taken to carry out a specified (often unconscious) mental process. *See also* SUBTRACTION METHOD.

mental construct. A concept.

mental contagion. A synonym for CONTAGION.

mental deficiency. The condition of having a low IQ (below 80). The following breakdown of IQ is sometimes used: 70–79, borderline deficiency; 50–69, moron; 20–49, imbecile; below 20, idiot. The expression MENTAL RETARDATION is now more commonly used.

mental discipline. *See* FORMAL DISCIPLINE.

mental disorder. The fashionable term for mental illness; it leaves open the question how far 'illness' is involved.

mental element. Any mental entity that cannot be divided into parts; e.g. Locke thought sensation was made up of such indivisible elements.

mentalese. The hypothetical set of non-linguistic propositions in which concepts are represented in the mind: to understand a sentence, one must translate it into mentalese.

mental handicap. A deficiency in intelligence sufficient to impair the individual in his functioning.

mental illness. The state of having severely disordered behaviour, thoughts, or feelings, usually taken to exclude cases where the disorder arises from low intelligence or as a result of strokes or other direct brain injury.

mental image. *See* IMAGE (2).

mentalism. The doctrine that the mind cannot be wholly explained in physical terms.

mental level. 1. Degree of mental ability, usually as measured by an intelligence test. 2. In Jung, the three levels of the psyche – consciousness, personal unconscious, and collective unconscious.

mental lexicon. The system in which all the words known to a person are stored. The words there can be accessed in many ways, e.g. by perceiving the word in auditory or written form, by thinking of the object a word represents, by association from other words, etc.

mental measurement. *See* MENTAL TEST.

mental models. A mental representation that has the same structure as whatever is represented. Propositions are therefore not mental models, but imagery is. Understanding speech or text may depend on building such representations. Johnson-Laird has proposed that everyday inference (including deduction) depends on constructing and manipulating such representations. He argues that a given proposition can give rise to many different mental models. If none of these is incompatible with a given conclusion, it can be inferred that the conclusion is true. E.g. from the proposition 'A is to the left of B, B is to the left of C and C is to the left of D', it might be inferred through picturing four men in a row that A is to the left of D. The same conclusion follows logically from the transitivity of the relationship 'left of'. A different mental model representing A, B, C and D as seated round a bridge table leads to a different conclusion: A is to the right of D.

mental retardation. (DSM III) The possession of an IQ below 70, manifesting itself before adulthood; mental retardates cannot function normally and usually need to be cared for; they are divided into mild (IQ 55–69), moderate (IQ 40–54), severe (IQ 25–39), and profound (IQ below 25). *Compare* MENTAL DEFICIENCY.

mental rotation. The rotation of the mental image of an object or shape; if a person has to decide whether a rotated letter R is a genuine R or a mirror image of R, a mental image of it is formed and is rotated to an upright position in order to make the comparison; there is evidence that the image passes through all intermediate positions.

mental set. *See* SET.

mental state. The mental condition of a patient including his appearance, speech, motor coordination, memory, intelligence, and so on.

mental test. Any test purporting to measure one or more mental aptitudes or abilities. *See* QUESTIONNAIRE.

menticide. A rare synonym for BRAINWASHING.

mere exposure effect. The phenomenon that the more frequently an item is exposed to a person, the more attractive it seems (even when he cannot remember it being presented).

merger state. A state in which a person's consciousness feels fused with another person or with an object.

meridian. (Vision) A segment of a great circle on the retina. The vertical meridian is the line bisecting the retina into its left and right halves.

meridional astigmatism. The phenomenon that visual acuity and the difference threshold in tilt judgements is lowest for vertical and horizontal lines; this effect is caused by the nervous system, not the eye's optics.

Merkel cell-neurite complex, Merkel's discs. Synonyms for TACTILE MENISCI.

Merkel's law. The incorrect assumption that equal differences between sensations are produced by equal differences between stimuli. *Compare* WEBER'S LAW.

Merrill–Palmer Scale. An intelligence test for children aged 2–5.

mescaline. A hallucinatory drug derived from the cactus plant, peyote.

mesencephalon. A synonym for MIDBRAIN. *See also* BRAIN.

Mesmerism. An obsolete synonym for HYPNOTISM.

mesocephalic. Having a medium ratio of head breadth to length. *See* CEPHALIC INDEX.

mesoderm. The middle of the three layers of the embryo, which develops into bone and muscle, and some internal organs.

mesokurtic. Of a statistical distribution that has a moderately sharp peak, as e.g. the normal distribution.

mesomorphy. A body type (stocky, muscular) in SHELDON'S CONSTITUTIONAL THEORY. It is said to be derived from the embryonic mesoderm and to be associated with SOMATOTONIA.

mesopic vision. Vision in a light intensity that lies on the border between SCOTOPIC VISION and PHOTOPIC VISION, at which point rods and cones are contributing about equally.

mesosomatic. On Eysenck's categorization, having a body build that is approximately average.

message. (Information theory) Information passed from a transmitter to a receiver.

messenger RNA. *See* RIBONUCLEIC ACID.

meta-analysis. A method of quantifying the results of a large number of studies in a given topic by calculating the effects of the independent variable in terms of the standard deviation of a control group. In assessing the effects of treatment on psychiatric disorder, it is possible through this technique to examine the overall effects of a large number of variables such as type of therapy, length of training of the therapist, number of hours spent on therapy, etc.

metabolism. The chemical processes occurring in the body, particularly those having to do with the storage and release of energy. *Compare* ANABOLISM and CATABOLISM.

metacognition. A person's knowledge about his own cognitive processes, e.g. knowing that his memory for an experience will tend to decay with time or knowing that he is bad at mathematics.

metacommunication. 1. Non-linguistic cues used to modify oral utterances, e.g. smiling or frowning. 2. (Ethology) A communication that modifies the meaning of other communications. E.g. a baboon may take a large bite out of another baboon, and then grin to show that the bite should not be taken seriously.

metacontrast. A form of backward VISUAL MASKING in which the masking figure is presented after the one that is masked, with its contours surrounding or flanking those of the masked figure. Both figures are presented only briefly. The masking figure reduces or eliminates the visibility of the masked figure. *Compare* PARACONTRAST.

metaevaluation. In evaluation research, the assessment of the evaluation processes themselves.

metakinesis. The rudimentary conscious processes that some think occur in lower organisms.

metalanguage. Any language used to make statements about another language (including formal languages like logical systems). In the proposition '"Black" is an adjective', English is both the metalanguage and the **object language** since a statement in English is being made about the English word 'black'. When object language and metalanguage are the same, paradoxes (e.g. the LIAR PARADOX) may arise.

metalinguistics. The study of the way in which language is related to other aspects of behaviour within a culture, what it is used for, etc.

metallophobia. A morbid fear of metal.

metamemory. Knowledge of the processes of memory, e.g. of mnemonics or knowing that one is likely to forget something and should therefore write it in one's diary.

metameric matching. The adjustment of a comparison stimulus until it appears exactly like a standard stimulus when the physical composition of the two stimuli is different; the expression is applied particularly to matching a colour made up of any combination of wavelengths by adjusting the proportions of three monochromatic wavelengths (*see* PRIMARY (1)), forming a second coloured patch.

metamorphopsia. A visual disorder in which the apparent shapes or sizes of objects are distorted; it can occur in migraine, epilepsy, or after certain brain lesions.

metamotivation. Maslow's term for the motive whose fulfillment is self-actualization.

metaneeds. Maslow's term for high-level needs connected with self-actualization. Eating is not a high-level need, but the pursuit of knowledge, artistic endeavour, etc. are. Maslow is the judge of what constitutes a metaneed.

metaphor. The use of a word or phrase in a non-literal analogical way to imply that an object, property, or action has some quality suggested by the word or phrase: e.g. 'Jones is a rat' means not that Jones is literally a rat but that he has rat-like qualities. In metaphor, the analogy is not explicitly marked as such, while in SIMILE it is.

metaphysics. The philosophical study of first principles (e.g. the basis of induction) or of those aspects of reality that are not captured by empirical observation (e.g. the purpose of the universe – if any).

metapsychiatry. The psychiatric study of unusual mental phenomena, like mystical experiences or psychic happenings.

metapsychology. 1. Freud's term for the investigation of unconscious processes. 2. (Psychology) The study of the principles governing the practice of psychology, its theories, and its techniques.

metathesis. The transposition of sounds within a word or series of words, e.g. 'metesathis' for 'metathesis'.

metathetic continuum. A continuum of sensation that changes qualitatively with changes in a physical dimension of the stimulus; e.g.

hue changes qualitatively with changes in wavelength. *Compare* PROTHETIC CONTINUUM.

metazoa. All animals having more than one cell.

metempirical. Incapable of empirical investigation (of ideas, propositions, etc.).

metempsychosis. Reincarnation.

metencephalon. The more rostral (upper) of the two divisions of the HINDBRAIN, lying above the MEDULLA and below the DIENCEPHALON. It contains the PONS and the CEREBELLUM. *See* Appendix 5. *See also* BRAIN.

met-enkephalin. *See* ENKEPHALIN.

methadone. A synthetic narcotic, used as a pain killer and also as a substitute for heroin in an attempt to wean heroin addicts from their addiction.

methodological behaviourism. The adoption of a behaviouristic approach because it is the best way to proceed (i.e. because others' thoughts are not observable), but without commitment to the status or existence of mental events.

methodological individualism. (Social psychology) The doctrine that explanations of all psychological phenomena, including the behaviour of groups, are only valid if they are couched in terms of processes within the individual.

methodological solipsism. (Philosophy) The doctrine that the study of mental states and processes should disregard the environment, and that the formal operations undertaken by the mind should be investigated without being interpreted, just as one might study the formal properties of a computer program without reference to the task for which it is used. *Compare* NATURALISTIC INDIVIDUALISM.

methodology. (Psychology) The study of how best to acquire systematic knowledge (e.g. by good experimental design). It is often the resort of psychologists who don't know what to find out.

methoxyhydroxyphenylglycol (MHPG). A metabolite of epinephrine; there is some evidence that its level in urine is low in some kinds of depression and high in mania, suggesting that adrenergic activity is low in depression and high in mania.

methylphenidate. A drug which, like amphetamine, arouses the sympathetic system; it has been widely used to treat children with MINIMAL BRAIN DYSFUNCTION.

metonymy. 1. The substitution of the attribute of a thing for the thing that is meant (e.g. the use of 'crown' to mean 'king'). 2. The use of words that are wrong but are related to what the speaker intends to say (e.g. 'knife' for 'spoon'); it can occur in schizophrenia and in some forms of aphasia.

metrazol. A drug that induces convulsions and coma, once used in SHOCK TREATMENT for the mentally ill.

metre candle. An obsolete measure of luminance, approximately equal to one candela per square metre.

metronoscope. A device for presenting printed text at a constant rate.

Mexican hat. A synonym for DIFFERENCE OF GAUSSIANS, derived from the appearance of the graphic representation of the distribution of excitation and inhibition in retinal ganglion cells.

MFB. An abbreviation for MEDIAL FOREBRAIN BUNDLE.

MHPG. An abbreviation for METHOXY-HYDROXYPHENYLGLYCOL.

microcephalic. Having a very small head.

microcosm. 1. Something which models in miniature a larger entity. 2. Sometimes used to mean the self as opposed to the environment.

microelectrode. An electrode with a minute tip (down to one micron in diameter) that is used to record the activity of single cells.

microglia. Very small thread-like glial cells originating from macrophages and thought to act as phagocytes.

microlesion. A very small brain lesion which either selectively destroys cell bodies (but not axons in the vicinity) or that blocks only one specific kind of synapse. *See* APB and APO.

micromolar theory. Logan's theory that in learning a response the animal learns the optimal speed and amplitude and that therefore these response parameters are not measures of response strength.

micron (μ). One millionth of a metre.

microneurography. Recording from the axon of a single skin receptor while probing its receptive field.

microphobia. A morbid fear of anything small.

microphonia. A very weak voice.

microphonic. Short for COCHLEAR MICROPHONIC.

micropipette. A pipette with a minute aperture that can be used to inject or take up very small quantities of chemicals in a tiny part of the brain (or other organ).

micropsia. Seeing objects as much smaller than they really are; it can be caused by eye disease, hysteria, epilepsy, or experimental manipulation (e.g. placing atropine on the eye).

microsaccade. A very small involuntary flick of the eye made while fixating. *See* PHYSIOLOGICAL NYSTAGMUS.

microsecond (μsec). One millionth of a second.

microsleep. A very brief interval of sleep, which occurs when a person is ostensibly awake, and which he may not notice.

microsocial engineering. The establishment of a contract between family members outlining agreed responsibilities etc., in an attempt to reduce friction.

microsomatognosia. The perception of one's body or parts of it as abnormally small.

microspectrophotometer. A device for measuring the absorption spectrum of cones (or rods), by shining a tiny beam of light through a single cone in a freshly excised retina and measuring the light absorbed at different wavelengths.

microstructure. (Vision) Variations in the reflectance of a surface, occurring over very small areas, e.g. the texture of a piece of black card which is likely to contain tiny points of white. The microstructure is an important cue to BRIGHTNESS CONSTANCY, since the darker parts of a surface must lie toward black and the brighter points toward white.

microtome. A device for sectioning very thin slices of tissue, e.g. brain tissue, for examination under a microscope.

microtremor. See PHYSIOLOGICAL NYSTAGMUS.

microworld. A small fragment of the world, simulated in an artificial intelligence program in an attempt to learn how knowledge can be acquired, represented, and used, e.g. the simulated world of toy blocks which are rearranged by the computer on command in Winograd's program, SHRDLU.

midbrain. The middle of the three major divisions of the brain; it contains the colliculi, the tegmentum, part of the reticular formation, and numerous sensory and motor tracts. *See* Appendix 5. *See also* BRAIN and NEURAL TUBE.

middle ear. The air-filled chamber between the eardrum and the cochlea that contains the ossicles.

middle frontal gyrus. *See* Appendix 1.

middle premise. *See* SYLLOGISM.

middle temporal gyrus. *See* Appendix 1.

middle temporal sulcus. *See* Appendix 1.

middle term. *See* SYLLOGISM.

midget cell. A small retinal ganglion cell with centre-surround organization. The centre receives input from only one type of cone (low, medium, or high wavelength) and the sur-round from other cones forming a blue–yellow or red–green opponency system. It is part of the PARVOCELLULAR SYSTEM.

mid-life crisis. The difficulty that people sometimes have in adjusting to changes in their life between the ages of approximately 45 and 60.

midline nucleus. A thalamic nucleus relaying information from the reticular formation to other thalamic nuclei.

mid-phoneme. A phoneme uttered with the tongue neither lowered nor raised.

midrange. The mean of the highest and lowest of a set of numbers, a crude estimate of CENTRAL TENDENCY (1).

midsagittal plane. The vertical plane that divides the body into symmetrical left and right halves.

Midtown Manhattan Study. A psychiatric study carried out in 1962 and based on interviews in an area of New York City. It revealed that about 20 per cent of the population were severely impaired by mental illness, and that only one-third of those who were incapacitated by mental illness were receiving psychiatric help.

Mignon delusion. A child's fantasy that his parents are not really his biological parents and that his true parents are highly distinguished.

migraine. A severe, recurrent headache, often limited to one side only, commonly accompanied by scotomata, by visual hallucinations of colours and patterns, and also by nausea.

migration. An instinctive change of habitat, undertaken by members of a species, some of which travel distances of hundreds or thousands of miles; it is common in birds and fishes.

mil. A unit used in the construction of scales of apparent pressure. It is the pressure produced by a rod of one millimetre diameter pushed one millimetre into the centre of the palm of the hand.

mild mental retardation. The possession of an IQ of between 55 and 69. *See* MENTAL RETARDATION.

milieu therapy. The attempt to alter the social setting (in or out of hospital) of a mentally ill patient in such a way as to promote recovery.

Miller's Behavioural Style Scale. A personality test in which people are asked to imagine stressful situations (e.g. going to the dentist, being held by a terrorist group) and then have to indicate their agreement with statements about what they would do in that situation. The questions reveal whether they have a tendency to BLUNTING or MONITORING.

millilambert. A measure of luminance that is 0.001 of a LAMBERT.

millimicron (mμ). One thousand millionth (10^{-9}) of a metre, more commonly known as a nanometre (nm).

milliphot. A measure of luminance that is one thousandth of a PHOT.

millisecond (msec). One-thousandth of a second.

mimesis. Imitation.

mimicry. (Biology) The mimicking of the appearance of one species by another, developed for its evolutionary advantage. *See* AGGRESSIVE MIMICRY, BATESIAN MIMICRY, and MULLERIAN MIMICRY.

mind–body problem. The insoluble philosophical question of how the body and mind are related.

mineralocorticoids. A group of steroid hormones (e.g. aldosterone) released by the adrenal cortex that play a role in governing the balance of water, salt, and potassium in the body.

minimal attachment principle. The principle that in grammatical parsing each new word should be added to the phrase structure already formed using the least possible number of new syntactic nodes.

minimal audible angle. The difference threshold for detecting a difference in the direction of a sound source in the horizontal plane. It varies with the direction of the standard stimulus and with the frequency of the sound, but can be as low as 1° of arc.

minimal audible field (MAF). The sound pressure level of a tone at threshold in a FREE SOUND FIELD with the subject facing the tone. The pressure level is measured at the location of the centre of the subject's head after he has removed himself.

minimal audible pressure (MAP). The sound pressure of a tone at threshold as measured (or inferred) at the tympanic membrane.

minimal brain dysfunction, minimal brain damage (MBD). An alleged syndrome affecting children of normal or good intelligence who misbehave in a variety of ways, e.g. by failure to attend or concentrate, by fidgeting, moving around, etc. At one time the expression 'minimal brain damage' was used, but since there is no evidence of brain damage, it has been largely dropped. Nowadays it is sometimes called ATTENTION-DEFICIT DISORDER, an expression that is more pompous but less questionable.

minimal change, method of. A synonym for LIMITS, METHOD OF.

minimal group experiment. An experiment in which strangers are arbitrarily divided into different groups, in order to discover whether such arbitrary group membership increases liking between members within a group, whether treating the groups differently will increase in-group liking and decrease liking for out-group members, etc.

minimal pair. Two words of different meaning whose sounds differ only in a single articulatory element, e.g. 'big' and 'pig'. Such pairs can be used to establish the existence of a pair of separate phonemes.

minimax principle. (Game theory) A normative strategy for a two-person game, based on ranking one's own moves by the minimum value of their outcomes, i.e. the value each move would have if the opponent makes the best possible move in reply. The player should pick the move with the highest minimum value. For a method of implementing this principle, *see* ALPHA–BETA PRUNING.

minimum audible field. A synonym for MINIMAL AUDIBLE FIELD.

minimum audible pressure. A synonym for MINIMAL AUDIBLE PRESSURE.

minimum change therapy. Psychotherapy intended to bring about only a very limited change in a person, with no attempt to alter his basic personality.

minimum principle. (Vision) A Gestalt law to the effect that we see everything in the simplest way possible.

minimum separable. A measure of visual acuity based on the smallest detectable gap between two lines (with the breadth of the gap kept equal to that of the lines). Under optimal conditions a gap of about 30″ arc can be detected. Nowadays gratings are usually used.

minimum visible. A measure of visual acuity based on the thinnest hair-line (or smallest diameter dot) that can be detected. Under optimal conditions the threshold is about 0.5″. The technique is more a measure of the brightness difference threshold than of the accuracy with which stimuli can be located.

Minnesota Multiphasic Personality Inventory (MMPI). A battery of 550 questions requiring 'yes' or 'no' answers, and purporting to measure many aspects of personality and mental illness. The results can be summarized in terms of ten basic scales such as depression, masculinity, psychopathy, and schizophrenia.

minor epilepsy. A synonym for PETIT MAL.

minor hemisphere. The opposite hemisphere to the dominant hemisphere, i.e. the hemisphere in which language is not located; it is usually the right hemisphere.

minority group. Strictly, a homogeneous group in a society whose number is considerably smaller than that of the society as a whole. In practice the expression is only used of groups that are disadvantaged or think they are. Paradoxically, the expression is sometimes used of majority groups (like women) who believe themselves to be disadvantaged.

minority influence. In the ASCH SITUATION, the influence on a subject's judgement of a minority of people who disagree with the majority's view. Even one or two people disagreeing has a large effect. *Contrast* MAJORITY INFLUENCE.

minor premise. *See* SYLLOGISM.

minor term. *See* SYLLOGISM.

minor tranquillizers. Drugs that have a mild sedative action and relieve tension and anxiety. Today the BENZODIAZEPINES are the most commonly used class of such drugs.

mirror drawing test. The task of drawing an object correctly when it is viewed in a mirror.

mirror focus. A secondary focus occurring in the same part of the opposite hemisphere to the position of the main epileptic focus; similarly a brain lesion in one hemisphere can be followed by some degeneration in the corresponding site of the opposite hemisphere.

mirror phase. Lacan's term for the alleged phenomenon that at about one year old infants become fascinated by the sight of themselves in mirrors or other reflective surfaces; according to him the child seizes on its image as being its true self and for unexplained reasons finds this alienating.

mirror technique. A psychodrama technique in which a person is encouraged to see himself as others see him by having someone else enact him.

misologia. An avoidance of speaking; it can occur in schizophrenia.

miss. In SIGNAL DETECTION THEORY, failure to detect a signal when one is present.

missing fundamental. The missing fundamental may be heard when two conditions are met: (i) a complex tone consisting of tones equally spaced is sounded; (ii) each is an integer multiple of the interval between them. The pitch of the complex tone is heard at the difference frequency: this pitch is the missing fundamental. E.g. a complex tone containing harmonics at 600, 800, and 1,000 Hz will have a pitch of 200 Hz. The situation outlined is the standard case in which the missing fundamental appears, but some complex tones not fulfilling the two conditions given (e.g. a complex tone with energy at 500, 700, and 900 Hz) are heard at a pitch below that corresponding to the frequencies of their components.

mitochondria. Small structures within cells that produce adenosine triphosphate (a source of energy) from sugars and fats.

mitosis. The splitting of a cell containing paired chromosomes into two daughter cells, each with the same number of chromosomes as the parent cell; all processes of growth, tissue repair, etc. depend on mitosis. *Contrast* MEIOSIS.

mitral cell. A pyramidal cell in the olfactory lobe that receives an input from the olfactory nerve.

Mitwelt. (Existentialism) A person's relationship with others. *Compare* EIGENWELT and UMWELT (2).

mixed. (Psychiatry) Of psychiatric disorders, not displaying the standard pattern of symptoms laid down in any one diagnostic classification.

mixed laterality. The state in which a person prefers to use the members of one side of the body for some activities and those of the other side for others, or the state in which neither hemisphere is dominant.

mixed-list design. *See* BLOCK DESIGN (2).

mixed-motive game. (Game theory) A game in which some combination of moves will bring a positive payoff to one player and a negative one to the other, while other combinations result in a small gain to both. Such games are both competitive and cooperative. *See also* PRISONER'S DILEMMA.

mixed nerve. A nerve containing both afferent and efferent fibres.

mixed schedule. A REINFORCEMENT SCHEDULE in which two or more simple schedules are presented with no signal to inform the animal which schedule is operating.

mixed schizophrenia. A form of schizophrenia in which the symptoms of more than one of the four basic divisions (catatonic schizophrenia, hebephrenic schizophrenia, paranoid schizophrenia, and simple schizophrenia) are present.

mixed strategy. *See* EVOLUTIONARILY STABLE STRATEGY.

mixed transcortical aphasia. Aphasia caused by damage to the zone bordering the frontal, parietal and occipital lobes. There is almost complete loss of all language function.

MLD. *See* BINAURAL MASKING LEVEL DIFFERENCE.

MMPI. An abbreviation for MINNESOTA MULTIPHASIC PERSONALITY INVENTORY.

mμ. An abbreviation for millimicron, which is more often called a nanometre (nm). 1 mμ equals 10^{-9} metre.

mneme. A synonym for MEMORY TRACE.

mnemonic. Any technique used to improve memory; most mnemonics depend on forming additional associations or on associating new material with material already in memory. *Compare* LOCI, METHOD OF and PEGWORDS.

mobbing behaviour. (Ethology) The harassment by a large number of small animals of a predator in order to drive it away; it occurs mainly in birds.

mobility. (Sociology) The extent to which in a given society individuals tend to move upwards or downwards from one social class to another.

MOC curve. An abbreviation for MEMORY OPERATING CHARACTERISTIC CURVE.

modality. 1. (Psychology) A sensory system, e.g. vision, hearing, the temperature sense. 2. (Linguistics) A synonym for MOOD (2).

modality effect. In general, any differential effect of presenting the same material in different modalities, and in particular the finding that when a list of words is presented for immediate free recall, subjects do better on the last word or two with auditory presentation than with visual.

modal logic. A branch of formal logic, originally devised to handle inferences based on the concepts of necessity and possibility, and containing more than the two standard truth values ('true' and 'false').

modal verb. An auxiliary verb, like 'may', 'can', 'must', that changes the MOOD (2) of the sentence.

mode. 1. (Statistics) The value from a distribution of values that has the highest frequency; it is a measure of CENTRAL TENDENCY (1). 2. (Psychology) A rare synonym for modality.

model. 1. (Science) A representation, whether concrete (e.g. a map) or abstract (e.g. a mathematical theory) of a complex structure used to understand how the structure's parts are articulated, and (in the case of the nervous system) how the input is transformed to produce the output. 2. (Biology) A species or an organ of a species in which it is particularly easy to investigate a feature common to many species; e.g. the giant axon of the squid was particularly easy to investigate because of its size, and was used as a model for the conduction of the nerve impulse. 3. (Social psychology) Anyone whose behaviour is imitated by someone else.

modelling. A behaviour therapy technique in which the therapist performs activities that the patient finds difficult while persuading the patient to copy him; e.g. in treating someone with a phobia of spiders, the therapist may move closer and closer to a spider with the patient following him. More generally, basing one's own behaviour on that of others.

model psychosis. A psychosis produced artificially (usually by drugs) for experimental purposes.

model-referenced control. A hypothesis about how movements, particularly those used in speech, are generated, postulating that given the initial position of the muscles the movements requiring the least energy to bring them to the target are computed and then executed.

model theoretic semantics. A theory of semantics that equates the meaning of a word or expression with a set-theoretic construction based on various kinds of primitives, usually including truth values, individuals, and POSSIBLE WORLDS. *Compare* TRUTH CONDITIONAL SEMANTICS.

modem. A device to link a computer to a telephone line.

moderate mental retardation. The possession of an IQ between 40 and 54. *See* MENTAL RETARDATION.

moderator gene. A gene that regulates the way another gene expresses itself.

moderator variable. An independent or intervening variable that influences the interaction between two or more other variables. The term is used particularly in personality research, e.g. the relation between two traits is often different between men and women – sex is therefore a moderator variable.

modified whole method of learning. *See* WHOLE METHOD OF LEARNING.

modifier. A phrase that is not an ARGUMENT but which adds information to a sentence or clause. E.g. 'He lit his cigarette *with a match.*'

modifier gene. A synonym for MODERATOR GENE.

modiolus. A cavity running through the centre of the cochlea around which the rest of the cochlea spirals. It contains the axons from the spiral ganglia and blood-vessels.

modular architecture. (Computing) The structure of a computer program that exhibits MODULARITY.

modularity. The extent to which an information processing system is broken down into self-contained units each functioning in its own way, but having some connection with other units. Modular computer programs are easier to debug and to alter than non-modular ones and there is evidence that the brain is to a considerable extent modular.

modulation. A periodic change in any dimension of a stimulus, e.g. in brightness or frequency.

modulation transfer function (MTF). The ratio of the amplitude of a system's output to that of its input, measured as a function of the frequency of a sinusoidal input signal.

modulator. Granit's term for a ganglion cell that responds to a relatively narrow range of spectral wavelengths. *Contrast* DOMINATOR.

module. (Computing) A part of a program carrying out a specific task, and functioning largely independently of the rest.

modus ponens. The valid deduction from the truth of a conditional proposition's antecedent that the consequent is true.

modus tollens. The valid deduction from the falsity of the consequent of a conditional proposition that the antecedent is false.

mogigraphia. Writer's cramp.

mogilalia. Difficulty in speaking.

moiré patterns. The patterns that appear when one repetitive pattern is almost but not quite aligned with another.

molar. Pertaining to the whole of anything rather than to the separate parts. *Compare* HOLISM.

molar behaviour. A sequence of responses that are organized together (e.g. to achieve a goal) when viewed as a whole.

molecular. Pertaining to the analysis of a system into its separate components.

molecular layer. 1. A synonym for the PLEXIFORM LAYER (1), one of the six CORTICAL LAYERS. 2. The outermost of the three layers of the cortex of the CEREBELLUM.

Molyneux's question. The question of whether someone born blind who has learned to recognize objects by touch could recognize them by sight if he were suddenly able to see.

molysmophobia. A morbid fear of being contaminated.

moment (μ). 1. (Statistics) The first moment of a distribution is the arithmetic mean. Higher moments are given by the formula $\Sigma(x_i - M) - /N$, where x_i represents the individual values and M is their mean. In the **second moment** r is 2, in the **third moment** 3, and in the **fourth moment** 4. Moments enter into the description of various properties of a distribution. Thus, the VARIANCE is the second moment (μ_2), SKEWNESS is $\mu_3/\mu_2^{3/2}$, and KURTOSIS is μ_4/μ_2^2. 2. *See* PSYCHOLOGICAL MOMENT.

momentary reaction potential ($_s\dot{E}_R$). Hull's expression for the effective strength of a response after modifying NET REACTION POTENTIAL by the current state of BEHAVIOUR OSCILLATION. *See* HULLIAN THEORY.

monaural. Pertaining to or affecting only one ear. *Contrast* BINAURAL.

mongolism. An obsolete synonym for DOWN'S SYNDROME.

monism. The philosophical hypothesis that there is only one kind of entity, which is either physical (materialism) or mental (idealism).

monitoring. In trying to cope with a stressful situation, thinking about it a lot and pondering its implications. *Contrast* BLUNTING and *compare* MILLER'S BEHAVIOURAL STYLE SCALE.

monoamine. A class of amine compounds containing a single amine; some are neurotransmitters. *See* BIOGENIC AMINES.

monoamine oxidase (MAO). An enzyme that breaks up monoamines mainly within a cell. *Compare* CATECHOL-O-METHYL-TRANSFERASE.

monoamine oxidase inhibitor (MAOI). A class of antidepressant drugs that raises the activity of monoamine transmitters by inhibiting monoamine oxidase, thus preventing it from breaking them up.

monochromatism, monochromacy. Inability to see HUE; a rare condition afflicting about 3 in 100,000 people. Those with **cone monochromatism** have normal photopic luminosity curves and normal acuity; those with **rod monochromatism** do not have functional cones and hence have very poor photopic vision.

monocular. Pertaining to one eye.

monocular suppression. The suppression of vision in all or part of one eye, caused by a different pattern falling on the other eye; also complete suppression of vision in one eye caused by the other eye being very dominant. *See* BINOCULAR RIVALRY and STRABISMUS.

monoideism. Excessive preoccupation with a single thought or idea.

monomyoplegia. Paralysis of a single muscle.

monophobia. A morbid fear of being left alone.

monoplegia. The paralysis of one part of the body only.

monopolar. A synonym for unipolar.

monoptic. Pertaining to the presentation of two or more stimuli to the same eye (usually in succession). *Compare* MONOCULAR. *Contrast* DICHOPTIC.

monosynaptic reflex. A reflex mediated by two neurons (or two sets of neurons) in series, and therefore containing only one synapse (or several synapses all at one level), e.g. a spinal reflex in which sensory neurons end directly on motor neurons with no intervening neuron.

monothetic classification. A classification in which all members of a given class have one or more attributes in common that are not possessed by members of the other classes. In **polythetic classification** this is not true (e.g. classification may be made by grouping attributes each of which may be present in other classes).

monotic. Pertaining to the presentation of two or more stimuli to the same ear. *Contrast* DICHOTIC.

monotonic. The property of an ordered series of values, each of which is greater than (**monotonic increasing**) or less than (**monotonic decreasing**) its immediate predecessor.

monotonic logic. A logic in which the validity of an inference from a given premise is unaffected by adding other premises. In practice this comprises all formal logics. *See also* NON–MONOTONIC LOGIC.

monozygotic twins. Twins born from the division of a single fertilized egg and therefore having identical genes.

Montague grammar. A system of grammar containing a semantic as well as a syntactic component. The syntax contains rules that define syntactic categories on which a phrase-structure grammar is based. These categories map on to semantic categories which yield a MODEL THEORETIC SEMANTIC interpretation of sentences.

Monte Carlo procedure. The simulation of a stochastic model, e.g. by running simulated subjects through probabilistically determined stages, usually by means of a computer program. The procedure is used when the outcome of such a model cannot be determined mathematically. *Compare* STAT RAT.

mood. 1. A temporary disposition to behave and feel in a certain way. 2. (Linguistics) Contrasting forms of the same verb (other than changes in person, tense or aspect), determined either by inflection or the use of an auxiliary. In English the moods are indicative, imperative, and subjunctive, but in addition auxiliaries are used to change the certainty (e.g. 'may'), or possibility (e.g. 'must') of what is being said. 3. *See* SYLLOGISM.

Mooney Problem Check List. A personality inventory containing a list of problems that may arise in life; the testee has to tick those that apply to him.

moon illusion. The phenomenon that the horizon moon looks larger than the zenith moon, although they are effectively the same retinal size. It is probable that at some level of the visual system the horizon moon is interpreted as farther away than the zenith and hence through size constancy looks larger. However, at a conscious level the horizon moon is seen as nearer – perhaps because it is seen as too large.

moral anxiety. (Psychoanalysis) Anxiety arising from actions or contemplated actions prohibited by the superego. *Contrast* NEUROTIC ANXIETY and REALITY ANXIETY.

moral independence. Piaget's term for the stage in moral development (the autonomous stage) when the child has realized that, in judging the morality of an act, subjective factors like intention must be taken into account.

morality of constraint. Piaget's expression for the alleged phenomenon that, until about 10 years old, the child's concept of morality is unquestioning obedience to his parents.

morality of cooperation. Piaget's expression for the alleged phenomenon that children of about 11 regard morality as a set of conventional rules that can be questioned and, with the consent of a second party, broken.

moral realism. Piaget's expression for the alleged phenomenon that, until about 8 years old, children judge the morality of an action only by its consequences, ignoring intention, etc.

moral relativism. A synonym for MORAL INDEPENDENCE.

Morgan's canon. Short for LLOYD MORGAN'S CANON.

moria. A compulsive or morbid desire to joke, particularly in inappropriate circumstances, such as writing dictionary entries.

Morita theory. A form of Japanese psychotherapy that encourages the patient to behave well and to take responsibility for his behaviour, while teaching that feelings cannot be governed and neither shame nor pride can be attached to them.

moron. *See* MENTAL DEFICIENCY.

Moro reflex. The STARTLE REFLEX exhibited by infants in their first year, consisting mainly of drawing their arms across their chest.

morpheme. The smallest linguistic unit that has meaning: e.g. 'kicked' contains two such units – 'kick', which specifies the action, and '-ed', which indicates it took place in the past.

morphine. An addictive narcotic, derived from the opium poppy, whose structure is similar to that of certain naturally occurring neurotransmitters. *See* OPIATE.

morphogenesis. (Systems theory) The controlled growth or development of a system, e.g. of relationships within a family. *Compare* MORPHOSTASIS.

morphological index. Any measurement of body build.

morphology. 1. (Zoology) The study of the form or structure of organisms. 2. (Linguistics) The study of the composition of words, including their inflections.

morphophonemics. (Linguistics) The study of how morphemes are converted to their phonological forms.

morphostasis. (Systems theory) The preservation of the current state of a system by homeostatic mechanisms. *Compare* MORPHOGENESIS.

mortido. (Psychoanalysis) The drive underlying THANATOS. *Compare* LIBIDO which underlies Eros.

mosaic test. A projective test in which the testee is given about 400 differently shaped and coloured pieces and told to make anything he likes from them.

mossy fibre. An input fibre to the cerebellum that ends in the granular layer.

motherese. Baby talk as spoken to infants by the parents and others.

mother figure. Anyone who takes the place of a mother in someone's eyes.

motion aftereffect (MAE). The illusion of motion that occurs after exposing a part of the retina for half a minute or so to continuous motion in the same direction; the illusory motion occurs in the opposite direction. *Compare* SPIRAL AFTEREFFECT.

motion constancy. The tendency to see objects moving at their real speed despite variations in the speed at which they move in the retinal image.

motion detector. Any cell in the visual system that responds selectively to movement in a particular direction within its receptive field.

motion parallax. A cue to depth, based on the relative changes in the position of objects at different depths that occur when the observer moves. E.g. with fixation on the horizon, a lateral movement of the head will sweep all objects in the opposite direction in the visual field – the nearer an object is the faster and further it will move. The expression is also sometimes used to include the depth cues afforded when the observer is stationary and an object moves. *See* PARALLAX and *compare* KINETIC DEPTH EFFECT.

motion perspective. Gibson's term for the patterns of flow in the visual field caused by MOTION PARALLAX.

motion sickness. Nausea and dizziness caused by exposure to uncontrollable motion of the body, as on board a ship.

motivation. The internal forces that determine the goals of a person or animal.

motivation research. In consumer research, the study of the motives that cause consumers to buy a product or products. Its aim is to produce a product, package, or advertising campaign that appeals to these motives.

motokinaesthetic method. A speech therapy technique in which the therapist indicates the desired movements of the vocal tract by touching and manipulating it.

motoneuron. A synonym for MOTOR NEURON.

motoneuron pool. All motor neurons, which may come from several segments of the spinal cord, that innervate a single muscle.

motor. Pertaining to muscles or to glandular secretion.

motor amusia. Pathological inability to reproduce music or rhythm, often with an impaired capacity to recognize music. The syndrome affects many pop groups.

motor aphasia. Severe impairment in the ability to speak, caused by brain damage particularly to the motor areas controlling speech, or to the neighbouring BROCA'S AREA.

motor apraxia. A form of apraxia in which the patient at some level seems to know what movements are required to execute a task, but is unable to carry them out because of a failure of the motor command system. Movements are extremely clumsy; patients may commence an action and then perseverate with a component of it for a long time (e.g. grasping a glass and holding on to it instead of raising it to the lips). It is probably caused by damage to the motor cortex.

motor cortex, motor area (M1). The parts of the cortex directly implicated in the control of the muscles. *See* PRIMARY MOTOR CORTEX, SECONDARY MOTOR CORTEX, SUPPLEMENTARY MOTOR CORTEX and MOTOR HOMUNCULUS.

motor end plate. The flattened end of an efferent fibre at its synapse with a muscle.

motor equivalence. The phenomenon that the same action can be performed by using the motor system in completely different ways, e.g. a rat can depress a bar with its paw or by sitting on it.

motor homunculus. The mapping in the PRIMARY MOTOR CORTEX of the muscles of the body. The mapping is sequential, with the feet next to the central sulcus, and trunk, hands and face descending the lateral side of the cortex. Although the muscles from neighbouring parts of the body are represented in neighbouring parts of the cortex, the map is distorted since the parts of the body that have many finely controlled muscles occupy relatively more space than parts that have few. It is now known that there are similar maps in other motor areas. *Compare* SENSORY HOMUNCULUS.

motor neuron. A neuron terminating on a muscle or gland; such neurons have their cell bodies either in the brain or in the spinal cord: *See* ALPHA MOTOR NEURON and GAMMA MOTOR NEURON.

motor neurosis. A neurosis in which the main symptom is a motor disturbance, like tics or hyperactivity.

motor primacy theory. The hypothesis that motor functions develop before sensory ones.

motor skills. All skills that are mainly dependent on the ability to regulate muscular movements or to regulate them in coordination with the input to another sense such as vision. They have been much studied but are poorly understood.

motor system. All parts of the nervous system directly involved in the control of muscles and the muscles themselves.

motor theory of speech perception. The theory that speech is perceived by mapping the acoustic input onto a system that represents the articulatory movements made in speech. Unfortunately, nobody has been able to specify how such a mapping could be achieved, thus the basic problem of speech perception remains unresolved.

motor theory of thinking. The behaviourist theory, long since discredited, that thinking is a series of conditioned reflexes in which minimal movements of parts of the body (mainly the speech muscles) successively trigger further movements. *Compare* PERIPHERALISM.

motor unit. A MOTOR NEURON and the set of muscle fibres it stimulates.

mouches volantes. A synonym for MUSCAE VOLITANTES.

mouse scan. A synonym for DEPTH-FIRST SEARCH.

movement. 1. (Linguistics) The main transformation in transformational grammar. It moves a phrase from its position in deep structure to another place. 'You will come' can become 'Will you come?' 2. *See* **motion.**

movement response. A Rorschach test response in which movement of part of the inkblot is seen.

moving window technique. Showing a subject a limited number of consecutive letters from a text at any one time; the string is changed during saccades so that a given number of letters before and after each fixation point are displayed. No gain in reading speed or accuracy occurs if more than four letters before the fixation point or more than 14 after it are presented.

MR. An abbreviation for MENTAL RETARDATION.

MRI. An abbreviation for MAGNETIC RESONANCE IMAGING.

mRNA. An abbreviation for messenger RNA. *See* RIBONUCLEIC ACID.

msec. An abbreviation for MILLISECOND.

MSH. An abbreviation for MELANOCYTE-STIMULATING HORMONE.

M-system. An abbreviation for MAGNOCELLULAR SYSTEM.

MT (M5). A visual association area which in humans probably lies in Brodmann's areas 19 and 39; *see* Appendix 3. It contains a topographical map of the retina with cells responsive to movement in a selective direction, and to retinal disparity.

MTF. An abbreviation for MODULATION TRANSFER FUNCTION.

mu (μ). An abbreviation for the POPULATION MEAN.

μ-second. An abbreviation for microsecond, one-millionth of a second.

Müller effect. The phenomenon that when an observer views a luminous vertical rod in the dark, it appears to be tilted out of vertical in the same direction as the head. This effect only occurs with small tilts of the head. *Contrast* AUBERT EFFECT.

Müllerian mimicry. The sharing by a number of noxious species of the same coloration and shape; this is of advantage to all the species since once a predator has attacked one member of one species it will tend not to attack members of any of the other species. *Compare* BATESIAN MIMICRY.

Müller–Lyer illusion. The geometric illusion illustrated below: the line between the inward pointing arrowheads looks shorter than that between the outward ones.

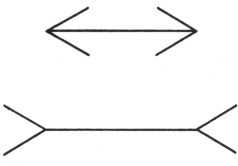

Müller–Lyer illusion

Müller–Schumann law. The principle that, when an association between two terms has been learned, it is subsequently more difficult to associate either with another term.

Müller's fibre. A type of glial cell that seems to support the layers of the retina.

multiattribute utility theory. (Decision theory) A form of UTILITY THEORY in which different dimensions of the possible outcomes are each given a weight (w) representing their importance. For each possible outcome the EXPECTED UTILITY is the sum of its value (v) on each dimension multiplied by the weight of that dimension multiplied by the probability of the outcome occurring (p). The dimensions on which the utility of a car is measured might be petrol consumption, comfort, acceleration etc.

multidimensional. Pertaining to or having more than one dimension. *Contrast* UNIDIMENSIONAL.

multidimensional scaling (MDS). The construction by mathematical techniques of a multidimensional space that will fit a given body of data, usually judgements of similarity. E.g. judgements of similarity between all pairs of a group of items may be submitted to multidimensional scaling to yield an estimate of the number of dimensions of similarity. *Compare* KRUSKAL–SHEPARD SCALING.

multifactorial inheritance. The inheritance of a trait that is determined by many different genes.

multiframe task. A VISUAL SEARCH task in which different stimuli are presented in successive displays. *Contrast* SINGLE FRAME TASK.

multimodal. Pertaining to a distribution of values that has more than one peak.

multimodal perception. The perception of stimuli arriving simultaneously from more than one modality.

multimodal psychotherapy. Psychotherapy in which the practitioner uses techniques and ideas borrowed from different schools of therapy. Multimodal therapy has itself become a school. It focuses on the whole person in his social network, but also pays detailed attention to any idiosyncrasies he may exhibit.

multiple-choice test. Any test in which a person or animal has to choose one of three or more alternatives.

multiple correlation coefficient (R). *See* MULTIPLE REGRESSION.

multiple discriminant function. *See* DISCRIMINANT FUNCTION.

multiple personality. A dissociative disorder in which a person exhibits in turn different personalities; when exhibiting one personality, he may have no knowledge of the others and no memory for his experiences under a different personality.

multiple regression. A technique which determines the optimum weighting of a number of independent variables in order to predict a single dependent variable. The measure of the degree of fit is the **multiple correlation coefficient**.

multiple schedule. A REINFORCEMENT SCHEDULE in which two or more simple schedules are given with a signal to indicate to the animal which schedule is currently operating.

multiple sclerosis. A progressive disease of the central nervous system in which parts of the myelin sheath are destroyed.

múltiple threshold model. (Psychiatry) The theory that psychosis is caused by the sum of genetic and environmental factors and that with increasing values of this sum the disorder caused will be unipolar manic-depressive illness, bipolar manic-depressive illness and schizophrenia.

multipolar neuron. A neuron with a single axon and with one or more long dendritic processes emanating from the cell body.

multisensory method. A synonym for VAKT PROCEDURE.

multistore memory model. Any theory of memory postulating that there are three (or more) memory stores – sensory, short-term and long-term memory.

multisynaptic arc. A neural pathway containing two or more synapses in series.

multivariate analysis. Any statistical technique that involves the analysis of data which are multivariate, i.e. each member of a sample bears the values of several variables. Some of the principal techniques are FACTOR ANALYSIS, ANALYSIS OF VARIANCE, and the multivariate analogue of the T-TEST.

Munchausen syndrome. The repeated simulation of illness in order to gain medical attention or be admitted to hospital.

Munsell system. An atlas of chromatic and achromatic colours varying in subjectively equal steps of brightness, hue, and saturation.

Münsterberg illusion. The geometric illusion illustrated below. The physically vertical

Münsterberg illusion

black and white lines appear to be slightly off vertical with alternate ones tilted in opposite directions.

muricide. The killing of mice, particularly by cats and some rats.

muscae volitantes. Dark spots seen floating in front of the eyes, caused by opaque bodies in the vitreous humour.

muscarinic receptors. One of two types of synaptic receptors for ACETYLCHOLINE; they can be excitatory or inhibitory and are found both in parts of the central nervous system and in the peripheral parasympathetic system. *Compare* NICOTINIC RECEPTORS.

muscle. An organ that can contract. *See* SMOOTH MUSCLE and STRIATED MUSCLE.

muscle action potential. An ACTION POTENTIAL in a muscle fibre, normally caused by the firing of a motor neuron, as a result of which the fibre contracts.

muscle fibres. The EXTRAFUSAL FIBRES and INTRAFUSAL FIBRES. The expression can refer to both kinds of fibre together, but is also used to mean only the extrafusal fibres.

muscle spindle. A bundle of about two to twelve INTRAFUSAL FIBRES, which are jointly attached at both ends to EXTRAFUSAL FIBRES. They contain annulospiral flower spray receptors which fire when the extrafusal fibres are passively stretched and which through a spinal loop cause firing in alpha motor neurons, thus exciting the extrafusal fibres and preserving the right degree of tension in the muscle.

muscle tonus. The slight tension that normally exists in a muscle when it is relaxed and not in use.

muscular anal. *See* ERIKSON'S PSYCHOSOCIAL DEVELOPMENTAL STAGES.

muscular dystrophy (MD). A group of inherited diseases characterized by progressive atrophy and weakening of the muscles.

mussitation. Unintelligible murmuring or lip movements.

mutagen. Any agent that increases the rate of mutation, e.g. X-rays.

mutation. A change in DNA, such as a change in the composition of a gene (**gene mutation**), a change in the sequence of genes in a single chromosome (**inversion**), a change in a chromosome through transfer of material from one paired chromosome to the other (**translocation**), the **deletion** of a sequence from a chromosome, or the **duplication** of a sequence in a chromosome. Evolution is thought to depend on such random mutations.

mute. Unable to speak.

mutuality. Erikson's term for the capacity to give and receive help and support.

myasthenia. Muscular weakness caused by disease.

myasthenia gravis. A progressive disease of the neuromuscular system, producing weakness or paralysis of the muscles.

mydriasis. Extreme dilation of the pupil, which can be caused by drugs like atropine.

myelencephalon. The more caudal of the two divisions of the hindbrain (the other being the METENCEPHALON). It comprises only the MEDULLA OBLONGATA. *See* BRAIN.

myelin. A white fatty substance that surrounds and insulates many large axons, thus increasing the velocity of conduction of the nerve impulse.

myelincephalic encephalitis (ME). A purported illness characterized by fatigue and inertia, currently fashionable among the managerial classes.

myoaesthesia. The muscle sense.

myoclonic movement. Involuntary movement of skeletal muscles, e.g. through a spasm or an epileptic attack.

myoesthesia. An alternative spelling for MYOAESTHESIA.

myograph. A device for measuring muscular strength.

myoneural junction. A synonym for NEUROMUSCULAR JUNCTION.

myopia. Short-sightedness, i.e. inability to accommodate correctly for distant objects; in this condition, even when the lens is fully relaxed, distant objects are brought into focus in front of the retina. It is caused by the distance from lens to retina being abnormally long. It can be corrected by concave glasses. *Contrast* HYPEROPIA.

myosin. *See* ACTIN and EXTRAFUSAL FIBRES.

myosis. Abnormally extreme contraction of the pupil.

myotactic reflex. A synonym for STRETCH REFLEX.

myotonia. An impairment of muscle tone, e.g. prolonged spasm or rigidity.

mysophilia. The obtaining of sexual excitement from dirt, a fetish.

mysophobia. A morbid fear of dirt.

mystification. The process by which parents may cause their children to doubt their own feelings and perceptions and the imposition of DOUBLE BINDS; it is thought by some to be one of the causes of schizophrenia.

myxoedema, myxedema. A disease caused by an underactive thyroid and characterized by weakness, fatigue, and an abnormally low metabolic rate.

MZ twins. An abbreviation for MONOZYGOTIC TWINS.

MZa. An abbreviation for MONOZYGOTIC TWINS reared *a*part.

MZt. An abbreviation for MONOZYGOTIC TWINS reared *to*gether.

N

N. An abbreviation for 1. number, particularly for the number of scores in a sample or the number of observations made; 2. NOUN; 3. number of reinforced trials in HULLIAN THEORY.

n. An abbreviation for number of trials to extinction in HULLIAN THEORY.

n-Ach. An abbreviation for NEED FOR ACHIEVEMENT.

naive physics. The beliefs about the physical world held by the ordinary man; e.g. he is likely to believe that a ball dropped by a moving person will fall straight down.

naive realism. (Philosophy) The hypothesis that people directly perceive the real qualities of objects in the world, not merely their appearances. *Compare* SENSE DATA.

naive subject. A subject who has no previous experience of the experimental situation and has no technical knowledge from which he could infer the nature or purpose of the experiment; an unfortunate expression.

nalorphine. An opiate that blocks OPIATE RECEPTORS but that when used in the absence of opiates has an opiate-like effect.

naloxone. An opiate ANTAGONIST that blocks OPIATE RECEPTORS; it can be used to aid recovery from an overdose of heroin or morphine.

Nancy school. A 19th-century school of psychiatrists who held that hypnosis was based on suggestibility and was a normal phenomenon. *Compare* PARIS SCHOOL.

nanism. Dwarfism.

nanometre (nm). One-thousand-millionth (10^{-9}) of a metre.

narcissism, narcism. (Psychoanalysis) Excessive love of oneself. Freud distinguished **primary narcissism**, which is normal and occurs in the oral and anal stages when the child is concerned mainly to gratify its own bodily functions and **secondary narcissism**, a neurotic trait, occurring in later life as a result of withdrawing the libido from external objects.

narcissistic personality disorder. (DSM-III) The possession of a set of egocentric traits, including a strong desire for admiration, indifference to criticism, and an exaggerated opinion of oneself.

narcissistic type. (Psychoanalysis) A personality type in which the libido expresses itself mainly through the ego; the person is selfish and does not care for others. This type is associated with psychosis and antisocial disorders.

narcoanalysis. Analysis carried out under a narcotic or sedative drug to relax the patient and help him to speak freely by reducing his inhibitions.

narcohypnosis. Hypnosis induced with the aid of a narcotic drug.

narcolepsy. An illness in which the patient cannot stop falling asleep, even in the daytime.

narcosis. A state of unconsciousness or extreme drowsiness induced by a narcotic drug.

narcosynthesis. A synonym for NARCOANALYSIS.

narcotic. Any drug that dulls sensibility to pain and induces sleep, usually, but not solely, used of the OPIATES.

narcotic antagonist, narcotic blocking agent. Any drug that reduces the effects of a NARCOTIC (particularly of opiates), usually by occupying the same receptor sites.

nares. Nostrils.

narratophilia. The use of pornographic writing as the sole means of achieving sexual arousal.

nasal. (Phonetics) A speech sound produced by passing air through the nose, e.g. the 'nk' in 'ink'. It results from having the soft palate open.

native. A synonym for innate.

nativism. The doctrine that all or most human abilities are inherited rather than formed by experience. *Contrast* EMPIRICISM.

natural category. 1. A category imposed by the innate organization of the senses, e.g. the division of hues into red, blue, green, yellow, or of skin sensations into itching, burning, pressure, pain, etc. 2. Sometimes also used as a misnomer for BASIC LEVEL CATEGORY.

naturalistic individualism. (Philosophy) The doctrine that the operations carried out in the mind can only be understood by taking into account their connection with the world. *Contrast* METHODOLOGICAL SOLIPSISM.

natural language. Any human language that has evolved naturally and not by design (unlike e.g. predicate calculus), and in particular the language a child first learns.

natural-response theory of language. The theory that language evolved from natural oral responses made to events.

natural selection. The Darwinian doctrine that which species, or variants within species, survive, and which are eliminated is determined by their fitness to survive in their environment.

natural sign. Anything which for natural reasons indicates the occurrence of something else, e.g. black clouds are a natural sign for rain.

nature–nurture controversy. The dispute between those who believe that behaviour is mainly determined by inheritance (nature) and those who believe it is mainly determined by experience (nurture).

Nauta stain. A silver stain that is taken up by degenerating axons, and hence · identifies dead or degenerating neurons.

N-dimension. An abbreviation for NEUROTICISM DIMENSION.

NE. An abbreviation for NOREPINEPHRINE.

near point of accommodation. The nearest point at which an object can be brought into sharp focus by the lens.

near point of convergence. The nearest point at which the image of an object can be imaged on the centre of both eyes through maximum convergence.

near-sightedness. A synonym for MYOPIA.

near vision. Vision for points less than two feet away.

necessary condition. A condition that must be fulfilled if a given event is to occur. *Contrast* SUFFICIENT CONDITION.

necessary proposition. A proposition that is true a priori, e.g. '2 × 2 = 4' or 'red is a colour'.

Necker cube. The ambiguous figure illustrated below. Two different sides can be seen as lying at the front: they tend to oscillate.

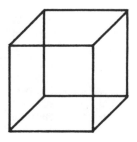

Necker cube

necromania. Pathological fascination with the dead or death.

necrophilia. Obtaining sexual pleasure from corpses.

necrophobia. A morbid fear of the dead or of things to do with death.

need. 1. The lack of something necessary for survival or well-being. In this sense there may be a need without a corresponding drive. 2. A motivational state (drive) set up by the absence of something, either genuinely needed for the organism's well-being or mistakenly thought to be needed. It is regrettable that 'need' has come to be used in this second sense, for which 'drive' is a more appropriate term. Failure to differentiate between the two senses has caused much confusion. *See also* PHYSIOLOGICAL NEED.

need for achievement (n-Ach). The drive to be successful, to master difficult tasks, and to meet exacting standards.

need for affiliation. The drive to interact or socialize with other people.

need-hierarchy theory. Maslow's doctrine that there is a hierarchy of needs, which are (beginning at the lowest level) physiological needs; the need for safety; the need for love; the need to be respected; the self-actualization needs, including the need for knowledge, aesthetic needs, etc.

need-press. A synonym for PRESS-NEED.

need reduction. The reduction of a NEED (2), usually by consummatory behaviour, sometimes thought to be the basis of all reinforcement.

needs-press method. A technique for analysing the stories told in the Thematic Apperception Test in terms of the needs of the main character and the pressure of the environment on him.

neencephalon. A synonym for NEOCORTEX.

negation. A logical connective meaning 'not true', usually written ∼.

negative acceleration. *See* DERIVATIVE.

negative adaptation. A gradual loss of sensitivity or the gradual weakening of a response, caused by prolonged stimulation.

negative afterimage. *See* AFTERIMAGE.

negative assortative mating. The tendency in a population for dissimilar individuals to mate with one another. *Contrast* ASSORTATIVE MATING and PANMIXIA.

negative cathexis. A dislike for, or wish to avoid, anything.

negative correlation, negative correlation coefficient. A correlation coefficient indicating that as one variable increases the other decreases.

negative feedback. *See* FEEDBACK.

negative goal gradient. The decrease in the tendency to move away from a punishing stimulus with increased distance from it. *Compare* GOAL GRADIENT.

negative incentive. An aversive stimulus. *See* INCENTIVE.

negative induction. *See* INDUCTION (2).

negative law of effect. Thorndike's law that responses followed by 'an annoying state of affairs' are less likely to recur. He subsequently pointed out that the negative law of effect differs from the LAW OF EFFECT in that punishment suppresses a response rather than causing it to be unlearned.

negatively accelerated. Having a decreasing rate of acceleration, e.g. of a curve, or of rate of physical growth.

negative Oedipus complex. (Psychoanalysis) A complex in which the son desires the father and is jealous of the mother.

negative phototaxis. *See* PHOTOTAXIS.

negative practice. The deliberate repetition of an error in an attempt to eliminate it. *Compare* PARADOXICAL INTENTION.

negative priming. Increased reaction time to a stimulus as a result of previously being made to attend to a different class of stimuli.

E.g. if someone has to respond to any fruit and is shown 'dog' and 'apple', and on the next trial has to respond to any animal and is shown 'cat' and 'orange', the response to 'cat' is delayed.

negative recency effect. In a series of stimuli (or responses) the tendency to predict a stimulus (or to make a response) that has not occurred recently. E.g. if a coin has come down heads ten times in a row, many people think it is more likely to come down tails next time. Such effects must be guarded against in questionnaires: if someone has answered 'yes' several times in a row, the probability of his answering 'no' to the next question is increased. *Contrast* POSITIVE RECENCY EFFECT.

negative reference group. A REFERENCE GROUP disapproved of by a person to such an extent that he tends to adopt the opposite values, beliefs, and attitudes to those of the group. *Contrast* POSITIVE REFERENCE GROUP.

negative reinforcement. The strengthening of a response by the cessation (ESCAPE LEARN-ING) or elimination (AVOIDANCE LEARNING) of an aversive stimulus after the response has been made. *Compare* POSITIVE REINFORCE-MENT.

negative reward. A synonym for PUNISHMENT (note the difference from NEGATIVE REINFORCEMENT).

negative stimulus (S–, S△). 1. A DISCRIMINA-TIVE STIMULUS signalling in successive dis-crimination learning that no reinforcement is available and in simultaneous discrimination learning that no reinforcement will be ob-tained if the animal selects that stimulus. 2. A stimulus signifying that the organism will be punished if it approaches or carries out some specific act.

negative symptoms of schizophrenia. Com-paratively mild schizophrenic symptoms that are exaggerations of normal traits, e.g. apathy, emotional blunting and im-poverished speech. *Contrast* POSITIVE SYMPTOMS OF SCHIZOPHRENIA.

negative taxis. *See* TAXIS.

negative therapeutic reaction. A worsening of the patient's condition during psychoana-lysis, a not uncommon occurrence; it is usually attributed to the patient's need to suffer, rather than to any fault of the therapist. The expression 'negative therapeutic treatment' would in most cases be more appropriate, but for some reason has not been adopted.

negative time error. An error in the judgement of the intensities of two successive stimuli, in which the magnitude of the first stimulus is underestimated relative to that of the second. This is the more frequently found direction of time error. *Compare* POSITIVE TIME ERROR.

negative transfer. The impairment of per-formance on one task as a result of practice on another. *Compare* PROACTIVE INTERFER-ENCE and RETROACTIVE INTERFERENCE.

negative transference. (Psychoanalysis) A patient's hostility towards his analyst, alleged to be a displacement of his attitudes to his parents, however justifiable it may be.

negative triad. A synonym for COGNITIVE TRIAD.

negative trial. In successive discrimination learning, any trial on which the NEGATIVE STIMULUS is presented.

negative tropism. A tendency for an organism to move away (or orientate itself away) from a specific stimulus.

negative valence. *See* VALENCE.

negativism. Resistance to the ideas and suggestions of other people.

neoassociationism. Any modern variant of associationism; e.g. cognitive psychologists may use directed graphs to represent the associations between concepts.

neobehaviourism. Any school of BE-HAVIOURISM after Watson. More specifically, the thesis that although psychology can only study stimuli and behaviour it is legitimate to infer intervening covert processes. In prac-tice there were three main schools, HULLIAN BEHAVIOURISM, PURPOSIVE BEHAVIOURISM, and RADICAL BEHAVIOURISM. *See also* METHODO-LOGICAL BEHAVIOURISM.

neocerebellum. The dorsal part of the cerebellum, which communicates with the pons; it developed in phylogeny after the PALAEOCEREBELLUM.

neocortex. The part of the cerebral cortex most recently developed in mammals; it excludes the older PALAEOCORTEX and ARCHICORTEX, which have fewer layers of cells than the six of the neocortex.

neoendorphin. *See* ENDORPHIN.

neo-Freudian. A psychoanalyst who accepts Freud's basic ideas, but with modifications. The expression is mainly used of those who reject his view of the overriding importance of the libido, and who stress the importance of social and cultural factors (e.g. Horney and Sullivan).

neolalia. Speech containing many neologisms.

neologism. A newly created word, including the nonsense words spoken by schizophrenics.

neomnesis. Memory for the recent past.

neonatal. Pertaining to the period in the offspring immediately after birth. *Compare* POSTPARTUM.

neonate. An infant of less than a month old.

neopallium. A synonym for NEOCORTEX.

neophasia. An elaborate language system with its own grammatical rules invented by e.g. schizophrenics or siblings at an early age. In **polyglot neophasia** a person invents and uses more than one such system.

neophobia. A morbid fear of novelty.

neostriatum. A recently evolved part of the CORPUS STRIATUM that contains the PUTAMEN and CAUDATE NUCLEUS.

neoteny. The retention in the adult of characteristics that were confined to the embryo in its ancestors, e.g. lack of body hair in man.

nerve. A bundle of AXONS running parallel to one another, usually outside the central nervous system (within it such bundles are usually called TRACTS).

nerve block. The blocking of nerve impulses, e.g. by drugs or by pressure on a nerve.

nerve cell. A synonym for NEURON.

nerve deafness. Hearing loss caused by damage to the auditory receptors or auditory pathways.

nerve ending. The receptive terminal of a sensory neuron in the somaesthetic and kinaesthetic senses, e.g. BASKET ENDING or FLOWER-SPRAY ENDING.

nerve felt. A synonym for NEUROPIL.

nerve fibre. Any long process of a neuron, usually an axon but it can refer to a long dendritic process. Peripheral nerve fibres are classified by size (i.e. diameter) into types A, B, and C. Type A is further broken down by size into three afferent and three efferent groups. The three groups of **A afferent fibres** are: **AI fibres**, the largest, which include primary sensory fibres from muscle spindles and tendon organs; **AII fibres**, of intermediate size, which include cutaneous fibres and afferent fibres serving larger hair follicles; **AIII fibres**, the smallest, which are fibres mediating sharp, bright pain and fibres serving small hair cells. The three groups of **A efferent fibres** are: **Aα fibres**, the largest, which are motor neurons; **Aβ fibres**, of intermediate size, which are efferents to slow twitch muscles; **Aγ fibres**, the smallest, which are efferents to the intrafusal fibres. **B fibres** are fibres of the preganglionic autonomic system. **C fibres** are very slow unmyelinated fibres, including postganglionic autonomic fibres, some visceral and somatic sensory fibres, and fibres mediating dull long-lasting pain.

nerve growth factor. A hormone present in the saliva and elsewhere that is absorbed by some nerve endings, is transported in a retrograde direction, and is essential for the survival of the neuron.

nerve impulse. *See* IMPULSE (2).

nerve root. A collection of neurons at the point where they join the spinal cord.

nervism. Pavlov's doctrine that all behaviour is under the control of the nervous system.

nervous breakdown. A non-technical expression meaning the inability to function due to a mental disorder.

nervous system. All the nerve cells in the body. It is divided into the CENTRAL NERVOUS SYSTEM and the PERIPHERAL NERVOUS SYSTEM, which in turn is divided into the SOMATIC NERVOUS SYSTEM and the AUTONOMIC NERVOUS SYSTEM.

nesting. (Linguistics) In generative grammar, the insertion of one or more linguistic constituents within another of the same type. E.g. in 'The man in the pub', 'the pub' is a noun phrase nested within the noun phrase 'the man in the pub'. *Compare* EMBEDDING, which is restricted to a sentence inserted in another sentence.

net reaction potential ($_s\bar{E}_R$). Hull's expression for response strength as determined by GENERALIZED REACTION POTENTIAL with the AGGREGATE INHIBITORY POTENTIAL deducted. *See* HULLIAN THEORY.

NET talk. A neural net that learns English pronunciation by being fed letters making up words and being taught by the back-propagation of the correct simulated phonemes.

network. Any collection of units that may activate (and sometimes inhibit) one another through their interconnections. For examples, *see* PARALLEL DISTRIBUTED PROCESSING, SEMANTIC NETWORK, and STRUCTURAL DESCRIPTION.

neural. Pertaining to neurons or nerves.

neural arc. A chain of neurons usually starting with a RECEPTOR and ending with an EFFECTOR.

neural auto-inhibition. A reduction in the amount of NEUROTRANSMITTER that can be released from the presynaptic cell, caused by an active mechanism triggered by an immediately preceding release of the transmitter.

neural conduction. *See* CONDUCTION.

neural crest. The strip of cells running along the NEURAL TUBE of the vertebrate embryo, from which the central nervous system develops.

neural Darwinism. A theory of learning and of the development of the nervous system put forward by Edelman. It hypothesizes that the 'fittest' synapses survive and stresses the role of feedback loops in the brain. Many have found its exact content hard to divine.

neural discharge. The production of an IMPULSE (2) by a neuron.

neural excitation. *See* EXCITATION (1).

neural facilitation. An increase in the readiness of a neuron to fire, which can occur through TEMPORAL SUMMATION or SPATIAL SUMMATION.

neural fold. The layer of embryonic tissue on either side of the NEURAL PLATE that grows to enfold the neural groove.

neuralgia. Recurrent pain in the area served by a nerve, caused by damage to the nerve, or of unknown origin.

neural groove. A fissure that develops in the NEURAL PLATE of the embryo and that becomes the NEURAL TUBE.

neural impulse. *See* IMPULSE (2).

neural induction. The process by which the NEURAL PLATE in the embryo becomes committed to forming the central nervous system as a result of triggering substances being released.

neural network. 1. A system of neurons each connected to at least one other neuron. 2. (Artificial intelligence) *See* PARALLEL DISTRIBUTED PROCESSING.

neural plate. The embryonic ectodermal tissue that develops into the NEURAL TUBE. *See* NEURAL INDUCTION.

neural process. Any branch or filament of a neuron.

neural receptor. A synonym for RECEPTOR (2).

neural tube. A tube that develops in the NEURAL PLATE from which the central nervous system is developed. The posterior part becomes the spinal column and the anterior part the brain. Three bulges develop at the anterior end: the most anterior becomes the forebrain, the next the midbrain, and the most posterior the hindbrain.

neurasthenia. An obsolete term for a neurotic condition, marked by fatigue, weakness, headaches, etc.

neuraxis. The axis defined by the positions of the brain and spinal cord; neuroanatomical terms like anterior or dorsal are defined in relation to this axis.

neurilemma. The membrane covering the myelin sheath in peripheral axons.

neuroanatomy. The study of the structure of the nervous system, its constituents, and their connections.

neurobiology. The study of the nervous system and its role in behaviour.

neurobiotaxis. The growth of an axon in development to the point with which it has to connect.

neuroblast. A neuron in the embryonic form.

neurochemistry. The study of the chemistry of neurons.

neurocyte. A synonym for NEURON.

neuroeffector junction. The junction between an efferent neuron and the muscle or gland that it innervates.

neuroendocrine cell. A cell that functions both as a neuron and as an endocrine cell (e.g. some cells in the pituitary).

neuroendocrinology. The study of the relationship between the central nervous system and the endocrine system.

neurofibril. One of a number of thread-like structures running through nerve fibres; their function is not known.

neurogenesis. The growth of neurons.

neurogenetics. The study of the effects of mutations on the nervous system and the resulting changes in behaviour.

neurogenic drive. The automatic generation within the nervous system of a pattern of impulses, usually rhythmic, to control the activity of an organ, e.g. heart beat.

neuroglia. Cells found in the central nervous system that are thought to provide structural support and sustenance, and that may influence the firing of neurons. There are three main kinds. (i) ASTROGLIA (astrocytes) are thought to provide nutrition to neurons, to form scar tissue after injury and to dispose of dead cells. (ii) MICROGLIA act as phagocytes. (iii) OLIGODENDROGLIA provide the myelin sheath and may also guide the developing axon to its target.

neurogram. A synonym for ENGRAM.

neurohumour. Any chemical substance specifically secreted by neurons, particularly substances involved in synaptic transmission, such as neurotransmitters.

neurohypophysis. *See* PITUITARY.

neurolemma. An alternative spelling for NEURILEMMA.

neuroleptic. Any drug that has a therapeutic effect on schizophrenia in particular, and more generally on any overactivity or agitation that is a symptom of a psychotic illness (e.g. mania). The PHENOTHIAZINES (which include CHLORPROMAZINE) are one group of such drugs. These drugs are also known as MAJOR TRANQUILLIZERS since they have a large tranquillizing effect, though they have little effect on alertness.

neurolinguistics. The study of the neural basis of language, undertaken mainly by examining neurological cases with impaired language abilities.

neurology. A medical speciality dealing with the diagnosis and treatment of patients with damage to, or disorders of, the nervous system, and with the causation of the symptoms.

neurometrics. The study of EEG waves and evoked potentials.

neuromodulator. A chemical substance that modifies the synaptic action of a neurotransmitter, e.g. various peptides like SUBSTANCE P.

neuromuscular. Pertaining to the interactions of neurons and muscles.

neuromuscular junction. The interface between a motor nerve and a skeletal muscle.

neuron, neurone. A cell that transmits information by means of a change in the electrical polarization of its membrane. A neuron normally consists of DENDRITES (which receive information), the CELL BODY, and an AXON (which transmits information to another cell, or to a muscle or gland). There are three categories of neurons – RECEPTORS (1), INTERNEURONS, and MOTOR NEURONS. The structure of neurons is extremely varied.

neuron theory. The theory, substantiated by Cajal, that the brain is made up of separate neurons rather than being a continuum. *Contrast* RETICULARIST THEORY.

neuropathology. The study of diseases of the nervous system.

neuropathy. Any disease or disorder of the nervous system.

neuropeptide. A peptide (e.g. ACTH, ENKEPHALIN) that can be present in the synaptic cleft and acts as a NEUROTRANSMITTER or NEUROMODULATOR.

neuropeptide Y (NPY). A peptide, found in the sympathetic nervous system and in the brain. It is associated with norepinephrine; injecting it into the paraventricular nucleus is effective in producing eating.

neuropharmacology. The study of the effects of drugs on the nervous system.

neurophysiology. The study of the functioning of the nervous system and its components.

neuropil, neuroplexis. A network of nerve cells packed close together and containing cell bodies, dendrites, and axons, such as the cortical grey matter.

neuropsychiatry. A branch of medicine that studies how brain malfunctioning can cause mental disorders, and that attempts to devise physical methods of treating such disorders.

neuropsychology. The branch of psychology that studies (and treats) brain damaged patients, and that attempts to infer from their symptoms the brain mechanisms underlying both normal and impaired behaviour. Unfortunately, the term is sometimes used more widely as a synonym for PHYSIOLOGICAL PSYCHOLOGY.

neuropsychotropic. A synonym for PSYCHOTROPIC.

neuroreceptor. *See* RECEPTOR (2).

neuroregulator. A generic term for a substance that is a NEUROTRANSMITTER or a NEUROMODULATOR.

neuroscience. A fashionable catch-all phrase that includes all disciplines that directly study the nervous system (e.g. neuroanatomy, neurochemistry, and neuropharmacology) and all that attempt to relate behaviour to the nervous system (e.g. physiological psychology). *Contrast* COGNITIVE SCIENCE, an equally fashionable term, comprising a set of disciplines that barely overlap with neuroscience.

neurosecretory cell. A neuron that secretes a hormone into the extracellular fluid, found for example in the neurohypophysis.

neurosis. A mental disorder, mild as compared with a PSYCHOSIS, in which the patient does not lose contact with reality, and which is thought not to be due to a brain disorder. It is usually accompanied by anxiety. *See* ANXIETY NEUROSIS, EXPERIMENTAL NEUROSIS, HYPOCHONDRIASIS, HYSTERIA, NEURASTHENIA, NEUROTIC DEPRESSION, OBSESSIVE–COMPULSIVE DISORDER, and PHOBIA.

neurosurgery. The medical speciality concerned with operations on the nervous system, particularly on the brain.

neurotendinal spindle. A synonym for GOLGI TENDON ORGAN.

neurotensin. A peptide that, though not an opiate, appears to act as a reinforcer when injected into the ventral tegmental area.

neurotic anxiety. (Psychoanalysis) The fear that the instincts of the id will get out of control. *Contrast* MORAL ANXIETY and REALITY ANXIETY.

neurotic character. Adler's expression for the personality traits developed to shield a person from inferiority feelings.

neurotic defence. Horney's expression for a set of maladaptive strategies used to guard against anxiety aroused by repressed wishes; they include a mixture of dependence on others, and the assertion of one's own desires.

neurotic depression. A neurosis in which the main symptom is depression; in severe cases it is indistinguishable from UNIPOLAR MANIC-DEPRESSIVE DISORDER.

neurotic disorder. A fashionable but lengthy expression for NEUROSIS.

neurotic fiction. 1. Adler's term for a belief about oneself, particularly about one's capabilities, that is completely wrong and that is held to reduce anxiety about oneself. 2. Any novel by Iris Murdoch.

neuroticism. Proneness to neurosis.

neuroticism dimension. One of the personality dimensions measured in the EYSENCK PERSONALITY QUESTIONNAIRE. Those high in neuroticism are emotionally unstable, anxious, shy, moody, and depressed, and have low self-esteem. It is thought to correlate with neurosis.

neurotic nucleus. A set of traits thought by some to be common to all neurotics, e.g. sensitivity to stress, and tendency to feel anxious.

neurotic paradox. (Psychoanalysis) The alleged refusal of the neurotic to give up maladaptive defence strategies despite the distress they cause him.

neurotic process. The process by which repressed conflicts come to be expressed as neurotic symptoms.

neurotic process trait. Cattell's term for neuroticism, as measured by his own tests.

neurotic regression debility. One of Cattell's personality dimensions, characterized mainly by inflexibility.

neurotic sleep attack. An uncontrollable urge to sleep at an inappropriate time that is of psychogenic origin.

neurotic solution. Horney's expression for getting rid of a conflict by repressing it (which in some circumstances would seem the most sensible thing to do).

neurotransmitter. A chemical substance secreted at a neuron's axonal terminal, which attaches to the receptor of the postsynaptic cell, and has an excitatory or inhibitory effect upon it. Examples of neurotransmitters are ACETYLCHOLINE, DOPAMINE, EPINEPHRINE, GLUTAMATE, NOREPINEPHRINE, SEROTONIN, and various NEUROPEPTIDES.

neurotropism. The tendency of developing or regenerating axons to grow in a particular direction.

neurovegetative system. A synonym for PARASYMPATHETIC SYSTEM.

neutral colour. A colour lacking HUE, i.e. black, grey, or white.

neutral density filter. An achromatic filter that reduces the light transmitted equally at all wavelengths.

neutralization. (Psychoanalysis) The conversion of libidinal drives into non-sexual activities like writing dictionaries.

neutralizer. A member of an ENCOUNTER GROUP who tries to control the aggressive or destructive behaviour of the others.

neutral stimulus. 1. (Classical conditioning) Any stimulus that in the absence of training excites neither the response to be conditioned nor an antagonistic response. 2. (Operant conditioning) Any stimulus that does not control behaviour at a given stage of learning.

neutral vowel. A synonym for SCHWA.

new information. (Linguistics) The novel information in a sentence, as opposed to the GIVEN INFORMATION.

New Look School. The forlorn attempt of Bruner and others to show that perception is influenced by motivation.

Newman–Keuls test. (Statistics) An A POST-ERIORI TEST that assesses the significance of the difference between all pairs of a set of means, and sorts them into homogeneous subsets. The means are ranked and the difference in the absolute values of means having extreme ranks is compared with the difference for means having adjacent ranks.

newton. The SI unit of force; it is the force required to accelerate one kilogram mass through one metre per second per second.

nexus. 1. A connection. 2. Several entities connected together.

nicotine. An alkaloid present in tobacco that increases alertness by its stimulating effect on the nervous system, probably through mimicking ACETYLCHOLINE; in larger quantities it may have a depressant effect. *See also* NICOTINIC RECEPTORS.

nicotine replacement therapy. *See* RE-PLACEMENT THERAPY (2).

nicotinic receptors. One of two types of excitatory synaptic receptor for ACETYL-CHOLINE. They are found in the central nervous system, at the ganglionic autonomic synapses, and in motor fibres innervating skeletal muscle; they can be stimulated by NICOTINE. *Compare* MUSCARINIC RECEPTORS.

nictitating membrane. A transparent fold of skin lying next to the cornea and forming a second eyelid. It occurs in some amphibia and birds, and a few mammals (e.g. cats and rabbits). Its closure has been widely used as the unconditioned response in studies of classical conditioning in the rabbit.

nictophobia. A synonym for ACHLUOPHOBIA.

night blindness. A synonym for NYCTALOPIA.

night residue. Material from a dream that persists in one's daytime thoughts.

night vision. A synonym for SCOTOPIC VISION.

nigrostriatal bundle. A group of axons running from the SUBSTANTIA NIGRA to the CAUDATA NUCLEUS and PUTAMEN, thought to be implicated in hunger, thirst, and activity.

nihilism. (Psychiatry) A patient's delusion that he does not exist or is in a dream.

ninth cranial nerve. A synonym for GLOS-SOPHARYNGEAL NERVE.

Nissl bodies, Nissl granules. Small organelles containing RIBOSOMES, found in the cytoplasm of the cell bodies of neurons, and forming part of the ENDOPLASMIC RETICULUM. Nissl bodies are stained by thionine. *See* NISSL STAIN.

Nissl stain. A thionine stain that selectively colours NISSL BODIES and therefore shows up the cell body.

nit (nt). A largely obsolete synonym for CANDELA PER SQUARE METRE.

nitrazepam. A BENZODIAZEPINE used as a sleeping drug.

nitrous oxide. A mild NARCOTIC and anaesthetic, popularly called 'laughing gas'.

nm. An abbreviation for NANOMETRE.

NMDA (N-methyl-D-aspartate). A synthetic amino acid binding preferentially to one type of glutamate receptor (the NMDA RECEPTOR) and can therefore be used to identify that receptor.

NMDA channel. A membrane channel in a postsynaptic membrane that responds to NMDA and that allows ions through if and only if GLUTAMATE is released by the pre-synaptic cell and the potential across the postsynaptic cell is less negative than the RESTING POTENTIAL (i.e. if it is already partially excited). In addition to potassium and sodium ions, it admits calcium ions, which are thought indirectly to increase the strength of the synapse. The mechanism could be the basis of the HEBB SYNAPSE.

NMDA receptor. A GLUTAMATE receptor that also responds to NMDA.

N-methyl-D-aspartate. *See* NMDA.

NMR. An abbreviation for NUCLEAR MAGNETIC RESONANCE.

nociceptor. A sensory receptor sensitive to pain.

noctambulism. A synonym for SOMNAMBULISM.

nodal behaviour. In group therapy, the occurrence of highly emotional behaviour.

nodal point. The point at which unrefracted light rays from all directions intersect, which in the case of the eye is taken to be the centre of curvature of the cornea (the nodal point of the lens is very close to this point).

node. 1. (Anatomy) A knob or swelling. 2. A point in a network where one or more paths enter and one or more paths depart. Nodes can represent entities. An **open node** is one that merits a search, a **closed node** one that has been put aside. **Node expansion** is examining a node's successor nodes. 3. (Acoustics) *See* STANDING WAVES.

node of Ranvier. A gap in the myelin sheath which occurs at intervals along myelinated axons; it increases speed of conduction of the nerve impulse since the current jumps from one node to the next.

noesis. Conscious reasoning.

noise. 1. (Information theory) Any randomly occurring signals in a communication channel that do not form part of the message being conveyed, but can be confused with it; or any random distortions of the signals conveying the message. 2. (Hearing) An auditory stimulus having no clearly defined pitch. *See also* COLOURED NOISE, PINK NOISE, and WHITE NOISE.

noise masking. A synonym for PATTERN MASKING BY NOISE.

nominal aphasia. Aphasia in which the primary symptom is the inability to recover the right word in speaking and to recognize words in listening.

nominalism. (Philosophy) The doctrine that only individual objects exist and that general terms (like 'red', 'horse', 'beauty') have no meaning except in so far as they refer to the specific objects they denote.

nominal realism. Piaget's expression for the young child's belief that names are not arbitrary, but are an intrinsic characteristic of whatever they refer to.

nominal scale. A so-called scale in which individual items are divided into categories but in which there is no rank order; divisions of people by race or of patients by diagnostic category are nominal scales. *Compare* CATEGORICAL VARIABLE.

nominating technique. A sociometric method in which each member of a group selects another member according to some criterion, e.g. least liked.

nominative. The case of a noun or pronoun when used as the subject of the verb.

nomogram. 1. (Statistics) A graph containing a number of lines – usually three. The lines have graduated values and are drawn in such a way that a straight line intersecting all three will intersect each at the value it would have if the others had the values at which it intersects them. Hence if the values of two of the variables are known, that of the third can be determined. Nomograms are sometimes used instead of mathematical tables. 2. (Vision) A plot invented by Dartnall from which it is possible to calculate the absorption spectrum of any retinal pigment provided the wavelength at which its absorption is maximal is known.

nomological validity. The extent to which a test appears to measure what it purports to measure in the light of some overall theory. *Contrast* TRAIT VALIDITY.

nomology. (Science) The construction and study of scientific laws and principles.

nomothetic psychology. The attempt to

establish general laws, as opposed to those applying only to an individual. *Contrast* IDEO-GRAPHIC PSYCHOLOGY.

non-classical receptive field. *See* RECEPTIVE FIELD.

non-common effects principle. The principle that in inferring underlying motives or dispositions from a person's action, observers rely most on those (probable) effects of the action that differ most from those of other actions he might have performed.

non–contingent reinforcement. Reinforcement that is not contingent on a response. *See* AUTOSHAPING and SUPERSTITIOUS BEHAVIOUR.

non–continuity theory. The hypothesis that on a given trial organisms only learn about the stimuli to which they are attending, and that once they attend to the correct stimulus, they learn in a single trial. *Compare* HYPOTHESIS and *contrast* CONTINUITY THEORY.

non-correction method. *See* CORRECTION METHOD.

non–decremental conduction. The phenomenon that a nerve impulse travelling down an axon retains the same intensity.

non-determinate hard polynomial problem. *See* NP HARD PROBLEM.

non–directional statistical significance. The significance of a difference (e.g. between means) regardless of the direction of the difference. *Compare* TWO-TAILED TEST.

non-directional test. A synonym for a two-tailed test.

non-directive therapy. A form of psychotherapy originated by Rogers, in which the therapist encourages the patient to talk and reflect, but gives little or no guidance. Rogers believed that all patients were capable of self-actualization if the therapist treated them in a genuine, empathetic, and respectful manner: he was an optimist. *See* CARE.

Nonius method. A method of measuring the EMPIRICAL HOROPTER by projecting two vertical rods, one to each eye and one above the other, while the subject fixates another point.

One of the rods is moved sideways until they appear to the subject to be aligned. This yields a point on the empirical horopter.

non–metric scaling. The production of an original scale, e.g. by having subjects rank items without assessing intervals or ratios.

non–monotonic logic. A logic that allows for contradictions and the modification of inferences when contradictions occur. No such logics are satisfactory: they are an attempt to represent the way in which the mind works.

non–parametric statistics. (Statistics) Methods of testing hypotheses or setting up confidence intervals that do not depend on assumptions about the form of population distributions. Non–parametric statistics normally use either ranks or ordered scores (e.g. WILCOXON TEST, MANN–WHITNEY U TEST, and FRIEDMAN TEST). *Contrast* PARAMETRIC STATISTICS.

non-REM sleep. Any sleep other than REM sleep. *See* SLEEP.

non-reactive measures. A synonym for UNOBTRUSIVE MEASURES.

non–reversal shift. Any change in the stimulus to be rewarded that does not consist of reversing the positive and negative stimuli (reversal shift); e.g. an organism trained to take a black form and not white (ignoring shape) might be shifted to taking a square and avoiding a triangle while ignoring colour.

nonsense figure. A figure that has no meaning and no immediate associations; they are used in experiments on the memory for, and recognition of, two-dimensional figures.

nonsense syllable. A syllable that can be spoken or written, but has no meaning, e.g. 'bok', 'tul'. Nonsense syllables have been extensively used since Ebbinghaus as items to be learned. *Compare* CVC.

non–specific transfer. Transfer between two tasks having few elements in common: the general principles learned in one task may assist or impair performance on the other.

nonspectral hue. A synonym for EXRASPEC-TRAL HUE.

non–verbal behaviour. Usually used in the restricted sense of NONVERBAL COMMUNICATION.

non–verbal communication. Communication without the use of language, by gestures, facial expression, etc.

non–verbal language. Cues, inadvertently given by a person, that he is lying or trying to conceal something, e.g. through his facial expression, body posture etc.

nootropic. Any drug that improves memory, so far a null class.

noradrenaline. A synonym for NOREPINEPHRINE.

noradrenergic. Pertaining to transmission across a synapse based on NOREPINEPHRINE (or on substances that mimic its action).

norepinephrine. A CATECHOLAMINE hormone and NEUROTRANSMITTER secreted by the adrenal medulla. It is active in the postganglionic sympathetic system and in the pleasure centres. Underactivity of the norepinephrine system may be implicated in depression and overactivity in mania. The adjective is NORADRENERGIC.

norm. 1. (Mental testing) The value of a trait or capacity that is average for a population 2. (Social psychology) Any way of behaving or rule of conduct that is conventional in a given community. 3. (Perception) A stimulus that acts as an anchor point for a dimension, e.g. vertical or horizontal for tilt, a straight line for degree of curvature, etc. Difference thresholds are usually lower for stimuli that are norms than for other stimuli on the dimension. *See also* NORMALIZATION (2).

normal. Average within a group; but it sometimes takes on overtones of right or good, and it may mean free from mental or physical disorder. *Contrast* ABNORMAL.

normal curvature. The curvature of a line on a surface created by intersecting the surface by a plane containing the surface normal.

normal distribution. This can be considered as the limiting form of the BINOMIAL DISTRIBUTION, giving the theoretical frequency with which a probabilistic event will occur n times in an infinite number of samples, where n is continuous and ranges from zero to infinity. The distribution is symmetrical and bell-shaped, hence it has MEAN, MEDIAN, and MODE at the same point. It is characterized by its mean and STANDARD DEVIATION. Though seldom observed, it has remarkable statistical properties (*compare* CENTRAL LIMIT THEOREM) and is the most frequently assumed statistical distribution.

normalization. 1. (Statistics) Transforming data by mathematical operations to make them fit a preconceived pattern, e.g. that of having a normal distribution. Thus, the logarithm of reaction time scores is often computed to reduce the influence of the (usually rare) very long reaction times. 2. (Perception) A change in a NORM (3) to make it consistent with current stimulus conditions. E.g. after prolonged inspection, curved lines come to seem straighter than they are, and lines slightly off vertical or horizontal come to seem more vertical or horizontal. 3. (Social psychology) The process whereby a person comes to accept and act upon the NORMS (2) accepted by his society or group, or by others in his role.

normative. 1. Setting principles or standards for how people or other systems ought to behave; e.g. both GAME THEORY and SIGNAL DETECTION THEORY are normative since they describe how an ideal system would behave. 2. Pertaining to norms or to the establishment of norms.

normative influence. Conforming to group norms in order to secure approval from the group.

normative theory. An abstract theory that specifies the optimal performance on a task, e.g. INFORMATION THEORY or SIGNAL DETECTION THEORY.

normless suicide. A synonym for ANOMIC SUICIDE.

nortriptyline. A commonly used TRICYCLIC.

nosology. The study of the classification of diseases.

nosophobia. A morbid fear of illness.

notochord. 1. The evolutionary forerunner of the spinal cord. 2. In vertebrates, the embryonic forerunner of the spinal cord.

noun. A syntactic category of words. It is often defined as a word that refers to a person, place, or thing, but since 'philosophy' or 'sweetness' are also nouns, it is better defined in terms of its syntactic role – e.g. it can serve as subject or object, can be preceded by a preposition, etc.

noun phrase (NP). Any phrase that can serve as subject or object of a verb, e.g. 'The tall man at the bar'.

NP. An abbreviation for NOUN PHRASE.

NP hard problem (non-determinate hard polynomial problem). A synonym for INTRACTABLE PROBLEM.

NPY. An abbreviation for NEUROPEPTIDE Y.

NREM sleep. An abbreviation for NON-REM SLEEP.

nt. An abbreviation for NIT.

nuclear complex. (Psychoanalysis) The basic source of psychological conflict which is said to arise in infancy, e.g. according to Freud, the OEDIPUS COMPLEX, and according to Adler the INFERIORITY COMPLEX.

nuclear family. A family that consists of the parents and their children. *Contrast* EXTENDED FAMILY.

nuclear magnetic resonance (NMR). A non-invasive technique for measuring the density of tissue. A magnetic field is imposed, and causes some nuclei to align with it like dipoles. Radio waves are then used to excite these nuclei, which subsequently give off electromagnetic radiation at a radio frequency; this is measured. The technique can be used to produce a 3-D image of the density of tissue in the brain by recording strong signals received from hydrogen atoms, which are abundant in tissue. Spatial resolution is about 1 mm, but temporal resolution is poor, since it takes about 15 minutes to construct an image.

nuclear schizophrenia. A synonym for PROCESS SCHIZOPHRENIA.

nucleic acids. The complex acids composing DNA and RNA; they are made up of long sequences of NUCLEOTIDES.

nucleolus. An organelle in a cell's nucleus that manufactures RNA.

nucleoplasm. The material in the nucleus. *Contrast* CYTOPLASM.

nucleotide. A unit of DNA based on adenosine, cytosine, guanine, or thymine, or a unit of RNA based on adenosine, cytosine, guanine, or uracil. Which amino acid is to be introduced at a given point in a polypeptide chain is specified by a triplet of nucleotides.

nucleus. 1. (Cell biology) The central spherical structure in a cell body that contains the genetic material, and that directs the activities of the cell. 2. (Neurophysiology) A cluster of neuronal cell bodies in the central nervous system. 3. (Linguistics) *See* TONE GROUP.

nucleus accumbens. Part of the limbic system, receiving projections from the amygdala, hippocampus and limbic cortex in addition to a dopamine input from the ventral tegmental area. It is probably implicated in reinforcement.

nucleus cuneatus. A synonym for CUNEATE NUCLEUS.

nucleus gracilis. A synonym for GRACILE NUCLEUS.

nucleus of raphe. A synonym for RAPHE NUCLEUS.

null hypothesis. 1. (Statistics) The hypothesis under test in the application of inferential statistics, as distinct from the **alternative hypothesis**. Rejection of the null hypothesis can lead to a TYPE I ERROR. 2. The term is often used more specifically to mean the hypothesis that there is no difference between population values (e.g. means).

number. (Linguistics) A grammatical category that classifies words (e.g. nouns, verbs) as singular or plural (or in some languages dual or even more).

number-completion test. A test, often used in IQ testing, in which a person has to supply a missing number in a series of numbers arranged according to a rule. E.g. 'Supply the next number in the series 1, 9, 25, . . . '.

number factor. A postulated factor underlying the ability to manipulate numbers.

numerator. The dividend in a fraction, e.g. 3 in 3/4.

nurture. The environmental factors that influence both the physical and mental development of an organism. *Compare* NATURE–NURTURE CONTROVERSY.

NVC. An abbreviation for NON-VERBAL COMMUNICATION.

nyctalopia. Poor vision in low illumination (scotopic vision) with unimpaired photopic vision, usually caused by a defect in the rods. *Contrast* HEMERALOPIA.

nyctophilia. A liking for the dark.

nyctophobia. An alternative spelling of NICTOPHOBIA.

nymphomania. Excessive pursuit by women of sexual intercourse with men.

nystagmus. Any regular, repetitive involuntary movements of the eyes, usually alternating slow and fast movements (**jerk nystagmus**), but sometimes with movements of the same speed in each direction (**pendular nystagmus**). *See also* CALORIC NYSTAGMUS, CENTRAL NYSTAGMUS, LABYRINTHINE NYSTAGMUS, OPTOKINETIC NYSTAGMUS, PHYSIOLOGICAL NYSTAGMUS, and VESTIBULAR NYSTAGMUS.

O

O. An abbreviation for 1. observer; 2. organism; 3. BEHAVIOURAL OSCILLATION, when it is usually written $_sO_R$ (*see* HULLIAN THEORY); 4. OHM.

OBE. An abbreviation for OUT OF THE BODY EXPERIENCE.

object. 1. (Linguistics) The noun phrase specifying the recipient or target of an action, as in 'The man hurt *his leg*'. 2. (Psychoanalysis) Anything to which the libido is or may be attached, i.e. the object of a person's desires.

object assembly test. A test in which the parts of an object have to be put together.

object attitude. Concentration on the outside world rather than on one's state of mind, particularly as a result of experimental instructions. *Contrast* PROCESS ATTITUDE.

object blindness. A synonym for VISUAL AGNOSIA.

object cathexis. (Psychoanalysis) Investment of the libido (even in sublimated form) in something outside oneself. *Compare* EGO CARTHEXIS.

object-centred description. (Vision) A description of an object based on a coordinate system intrinsic to it. Marr suggested the axis of longest elongation as a possible intrinsic axis, but not all objects have a unique axis of longest orientation. *Contrast* VIEWER-CENTRED DESCRIPTION.

object choice. (Psychoanalysis) The selection of an object for cathexis.

object colour. Colour perceived to belong to the surface of an object and subject to COLOUR CONSTANCY. *Contrast* FILM COLOUR.

object constancy. The tendency for an object to be seen as it really is despite changes in the conditions of viewing. *Compare e.g.* COLOUR CONSTANCY, SHAPE CONSTANCY, and SIZE CONSTANCY.

objectivation. (Psychoanalysis) A defence mechanism in which a person fails to recognize his own traits or desires but recognizes them when they exist in other people. *Compare* PROJECTION.

objective altruisim. Any behaviour undertaken to benefit a conspecific with no survival value for the organism performing it.

objective anxiety. A synonym for REAL ANXIETY.

objective case. *See* CASE GRAMMAR.

objective test. A test scored according to rigorous rules so that no subjective judgements are required.

objectivism. (Ethics) The doctrine that there are correct objective moral standards applicable to all societies, whether or not they observe them.

object language. *See* METALANGUAGE.

object libido. Those aspects of the LIBIDO that are directed to an external OBJECT (2). *Contrast* EGO LIBIDO.

object loss. (Psychoanalysis) The loss of someone to whom a person has been strongly attached, or the loss of his love.

302

object permanence. The fact that objects continue to exist even when they pass out of sight, which according to Piaget the child only comes to understand towards 2 years of age.

object recognition. The identification of a 3-D body as a particular individual object or as belonging to a particular class of objects, a task that can usually be performed regardless of viewpoint or the orientation of the object relative to the body. Note that more is involved in recognition than merely vision – a perfect visual replica of Mae West is still not Mae West. *Compare* PATTERN RECOGNITION.

object relations theory. A psychoanalytic theory, originated by Klein, that holds a person relates to others not, as Freud held, to satisfy his instincts, but rather to develop himself and to differentiate himself from others. The theory stresses the effects of social relations on a person. It has heavily influenced family therapy.

object selection. (Psychoanalysis) A person's relationships with anybody or anything about which he has strong feelings; the term is used by writers like Klein to stress the importance of the objects on which the libido focuses for the dynamics of the mind.

object superiority effect. The phenomenon that a stimulus can be easier to detect when it is a unit contained in a larger stimulus than when it is presented on its own. The best known example is the WORD SUPERIORITY EFFECT.

oblique décalage. *See* DECALAGE.

oblique muscles. The INFERIOR OBLIQUE and SUPERIOR OBLIQUE.

oblique projection. A PROJECTION SYSTEM in which points in space are connected to the picture plane by parallel lines that strike it obliquely. In a **horizontal oblique projection**, the rays strike the picture plane at an oblique angle along the horizontal axis and at a right angle along the vertical axis. In a **vertical oblique projection**, the rays strike the picture plane at an oblique angle along the vertical axis and at a right angle along the horizontal axis. *Compare* ORTHOGRAPHIC PROJECTION.

oblique solution. A solution to a factor analysis in which some of the factors obtained are correlated with one another. *Contrast* ORTHOGONAL SOLUTION.

oblongata. Short for MEDULLA OBLONGATA.

OBS. An abbreviation for ORGANIC BRAIN SYNDROME.

observational learning. Learning by watching a conspecific, taking into account not merely what he does but whether he is rewarded or punished for it.

observed score. A synonym for RAW SCORE.

observer drift. The tendency for the judgements of two or more observers working together to become more and more similar, thus giving a false impression of being reliable.

observing response. 1. (Generally) Any response that exposes a part of the environment to the system's senses. *See* VICARIOUS TRIAL AND ERROR. 2. (Animal learning) A response selected from two or more responses that provides a signal informing the organism of whether it will be reinforced; the organism may have the same probability of being reinforced regardless of whether the observing response is made, but nonetheless it normally learns to make it.

obsession. A thought or idea, usually of an upsetting nature, that preoccupies a person for long periods of time, and that he cannot get rid of. *See* OBSESSIVE–COMPULSIVE DISORDER.

obsessional character. A personality type marked by overconscientiousness, rigidity, intolerance, and excessive orderliness; such people are prone to OBSESSIVE–COMPULSIVE DISORDER.

obsessional neurosis. A neurosis in which the dominant symptom is obsessions.

obsessional type. In Freudian theory, a personality type in which the libido expresses itself mainly through the superego, thus producing the traits of the OBSESSIVE PERSONALITY.

obsessive–compulsive disorder (OCD). A neurosis marked by extreme and destructive obsessions, and/or repetitive compulsions; e.g. a patient may be so preoccupied with cleanliness that he spends many hours each day washing, or be so absorbed by orderliness that he takes hours going to bed because he has to check the position of his clothes over and over again.

obsessive personality, obsessive–compulsive personality. A personality marked by excessive rigidity, orderliness, and intolerance.

obstacle sense. The ability developed by some blind people to detect obstacles in their path using the other senses.

obstruction box. An apparatus sometimes used in experiments on animal learning, in which the animal has to overcome an obstacle in order to reach a reward.

obstruction method. A technique that can be used for measuring the relative strength of drives in which an animal has to overcome an obstruction (e.g. cross an electrified grid) in order to reach the goal of a given drive (e.g. to reach food when hungry). The delay before crossing and the maximum intensity of shock tolerated can be used to assess the drive's strength.

obtained mean. A synonym for SAMPLE MEAN.

obtained score. A synonym for RAW SCORE.

obtrusive measure. (Social psychology) Any way of recording behaviour that the subject is aware of, particularly when it may alter the way he behaves, e.g. the presence of a social psychologist in his sitting room making notes on his interaction with his wife and children. *Compare* UNOBTRUSIVE MEASURE.

Occam's razor. The principle that other things being equal, the best explanation of something is the one that makes the fewest assumptions, or, more generally, is the simplest.

occasionalism. A synonym for PSYCHOPHYSICAL PARALLELISM.

occasion setter. When conditioning has occurred, a stimulus given with the CS that is never followed by the US (or is always followed by the US if extinction has occurred) and similarly *mutatis mutandis* for instrumental learning.

occipital lobe. One of the four main lobes of the cerebral cortex, which is at the back of the brain and is concerned largely with vision. It comprises Brodmann's areas 17–19; *see* Appendices 3 and 4.

occipital pole. The posterior tip of the occipital lobe.

occlusion. (Perception) A synonym for INTERPOSITION.

occupational interest inventory. A synonym for INTEREST INVENTORY.

occupational norm. The average score obtained by people in a particular job on a given test or tests.

occupational psychology. A synonym for INDUSTRIAL PSYCHOLOGY.

occupational therapy. The provision of tasks (e.g. basket weaving, painting, play reading) to keep a patient employed, to distract him, or (in the case of neurological patients) to help him recover function. Since boredom is one of the most distressing symptoms of much mental illness, occupational therapy is often more helpful than psychotherapy.

OCD. An abbreviation for OBSESSIVE–COMPULSIVE DISORDER.

ochlophobia. A morbid fear of crowds.

Ockham's razor. An alternative spelling for OCCAM'S RAZOR.

OCP. An abbreviation for OBSESSIVE–COMPULSIVE PERSONALITY.

OCR. An abbreviation for OPTICAL CHARACTER RECOGNITION.

octave. The frequency interval between two tones, one of which is twice the frequency of the other.

ocular. Of the eyes, visual.

ocular dominance. 1. The extent to which a cell in the visual cortex responds primarily to one or other eye. Traditionally seven degrees of ocular dominance have been distinguished: the fourth indicates no dominance and the first and seventh indicate that the cell is only receptive to the left or right eye respectively; the others indicate intermediate degrees of dominance. 2. A synonym for EYE DOMINANCE.

ocular dominance column. A slab in one of the visual areas within which the input to cells is mainly from one eye; from one such slab to the next the left and right eyes dominate alternately. It is a CORTICAL COLUMN with a width of about 0.5–1 mm. *See also* HYPERCOLUMN and *compare* ORIENTATION COLUMN.

ocular nystagmus. A synonym for NYSTAGMUS.

ocular pursuit movements. A synonym for PURSUIT MOVEMENTS.

oculocentric judgement. *See* EGOCENTRIC JUDGEMENT.

oculogravic illusion. An illusion caused by placing a subject in a centrifuge. This produces a Coriolis force: the subject will feel his body tilted in a direction determined by the average of the vector of the Coriolis force and that of gravity. Since he misperceives his body tilt with respect to gravity, he misperceives the orientation of lines and edges with respect to gravity.

oculogyral illusion. Any illusion of visual motion caused by rotation of the body, including illusions caused by the aftereffect of bodily rotation. E.g. if the body is rotated about a vertical axis in darkness, but with a small light present that rotates with the body, horizontal movement of the light with respect to the head is often seen, because the subject misperceives his own rate of rotation, e.g. through adaptation of the vestibular receptors.

oculomotor apraxia. Impairment of the ability to make eye movements, usually caused by brain damage.

oculomotor nerve. The third CRANIAL NERVE,

which is one of the three EXTRAOCULAR NERVES.

oculo-vestibular reflex. A synonym for VESTIBULO-OCULAR REFLEX.

oddity problem. A discrimination task in which a number of stimuli are displayed and the organism must learn always to select the one that differs from all the others. In the **generalized oddity problem**, the organism must learn to solve problems involving completely new stimuli on the basis of what it has learnt in a series of oddity problems. This is an example of SERIAL LEARNING.

odontophobia. A morbid fear of teeth.

odorimetry. The measurement of odours.

odour prism. A method of classifying smells put forward by Henning. It places six supposedly primary odours (fragrant, etherial, spicy, resinous, burnt, and putrid) at the corners of a prism with other smells placed in the prism in the positions governed by the proportions of the primaries they contain. *See also* ODOUR SQUARE and *contrast* CROCKER–HENDERSON SYSTEM.

odour square. The front face of Henning's ODOUR PRISM, also called the **FERS odour square** since the primary odours represented at the corners are *F*ragrant, *E*therial, *R*esinous, and *S*picy.

oedema. An excessive accumulation of fluid between cells. Brain damage can be followed by oedema and the resultant intracranial pressure can cause malfunction outside the region of the initial damage.

Oedipal complex. A synonym for OEDIPUS COMPLEX.

Oedipal phase. (Psychoanalysis) A synonym for the PHALLIC STAGE of development (lasting from about 3 to 7 years of age), when the Oedipus complex is alleged to develop.

Oedipus complex. (Psychoanalysis) The alleged desire of a boy for his mother (starting between about 3 to 5 years of age). It is compounded by jealousy and even hatred of the father. The expression is also used of the daughter's incestuous desire for her father (sometimes called the ELECTRA COMPLEX). According to Freud it is the most basic and universal complex, which if not resolved causes neurosis in later life.

OEE. An abbreviation for OVERTRAINING EXTINCTION EFFECT.

oestradiol. The main form of OESTROGEN produced by the human ovary and adrenal cortex and found in the brain. TESTOSTERONE converts to oestradiol on contact with neurons: it is responsible for androgenizing the developing animal.

oestrogen. A group of hormones secreted by the ovary and adrenal cortex; they play a role in the development of secondary female characteristics, the onset of oestrus, ovulation, lactation, and physical growth. *See* MENSTRUAL CYCLE.

oestrous cycle. The ovarian cycle in female mammals below primates.

oestrus. The period when the female is most sexually receptive.

off-centre on-surround cell. A cell with a circular visual receptive field, having an inhibitory centre and an excitatory surround. Such receptive fields (and their reverse which belong to ON-CENTRE OFF-SURROUND CELLS) are found in ganglion cells, lateral geniculate cells, and a small proportion of cells higher up the visual system.

ogive. A rising curve, at first positively accelerated then negatively accelerated, rather like the letter S. It frequently occurs in a cumulative frequency distribution.

ohm (O). A measure of the resistance to the passage of electricity. *See* OHM'S LAW.

Ohm's acoustic law. The principle that the auditory system decomposes a complex tone into its separate frequencies, each of which can be heard.

Ohm's law. The principle that the electric current passing through a conductor is directly proportional to the potential difference across it and inversely proportional to its resistance, i.e. $I = V/R$, where I is current in amperes, V is potential difference in volts, and R is resistance in ohms.

oikophobia. A morbid fear of being at home.

olfactie. A psychophysical unit on an odour intensity scale. It is the amount of a substance that yields the absolute olfactory threshold.

olfaction. The sense of smell.

olfactometer. A device for measuring the acuteness of a person's sense of smell.

olfactophobia. A synonym for OSMOPHOBIA.

olfactory areas. The parts of the brain serving the sense of smell; they include the OLFACTORY BULBS and some other parts (not yet well specified) of the RHINENCEPHALON.

olfactory bulb. A bulb-like structure on the undersurface of each frontal lobe that forms part of the RHINENCEPHALON. The olfactory nerve terminates there and the olfactory tract exits from it. *See* Appendix 5.

olfactory epithelium. A layer of cells in the roof of the nasal passages which contains the OLFACTORY RECEPTORS and which is covered by mucus.

olfactory lobe. A synonym for OLFACTORY BULB.

olfactory nerve. The first CRANIAL NERVE, which transmits information from the OLFACTORY RECEPTORS to the OLFACTORY BULB.

olfactory receptors. Cells ending in cilia and thought to contain receptor sites for the molecules that produce smell; they are located in the OLFACTORY EPITHELIUM. Nothing is known about the differential sensitivity of different receptors to different molecules.

olfactory tract. A bundle of nerve fibres that conducts olfactory signals from the OLFACTORY BULB to the PRIMARY OLFACTORY CORTEX, and other parts of the RHINENCEPHALON, including the amygdala.

oligodendroglia, oligodendrocyte. A glial cell that wraps itself around axons in the central nervous system, providing them with a myelin sheath. The same function is performed in the peripheral nervous system by the SCHWANN CELLS. *See* NEUROGLIA.

oligoencephaly. A form of mental deficiency associated with having a very small head.

oligophrenia. A rare term for mental retardation.

olivary body. A mass of grey matter in the medulla, containing many cell bodies. *See* INFERIOR OLIVE and SUPERIOR OLIVE.

olivocochlear bundle. An efferent pathway running from the inferior olive to the cochlea that may exert control over the auditory input.

ombrophobia. A morbid fear of rain.

omega effect. In a stroboscopic motion experiment in which a bright light alternates between two positions, the phenomenon that the dark afterimage of the light is seen in apparent motion in the opposite direction to the light.

omission schedule. In classical conditioning, failure to give the unconditioned stimulus whenever the conditioned response is made to the conditioned stimulus but giving it at other times. Even when the unconditioned stimulus is rewarding (e.g. food) the conditioned response may still be learned (though this prevents the animal obtaining reinforcement). *See* AUTOSHAPING.

ommatidium. A unit of a COMPOUND EYE that conducts light down a tube to a small number of receptors at its base (the RHABDOME). Ommatidia are directionally sensitive, since light entering them obliquely is absorbed by dark pigments. In some species each ommatidium has a smell lens at the top.

on-centre off-surround cell. A cell with a circular visual receptive field, having an excitatory centre and an inhibitory surround. *See also* OFF-CENTRE ON-SURROUND CELL.

one-element model. A synonym for ALL-OR-NONE LEARNING THEORY.

oneirism. A dream-like state occurring in someone awake.

oneirology. The study of dreams.

one-tailed test. A test of a hypothesis using a region of rejection located only at one end of the distribution of the test statistic. In consequence, the null hypothesis cannot be rejected if there is a difference, however large, in the direction opposite to that anticipated. *Contrast* TWO-TAILED TEST.

one-to-one mapping. *See* MAPPING.

one-trial learning theory. The theory, largely discredited, that associations are not gradually strengthened over trials, but that a given association is either fully learned on a given trial or is not strengthened at all.

one-way mirror, one-way screen. A sheet of glass that both transmits and reflects light; if a subject is placed in bright light on one side of it and the experimenter in dim light on the other, the experimenter can observe the subject without the subject seeing him.

on-line. Pertaining to a computer peripheral that is directly connected to the computer, or to a process making use of such a direct connection.

onomatomania. Uncontrollable or obsessive intrusion of a name or word into someone's thoughts.

onomatophobia. A morbid fear of a word.

onomatopoeia. Similarity between the sound of a word and the sound made by the referent of the word; e.g. the word 'hiss' is onomatopoeic.

ontogeny, ontogenesis. The development of the individual. The term 'ontogeny' tends to be used for development in general, 'ontogenesis' for the development of a particular aspect of the individual. *Contrast* PHYLOGENY.

ontology. The philosophical study of existence and of what can correctly be said to exist; among other problems ontology deals with the distinction between reality and appearance, and with the sense in which numbers or other abstract entities can be said to exist.

oogenesis. Development of the ovum.

open-class word. A synonym for CONTENT WORD.

open economic system. See CLOSED ECONOMIC SYSTEM.

open-ended question. A question that someone must answer in their own words rather than by selecting one of a number of alternative answers provided. *Contrast* CLOSE-ENDED QUESTION.

open-ended test. A test consisting of OPEN-ENDED QUESTIONS.

open-field test. An enclosed area (usually square) with a floor made up of black and white squares. When a rat or other animal is let loose in it, its activity can be measured by counting the number of squares it crosses over a period of time.

open instinct. An instinct in which the associated behaviour can be modified by experience; e.g. the way the human sex drive is expressed is highly modifiable through learning.

open loop. (Cybernetics) A system in which the output does not affect the input, e.g. a ballistic movement. *Contrast* CLOSED LOOP.

open node. See NODE (2).

open study. A study in which the experimenter and the subjects know what experimental condition the subject is in, and what the purpose of the experiment is. It is usually only a pilot study. *Contrast* DOUBLE-BLIND PROCEDURE and SINGLE-BLIND PROCEDURE.

open system. A system that can influence or be influenced by its environment. *Contrast* CLOSED SYSTEM.

open word. See PIVOT GRAMMAR.

operand. A synonym for MANIPULANDUM.

operant. Any behaviour spontaneously emitted by an organism (i.e. any behaviour other than an instrumental response or an uncondi-tioned or conditioned reflex). An operant is classified not by the muscle movements made, but by its effects on the environment, e.g. the depression of a panel or bar. *Compare* RESPONSE TOPOGRAPHY and *contrast* RESPONDENT.

operant conditioning. Skinner's term for INSTRUMENTAL LEARNING, i.e. learning in which the animal has to make a spontaneous action to obtain reinforcement, as opposed to CLASSICAL CONDITIONING, in which the response to be learned is elicited by the unconditioned stimulus; the reinforcement increases the frequency with which the operant response is made to the stimulus that precedes it. *See also* FREE OPERANT.

operant level. In operant conditioning the rate at which an organism emits the response to be learned before any training has taken place.

operant reserve. The rate at which an operant is emitted either before any training has been given or after extinction has been completed. *Compare* REFLEX RESERVE.

operation. 1. (Computing science) The execution of an instruction. 2. (Piaget) Any mental process that a person can execute in reverse.

operational definition. The definition of an expression (usually a theoretical one) in terms of the operations and observations to which it refers. *See* OPERATIONALISM.

operationalism. (Philosophy of science) The doctrine that a theoretical concept can and should mean no more than the operations that measure it, e.g. intelligence can be defined as how well people do on intelligence tests, or hunger as the length of time since last eating.

operational knowledge. Piaget's expression for knowledge acquired through OPERATIONAL THINKING, as opposed to FIGURATIVE KNOWLEDGE (the memory for facts).

operational research. A synonym for OPERATIONS RESEARCH.

operational stage. Piaget's expression for the

stage when the child conducts OPERATIONAL THINKING (from about seven years of age onwards).

operational thinking. Piaget's expression for the rational manipulation of concepts; the child's manipulation of physical concepts begins at about seven years of age (*see* CONCRETE OPERATIONAL STAGE) and of abstract or logical ones about twelve (*see* FORMAL OPERATIONAL STAGE).

operationism. An alternative spelling of OPERATIONALISM.

operations research. The scientific and mathematical analysis of a complex system with a view to maximizing its efficacy: the systems analysed can vary from the transit of convoys in war to the running of a hospital.

operator. In mathematics and logic, any symbol that specifies the operations to be conducted on other symbols e.g. × ('multiply'), ∨ ('or'), and, by analogy, in AI any function that transforms data in a specified way.

operatory knowledge. A synonym for OPERATIONAL KNOWLEDGE.

ophidophobia. A morbid fear of snakes.

ophthalmic nerve. *See* TRIGEMINAL NERVE.

ophthalmology. The branch of medicine dealing with the eye.

ophthalmometer. A synonym for KERATOMETER.

ophthalmoscope. An instrument that makes it possible to examine the retina through the pupil.

opiate. Any substance that attaches to and stimulates an OPIATE RECEPTOR, including substances produced by the brain (opioid peptides), morphine and its derivatives, and synthetic substances like methadone. *See* OPIOID.

opiate receptors. The neural receptors that receive the OPIATES.

opinion molecule. An organized mental unit comprising a belief and an attitude, and the perception that these are supported by other people.

opioid. Any OPIATE produced in the brain, and excluding opiates not produced by the brain. The term is sometimes used as equivalent to opiate, but it is better to confine it to the more restricted sense given above.

opioid peptides. A class of PEPTIDES that bind to opiate receptors in the central nervous system and act as NEUROTRANSMITTERS and NEUROMODULATORS. They are found in the LIMBIC SYSTEM, and elsewhere in the brain and spinal cord. Like opium itself, they are thought to reduce pain and give a sense of well-being. They currently include the ENKEPHALINS, ENDORPHINS, and DYNORPHINES.

opium. A narcotic and analgesic opiate obtained from poppy seeds.

Oppel–Kündt illusion, Oppel illusion. The illusion, illustrated below, that an extent of space looks larger if it is filled than if it is empty; e.g. two vertical lines look further apart when a series of other vertical lines is placed between them than when there is nothing between then.

| ı ı ı ı ı ı ı ı ı |

Oppel–Kündt illusion

opponent process theory of colour vision. Hering's theory of colour vision (and subsequent modifications of it), which postulates that the visual system contains three antagonistic processes – blue versus yellow, red versus green, and black versus white. The theory is in essence correct above the level of the receptors. *Contrast* TRICHROMATIC THEORY.

opponent process theory of motivation. A theory put forward by Solomon, postulating that any extreme of emotion (especially hedonic extremes) tends to produce an opposing process, which will dominate when the stimulus that gave rise to the original extreme is withdrawn; the theory purports to explain tolerance to narcotics and other forms of addiction since the dose has to be continually increased to overcome the opponent process. In practice the theory does little more than summarize the observed phenomena.

opposites test. A test in which a person has to give the opposite of a word supplied.

opsin. A protein that in combination with RETINENE forms VISUAL PHOTOPIGMENT; the opsin in the rods is sometimes known as **scotopsin**, and that in the cones as **photopsin**.

optic agnosia. The inability to name objects when seen, but with an intact ability to perceive and name them by touch.

optical axis. In an optical system, the line that is normal to all optical surfaces in the system, which in the case of a lens passes through its centre of curvature. In the human eye this axis corresponds approximately to the PUPILLARY AXIS, but not to the PRIMARY LINE OF SIGHT. *Contrast* VISUAL AXIS.

optical character recognition. The recognition of written or (more usually) printed characters by computer, using a camera or other light-sensitive device.

optic ataxia. (Neuropsychology) Impairment of the capacity to reach for or touch visually presented objects, caused by brain damage. It can be limited to one side of the visual field or to one hand and is usually associated with oculomotor defects. *Compare* BALINT'S SYNDROME.

optical flow. The instantaneous velocity at each point of the retinal image, caused either by an object moving or by movement of the head or eyes.

optical illusion. Any visual illusion, including, among others, GEOMETRIC ILLUSIONS.

optical image. A synonym for IMAGE (1).

optical projection. A mapping of one set of points in space onto a picture plane, or the mapping of an image (particularly the retinal image) onto the set of points in space that produces it. *Compare* PROJECTION SYSTEM and PERSPECTIVE.

optic array. The patterning of ambient light as determined by the nature of the incident light and the surfaces from which it is reflected, which is sampled by the observer according to the position of his head and eyes. Gibson thought the information in the optic array was sufficient to specify unequivocally the 3-D nature of the environment. He also thought it was 'picked up' by the observer and used in vision directly and without processing; the latter view has misled many workers in vision.

optic chiasm. The point at which fibres from the nasal half of each retina cross to the opposite side of the brain joining the fibres from the opposite temporal retina.

optic disc. A circular region of the RETINA about 18° nasally from the FOVEA where the axons of ganglion cells exit to form the OPTIC NERVE and where blood-vessels enter: because there are no receptors there, the eye is blind at this point.

optic flow. An alternative spelling of OPTICAL FLOW.

optic nerve. The second CRANIAL NERVE, which runs from the retina to the optic chiasm; there is no synapse there but the continuation of the pathway to the lateral geniculate is known as the OPTIC TRACT.

optic nystagmus. A synonym for OPTOKINETIC NYSTAGMUS.

optic papilla. A synonym for OPTIC DISC.

optic radiations. Fibres of the visual system originating in the lateral geniculate and terminating in the visual cortex.

optics. The physical study of the behaviour of light, as affected by lenses, mirrors, and prisms.

optic tectum. The part of the TECTUM in fish, reptiles, amphibia, and birds reponsible for vision; it developed into the superior colliculus in mammals.

optic tract. The pathway from the optic chiasm, which carries visual information to the lateral geniculate.

optimal apparent motion, optimal motion. The appearance of motion in a stationary stimulus caused by exposing the stimulus briefly at discrete times and positions, as occurs e.g. in the cinema. If the duration of each exposure and the interstimulus interval are correctly adjusted, the appearance of motion is indistinguishable from that of a stimulus genuinely moving, hence the word 'optimal'. *Compare* KORTE'S LAWS, PART MOTION, and PHI PHENOMENON.

optional stopping. Stopping an experiment at a point not determined in advance; the experimenter may stop it when the results are favourable to his own hypothesis and obtain a statistically significant result that is an artefact since a different result might have been obtained had he stopped earlier or later.

optogram. The pattern of bleached pigment caused by light from an object falling on the eye.

optokinetic. Pertaining to eye movements triggered by the input to the eye.

optokinetic nystagmus. The alternation of SMOOTH FOLLOWING MOVEMENTS and SACCADES in the opposite direction that occurs when the visual field is in continuous motion past the observer (e.g. on a moving train). The smooth movements allow the observer to retain fixation for as long as possible; the saccades allow him to fixate new stimuli, when those currently being fixated are swept out of view.

optometer. Any device for measuring the refractive powers of the eye.

optometry. The measurement of the refractive powers of the eye, usually with a view to correcting defects by supplying glasses.

optomotor response. The response whereby an animal, particularly an insect, keeps itself oriented to the same part of the visual world by turning (both in flying and in walking) to compensate for movement of the visual field on the eyes.

OR. An abbreviation for OPERATIONS RESEARCH.

or (v). A logical connective in the propositional calculus. *See* DISJUNCTION.

oral. 1. Pertaining to the mouth. 2. Pertaining to spoken language. *Contrast* VERBAL.

oral-aggressive character, oral-aggressive personality. (Psychoanalysis) A personality formed by sublimating the drive to bite which is present in the latter part of the ORAL STAGE; it is marked by ambition, envy, aggression, and the exploitation of others. *See* ORAL CHARACTER.

oral biting period. (Psychoanalysis) A synonym for aggressive oral phase; *see* ORAL STAGE.

oral character. (Psychoanalysis) A personality alleged to originate in the ORAL STAGE; if a person was satisfied during that stage the personality traits shown are friendliness, optimism, generosity, and dependence (the ORAL-RECEPTIVE CHARACTER); if he was not satisfied he develops an ORAL-AGGRESSIVE CHARACTER.

oral dependence. (Psychoanalysis) Dependence on others derived from dependence on the mother in the ORAL STAGE.

oral eroticism. (Psychoanalysis) Libidinal pleasure derived from sensations from the lips and mouth, e.g. chewing, kissing, smoking, talking.

oral eroticism phase. A synonym for ORAL STAGE.

oral erotism. A synonym for ORAL EROTICISM.

oral-incorporation stage. (Psychoanalysis) Part of the ORAL STAGE when the child is alleged unconsciously to be trying to incorporate the mother into itself by sucking.

oral method, oralism. A method of teaching language to the deaf mainly through lip reading and training them how to shape their vocal tract to produce words. There is a controversy over whether it is best to teach the deaf to communicate by this method or by SIGN LANGUAGE.

oral orientation. A tendency to use the mouth in reacting to the external world, e.g. by putting objects to it as infants do, etc.

oral-passive type. A synonym for ORAL CHAR-ACTER.

oral phase. A synonym for ORAL STAGE.

oral primacy. (Psychoanalysis) The alleged phenomenon that the libido is at first concentrated on the mouth.

oral reading. Moving the lips while reading silently, a habit that slows down reading and is suppressed by most people.

oral-receptive character. A personality formed at the passive oral phase and marked by dependence, optimism, and generosity. *See* ORAL CHARACTER.

oral-receptive phase. A synonym for passive oral phase. *See* ORAL STAGE.

oral sadism. (Psychoanalysis) The infliction of pain by the mouth, e.g. by biting.

oral-sadistic phase. A synonym for aggressive oral phase: *see* ORAL STAGE.

oral-sensory. *See* ERIKSON'S PSYCHOSOCIAL DEVELOPMENTAL STAGES.

oral stage. (Psychoanalysis) The first of Freud's five LIBIDINAL STAGES (lasting from birth to about 18 months) in which the libido is concentrated on the mouth. It is divided into an early **passive oral phase** (from birth to about 8 months) in which the infant passively takes milk from the breast, and a later **aggressive oral phase** in which the child begins to be independent and expresses anger by biting and chewing.

oral triad. (Psychoanalysis) The alleged three main wishes of the infant in the PASSIVE ORAL STAGE – to suck at, to be devoured by, and to sleep with the breast.

orange. *See* SPECTRAL HUES.

ora terminalis. The extreme edge of the retina.

Orbison figures. Geometrical illusions that are produced through the simultaneous tilt illusion, by radiating lines or circular lines crossing straight lines at different angles. They are variants of the HERING ILLUSION and the EHRENSTEIN ILLUSION. The best known Orbison illusion is shown in the illustration below.

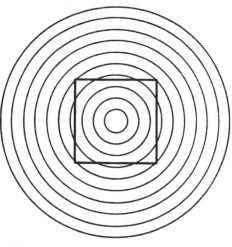

Orbison figure

orbit. The bony cavity containing the eye.

orbital cortex, orbitofrontal cortex. Brodmann's area 47; *see* Appendix 3. It is in the prefrontal cortex lying just behind and slightly above the orbit of the eye; it is separated from the temporal lobe by the LATERAL SULCUS. Damage to it leads to extreme flattening of affect.

order. *See* TAXONOMY.

ordered metric scale. A scale in which the magnitudes of the intervals can be rank ordered, but in which the intervals cannot be equated to give an interval scale.

ordered recall. A synonym for SERIAL RECALL.

order effect. In experiments the effect (usually unwanted) of a prior condition (or set of trials) on performance in a later condition (or set of trials).

orderly change theory. Any theory of psychological development postulating systematic and ordered changes from one stage to another, e.g. GENETIC EPISTEMOLOGY.

order of magnitude. 1. A factor of about ten: two sets of scores would be said to differ by an order of magnitude if one was about ten times as high as the other. 2. The rank order of a set of values.

order statistics. Statistical tests that use only ordered properties of the observations.

ordinal position. The rank assigned to an item in an ORDINAL SCALE.

ordinal scale. A scale in which items are arranged in order of magnitude. From such a scale it is possible to determine whether one item has a larger value than another but not the size of the difference in values.

ordinate. The vertical coordinate of a graph, conventionally called the y-axis. *Compare* ABSCISSA.

ORE. An abbreviation for OVERTRAINING REVERSAL EFFECT.

Orestes complex. (Psychoanalysis) The son's wish (conscious or unconscious) to kill his mother.

orexis. The aspects of an act that have to do with conation or drive rather than with reasoning.

organ eroticism. (Psychoanalysis) The concentration of the libido on a specific organ.

organic. (Psychiatry) Pertaining to a condition that is known to have a physical cause, used particularly of mental illnesses. *Contrast* FUNCTIONAL.

organic affective syndrome. Disturbance of mood due to organic causes.

organic anxiety. Anxiety about a physical disorder.

organic brain syndrome. (Psychiatry) Any mental or neurological disorder known to be caused by brain damage or malfunctioning. The expression is sometimes misleadingly used to refer to disorders thought without evidence to be caused by brain malfunctioning (e.g. minimal brain damage).

organic-delusional syndrome. The occurrence of delusions for a known physical cause, e.g. taking cannabis or having temporal lobe epilepsy.

organic drivenness. Hyperactivity caused by brainstem damage.

organicism. Herbert Spencer's theory that society is like a living being, with its parts interacting in the way bodily organs do.

organicity. Brain damage or malfunctioning.

organicity assessment. The evaluation of the effects of brain damage or disorder.

organic mental disorder. Any mental disorder known to be caused by damage to or malfunctioning of the brain (e.g. as a result of taking amphetamines or through senile dementia). The distinction between organic and FUNCTIONAL MENTAL DISORDERS (non-organic ones) is becoming tricky, since evidence is accumulating that abnormal functioning of NEUROTRANSMITTERS is implicated in the functional psychoses.

organic personality disorder. A disorder marked by a change in personality or behaviour and caused by specific brain damage.

organic psychosis. Effectively a synonym for ORGANIC MENTAL DISORDER, which is nowadays the preferred expression.

organic repression. An unfortunte expression meaning retrograde amnesia caused by brain damage. It has no relation to the Freudian term 'repression'.

organic sensations. A synonym for VISCERAL SENSATIONS.

organic therapies. Physical methods of treatment in psychiatry, e.g. electroconvulsive shock treatment, psychosurgery, and drugs.

organic variable. Any internal factor in an organism that affects its behaviour, e.g. hunger.

organ inferiority. Adler's expression for any physical defect in a person (whether real or imaginary) that makes him feel inferior, and hence try to compensate.

organismic. Pertaining to a theoretical approach that emphasizes the whole organism and makes no distinction between mind and body; a vague word that has more sound than meaning.

organizational dynamics. (Industrial psychology) The interactive processes that determine the functioning of an organization.

organizational psychology. The study of the interaction between people in an organization, e.g. in industry, the armed forces, etc. It is usually undertaken with a view to making the organization more efficient, e.g. by improving relations between management and workers, improving communication channels, improving decision making processes, etc.

organ jargon. Adler's expression for a somatic symptom (like constipation) arising from a neurosis and forming part of the masculine protest against feminine traits.

organ language. (Psychoanalysis) The physical expression of an underlying disturbance, e.g. constant sniffing may signify distaste for a situation.

organ libido. A synonym for ORGAN EROTICISM.

organ neurosis. (Psychoanalysis) A psychosomatic illness.

organ of Corti. A structure in the COCHLEA, which rests on the BASILAR MEMBRANE and is set in motion as a result of movements in the fluid of the SCALA TYMPANI; it contains the auditory receptors, the HAIR CELLS, whose tips are embedded in the tectorial membrane.

organogenic. A synonym for SOMATOGENIC.

organ speech. A synonym for ORGAN LANGUAGE.

orgasmic dysfunction. Difficulty in obtaining an orgasm, used mainly of women. It is called **primary orgasmic dysfunction** when a woman never has an orgasm and **situational orgasmic dysfunction** when she is unable to obtain an orgasm only in certain situations.

orgasmic impotence. In males, inability to ejaculate. The term is occasionally used of females to mean ORGASMIC DYSFUNCTION.

orgasmic phase. *See* SEXUAL RESPONSE CYCLE.

orgasmic reconditioning. A behaviour therapy technique aimed at reducing or eliminating perversions; pictures of the client's perversion are shown while he masturbates, but are replaced by pictures of 'normal' heterosexual activity just before orgasm.

or gate. An electronic unit that has two inputs and that gives an output if either or both are on.

orgone. Reich's term for a hypothetical blue particle, charged with life energy, which exists everywhere and is needed for mental health and the sexual act.

orgone accumulator, orgone box. A box, devised by Reich, composed of layers of different metals, which he claimed collected orgones and thus concentrated them on the person sitting inside, much to the benefit of their sex-lives. If it worked, it would be in great demand.

orgone therapy. Reich's therapy derived from his view that the discharge of orgones through the sexual act was necessary both to avoid and overcome mental disorder; the therapy included massage, the correction of poor bodily postures, and sometimes the use of the ORGONE ACCUMULATOR.

orgonomy. Reich's theoretical system based on his belief in orgones, the value of good and regular orgasms for maintaining mental health, and the idea that tension and bad posture are inimical to adequate orgasms. *See also* CHARACTER ARMOUR.

orientation. 1. (Psychiatry) Knowledge of one's immediate environment, e.g. of time, position, who the other people in the environment are, how to react to them, etc. 2. (Ethology) A synonym for TAXIS. 3. (Generally) Set or attitude.

orientation column. A CORTICAL COLUMN of cells in a visual area within which all cells have receptive fields maximally sensitive to lines and edges in the same orientation; with a few exceptions each column is sensitive to an orientation differing only slightly from that to which its neighbour is sensitive. *Compare* OCULAR DOMINANCE COLUMN.

orientation constancy. The tendency to judge the gravitational orientation of a line correctly when the vertical meridian of the eye is not vertical with respect to gravity (e.g. because of eye torsion or head tilt).

orienting response, orienting reflex. The behaviour invoked by a novel or threatening stimulus, which consists of attending to it and pointing the body towards it in addition to the arousal of the reticular activating system and the sympathetic system.

origin. The point in a graph at which the coordinates meet.

original response. An unusual (occurring less than 1 per cent of the time) response in a Rorschach test.

ornithophobia. A morbid fear of birds.

orthodox sleep. A synonym for NON-REM SLEEP.

orthogenesis. The theory that the development of a system is pre-set from the start; the idea has been applied mainly to evolution, but also to the development of the individual and of societies.

orthogenital. Pertaining to normal sexual behaviour.

orthognathy. The possession of a jaw that does not project beyond the line of the forehead. Orthognathy is a characteristic of modern man. *Contrast* PROGNATHY.

orthogonal. At right angles.

orthogonal dimension. A dimension whose values do not correlate with the values of another dimension.

orthogonal projection. A synonym for ORTHO-GRAPHIC PROJECTION.

orthogonal solution. A factor analysis in which all the factors are at right angles to one another, i.e. there is no correlation between them. *Contrast* OBLIQUE SOLUTION.

orthographic projection. A PROJECTION SYSTEM in which points in space are connected to the picture plane by parallel lines perpendicular to it. It is commonly used in engineering drawings. *Compare* OBLIQUE PROJECTION.

orthography. A writing system, e.g. an alphabet or a syllabary.

orthomolecular psychiatry. Pauling's theory that all mental illness is due to biochemical deficiencies and should be treated with remedial drugs, particularly with vast doses of vitamins.

orthophoria. The state of having the eyes aligned with one another when one eye is receiving no visual input. *See* PHORIA.

orthopsychiatry. The study and practice of how to prevent mental illness.

orthoptics. A treatment for patients with unbalanced extraocular muscles based on a series of eye-movement exercises.

orthostasis. The act of standing up.

oscillation. *See* BEHAVIOURAL OSCILLATION.

oscillograph. An instrument to record in graphic form changes in electrical potentials occurring over time, e.g. to record a muscle potential.

oscilloscope. An instrument for displaying rapid changes in electrical potentials on a fluorescent screen. Provided they are first converted into potential changes, it can display waveforms of any kind, and may be used to investigate electrical activity in the nervous system.

osmometric thirst. Thirst caused by there being a higher concentration of salt in the extracellular fluid than in the intracellular fluid. *Compare* VOLUMETRIC THIRST.

osmophobia. A morbid fear of smells.

osmoreceptor. Receptors in the HYPO-THALAMUS that are sensitive to intracellular fluid loss, thus indicating dehydration of the blood. They exert control over thirst and cause the release of ANTIDIURETIC HORMONE.

osmosis. The diffusion of water (or any other solvent) through a semipermeable membrane to the side on which there is a greater concentration of a solute, thus tending to equalize the concentration of the solute on either side.

osmotic pressure. The pressure required to prevent the flow of water through a semipermeable membrane to the side on which there is a greater concentration of a solute.

osphresiolagnia. A morbid or fetishistic interest in odours (often body odours).

osphresiophobia. A morbid fear of smells.

osphresis. Olfaction.

osseous labyrinth. A synonym for BONY LABYRINTH.

osseous spiral lamina. A bony ledge in the inner part of the cochlea that spirals round the MODIOLUS. The basilar membrane is attached to it and runs parallel to it.

ossicles. Any small bones, but particularly the three tiny bones in the middle ear – the MALLEUS, INCUS, and STAPES – that transmit the sound vibrations received by the eardrum to the oval window of the cochlea.

Othello syndrome. Morbid jealousy without sufficient cause.

other behaviour. (Operant conditioning) Any behaviour emitted in an experiment that is not being systematically reinforced or punished.

other directedness. (Sociology) Reisman's expression for the tendency to accept outside standards for one's own behaviour (e.g. those of the group) rather than working out for oneself how to behave.

otic. Pertaining to the ear.

otogenic tone. A tone caused by the auditory system itself and not present at the ear. *See also* COMBINATION TONE and MISSING FUNDAMENTAL.

otoliths. Crystals of calcium carbonate in the endolymph of the labyrinth that touch the tips of the hair cells in the VESTIBULAR SACS, and hence stimulate them when the endolymph is set in motion by head movements.

otology. The branch of medicine dealing with the ear.

Ouija board. A device used in parapsychology, consisting of a board containing numbers and letters, and a pointer, which, it is claimed, can in the right hands spell out messages from the dead.

outcome research. Research intended to test the efficacy of one or more therapies or techniques.

outer boundary. A synonym for EGO BOUNDARY.

outer directedness. A synonym for OTHER DIRECTEDNESS.

outer hair cells. *See* AUDITORY RECEPTORS.

outer layers of retina. *See* RETINA.

outer limiting membrane. A transparent membrane that runs over the whole retina and splits the receptors into OUTER SEGMENTS and INNER SEGMENTS. The inner segment is the part nearer to the lens.

outer nuclear layer. The layer of the retina in which the cell bodies of the receptors lie.

outer plexiform layer. *See* PLEXIFORM LAYER (2).

outer segment. The pigment bearing part of a rod or cone; it lies furthest from the lens.

outflow theory. *See* CANCELLATION THEORIES.

out-group. Everyone not belonging to a particular IN-GROUP.

out of the body experience (OBE). (Parapsychology) The conviction that one has left one's body and is floating or moving outside it, while perceiving the environment from the new position.

output. Information or energy emitted from a system, often used of computers.

ova. Plural of OVUM.

oval window. The window in the COCHLEA to which the stapes is attached and which therefore provides the input.

O variable. An abbreviation for ORGANIC VARIABLE.

ovarian follicle. The tiny sac in the ovary, in which the ovum develops and from which it is released at ovulation.

ovary. One of two sacs in the female that produce the ova, which at ovulation are deposited in the FALLOPIAN TUBE, through which they travel towards the UTERUS. The ovaries also act as ENDOCRINE GLANDS and secrete OESTROGEN and PROGESTERONE.

overachiever. Anyone who achieves more than would be expected. The term is often used of a student who does better than would be expected on the basis of objective tests; its perjorative overtones doubtless reflect the annoyance of those who set the tests that someone should dare to do better than they predict.

overanxious disorder. Persistent anxiety without external cause often involving shyness, worry about appearance or ability, and overconcern about the future. The expression is usually used only of children.

overcompensation. Adler's term for extreme striving for success and power, motivated by an inferiority complex.

overconstancy. The tendency for a distant object to be judged as bigger than it really is, and in general overcompensation in PHENOMENAL REGRESSION TO THE REAL OBJECT.

overdetermination. (Psychoanalysis) The existence of many different causes for a dream or action (e.g. a slip of the tongue); thus, according to Freud, the same dream or even the same symbol in a dream may express many different wishes. See CONDENSATION.

overdiscrimination. Including too narrow a class of exemplars in a category.

overextension. A synonym for OVERGENERALIZATION.

overflow activity. (Ethology) A synonym for VACUUM ACTIVITY.

overgeneralization. 1. The use of a word or category to cover too broad a range of things. It is common in children, e.g. they may call all animals 'doggy'. *Contrast* UNDERGENERALIZATION. 2. The tendency in depressives to draw too broad conclusions from bad events, e.g. to think that being rejected in love once means they will always be rejected; the term is used by cognitive therapists.

overinclusiveness. Using concepts too broadly, so that irrelevant thoughts and ideas intrude in speech; it is common in schizophrenics.

overjustification. (Social psychology) The provision of reinforcement for performing a task that the person thinks worth doing in its own right. The reinforcement may diminish his liking for the task.

overlapping factor. Any factor that accounts for the results of two or more tests.

overlearning. The process occurring when additional trials or practice on a task are given after the organism has already mastered it to a high criterion. Although performance is not necessarily improved by overlearning, long-term memory for the task often is. But *see* OVERTRAINING EXTINCTION EFFECT and OVERTRAINING REVERSAL EFFECT.

overload. *See* INFORMATION OVERLOAD.

overprotection. The tendency to pamper and shelter a child too much, so that it fails to become independent; nobody knows how much is 'too much'.

overreaction. An emotional reaction stronger than the occasion seems to warrant; it is sometimes thought, particularly by psychoanalysts, that overreaction is a sign of conscious or unconscious insecurity.

overregulation. The production of words, particularly by children, that are incorrect but are based on genuine rules in the language, e.g. a child may say 'rided' for 'rode'.

overshadowing. The reduction in the strength of conditioning to a weak conditioned stimulus that occurs when it is conditioned in COMPOUND CONDITIONING with a more salient conditioned stimulus, as compared with the strength of conditioning it would have acquired had it been always presented on its own. *Compare* BLOCKING.

oversufficient justification. A synonym for OVERJUSTIFICATION.

overtone. Any PARTIAL TONE produced by a vibrating body, excluding the FUNDAMENTAL. The numbering of HARMONIC overtones is confusing, since the first overtone is twice the frequency of the fundamental, the second is three times the frequency of the fundamental, etc. (the numbering of partial tones is more consistent). Non–harmonic overtones are non-integral multiples of the fundamental.

overtraining. The continuation of training, usually for many trials, after the organism has reached asymptote.

overtraining extinction effect (OEE). The finding that animals given considerable OVERTRAINING extinguish faster after reinforcement is withdrawn than do those not given overtraining.

overtraining reversal effect (ORE). The finding that when on a discrimination task the positive and negative stimuli are exchanged so that the animal must reverse its responses, animals that have been overtrained often learn the reversal task faster than those not overtrained.

ovisophobia. Pathological fear of birds.

ovulation. The release of a mature ovum into the FALLOPIAN TUBE.

ovum. The female GAMETE.

own-control design. An experimental design in which each subject is given each condition so that each subject is his own control.

oxazepam. A minor tranquillizer, one of the BENZODIAZEPINES.

oxygen debt. A deficit of oxygen in the blood, caused by its having been used by the muscles during heavy exertion; the blood level must be restored by heavy breathing after the exertion is finished.

oxygen regulation. The maintenance of the oxygen level in the blood at around the correct level; this is achieved by receptors that monitor carbon dioxide levels, which tend to vary inversely with those of oxygen.

oxyopia. Unusually acute vision.

oxytocin. A HORMONE secreted by the POSTERIOR PITUITARY which strengthens uterine contractions, stimulates the ejection of milk from the mammary glands, and, by producing smooth muscle contractions in the uterus, facilitates the ascent of sperm after intromission.

P

P. An abbreviation for P DIMENSION.

P300. *See* P300 WAVE.

p. Probability, particularly the statistical probability of the null hypothesis being true.

p(A/B). The CONDITIONAL PROBABILITY of A given B.

pacing. 1. Structuring education so that new material is introduced only when the student is ready for it. 2. Controlling the speed at which an act (e.g. reading) is performed.

Pacinian corpuscle. A receptor with a bulbous ending lying in the deeper parts of the skin; it is sensitive to pressure.

paederasty. Anal intercourse with a boy.

paediatrics. The medical speciality concerned with childhood diseases and disorders.

paedicatio. A synonym for PAEDERASTY.

paedolalia, paedologia. Infant speech.

paedomorphism. The attribution to adults of childish traits. *Contrast* ENELICOMORPHISM.

paedomorphosis. (Ethology) The retention of formerly juvenile characteristics by adult descendants.

paedophilia. Obtaining sexual excitement from prepubertal children, usually of the opposite sex.

pain. *See* following entries and REFERRED PAIN.

pain pathways. The pathways that transmit pain; the AIII afferent fibres with free nerve endings yield sharp, bright pain, and the C fibres dull long-lasting pain (*see* NERVE FIBRE). The AIII fibres terminate in the substantia gelatinosa, the second order fibres run through the lateral spinal tract to the ventral posterior nucleus of the thalamus; further neurons project via the internal capsule to the somaesthetic cortex. Pain in the head and face is mediated by the trigeminal nerve; after a single synapse its messages are also conveyed to the ventral posterior nucleus of the thalamus. *See also* GATE CONTROL THEORY.

pain principle. Freud's hypothesis, put forward late in his career, that people seek to destroy or hurt themselves because of the THANATOS instinct.

pain spot. A tiny area of skin that is especially sensitive to pain.

pair bond. (Ethology) An enduring union between a male and a female conspecific.

paired associate learning (PAL). Learning to respond with the second member of a pair of items when presented with the first. Usually a list of pairs is presented in random succession; the subject is asked to respond to the first member of each pair by giving the second; after responding he is shown the second.

paired comparisons, method of. A psychophysical scaling method in which the subject ranks the members of all pairs of items presented, with each item in the set paired with every other item. An ordinal scale is produced. *See also* MULTIDIMENSIONAL SCALING METHODS, which may be employed on the results.

paired comparison test. (Statistics) A

319

significance test in which two sets of scores can be grouped into pairs (e.g. if the same subjects perform under two conditions, the scores of each subject on each condition can be paired). Such tests can assess whether the mean difference between the paired scores is significantly different. Since the variability between conditions is not influenced by the variable that is paired (e.g. subjects), such a significance test is more sensitive to variations caused by the independent variable than one using an UNPAIRED COMPARISON TEST.

PAL. An abbreviation for PAIRED ASSOCIATE LEARNING.

palaeocerebellum. The anterior lobe of the CEREBELLUM, which developed phylogenetically after the ARCHICEREBELLUM and before the NEOCEREBELLUM.

palaeocortex. The portion of the medial temporal lobe that developed phylogenetically before the ARCHICORTEX and NEOCORTEX. It has only three layers (or even no discernible layers), and includes the RHINENCEPHALON and parts of the LIMBIC SYSTEM.

palaeological thinking. Thinking based on fantasy and random associations with no reasoning, which is found in young children and schizophrenics.

palaeomnesis. A person's ability to recall events from his distant past.

palaeopallium. A synonym for PALAEO-CORTEX.

palaeopsychology. The study of the characteristics of our distant ancestors or of their influence on mental processes now, e.g. on the form of language or on the archetypes posited by Jung. The enterprise is highly speculative.

palaeostriatum. A synonym for GLOBUS PALLIDUS.

palaeosymbol. A private neologism of the sort sometimes used by schizophrenics.

palatal. (Phonetics) Pertaining to a speech sound (e.g. the 'sh' in 'shin', the 'ch' in 'chin', and the 'g' in 'gin') produced with the tongue against the roof of the mouth just above the alveolar ridge.

palate. The roof of the mouth, comprising the **hard palate** at the front and the SOFT PALATE at the back.

palato-alveolar. (Phonetics) Pertaining to a speech sound produced with the blade of the tongue in contact with the alveolar ridge and the front of the tongue raised towards the hard palate (e.g. the 'sh' in 'ship').

PA learning. An abbreviation for PAIRED ASSOCIATE LEARNING.

paleocerebellum. An alternative spelling for PALAEOCEREBELLUM.

paleocortex. An alternative spelling for PALAEOCORTEX.

paleological thinking. An alternative spelling for PALAEOLOGICAL THINKING.

paleomnesis. An alternative spelling for PALAEOMNESIS.

paleopallium. An alternative spelling for PALAEOPALLIUM.

paleopsychology. An alternative spelling for PALAEOPSYCHOLOGY.

paleostriatum. An alternative spelling for PALAEOSTRIATUM.

paleosymbol. An alternative spelling for PALAEOSYMBOL.

paligraphia. Obsessive repetition of letters, words, or phrases in writing.

palilalia. A speech disorder in which material is repeated over and over again; it can occur in e.g. Alzheimer's disease.

palilexia. Abnormal repetition of words or phrases.

palilogia. A synonym for PALILALIA.

palinacousis. (Neuropsychology) Hearing again voices or other sounds that have just occurred or that occurred up to 24 hours previously, a rare condition associated with temporal lobe lesions.

palindrome. A word, like 'nun', that is the same whether read backwards or forwards.

palingraphia. Writing with left and right directions reversed so that the writing appears as normal writing would if held before a mirror.

palinlexia. Reading backwards either by reversing the letters in a word or by reversing the order of words.

palinopsia, palinopia. Persistence of vision for a stimulus for some time after it is no longer present, a rare condition sometimes caused by damage to the visual cortex.

palinphrasia. Involuntary repetition in speaking.

pallaesthesia, pallesthesia. The sense of vibration.

pallidum. A synonym for GLOBUS PALLIDUS.

pallium. An obsolete term for the white matter of the cortex.

pallesthesia. An alternative spelling of PALLAESTHESIA.

palmar reflex. A grasping reflex made when the palm is scratched, which occurs in young children.

palmesthesia. An alternative spelling of PALLAESTHESIA.

P-alpha group. Another term for the retinal ganglion cells in the MAGNOCELLULAR SYSTEM.

palsy. An obsolete synonym for PARALYSIS.

PAM. An abbreviation for PRECATEGORICAL ACOUSTIC MEMORY.

pancreas. An ENDOCRINE GLAND behind the stomach, which secretes INSULIN, GLUCAGON, and various digestive hormones.

pandemic. (Epidemiology) Occurring everywhere or over a large geographical area, mainly used of disease.

Pandemonium. (AI) A proposed letter-recognition system, operating in three stages. (a) Templates detect features of the letter (e.g. a horizontal line). (b) Their output is fed to letter detectors. (At both these stages the better the fit, the stronger the detectors fire.) (c) The decision of which letter is present is based on which letter detector is firing most strongly.

pangenesis. A false doctrine to explain inheritance, positing that each part of the body gives off a specific essence that is collected in the gene cell.

panglossia. Pathological talkativeness.

panic disorder. Any neurosis marked by extreme recurrent panics.

panmixia. The attribute of a population in which mating occurs randomly. *Contrast* ASSORTATIVE MATING.

pan-neurosis. A syndrome in which the symptoms of many different neuroses are present, e.g. anxiety, conversion symptoms, phobias, and obsessive–compulsive symptoms; it occurs, e.g., in PSEUDONEUROTIC SCHIZOPHRENIA.

panphobia, panophobia. A morbid fear of everything.

panpsychism. The philosophical theory that all that exists is mental.

pansexualism. Reducing (or perhaps elevating) everything to sex (like Freud).

pantophobia. A synonym for PANPHOBIA.

pantry-check technique. (Market research) A check of the contents of people's houses to discover whether they are really using the products they say they use.

Panum's area. For a stimulus at a given locus on one eye, the area on the other eye over which a stimulus can be fused with the stimulus on the first eye. The area has a horizontal extent of about 10′ of arc at the fovea and is considerably broader in the periphery.

Panum's effect. A stereoscopic effect in which when two vertical lines (A, B) are shown to one eye and three (A', B', C) to the other lines A and B fuse with lines A' and B' and B is seen as lying in front of C.

Panum's limiting case. The projection of two vertical lines horizontally aligned to one eye and only one to the other. The two lines projected to one eye are seen as at different depths in a manner consistent with the line on the other eye having been fused with both of them. The case is 'limiting' because this is the smallest number of stimuli with which stereopsis can be produced.

Papez circuit. A hypothetical neural circuit in the LIMBIC SYSTEM possibly implicated in emotion and passing from the hypothalamus through the mammillary bodies, the anterior thalamus, the cingulate gyrus, the hippocampus, and the fornix, back to the hypothalamus. *See* Appendix 5.

papilla. (Anatomy) A small protuberance. The **lingual papillae** are protuberances on the surface of the tongue and contain the taste buds.

parabiosis. Living joined together, particularly of Siamese twins.

parabiotic preparation. A preparation in which two genetically similar animals have their blood circulations joined; it is used to investigate the effects of hormones or other substances in the blood of one animal on the state of the other.

parabulia. A pathological disorder of the will in which one act tends to negate another; e.g. a person may be putting on his shoe and suddenly throw it away.

paracentral lobule. *See* Appendix 2.

paracentral vision. Vision using the area immediately surrounding the fovea. *Compare* PARAFOVEA.

parachlorophenylalanine (PCPA). A drug that prevents the synthesis of SEROTONIN by blocking the action of the enzyme tryptophan hydroxylase.

parachromatopsia. A synonym for colour blindness.

paracontrast. A form of forward VISUAL MASKING in which the masking figure is presented before the one that is masked with its contours surrounding or flanking those of the masked figure. Both figures are shown only briefly. The masking figure reduces or eliminates the visibility of the masked figure. *Compare* METACONTRAST.

paracusia. (Hearing) 1. Selective deafness to low-frequency tones. 2. The supposed ability of people with some forms of deafness to hear better when there is a background noise, which may be caused by speakers raising their voice in the presence of the noise. 3. Any abnormality of hearing, other than simple deafness, e.g. impairment of sound localization.

paradigm. 1. (Generally) A model or pattern. 2. (Linguistics) The set of all the inflected forms of a word. 3. (Psychology) A type of approach to a subject or to designing experiments (e.g. the Pavlovian paradigm).

paradigmatic. (Linguistics) Pertaining to the relation a linguistic constituent has to other constituents that can replace it in a given context; e.g. 'l' can be replaced by 'b' when followed by '-it' or 'the' can be replaced by 'a'. The role of a constituent can be defined in terms of its paradigmatic and SYNTAGMATIC relations with other constituents. *Compare* CONTRASTIVE DISTRIBUTION.

paradigmatic association. An association to a word that is related to it by meaning (e.g. black–white). *Contrast* SYNTAGMATIC ASSOCIATION.

paradoxical cold. A sensation of coldness experienced when a cold spot on the skin is stimulated by warmth (about 45°C).

paradoxical intention. 1. A psychotherapeutic technique in which the patient is told to magnify his fears or obsessive worries while behaving in defiance of them. 2. More generally, the deliberate practice of a neurotic habit in the hope that this will make it go away (a technique used by some behaviour therapists).

paradoxical sleep. A synonym for REM SLEEP.

paradoxical warmth. A sensation of heat experienced when a warm spot on the skin is stimulated by cold (about 10°C).

paraesthesia. Abnormal skin sensations, like tickling or burning, that are not caused by an external stimulus, but by e.g. drugs or brain damage.

parafovea. The part of the retina immediately surrounding the FOVEA.

parageusia. A distortion of or hallucination of taste.

paragnosia. A synonym for EXTRASENSORY PERCEPTION.

paragrammatism. A disturbance of speech, characterized by faulty grammar, such as may occur in schizophrenia or some forms of aphasia.

paragraphia. A disturbance of writing, in which letters, syllables, or words are transposed or omitted, and incorrect ones sometimes inserted.

parahippocampal gyrus. A cortical convolution in the limbic lobe. *See* Appendix 2.

parahypnosis. An abnormal type of sleep caused by an anaesthetic or hypnosis, in which a person may hear what is going on around him.

parakinesia. A clumsy movement.

parakinesis. A synonym for PSYCHOKINESIS (1).

paralalia. A speech defect in which one sound is substituted for another.

paralalia literalis. Difficulty in enunciating certain speech sounds correctly.

paralexia. A type of DYSLEXIA in which letters or words are misread or transposed.

paralinguistics. The study of communication through aspects of speech other than phonemes, syntax, and semantics, e.g. the study of tones of voice, pausing, emphasis, and gestures.

parallax. The change in the projected image of a scene that occurs when the viewpoint is shifted laterally, as produced by sideways head movements (*see* MOTION PARALLAX) or by the difference in the position of the two eyes (*see* STEREOPSIS). Parallax is an important cue to depth. The term is sometimes used more broadly to include changes in the image caused by other movements of the observer, e.g. moving forwards.

parallel distributed processing (PDP). Processing through a network of nodes (a NEURAL NETWORK), each connected to several other nodes in an excitatory or inhibitory way, usually with different strengths of connection. In such a network no single node represents a single concept or entity; each node will fire to many different inputs, but the ensemble of nodes firing to a given input may come to represent a given concept. Learning depends on changes in the strengths of the connections. Some such systems have generalized from the input in interesting ways, and given rise to what appear to be new concepts. The systems can exhibit associative learning and learning based on knowledge of results (*see* BACK-PROPAGATION ALGORITHM). They have the advantage over most other forms of computer simulation that they work in parallel, and exhibit the same sloppiness and lack of predictability as does the human mind. Some believe they are the most important revolution in our understanding of the mind since Aristotle, or at least since the advent of the digital computer.

parallel fibres. The processes of the granule fibres that run horizontally across the molecular layer of the cerebellum, making contact with the dendrites of the Purkinje cells.

parallel forms reliability. A measure of the reliability of a test based on giving two different but similar versions of it to the same subjects, and measuring the correlation between the scores on each form.

parallelism. *See* PSYCHOPHYSICAL PARALLELISM.

parallel law. Fechner's hypothesis that, when two stimuli of different intensity are presented for a period of time, although through adaptation the apparent magnitude of each will lessen, the ratio of their apparent magnitudes will remain the same.

parallel play. The play of two or more children in the same locality and often using the same materials, but without any interaction between them. It develops after SOLITARY PLAY and before COOPERATIVE PLAY.

parallel processing. (Computing) The execution of several (usually many) different operations simultaneously; much parallel processing occurs in the brain (e.g. in the early levels of the visual system). *Contrast* SERIAL PROCESSING.

parallel search. A search through memory in which several (usually many) items are examined simultaneously.

paralog. A rare term for a nonsense syllable having two syllables, e.g. 'latuk'.

paralogia. Incoherent and illogical speech, as e.g. in schizophrenia.

paralogism. An unintentional error in reasoning.

paralysis. Impairment of motor functioning, usually caused by damage to the nervous system, though it can be hysterical.

paralysis agitans. A synonym for PARKINSON'S DISEASE.

paralytic dementia. A synonym for GENERAL PARESIS.

parameter. 1. (Mathematics) An unspecified constant or a constant in a function other than the argument that needs to be set to evaluate the function. 2. (Statistics) A statistical property of a population, as opposed to a SAMPLE STATISTIC. Thus the mean or standard deviation of a population may not correspond to the mean or standard deviation of a sample from it. Greek letters are often used for parameters (e.g. μ for mean, σ for standard deviation) and English ones for sample statistics (e.g. M or s). 3. (Experimental research) Any independent variable in an experiment other than the main one, e.g. in measuring food consumption with different lengths of food deprivation, time since last allowed access to water might be a parameter. In recording results in graphic form the values of the main independent variable are usually placed along the horizontal axis and separate lines are drawn to represent the effects of a parameter. 4. (Psychoanalysis) Any technique not derived from psychoanalytic theory, e.g. reassurance.

parameter dragging. The use of a parameter value estimated in one experiment to provide a value to apply to the data of another experiment, usually as part of an equation.

parametric statistics. Statistical methods that involve assumptions about population parameters other than those under test, e.g. the assumption that a population has a particular normal distribution. *See* NON–PARAMETRIC STATISTICS.

paramimia. A type of apraxia in which the ability to gesture is impaired.

paramnesia. A distorted or incorrect memory.

paranoia, paranoid disorder. A mental disorder marked by systematized delusional beliefs, e.g. the belief that one is being plotted against, or extreme and groundless sexual jealousy, but with the personality and thought processes otherwise intact; the term is not limited to persecutory delusions, although it is often used in this way in everyday life.

paranoid personality disorder. A personality disorder marked by extreme distrust, jealousy, and suspicion of others.

paranoid schizophrenia. (DSM-III) A form of schizophrenia in which, in addition to other symptoms, the patient has delusions of grandeur, persecution, or reference, or delusional jealousy, but with most of the rest of his behaviour relatively unaffected.

paranormal. Pertaining to events that can have no ordinary explanation, e.g. telepathy, witchcraft. *See* PARAPSYCHOLOGY.

paranosis. Any side benefit to be gained from an illness, e.g. being relieved of responsibility at work, or (according to Freud) relief from anxiety through the development of a neurosis.

paraphasia. The habitual use of inappropriate words (and particularly of words associated with the correct word), commonly found when people with RECEPTIVE APHASIA are asked to repeat another's speech.

paraphemia. Habitual errors in the use of words and phonemes in speech.

paraphilia. Gaining sexual excitement by a method that is abnormal in one's society (e.g. in Western society, exhibitionism, frottage, sadism).

paraphobia. A mild form of phobia, of the sort many people suffer from, e.g. of taking examinations or of writing dictionaries.

paraphonia. An abnormal or pathological quality of voice.

paraphrase. A sentence with the same meaning as another (e.g. 'John was hit by Mary' is a paraphrase of 'Mary hit John'), or, more generally, any passage of language that has the same sense as another.

paraphrasia. A synonym for PARAPHASIA.

paraphrenia, paraphrenic schizophrenia. Synonyms for PARANOID SCHIZOPHRENIA (obsolete).

paraphresia. A synonym for PAROSMIA.

paraplegia. Paralysis of the lower part of the body including the legs and often the lower part of the trunk.

parapraxis. A minor mistake made in speaking or action (e.g. trying to open a door with the wrong key). Freud thought such errors were caused by repressed wishes expressing themselves in devious ways.

parapsychology. The study of alleged psychic phenomena, like TELEPATHY, CLAIRVOYANCE, PRECOGNITION, and PSYCHOKINESIS.

parasagittal. Pertaining to a plane parallel to the SAGITTAL PLANE.

parasexuality. Sexual perversion.

parasitic superego. A temporary SUPEREGO that accepts different moral principles from those instantiated in a person's normal superego, e.g. it may accept the principles of a mob of which a person finds himself a part.

parasitophobia. A morbid fear of parasites.

parasocial speech. A synonym for EGOCENTRIC SPEECH.

parasol cell. A large retinal ganglion cell with centre-surround organization, without colour opponency and with an input to the centre from several cones. It is part of the MAGNOCELLULAR SYSTEM.

parasomnia. Any disorder of sleep, e.g. insomnia, sleepwalking, or enuresis.

parastriate cortex. An obsolete term for Brodmann's area 19; see Appendix 3. An area of the occipital lobe lying immediately anterior to the prestriate cortex, and containing retinotopic projections.

parasuicide. A feigned or unsuccessful attempt at suicide.

parasympathetic system. One of the two divisions of the AUTONOMIC NERVOUS SYSTEM; it stems from ganglia in the 3rd, 7th, 9th, 10th, and 11th cranial nerves and in the 2nd, 3rd, and 4th segments of the sacral part of the spinal cord. In general, it serves an anabolic function by promoting the storage of energy. It helps to control respiration and heart beat, and to promote digestion and the elimination of waste products.

parataxic distortion. (Psychoanalysis) Any attitude towards someone else that is distorted because of one's underlying drives; in particular a reaction to someone as though he were an important figure (e.g. one's father) in one's early life.

parataxis. 1. (Linguistics) The placing of words or phrases together with no intervening conjunctions, e.g. 'Now, then, always'. 2. (Psychoanalysis) Sullivan's term for a failure to integrate thoughts, goals, and emotions. *Compare* SYNTAXIS.

parathormone. A hormone secreted by the PARATHYROID GLANDS that controls calcium and phosphorus metabolism.

parathymia. Making inappropriate emotional responses, e.g. laughing at a personal calamity; it can be a symptom of schizophrenia.

parathyroid glands. Two pairs of pea-sized glands attached to the thyroid that secrete PARATHORMONE.

paratype. All the environmental influences to which a person has been exposed; they act upon his GENOTYPE to make him what he is.

paratypic. Environmentally caused.

paraventricular   nucleus   (PVN).   A hypothalamic nucleus anterior to the medial hypothalamus that, when injected with nor-epinephrine or neuropeptide-Y, produces eating.

paraverbal communication. A synonym for NON–VERBAL COMMUNICATION. *See also* PARA-LINGUISTICS.

paravertebral ganglia. The ganglia of the sympathetic system; they lie in a chain outside the spinal cord.

parental investment. (Sociobiology) Any contribution to the INCLUSIVE FITNESS of an offspring made by a parent at its own expense.

parergasia. The performance of an action other than that intended, e.g. blowing instead of sucking.

paresis. 1. Partial paralysis. 2. An organic mental disorder, marked by paralysis and dementia, occurring in tertiary syphilis.

paresthesia. An alternative spelling for PAR-AESTHESIA.

Pareto analysis. (Economics) The percentage of a population associated with a given percentage of a property that varies between members of the population. E.g. 20 per cent of British adults own 80 per cent of the country's wealth.

Pareto frontier. (Decision theory) The subset of options that dominate other options, i.e. they have utility values on all dimensions that are better than or equal to all other options; the latter options can be discarded from further consideration.

parietal lobe. One of the four main divisions of the cortex. It lies at the upper middle part of the head and is above the TEMPORAL LOBE, behind the FRONTAL LOBE, and in front of the OCCIPITAL LOBE; it is involved in a variety of functions including somaesthesis (*see* SOMATOSENSORY CORTEX) and spatial organization. It comprises Brodmann's areas 1, 3, 5, 7, 39, and 40; *see* Appendices 3 and 4.

parieto-occipital sulcus. *See* Appendices 1 and 2.

Paris school. The psychiatrists of the late 18th century to the early 20th century at the Salpêtrière in Paris, particularly Pinel, who first practised more liberal treatment of the mentally ill, and Charcot, who advocated the use of hypnosis in psychotherapy, and who attempted to relate neurological symptoms to the locus of brain damage. Their approach to hypnosis, started mainly by Charcot, and current in Paris in the late 19th century, was based on the belief that it was allied to hysteria. *Compare* NANCY SCHOOL.

Parkinsonism. Any disorder with similar symptoms to PARKINSON'S DISEASE; the symptoms may be caused by neuroleptics, a brain tumour, carbon monoxide poisoning, etc.

Parkinson's disease. An insidious and progressive illness resulting from degeneration of the nervous system in older people; it is marked by poor motor coordination, tremor, a mask-like face, and inability to initiate voluntary actions. It is probably caused by impaired dopamine activity in the basal ganglia. Similar symptoms can be produced by long-term use of neuroleptics.

parole. (Linguistics) Saussure's term for the corpus of utterances actually produced by an individual speaker in a community. *Contrast* LANGUE.

parorexia. A pathological craving for strange foods.

parosmia, parosphresia. Any disorder of the sense of smell.

parotid glands. The largest of the three salivary glands; they lie inside the cheeks, below and in front of the ears.

paroxysm. A spasmodic convulsion.

parsimony, principle of. A synonym for LLOYD MORGAN'S CANON.

parsing. Inferring (usually unconsciously) the syntax of a sentence.

parthenogenesis. The reproduction of offspring from an unfertilized female egg, which occurs, e.g. in some insects.

partial. A synonym for PARTIAL TONE.

partial aim. (Psychoanalysis) The pursuit of sexual gratification without copulation that occurs before the GENITAL STAGE.

partial correlation. (Statistics) The correlation between two variables that remains when a correction has been made for the correlation of other variables with the original variables.

partial instinct. (Psychoanalysis) Any component of the full libidinal instinct, e.g. the oral, anal, or genital instinct.

partialism. Obtaining sexual pleasure from touching a part (e.g. a leg) of another person.

partial reinforcement (PR). Reinforcing an organism for making a response on only some randomly chosen trials. *Contrast* CONTINUOUS REINFORCEMENT.

partial reinforcement effect (PRE). The phenomenon that when organisms are trained with partial reinforcement, they tend to take longer to extinguish.

partial report method. A synonym for PART REPORT METHOD.

partial tone. Any pure tone that forms part of a complex tone, i.e. the FUNDAMENTAL and the OVERTONES. The numbering of HARMONIC partials is as follows: the first partial is the fundamental, the second partial is twice the frequency of the fundamental, the third partial is three times the frequency of the fundamental, etc; *compare* OVERTONE. Non-harmonic partials are non-integral multiples of the fundamental.

participant observation. The study of a group by an observer who pretends to belong to it. *Compare* PSEUDOPATIENT.

participant observer. An observer who is also taking part in the activities of a group.

participation. Piaget's term for the child's tendency to think that events with an external cause are caused by him.

participle. A verb form that must be used with an auxiliary or other verb, e.g. 'gone'.

particle. (Linguistics) A function word that does not readily fit into any other grammatical category, e.g. 'to' (when used in an infinitive) and 'not'.

particular complex. (Psychoanalysis) A complex peculiar to a given person, and not, unlike e.g. the Oedipus complex, universal.

partile. (Statistics) A score that divides a distribution into parts in which each part has the same percentage of the total number of ordered scores. Thus DECILES divide sets of scores into tenths, and QUARTILES into fourths.

part instinct. A synonym for PARTIAL INSTINCT.

partition scaling. Any psychophysical scaling method in which the subject has to assign stimuli to categories, keeping the apparent distance between categories the same, e.g. EQUAL-APPEARING INTERVALS METHOD. It yields an interval scale.

part method of learning. Learning a block of material one part at a time, instead of learning all of it at once. *Contrast* WHOLE METHOD OF LEARNING.

part motion. A form of apparent motion in which two successively presented stationary stimuli displaced from one another in space appear to move towards one another without meeting. This occurs when the pause or spatial separation between the stimuli is too short for the observer to see OPTIMAL APPARENT MOTION.

part object. Any part (e.g. the breasts) of a person that satisfies the libidinous needs of another. *Compare* WHOLE OBJECT.

part of speech. The syntactic category of a word: NOUN, PRONOUN, VERB, ADJECTIVE, PREPOSITION, ADVERB, CONJUNCTION, PARTICLE.

part report method. An experimental technique in which the subject is shown a display and is subsequently told to report a selected part of it. It is used in the study of ICONIC MEMORY, which only lasts for about 0.5 sec. It yields a more accurate estimate of how much material a subject can remember after a very short interval than does the WHOLE REPORT METHOD, since some material may be forgotten while the subject is reporting the remainder.

parturiphobia. A morbid fear of childbirth.

parvocellular layers. The four dorsal layers of the LATERAL GENICULATE NUCLEUS. They contain P CELLS. *Contrast* MAGNOCELLULAR LAYERS.

parvocellular system (P system). A visual pathway containing small ganglion cells in the retina and the dorsal four layers of the lateral geniculate. It has small slow conducting axons. It responds to fine detail and to colour. *See also* X CELLS, which are almost certainly identical with **parvocellular cells**.

PAS. An abbreviation for PRECATEGORICAL ACOUSTIC STORE.

passing stranger effect. The tendency of some people to relate the most intimate details of themselves to a casual stranger, better known as the **ancient mariner syndrome**.

passive-aggressive personality disorder. (DSM-III) A personality disorder in which the person resists social demands passively – e.g. by forgetting appointments, being inefficient, etc.; it is thought to reveal an underlying aggression.

passive analysis. A psychoanalysis in which the analyst makes the minimum of interventions.

passive avoidance learning. Learning *not* to do something in order to avoid punishment. *Contrast* ACTIVE AVOIDANCE LEARNING.

passive-dependent personality. A synonym for DEPENDENT PERSONALITY DISORDER.

passive learning. A synonym for INCIDENTAL LEARNING.

passive oral phase. *See* ORAL STAGE.

passive therapy. Psychotherapy in which the therapist intervenes as little as possible. *Contrast* ACTIVE THERAPY.

passive transport. Movement of a substance through a semipermeable membrane by DIFFUSION or by OSMOSIS.

passive vocabulary. All the words a person can understand, including those he never utters himself. *Contrast* ACTIVE VOCABULARY.

passive voice. A category applied to sentences, clauses, and verb forms in which the grammatical subject is the recipient or target of the action e.g. 'He was shot'.

past perfect tense. A synonym for PLUPERFECT TENSE.

past pointing. 1. The tendency to be inaccurate in pointing to a part of the body, caused by some forms of brain damage. 2. The tendency to point at the environment inaccurately for a short time after being spun with an accelerated or decelerated motion; it is caused by the aftereffects of such motion on the VESTIBULAR SYSTEM.

past tense. Any TENSE used of an action or event completed or begun before the time of utterance, e.g. the AORIST, IMPERFECT TENSE, and PERFECT TENSE.

patch clamping. A method of investigating ION CHANNELS by picking up a small section of cell membrane with a tiny pipette and measuring the current passing through the channel when it opens. The effects of neurotransmitters and of the voltage across the membrane can be studied.

patellar reflex. A spinal reflex in which the lower leg rises sharply when the patellar tendon is tapped just below the knee.

path analysis. The attempt to establish a causal chain, usually by the use of MULTIPLE REGRESSION.

pathetic nerve. A synonym for TROCHLEAR NERVE.

pathobiography. A biography that attempts to give a psychoanalytic account of a person, based on historical data, e.g. Freud's wildly inaccurate biography of Leonardo.

pathocure. The cessation of a neurosis when a physical illness starts. *Contrast* PATHONEUROSIS.

pathogenesis. The origin and course of a disease.

pathognomonic. Indicative of, or characteristic of, a given illness, usually used of symptoms.

pathognomy. 1. The study of how to recognize an illness from its symptoms. 2. A symptom or symptoms of an illness.

pathohysteria. A form of CONVERSION HYSTERIA in which chronic illness gives rise to hysterical symptoms.

pathology. 1. The study of all aspects of illnesses. 2. A disease or disorder.

pathomimesis. A synonym for PATHOHYSTERIA.

pathomimicry. Simulating the symptoms of a disease whether deliberately (MALINGERING) or without intent (FACTITIOUS DISORDER).

pathomorphism. Abnormal or extreme body build.

pathoneurosis. Any neurotic reaction to a physical disease or disorder; it may consist of gross underestimation or overestimation of the disability the disease causes, or of the hysterical continuation of the symptoms of a disease that has been cured. *Contrast* PATHOCURE.

pathophobia. A synonym for NOSOPHOBIA.

patrilineal. Pertaining to inheritance through the male line.

pattern discrimination. The ability to discriminate between two or more patterns, i.e. to make consistently different responses to each pattern. This does not imply recognition of the pattern as a whole, since discrimination may be based on a single feature (e.g. a square and a triangle base down can be discriminated merely by the difference between the straight line and the point at the top).

patterning. Systematic teaching of sensory-motor actions to brain-damaged patients, especially brain-damaged children who may be taught in sequence the normal developmental series of sensory-motor abilities.

pattern masking. Reducing the visibility of a brief visual stimulus by presenting a pattern in close temporal and spatial proximity (as opposed to BRIGHTNESS MASKING). For different kinds of pattern masking *see* METACONTRAST, PARACONTRAST, PATTERN MASKING BY NOISE, and PATTERN MASKING BY STRUCTURE.

pattern masking by noise. PATTERN MASKING in which the masking stimulus is visual noise, e.g. a random array of black and white squares.

pattern masking by structure. PATTERN MASKING in which the masking stimulus is a random array of elements each of which is similar to the elements in the figure being masked.

pattern recognition. The ability to recognize a pattern as the same, despite changes in it (e.g. a melody has the same pattern even if transposed through an octave), and despite changes in the proximal stimulus to which it gives rise (e.g. changes caused by different view points). If the pattern itself is changed (e.g. in visual patterns, by being rotated, changed in size, or even changed in shape as in different versions of a given lower case letter), the question arises of what is to count as the same pattern. In general we recognize as the same pattern, patterns that have the same significance for us (e.g. a given letter) but the allowable transformations on the pattern then depend on the other patterns that must be discriminated from it and on context. In vision the expression is usually confined to two-dimensional patterns. *Compare* OBJECT RECOGNITION.

pattern theory. (Skin senses) The hypothesis that information about individual somaesthetic continua (e.g. touch, pressure, and pain) is carried not so much by the type of neuron firing but by the spatio-temporal configuration of firing of all the different types. *Contrast* SPECIFICITY THEORY.

Pavlovian conditioning. A synonym for CLASSICAL CONDITIONING.

Pavlovianism. The doctrine that all behaviour can be explained by conditioned reflexes, which in turn can be explained in terms of the physical working of the brain.

pavor diurnus. Terror, usually in a child, occurring in a daytime nap; it is normally caused by a bad dream.

pavor nocturnus. Terror, usually in a child, occurring at night during sleep; it is normally caused by a bad dream.

payoff. The cost or benefit of a given course of action, used especially in situations that can be analysed by GAME THEORY.

P300 component. *See* P300 wave.

P-beta group. Another term for retinal ganglion cells in the PARVOCELLULAR SYSTEM.

P cell. An abbreviation for parvocellular cell (*see* PARVOCELLUAR SYSTEM).

PCP. A hallucinogenic drug commonly known as **angel dust**.

PCPA. An abbreviation for PARA-CHLOROPHENYLALANINE.

P dimension. An abbreviation for PSYCHOTICISM DIMENSION.

PDP. An abbreviation for PARALLEL DISTRIBUTED PROCESSING.

PE. An abbreviation for PROBABLE ERROR.

Peabody Picture Vocabulary Test. A test, mainly for preliterate children, in which the subject has to select from four pictures the one that corresponds to a spoken word.

peak amplitude. *See* AMPLITUDE.

peak clipping. The elimination of the high amplitude parts of a waveform by cutting off its highest and lowest sections. If a speech wave is transformed in this way, it makes little difference to its intelligibility.

peak experience. A moment of extreme awe or ecstasy.

peak shift. (Animal learning) The phenomenon that, if an organism is given discrimination training to a positive and a negative stimulus lying on the same dimension, when it is subsequently tested with other stimuli on that dimension, it responds maximally not to the original positive stimulus, but to a stimulus shifted away from it in the opposite direction to that of the negative stimulus.

peak-to-peak amplitude. *See* AMPLITUDE.

Pearson product moment correlation. *See* PRODUCT-MOMENT CORRELATION.

PEC. A scale measuring political and economic conservatism.

peccatophobia. A morbid fear of sinning.

pecking order. (Ethology) A synonym for DOMINANCE HIERARCHY.

pecten. A comb-like structure of blood-vessels in the eye of birds or reptiles; its function may be to protect receptors from the direct image of the sun.

pederasty. An alternative spelling of PAEDERASTY.

pediatrics. An alternative spelling of PAEDIATRICS.

pedicatio. An alternative spelling of PAEDICATIO.

pedolalia. An alternative spelling for PAEDOLALIA.

pedalogia. An alternative spelling for PAEDOLOGIA.

pedomorphism. An alternative spelling of PAEDOMORPHISM.

pedomorphosis. An alternative spelling of PAEDOMORPHOSIS.

pedophilia. An alternative spelling of PAEDOPHILIA.

peduncle. Any bundle of nerve fibres in the brain.

peer group. A group composed of people of about the same age and status.

pegboard test. A test of sensory motor skill in which pegs have to be placed in holes as fast as possible.

pegwords. A prelearned list of words with which new items can be associated to assist memory. E.g. someone who knows the peg words 'one bun, two shoe, three tree', etc. can associate the first item in a list to be learned with bun, the second with shoe, etc. *Compare* MNEMONIC.

pendular nystagmus. *See* NYSTAGMUS.

pendular whiplash illusion. An illusion caused by observing a moving pendulum with two luminous points attached by a horizontal rod, each at the same distance out from it. If an observer tracks one of them, the other appears to move faster and through a larger angle. *Compare* AUBERT–FLEISCHL PARADOX.

penetrability. *See* COGNITIVE PENETRABILITY.

penetrance. (Genetics) The proportion of organisms bearing a particular dominant gene or that are homozygous for a particular recessive gene in which the trait produced by that gene is manifested.

penetration response. A response to a projective test that suggests the testee is vulnerable or weak.

penilingus. A synonym for FELLATIO.

penis envy. Freud's idea that women envy the penis because they are incomplete men, for which he has of late been much castigated.

Penrose triangle. An IMPOSSIBLE FIGURE that tends to be seen as a three-dimensional triangle, *see* illustration below. Closer inspection shows that it cannot be because if it were the lines depicting edges could not be connected as they are.

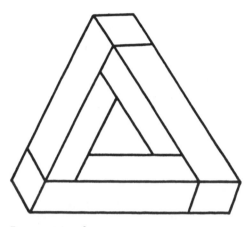

Penrose triangle

pentobarbital. A fast-acting BARBITURATE.

penumbra. The region at the edge of a shadow where there is a gradual increase in light intensity.

Pepper's ghost. A visual effect produced by a half-silvered mirror or sheet of glass: in it two objects can be seen superimposed (one through the mirror, the other reflected by it). If one object is brightened and the other dimmed, the first object will be seen to take the place of the second. The device is used to create stage ghosts.

peptide. A molecule composed of a short sequence of amino acids. *See also* NEUROPEPTIDE.

peptide bond. A bond joining amino acids to form PEPTIDES or proteins.

perceived locus of control. *See* LOCUS OF CONTROL.

percentile. 1. Any of the 99 points that divide rank ordered scores up into 100 sets, each containing an equal number of scores. The first percentile is the point dividing the highest 1 per cent of scores from the rest, and the 99th percentile is the point above which 99 per cent of the scores fall. 2. The term is sometimes used to mean the range of scores within a set, e.g. the first percentile would be the highest 1 per cent of scores.

perception span. A synonym for SPAN OF APPREHENSION.

perceptron. (AI) A system for recognizing patterns, into which the features of a pattern are input. The inputs are weighted, and if the combined weights exceed a certain threshold, the perceptron 'fires' (decides the pattern is present). The device can learn by increasing weights for features active when the pattern is there, and decreasing those active when a false alarm occurs. It works in parallel. It has been shown that a two-layered perceptron (input units directly connected to output units) cannot distinguish certain classes of pattern (e.g. patterns containing a closed line versus patterns not containing one) but these restrictions do not apply to perceptrons having more layers.

perceptual defence. The raising of the absolute threshold for perceiving a stimulus because it is threatening or unpleasant, a phenomenon that is in doubt. *Contrast* PERCEPTUAL SENSITIZATION.

perceptual extinction. Failure to sense a stimulus when it is presented with another stimulus, a phenomenon that can be caused by brain damage.

perceptual field. All the perceptions a person has at an instant in time.

perceptual learning. Learning how to perceive or how to improve one's perception, e.g. by finer differentiation. There are many possible forms of perceptual learning; one is to learn the general structure of a class of visual objects (e.g. faces), thus making it easier to record the differentiating features of a new example, and hence to recognize it again as an individual object.

perceptual rearrangement. 1. Any systematic change in the input to the senses from the real world, e.g. wearing wedge prisms that shift the visual image on the eye, looking at the world through a horizontal mirror above the eye that inverts it on the eye, etc. 2. The rearrangement of the perceptual control of the muscles that can occur as a result of adaptation to PERCEPTUAL REARRANGEMENT (1). *Compare* PRISM ADAPTATION.

perceptual reversal. The reversal in depth of a REVERSIBLE FIGURE.

perceptual sensitization, perceptual vigilance. A set to perceive certain objects, which may result in lowered thresholds for them, and sometimes in perceiving them when they are not there.

perdeviation effect. When a part of the body is maintained in an eccentric position, the experience that the posture is less eccentric than it is. *Compare* POSTURAL AFTEREFFECT.

perfect pitch. A synonym for ABSOLUTE PITCH.

perfect tense. A tense signifying that an action has been completed before a given moment in time, and that it has some relevance to that moment in time. In English there are three perfect tenses – the perfect tense ('I have come'), the **pluperfect tense** ('I had come'), and the **future perfect tense** ('I will have come').

performance. 1. (Linguistics) The actual utterances made by native speakers of a language, which because of memory limitations, inadequate grasp of syntax or semantics, absent-mindedness, etc., will not conform exactly to an idealized grammar (COMPETENCE). 2. (Psychology) The execution of a task on a particular occasion, as opposed to what has been learnt about that task.

performance anxiety. Anxiety about not being able to perform a task such as taking an examination or having sexual intercourse.

performance neurosis. A temporary emotional disturbance caused by having to perform a difficult task, like taking an examination.

performance operating characteristic (POC). A graph showing performance on one task plotted against performance on another when both are performed concurrently. In general, the better a subject does at one task, the worse he will do at the other.

performance resource function. Performance on a task plotted against the percentage of resources allocated to that task: such plots are largely hypothetical since we cannot know the percentage of resources allocated. *Compare* ATTENTION OPERATING CHARACTERISTIC.

performance test. Any non-verbal test of an ability.

performative. (Linguistics) A speech act the making of which changes the state of the world in some way, e.g. promising ('I promise'), entering into a marriage contract ('I thee wed'), etc.

perhaps neurosis. An obsessional neurosis in which someone is preoccupied with what might have happened had he acted differently.

periamygdaloid cortex. Part of the PYRIFORM LOBE.

perikaryon. A synonym for CELL BODY.

perilymph. The fluid between the bony labyrinth and the membranous labyrinth of the inner ear. *See* LABYRINTH.

perimacular vision. Vision using the area of the retina immediately surrounding the MACULA.

perimeter. A device for measuring the sensitivity of each part of the retina, consisting of a hemisphere on to any part of which a visual stimulus can be projected; the subject fixates the centre of the hemisphere and reports whether he has seen the stimulus.

periodicity theory. (Hearing) A synonym for FREQUENCY THEORY.

periodic reinforcement schedule. Any schedule of reinforcement in which reinforcement is made available at regular time intervals.

period prevalence. *See* PREVALENCE.

peripheral. Any device attached to a computer but not forming part of the central processor or core store, e.g. a disk, printer, or visual display unit.

peripheralism. The behaviourist fallacy that higher mental processes can be explained in terms of feedback from peripheral parts of the body, such as the vocal cords. *Compare* MOTOR THEORY OF THINKING.

peripheral nervous system. Those parts of the nervous system lying outside the brain and spinal cord. The peripheral nervous system is divided into the SOMATIC NERVOUS SYSTEM and the AUTONOMIC NERVOUS SYSTEM. *Contrast* CENTRAL NERVOUS SYSTEM.

peripheral route persuasion. The attempt to persuade by indirect methods, e.g. by showing in an advertisement for a brand of drink a well-known footballer drinking it with gusto.

peripheral store. (Computing) A memory store on a device attached to a computer (e.g. a disk). Access is slower than to CORE STORE.

peripheral theory of drive. The theory that physiological drives are controlled by peripheral sensations, e.g. that thirst is turned on by dryness of the mouth or hunger by stomach contractions.

peripheral vision. Vision for those parts of the visual field falling on the periphery of the retina.

periphery. (Vision) The outer parts of the retina, where there are few cones. The boundary is vague, though it is sometimes taken to include all the retina further out than the macula.

peristriate cortex. A synonym for PARASTRIATE CORTEX.

perisylvian. The region lining the sylvian fissure. It is thought to contain most of the brain areas serving language.

periventricular. Near the ventricles of the brain.

periventricular system (PVS). A pathway running through the LIMBIC SYSTEM and passing from the forebrain to the brainstem. Stimulation of it is punishing. *Compare* MEDIAL FOREBRAIN BUNDLE.

Perky effect. Mistakenly taking a sensation produced by a stimulus for an internal mental image; if someone is asked to image something (e.g. a banana) and a very faint picture of the object is shown, he tends to construct the image in the same location and orientation as the physical stimulus. He must therefore in some sense be seeing the stimulus.

perlocutionary force. The effect of a speech act on the hearer, e.g. gratification, fear, discomfort, concern, etc.

permanence. *See* OBJECT PERMANENCE.

perseveration. The prolonged and sometimes pathological repetition of an act, thought, or speech sound; it can be caused by brain damage or schizophrenia.

perseverative error. 1. Any response that occurs later in a sequence of responses than it should have done. *Contrast* ANTICIPATORY ERROR. 2. Any error that is persistently repeated.

perseverative trace. Hull's term for the continued firing of neurons in the sensory system after cessation of the stimulus, invoked to explain such phenomena as TRACE CONDITIONING.

person. A grammatical category applying to pronouns (and verb forms) depending on whether the speaker is referred to, or someone addressed by the speaker or some other person (or object). In English, it is the difference between 'I', 'we' (first person), 'you' (second person), and 'he', 'she', 'they', 'it' (third person).

persona. Jung's term for the outer characteristics displayed by a person in an attempt to adapt to society and its demands; these characteristics may not correspond to his true self. *Contrast* ANIMA (1).

personal construct. Kelley's expression for any of the set of dimensions or categories used by a given person in describing or explaining the personality and behaviour of others (or of himself). The basic idea is that different people will use consistently different categories. The ROLE CONSTRUCT REPERTORY TEST and the REPERTORY GRID TEST were devised to assess a person's personal constructs.

personal disjunction. The disparity between what a person would like to be or achieve and what he sees himself as being or achieving.

personal distance zone. The physical distance a person tries to maintain between himself and others which tends to decrease with increasing intimacy.

personal equation. A method, developed by an astronomer, of correcting for individual differences in reaction time so that observations of the transit times of stars would be consistent. *Compare* PRIOR ENTRY, LAW OF.

Personal Experience and Attitude Questionnaire. A test designed to reveal psychopathic tendencies.

personal fitness. The probability of the replication of an organism's genes through its own descendants. *Contrast* INCLUSIVE FITNESS.

personal growth. A slogan of humanistic psychology directed towards developing a mature personality, achieving self-fulfilment, etc. In practice the phenomenon is rarely observed.

personal growth group. A form of encounter group, whose fashionable aim is personal growth; although one might expect this to include growing more sensitive to others' feelings, more noble, etc., it often seems to result merely in increased selfishness.

personalism. 1. The idea that psychology should be based on the concept of the individual person. 2. Bias in interpreting the actions of others, caused by seeing them as directed towards oneself.

personalistic psychology. An approach to psychology holding that psychological principles only have meaning if they reflect individual experience.

personality. All the traits that characterize an individual over a relatively long period.

personality disorder. Any disorder unaccompanied by severe anxiety in which someone consistently adopts maladaptive patterns of behaviour, e.g. by being too selfish, too unselfish, too exhibitionistic, too dependent, etc.

personality inventory. A questionnaire put to a person with the intention that his answers will directly or indirectly reveal his personality.

personality typology. Any systematic method of dividing people into different personality types; such typologies are usually based on the assumption that traits go together in clusters. Sheldon and others have argued that there is a correlation between personality type and body build.

personal pronoun. *See* PRONOUN.

personal space. The area around a person's body within which he tries not to allow others to intrude.

personal unconscious. Jung's expression for all the unconscious memories, wishes, etc. that are peculiar to a person. *Contrast* COLLECTIVE UNCONSCIOUS.

person-centred therapy. A synonym for NON-DIRECTIVE THERAPY.

personnel psychology. A branch of applied psychology dealing with the selection, promotion, and treatment (in the wide sense) of personnel.

personnel selection. The process of selecting employees, particularly when based on methods devised by psychologists, like structured interviews and objective tests of abilities or personality.

personology. Murray's term for his holistic theory of personality and social behaviour, which held that a person's needs and personality are integrated and cannot be considered apart – surprise, surprise.

person perception. An area of social psychology that studies how a person sees others.

perspectival projection. A PROJECTION SYSTEM in which points in space are connected to the picture plane by converging lines that meet at a point in front of or behind it. Normally the lines meet behind the picture plane, but two other variants are recognized: (i) **inverted perspective** occurs when the rays cross in front of the picture plane, as is the case with the retina; (ii) **synthetic perspective** is the perspectical mapping of points in space onto a curved surface, as in the retinal image.

perspective. The mapping of points in space onto a picture plane where all points are connected to it by straight lines which converge to a point in front of or behind the picture plane. Since the mapping of the visual world onto the retina is a perspective projection, pictures drawn in perspective are realistic, and perspective is a powerful cue to depth. Perspective is sometimes called **linear perspective** to distinguish it from **aerial perspective**. The most commonly cited aspect of perspective is that parallel lines receding in depth in the scene converge in the picture plane, but it has many other aspects, e.g. objects of the same physical size project smaller images, the further away they are. *See also* PROJECTION SYSTEM and PERSPECTIVAL PROJECTION, and *compare* HEIGHT IN THE VISUAL FIELD and TEXTURE GRADIENT.

persuasive therapy. Psychotherapy in which the therapist plays an active role by attempting to make the patient modify maladaptive behaviour, attitudes, etc.

pervasive developmental disorder. (DSM-III) A group of childhood disorders in which there are disturbances of several functions, e.g. language, social skills, perception, motor control; the disorders include KANNER'S SYNDROME and CHILDHOOD-ONSET PERVASIVE DEVELOPMENTAL DISORDER.

PET. An abbreviation for PHOTON EMISSION TOMOGRAPHY and POSITRON EMISSION TOMOGRAPHY.

pethidine. A synthetic NARCOTIC.

petit mal. A form of EPILEPSY in which the person loses consciousness for brief spells, but does not fall or have a convulsion. *Contrast* GRAND MAL.

peyote. The cactus from which MESCALINE is derived.

16PFQ. An abbreviation for SIXTEEN PERSONALITY FACTOR QUESTIONNAIRE.

PGO spikes. Large spikes in the brain waves recorded from the pons, lateral geniculate, and occipital cortex during REM SLEEP.

PGR. An abbreviation for PSYCHOGALVANIC RESPONSE.

pH. A measure of the degree of acidity or alkalinity of a fluid, specifically the negative logarithm of the ratio of H^+ ions to OH^-. A value of 7 is neutral; higher values are alkaline, lower are acid.

phacoscope. An instrument for observing the changes in the reflections from the lens during accommodation.

Phaedra complex. The incestuous love of a mother for her son.

phagophobia. A morbid fear of eating.

phallic character. (Psychoanalysis) A person with traits connected with potency, such as boastfulness, arrogance, exhibitionism, or aggression. It is supposed to originate in the PHALLIC STAGE.

phallic love. (Psychoanalysis) A boy's love of his penis or a girl's of her clitoris.

phallic mother. (Psychoanalysis) A boy's fantasy that his mother has a penis; discovery of the true state of affairs can, according to Freud, lead to impotence or homosexuality.

phallic phase. A synonym for PHALLIC STAGE.

phallic pride. (Psychoanalysis) The sense of superiority a boy obtains from knowing that he has a penis while a girl does not.

phallic primacy. (Psychoanalysis) The concentration of the libido on a person's own sexual organs; this starts in the phallic stage.

phallic stage. (Psychoanalysis) The third of Freud's LIBIDINAL STAGES, occurring from about three to seven years of age, in which the LIBIDO is concentrated on the child's own sexual organs and masturbation occurs. In addition, the child is sexually attracted by the parent of the opposite sex, and becomes jealous of, or hostile to, the parent of the same sex.

phallic symbol. (Psychoanalysis) Any object that could symbolize a penis, i.e. most objects, but particularly elongated ones.

phallic woman. (Psychoanalysis) A woman with traits originating in the phallic stage, who tends to be aggressive and dominating, and inclined to castrate men – metaphorically.

phallocentric. Based on the phallus or penis.

phallophobia. A pathological fear of the penis.

phallus. 1. The penis as a symbol of potency or power. 2. An object designed to represent the penis.

phantom colour. If the inducing part of a Kanisza figure has a chromatic hue, the part that is seen to stand out will appear to be of the same hue but very desaturated. This apparent hue is known as a phantom colour.

phantom grating. A non-existent grating seen in a central square that occludes part of a real sinusoidal grating in motion.

phantom limb. The sensation that a missing limb is still there.

pharmacodynamics. The study of the biochemical and physiological effects of drugs.

pharmacodynamic tolerance. Tolerance for a drug caused by a decrease in the response of the body's tissues to the drug. *Compare* PHARMACOKINETIC TOLERANCE.

pharmacogenetics. The study of the biochemical transformations through which a gene or genes determine an organ or behaviour.

pharmacokinetics. The study of the absorption, distribution, excretion, and chemical transformations of drugs.

pharmacokinetic tolerance. A reduction in the effect of a drug caused by its being broken down or excreted more rapidly. *Compare* PHARMACODYNAMIC TOLERANCE.

pharmacological antagonism. *See* ANTAGONIST (3).

pharmacology. The study of drugs and their effects.

pharmacophobia. A morbid fear of medicine.

pharmacotherapy. The treatment of a disorder by drugs.

pharyngeal. (Phonetics) Pertaining to a speech sound made by contraction of the pharynx; such sounds are not used in English.

pharynx. The cavity, with its surrounding membranes and muscles, that lies behind the mouth, and connects the mouth to the nostrils, oesophagus, and larynx.

phase. Of a waveform, the time at which a particular part of it occurs, usually relative to that of an identical waveform. *See also* PHASE DIFFERENCE.

phase angle. *See* PHASE DIFFERENCE.

phase cue. An auditory cue to localization, consisting of a small PHASE DIFFERENCE at the two ears in the sound wave produced from a single source; the cue is only effective for low-frequency sounds (below 800 Hz).

phase difference. The difference in the timing of two identical waveforms; if they are in synchrony, they are said to be 'in phase'. For sinusoidal waves the phase difference is measured in degrees as a **phase angle**; if the troughs of one waveform correspond to the peaks of another, they are 180° out of phase.

phase locking. The synchronization of the phase of one waveform to that of another, particularly the phenomenon that at low sound frequencies auditory receptors change their receptor potential in phase with the movement of the basilar membrane that stimulates them. Above about 4,000 Hz, the receptor potential becomes almost steady because the cell does not have time to recover its resting potential between successive movements of the basilar membrane. Hence the periodicity of the firing of the auditory ganglion cells cannot be used to determine pitch above this frequency.

phase sequence. Hebb's term for a set of CELL ASSEMBLIES that contain closed loops so that the different assemblies excite one another, thus producing reverberatory activity. He hypothesized that this activity

was the basis of CONSOLIDATION. *See* REVERBERATORY CIRCUIT.

phase shift. 1. A change in the phase of a waveform, particularly a shift in its phase relative to that of another. 2. A change in the phase of the diurnal rhythm caused, e.g. by doing night work or passing through several time zones.

phenazocine. A synthetic OPIATE.

phencyclidine. A HALLUCINOGEN.

phengophobia. A pathological fear of the daytime.

phenobarbital. A long-acting BARBITURATE.

phenocopy. A trait that resembles an inherited trait, but is produced by environmental influences (e.g. dark skin in a white person caused by exposure to sunlight).

phenomenal. (Psychology) Pertaining to experience or to the contents of the mind, in contrast to physical reality; often synonymous with 'apparent'.

phenomenal field. A synonym for PHENOMENOLOGICAL FIELD.

phenomenalism. 1. (Philosophy) The doctrine that the external world is to be analysed in terms of the sensations, actual or possible, that it produces. According to Mill objects are permanent possibilities of sensation. 2. (Psychology) A synonym for PHENOMENOLOGY (2).

phenomenal motion. A synonym for APPARENT MOTION.

phenomenal regression to the real object, phenomenal regression. The phenomenon that people tend to see things approximately the way they physically are despite variations in their projections on the retina, and in particular the phenomena of CONSTANCY; constancy may not be complete, hence the term 'regression'.

phenomenistic causality. Piaget's expression for the tendency, particularly in children, to attribute a causal relationship between two phenomena occurring together or in close succession.

phenomenological field. The total contents of consciousness at any one time.

phenomenology. 1. (Psychology) The doctrine that psychology should focus on the contents of the mind, and that its task is to explain them rather than to explain behaviour. In this sense, introspectionist schools of psychology were phenomenologists, and so were the Gestalt psychologists who investigated the effects of external stimuli on mental processes. 2. (Philosophy) Husserl's doctrine that philosophy must start from the scrutiny of one's own intellectual processes.

phenomenon. Any event (or pattern of events) that has been observed; it is sometimes used to mean any event that can in principle be observed.

phenothiazines. A group of NEUROLEPTIC drugs, which includes CHLORPROMAZINE and THIORIDAZINE, used to treat schizophrenia and to tranquillize overexcited patients; among other effects, they reduce CATECHOL-AMINE activity.

phenotype. The characteristics of an organism, particularly in so far as they derive from the GENOTYPE (genetic make-up), though making allowances for the fact that because of environmental influences the same genotype may give rise to different phenotypes.

phentolamine. *See* ADRENERGIC RECEPTOR.

phenylketonuria (PKU). An inherited disease in which phenylalanine cannot be metabolized because of the absence of the necessary enzyme; unless from a very early age sufferers are given a diet containing no phenylalanine, it causes mental retardation.

pheromone. A chemical released as a signal to other members of the species, e.g. to mark territories or attract members of the opposite sex.

phi. *See* PHI PHENOMENON.

phi coefficient (Φ). (Statistics) A correlation or coefficient of association between two dichotomous variables. E.g. it could be used to describe the degree of association between the presence and absence of mental illness and sex. *See also* TETRACHORIC CORRELATION, which has a narrower use.

phi-gamma function. The S-shaped curve obtained when, in a psychophysical experiment, the frequency of detection of a stimulus is plotted against its intensity (absolute threshold) or the frequency of detecting a difference is plotted against the size of the difference between two stimuli (difference threshold).

phi-gamma hypothesis. (Psychophysics) The hypothesis that when probability of detection is plotted against stimulus intensity near threshold, the resultant curve will correspond to the cumulative distribution of a normal curve.

philology. The study of the history and development of languages.

philosophical psychotherapy. Any form of psychotherapy (e.g. existential psychotherapy) that starts from the doctrine that behaviour and attitudes stem from an overall belief system that must be altered if a client is to be helped.

philosophy. The study of concepts and of their interactions, particularly abstract concepts like 'cause' and 'existence', and including scientific, moral, aesthetic, logical, and mathematical concepts.

phi neuron. One of two classes of neuron hypothesized by Freud, which lies towards the periphery of the nervous system and does not store information. *Compare* PSI NEURON.

phi phenomenon. The illusion that movement is taking place but that nothing is moving, which occurs when two identical stationary stimuli slightly displaced from one another are presented in rapid succession with too large a pause or spatial separation for the observer to see OPTIMAL APPARENT MOTION. Strictly speaking, the term 'phi' should be reserved for this phenomenon, but it is nowadays often used for all forms of STROBO-SCOPIC MOTION and strict phi is commonly referred to as 'pure phi'.

phlegmatic. *See* HUMOUR (2).

phobia. A morbid, irrational and often incapacitating dread of something which the sufferer usually realizes is unrealistic, although it remains uncontrollable. *See* PHOBIC DISORDER and *compare* e.g. AGORAPHOBIA or CLAUSTROPHOBIA.

phobic anxiety. Freud's term for the anxiety apparently generated by the object of a phobia, but which according to him is merely displaced from its real source (e.g. the dread of satisfying a repressed wish) in the unconscious.

phobic character. (Psychoanalysis) Someone who deals with neurotic problems by avoiding situations of which he has a neurotic dread.

phobic disorder. DSM-III's pleonastic expression for PHOBIA, which has three categories – AGORAPHOBIA, SIMPLE PHOBIA, and SOCIAL PHOBIA.

phobic reaction. The intense fear and distress that anyone suffering from a phobia feels on being confronted with the object of the phobia.

phobophobia. A morbid fear of being afraid.

phon. A unit in a scale of loudness, measured in dB. The phon level of a sound is the number of dB needed to match the loudness of the sound.

phonation. The production of speech sounds by vibrating the vocal cords.

phone. (Linguistics) The smallest discrete sound unit in speech that is discriminable from other sounds; the same PHONEME may be represented on different occasions by different phones.

phoneme. (Linguistics) The smallest unit in speech that serves to differentiate one word from another in a given language (e.g. /b/ and /c/ occurring in 'but' and 'cut'). The same phoneme may be represented by different phones depending on the context in which it occurs or the dialect being used. The different versions of the same phoneme are ALLOPHONES and it is critical to the concept of a phoneme that the replacement of one of its allophones by another does not alter the meaning or interpretation of the word uttered.

phoneme grapheme correspondence rules. (Linguistics) The rules by which phonemes are mapped onto graphemes; writing could be assisted by using these rules, but many phonemes do not specify a unique grapheme, e.g. the same sequence of phonemes maps onto both 'rough' and 'ruff'.

phonemic alphabet. An alphabet in which all the phonemes of a language can be represented. The symbols representing the sounds are normally enclosed in oblique strokes. Such an alphabet does not need to make so many distinctions as a PHONETIC ALPHABET.

phonemic dyslexia. A synonym for PHONOLOGICAL DYSLEXIA.

phonemic paraphasia. A form of EXPRESSIVE APHASIA in which, in speaking, syllables or phonemes are transposed or substituted.

phonemic restoration effect. The phenomenon that if a single phoneme is deleted from a sentence and replaced with a click (or other brief noise), the listener is unaware that the phoneme is missing; he hears the click, though usually as being in a different part of the sentence from that in which it actually occurred.

phonemics. (Linguistics) The study and identification of the phonemes of a given language. *See also* PHONETICS.

phonetic alphabet. An alphabet in which speech sounds differing from one another in articulation and sound can be represented. In such an alphabet, the symbols representing the sounds are normally enclosed in square brackets. Since it makes more distinctions than a phonemic alphabet, it uses more symbols. *See* INTERNATIONAL PHONETIC ALPHABET and *contrast* PHONEMIC ALPHABET.

phonetic method. A method of teaching people, particularly the deaf, how to make speech sounds by showing them how to place the parts of the vocal tract.

phonetics. (Linguistics) The study and description of speech sounds, their acoustic and auditory properties, and the ways in which they are produced by the vocal tract. *Compare* PHONOLOGY.

phonic method. Teaching people to read by teaching them how to translate letters or letter strings into phonemes. *Contrast* WHOLE WORD METHOD.

phonism. The hearing of sounds in response to stimulation of other modalities, a form of SYNAESTHESIA.

phonography. Any writing system in which the symbols represent speech sounds.

phonological dyslexia. A form of ACQUIRED DYSLEXIA marked by an inability to read the phonemes of non-words (e.g. 'sim') with the ability to read real words (e.g. 'dim') more or less intact.

phonological similarity effect. In recall, substituting a similar sounding word for the word to be remembered (e.g. 'five' for 'nine') or transposing similar sounding words.

phonology. The study of the structure of sound systems of languages, including their evolution and the comparative study of the sounds in different languages. Phonology focuses on the SYNTAGMATIC and PARADIGMATIC patterns of sounds within a language, whereas PHONETICS studies the individual sounds.

phonopathy. Any disorder of the voice.

phonophobia. 1. A morbid fear of failure in any vocal activity, like acting or singing. 2. A morbid fear of sounds.

phonoscope. Any device that converts sound waves into a visual representation.

phonotactic rule. (Linguistics) A rule governing the permissible sequence of phonemes in a language, e.g. in English initial /t/ may be followed by /r/ but not by /l/.

phoria. The relative position of the two eyes while one is fixating a point and the other is occluded. *See also* HETEROPHORIA.

phosphene. A visual sensation that may be produced by applying pressure to the eye, by a bang on the back of the head, or by other forms of abnormal stimulation.

phosphorylation. The bonding of a phosphate ion to a protein which changes the protein's shape and can thus lead to the opening or closing of a membrane CHANNEL (2).

phot. An obsolete measure of ILLUMINANCE, being the LUMENS falling on one square centimetre of a surface.

photerythrous. Having abnormally high sensitivity to red light.

photic driving. The entrainment of the EEG by regularly flickering light, which can cause epileptic seizures in those susceptible.

photism. 1. The experience of visual sensations in response to stimuli in other modalities, a form of SYNAESTHESIA. 2. The perception of light in its absence.

photobiology. The study of the effects of light on the organism.

photochemical. A substance sensitive to light, e.g. the pigments in the VISUAL RECEPTORS.

photochromatic interval. The range of stimulus intensity over which light but not hue may be seen, i.e. the range too low to stimulate the cones.

photogenic epilepsy. Epilepsy induced by a flickering light.

photokinesis. Activity induced by light, mainly occurring in lower organisms.

photoma. A hallucination of seeing a flash of light.

photometer. Any instrument for measuring light intensity. One device contains a comparison stimulus of variable and known luminance, and the field to be measured (the standard) is projected adjacent to it. The observer sets the comparison field to the same brightness as the standard, and reads off the luminance value of the setting. This works well when the standard and comparison fields are both white, but poorly when they are of different hues. The **heterochromatic flicker photometer** (abbreviated to **flicker photometer**) overcomes this problem by projecting the two fields in the same place and rapidly alternating them. At fast rates of flicker, the colour of the two fields looks nearly equal and the observer alters the luminance of the comparison field until the apparent flicker is minimized, which will occur when both fields are of the same brightness. *See* PHOTOMETRY.

photometric unit. Any unit in which the apparent brightness of light is measured, e.g. CANDELA, LUMEN, or LUX.

photometry. The measurement of light in terms of its apparent brightness for a standard observer. This does not correspond to the physical power of the light, because the eye is more sensitive to certain wavelengths than to others. If the physical specification of the light is known, it can be converted to a photometric measurement by multiplying the power at each wavelength by the appropriate factor and summing (*see* LUMINOUS EFFICIENCY FUNCTION and GRASSMAN'S LAWS). In practice, instead of working from physical measurements of the light, it is usually easier to use a PHOTOMETER, which is calibrated in PHOTOMETRIC UNITS, and can be set to equal the brightness of the light to be measured. Photometric units form ordinal scales, not ratio scales; a source of light having twice as many photometric units as another will not look twice as bright. Photometric units are based on a source of one candlepower – a point source radiating at 540 nm with a power of 1/683 watts per STERADIAN is one CANDELA, a measure of LUMINOUS INTENSITY. LUMINOUS FLUX is the total power of the light from a point source emitted in all directions, and is measured in LUMENS; one lumen is 4π candela (since a steradian is 1/4π of the area of a sphere). The amount of light falling on a surface is ILLUMINANCE: it is measured in LUX, which are lumens per square metre; hence the illuminance on a surface receiving one lumen per square metre is one lux. LUMINANCE is light given off by an extended source, and is measured in candela per square metre. This can be rewritten as lumens per square metre per steradian, because the lumens per steradian (i.e. candela) can be estimated from a small area and the result multiplied by

the ratio of one square metre to the size of the area used in the measurement, to yield candela per square metre.

photon. 1. A QUANTUM of electromagnetic energy; light is made up of a discrete number of photons. 2. An obsolete synonym for TROLAND.

photon emission (computer) tomography (PET). A technique for measuring REGIONAL CEREBRAL BLOOD FLOW, which detects the distribution in the brain of a radioactive substance that has been injected or inhaled by counting the photons emitted.

photophobia. Extreme, and often painful, sensitivity of the eye to light, as found in albinos.

photopic. Pertaining to vision in light bright enough for the cones to function well, as in daylight.

photopic luminosity curve. *See* LUMINOSITY CURVE.

photopic vision. Vision in light sufficiently bright for the cones to be functioning, e.g. daylight vision. *Contrast* SCOTOPIC VISION.

photopsin. The OPSIN in cones.

photopsy. A synonym for PHOSPHENE.

photoreceptor. Any receptor that is excited specifically by light, e.g. the rods and cones of the human retina.

phototaxis, phototropism. The orientation of an organism controlled by light and usually directed either towards it (**positive phototaxis**) or away from it (**negative phototaxis**).

phrase. Several words constituting a constituent of a sentence lower than a clause, e.g. a noun phrase, like 'The hungry farmer'.

phrase marker. (Linguistics) Any way of exhibiting the hierarchical structure of the elements in a sentence as determined by a phrase-structure grammar, e.g. by a downward-branching tree with 'Sentence' at the top node and words at the bottom, or by a nested and labelled bracketing of the sentence.

phrase-structure grammar. A GENERATIVE GRAMMAR in which a set of rules defines how, starting with one element (e.g. 'Sentence'), individual elements can be rewritten as other elements, until at the lowest level a string of words forming a sentence is reached. Typical rewrite rules are 'Sentence → Noun Phrase + Verb Phrase', 'Noun Phrase → Determiner + Noun', 'Verb Phrase → Verb + Noun Phrase'. Such grammars exhibit the structure of a sentence, but they do not take account of the presumed similarity of derivation of e.g. active and passive sentences with the same meaning. *Compare* TRANSFORMATIONAL GRAMMAR.

phrenaesthesia, phrenesthesia. An obsolete term for mental deficiency.

phrenic nerve. The spinal nerve innervating the heart and diaphragm.

phrenology. The false doctrine that the strength of each mental faculty can be determined by feeling the skull; it is based on the assumption that each faculty is mediated by a different part of the brain.

phrenophobia. A morbid fear of having to think, endemic in politicians, or a morbid fear of losing one's mind.

phrenotropic. A synonym for PSYCHOTROPIC.

phthisiophobia. A morbid fear of tuberculosis.

phylogenetic principle. A synonym for RECAPITULATION THEORY.

phylogeny, phylogenesis. The evolutionary origins and development of a species. *Contrast* ONTOGENY.

phylum. *See* TAXONOMY.

physical anthropology. The study of the physical structure of man, particularly with a view to establishing the interrelationship between modern man and his evolutionary ancestors.

physical dependence. A synonym for PHYSIOLOGICAL DEPENDENCE.

physicalism. 1. The philosophical doctrine that all scientific explanations can be reduced to physics. 2. A synonym for IDENTITY THEORY OF MIND.

physical stimulus. A synonym for PROXIMAL STIMULUS.

physiodynamic therapy. Any psychiatric therapy that directly interferes with the brain, other than drug therapy (e.g. EEG and psychosurgery).

physiognomic. 1. Pertaining to PHYSIOGNOMY. 2. Pertaining to the ascription of human qualities to inanimate objects, as in children's thinking.

physiognomy. 1. The attempt to infer character from a person's face. 2. The shape of a person's face.

physiological age. The average age at which people reach the state of physiological development or deterioration that a given person has reached.

physiological antagonism. *See* ANTAGONISM (3).

physiological dependence. A state produced by repeatedly taking an addictive drug, in which physiological adaptation to the drug has occurred, and withdrawal produces physiological symptoms. *See* TOLERANCE and *compare* PSYCHOLOGICAL DEPENDENCE.

physiological drive. Any drive whose goal satisfies a PHYSIOLOGICAL NEED (e.g. hunger, sex); most if not all physiological drives are thought to be innate. Whereas hunger and thirst are clearly physiological drives, it is less clear that higher species have a physiological drive to mother or to build shelter, let alone to explore the environment. It might be better to distinguish only innate from learned drives and to discard the contrast between physiological and non-physiological drives.

physiological maintenance. The provision of an environment (e.g. in a factory) that is safe and comfortable.

physiological motive. A synonym for PHYSIO-LOGICAL DRIVE.

physiological need. 1. The lack of something necessary for the survival of the organism or for the survival of its genes. 2. An inborn drive based on such a need. The two definitions differ in that the existence of a need (1) does not logically imply the existence of a need (2): in fact all animals have a need (1) for oxygen, but there is no directly corresponding need (2) (drive) since breathing is regulated by the amount of carbon dioxide in the blood. *See also* NEED.

physiological nystagmus. Small involuntary eye movements occurring constantly during fixation and made up of short DRIFTS (up to 5' of arc), MICROSACCADES (of from 1' to 20' of arc) and a high frequency TREMOR (2) (sometimes called a **microtremor**) of about 60 Hz with an amplitude of about 30" of arc. The drifts and tremor are random, but the microsaccades tend to return the eye to the fixation point.

physiological psychology. The branch of psychology that studies the relation between the physiology (particularly the neurophysiology) of the organism and its behaviour, and attempts to explain behaviour by physiological mechanisms.

physiological scotoma. The absence of vision for stimuli falling on the OPTIC DISC.

physiological time. The portion of a reaction time taken up by passing a signal from the receptor to the brain and from the brain to the muscles.

physiological zero. The temperature at which a probe applied to the skin feels neither warm nor cold.

physiology. The study of how the body and its parts work.

physiotherapy. Treatment of illness by external manipulation of the body, e.g. by massage, body exercises, or the application of heat.

PI. An abbreviation for 1. PROACTIVE INHIBITION; 2. PROACTIVE INTERFERENCE.

Piaget's stages. Piaget postulated four stages of intellectual development which were, beginning with the earliest: SENSORY–MOTOR STAGE, PREOPERATIONAL STAGE, CONCRETE OPERATIONAL STAGE, and FORMAL OPERATIONAL STAGE. *See also* GENETIC EPISTEMOLOGY.

pia mater. The innermost of the three membranes covering the brain and spinal cord. *See* MENINGES.

piano theory. (Hearing) A synonym for PLACE THEORY.

piblokto. A syndrome specific to Eskimos, in which the person runs around naked and screaming in the snow.

pica. The repeated eating of a non-nutritive substance (e.g. clay) for at least a month, a pathological disorder. *Compare* ALLOTRIOPHAGY.

Pick's disease. A degenerative disease of the brain occurring about 45 or 50 years of age; it is more common in women than men. The symptoms include incoherent thinking, stereotyped behaviour, and eventually the collapse of all mental faculties.

pictograph. The representation of an object or situation by a symbol that depicts it; the use of pictographs is the most primitive form of writing.

pictorial depth cue. Any depth cue that can function as a cue in a stationary 2-D picture, e.g. perspective, shadows, interposition, or aerial perspective, but not motion parallax or stereopsis.

picture anomalies test. A test of intelligence in which a person has to spot what is wrong in each of a series of pictures.

picture arrangement test. A test of intelligence in which a person has to arrange scrambled pictures in order so that they make up a story.

picture completion test. A test of intelligence in which a person is shown incomplete pictures and has to say what is missing.

picture frustration test. A projective test in which a person is shown pictures depicting frustrating situations and asked what he would do in those situations.

picture interpretation test. Any test in which a person is required to interpret a picture.

picture world test. A projective test of children in which they make up a story about a toy scene that they can manipulate.

Piderit drawings. A set of drawings of the face with different expressions, which are cut into pieces that can be reassembled to form different faces.

pidgin. Any language that is not native to anyone, formed by a mixture of two languages whose speakers are trying to communicate with one another. It has an impoverished grammar and vocabulary. *Compare* CREOLE.

piecemeal activity, law of. Thorndike's principle that a learned response may still be given when only part of the original stimulus situation is presented.

pigment layer. The layer of the retina, lying next to the choroid layer, in which the pigments of the receptors are located.

pillars of Corti. Columns in the COCHLEA that keep the TECTORIAL MEMBRANE from collapsing onto the BASILAR MEMBRANE.

piloerection. The state of having one's hair standing up.

pilomotor response. Small bumps in the skin, caused by the contraction of the muscles that erect hairs (commonly known as goose-flesh).

pilot study. A small-scale experiment undertaken in order to discover the conditions under which a fuller study would be feasible.

pincushion distortion. A distortion of the retinal image caused by ANISEIKONIA in which the sides of the image of a square are bowed inwards. *Compare* BARREL DISTORTION.

pineal gland, pineal body. A small gland lying in the centre of the brain, behind the thalamus and above the midbrain. In some amphibians and reptiles it contains photo-receptors and may play a role in regulating diurnal rhythms both in them and mammals. In man it contains a high concentration of melatonin and serotonin. Descartes thought it was the seat of the soul.

pink noise. A signal (usually an audio signal) having both random frequency and amplitude, with equal power for each octave. *Compare* WHITE NOISE.

pink spot. A reaction occurring when dimethoxyphenethylamine is treated with reagents; the reaction was once thought to occur specifically in the urine of schizophrenics but later studies have produced contradictory results.

pinna. The external part of the ear.

Piper's law. The principle that perceived brightness and the absolute brightness threshold depend on the luminance (L) multiplied by the square root of the retinal area (A) of the stimulus, i.e. brightness is equal to $L.\sqrt{A}$. The law applies to stimuli of intermediate area: for smaller stimuli RICCO'S LAW applies; for larger ones the area ceases to be of importance.

piriform lobe. An alternative spelling for PYRIFORM LOBE.

pitch. The subjective dimension of hearing that varies mainly with changes in the frequency of the sound wave. *See also* FREQUENCY THEORY and PLACE THEORY.

pitch contour. (Linguistics) The pattern of pitch changes occurring in an utterance. *See also* TONE GROUP.

pituitary. An ENDOCRINE GLAND attached by a stalk (the INFUNDIBULUM) to the base of the HYPOTHALAMUS. It has three lobes – anterior, intermediate, and posterior. The **anterior pituitary** (the **adenohypophysis**) secretes GROWTH HORMONE, ADRENOCORTICOTROPHIN, THYROID-STIMULATING HORMONE, FOLLICLE-STIMULATING HORMONE, LUTEINIZING HORMONE, and PROLACTIN. The secretion of these hormones is regulated by secretions from the hypothalamus carried in the blood through the infundibulum to the pituitary. The **intermediate pituitary** secretes MELANOCYTE-STIMULATING HORMONE. The

posterior pituitary (the **neurohypophysis**) secretes OXYTOCIN and VASOPRESSIN.

pivot grammar. A loose grammar purporting to account for young children's speech in which there are many two-word sentences. One of the two words (the **pivot word**) is the more frequently used, the other word (the **open word**) is usually more rarely used; e.g. in 'Daddy gone', 'gone' is the pivot, 'Daddy' the open word.

pivot word. *See* PIVOT GRAMMAR.

pixel. (AI) The area over which light is integrated when a picture is transduced into an array of discrete units. The units may be photoelectric cells, in which case the pixel would correspond to the size of an individual cell. In the eye the pixels correspond to individual rods and cones. It is often convenient to specify the length of a feature in a digitized picture in terms of the number of pixels it subtends.

PK. An abbreviation for PSYCHOKINESIS (1).

PKC. *See* PROTEIN KINASES.

PKU. An abbreviation for PHENYL-KETONURIA.

placebo. An inert substance given instead of a drug to a control group to make sure that the effects of the genuine drug are not merely due to suggestion. By extension, a form of interaction with a patient in psychotherapy used as a control and intended to simulate the psychotherapeutic treatment being tested, but omitting what are thought to be the crucial features of the psychotherapy.

placebo effect. Any improvement in a patient's condition caused by being given a placebo or placebo treatment. It is said that the only reliable result obtained from studies of the efficacy of psychotherapy is the placebo effect, which is invariably present.

place of articulation. (Linguistics) The place at which the vocal tract is closed or constricted in the production of a phoneme. *See also* ALVEOLAR, BILABIAL, DENTAL, LABIODENTAL, LABIOVELAR, PALATAL, and VELAR.

place learning. Learning to go in a given direction relative to the environment or learning to go towards a particular place rather than learning to make a specific turn (RESPONSE LEARNING). Consider a rat that is run in a maze with the shape of a cross, that is always started from the same point, and that is trained always to turn left at the intersection. If it is now started from the position opposite its original starting point, place learning has occurred if it turns right at the intersection hence going to the same place; if it turns left there, then it shows response learning.

place theory. (Hearing) The hypothesis that sound freqency is coded in the auditory nerve by which fibres fire most strongly (i.e. those innervating the point of maximal displacement of the BASILAR MEMBRANE). Place is probably the sole coding for high-frequency sounds (greater than about 4,000 Hz) though it may play some role at lower frequencies. *Contrast* FREQUENCY THEORY and VOLLEY THEORY.

place token. A record in the visual system of the position of an entity, e.g. a blob or line segment, on the retina.

placing reflex. A positional reflex of an animal (e.g. a cat) consisting of placing the forefeet on a surface which it is approaching (e.g. by jumping).

planarian. A flatworm sometimes investigated by physiological psychologists because its nervous system is simple and regenerates well.

plan-based understanding. Understanding a narrative by appreciating the characters' goals and using a general knowledge of how goals can be realized.

planchette. A small tripod used to produce AUTOMATIC WRITING.

plane. A flat two-dimensional, infinitely thin, imaginary surface. *See also* FRONTAL-PARALLEL PLANE and SAGITTAL PLANE.

planned comparison test. The assessment by a statistical test of the significance of the difference between two or more experimental groups that was planned before the experiment was undertaken.

planophrasia. An obsolete synonym for FLIGHT OF IDEAS.

plan recognition. Inferring from a person's speech or actions what his intentions are.

plantar reflex. Flexion of the toe to stroking of the sole of the foot; the reflex is present in infants but is a sign of brain damage if it appears in adults.

plasma. The straw coloured fluid in which blood cells are immersed.

plasticity. The capacity of the brain to alter in such a way as to produce learning or adaptation or to recover from damage.

plateau. 1. In a graph, the region over which a curve remains flat. 2. In learning experiments, a period over which no improvement takes place, e.g. because the subject has reached ASYMPTOTE (2).

Plateau spiral. A rotating spiral that seems to be continuously expanding or contracting. When the centre is fixated for about 30 sec and the spiral is then suddenly stopped a strong motion aftereffect is seen.

platoon-volley theory. (Hearing) A synonym for VOLLEY THEORY.

platycephalic. Flat-headed.

platykurtic. (Statistics) A frequency distribution flatter than the normal distribution.

platyrrhines. New World monkeys. *Compare* CATARRHINES.

play therapy. A form of psychotherapy used mainly with children, in which they are encouraged to play with materials provided; it is used both for diagnostic and therapeutic purposes.

pleasure centre. Any area or locus in the brain in which implanted electrodes can lead to SELF-STIMULATION; such areas are particularly common in the LIMBIC SYSTEM.

pleasure principle, pleasure–pain principle. (Psychoanalysis) The rule that people seek pleasure by discharging drives or tensions (whose build-up causes anxiety). Freud thought it began to operate later than REPETITION-COMPULSION but before the REALITY PRINCIPLE which modifies it; much of the activity governed by the pleasure principle can be in the form of fantasy.

pleiotropic. Pertaining to a gene that influences more than one trait.

pleniloquence. A compulsion to talk too much, a characteristic of clergymen and politicians.

pleonasm. The use of words that add nothing to the content of what is being said, e.g. 'a male father'.

pleonexia. Abnormal covetousness.

plethysmograph. Any device for measuring the volume of an organ (e.g. the penis) or changes in its volume; such changes are usually caused by changes in blood supply.

plexiform layer. 1. The first (outermost) layer of nerve cells in the cerebral cortex containing many fibres but few cell bodies. *See also* CORTICAL LAYERS. 2. Either of two layers in the retina. The **outer plexiform layer** contains the horizontal cells and the synapses between receptor and bipolar cells; the **inner plexiform layer** contains amacrine cells and the synapses between bipolar and ganglion cells.

plexus. A network of neurons or blood-vessels.

plosive. (Phonetics) A speech sound made by building up pressure in the vocal tract and suddenly releasing it, e.g. [b], [d], [g], [k], [p], [t]. *See also* VOICE-ONSET TIME.

pluperfect tense. *See* PERFECT TENSE.

pluralism. 1. (Philosophy) The doctrine that there are several (more than two) kinds of substance, or that there are several kinds of attribute. 2. (Psychology) The doctrine that a mental event or an action usually has many different causes, as in Freudian theory. *Compare* OVERDETERMINATION.

pluralistic ignorance. The mistaken belief of bystanders witnessing an emergency that the other bystanders think the occurrence is harmless.

plurel. (Social psychology) A group or class of people with more than one member.

PMA. An abbreviation for PRIMARY MENTAL ABILITIES.

PMLD. *See* BINAURAL MASKING LEVEL DIFFERENCES.

PMS, PMT. Abbreviations for PRE-MENSTRUAL SYNDROME and PREMENSTRUAL TENSION.

pneumoencephalography. Taking an X-ray picture of the brain after injecting air into the spinal fluid in the SUBARACHNOID SPACE. The air rises into the ventricular system revealing any distortions of it, due e.g. to a tumour.

pneumograph. A recording of the state of the lungs or of their activity.

pneumophobia. A morbid fear of being smothered.

pneumophonia. Excessive breathing while speaking.

POC. An abbreviation for PERFORMANCE OPERATING CHARACTERISTIC.

Poetzl effect. The alleged appearance in dreams or waking images of material previously perceived subliminally. *See* SUBLIMINAL PERCEPTION.

Poggendorff illusion. A geometrical illusion. The two oblique lines are colinear, but they look as though they would not meet if continued. It may be an example of the SIMULTANEOUS TILT EFFECT, but this is disputed.

poiesis. The construction of a neologism, particularly by schizophrenics.

poikilotherm. An animal whose body

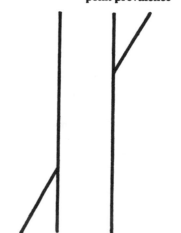

Poggendorff illusion

temperature varies with the environmental temperature (i.e. a cold-blooded animal).

poinephobia. A morbid fear of punishment.

point biserial correlation. (Statistics) The correlation between two variables one of which is in principle continuous (e.g. intelligence) and the other dichotomous (e.g. sex); it can be calculated as a product moment correlation by setting the values of the dichotomous variable to 0 and 1.

point estimate. (Statistics) A single estimate of a population parameter. *Contrast* INTERVAL ESTIMATE.

point localization. The ability to determine which point on the skin is being stimulated by a fine point.

point mutation. The mutation of a single NUCLEOTIDE.

point of regard. A synonym for FIXATION POINT.

point of subjective equality (PSE). The setting at which a comparison stimulus appears the same along a given dimension as the standard stimulus. Because of time errors and other factors, the comparison stimulus will not necessarily be set to objective equality with the standard.

point prevalence. *See* PREVALENCE.

point source. A source of light sufficiently small in area to be treated as a point for practical purposes.

point spread function. (Vision) The distribution on the retina of the light from a point source.

Poisson distribution. A limiting case of the binomial distribution that occurs where there are a large number of trials in which the probability of the event occurring is low. It applies to such phenomena as the number of particles emitted by a radioactive substance in a given time or the number of accidents a person has in a given time.

polar continuum. Any continuum with opposite attributes at each end (e.g. loud–quiet or extraversion–introversion).

polar coordinates. A method of specifying position on a two-dimensional plane using two coordinates, one for the distance out from a fixed point along a radius, and the other for the direction of the radius. The method can be extended to spaces of higher dimensions. *Contrast* CARTESIAN ' CO-ORDINATES.

polarity. The property of having two opposite poles, as in a magnet or an electric circuit. In psychology the term is often used of the presence of two opposite emotions, e.g. 'a love–hate relationship'.

polarization. 1. (Neurophysiology) The difference in potential between the inside and outside of a nerve cell's membrane. 2. (Light) The restriction of the direction in which light waves vibrate to a single direction or to a segment of the 180° over which vibration is possible. The polarization of light can be detected by many insects, but not by vertebrates. 3. *See* GROUP POLARIZATION.

pollyanaism. The allegedly greater ease with which people process pleasant material than unpleasant; e.g. the words 'joy' and 'pain'.

poltergeist. (Parapsychology) An agency alleged to haunt a house; it remains unseen but plays mischievous pranks by throwing things, moving objects around, overturning furniture, etc. These phenomena are often alleged to be associated with the presence of a child or adolescent, which is perhaps not surprising.

polyandry. A system of marriage in which a wife can have more than one husband simultaneously.

Polycrates complex. (Psychoanalysis) Unconscious guilt and a feeling of needing to be punished, alleged to arise in some successful people.

polydipsia. The consumption of abnormally large amounts of water.

polygamy. Marriage with more than two partners. *Compare* POLYANDRY and POLYGYNY.

polygenic. Pertaining to or caused by many genes.

polyglot amnesia. A form of amnesia in which the person cannot speak the langauage he has been using but can speak another language previously learned.

polyglot neophasia. *See* NEOPHASIA.

polygraph. An apparatus that records data from several sources simultaneously; the term is often used to mean LIE DETECTOR, since the information about breathing, heart rate, GALVANIC SKIN RESPONSE, and voice can be recorded on a polygraph.

polygyny. A system of marriage in which a husband may have more than one wife simultaneously.

polylogia. Incessant incoherent speech.

polymorphism. The existence within a species of individuals having different characteristics.

polymorphous perverse. (Psychoanalysis) Pertaining to the ability to obtain sexual pleasure in many different ways, both in normal children through several orifices (genitals, anus, and mouth), and in adults who have sexual perversions.

polymorphous strategy. *See* EVOLUTIONARILY STABLE STRATEGY.

polynomial. A mathematical expression, in which there is a series of terms each being the product of a constant and one or more variables raised to an integral power. E.g. where x is a variable $2x^3 + 5x^7 + \ldots$

polyonomy. The existence in a language of many words describing different aspects of something (e.g. Eskimos have words for many different states of snow).

polyopia, polyopsia. The existence of two or more images on the same retina resulting from defects in the optics of the eye. *Compare* DIPLOPIA.

polypeptide. A molecule made up of several PEPTIDES.

polyphagia. Eating too much.

polyphobia. A morbid fear of many different things.

polyphony. The representation by a single grapheme of two or more different sounds, as in English 'c' which can be hard (as in 'cash') or soft (as in 'cite').

polyphrasia. A synonym for LOGORRHEA.

polysemy. The possession by the *same* word of more than one meaning, e.g. 'nice' can mean either 'pleasant' or 'subtle'. Distinguish from HOMONYM, in which *different* words happen to have the same pronunciation and spelling.

polysynaptic. Having more than one synapse, used of reflexes and of other neural arcs.

polythetic classification. *See* MONOTHETIC CLASSIFICATION.

polyuria. Excessive secretion of urine.

ponder. A unit of subjective weight, used in the construction of scales of apparent heaviness.

pongids. A synonym for ANTHROPOID APES.

ponophobia. A morbid fear of work, common in students.

pons. A region of the hindbrain that connects the medulla and cerebellum to the midbrain; it contains ascending and descending tracts, part of the reticular formation, and some nuclei such as the vestibular and cochlear nuclei. *See* Appendix 5.

Ponzo illusion. The geometrical illusion that when lines of equal length are drawn between two converging lines, the nearer they are to the point of convergence, the longer they appear.

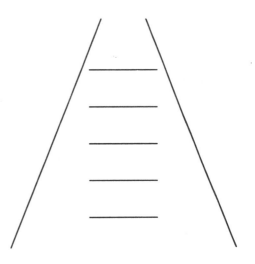

Ponzo illusion

pooh-pooh theory. A synonym for INTERJECTIONAL THEORY.

pooling. Combining data from different sources, e.g. different tests or different experimental groups.

pop-out effect. The phenomenon that in an array of items, one may be immediately noticed without serial search either because it has a unique primitive feature or because the person is looking for a particular primitive feature.

popular response. A common response to a stimulus, particularly to a Rorschach stimulus.

population. 1. (General) All people (or other kinds of organism) in a particular area of the world. 2. (Statistics) The whole set of values from which a sample is drawn. In this sense a population may be finite or infinite.

population mean (μ). (Statistics) The mean of the set of values in a population; unless a value is obtained for every member of the population, it can only be estimated. *Contrast* SAMPLE MEAN.

population parameter. *See* PARAMETER (2).

poriomania. A compulsion to wander away, sometimes found in epileptic or demented patients, or in a fugue.

pornographomania. A morbid impulse to write obscenities.

pornolagnia. A desire to have sexual intercourse with prostitutes.

porphyropsin. A rod photopigment found particularly in freshwater fish, having a peak sensitivity between about 520 and 540 nm. It is the A2 analogue of RHODOPSIN, and decomposes into OPSIN and 3-DEHYDRO-RETINAL.

porropsia. (Vision) The perception of objects as being more distant than they are.

Portage programme. A systematic method of teaching parents how to train their children, particularly mentally retarded children, in a variety of skills (e.g. cognitive, motor, and social skills), using some of the methods of behaviour therapy.

Porter's law. A synonym for FERRY–PORTER LAW.

Porteus maze test. A test of spatial intelligence, in which the subject has to solve a series of mazes presented with all paths visible.

portfolio theory. (Decision theory) The hypothesis that preference among alternatives is determined by their expected value and their perceived risk: the higher the stakes, the higher is the perceived risk and therefore the less likely is a gamble to be accepted.

position constancy. The phenomenon that objects appear to be stationary when their images change position on the eye as a result of eye or body movement.

position preference, position habit. Any preference exhibited over a period of time for selecting a particular spatial position. The term is particularly used of performance in two-choice discrimination tasks and mazes, where the organism may continually select one position on almost every trial even after its latencies reveal that it has learned to recognize whether the positive or negative stimulus is in the preferred position.

positive acceleration. *See* DERIVATIVE.

positive afterimage. *See* AFTERIMAGE.

positive correlation coefficient. A CORRELATION COEFFICIENT indicating that the correlated variables vary together in the same direction.

positive discriminative stimulus. A synonym for POSITIVE STIMULUS.

positive feedback. *See* FEEDBACK.

positive induction. *See* INDUCTION (2).

positively accelerated. Of a curve, accelerating upwards.

positive phototaxis. *See* PHOTOTAXIS.

positive recency effect. The tendency, when a series of events is presented, to predict that the next event will be the same as the last one; this tendency can appear in gambling. *Contrast* NEGATIVE RECENCY EFFECT. *See also* RECENCY EFFECT.

positive reference group. A REFERENCE GROUP with which a person identifies and whose standards and values he adopts. *Contrast* NEGATIVE REFERENCE GROUP.

positive reinforcement. Any reinforcement other than that provided by the cessation or avoidance of a noxious stimulus (NEGATIVE REINFORCEMENT); positive reinforcement is associated with pleasure (e.g. eating) whereas in negative reinforcement pain is diminished. The distinction is not clear-cut – consider the masochist or the elimination of hunger pangs by eating.

positive reinforcer. A synonym for POSITIVE REINFORCEMENT.

positive stimulus (S+, S^D). In DISCRIMINATION LEARNING the stimulus that signals the presence of reinforcement if the organism approaches it or responds to some other manipulandum. In SUCCESSIVE DISCRIMINATION TRAINING the distinction between the positive and negative stimuli is clear, but in SIMULTANEOUS TRAINING it is less clear, since the negative stimulus can act as a signal that the organism must go to the other stimulus to obtain reinforcement.

positive symptoms of schizophrenia. Those symptoms of schizophrenia that appear qualitatively different from any normal traits, e.g. hallucinations and delusions.

positive taxis. See TAXIS.

positive time error. An error in the judgement of the intensities of two successive stimuli, in which the second is judged to be less intense than it really is relative to the first. Contrast NEGATIVE TIME ERROR.

positive transfer. See TRANSFER.

positive transference. See TRANSFERENCE.

positive tropism. See TROPISM.

positive valence. See VALENCE.

positivism. (Philosophy) The doctrine, originating with Compte, that it is possible to have knowledge only about things that can be observed, and that are therefore amenable to scientific investigation; the doctrine eliminates all metaphysical knowledge, knowledge of ultimate causes, etc.

positron emission tomography (PET). A technique for measuring metabolic rate in different parts of the brain, based on administering a radioactive isotope of e.g. glucose and measuring with a sphere of detectors placed near the head the gamma rays that result from positrons colliding with electrons; the technique gives the 3-D location of the concentration of the radioactive glucose throughout the brain; this correlates with how active the neurons are in each part. The resolution is about 8 mm.

possessive pronoun. See PRONOUN.

possible world. Any possible universe different from our own. It has been suggested that referring expressions with no actual referent (e.g. 'The present King of France . . .') and COUNTERFACTUALS refer to possible worlds.

post–ambivalent stage. (Psychoanalysis) The final phase of libidinal development, in which the person becomes capable of loving someone else. See LIBIDINAL STAGES.

post–categorical acoustic store. A memory store for words or phrases that have already been categorized into syllables, words etc. Compare PRECATEGORICAL STORE.

post–central gyrus. A strip of parietal cortex lying behind the central fissure; it includes the SOMATOSENSORY CORTEX. See Appendix 1. It comprises Brodmann's areas 1, 3, 5, and 7; see Appendix 3.

post–central sulcus. See Appendix 1.

post–concussional syndrome. A set of symptoms that may follow a head injury, including dizziness, headaches, anxiety, insomnia, and inability to concentrate.

post–conventional level. The highest of Kohlberg's three stages of moral development, which is itself divided into two stages: in stage 5 people are concerned with the balance between individual rights and the needs of the community, and in stage 6 with their own moral principles. See also PRECONVENTIONAL LEVEL and CONVENTIONAL LEVEL.

post–decision model. See PRIOR-DECISION MODEL.

post–deviation effect. A synonym for POSTURAL AFTEREFFECT.

post–emotive schizophrenia. A schizophrenic episode triggered by an emotional crisis.

posterior. (Anatomy) Toward the back of the body or brain. In upright species it is synonymous with DORSAL when used of the body but not when used of the brain. Contrast ANTERIOR.

posterior commissure. A bundle of myelinated fibres that connect across the midline various structures below the level of the cortex including the THALAMUS and COLLICULI.

posterior hypothalamic area. An area of the hypothalamus, stimulation of which tends to arouse the sympathetic system, and damage to which causes sleep.

posterior parietal cortex. A synonym for SECONDARY SOMATOSENSORY CORTEX.

posterior pituitary. *See* PITUITARY.

post–ganglionic autonomic neurons. The fibres of the autonomic system that are peripheral to the ganglia and that innervate visceral and other organs.

post hoc. 1. Pertaining to the (false) inference that because X followed Y, X caused Y. 2. Pertaining to explanations involving HINDSIGHT BIAS.

post hoc **test.** A synonym for A POSTERIORI TEST.

post–hypnotic suggestion. A suggestion given by a hypnotist during hypnosis that the person hypnotized will behave in a certain way after the hypnosis is over; such suggestions are often obeyed without the person recalling that he had been told to do something.

post–ictal. Following an apoplectic stroke or an epileptic seizure.

post–partum. Pertaining to the period in the mother immediately after birth, during which the reproductive system returns to the condition it was in before pregnancy. *Compare* NEONATAL.

postremity principle. Guthrie's principle that an organism always does what it last did in a given stimulus situation.

post–rotational nystagmus. The NYSTAGMUS that occurs when rotation of the body is suddenly stopped.

post–synaptic. Pertaining to a cell or any of its parts or activities that are affected by the firing of another cell whose terminals end on it. *Compare* PRESYNAPTIC.

post–synaptic potential (PSP). Any change in the polarization of the membrane of a cell induced by the firing of other cells. *See* EXCITATORY POSTSYNAPTIC POTENTIAL, and INHIBITORY POSTSYNAPTIC POTENTIAL.

post-test. Any test given after conducting an experiment or training procedure to compare performance after the procedure with that before it.

post-tetanic potentiation (PTP). An increase, lasting for about a minute, in the likelihood of a presynaptic cell firing a postsynaptic one, resulting from tetanic (heavy and repeated) stimulation of the presynaptic cell; it is thought to be caused by an increase in the amount of neurotransmitter available. *Compare* LONG-TERM POTENTIATION.

post-traumatic amnesia (PTA). Inability to recall events connected with a severely stressful experience.

post-traumatic stress disorder (PTSD), post-traumatic syndrome (PTS), post-traumatic neurosis. A syndrome occurring after a major psychological trauma, characterized by e.g. anxiety, sleeplessness, vivid and frequent images of the event, incessant thinking about it, numbness, a lack of interest in the world, and a tendency to be readily startled.

postulate. A synonym for AXIOM or assumption.

postural aftereffect. After a part of the body has been held in an eccentric posture for some time and has been returned to its normal position, the subjective feeling that it is now located away from normal in the opposite direction to that in which it was originally positioned. *Compare* PERDEVIATION EFFECT.

postural reflexes. The reflexes, both innate and acquired, that maintain body posture.

posturology. The study of the relation between psychological state and body posture.

potential. Short for POTENTIAL DIFFERENCE or voltage.

potential difference. The difference in electric charge at two points, especially between the inside and outside of the membrane of a cell, which in the resting state is about -70 millivolts (with the inside negative). *See also* ACTION POTENTIAL, EVOKED POTENTIAL, and GENERATOR POTENTIAL.

potentiation. *See* LONG-TERM POTENTIATION.

potlatch. A ceremonial feast held by some Indian tribes in north-west America, at which prestige is acquired by destroying or giving away possessions.

Pötzl effect. *See* POETZL EFFECT.

power. 1. (Mathematics) Either the product of a number multiplied by itself a given number of times, or the number of times the multiplication is to be carried out. *See* EXPONENT. 2. (Physics) The rate at which energy is expended or work done. The SI unit is the watt, which is equal to one JOULE per second. 3. (Statistics) The power of a statistical test is the probability that it will reject the null hypothesis when the alternative hypothesis is true (i.e. not make a TYPE II ERROR). In general the more details of the data are taken into account by the test, the greater its power. Thus parametric tests tend to be more powerful than non–parametric tests.

power coercive strategy. (Social psychology) The attempt to obtain what one wants by coercion, e.g. through strikes, lock-outs, or refusal of marital rights.

power complex. Jung's term for the attempt to make the ego dominate all other influences, both external and internal.

power field. Lewin's term for the parts of the life space (perceived environment) which a person can control.

power function. A function of the form in which a variable (x) is raised to a constant power (n), e.g. $y = 4x^n$. *Contrast* EXPONENTIAL FUNCTION.

power law. (Psychophysics) The generalization that the apparent intensity (A) of a stimulus is a power function of its physical intensity (I) for prothetic continua $(A = kI^r)$, like brightness, pitch, or weight. The generalization is open to doubt, since the result could be an artefact of the questionable scaling methods that have been employed.

power law of practice. The law that the time taken to perform a mental task decreases as a fractional power of the number of trials.

power spectrum. A graph of the power of the frequency components of a waveform.

power test. An ability test in which speed is not important, often with questions arranged in ascending order of difficulty. *Contrast* SPEED TEST.

p-o-x triad. Two people (p and o), known to one another, and an object (x) to which both people have positive or negative attitudes. In BALANCE THEORY the triad is balanced if both people like one another and have the same attitude to the object, unbalanced if they both like one another but have different attitudes to the object, etc.

pp. An abbreviation for PREPOSITIONAL PHRASE.

pq4r. A method that purports to improve understanding and memory for textual material. It involves *p*reviewing the material, making up *q*uestions about it, *r*eading it, while using it to answer the questions posed, *r*eflecting upon it, *r*eciting each section to oneself, and finally *r*eviewing it.

PR. An abbreviation for PARTIAL REINFORCEMENT.

practice effect. Any improvement in performance caused by practising a task; in some tests (e.g. IQ tests) it is desirable to take account of the effects of previous practice on current performance.

practice theory of play. The hypothesis that the function of play is to give the organism practice on tasks that it will have to perform in earnest in later life.

Praegnanz. An alternative spelling of PRAGNANZ.

pragmatics. (Linguistics) All factors affecting language use and understanding other than syntax and semantics; in particular the effects on language of the situation in which it is used. *See also* CONVERSATIONAL IMPLICATURE, SPEECH ACT, and DEIXIS.

pragmatism. The doctrine, put forward by Peirce and William James, that the truth of an idea depends on its practical and predictive consequences, and that the purpose of thought is to achieve better adjustment to the environment. They also held that truth can only be discovered by the systematic use of the scientific method.

Prägnanz, law of. The Gestalt principle that stimuli are perceived and remembered as coherent wholes (often as more coherent than they are), and are organized in perception in as stable, symmetrical, simple, and meaningful a way as possible. E.g. an incomplete circle briefly exposed may be seen as complete. The law of Prägnanz has many more specific aspects, *see* e.g. CLOSURE, LAW OF, COMMON FATE, LAW OF, GOOD CONTINUATION, LAW OF, PROXIMITY, LAW OF, SIMILARITY, LAW OF and SYMMETRY, LAW OF.

prandial drinking. Drinking that is triggered by eating.

praxis. Action.

PRE. An abbreviation for PARTIAL REINFORCEMENT EFFECT.

preattentive processing. Processing in which only low level features (e.g. line orientation, presence of curvature) are analysed, and in which there is no recognition of complex symbols or objects; if someone is searching for the letter O in an array of letters, none of which contain curves, he can race through the other letters until he reaches the O without being aware of what letters he is looking at.

precategorical acoustic memory (PAM), precategorical acoustic store (PAS). A rapidly decaying acoustic memory in which the raw features of a speech sound are preserved, without its being categorized (e.g. as a given syllable). The concept was suggested to explain the STIMULUS SUFFIX EFFECT but it does not differ from ECHOIC MEMORY.

precausal thinking. Piaget's expression for the young child's tendency to perceive the natural world anthropomorphically.

precedence effect. The phenomenon that when the same sound or pattern of sounds recurs on the ear after a short delay (up to 50 msec) the sound pattern is only heard at its first occurrence. Echoes are therefore eliminated, and the sound is heard as originating from its original source.

precentral area. A strip of cortex in front of the central fissure, containing the MOTOR CORTEX. It comprises Brodmann's areas 4 and 6; *see* Appendix 3.

precentral gyrus. Brodmann's area 4; *see* Appendices 1 and 3. The MOTOR CORTEX.

precentral sulcus. *See* Appendix 1.

precentre. To make a subject fixate a point in advance of presenting the experimental stimulus, so that the stimulus can be presented to any point of the retina.

precision. (Statistics) A term sometimes used to mean the reciprocal of the variance, i.e. a measure of the narrowness of a distribution.

precision law. A synonym for PRAGNANZ, LAW OF.

precocity. The early development of a trait in ontogeny; more specifically in biology, the ability of the young of a species to fend for themselves when born.

precognition. (Parapsychology) Paranormally acquired knowledge of the future.

preconcept. Piaget's term for the concrete or action-based concepts characterizing the preoperational stage of development.

preconditioning. *See* SENSORY PRECONDITIONING.

preconscious. (Psychoanalysis) All the contents of the mind that are not currently in consciousness, but that can readily be brought into consciousness; the contents of the UNCONSCIOUS are thus excluded from the preconscious.

preconventional level. The first of Kohlberg's three stages of moral development, which is itself divided into two stages. In stage 1 morality is determined only by expectations of reward and punishment; in stage 2 in addition to using hedonistic considerations, the child tends to do friends favours. *See also* CONVENTIONAL LEVEL and POSTCONVENTIONAL LEVEL.

precursor. (Pharmacology) A substance that forms the basis for the synthesis of a biochemical molecule.

precursor load strategy. The provision of the PRECURSOR of a substance in order to increase its amount or availability, often undertaken because the substance itself will not cross the BLOOD–BRAIN BARRIER, while the precursor will; e.g. treating Parkinson's disease with L-dopa, a precursor of dopamine, deficiency of which is thought to cause the illness.

predelay reinforcement procedure. An experimental procedure in which the animal is reinforced at a particular spot, and after a delay has to find its way back to the same place to obtain a further reinforcement.

predementia praecox. An early stage of schizophrenia, in which someone is preoccupied with fantasies and daydreams, and cannot cope with difficulties.

predicate. The part of a sentence that makes an assertion about the subject; e.g. in 'John fell down', the predicate is 'fell down'.

predicate calculus. A branch of formal logic that embodies propositional calculus but also contains axioms and deductive rules for the use of QUANTIFIERS and predication: it contains operators roughly corresponding to the English words 'all', and 'some'. Propositions are translated into a form that facilitates deduction, e.g. the sentence 'All men are mortal' would be written as 'for all x, if x is a man, x is mortal'.

predicate thinking. The tendency to consider two things identical because they have attributes in common. According to psychoanalysts, it is characteristic of the ratiocinations of the ID; according to Piaget, it is characteristic of the thinking of the preoperative child.

predication. The attaching of a predicate to a subject, or the assignment of an attribute to an entity or of a relationship between entities.

predictive efficiency. The extent to which a test or theory makes accurate predictions.

predicative thinking. A synonym for PREDICATE THINKING.

predictive validity. The extent to which a test predicts performance on a variable that is closely related to whatever it purports to measure. This is the only secure way of validating selection tests.

predictor. Anything (e.g. a symptom) used to predict (or to retrodict) something (e.g. an illness).

predictor variable. A variable that predicts or is thought to predict the values of a dependent variable. The expression is usually used when the predictor variable cannot be directly manipulated. E.g. in studying effects of life events on mental illness, the number of life events might be called a predictor variable rather than an INDEPENDENT VARIABLE.

predisaster adaptation. The measures taken by people warned of a disaster such as an earthquake.

predisposition. Disposition, particularly the disposition to have certain characteristics caused by genetic make-up.

prefix. (Linguistics) A morpheme placed before another morpheme to form a word and modifying the meaning of the second morpheme, e.g. 'un-' or 'para-' as in 'unhappy' or 'parapsychology'. In some languages (e.g. German) prefixes are used as INFLECTIONS (1).

preformationism, preformism. The doctrine that all the characteristics of an organism are contained in the GERM CELLS at conception and merely have to be unfolded thereafter.

prefrontal cortex. A synonym for PREFRONTAL LOBE.

prefrontal leucotomy. A synonym for FRONTAL LEUCOTOMY.

prefrontal lobe. The area of the frontal lobe anterior to the precentral area, comprising Brodmann's areas 8–11 and 44–7; see Appendices 3 and 4.

prefrontal lobectomy. A synonym for FRONTAL LOBECTOMY.

prefrontal lobotomy. A synonym for FRONTAL LOBOTOMY.

pregenital stage. (Psychoanalysis) All stages of libidinal development preceding the genital stage.

Pregnanz. An alternative spelling of PRAGNANZ.

prelogical thinking. Irrational thought processes, characteristic of childhood, an expression mainly used by psychoanalysts to describe thinking dominated by the PLEASURE PRINCIPLE rather than the REALITY PRINCIPLE.

Premack principle. The generalization that performing the more probable of two responses will reinforce the less probable; e.g. if a rat is not hungry, eating may be reinforced if it is followed by an opportunity to explore.

premature ejaculation. An ejaculation that occurs too quickly (i.e. before the man or his partner are ready for it). The term is sometimes restricted to ejaculation occurring before penetration has taken place.

premenstrual syndrome (PMS), premenstrual tension (PMT). The tendency for some women to feel unusually tense and irritable from about the third day before menstruation to about four days after it. It may be caused by the high ratio of TESTOSTERONE TO OESTRADIOL or by the drop in opiates that occurs at that point in the menstrual cycle.

premise. A proposition from which a conclusion is deduced. See SYLLOGISM.

premoral stage. The stage of infancy (up to 18 months) when, according to Kohlberg, the infant has no morality. It is followed by the PRECONVENTIONAL STAGE.

premotor cortex. An area of the frontal lobes lying immediately anterior to the motor cortex and extending ventrally to the cingulate gyrus. It contains a topographical map of the motor system, and is thought to be implicated in the learning of motor skills. It comprises Brodmann's area 6 and parts of areas 8, 44, and 45; see Appendix 3.

prenatal. Before birth.

preoperational stage. The second stage of PIAGET'S STAGES of child development, lasting from about two to seven years of age, in which children become more reflective and can think about things not present, though only in an unsystematic and often contradictory way – e.g. they are supposed to lack conservation.

preoptic area. The part of the hypothalamus above the optic chiasm.

preparation. (Physiology) An organism or part of an organism prepared for an experiment or series of observations, e.g. a cat with microelectrodes in the visual cortex. An **acute preparation** is one studied briefly (and then usually destroyed); a **chronic preparation** (e.g. an animal with a brain lesion) is studied over a longer period of time.

preparatory interval. In experiments on REACTION TIME, the interval between presenting the warning signal and the stimulus to which the organism is to respond.

preparatory response. Any response (usually belonging to a chain of responses) that in a given situation consistently precedes the consummatory response; the expression is also used of OBSERVING RESPONSES.

preparedness. The extent to which, as a result of past experience or inheritance, an organism has a tendency to associate a given reinforcer with a given stimulus, or a given response with a given stimulus. E.g. as a result of preparedness, many animals who taste a new food and are made sick, even hours later, associate the taste of the food with sickness, and subsequently avoid food having that taste. Again, there are certain stimuli like snakes and worms to which people are predisposed to develop an avoidance response or phobia.

preperception. A vague term for the mental processes immediately preceding the perception of a stimulus.

prephallic stage. (Psychoanalysis) All stages of sexual development before the PHALLIC STAGE.

prepiriform cortex. An alternative spelling for PREPYRIFORM CORTEX.

preposition. (Linguistics) A word occurring before a noun phrase that relates it to the rest of the sentence both grammatically and semantically, e.g. 'in', 'to', 'up'.

prepositional phrase (pp). A preposition and the words governed by it.

prepotent. Pertaining to a reflex (or response) that is more likely to occur in a given stimulus situation than any other, or pertaining to a stimulus that is more likely to gain control of responding than any other.

prepyriform cortex. An area lying immediately dorsal to the ENTORHINAL CORTEX, and forming part of the primary olfactory area.

presbyacusis. Loss of auditory sensitivity, caused by old age.

presbyophrenia. A synonym for WERNICKE'S DEMENTIA.

presbyopia. (Vision) The inability of many older people to accommodate correctly for near objects, caused by hardening of the lens.

presenile dementia. A syndrome, usually starting after 65 years of age, marked by impaired memory, judgement, and intellect, and by withdrawal and apathy; it has no specific cause.

presentational rituals. (Sociology) A cumbersome expression meaning conventional acts of politeness, e.g. greetings.

Present State Examination (PSE). A structured psychiatric interview containing about 400 items, and intended to have diagnostic power.

present tense. Any TENSE used of an action or event occurring at the same time as the utterance; this tense can also be used when the speaker does not want to make the time of occurrence explicit.

presolution period. (Animal learning) The initial period of practice on a discrimination problem, during which the animal performs entirely at chance level. According to Lashley the animal does not respond to the correct cue during this period, but once it latches on to it, performance improves very rapidly.

presolution reversal. In two-choice discrimination learning, reversing the positive and negative stimuli during the PRESOLUTION PERIOD. It is claimed that this procedure does not increase the trials needed to learn the discrimination. *See* HYPOTHESIS.

press. Murray's term for the aspects of the environment that determine behaviour, e.g. poverty, the constraints of a job, etc.

press-need. Murray's expression for the needs aroused by the environment, e.g. somebody poor may have a need for money, somebody rich may develop a need to alleviate boredom.

pressure. Force divided by the area to which the force is applied, it may be measured in dynes per square centimetre. *See also* SOUND PRESSURE.

pressure gradient. Differences in pressure on the skin within a small region, such as occur around a point poked into the skin, or along a felt edge; the pressure sense responds mainly to such differences rather than to changes in overall pressure.

pressure receptor. Any receptor sensitive to pressure; *see* FREE NERVE ENDINGS, MEISSNER'S CORPUSCLE, and PACINIAN CORPUSCLE.

pressure sensitive spot. Any small spot on the skin that is more sensitive to pressure than the surrounding area.

prestige suggestion. The attempt to persuade others to adopt a belief by associating it with prestigious people.

prestriate cortex. An obsolete term for Brodmann's area 18 (*see* Appendix 3), which lies immediately in front of the STRIATE CORTEX: it is part of the VISUAL CORTEX and contains a retinotopic projection.

presupposition. An unstated assumption on which an argument is based; in particular, in linguistics, an assumption underlying a fragment of conversation, e.g. the sentence 'Open the door' presupposes that there is only one door and that the hearer is in a position to open it. *Compare* GIVEN INFORMATION and NEW INFORMATION; given information is presupposed.

presynaptic. Pertaining to a neuron (or to its parts or processes) that can influence the firing of another (POSTSYNAPTIC) neuron through its axonal terminals.

presynaptic inhibition. Inhibition produced at an axodendritic synapse as a result of the presynaptic axon's SYNAPTIC BUTTON being stimulated by the axon of a third cell (axoaxonic conduction) which reduces the probability of transmission across the axodendritic synapse. The term 'presynaptic' signifies that the inhibition is caused by a change in the presynaptic axon rather than by a change in the postsynaptic dendrites or cell body.

pretest. A practice run on a task; it is given either to familiarize the subject with the task before it is undertaken in earnest, or to obtain data against which improvement on the task with further practice can be measured.

prevalence. (Epidemiology) The proportion of a given population having a particular illness or disorder at one moment of time (**point prevalence**) or over a specified period of time (**period prevalence**). *Contrast* INCIDENCE.

preventive ritual. A compulsion (e.g. checking) undertaken to prevent future guilt. *Compare* RESTORATIVE RITUAL.

primacy effect. 1. (Learning) The finding that in free recall learning, the first items to be presented are more likely to be recalled than items towards the middle of the list. 2. (Social psychology) The phenomenon that material presented early on in a sequence tends to have a bigger effect on changing a person's attitudes than material presented later. E.g. people's views of another person tend to be heavily biased by first impressions. Unfortunately, the same is true of diagnostic judgements in psychiatry. *Contrast* RECENCY EFFECT.

primacy zone. The erotogenic zone on which the libido is mainly focused at a particular point in a person's development.

primal anxiety. (Psychoanalysis) The anxiety associated with birth, based on the shock of leaving the womb and being subjected to massive stimulation from the environment; it is thought by some to be the root of all further anxiety.

primal father. (Psychoanalysis) The head of the PRIMAL HORDE.

primal horde. (Psychoanalysis) Freud's expression for the hypothesized primordial society in which there was an alleged dominance hierarchy between males, the dominant male keeping for himself a number of selected females.

primal repression. *See* REPRESSION.

primal scene. (Psychoanalysis) Copulation between parents, witnessed or fantasized by a child.

primal scream. *See* PRIMAL THERAPY.

primal sketch. Marr's term for the explicit representation at a low level of the visual system of oriented lines and edges, of the extent of the blur gradient at their boundaries, and of luminosity differences at lines or edges. The **raw primal sketch** consists of blobs, oriented line and edge segments, and terminations. In the **full primal sketch** line segments are joined together where appropriate by grouping operations; other similar entities (e.g. a row of dots) are also grouped together; in addition boundaries are located. The information in the primal sketch forms, according to Marr, the basis for all further visual processing.

primal therapy. A form of psychotherapy, initiated by Arthur Janov, in which the patient is encouraged to recall the **primal trauma**, i.e. traumatic events from his childhood, usually involving his parents, and to recapture and vent his agony and anger by the allegedly therapeutic **primal scream**.

primal trauma. *See* PRIMAL THERAPY.

primary. 1. Any of the comparison colours, usually three in number (or strictly speaking the corresponding monochromatic wavelengths), mixtures of which produce METAMERIC MATCHING; the colours are monochromatic, and to make metameric matching possible must be chosen in such a way that no mixture of any two can produce a match to the third, but within this constraint there are a large number of possible triples that can serve as primaries. *See* RGB SYSTEM. 2. A synonym for UNIQUE HUE (which is the better expression).

primary abilities. Short for PRIMARY MENTAL ABILITIES.

primary amentia. Genetically-caused mental deficiency.

primary anxiety. (Psychoanalysis) Anxiety caused by the failure of the EGO to deal with the demands of the ID. *Compare* SIGNAL ANXIETY.

primary area. A synonym for PRIMARY CORTEX.

primary attention. Attention determined by the arresting qualities of an extraneous stimulus, rather than attention directed from within. *Contrast* SECONDARY ATTENTION.

primary auditory cortex. Brodmann's area 41 and parts of 42 and 52; *see* Appendix 4. In man, it is part of the medial TEMPORAL LOBE lying largely buried in the SYLVIAN FISSURE. It receives the largest projection from the COCHLEA (by way of the medial geniculate), and contains a map of sound frequency, orthogonal to which is a binaural map representing different proportions of input from the two ears.

primary circular reaction. Piaget's expression for ineffective repetitive behaviour, like putting the hand to the mouth again and again. It develops in the second phase of the SENSORY-MOTOR STAGE. *See also* SECONDARY CIRCULAR REACTION and TERTIARY CIRCULAR REACTION.

primary cognition. The early thought processes of infants, in which the self and the environment are not differentiated. *Compare* PRIMARY INTEGRATION.

primary colour. A synonym for PRIMARY.

primary control. Coping by changing the external world rather than oneself. *Contrast* SECONDARY CONTROL.

primary cortex. The cortex that receives the largest projection from sensory receptors in a given modality, or that has the largest efferent projection (motor cortex). For discussion *see* ASSOCIATION CORTEX.

primary drive. Any unlearned drive. *See* PHYSIOLOGICAL DRIVE. *Contrast* SECONDARY DRIVE.

primary factor. Any factor uncovered in a factor analysis that accounts for a significant amount of the variance.

primary function. The sensation immediately caused by a stimulus. *Contrast* SECONDARY FUNCTION.

primary gain. (Psychoanalysis) The relief from anxiety allegedly produced at the onset of a neurosis by e.g. a reduction in conflicting impulses. *Contrast* SECONDARY GAIN.

primary generalization. Short for PRIMARY STIMULUS GENERALIZATION.

primary group. Any group to which someone gives his main allegiance, and to whose values etc. he is highly committed. *Contrast* SECONDARY GROUP.

primary hue. A synonym for PRIMARY COLOUR.

primary identification. (Psychoanalysis) The identification the infant makes with its mother (or sometimes with its father or a surrogate for a biological parent).

primary integration. (Psychoanalysis) The child's recognition that it is a single, unique entity that is separate from the environment.

primary line of sight. The line passing from the point fixated through the centre of the pupil; this line is usually about 5° displaced nasally in the visual world from the PUPILLARY AXIS and falls on the centre of the fovea.

primary memory. The current contents of consciousness that are derived from memory, rather than from immediate perception. *Compare* SECONDARY MEMORY; *see also* WORKING MEMORY.

primary memory image. A synonym for EIDETIC IMAGE.

Primary Mental Abilities Test. A measure of putative PRIMARY MENTAL ABILITIES, namely verbal memory, word fluency, numerical ability, spatial relations, memory, perceptual speed, and reasoning.

primary mental abilities (PMA). The alleged separate abilities that contribute to intelligence (e.g. verbal and spatial ability), which psychologists claim to discover by factor analysing intelligence test items to find which set of factors account best for the variance of the results. In fact there is no general agreement about what the primary mental abilities are.

primary mental deficiency. Genetically-caused subnormal intelligence.

primary motivation. A synonym for PRIMARY DRIVE.

primary motor cortox (M1). Brodmann's area 4; *see* Appendix 3. It is a vertical strip lying at the rear of the FRONTAL LOBES and in front of the CENTRAL SULCUS. It contains a topographical map of the body (the MOTOR HOMUNCULUS). Electrical stimulation produces firing of discrete muscles or muscle groups. *See* MOTOR CORTEX.

primary narcissism. (Psychoanalysis) *See* NARCISSISM.

primary need. A synonym for PHYSIOLOGICAL NEED.

primary object. (Psychoanalysis) The first external object (usually the mother) to which the LIBIDO is directed.

primary odour. Any of the odours forming the ODOUR PRISM, i.e. spicy, burned, resinous, ethereal, putrid, and fragrant.

primary olfactory cortex. An area of the RHINENCEPHALON on which some fibres from the OLFACTORY TRACT terminate, and which includes the UNCUS, the rostral PARAHIPPOCAMPAL GYRUS, the PERIAMYGDALOID CORTEX, and the PREPYRIFORM CORTEX.

primary orgasmic dysfunction. *See* ORGASMIC DYSFUNCTION.

primary position. (Vision) The position of the eye from which no torsion occurs if a horizontal or vertical eye-movement is made. This is usually the position of the eyes when directed straight in front with their optic axes parallel.

primary process. (Psychonanalysis) The mental processes occurring in the ID, which Freud thought were unconscious, irrational, not based on reality, and dominated by the PLEASURE PRINCIPLE.

primary punisher. A stimulus that is innately aversive to an organism, such as an electric shock.

primary punishment. 1. A PRIMARY PUNISHER. 2. The process by which a PRIMARY PUNISHER leads to aversion.

primary quality. (Philosophy) A quality of an object that exists regardless of the observer (e.g. extension, solidity) as opposed to a SECONDARY QUALITY which depends on a reaction of the observer to some quality of the object (e.g. sound, taste). The distinction is less easy to maintain than was once thought.

primary reaction tendency. The characteristic way in which an individual responds to stress, e.g. by insomnia, indigestion, or a skin rash.

primary reinforcer. A stimulus that provides innate REINFORCEMENT (1).

primary reinforcement. 1. A PRIMARY REINFORCER. 2. The process of being reinforced by a primary reinforcer. *Compare* SECONDARY REINFORCEMENT.

primary relationship. A relationship in which two people are very much involved with one another.

primary repression. (Psychoanalysis) The repression of unconscious material before it has even emerged into consciousness.

primary saccade. *See* SACCADE.

primary scaling. A hypothetical mechanism that affects the apparent size of objects, tending to produce some SIZE CONSTANCY; it is alleged to depend directly on perspective cues with no reference to apparent distance. Gregory, following Tausch, thought many of the geometrical illusions were caused by primary scaling. **Secondary scaling** is the influence of apparent depth on perceived size.

primary sex characteristics. *See* SEX CHARACTERISTICS.

primary signalling system. A synonym for FIRST SIGNAL SYSTEM.

primary somatosensory cortex (SmI). Brodmann's areas 1–3; *see* Appendix 3. A strip of cortex lying in the parietal lobe immediately behind the central gyrus. It receives a topographical projection from the somatosensory system. *See* HOMUNCULUS (2).

primary stimulus generalization. Stimulus generalization caused by similarity between stimuli rather than by a mediating process such as SEMANTIC GENERALIZATION. *Contrast* MEDIATED GENERALIZATION.

primary symptoms. A synonym for FUNDAMENTAL SYMPTOMS.

primary territory. (Ethology) The territory which one or more members of a species allocate to themselves and which they will defend against encroachment by conspecifics.

primary thought process. A synonym for PRIMARY PROCESS.

primary tone. A tone that is physically present at the ear, in contrast to a COMBINATION TONE.

primary visual cortex. A synonym for STRIATE CORTEX.

primary zone. (Psychoanalysis) The bodily region on which the libido is directed at a given stage of development, i.e. (in succession) the mouth, the anus, and the genitals.

prime. 1. (Hearing) A synonym for FUNDAMENTAL. 2. (Mathematics and Logic) A symbol (′) used to modify another symbol, e.g. d′ (*see* e.g. D-PRIME). 3. (Mathematics) A number divisible without remainder only by itself and one.

priming. 1. (Psychology) The facilitation of a particular association or response by giving a prompt. E.g. presenting the word 'fruit' may prime subsequent responses like 'orange' or 'banana'. (*See also* NEGATIVE PRIMING). 2. (Neurophysiology) Giving a burst of electrical stimultion to a 'pleasure centre' in the brain at the start of a session, which facilitates the self-stimulation response; animals are often slow to make it without this priming. *See also* NEGATIVE PRIMING.

primitives. The basic elements out of which a description or representation is formed. E.g. generalized cones and their axes were the primitives chosen by Marr for the representation of 3-D objects; letters are the primitives for written words and strokes, curves, etc. are the primitives for letters.

primitivization. (Psychoanalysis) Loss of rational functioning alleged to be a reversion to more primitive modes of functioning based on the id. *Compare* REGRESSION (1).

primordial. Occurring first or early on in a temporal sequence, used particularly of the development of human societies.

primordial image. Jung's term for the image or idea of an ARCHETYPE.

primordial thinking. A synonym for PRIMARY PROCESS.

principal component method. (Statistics) A technique of factor analysis in which the factor that accounts for the maximum amount of the observed variance is first extracted, and orthogonal factors then successively chosen to account for the maximum amount of the remaining variance at each step.

principal curvatures. The curvatures that are greatest and least around a point on a surface. They are always at right angles to one another.

principal factor method. A variation of the PRINCIPAL COMPONENT METHOD.

principal focus. See FOCAL POINT.

principal sulcus. See SULCUS PRINCIPALIS.

principled stage. Stage 6 of KOHLBERG'S STAGES OF MORAL JUDGEMENT and the second stage of the POSTCONVENTIONAL LEVEL; at this stage the person is supposed to be concerned with his conscience and with arriving at universal moral principles.

principle of X. See under X, PRINCIPLE OF.

prior-decision model. (Psycholinguistics) The hypothesis that when a polysemous word occurs, people immediately interpret it in one way even if they may have to revise their interpretation in the light of what follows. The **post-decision model** holds that all interpretations are processed when the word occurs, the correct one being determined later.

prior entry, law of. The principle that if a subject is attending to one of two possible stimuli and if they occur simultaneously, the one to which he is attending tends to be perceived as having occurred before the other. The law accounts for variations in observers' estimation of the transit times of stars; some attend to the clock, others to the stars.

prior entry effect. (Social psychology) The phenomenon that the first impressions of a person tend to dominate, and are not easily changed by further acquaintance.

prior probability. The frequency with which a given characteristic or event appears in the members of a POPULATION. *Contrast* CONDITIONAL PROBABILITY.

prism. In optics, a wedge-shaped transparent body that can be used to deviate incident light and separate it into its component wavelengths (since different wavelengths are refracted through different angles).

prism adaptation. Adaptation to the displacement of the visual image (usually horizontally through about 10°), caused by wearing wedge-shaped prisms on the eyes. At first, subjects, if making ballistic movements or if unable to see their hand, reach for visually perceived objects incorrectly, but with sufficient experience they come to reach correctly. There are other forms of prism adaptation, e.g. to the slight curvature induced and to the colour fringes occurring at edges.

prisoner's dilemma. (Game theory) A situation in which each of two people have to make a choice between two alternatives (A and B) without knowing which alternative the other will choose. If both choose A they each receive a modest reward; if both choose B they receive little or no reward; while if one chooses A and the other B, the one choosing A receives a substantial punishment, and the one choosing B receives a large reward. The dilemma is knowing whether to cooperate by choosing A, which is safe provided the other player does so, but disastrous if he does not. The problem is based on a hypothetical situation in which either of two prisoners can go free by confessing, provided they do not both confess.

private acceptance. A person's acceptance of a belief without letting others know he has accepted it; only if others know that a person has accepted a belief will they expect him to act on it.

proactive inhibition (PI). 1. A synonym for PROACTIVE INTERFERENCE. 2. The process underlying PROACTIVE INTERFERENCE.

proactive interaction. The phenomenon that people choose the situations in which they engage and that these situations may partially determine their personality and abilities. *Compare* EVOCATIVE INTERACTION and REACTIVE INTERACTION.

proactive interference (PI). The impairment in learning or remembering material or in performing a task caused by having previously learned similar material or a similar task. *Compare* REPRODUCTIVE INTERFERENCE and RETROACTIVE INTERFERENCE.

pro-attitudinal behaviour. Behaviour that is in accordance with a person's own attitudes. The term is usually used where the behaviour has been externally imposed. Behaviour that is performed under persuasion or sanctions and that a person does not want to carry out is **counter-attitudinal** behaviour, e.g. not smoking in an area where smoking is banned.

probabilism. The doctrine that events cannot be predicted with certainty but only with some degree of probability.

probabilistic functionalism. The doctrine, as put forward by Brunswik, that the veracity of perception and of all beliefs is probabilistic. *See* ECOLOGICAL PERCEPTION (2).

probability. A measure of how likely something is to occur expressed as a decimal lying between 0 (cannot occur) and 1.0 (certain to occur). The probability of an occurrence of an instance of a particular kind is the ratio of instances of that kind to the size of the population containing them. This is the frequency theory of probability, but there are many others, some of which are completely cranky. *See also* PRIOR PROBABILITY and SUBJECTIVE PROBABILITY.

probability curve. A graph showing the probability of occurrence of the different values of a variable.

probability density. The probability of occurrence of any value of a continuous variable that lies within a specified range of values (e.g. between 9.0 and 9.99).

probability distribution, probability function. The probability of occurrence of each value (or range of values) in a category.

probability learning. Discrimination learning in which the subject has to choose between two (or more) alternatives, and in which the probability of reward is less than 1.0 on each alternative; the probabilities are usually made to sum to 1 (e.g. 0.7 on one alternative,

0.3 on the other), so that a reward is available on one or other alternative on every trial. Animals rarely adopt the best strategy, which is to select the more favourable alternative on every trial. *See* PROBABILITY MATCHING.

probability matching. The selection of each alternative with the same probability with which it is rewarded in a PROBABILITY LEARNING experiment. Individual animals rarely show probability matching, but when the scores of many animals are grouped together they may correspond to probability matching.

probability of response. The probability with which an organism makes a response when exposed to a given situation; this traditional measure of strength of learning can only be used in a DISCRETE TRIALS EXPERIMENT, and not in a FREE OPERANT EXPERIMENT.

probability paper. A synonym for PROBIT PAPER.

probability ratio. (Statistics) The ratio of the number of occurrences of a particular type of event to the total number of occasions on which it might have occurred.

probability sampling. (Statistics) A technique of sampling in which the frequency with which members of each group in a population are sampled is proportional to the size of each group relative to the size of the population.

probable error (PE). (Statistics) A measure of dispersion equivalent to half the INTERQUARTILE RANGE. Although historically used, it has been supplanted by the STANDARD DEVIATION.

proband. An individual with a particular trait (or illness), whose blood relatives are investigated in order to obtain evidence about the genetic transmission of the trait.

probe technique. An experimental technique in which the subject is given a list of items to remember; he is then presented with one of them and has to respond with the item that came after it in the list.

probit paper. Paper on which the frequencies plotted on the ordinate are spaced out at extreme frequencies, and are close together at intermediate ones in such a way that the cumulative distribution of a normal curve will yield a straight diagonal line.

problem box. A synonym for PUZZLE BOX.

problem-focused coping. Reducing anxiety by changing or avoiding the situation that causes it. *Contrast* EMOTION-FOCUSED COPING.

problem solving. An expression used by psychologists to refer mainly to well defined problems that are solved by making a sequence of operations having a clear solution (e.g. the TOWER OF HANOI PROBLEM or WATER JAR PROBLEMS). If the problem is drawn from mathematics or formal logic, the subject is usually said to be **reasoning**, but the rationale for this is obscure.

problem space. In a well defined problem, all the possible states that can be attained by making sequences of permissible operations (e.g. all possible positions in chess).

procedural knowledge. Knowing how to do something.

procedural memory. The part of memory containing information to which there is no conscious access, but which is used in performing certain skills (e.g. speaking or riding a bicycle). *Compare* DECLARATIVE MEMORY and EPISODIC MEMORY.

procedural semantics. An approach to semantics based on the theory that to know the meaning of a sentence is to have a set of procedures for establishing its truth or falsity, or for establishing internal models of the state of affairs referred to.

proceeding. Murray's vague term for a unit of behaviour in which a person either interacts with another person or with some part of the world.

proceptive period. The period over which a female animal is ready to mate.

process. 1. (Generally) Any mechanism that brings about some outcome. 2. (Anatomy) Any fine thread-like structure of a cell, particularly axons and dendrites and their branches.

process analysis. (Evaluation research) An analysis of a system's individual processes and their interactions, with a view to improving them.

process attitude. Concentration on one's mental state (even when performing an external task) particularly as a result of experimental instructions. *Contrast* OBJECT ATTITUDE.

process tracing method. Any experimental method that attempts to discover intervening processes by making them as directly observable as possible, e.g. by PROTOCOL ANALYSIS or by recording eye-movements.

processor. A synonym for CENTRAL PROCESSING UNIT.

process schizophrenia. Schizophrenia that develops gradually and without any clear precipitating event. The prognosis is poor. *Contrast* REACTIVE SCHIZOPHRENIA.

proctophobia. A morbid fear of the anus and anything associated with it.

prodrome. An early symptom of an illness, e.g. the aura preceding epilepsy.

product image. A synonym for BRAND IMAGE.

production. 1. (Psycholinguistics) The output of written or spoken language, as opposed to its reception and comprehension. 2. (Psychophysics) *See* PRODUCTION, METHOD OF.

production, method of. A psychophysical scaling method in which the subject is asked to select or produce by adjustment a stimulus that appears to differ from the standard by a given proportion (e.g. twice as big, one-half the size), thus producing a ratio scale.

production system. (AI) A high-level language devised by Newell in which commands are written as conditional instructions (e.g. 'If y is greater than 100, then set x to 11') and assigned an order of priority; whenever its condition is met, a command will be executed (if it has the highest priority for that condition).

product moment correlation (r). (Statistics) A measure of the extent to which there is a linear relationship between two continuous variables, computed by the formula $\Sigma(z_xz_y)/N$ where z_x and z_y are the differences of the individual scores on each dimension from their means divided by their standard deviations and N is the number of scores. It can also be defined as the covariance between two variables divided by their standard deviations. *See also* CORRELATION COEFFICIENT.

profile. 1. A graph (usually a histogram) of a set of quantified characteristics, e.g. personality traits. 2. (Linguistics) *See* BASE.

profile analysis. The statistical analysis of a set of PROFILES or of the differences between sets of profiles; it is a branch of multivariate statistics.

profile matching system. A method of personnel selection in which the profiles of applicants for a job are compared with the profiles of employees who do the job well.

profound mental retardation. Mental retardation in which the IQ is below 25; motor coordination is severely impaired.

progesterone. A hormone secreted by the CORPUS LUTEUM that brings about the changes to the uterus that occur in pregnancy and also aids prolactin to prepare the mammary glands for suckling.

progestin. A synthetic substance that has similar effects to PROGESTERONE.

prognathy. The possession of a jaw projecting beyond the line of the forehead. *Compare* ORTHOGNATHY.

program. (Computing) A set of instructions to a computer, which when they are run implement some task. In the UK 'program' in this sense ends with a single 'm', while in all other uses the word is spelled 'programme'. In the USA only the former spelling exists.

programmed instruction, programmed learning. Any systematic teaching method in which the material is carefully graded for difficulty, and in which the subject has to answer questions at one stage before moving on to the next; the material to which he is directed at any point may depend on the answers he has given to previous questions. Such instruction may be implemented in a book or on a computer.

programming language. (Computing) Any formal language in which computer programs can be written, ranging from machine code to high level languages containing complex functions. *See* e.g. LIST PROCESSING LANGUAGE and PRODUCTION SYSTEM.

progredient neurosis. A neurosis in which the symptoms become progressively more severe; e.g. a fear of entering shops may become generalized to the point where the person cannot leave his house.

progression. (Mathematics) A series in which successive terms are governed by a specifiable mathematical relationship to one another. In **arithmetic progression** (e.g. 1, 5, 9, 13 . . .) the relation consists of adding or subtracting a constant; **geometric progression** consists of multiplying or dividing by a constant (e.g. 1, 3, 9, 27 . . .).

progression law. The principle that sensations increase in arithmetic progression when the intensity of the stimulus is increased in geometric progression.

progressive. (Linguistics) An ASPECT of verbs that indicates that an action is continuous (e.g. 'I am walking').

progressive matrices. *See* RAVEN'S PROGRESSIVE MATRICES.

progressive relaxation. A technique, sometimes used in therapy, for producing relaxation, in which the person is taught to tighten and relax different muscle groups with the aim of teaching him to relax his whole body at will.

prohormone. A large molecule (e.g. 31-K or 50-K) produced by the body that can be broken down into fragments that are themselves hormones. 50-K is manufactured in the adrenal gland and contains ENKEPHALIN, among other hormones.

projection. 1. (Psychoanalysis) A defence mechanism in which a person conceals from himself that he has a trait or disposition of which he is unconsciously ashamed, by falsely seeing its presence in others. *Compare* OB-JECTIVATION. 2. (Generally) Interpreting the world in terms of one's own needs and wishes. 3. (Neurophysiology) The locality at which axons arising in one part of the nervous system terminate. 4. (Anatomy) A protuberance on a cell or organ. 5. *See also* OPTICAL PROJECTION and PROJECTION SYSTEM.

projection area, projection cortex. Short for SENSORY PROJECTION AREA.

projection system. Any method of mapping points in space onto a picture plane by projective geometry. *See* ISOMETRIC PROJECTION, OBLIQUE PROJECTION, ORTHOGRAPHIC PROJECTION, and PERSPECTIVAL PROJECTION.

projective test. Any personality test in which the subject is required to respond freely to material that can be interpreted in different ways. The assumption is that his responses will reveal needs, wishes, or ways of seeing the world that he will not explicitly disclose because of psychoanalytic repression, because he is only vaguely aware of some of his feelings, or because, although aware of them, he does not wish to reveal them. The value of the technique is in doubt, since the interpretation of the testees' responses is necessarily subjective. The interpretations made could themselves form a useful projective test executed on the tester. *See also* RORSCHACH TEST and THEMATIC APPERCEPTION TEST.

prolactin. A HORMONE secreted by the ANTERIOR PITUITARY to stimulate the production of milk by the mammary glands.

prompt. A hint given to help someone perform a task.

prompting and fading. A behaviour therapy technique in which the therapist first guides the client's behaviour and then gradually withdraws the guidance.

pronoun. (Linguistics) A closed word that can be used in place of a noun phrase. There are several types: **personal pronouns** (e.g. 'I', 'me') replace a person in the nominative or accusative case; **possessive pronouns** ('my', 'mine') replace a person in the genitive case; **demonstrative pronouns** ('this', 'that') are deictic; **interrogative pronouns** ('who', 'which') signify a question; **reflective pronouns** ('myself', 'yourself') stand for the object when subject and object are the same entity; **indefinite pronouns** ('anyone', 'nobody') refer to an unspecified entity; **relative pronouns** ('who', 'whom') indicate a subordinate clause modifying the noun to which the pronoun refers.

pronouncedness. (Vision) The SALIENCE of a colour (including an achromatic colour).

proof-readers' illusion. Either failure to notice in proof-reading a low-level error like an incorrect letter, or failure to notice a higher-level one, like a faulty argument. The first kind of error is thought to arise because text is normally read for its sense and there is a tendency to see what one expects to be there. The second kind arises from the difficulty of reading for both low-level and high-level errors simultaneously.

propaedeutic task. Any task that imparts the preliminary knowledge needed for further learning, particularly in the instruction of the mentally retarded.

propagation. (Neurophysiology) The conduction of a nerve impulse down an axon.

property list theory. The hypothesis that the meaning of a word is encoded as a list of properties of the item referred to, e.g. 'wing', 'feathers' etc. for bird. *Contrast* PROTOTYPE THEORY.

proposition. That which is asserted by a declarative sentence. The same proposition may be asserted by different sentences, e.g. 'John hit the cat' and 'The cat was hit by John'.

propositional. (Experimental psychology) Pertaining to a mental representation of the world couched in discrete symbols. One such representation is natural language, but there must be higher-level representations than that. A propositional representation differs from an ANALOGUE representation in not being continuous, and in using structures that do not directly reflect the structure of whatever is represented.

propositional attitude. (Philosophy) Any

proposition expressing an attitude towards some aspect of the world, e.g. a belief, hope, fear, doubt, wish, etc. *See also* IN-TENTIONALITY. *Contrast* QUALE.

propositional calculus. A system of formal logic containing axioms, rules of deduction (e.g. MODUS PONENS), and rules for constructing well-formed expressions from the combination of propositions by propositional CONNECTIVES (whose English equivalents are terms such as 'and', 'or', 'not' etc.)

propositional network. A synonym for SEMANTIC NETWORK.

propositional syllogism. *See* SYLLOGISM.

propranolol. *See* ADRENERGIC RECEPTOR.

proprioception. The senses that provide information about the positions of parts of the body relative to one another and to gravity, and about changes in these positions, particularly sensations from receptors in the muscles, tendons, and joints, and from the vestibular system.

proprioceptor. Any receptor mediating proprioception.

proprium. Allport's term for the individuating features of the self.

prosencephalon. A synonym for FOREBRAIN.

prosocial. Socially helpful.

prosodic features. (Linguistics) The aspects of utterance that determine PROSODY.

prosody, prosodics. 1. (Linguistics) The variations, made while speaking, in pitch, loudness, tempo, and rhythm; prosody has a variety of uses, including distinguishing NEW INFORMATION from GIVEN INFORMATION, and indicating the MOOD (2) of a sentence. Some authorities confine the term to changes in rhythm and stress, using INTONA-TION for changes in pitch. 2. (Generally) The study of stress, rhythm, and intonation; or their pattern in a language or segment of a language.

prosopagnosia. An inability to recognize faces, which can be congenital or due to brain damage.

prospective memory. The ability to take an action planned some time before, e.g. remembering to take one's pills at the right time.

prospective study, prospective research. Research undertaken on a cohort of people who are systematically observed over a period of time in order to discover which conditions lead to the subsequent development of a particular trait or illness. The method is more satisfactory but more time consuming than a RETROSPECTIVE STUDY.

prospect theory. (Decision theory) An algebraic theory that attempts to explain departures from EXPECTED UTILITY THEORY. It postulates: (a) people overweight outcomes that are certain (**certainty effect**); (b) they tend to reverse their preferences when equivalent losses are substituted for gains by accepting greater risks to avoid a loss than to make a gain (**reflection effect**); (c) they tend to simplify choices by disregarding components that the alternatives have in common, which can lead to inconsistent decisions (**isolation effect**).

prosthesis. A device used to compensate for the loss of, or for a defect in, a bodily organ or member.

protan. A person who is protanomalous or protanopic.

protanomaly. A form of colour blindness in which trichromacy is preserved but metameric matches are abnormal. There is some loss of sensitivity for high wavelengths; it may be caused by the possession of an abnormal wavelength cone pigment or by some deficiency in it.

protanope. A person with PROTANOPIA.

protanopia. A form of dichromatic colour blindness in which it would appear that the high wavelength receptor system is not functional so that colours in this region of the spectrum cannot be discriminated.

protasis. A synonym for ANTECEDENT (1).

protein. A molecule composed of a long sequence of AMINO ACIDS.

protein kinases. Enzymes that catalyse phosphorylation, one of which (**PKC**) is specifically activated by calcium.

protensity. Titchener's term for the experience of the duration of a stimulus.

prothetic continuum. Any continuum of sensation that does not change qualitatively with changes in the physical dimension of the stimulus (e.g. loudness). *Contrast* META-THETIC CONTINUUM.

protocol analysis. The analysis of a subject's thought processes elicited from him while he is performing a mental task.

protocols. The original notes or records made of an experiment or of a systematic series of observations.

protopathic. Pertaining to the ability of some skin receptors to respond only to gross differences in pressure and temperature. The distinction between protopathic and EPICRITIC was first made by Head.

protoplasm. The semifluid substance inside a cell membrane, including the CYTOPLASM and NUCLEOPLASM, but excluding large vacuoles, injected material, and material to be secreted.

prototype. The most characteristic member of a class, e.g. a sparrow is a prototypical bird, an ostrich or pelican is not. In some cases the prototype may be abstract and not actually exist: e.g. subjects shown variations of a geometric form may subsequently pick as the most typical (i.e. the prototype) a form which they have never seen but which most closely shares the common properties of those they have seen. *See* CORE.

prototype theory. The hypothesis that categories are formed by constructing a PROTO-TYPE from exemplars. New items are classified by their similarity to the prototype.

protozoa. Organisms consisting of a single cell.

pro-verb. (Linguistics) A verb which takes the place of another verb, e.g. in response to 'May I come in?', 'Please *do*.'

proverb test. An ability test in which a person is asked to explain the meaning of a proverb.

proxemics. The study of the physical spacing of organisms and its effects including territoriality, interpersonal distance, and crowding.

proximal. (Anatomy) Towards the centre of the body or of an organ. *Contrast* DISTAL.

proximal development zone. The difference between a child's actual ability and the ability it is capable of developing under instruction, one of Vygotsky's concepts.

proximal response. A response occurring inside an organism, e.g. a change in heart rate. *Contrast* DISTAL RESPONSE.

proximal stimulus. The pattern of physical energy that stimulates an organism's receptors, as it exists at the interface between the receptors and the environment. *Contrast* DISTAL STIMULUS.

proximity, law of. The Gestalt law of grouping stating that the nearer together visual forms are, the more likely they are to be seen as belonging together.

proximodistad development, proximodistal development. The progression of physical and behavioural development from the centre of the body outwards, which occurs in the later fetal stages and soon after birth. *Compare* CEPHALOCAUDAD DEVELOPMENT.

Prozac. *See* SSRI.

PRP. An abbreviation for PSYCHOLOGICAL REFRACTORY PERIOD.

PSE. An abbreviation for 1. POINT OF SUBJECTIVE EQUALITY; 2. PRESENT STATE EXAMINATION.

pseudaesthesia, pseudesthesia. An illusory sensation in the skin or proprioreceptive senses, e.g. the feeling of having a phantom limb.

pseudoanhedonia. An attitude of withdrawal and not caring, seen in the old, which is assumed to be assumed.

pseudochromaesthesia, pseudochromesthesia. Synonyms for CHROMAESTHESIA.

pseudoconditioning. The increase in the strength of a response to a stimulus caused by SENSITIZATION, i.e. merely by the occurrence of the CS alone not by its proximity to the US. In conditioning experiments it is desirable to control for this effect to make sure that any response given to the US is caused by conditioning, not by sensitization.

pseudoconvulsion. A seizure caused by hysteria.

pseudodementia. Temporary disorientation and severe intellectual impairment, caused by an emotional shock or depression.

pseudogeusia. Any illusion of taste.

pseudohallucination. A hallucination recognized as such by the person having it.

pseudoimbecility. Simulated mental defect.

pseudoindependent personality. A person who pretends to be self-reliant and independent, but who underneath wants to be cared for by others.

pseudoisochromatic charts. Plates containing figures or designs, picked out in colours equated for brightness; they are used to test colour vision. *Compare* ISHIHARA PLATES.

pseudolalia. Nonsensical babbling.

pseudologia fantastica. A syndrome marked by the production of fabrications or tall tales, which the person only believes for a short time.

pseudomania. A symptom in which the patient confesses to crimes or evil deeds that he has not committed.

pseudomemory. A synonym for PARAMNESIA.

pseudoneurotic schizophrenia. A form of schizophrenia characterized by pervasive anxiety and other neurotic traits together with psychotic symptoms like extreme withdrawal and thought disturbances.

pseudonomania. Lying to an abnormal extent, a characteristic of British prime ministers and American presidents.

pseudoparkinsonism. Parkinsonism caused by drugs.

pseudopatient. A social scientist who poses as mentally ill, usually in order to gain admission to a mental hospital in order to observe what happens there. The pseudopatient has become the psychiatrist's worst occupational hazard.

pseudophone. A device that sends to the left ear the sound pattern that would normally enter the right ear and vice versa; it has been used to study sound localization.

pseudopsychology. The theories and experiments of any psychologist whose views differ from your own.

pseudopsychopathic schizophrenia. A form of schizophrenia in which there are strong antisocial and asocial tendencies.

pseudopsychosis. A synonym for FACTITIOUS DISORDER WITH PSYCHOLOGICAL SYMPTOMS.

pseudoretardation. Mental defect caused by environmental factors (e.g. maternal deprivation) rather than by congenital ones.

pseudoscience. Scientific work undertaken by anyone of whom one disapproves.

pseudoscope. A device for transposing the images on the two eyes, thus giving rise to an impression of reversed depth.

pseudoword. A letter string that, like a word, can be pronounced but is not a word (e.g. 'cantost').

pseudoword superiority effect. The phenomenon that when a PSEUDOWORD is displayed, any letter in it is identified faster than if the letter is shown on its own. *Compare* WORD SUPERIORITY EFFECT.

psi. Any paranormal ability or process.

psi function (ψ function). A synonym for PSYCHOMETRIC FUNCTION.

psilocybin. A HALLUCINOGEN.

psi-missing. Pertaining to any paranormal ability that works in reverse, like paranormal guessing at cards that scores below chance expectation.

psi neuron. One of two classes of neuron hypothesized by Freud. He alleged that it lies in the brain, particularly in the grey matter, and that it stores memories in the form of energy. *Compare* PHI NEURON.

psopholalia. Babbling or meaningless speech.

PSP. An abbreviation for POSTSYNAPTIC POTENTIAL.

psychalgia. Psychosomatic or hysterical pain having no organic cause.

psychasthenia. An obsolete synonym for MENTAL RETARDATION.

psychedelic. Pertaining to altered states of consciousness (e.g. hallucinations, changes in the perception of time, transcendental feelings), particularly as produced by PSYCHEDELIC DRUGS.

psychedelic drugs. Drugs, such as LSD, that produce an altered state of consciousness.

psychiatry. The medical speciality that deals with mental disorders.

psychic. 1. Pertaining to the mind. 2. Paranormal.

psychical. A synonym for PSYCHIC (2).

psychic apparatus. Freud's expression for the alleged division of the mind into SUPEREGO, EGO, and ID.

psychic blindness. A synonym for VISUAL AGNOSIA.

psychic energy. (Psychoanalysis) The energy originating in the libido that according to Freud drives all mental processes.

psychic equivalent. A synonym for PSYCHOMOTOR EPILEPSY.

psychic inertia. (Psychoanalysis) Fixation at an early stage of libidinal development, an alleged characteristic of neurotics.

psychic reality. (Psychoanalysis) The reality to the individual of his thoughts, feelings, wishes, and fears as opposed to the reality of external events.

psychic research. Research in PARAPSYCHOLOGY.

psychic resultants, law of. Wundt's principle that through apperception, a creative synthesis of the elements of the mind occurs out of which something new arises.

psychic secretion. Pavlov's term for the saliva elicited by the conditioned stimulus after salivary conditioning has taken place.

psychoacoustics. The study of hearing taking into account the relevant physiology and the physical properties of the sound wave.

psychoactive. A synonym for PSYCHOTROPIC.

psychoanaleptic. A psychotropic drug that produces a euphoriant or antidepressant action, e.g. the tricyclics. *Compare* ANALEPTIC.

psychoanalysis. 1. Originally, a comprehensive dynamic theory proposed by Freud to account for human personality, motivation, dreams, and mistakes, based on the assumption that motives are determined by the LIBIDO, and that their expression is controlled by unconscious forces in which there is a conflict between libidinal urges and social training. The term includes the many variations on Freudian theory, such as Jung's (usually called ANALYTIC PSYCHOLOGY), Adler's (usually called INDIVIDUAL PSYCHOLOGY), and those of a host of NEO-FREUDIANS. 2. A method of treating mental disorders based on one or other form of psychoanalytic theory, in which an attempt is made to give patients insights into the workings of their unconscious minds by interpreting their dreams, fantasies, free associations, mistakes, and attitudes. It is unclear why such insights should help to overcome neurosis, and frequently they do not. Nowadays, normal people often seek psychoanalysis in the hope that it will give them insight into themselves and help to resolve their personal problems.

psychoanalyst. A person who takes money from another on the pretence that it is for the other's own good.

psychoasthenia. A synonym for MENTAL RETARDATION.

psychobiology. 1. Myer's approach to mental illness, in which he emphasized the integration of the social, psychological, and biological aspects of a person (obsolete). 2. The study of behaviour and the mind with special emphasis on their biological determinants.

psychochemistry. The study of the influence of chemical substances (e.g. hormones, neurotransmitters, and psychotropic drugs) on behaviour and the mind.

psychodrama. A psychotherapeutic technique in which patients are asked to act, usually in front of a group, the part of themselves or of people close to them in the hope that they will gain insight into their conflicts and methods of behaving.

psychodynamic. Pertaining to dynamic accounts of motivation or personality.

psychodysleptics. Psychotropic drugs that cause disintegration of the mind, e.g. lysergic acid or mescaline.

psychoendocrinology. The study of the interactive relations between hormones and behaviour, as mediated by the nervous system.

psychogalvanic response (PGR). A synonym for GALVANIC SKIN RESPONSE.

psychogalvanic skin resistance audiometry. A method of testing auditory acuity in infants and suspected malingerers, by recording changes in skin-resistance in response to tones.

psychogalvanometer. An instrument for measuring the GALVANIC SKIN RESPONSE.

psychogenesis. The origin and development of personality, behaviour, and mental processes.

psychogenetic. A synonym for PSYCHOGENIC.

psychogenetics. A synonym for BEHAVIOUR GENETICS.

psychogenic. Produced by the mind.

psychogenic amnesia. Pathological forgetting occurring for psychological causes, as in e.g. a fugue.

psychogenic pain. Pain produced by psychological not physical causes.

psychogeriatrics. The study and treatment of mental disorders in old people.

psychograph. A profile of a person's traits usually as measured by tests.

psychohistory. The attempt to understand historical events in terms of the psychology of the people involved; in practice this usually comes down to applying or misapplying psychoanalytic theory.

psychoinfantilism. The presence in an adult of traits that normally only appear in children.

psychokinesis. 1. (PK) (Parapsychology) Control of external events (e.g. the fall of a die) by paranormal means. 2. (Psychiatry) A rare term for manic behaviour.

psycholagny. Sexual excitement induced by the imagination.

psycholepsy. A sudden drop in psychological tension occurring after a period of excitement; it is accompanied by depression and morbid thoughts, and is said sometimes to result in an epileptic fit.

psycholinguistics. The study of the mechanisms underlying the production and comprehension of language, based largely on experiments. Linguistics studies the COMPETENCE of a native speaker, i.e. the idealized rules governing the use of language, psycholinguistics studies PERFORMANCE, which includes errors, and the processes and mechanisms instantiated in the brain that underlie performance.

psychological dependence. A strong need for a psychoactive drug (such as nicotine or coffee) based on the sense of well-being it provides, but without the existence of physical tolerance to the drug or the occurrence of physiological withdrawal symptoms if the drug is withdrawn. The distinction between psychological and physical dependence is by no means clear-cut. *See* PHYSIOLOGICAL DEPENDENCE.

psychological distance. 1. (Social psychology) A synonym for SOCIAL DISTANCE. 2. Adler's expression for the concealment of weakness by erecting a barrier between oneself and others, e.g. by feigned illness, indecision, or avoiding others in other ways.

psychological factors affecting physical condition. (Psychiatry) Any psychological event (e.g. divorce) that affects some aspect of a person's physical condition, i.e. produces psychosomatic effects.

psychological field. Lewin's expression for the self and the environment as perceived by a person.

psychological moment. The period of time (perhaps sometimes as much as 100 msec) over which successive stimuli are integrated and are perceived as a whole.

psychological motive. A synonym for SECONDARY DRIVE.

psychological refractory period (PRP). A period following the receipt of a stimulus to which a response has to be made, during which the reaction time to a second stimulus is longer than normal. The reaction time is often the normal reaction time added to the time elapsing between the second stimulus and the first response, i.e. it is as though the processing of the second stimulus did not start until the first response had been emitted.

psychological time. The subjective impression of duration, which varies with the conditions, both internal and external.

psychological zero. The intensity at which a stimulus is not experienced, e.g. on the body a probe of about 32°C is not felt as either hot or cold.

psychologism. The view, held only by psychologists, that psychology is or should be the most basic science on which all else depends.

psychology. The systematic study of behaviour and the mind in man and animals, a discipline which has as yet little coherence. It has many different branches, of which some provide explanations little, if at all, advanced from common sense; others put forward reasonably rigorous scientific theories. Almost all branches are united by their faith in the value of experiments, regardless of the importance or replicability of the results.

psychology of individual differences. The attempt to describe and to measure the differences in people's traits and to make theoretical sense of these differences, e.g. by attempting to account for differences in many surface traits by postulating a few underlying traits or by investigating the effects of nature and nurture.

psycholytic. Pertaining to hallucinogenic or psychedelic drugs.

psychometric function. Any function in which behaviour or experience is one of the arguments, including PSYCHOPHYSICAL FUNCTIONS.

psychometric intelligence. *See* INTELLIGENCE.

psychometrics. The attempt to measure any aspects of the functioning of the mind, particularly by the use of ability or personality tests, but also by psychophysical methods and by the application of mathematics (e.g. SIGNAL DETECTION THEORY) to psychological findings.

psychometrizing. (Parapsychology) Obtaining information about someone by touching an object (e.g. a handkerchief) associated with him.

psychometry. A synonym for PSYCHOMETRICS.

psychomimic syndrome. The appearance, without physical cause, in a person of the symptoms of an illness suffered by a friend or relative, often one who has died of the illness.

psychomotility. The influence of the mind on a motor action, particularly a disruptive one, such as stammering.

psychomotor. Pertaining to the control of the muscles by the mind or brain.

psychomotor agitation. Restlessness expressed in movement, e.g. fidgeting or pacing up and down; it occurs in agitated depression.

psychomotor epilepsy. Recurrent epileptic disturbances, including the automatic performance of organized movements, often with confusion but no loss of consciousness, and with retroactive amnesia for the attack; incontinence is common. Most psychomotor epileptics have GRAND MAL attacks but few have PETIT MAL.

psychomotor hallucination. The illusory sensation that parts of the body are moving or being moved when they are not.

psychomotor retardation. A gross reduction in physical activity accompanied by a slowing down of thought processes. The sufferer may sit vacantly in a chair for hours without moving; it can accompany depression and catatonic schizophrenia.

psychomotor stimulants. Drugs that increase activity, e.g. amphetamine and caffeine.

psychoneural parallelism. A synonym for PSYCHOPHYSICAL PARALLELISM.

psychoneuroimmunology. The study of the deleterious effects of low mood and stress on the immune system and of the resulting proneness to illness.

psychoneurosis. (Psychoanalysis) A neurosis brought about by conflict between the ego and the id. Freud used the term particularly of hysteria, phobias, and obsessive–compulsive disorders, in contrast with ACTUAL NEUROSIS. Today it is usually used as a synonym for NEUROSIS.

psychonomic. Pertaining to the discovery of rigorous scientific laws in psychology, particularly quantifiable ones.

psychonosology. The systematic classification of mental disorders.

psychopaedics. Psychological treatment for children.

psychopathology. The study of mental disorders from all aspects.

psychopathy. 1. A snappier term for ANTISOCIAL PERSONALITY DISORDER. 2. Any undiagnosed mental disorder of unknown origin.

psychopedics. An alternative spelling for PSYCHOPAEDICS.

psychopharmacology. The study of the effects of drugs on behaviour and the mind and of the mechanisms underlying their effects.

psychopharmacotherapy. Drug therapy for mental disorders.

psychophobia. A morbid fear of the mind or of thinking, common among students.

psychophysical. 1. Pertaining to PSYCHOPHYSICS. 2. Pertaining to the relationship between the mental and the physical.

psychophysical dualism. See DUALISM.

psychophysical function. Any mathematical function relating variations in physical stimuli to variations in sensations, e.g. WEBER'S LAW.

psychophysical methods. The techniques of PSYCHOPHYSICS. They are used to establish absolute or difference thresholds; see e.g. AVERAGE ERROR, METHOD OF, CONSTANT STIMULI, METHOD OF, LIMITS, METHOD OF, STAIRCASE METHOD, or for scaling a subjective dimension see PSYCHOPHYSICAL SCALING METHODS.

psychophysical parallelism. The philosophical doctrine that for each mental event there is a corresponding physical event in the brain, and that the two kinds of event exist in parallel with no causal interaction between them.

psychophysical power law. *See* POWER LAW.

psychophysical scaling methods. Techniques for forming a scale of the subjective differences between stimuli along a dimension (e.g. brightness, loudness, or pitch); the scale formed may be an ordinal scale, an interval scale, or a ratio scale. **Direct scaling** is based on the subjects' estimate of the position of a stimulus on the scale (e.g. MAGNITUDE ESTIMATION, METHOD OF), **indirect scaling** on a judgement from which its position can be inferred (e.g. BISECTION, METHOD OF). *See also* CROSS-MODALITY MATCHING, METHOD OF, EQUAL-APPEARING INTERVALS, METHOD OF, and PRODUCTION, METHOD OF.

psychophysical tuning curve. The auditory TUNING CURVE for a response to a sine wave of given frequency (the signal). It is determined by measuring the strengths of masking tones of neighbouring frequencies needed to mask the signal.

psychophysics. The measurement of the effects of variation in the stimulus on sensation, and in particular the determination of thresholds and psychophysical scales.

psychophysiologic. A synonym for PSYCHOSOMATIC.

psychophysiological disorder. A new and clumsy term for PSYCHOSOMATIC DISORDER.

psychophysiology. A fashionable synonym for PHYSIOLOGICAL PSYCHOLOGY.

psychorrhea. The utterance of vague and disorganized philosophical theories, a symptom of hebephrenic schizophrenics and existentialists.

psychose passionelle. The delusion that another person, usually a celebrity, is in love with one.

psychosexual. Pertaining to the relation, if any, between sexuality and the mind.

psychosexual development. (Psychoanalysis) The development of the libido through its five stages. *See* LIBIDINAL STAGES.

psychosexual disorder. Any sexual disorder caused by psychological factors, e.g. GENDER IDENTITY DISORDER, the PARAPHILIAS, PSYCHOSEXUAL DYSFUNCTION, or EGO-DYSTONIC HOMOSEXUALITY.

psychosexual dysfunction. A sexual disorder due to malfunction in one of the four phases of sexual excitement: loss of desire (appetitive phase); loss of sexual excitement, i.e. absence of tumescence or of vaginal lubrication (excitement phase); failure to obtain orgasm (orgasmic phase); or failure to relax after orgasm (resolution phase). *See* SEXUAL RESPONSE CYCLE.

psychosexual stages. 1. (Psychoanalysis) A synonym for LIBIDINAL STAGES. 2. A synonym for SEXUAL RESPONSE CYCLE.

psychosis. A severe mental disorder, marked by lack of contact with some aspects of reality, e.g. by delusions, hallucinations, or incoherent thought. Psychoses may be organic (e.g. DRUG-INDUCED PSYCHOSIS or SENILE DEMENTIA), or functional (e.g. MANIC-DEPRESSIVE DISORDER or SCHIZOPHRENIA), though it now seems likely that even the functional psychoses are at least in part caused by organic malfunctioning.

psychosocial. Pertaining to both psychological and social factors.

psychosocial stages. *See* ERIKSON'S PSYCHOSOCIAL DEVELOPMENT STAGES.

psychosomatic. In general, pertaining to something that has both bodily and mental components, but usually used more specifically of a physical symptom caused partly or wholly by psychological factors.

psychosomatic disorder. Any physical disorder whose cause is wholly or partly psychological. Whether a given disorder should be called psychosomatic is often unclear and depends how far back in the chain of causation the precipitating psychological causes are. Thus indigestion produced by anxiety is clearly psychosomatic, but lung cancer caused by smoking would not normally be called psychosomatic. *Compare* FACTITIOUS DISORDER and SOMATOFORM DISORDER.

psychostimulant. A synonym for STIMULANT.

psychosurgery. Any operation on brain tissue not known to be diseased, with the aim of changing the mental state of the patient. *See* AMYGDALECTOMY, FRQNTAL LOBOTOMY, and TRANSORBITAL LOBOTOMY.

psychotechnics, psychotechnology. Synonyms for APPLIED PSYCHOLOGY.

psychotherapy. Any systematic attempt to alleviate mental disorder by psychological means. There are over a hundred different kinds of psychotherapy currently being practised, most of them of doubtful value. Described by Laing as 'a conversation between two people, one of whom is sane by mutual consent'.

psychotic disorder. A euphemism for PSYCHOSIS.

psychotic episode. The manifestation of a psychosis that lasts for a limited period.

psychoticism dimension. One of the three factors extracted from the EYSENCK PERSONALITY QUESTIONNAIRE, the other two being NEUROTICISM and the EXTRAVERSION–INTROVERSION DIMENSION; people with high loadings on psychoticism are aggressive, cold, impulsive, antisocial, tough-minded, and creative.

psychotogenic. Tending to produce psychosis or psychotic symptoms; the term is used, e.g. of certain drugs.

psychotomimetic. Pertaining to a drug whose effects resemble the symptoms of a psychosis (e.g. amphetamine or LSD).

psychotropic. Pertaining to a drug that changes one's state of mind or alters one's behaviour.

psylocykin. A hallucinatory drug.

P-system. Short for PARVOCELLULAR SYSTEM.

PTA. An abbreviation for POST-TRAUMATIC AMNESIA.

pteronophobia. A morbid fear of feathers.

ptosis. The sinking or drooping of an organ or bodily part, used particularly of paralysed eyelids.

PTP. An abbreviation for POST-TETANIC POTENTIATION.

PTS, PTSD. Abbreviations for POST-TRAUMATIC SYNDROME and POST-TRAUMATIC STRESS DISORDER.

puberty. The period of life when the sex organs become fully functional and the SECONDARY SEX CHARACTERISTICS develop. In females it begins at the onset of menstruation. It lasts from roughly 11 to 15 years of age, but the ages vary between individuals and its end is ill-defined.

public distance zone. The distance preserved between people on formal occasions.

public territory. Territory open to all comers.

puer aeternus. Jung's term for the archetype of eternal youth.

puerperism. The period from childbirth until the return of the womb to its normal condition (about six months).

Pulfrich pendulum. A pendulum that is viewed binocularly but with an achromatic filter over one eye. It appears to traverse an elliptical path. One explanation is that the effect of the filter is to increase the time taken by impulses from that eye to reach the cortex, thus producing a stereoscopic effect since rays from the pendulum in one position on one eye are being integrated with rays from a different position on the other, creating binocular disparity. *Compare* MACH–DVORAK PHENOMENON.

pulsation threshold. The minimum change in a sound that can be detected as a pulsation, usually with the change occurring at about 4 Hz.

pulvinar. A large thalamic nucleus containing several retinotopic maps. It is thought to play a role in visual attention, particularly the suppression of irrelevant stimuli. Part of it may be concerned with the other senses.

punctate stimulus. A stimulus applied to a single point on the skin.

punctuated equilibrium. A theory of evolution postulating that evolution occurred in bursts with long periods of little change between them.

punishment. (Learning theory) Any event that an organism tends to escape or avoid. The definition, as has often been pointed out, is circular, but the circularity is not overcome by defining punishment as a noxious stimulus. Note the difference from NEGATIVE REINFORCEMENT, which is the cessation (or avoidance) of a punishment.

pupil. An opening in the iris of the eye of adjustable size (its diameter is between about 2 mm and 8 mm in man) through which light is admitted to the lens and retina.

pupillary axis. The line passing through the centre of the pupil and the centre of curvature of the anterior surface of the cornea; the pupillary axis is normally about 5° displaced temporally in the visual field from the PRIMARY LINE OF SIGHT; it corresponds approximately to the OPTICAL AXIS.

pupillary reflex. Any change in the size of the pupil produced by alterations in light intensity, fixation, or the significance of the stimulus fixated.

pure hue. 1. The hue produced by monochromatic light. 2. Prototypical blue, green, yellow or red light.

pure line. A strain of organisms so inbred that they all have the same genes; all differences between individuals are therefore environmentally determined.

pure meaning. Vigotsky's expression for the cohesion between language and thought achieved in adult reasoning.

pure phi. *See* PHI PHENOMENON.

pure stimulus act. Hull's term for an act that does not bring an organism nearer the goal, but which may facilitate goal directed behaviour, e.g. an observing response.

pure strategy. *See* EVOLUTIONARILY STABLE STRATEGY.

pure tone. The tone produced by a sinusoidal sound wave of a single frequency.

purines. A class of compounds that includes ADENINE, GUANINE, and ATP (and its breakdown products such as ADENOSINE). Some of these compounds are thought to be neurotransmitters, particularly in the autonomic system and in the dorsal root ganglion cells of the spinal cord.

purinergic. Pertaining to synaptic transmission mediated by PURINES.

Purkinje afterimage. A synonym for PURKINJE IMAGE.

Purkinje cell. A large nerve cell with extensive dendritic spread, found in the middle layer of the cerebellar cortex and providing the output from it.

Purkinje effect. *See* PURKINJE SHIFT.

Purkinje figure. The network of blood-vessels that can be observed as shadows by projecting them on to one's own retina and wiggling a small light against the lower eyelid in a darkened room.

Purkinje image. A positive AFTERIMAGE, occurring after the first negative afterimage and lasting about 0.2 sec. It is sometimes seen in complementary colours to the original stimulus.

Purkinje layer. The middle of the three layers of the cerebellum.

Purkinje network. A synonym for PURKINJE FIGURE.

Purkinje–Sanson images. Up to four different reflected images of an object that a person is viewing, which can be seen by looking into his eye; one is reflected from the corneal surface, the second from its back, the third from the front surface of the lens, and the fourth from its rear surface.

Purkinje shift. The phenomenon that under scotopic conditions green and blue hues look brighter relative to reds and oranges than under photopic conditions; the effect is produced because rods are maximally excited by light of a lower wavelength (500 nm) than that which maximally excites cones (555 nm).

purple. A hue, lying outside the spectrum, that is produced by an additive mixture of blues and reds.

purposive behaviourism, purposive psychology. Tolman's expressions for his approach to psychology. Although he believed only stimuli and responses could be observed, he thought that the behaviour of organisms could only be explained by inferring goals, needs, and cognitions. He was silent on the question of how far these intervening variables may be identified with the contents of consciousness.

pursuitmeter. Any device for measuring how closely a subject can track a moving target. *See* PURSUIT ROTOR.

pursuit movement. A synonym for SMOOTH FOLLOWING MOVEMENT, but sometimes used to include CATCH-UP SACCADES.

pursuit rotor. One kind of pursuitmeter consisting of a rotating drum on the surface of which a target is marked; as the drum rotates around a vertical axis, the subject views the target through a slit and has to track its changes in height.

pursuit tracking. The task of keeping a pointer on a moving target. *See* TRACKING.

push-down stack. *See* STACK.

putamen. A nucleus of the BASAL GANGLIA and part of the CORPUS STRIATUM; it is implicated in motor function.

putrid odour. One of the six so-called primary odours, reminiscent of the smell of decay. *See also* ODOUR PRISM.

puzzle box. Any box with a locking device which an organism must discover how to open in order to escape from it or to obtain a reward.

PVN. An abbreviation for PARAVENTRICULAR NUCLEUS.

PVS. An abbreviation for PERIVENTRICULAR SYSTEM.

P300 wave. A positive wave in the electro-encephalogram that tends to occur when a stimulus is unexpected; its latency suggests that it occurs when the stimulus has been evaluated.

Pygmalion effect. 1. The tendency for people to behave in the way others expect them to. 2. A synonym for PYGMALIONISM.

pygmalionism. The tendency to fall in love with one's own creations.

pyknic type. A bodily type (short, thickset) in KRETSCHMER'S CONSTITUTIONAL THEORY, alleged to be associated with CYCLOTHYMIA. *Compare* ATHLETIC TYPE and ASTHENIC TYPE.

pyramidal cell. A neuron having a pyramid-shaped cell body and extensive dendritic processes. Pyramidal cells are widely distributed in the cortex, and are the main outputs from it to subcortical structures, to the spinal cord, and from one part of the cortex to another. They have a long dendritic process that often rises to the top layers of the cortex. In the motor cortex there are very large pyramidal cells (BETZ CELLS) that project directly to motor neurons. *See* PYRAMIDAL SYSTEM.

pyramidal layer. Either of two layers of nerve cells in the cerebral cortex; numbered from the surface inwards, the **external pyramidal layer** is the third, and contains many small- to medium-sized PYRAMIDAL CELLS. The **internal pyramidal layer** is the fifth: it contains many pyramidal cells. *See also* CORTICAL LAYERS.

pyramidal system, pyramidal motor system. Two descending pathways relaying impulses from the motor cortex and elsewhere: the CORTICOBULBAR TRACT ends in the medulla on the motor neurons of the cranial nerves, while the axons of the CORTICOSPINAL TRACT synapse throughout the length of the spinal cord. About 5 per cent of them synapse directly on motor neurons. The system contains efferents from other areas of the cortex, including the somatosensory cortex, and the basal ganglia. It is thought to mediate voluntary control of movement.

pyramidal tract. A synonym for CORTICOSPINAL TRACT.

pyriform lobe. A lobe in the rhinencephalon that includes the entorhinal cortex and the periamygdaloid cortex. It comprises Brodmann's areas 23, 27, 28, 34, and 35; *see* Appendix 4.

pyrolagnia. The arousal of sexual excitement by fires.

pyromania. A compulsive desire to set fire to things.

pyrophobia. A morbid fear of fire.

Q

Q. An abbreviation for 1. QUARTILE DEVIATION; 2. with a subscript (e.g. Q_2) the QUARTILE indicated by the subscript; 3. question; 4. QUESTIONNAIRE.

QALY. An abbreviation for QUALITY ADJUSTED LIFE YEAR.

Q-data. Data obtained from a questionnaire. *Compare* L-DATA and T-DATA.

Q sort. A technique for assessing personality in which the subject sorts statements about himself, his ideal self, relationships, etc., into categories ranging from 'most characteristic' of himself to 'least characteristic'. The subject is forced to distribute the statements into categories in such a way as to yield a normal distribution.

Q technique. The factor analysis of the correlations between subjects rather than tests. It groups subjects into clusters. *Contrast* R TECHNIQUE.

Q test. Short for COCHRAN Q TEST.

quadrangular therapy. MARITAL THERAPY conducted with husband, wife, and both their therapists all together.

quadrant. A quarter of the retina (or visual field); each of the four quadrants is bounded by the horizontal and vertical axes passing through the fovea, and by the edge of the retina.

quadrantopsia, quadrantic hemianopsia. Loss of vision in one quadrant of the visual field, which may be caused by damage to part of the optic radiations.

quadriplegia, quadriparesis. Paralysis of all four limbs.

quale. The singular of QUALIA.

qualia. (Philosophy) The subjective qualities of a mental experience, e.g. the appearance of a particular shade of red. Unlike beliefs etc., qualia do not have INTENTIONALITY, since they do not refer to anything in the external world. Many philosophers hold that no matter how closely computers simulated human behaviour they would not have qualia (the argument from **absent qualia**). Moreover, the possibility that someone might see red the way others see green and vice versa is used to show that consciousness is not a physical entity (the argument from **inverted qualia**). *Compare* SENSE DATA and *contrast* PROPOSITIONAL ATTITUDE.

qualitative identity conservation. Piaget's expression for the ability to recognize that an object remains the same object when some of its attributes are changed (e.g. recognition of the child's mother when she dresses differently).

Quality Adjusted Life Year (QALY). A measure of the subjective severity of a disability obtained by asking people how many years of life with the disability they would exchange for one year without it. E.g. if someone would exchange two years with for one year without, two years with the disability are counted as one life year. The measure can be used in COST–BENEFIT analysis of the value of different treatments.

quantal hypothesis. The theory that as stimulus intensity is increased continuously, sensation and/or the underlying neural activity increases in discrete jumps.

quantifier. A term assigning number to a noun or noun phrase (e.g. 'all', 'some', 'few', 'each'). The use of 'all' or 'some' determines the set relationships between the subject and predicate and the syllogism is based on these relations. Two quantifiers are used in predicate calculus – the **universal quantifier** (basically equivalent to 'all') and the **existential quantifier** (basically equivalent to 'some' or 'there exists a'), each of which, with the help of negation, may be defined in terms of the other.

quantitative conservation. The ability to see that the number of items (or amount of material) remains the same when their positions (or shape) are changed. *See* CONSERVATION.

quantitative equivalence conservation. Piaget's expression for the ability to understand that an attribute that is equal in two different objects is still equal when one or other object is transformed without affecting that attribute.

quantum. A particle that has the smallest possible amount of energy. A quantum of light is a PHOTON.

quantum fluctuation. (Vision) Random and unpredictable variations in the positions on the retina on which a quantum of light will impinge.

quantum hypothesis. (Psychophysics) The hypothesis that as stimulus magnitude is increased, the strength of the sensation increases not continuously, but in quantum leaps, i.e. no increase in sensation is produced until the change in stimulus magnitude is sufficient to produce a sharp change in sensation.

quartile. 1. One of the three values that partition a distribution of scores into four sets, each containing an equal number of scores; the first, or upper, quartile is the score above which 25 per cent of all the scores lie. 2. Any of the four sets of scores created in this way. In this sense the first quartile would be the top 25 per cent of scores.

quartile deviation. One-half of the difference between the first and third QUARTILES. It is a measure of variability that in a normal distribution corresponds to the probable error.

quasi-experimental research. Research conducted without full control over all the independent variables, e.g. most research in natural situations, including much outcome research on psychotherapy.

quasi group. A collection of people, not yet a proper group, but with the capacity to become one.

quasi need. Lewin's term for a SECONDARY NEED.

questionnaire. Any set of questions deliberately designed to reveal something about a person's attitudes or traits. Although devices to measure intelligence, abilities, or aptitudes may consist of questions, they are called mental tests, and not questionnaires.

question stage. A stage at which many young children (about three years old) continually ask questions.

Quick Test. A short intelligence test, useful for screening and for the mute since subjects may respond by nodding, etc.

quiet biting, quiet attack. Attacking or biting without vocalization – a reaction seen in some animals to stimulation of the medial forebrain bundle. *Compare* DEFENCE RESPONSE.

quiet sleep. Stages 2–4 of SLEEP.

quota sampling. Selecting a sample by taking a specified number of cases from each category of a population (e.g. categories of age, sex, and educational level), usually keeping the number of people sampled from each category proportional to the frequency of people in the category in the whole population.

quotient. The result of dividing one number by another, e.g. 3 is the quotient obtained by dividing 6 by 2.

R

R. An abbreviation for 1. RESPONSE; 2. a hypothesized primary mental ability having to do with reasoning.

R^2. The value of a multiple correlation coefficient.

R_c. A rare abbreviation for CONDITIONED RESPONSE.

R_u. A rare abbreviation for UNCONDITIONED RESPONSE.

r. 1. An abbreviation for the value of the product moment correlation coefficient. 2. In Hull's theory, an abbreviation for a response, not necessarily overt, that produces stimulus feedback that may serve as the stimulus for a further response. *Compare* FRACTIONAL ANTEDATING GOAL RESPONSE and PURE STIMULUS ACT.

r_G. In Hull's theory, an abbreviation for the GOAL RESPONSE or CONSUMMATORY RESPONSE, e.g. eating or drinking.

r_{xy}. The product-moment correlation coefficient between the variables x and y.

race. A loosely applied term used to distinguish major groups of people according to their ancestry and distinguishing physical characteristics.

racial memory, racial unconscious. Synonyms for COLLECTIVE UNCONSCIOUS.

radian. The angle between two radii of a circle that cut off an arc of the circumference of the same length as the radius. It equals approximately 57.3°.

radiance. The amount of radiant energy (e.g. light) that passes through a given area per unit time. It is usually measured in watts per square metre per steradian.

radiant energy. Electromagnetic energy, of which the part with wavelengths between about 380 and 750 nm is visible as light.

radiant flux. The total amount of light emitted per unit time from a source.

radiant intensity. The intensity of light emitted by a source per unit solid angle (steradian), usually measured in watts per steradian.

radiation. 1. The spread of energy through space. 2. A synonym for RADIANT ENERGY. 3. (Anatomy) The spreading out of nerve fibres to project on to an extended area, e.g. OPTIC RADIATIONS.

radical behaviourism. The belief that consciousness is either an epiphenomenon or even non-existent. It has the consequence that psychology can only be concerned with stimuli and responses (but it leaves open the possibility of physiological explanations for behaviour).

radical therapy. A form of therapy for mental disorders, influenced by the anti-psychiatry movement, and based on the idea that they are caused by society, and that it is necessary to change society by e.g. eliminating poverty and privileges.

radioactive isotope. A form of a chemical substance that emits radioactivity.

radioactive tracers. RADIOACTIVE ISOTOPES whose passage through the body is monitored by recording their radiation, e.g. ^{14}C, ^{15}N.

radioisotopic encephalography. A synonym for AUTORADIOGRAPHY.

radiometer. Any device for measuring radiant energy.

radula. A horny tongue with teeth on its surface that is found in some molluscs; it can act like a file to make a hole in hard material, e.g. in a shell.

railway illusion. A synonym for the PONZO ILLUSION.

RAM. An abbreviation for RANDOM ACCESS MEMORY.

ramus. (Neuroanatomy) 1. Any branch of a nerve, of a fissure, etc. 2. More specifically, the major branches of each of the spinal nerves, which are the **dorsal ramus** (supplying the back of the body), and the **ventral ramus** (supplying the front and sides). Distinguish from SPINAL ROOT. *See also* RAMUS COMMUNICANS.

ramus communicans. Any nerve leading from the spinal column to the sympathetic ganglia (**white ramus**) or from these ganglia to the organ innervated (**grey ramus**).

random. Impossible in principle to predict.

random access memory (RAM). A computer store from which items can be read directly into the central processor, and into which new items may be placed. *Contrast* ROM.

random control trial, random clinical trial. A test of the efficiency of a therapeutic method in which patients, matched for type of disorder and for its severity, are randomly assigned to a treatment group and a placebo group; ideally the final assessment should be made by someone who does not know to which group each patient belongs.

random dot kinematogram. An array of randomly placed dots, whose position changes from one presentation to the next, thus generating stroboscopic motion.

random dot stereogram. A stereogram made from two arrays of randomly positioned elements, usually of small black and white squares. The arrays are presented to opposite eyes and are so arranged that a region (or regions) of elements in one array is shifted laterally with respect to the other array. The lateral shift produces BINOCULAR DISPARITY, and the shifted region is seen at a different depth from the surrounding region.

random error. A synonym for VARIABLE ERROR.

randomization tests. (Statistics) Non–parametric tests of significance, based on the distributions obtained by permuting the actual observations. If the samples are large the number of permutations becomes prohibitive and approximations to the true distributions are used. These approximations often turn out to be well known distributions, such as the T-TEST and the F RATIO, and hence the use of these distributions can be justified inversely as good approximations to permutations or randomization tests.

randomize. To arrange items or events in an unpredictable order, not governed by any rule. The allocation of subjects to groups and the order in which different conditions are presented are often randomized in experiments. Such randomization is often not truly random, e.g. it may be convenient to ensure that of two experimental conditions each always occurs equally often over a block of trials.

random level. *See* LEVEL.

random noise. A synonym for WHITE NOISE.

random sample. A sample from a population drawn in such a way that each member of the population has the same probability of being selected.

random utility model. (Decision theory) The hypothesis that perceived values of different outcomes vary over time. Hence preferences will also vary.

random walk. A stochastic process consisting of a sequence of discrete steps in which the possible moves at each step are probabilistically determined, with the probability of the different moves remaining unchanged throughout the sequence. Random walks have wide application and have been used as models in decision theory. E.g. in a threshold task, the observer may accumulate successive pieces of probabilistically determined information, each of which successively alters the value of an internal variable. The decision is taken when that variable either exceeds one threshold or drops below another, i.e. when the random walk reaches a boundary.

range. (Statistics) 1. The interval between the highest and lowest scores in a distribution. 2. A crude measure of dispersion, in which the lowest score is subtracted from the highest.

range effect. Any effect on subjects' performance of the range of the stimuli presented. E.g. in psychophysical experiments there is a tendency to overestimate stimuli below the mean and underestimate those above the mean; similarly in pursuit tracking there is a tendency to undershoot with relatively large target movements and to overshoot with relatively small ones. *Compare* CENTRAL TENDENCY (2).

rank. The ordinal position of an item on a dimension as determined by counting the items from one or other end of the dimension until that item is reached. When applied to numerical data, ranking preserves no information about the size of the scores or of their differences. *See also* NON–PARAMETRIC STATISTICS and ORDINAL SCALE.

rank difference correlation. A synonym for RANK ORDER CORRELATION.

Rankian therapy. A synonym for WILL THERAPY.

ranking, method of. A psychophysical scaling method in which the subject is asked to rank all the items in a set along the subjective dimension to be scaled. An ordinal scale is produced.

rank order correlation. (Statistics) A nonparametric method for determining the correlation between the scores of two variables, based on ranking each set of scores and comparing the rank orders of pairs of scores. Examples are the SPEARMAN RANK ORDER CORRELATION and KENDALL'S TAU.

Ranschurgsches phenomenon. The phenomenon that in SERIAL RECALL a string of letters

(or other items) is better recalled if no letter (or item) is repeated than if there are repeats.

Ranvier's node. A synonym for NODE OF RANVIER.

raphe nucleus. A complex of nuclei in the reticular formation lying on the midline of the brainstem; it is connected to the thalamus and the grey nuclei of the spinal cord. It contains much serotonin and is probably implicated in the control of sleep.

rapid eye movements. The jerky eye movements that occur in REM SLEEP.

rapid eye movement sleep. *See* REM SLEEP.

rapid serial presentation. The successive presentation in the same place of consecutive words from a text. Subjects rapidly adapt to it and quickly come to read the material so presented as well as in normal reading.

rarefaction click. A TRANSIENT caused by a sudden drop in air pressure at the ear.

RAS. An abbreviation for RETICULAR ACTIVATING SYSTEM.

rate-dependence effect. The phenomenon that the effect of a drug (usually) depends on the prior value of the physical or psychological variable it effects, e.g. antidepressants may alleviate the mood of someone depressed, but have no effect on a non-depressed person.

rate of responding. A synonym for RESPONSE RATE.

rating, method of. Any technique for constructing a PSYCHOPHYSICAL SCALE based on the subjects rating the items on the dimension to be scaled.

rating scale. Any scale used to rate a person (or thing). Rating scales can contain lines with the end points labelled (e.g. 'bad' and 'good'), and the rater makes a mark along the line to indicate where the person being rated falls on this dimension; or they may contain a series of terms describing different positions along a dimension of personality of which the rater has to check one, and so on.

ratio estimation. A synonym for MAGNITUDE ESTIMATION.

ratio estimation, method of. A psychophysical scaling method, in which the observer has to estimate the ratio of the magnitudes of two stimuli presented, thus producing a ratio scale.

rational-emotive therapy (RET). A form of psychotherapy invented by Ellis, based on the idea that emotional disorders are caused by seeing the world falsely; the therapy attempts to change the patient's false attitudes and beliefs, and is highly directive. In some ways it resembles cognitive therapy (and behaviour therapy) but it is more confrontational and directive.

rational equation. An equation derived from a theory or from a set of plausible assumptions, rather than one designed *ad hoc* to fit a particular body of data. *Contrast* EMPIRICAL EQUATION.

rationalism. 1. The philosophical doctrine that holds that truth can be obtained by rational thought without experiments or observations. 2. The doctrine that some ideas or principles of reasoning are inborn.

rationalization. (Psychoanalysis) A defence mechanism in which spurious but plausible reasons are produced to explain aspects of one's behaviour or feelings, thus disguising the fact that they come from repressed wishes.

rational problem solving. Solving problems by rational thought rather than blindly by trial and error.

rational psychotherapy. Short for RATIONAL-EMOTIVE THERAPY.

rational type. *See* FUNCTION TYPES.

rational uniformity. Social compliance by an individual, based on the idea that in the long run such compliance will be good for everyone.

ratio production. *See* PRODUCTION, METHOD OF.

ratio reinforcement schedule. A REINFORCEMENT SCHEDULE in which reinforcement is delivered after a given number of responses (FIXED RATIO SCHEDULE) or after a variable number of responses usually with a constant mean (VARIABLE RATIO SCHEDULE).

ratio scale. A scale having a true zero, with equal intervals representing equal increments in magnitude of whatever is being measured. Length measured in metres is an example of such a scale. It is legitimate to carry out all arithmetic operations on a ratio scale.

ratio scaling. Any method of psychophysical scaling that yields a ratio scale, e.g. MAGNITUDE ESTIMATION, METHOD OF and PRODUCTION, METHOD OF.

ratio strain. The phenomenon that response rate drops with increasingly high ratio schedules: if they are high enough, responding ceases altogether.

Rat man. Freud's name for one of his most famous patients, who had an obsessional fear of rats. Despite Freud's claims, the treatment was a failure.

RATN. An abbreviation for RECURSIVE AUGMENTED TRANSITION NETWORK.

Raven's Progressive Matrices. An intelligence test mainly used for people of high IQ, in which a series of sets of related abstract figures are shown with one missing from each set; the testee has to select from several alternatives the drawing that completes the pattern exhibited by the relationships between those in the set presented. The problems become progressively more difficult over the series.

raw primal sketch. *See* PRIMAL SKETCH.

raw score. A score or aggregate of scores directly derived from an experiment or test and not transformed by e.g. being converted to a percentage, a logarithm, or units of standard deviation.

Rayleigh equation. An equation giving the relative amounts of a spectral red and green needed by someone with normal colour vision to match a spectral yellow. *Compare* ANOMALOSCOPE.

Rayleigh's disc. A method of determining sound intensity by measuring the torque on a disc suspended on a thread in the acoustic field.

RCBF. An abbreviation for REGIONAL CEREBRAL BLOOD FLOW.

RDC. An abbreviation for RESEARCH DIAGNOSTIC CRITERIA.

reactance theory. The hypothesis that a person will react against attempts to control his freedom of choice, both by coming to value more anything from which he is debarred and by adopting attitudes contrary to those being imposed upon him.

reaction. (Psychiatry) The pattern of symptoms in a mental disorder.

reaction chain. A synonym for CHAIN REFLEX.

reaction formation. (Psychoanalysis) A defence mechanism in which someone adopts an attitude diametrically opposed to his unconscious wishes. A standard case is the opponent of pornography, who gains a libidinous thrill from hunting it down.

reaction latency ($_st_r$). *See* HULLIAN THEORY.

reaction potential ($_sE_R$). Hull's term for the current strength of a learned response before generalization occurs. It is derived from HABIT STRENGTH, DRIVE STRENGTH, STIMULUS INTENSITY DYNAMISM, and INCENTIVE MOTIVATION. *See* HULLIAN THEORY.

reaction-specific energy. (Ethology) A synonym for ACTION-SPECIFIC ENERGY.

reaction threshold ($_sL_R$). In Hull's theory, the strength of the MOMENTARY REACTION POTENTIAL that must be reached for a response to be made. *See* HULLIAN THEORY.

reaction time (RT). The time, usually measured in milliseconds, between a stimulus and a person's reaction to it. *See also* COMPLEX REACTION TIME and SIMPLE REACTION TIME.

reaction type. 1. (Psychiatry) A syndrome classified by its predominating symptom or symptoms. 2. (Experimental psychology) The kind of reaction someone is making in a REACTION TIME experiment, in particular whether he is set to concentrate on the stimulus or on the response.

reactive. (Psychiatry) Pertaining to a mental illness caused by a trauma, as opposed to an ENDOGENOUS illness. Since external and internal factors are often simultaneously determinants of mental disorder, the distinction is insecure.

reactive attachment disorder of infancy. A ponderous synonym for HOSPITALISM.

reactive depression. Depression caused by an untoward external event.

reactive inhibition (I_R). Hull's term for the behavioural INHIBITION (1) caused by the work put into a response. The inhibition weakens the response strength only temporarily for it decays rapidly with time. It can, however, be conditioned to stimuli when it becomes CONDITIONED INHIBITION. *See* HULLIAN THEORY.

reactive interaction. The phenomenon that different people perceive and react to the same stimulus differently: hence it has different effects on them. *Compare* EVOCATIVE INTERACTION and PROACTIVE INTERACTION.

reactive measures. A procedure designed to obtain a measure of behaviour which itself changes the behaviour, e.g. openly observing someone.

reactive schizophrenia. Schizophrenia precipitated by a severe social or emotional crisis. *Contrast* PROCESS SCHIZOPHRENIA.

readiness, law of. Thorndike's principle that conduction across a 'conduction unit' is satisfying if it is ready to conduct; the meaning of 'conduction unit' is unclear, but the law appears to be a forerunner of the concept of PREPAREDNESS.

reading epilepsy. A form of epilepsy induced by reading.

reading quotient. A measure of reading ability obtained by dividing a child's score on a reading age test by his chronological age.

reading readiness. The extent to which a child has acquired the skills that will enable him to learn to read.

reading span. The number of words (in practice about three) that can be perceived in a single fixation while reading.

read-only memory (ROM). Memory stored in a computer that can be read but that cannot be altered or erased, e.g. the memory for the computer's operating system.

reafference. A change in stimulation caused not by a change in the environment but by a movement of the observer; e.g. a saccade to the right will cause movement of the visual world to the left. *Contrast* EXAFFERENCE.

real anxiety. Freud's expression for anxiety caused by an external threat, as opposed to anxiety caused by repressed wishes. *Contrast* MORAL ANXIETY and NEUROTIC ANXIETY.

realism. 1. In scholastic philosophy the doctrine that qualities have a real existence regardless of whether they are being perceived. 2. In modern philosophy, the doctrine that physical objects exist and are not merely constructs formed from sensations. *Contrast* IDEALISM.

realism of confidence. The extent to which a person's estimate of the probability of something being the case matches the objective probability.

realistic group conflict theory. The theory that conflict between groups and between societies arises only because they are competing for limited resources.

reality anxiety. A synonym for REAL ANXIETY.

reality orientation. (Psychotherapy) A technique to reduce confusion in disorientated patients by constantly reminding them of reality, e.g. of the time of day, where they are, etc.

reality principle. (Psychoanalysis) The control of behaviour to meet the constraints imposed by the external world, e.g. delaying gratification; this principle is embodied in the ego. *Compare* PLEASURE PRINCIPLE.

reality testing. (Psychoanalysis) The objective evaluation of the external world performed by the ego, which allows a person to distinguish between fact and fantasy.

real motion. Movement of a part of the external world which produces an impression of movement. *Contrast* APPARENT MOTION.

real self. Horney's term for that part of a person which is capable of growth and through which a person may be fulfilled.

real time. (Computing) Pertaining to a computation in which the computer processes external events at the same rate as they occur, rather than lagging behind. E.g. a program might be able to 'understand' a limited fraction of speech, but it would only be processing it in real time if it could respond as the speech arrived, rather than storing it and completing much of the processing later.

rearrangement. *See* PERCEPTUAL REARRANGEMENT.

reasoning. *See* PROBLEM SOLVING.

rebound effect. (Neurophysiology) The temporary strengthening of a process when an antagonistic process stops, e.g. a burst of firing (excitation) following a period of inhibition.

rebound illusion. The phenomenon that, if a moving object is being tracked by the eyes and suddenly stops, it appears to rebound backwards.

rebound insomnia. Insomnia caused by withdrawal from hypnotic drugs.

rebus. A symbol that represents a speech sound by depicting an object whose name has the sound to be represented; e.g. the word 'I' might be represented by a picture of an eye. Some writing systems originated in this way.

recall. Bringing material in memory to mind.

recall method. Testing memory by requiring the subject to recall the items to which he has been exposed. *See also* FREE RECALL and SERIAL RECALL, and *contrast* RECOGNITION METHOD.

recapitulation theory. The doctrine that in ontogenetic development organisms repeat the stages they went through in phylogenetic development.

received pronunciation (RP). The standard pronunciation of English by the upper-middle classes of southern England, as used until recently by BBC announcers; it is free from regional dialect and is posh without being too posh.

receiver. Any device that accepts a message and transduces it into a different form for further use.

receiver-operating characteristic curve (ROC curve). A plot of the data from the experiment designed for the application of SIGNAL DETECTION THEORY. The probability of a hit, given that the signal is present, is plotted on the vertical axis and the probability of a false alarm, given that the signal is not present, is plotted on the horizontal axis. A diagonal line drawn from the bottom left-hand corner represents chance performance (i.e. equal proportions of hits and false alarms); lines above this represent increasingly good detection; *see* figure below. Changes in the number of hits (and the concomitant change in the number of false alarms) can be manipulated by changing the setting of the RESPONSE

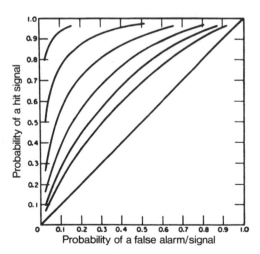

receiver-operating characteristic curve

CRITERION, e.g. by changing the payoff ratio of hits to correctly responding that the stimulus is not present.

recency, law of. The principle that the more recently material was learned the more likely it is to be remembered.

recency effect. 1. (Learning) The phenomenon that in free recall, the items presented at the end of a list have a higher probability of being recalled than those in the middle. 2. (Social psychology) The phenomenon that in forming attitudes the most recent events may have most influence. *Contrast* PRIMACY EFFECT.

receptive aphasia. Impairment or loss of speech comprehension, combined with some ability to speak. *See* WERNICKE'S APHASIA.

receptive behaviour. Female sexual behaviour (e.g. lordosis) made in response to courtship behaviour by a male to encourage or permit intercourse.

receptive character. Fromm's term for a passive, dependent personality.

receptive dysphasia. A synonym for RECEPTIVE APHASIA.

receptive-expressive aphasia. A synonym for GLOBAL ASPHASIA.

receptive fields. The retinal or sensory area that when stimulated can affect the firing of a particular higher order cell. Nowadays they are divided into the **classical receptive field** in which stimuli can directly excite or inhibit firing, and the surrounding **non-classical receptive field**, in which stimuli cannot directly excite or inhibit the cell, but can modulate the firing produced by stimuli in the classical receptive field, as e.g. in the case of END-STOPPED RECEPTIVE FIELDS.

receptive oral phase. A synonym for PASSIVE ORAL PHASE.

receptor. 1. A nerve cell that transduces a physical stimulus (whether of internal or external origin) into neural excitation or inhibition and that synapses with a higher-order nerve cell. The different receptor types are photic, mechanical, chemical, and thermal. 2. A molecular configuration on the surface of a nerve cell to which neurotransmitters (and other substances including some hormones and drugs) can attach, thereby increasing or decreasing the tendency of the cell to fire.

receptor potential. A synonym for GENERATOR POTENTIAL.

receptor site. A synonym for RECEPTOR (2).

recessive. (Genetics) Pertaining to an ALLELE which, when combined with another allele of a pair, does not express itself phenotypically; or pertaining to a trait that is produced only by two recessive genes. *Compare* DOMINANT.

recidives in schizophrenia. Schizophrenia with long periods of remission interspersed with acute episodes of the illness.

reciprocal altruism. Altruism based on an explicit or implicit pact that each individual will help the other.

reciprocal inhibition. 1. (Neurophysiology) A synonym for RECIPROCAL INNERVATION. 2. (Experimental psychology) Mutual inhibition between two responses. *See* RECIPROCAL INHIBITION THERAPY. 3. A synonym for RECIPROCAL INTERFERENCE.

reciprocal inhibition therapy. A behaviour therapy technique, in which an attempt is made to strengthen a response that is antagonistic to one which it is desired to eliminate. E.g. a phobic patient may be taught to relax in the presence of the phobic stimulus, since relaxation is incompatible with anxiety.

reciprocal innervation. Neuronal wiring that causes a system to work effectively by ensuring opposite inhibitory and excitatory effects on parts with opposing actions, e.g. by inhibiting contraction of a flexor muscle when the corresponding extensor muscle is contracted.

reciprocal interference. A reduction in the ability to perform two learnt tasks caused by the INTERFERENCE (1) of each on the other.

reciprocal punishment. Piaget's expression for the idea, entertained by children from about 8 years old, that the punishment should

fit the crime; e.g. a child who breaks another child's toy should have one of his own broken.

reciprocal translocation. The exchange of parts between two paired chromosomes.

reciprocity. In morality, the idea that good deeds should be reciprocated by other good deeds. It is also applied sometimes to bad deeds; *see* RECIPROCAL PUNISHMENT.

recognition method, recognition procedure. An experimental method for studying memory: the subject is asked which items he recognizes in a set containing items to which he has previously been exposed and ones to which he has not. *Contrast* RECALL METHOD.

recognition span. A synonym for READING SPAN.

recognition vocabulary. A synonym for PASSIVE VOCABULARY.

recombination. (Genetics) The combining of genetic material from different sources, e.g. from two parents.

reconditioning. 1. Strengthening a weak conditioned reponse by further conditioning. 2. Conditioning a new conditioned response to a conditioned stimulus to which some other conditioned response has been attached.

reconditioning therapy. A form of behaviour therapy in which RECONDITIONING (2) is attempted by conditioning a new and more adaptive response to a stimulus to which an unadaptive response has been conditioned, e.g. by conditioning the patient to relax in the presence of a phobic stimulus.

reconstruction. 1. (Psychoanalysis) The interpretation of information about a person's past in order to throw light on his present psychological state. 2. *See* MEMORY RECONSTRUCTION.

reconstruction method. An experimental technique for studying memory, by presenting the subject with some features of the material to be recalled and asking him to recall the whole.

recovery of function. Improvement in function impaired by damage to the central nervous system. It may occur for a variety of reasons, e.g. new learning, performance of the function by other parts of the nervous system, or reduction in oedema.

recovery time. A synonym for REFRACTORY PERIOD.

recruiting waves. EEG waves recorded in the cortex and caused by electrical stimulation of the thalamus; waves of increasing amplitude are generated with repeated stimulation.

recruitment. 1. (Neurophysiology) The increase in the number of nerve cells firing in response to an excitatory stimulus as the duration of the stimulus is prolonged. 2. (Experimental psychology) An abnormally rapid increase in the sensation of loudness occurring with an increase in the intensity of a sound that is just above the threshold for hearing; the condition often occurs in people with nerve deafness.

rectilinear relationship. A relationship between two variables that can be represented graphically by straight lines.

rectus muscles. *See* LATERAL RECTUS, MEDIAL RECTUS, SUPERIOR RECTUS, and INFERIOR RECTUS.

recurrent collateral. *See* COLLATERAL.

recurrent inhibition. Inhibition of a neuron produced by its own firing, e.g. an alpha motor neuron stimulates Renshaw cells, which in turn inhibit the motor neuron.

recurring-figures test. A test of visual memory in which a person is shown a series of figures; on subsequent presentations of those and other figures he has to say which he has seen before.

recursion. (Mathematics and Computing) A function defined in terms of itself or a programming routine that calls itself. E.g. factorial N ($f(N)$) may be computed by a routine in which n is initially set equal to N; if $n = 1$ or $n = 0 f(N) = 1$, otherwise $n = f(n \times (n - 1))$.

recursive augmented transition network (RATN). *See* AUGMENTED TRANSITION NETWORK.

red. *See* SPECTRAL HUE.

red cone. *See* CONE.

red–green colour blindness. Difficulty in distinguishing reds from greens. It can be caused by PROTANOPIA, DEUTERANOPIA, PROTANOMALY or DEUTERANOMALY.

redirected activity. (Ethology) The release of ACTION SPECIFIC ENERGY by directing the response to a stimulus other than the normal releasing stimulus. *Contrast* DISPLACEMENT ACTIVITY and VACUUM ACTIVITY.

red nucleus. A nucleus in the TEGMENTUM belonging to the EXTRAPYRAMIDAL MOTOR SYSTEM and receiving fibres from the CEREBELLUM.

reduced cue. A changed or weakened stimulus; after learning has taken place to the original cue, the reduced cue may be sufficient to evoke the learned response.

reduced vowel. A synonym for SCHWA.

reduction division. The production in MEIOSIS of gametes, each of which has half the number of genes of the parent cell.

reductionism. (Philosophy) The doctrine that it is always in principle possible to explain complex phenomena in terms of their less complex constituents, e.g. that behaviour may be explained in terms of the nervous system, the nervous system in terms of chemistry, chemistry in terms of physics. Although higher-level phenomena may in principle be reducible in this sense, understanding them involves developing concepts appropriate to explanation at the higher level. Such concepts often have no relevance to lower-level explanations, e.g. the concepts of memory search or receptive field have no relevance to physics.

reduction screen. A pin-hole in a screen through which the subject views a scene; this device removes many of the depth cues, e.g. accommodation, convergence, stereopsis and motion parallax.

reductive interpretation. Jung's expression for interpreting behaviour as symptomatic of some unconscious process.

redundancy. (Information theory) The extent to which (using optimal coding) a message could be shortened without losing any information. Language is redundant at all levels, e.g. in an English text the letters t h e i can only be followed by two of the total of 26 letters (to make 'their' or 'theism'). The more redundant a message is, the more predictable it is.

re-educative therapy. Psychotherapy in which one of the aims is to train people to deal more effectively with social interactions and personal relationships.

re-enactment. Re-experiencing with the appropriate emotions past events, usually from childhood, that are (or are thought to be) particularly significant in a person's life.

re-entrant. A pathway, especially in the nervous system, that, where one region provides an input to a second, returns from the second to the first. The function of such pathways is known only to Edelman and God.

reference. 1. The relationship between an expression or speech act and its REFERENT. *Contrast* SENSE. 2. A synonym for REFERENT; this usage should be discouraged. 3. *See* DELUSIONS OF REFERENCE.

reference axes. A synonym for REFERENCE VECTORS.

reference group. Any group (e.g. family, classmates, or profession) with which a person identifies, and whose beliefs and attitudes he tends to adopt. *See also* NEGATIVE REFERENCE GROUP and POSITIVE REFERENCE GROUP.

reference memory. A synonym for SEMANTIC MEMORY.

reference stimulus. A synonym for COMPARISON STIMULUS.

reference vectors. (Factor analysis) The positions to which the original factor axes have been rotated in order that the test projections onto them produce a SIMPLE STRUCTURE.

referent. The object, event or idea signified by an expression or by (a part of) a speech act. *Contrast* SENSE.

referred pain. A sensation of pain in a part of the body other than that from which the pain originates, e.g. pain in the upper arms caused by angina.

referred sensation. A sensation that is felt at a point of the body other than the one stimulated.

reflectance. The ratio of the luminance of a surface to its illuminance; i.e. the ratio of the intensity of light reflected to the intensity of incident light corrected by the chromatic sensitivity of the eye. *See also* REFLECTION SPECTRUM.

reflection. (Statistics) In factor analysis, the changing of the signs in some of the rows or columns of a matrix.

reflection densitometry. A synonym for RETINAL DENSITOMETRY.

reflection effect. (Decision theory) *See* PROSPECT THEORY.

reflection of feeling. In psychotherapy, particularly non-directive therapy, a statement by the counsellor that gives the essence of what the client has said in a form that will make him appreciate its true significance.

reflection spectrum. The proportion of incident light of each wavelength reflected from a given surface.

reflective pronoun. *See* PRONOUN.

reflex. 1. An innate and involuntary reaction, e.g. an eyeblink to an approaching object, leg withdrawal to pain on the sole of the foot, etc. 2. Any largely involuntary response whether innate or learned, e.g. a conditioned reflex; the blurring of the distinction between innate and learned responses is unfortunate.

reflect act. (Psychoanalysis) The process by which an external or internal stimulus provokes an action, so named by Freud to emphasize the (misleading) similarity with the neurophysiological concept of a reflex arc.

reflex arc. The nervous circuit mediating a REFLEX (1), e.g. an afferent neuron synapsing in the spinal cord with an effector neuron; interneurons may also be involved.

reflex association. Bekhterev's expression for CONDITIONED RESPONSE.

reflex epilepsy. Epilepsy triggered by a sensory stimulus, e.g. a flickering light.

reflex excitability. The degree to which the strength of a reflex varies depending on the organism's state, e.g. alert, drowsy, asleep.

reflex facilitation. An increase in the strength of a reflex caused by factors that do not directly produce it, e.g. grapsing an object hard increases the strength of the PATELLAR REFLEX.

reflex inhibition. A synonym for RECIPROCAL INNERVATION.

reflexology. The doctrine (an extreme form of behaviourism) that all behaviour can be explained in terms of innate and conditioned reflexes.

reflex relation. A relation in which it always follows that if xRy is true then yRx is true, where R is the relation and x and y its arguments, e.g. the relationship of being a sibling.

reflex reserve. The strength of the tendency to respond after operant learning, which determines the total number of responses an organism will make when extinction is given. It is one of Skinner's few intervening variables. *Compare* OPERANT RESERVE.

reflex sensitization. The increased likelihood of a response being made to a neutral stimulus after it has been repeatedly elicited by another stimulus.

refraction. The change in the direction of light that occurs when it passes from a medium of one REFRACTIVE INDEX to another. The angle through which the light is bent depends on the difference in the refractive

indices of the media, and on its angle of incidence to the surface through which it passes; the angular change is zero if the light falls perpendicularly on that surface and increases as it falls more obliquely. Different wavelengths are refracted through different angles (*see* CHROMATIC ABERRATION).

refractive error. Any blurring or degradation of an image caused by imperfections in the refractive properties of an optical system, such as the eye.

refractive index. The ratio of the speed of light in a vacuum to the speed of light in a given medium, which varies with wavelength. This ratio determines the angle through which light passing from one optic medium to another will be bent. The sine of the angle of incidence divided by the sine of the angle of refraction is equal to the refractive index of the second medium divided by the refractive index of the first.

refractory period, refractory phase. 1. (Neurophysiology) The brief period after a neuron has fired, during which its tendency to fire again is decreased. Immediately after firing, it cannot fire at all for about 1 or 2 msec (**absolute refractory period**), and for a further period of up to about 10 msec its tendency to fire is reduced, though it will fire to a sufficiently strong stimulus (**relative refractory period**). 2. *See* PSYCHOLOGICAL REFRACTORY PERIOD.

regional cerebral blood flow (RCBF). Blood flow in a part of the brain. Since it increases with increases in neuronal activity, the regions active during a given task can be determined by measuring it, using such methods as the PET scan.

region of rejection. (Statistics) A set of values such that if a test statistic falls within it the null hypothesis under test is rejected.

registration. The initial formation of a representation of a stimulus.

regnancy. Murray's term for all the brain processes occurring at one moment.

regression. 1. (Psychology) A return to an earlier (usually childish) mode of thinking, feeling or behaving, particularly in psycholanalysis where it implies abandoning the ego's grip on reality and returning to earlier methods of dealing with libidinal urges. *See also* HYPNOTIC REGRESSION and *compare* PRIMITIVIZATION. 2. (Statistics) Any technique enabling one to predict the values of one variable from a knowledge of those of other variables; e.g. the use of an equation (a REGRESSION EQUATION) to predict driving skill from blood alcohol. *See also* MULTIPLE REGRESSION. 3. *See* FILIAL REGRESSION. 4. *See* PHENOMENAL REGRESSION TO THE REAL OBJECT.

regression analysis. Any statistical analysis of REGRESSION (2).

regression coefficient. The coefficient of an independent or predictor variable in a REGRESSION EQUATION.

regression curve. A synonym for REGRESSION LINE.

regression equation. An equation describing a REGRESSION LINE or surface.

regression line. A line which predicts the values of one variable from those of another. A regression line may be fitted by eye or by the LEAST SQUARES METHOD.

regression time. The amount of time someone reading spends returning to words he has already read.

regression to the real object. Short for PHENOMENAL REGRESSION TO THE REAL OBJECT.

regression towards the mean. (Statistics) The principle that if the value of one variable is used to predict probabilistically the value of a second variable, the value of the predicted variable is likely to be closer to its mean than that of the predictor variable. *Compare* FILIAL REGRESSION.

regressive eye movement. In reading, an eye movement that carries the eye back to a point on the line or page that has already been fixated.

regret theories. (Decision making) Theories that account for some violations of utility theory in terms of the regret (or rejoicing) a person expects to feel for a given outcome compared with others. E.g. the CERTAINTY EFFECT may occur because the subject expects to feel regret if he chooses a gamble of high EXPECTED VALUE but comparatively low probability and the gamble does not come off.

rehabilitation. The restoration of function in a psychiatric or neurological patient by training, guidance, etc.

rehearsal. 1. Repeatedly going over material with a view to memorizing it or retaining it in memory. 2. Repeatedly bringing to mind the members of a list of (usually verbal) items in order to maintain them in the SHORT-TERM STORE.

rehearsal loop. A synonym for ARTICULATORY REHEARSAL LOOP.

reification. Treating an abstract idea as a real or concrete entity, a mistaken form of thinking common in children, schizophrenics, and psychologists.

Reil. *See* ISLAND OF REIL.

reinforcement. 1. Any stimulus or event that increases the probability of an organism repeating the response it has just made (INSTRUMENTAL LEARNING) or the unconditioned stimulus in classical conditioning (whose presence increases the probability of the conditioned response being evoked by the conditioned stimulus). 2. The process of strengthening a response as a result of the occurrence of a reinforcement (1). *See* NEGATIVE REINFORCEMENT, PRIMARY REINFORCEMENT and SECONDARY REINFORCEMENT. *See also* DELAYED REINFORCEMENT, DIFFERENTIAL REINFORCEMENT, GRADIENT OF REINFORCEMENT, PARTIAL REINFORCEMENT. It is a pity that the use of the term is not confined to sense (2), since another term (REINFORCER) is available for sense (1).

reinforcement density. The rate at which reinforcements are delivered on a REINFORCEMENT SCHEDULE.

reinforcement gradient. *See* GRADIENT OF REINFORCEMENT.

reinforcement schedule. Any experimental contingency under which the rate, number, or timing of an organism's responses are made to govern the availability of reinforcement. *See* SIMPLE SCHEDULE and HIGHER-ORDER SCHEDULE (the two major divisions).

reinforcer. A synonym for REINFORCEMENT (1).

Reissner's membrane. The membrane in the COCHLEA that separates the SCALA MEDIA from the SCALA VESTIBULI.

relational learning. A synonym for 1. CONFIGURATIONAL LEARNING; 2. TRANSPOSITIONAL LEARNING.

relative centrality. In a communication network, the centrality of a particular member, measured by dividing the sum of the distances from him to all others by the sum of all the distances in the network.

relative deprivation. The principle that in social exchange a person will feel satisfied if he is gaining as much (or losing no more than) those other people with whom he regards himself as comparable. *Compare* EXCHANGE THEORY.

relative motion. The difference in the motion of one part of the visual field from another (usually adjacent) part.

relative pronoun. *See* PRONOUN.

relative refractory period. *See* REFRACTORY PERIOD.

relativism. The doctrine that knowledge is not objective but is determined by culture and other adventitious factors; many accept the relativism of ethical or aesthetic beliefs, but some bounders have gone so far as to maintain that even scientific knowledge is relative.

relaxation principle. (Psychoanalysis) Ferenczi's method of treating patients in which he substituted an affectionate approach for the coldness of the traditional analyst, on the grounds that a more relaxed patient would allow repressed material to emerge more readily.

relaxation technique. (AI) A technique for assigning globally consistent labels or values to the nodes in a network, making use of local constraints by iteratively propagating them through the network. As an example, consider an array of nodes arranged in rows and columns with each node having an excitatory connection to neighbouring nodes in the same row and an inhibitory connection to neighbouring nodes in the same column. A subset of these nodes is excited by an external input. The strength of firing of each node as determined by the input and the internal connections is now calculated. Some excited nodes will have a decreased firing rate because of inhibition from neighbouring nodes. This decrease will alter the firing rate of nodes to which they are connected, so the calculation is iterated until all nodes settle into a stable state. *Compare* ANNEALING.

relaxation therapy. *See* PROGRESSIVE RELAXATION.

relearning method. A measure of memory for previously learned material, in terms of the savings in time or trials to relearn, compared to the original learning.

release from proactive interference. The improvement in learning that occurs when someone who has been learning one kind of material (e.g. names of animals) and therefore building up PROACTIVE INTERFERENCE is switched to learning another kind of material (e.g. names of flowers).

releaser. (Ethology) A stimulus that innately releases a species-specific response such as flight, courtship, or sexual activity; such stimuli are usually very simple, e.g. a male robin will respond with territorial behaviour to any object of about the size of a robin that has a red front. *See* INNATE RELEASING MECHANISM.

release therapy. Psychotherapy that encourages the client to give vent to his emotions on the grounds that this will help him.

releasing factor. Chemicals that stimulate the anterior pituitary to release a particular hormone or that inhibit its release.

releasing stimulus. A synonym for RELEASER.

reliability. Of psychometric tests, the extent to which the same test applied on different occasions, or different versions of the same test or different questions in the test, yield the same result. A test could be very reliable, i.e. completely consistent, while having low VALIDITY.

reliability coefficient. A correlation coefficient run on two sets of scores from the same test and therefore measuring the test's reliability.

reminiscence. (Learning) The phenomenon that after a task has been partially learnt, performance on it may be better when tested some time after learning has occurred than when tested immediately afterward. It occurs especially after MASSED PRACTICE.

remission. The temporary abatement of the symptoms of an illness.

remote association. A mental association between two items not presented contiguously (usually used of experiments on rote learning).

remote masking. Masking of low-frequency tones by high-frequency noise.

REM sleep. A commonly used abbreviation for **rapid eye movement sleep**. This kind of SLEEP is reached after descending to stage III or IV and then ascending through stage II. It occurs throughout the night with a periodicity of about 90 minutes. It is characterized by fast, jerky eye movements, dreams, a strong theta rhythm, and an absence of delta waves in the EEG.

renifleur. A person with a morbid interest in odours, especially one who derives sexual excitement from them.

renin. A hormone from the kidney, released on stimulation of the sympathetic system. It indirectly increases thirst.

Renshaw cell. A small neuron which is fired by a motor neuron and which has an inhibitory action on that neuron, thus preventing repeated firing and overcontraction of a muscle. *Compare* RECURRENT INHIBITION.

renunciation. (Psychoanalysis) The refusal of the EGO to yield to the ID's impulses.

repeated measures factorial design. A factorial design in which all subjects are presented with a succession of experimental conditions. Hence each subject is repeatedly measured: the saving in subjects and the belief that these designs control for individual differences has led to their widespread use by psychologists. Awareness of the highly restrictive assumptions behind the designs is not so widespread.

Repertory Grid Test. Kelley's modified form of the Role Construct Repertory Test in which respondents are asked in what respect two out of three persons (or objects or events) are the same as one another and different from the third. A grid is thus formed, with people (or events or objects) running horizontally, and the elicited constructs (in terms of bipolar opposites like loving hating, noisy quiet) plotted vertically. The technique is intended to reveal how a person sees the world and with what set of constructs he operates. Unlike most personality tests, this one uses only concepts or constructs emitted by the respondent, rather than ones presented to him. There are several modifications of the technique.

repetition, law of. A synonym for FREQUENCY, LAW OF.

repetition-compulsion. 1. (Psychoanalysis) The urge to re-experience emotional traumas from early life in different situations; a man may adopt the same attitudes to his wife that he exhibited earlier to his mother. 2. A compulsion to perform an act (e.g. washing) over and over again.

repetition effect. A modern (and for once helpful) synonym for RANSCHURGSHES PHENOMENON.

repetition priming. Better recognition of a word because of recent exposure to it, often without conscious awareness of the repetition.

replacement therapy. 1. (Neurology) Giving a substance (e.g. dopamine) thought to be underactive in the brain in order to restore a capacity (e.g. motor coordination). 2. (Addiction) Giving addicts an alternative substance that has the same effects as the substance to which they are addicted or giving the substance to which they are addicted by a less hazardous method. E.g. in **nicotine replacement therapy**, providing nicotine by a patch on the skin instead of through cigarettes.

replicate. 1. (Experimental psychology) To repeat someone else's experiments in the hope of proving him wrong, or an experiment of one's own in the hope of proving oneself right. 2. (Statistics) To repeat an experiment or survey so as to increase precision and reduce sampling error.

replication therapy. (Behaviour therapy) The reproduction of a situation close to real life in order to examine the patient's reaction or to train him to react more appropriately.

representation. A model or description of anything, particularly in the mind or in a computer program.

representation stage. Piaget's expression for the period from two to eleven years of age over which the child is learning to form and manipulate concepts of concrete things. It is composed of the PREOPERATIONAL STAGE and CONCRETE OPERATION STAGE.

representative. A SPEECH ACT in which the speaker gives his view about a proposition (e.g. by assenting, doubting, etc.).

representativeness heuristic. The tendency to classify something as a member of a class because it has many of the typical features of that class.

representative sample. A sample that matches the population from which it is drawn on all characteristics or (more usually) on those that are thought to be relevant to the study being undertaken.

representative score. (Statistics) The mean or some other measure of central tendency.

repression. (Psychoanalysis) The process of removing from consciousness, or preventing the emergence into consciousness, of material or wishes originating in the ID which would produce anxiety or guilt; it is the most important single defence mechanism. Three different kinds of repression have been distinguished: (i) in **primal repression**, wishes from the id are prevented from reaching

consciousness; (ii) in **primary repression**, anxiety-provoking material already in consciousness is removed and prevented from returning; (iii) in **secondary repression**, material in consciousness that might remind the person of material already repressed is removed from consciousness.

reproduction, method of. 1. (Memory) A procedure used in studying memory in which the subject has to reproduce the material learned. 2. (Psychophysics) a synonym for ADJUSTMENT, METHOD OF (1). 3. (Psychophysics) A synonym for PRODUCTION, METHOD OF.

reproductive interference. A decrement in the ability to reproduce learned material caused by the learning of other material. See PROACTIVE INTERFERENCE and RETROACTIVE INTERFERENCE.

REP test. An abbreviation for ROLE CONSTRUCT REPERTORY TEST.

reptilian brain. See TRIUNE BRAIN.

Rescorla–Wagner theory. A theory of classical conditioning, whose most basic postulate is that the increment in the CS–CR association on any one trial is a descreasing function of the predictability of the CS.

Research Diagnostic Criteria (RDC). A set of criteria (e.g. 'self-reproach', 'poor appetite') a specified number of which must be present in order to establish that the testee has a particular form of mental illness.

reserpine. An alkaloid that is a major tranquillizer. It was formerly employed as an antipsychotic but is no longer used since it can produce depression and seizures. It interferes with the synthesizing and storage of norepinephrine in the postganglionic terminals of the autonomic system.

residual schizophrenia. A diagnosis made when a person has had at least one episode of schizophrenia, and, although not currently psychotic, has some remaining symptoms such as illogical thinking or inappropriate affect.

residual variance. A synonym for ERROR VARIANCE.

residues. *See* DAY RESIDUES.

residue tone. A tone that can occur when a number of harmonics are sounded. The lower ones can usually be resolved as individual tones, but the higher ones cannot be resolved: the tone generated by them is the residue tone.

resinous odour. One of the six so-called primary odours of the ODOUR PRISM, reminiscent of the smell of resin. It is also one of the four odours of the ODOUR SQUARE.

resistance. 1. (Psychoanalysis) The attempt, usually unconscious, by the patient to prevent any of the contents of his unconscious being revealed, particularly in the course of psychoanalytic treatment. 2. The extent to which a medium opposes the flow of electric current. *See* OHM'S LAW.

resistance stage. *See* GENERAL ADAPTATION SYNDROME.

resistance to extinction. The strength of the tendency to continue to perform a learned response after reinforcement has been withdrawn, measured e.g. in terms of the number of trials taken before an organism ceases to respond.

resolution. A synonym for ACUITY.

resolution phase. *See* SEXUAL RESPONSE CYCLE.

resolution principle. A method of making inferences in the predicate calculus. The principle relies on demonstrating that if the conclusion to be proved is false, then there is a contradiction in the premises. All the premises are first translated into inclusive disjunctions. It is used in some AI programs, particularly in EXPERT SYSTEMS.

resolution stage. A synonym for RESOLUTION PHASE.

resolving power. Of an optical system, the extent to which it preserves fine detail. The expression is used of the visual system to mean either the resolving power of the eye's optics or VISUAL ACUITY.

resonance. Vibration in a body caused by vibration impinging on it. Depending on its properties, a body will vibrate at particular multiples of the frequency of the impinging vibration.

resonance theory. (Hearing) A synonym for PLACE THEORY.

resonant. (Phonetics) Any speech form in which the mouth resonates: it includes all vowels and [l], [r], [m], [n], [j], and [w].

resource allocation. When someone is performing two or more tasks simultaneously, the amount of processing capacity allocated to each.

respondent. 1. A person who is interviewed or who completes a questionnaire. 2. Any action elicited by a particular stimulus. *Contrast* OPERANT.

respondent conditioning. Skinner's expression for classical conditioning.

response (R). 1. Any of a set of behaviours elicited by a stimulus, all of which have the same effects on the environment (or on the internal milieu) as one another. A bar can be depressed or a letter posted by many different series of muscular contractions. 2. A specific series of muscular contractions, or a glandular secretion, elicited by a stimulus. The early behaviourists used the term in sense (2), mistakenly thinking that was what organisms learned; this use is now rare, though confusion between the two persists. *See also* CONDITIONED RESPONSE, DELAYED RESPONSE, DISCRIMINATIVE RESPONSE.

response amplitude. A measure of RESPONSE STRENGTH based on the response intensity, e.g. on its duration, force (if the response is muscular), or amount (e.g. amount of saliva secreted). *See* HULLIAN THEORY.

response bias. Any tendency to give a particular response or pattern of responses that is not determined by experimental or functional requirements. E.g. in a psychophysical experiment on absolute judgement someone may have a bias towards saying 'yes' too often, or in answering a questionnaire someone may be biased towards saying 'no' after a series of positive answers.

response class. All the RESPONSES (2) that produce the same external outcome. *See* RESPONSE (1).

response compression. The phenomenon that as the intensity of a stimulus is increased above adaptation level the increment in the neural response becomes less and less and eventually flattens off.

response criterion (beta). In SIGNAL DETECTION THEORY, the strength of the stimulus (whether made up of signal plus noise or noise alone), above which the subject makes a positive response, and below which he makes a negative response.

response differentiation. Learning to perform the correct differential responses to different stimuli, where the difficulty of the task lies mainly in learning the different responses rather than in learning to discriminate the stimuli.

response generalization, response equivalence. *See* GENERALIZATION.

response hierarchy. A number of RESPONSES (2) of different strengths that an animal may make in a situation in which learning has occurred; the concept is vague and fails to explain RESPONSE EQUIVALENCE.

response intensity. A rare synonym for RESPONSE AMPLITUDE.

response learning. Learning to solve a task by making a fixed response, rather than by constructing a model of the environment and using that model to plan what to do. The expression is used particularly in the context of maze learning by rats. Consider a rat placed in a cross maze, and always starting from the same point. If it is trained to turn left to reach the goal, and is then started from the end of the arm opposite to the original starting point, response learning is said to have occurred if it continues to turn left at the choice point, thus taking it away from the goal. *Contrast* PLACE LEARNING

response magnitude. A synonym for RESPONSE STRENGTH.

response probability. The probability that a response will be made at a particular stage of learning. It is a measure of RESPONSE STRENGTH.

response rate. The frequency with which a response is made over time, a measure of response strength used particularly in operant experiments.

response set. 1. A readiness to respond to a stimulus with a particular response, particularly if the subject is concentrating on the response he is to make rather than on the stimulus. *Contrast* STIMULUS SET (1). 2. Any tendency to respond to a situation or task in a particular way that is irrelevant to the demands of the situation. E.g. someone may give socially acceptable answers to a questionnaire rather than true ones.

response shock interval. In SIDMAN AVOIDANCE CONDITIONING, the interval between the animal making an avoidance response and the delivery of the next shock when no responses are made in the meantime.

response strength. The strength of a response or of the tendency to make that response. It can be measured in terms of reaction time, probability of occurrence, force, amount (e.g. amount of saliva secreted), duration, trials to extinction, etc. These measures do not always agree – animals can be trained to press a bar weakly, but still show many trials to extinction.

response time. A synonym for REACTION TIME.

response topography. In operant conditioning, the detailed specification of a response and the specification of how alternative responses may substitute for one another; e.g. a rat may press a bar strongly or weakly, and it may press with its forelimb, or rump, and so on.

response unit hypothesis. The hypothesis that the PARTIAL REINFORCEMENT EFFECT occurs because under partial reinforcement the organism has learnt to make a series of responses (a 'unit'). The explanation has some plausibility in free-operant learning, but has little in discrete trials learning.

response variable. The changes in responding (dependent variable) that are contingent on changes in the stimulus or state of the organism (independent variables).

resting potential. The difference in electric charge across a neuron's membrane when it has not been fired for at least a few milliseconds and is not being excited or inhibited by presynaptic neurons; this potential difference is about -70 millivolts, with an excess of negatively charged ions on the inside of the membrane.

restitutional schizophrenia. A stage of partial recovery from schizophrenia, in which the patient is beginning to have a better grasp of reality.

restorative ritual. A compulsion (e.g. constant washing) undertaken to avoid the changes associated with contact with something (e.g. dirt). *Contrast* PREVENTIVE RITUAL.

Restorff effect. *See* VON RESTORFF EFFECT.

restraining force. A synonym for EXTERNAL FORCE OF ORGANIZATION.

restricted code. Bernstein's expression for a way of speaking that tends to be limited to the immediate situation, to use a meagre vocabulary, to contain many pronouns and questions, and to make much use of intonation and gestures to convey meaning. Bernstein thought a restricted code was common among the poor, and alleged they were handicapped at school as a result. *Contrast* ELABORATED CODE.

resultant achievement motivation. The strength of a motive to succeed on a task (as measured by a THEMATIC APPERCEPTION TEST) minus the amount of worry over failing (as measured usually by the TEST ANXIETY QUESTIONNAIRE).

resynthesized speech. The alteration by a machine of human speech that is input to it; e.g. the speech might be altered by having the intonation pattern removed. *Compare* SYNTHESIZED SPEECH.

RET. An abbreviation for RATIONAL-EMOTIVE THERAPY.

retaliative distress. The fear of retaliation

sometimes experienced by a wrongdoer. *Compare* SELF-CONCEPT DISTRESS.

retardation. 1. (Psychiatry) A slowing down of any psychological process; e.g. a depressed person may move around, talk, and think abnormally slowly. 2. *See* MENTAL RETARDATION.

reticular activating system (RAS). Short for ASCENDING RETICULAR ACTIVATING SYSTEM.

reticular formation (RF). A large network of ascending and descending neurons running from the core of the brainstem through the midbrain to the thalamus, from which it projects diffusely to the cortex. It is implicated in arousal, sleep, and attention, bodily posture and visceral functions (e.g. breathing). *See also* ASCENDING RETICULAR ACTIVATING SYSTEM.

reticularist theory. The discarded theory that the brain is a network of continuous fibres, rather than being composed of separate nerve cells. *Compare* NEURON THEORY.

reticular nucleus. Any of several nuclei of the reticular formation lying in the medulla and pons.

reticular nucleus of the thalamus. A sheet of cells surrounding much of the thalamus. They receive excitation from cells passing to and from the cortex and they inhibit other cells in the thalamus. *Distinguish from* RETICULAR FORMATION.

retifism. A fetish in which sexual excitement is derived from shoes.

retina. A layered sheet of nerve cells and blood-vessels covering the central two-thirds of the inner part of the eyeball. In referring to depth in the retina, the layers furthest from the cornea are called **inner layers**, and the layers nearest to the cornea are called **outer layers**. Proceeding from inner to outer layers are the receptors (rods and cones), the bipolar cells, and the ganglion cells whose axons run across the retina to the optic disc where they exit from the retina in the optic nerve. The retina also contains cells whose processes run horizontally: the horizontal cells synapse with receptor and bipolar cells, and the amacrine cells synapse with the bipolar cells and ganglion cells.

retinal. 1. Pertaining to the retina. 2. A molecule based on vitamin A1, which together with OPSIN is a breakdown product of visual photopigment when bleached; it has two forms – *11-cis*-**retinal** which is changed by light into **all-*trans*-retinal**. Only the 11-*cis* form can combine with OPSIN to reform photopigment. **3-dehydroretinal** is a molecule with the same characteristics based on vitamin A2. In addition there is a further molecule, **3-hydroxyretinal** used in invertebrate eyes. A given species uses either A1 or A2 but not both. *See* RHODOPSIN, PORPHYROPSIN, and VISUAL PHOTOPIGMENT.

retinal densitometry. An ingenious method of measuring the spectral sensitivity of long and medium-wavelength cones by using a PROTANOPE, who lacks long-wave photopigment (or DEUTERANOPE who lacks medium wave), and comparing the amount of light of each wavelength reflected from the bleached and unbleached central fovea: the difference represents the light absorbed by the remaining (red or green) pigment. There are too few short-wavelength cells in the centre of the fovea to affect the result.

retinal disparity. A synonym for BINOCULAR DISPARITY.

retinal elements. An obsolete expression for the RODS and CONES.

retinal field. The part of the retinal image that produces a visual percept. In HEMIANOPIA the retinal field is reduced though the image is unchanged.

retinal grey. A synonym for IDIORETINAL LIGHT.

retinal illuminance. A photometric measure of the light falling on the retina, given by multiplying the area of the pupil by its illuminance; the unit of measurement is the TROLAND.

retinal image. The pattern of light on the retina which is the proximal stimulus for vision. *Compare* MENTAL IMAGE and note that, unless the context makes it clear which is meant, it is ambiguous to use the term 'image' without qualification.

retinal light. A synonym for IDIORETINAL LIGHT.

retinal rivalry. A synonym for BINOCULAR RIVALRY.

retinene. The molecule that combines with opsin to form a visual photopigment. The term is being replaced by RETINAL (2) (**retinene 1**) and **3-dehydroretinal** (**retinene 2**), but is useful as a generic term for either.

retinex theory. Land's theory of colour vision; he postulated three systems (retinexes) maximally sensitive to long-, medium-, and short-wavelength light respectively, with local inhibitory interactions between the systems, whose effects spread throughout the visual field. Because the colour seen is assumed to depend on the relative strengths of firing of the retinexes, and these in turn are influenced by interactions between different areas, Land claims to account for colour constancy among other phenomena. *See also* LAND EFFECT.

retinomotor response. The movement of pigment cells in the retina to screen the receptors from bright light or to expose them to dim light; also movements of the receptor cells themselves. These responses occur in fish and in some reptiles and birds.

retinoscope. A device for assessing refractive error, in which a streak of light is projected into the person's eye; its reflection is observed by the examiner, and trial lenses are inserted in the retinoscope until the reflection exactly fills the pupil, a sign that the light is correctly focused.

retinotopic. Pertaining to the topological mapping of the retina onto another area, i.e. neighbouring points on the retina are represented by neighbouring points in the other area. The mapping may be distorted; e.g. much more cortical space is devoted to a unit area of retina in the fovea than in the periphery.

retinula cell. Any of the seven or so receptor cells in the rhabdome of a compound eye.

retreat from reality. A synonym for FLIGHT FROM REALITY.

retrieval. The accessing and recovery of information from memory, whether in an organism or in a computer.

retrieval cue. A cue given to help someone recover an item from memory. E.g. both 'heavy' and 'musical' could serve as cues for 'piano'; which is more effective depends on how the subject originally coded the item to be remembered. *See* ENCODING SPECIFICITY HYPOTHESIS.

retrieving behaviour. The recovery by the parent of young who have strayed from the nest or lair.

retroactive association. A synonym for BACKWARD ASSOCIATION.

retroactive facilitation. Improvement in the performance of a previously learned task as a result of positive transfer from one learned later.

retroactive inhibition (RI). 1. A synonym for RETROACTIVE INTERFERENCE. 2. The process underlying RETROACTIVE INTERFERENCE.

retroactive interference (RI). The impairment of memory for previously learned material (or of performance on a previously learned task), caused by subsequently learning similar material (or a similar task). *Compare* PROACTIVE INTERFERENCE and REPRODUCTIVE INTERFERENCE.

retrograde amnesia. The forgetting of events that occurred before a trauma as a result of the trauma; e.g. a blow to the head often produces amnesia for events immediately preceding it, though some memories may return. *Contrast* ANTEROGRADE AMNESIA.

retrograde degeneration. The degeneration of an axon from the point where it has been damaged towards the cell body.

retrograde transportation. Transportation of substances in a neuron towards the cell body from the direction of the axonal terminals.

retrospective falsification. The unconscious distortion of memory to make the past fit better with present needs.

retrospective research. A synonym for RETROSPECTIVE STUDY.

retrospective study. Research on people who currently have a particular illness, character trait, etc., which aims by examining their past to discover the causal influences at work. For several reasons, such research cannot be as satisfactory as a PROSPECTIVE STUDY. The subjects may be influenced in what they say about the past by their present condition; it is difficult to establish an appropriate control group; and memory for the past, even that of a subject's friends and relatives, is notoriously fallible.

return sweep. In reading, an eye movement that carries the eye back to a point on the line or page that has already been fixated.

reuptake. The reabsorption of a substance, used particularly of the reabsorption of neurotransmitters by the neuronal endings from which they were released.

revealed difference technique. A method of studying interaction in a family by setting them a question and observing the processes by which they come to agree on an answer.

reverberatory circuit, reverberating circuit. A collection of neurons in the brain that contains re-entrant pathways and hence continues to fire for some time after the circuit has been stimulated; the concept, which is a possible explanation of short-term memory, was postulated by Hebb. *See also* CELL ASSEMBLY and PHASE SEQUENCE.

reversal. 1. (Psychoanalysis) An alleged change in libidinal desire to its opposite, e.g. love to hate, sadism to masochism. 2. A synonym for REVERSAL ERROR.

reversal error. Reading a letter or word as its mirror image (e.g. reading 'p' for 'q' or 'dim' for 'mid').

reversal learning. Learning to switch a previously learned discrimination response between two stimuli; e.g. an animal that has been trained to approach a triangle and avoid a square may subsequently be trained to avoid the triangle and approach the square. Depending on the conditions and the species, reversal learning can take more or less long than the original learning. *See also* SERIAL REVERSAL LEARNING.

reversal of affect. A synonym for REVERSAL (1).

reversal shift. The change in reinforcement contingencies that occurs in REVERSAL LEARNING.

reverse halo effect. *See* HALO EFFECT.

reverse tolerance. Increased sensitivity to a drug, occurring with persistent usage; it results in a smaller dose being needed to produce the same effect.

reversibility. *See* REVERSIBLE OPERATIONS.

reversible figure. A figure in which the apparent depth of the surfaces tends to reverse with prolonged inspection, e.g. the NECKER CUBE or the SCHROEDER STAIRCASE. *Compare* AMBIGUOUS FIGURE.

reversible operations. Piaget's expression for any series of mental processes that can be executed in reverse to restore the original state, e.g. addition and subtraction. He maintained that a grasp of these operations is needed for CONSERVATION to occur.

reversible perspective. The tendency for the parts of some ambiguous figures to reverse their apparent relative depth. *Compare* NECKER CUBE.

reversing lenses, reversing prisms. An optical device that reverses the retinal image, either from left to right or from up to down or both; when the device is worn constantly, remarkable adaptation to the reversal occurs over a period of a few days.

reversion. (Genetics) The appearance in one generation of a recessive genetic trait not expressed in the parents but expressed in some earlier generation.

revival. Recall of something hard to recall or not recalled for a long time.

reward. Anything that satisfies or gives pleasure; the meaning is very similar to that of REINFORCER or REINFORCEMENT (1), but whereas 'reinforcement' emphasizes the capacity of an event to strengthen a preceding response, 'reward' emphasizes its capacity to satisfy or give pleasure in return for an organism having made the response. **Negative reward** means PUNISHMENT, and not NEGATIVE REINFORCEMENT.

reward expectancy. Tolman's term for the expectation of a REWARD when an organism is in a situation in which it has previously been rewarded; his theory, unlike most other behavioural theories of learning, postulates that it is this expectancy that governs the organism's responses.

rewrite rule. (Linguistics) In formal grammars, a rule stating how a symbolic expression can or must be rewritten, e.g. $S \rightarrow NP + VP$ (a sentence can be rewritten as noun phrase plus verb phrase). The main aim of generative grammars is to construct rewrite rules that will produce any grammatical sentence and no non-grammatical ones.

RF, rf. An abbreviation for RETICULAR FORMATION.

RFT. An abbreviation for ROD AND FRAME TEST.

RGB system. A system, based on METAMERIC MATCHING, for describing colours in terms of three PRIMARIES (1) (usually at 460, 542, and 700 nm). To describe a given colour the amount of each primary needed is given, e.g. $rR + gG - bB$. The negative sign means that to obtain a match the amount specified has to be added to the colour being matched.

rhabdome. The light-sensitive area of an OMMATIDIUM, which usually contains about 6–8 receptor cells (RETINULA CELLS).

rhabdomere. The inner membrane of a RETINULA CELL, which contains light sensitive pigment.

rhabdophobia. A morbid fear of rods, particularly of being beaten by a rod.

rhathymia. A happy-go-lucky attitude.

rheobase. The minimum current that if applied indefinitely will excite a neuron or produce contraction in a muscle.

rheotaxis, rheotropism. A TROPISM in which the organism orientates itself in water against the direction of the current.

rhinal sulcus. A fissure on the medial surface of the temporal lobe that separates the uncus from the temporal lobe. *See* Appendix 2.

rhinencephalon. Literally, the 'smell brain', but since much of the cortex once thought to be involved in smell in fact has other functions, current usage is vague. It includes the olfactory bulb, the pyriform area, the amygdaloid area, the hippocampus and, according to taste, other parts of the archicortex and palaeocortex.

rhinolalia. Speech with abnormal nasal resonance.

rho (ϱ). (Statistics) 1. The correlation coefficient of a SPEARMAN RANK ORDER CORRELATION. 2. The correlation coefficient of the product-moment correlation of a bivariate normal population.

rhodopsin. The photopigment in the rods of most terrestrial species. It is responsible for SCOTOPIC VISION, and its peak sensitivity in man is at about 500 nm. It is based on vitamin A1 and when bleached decomposes into OPSIN and RETINAL. *Compare* PORPHYROPSIN.

rhombencephalon. A synonym for HIND-BRAIN.

rhypophobia. A morbid fear of faeces or dirt.

RI. An abbreviation for 1. RETROACTIVE INHIBITION; 2. RETROACTIVE INTERFERENCE.

ribonucleic acid (RNA). A nucleic acid made up of a string of nucleotides (adenine, cytosine, guanine, and uracil); it is responsible for the synthesis of amino acids and proteins. There are several kinds. **Messenger RNA** carries the genetic code from the DNA in the nucleus to the ribosomes where proteins are manufactured. 20 different kinds of **transfer RNA** assemble the 20 different amino acids, whose sequencing into proteins is governed by **ribosomal RNA**.

ribosomal RNA. *See* RIBONUCLEIC ACID.

ribosome. A small sac found in the cytoplasm of all cells which is the site at which proteins are constructed.

Ribot's law. The principle that in retrograde amnesia, the older the memory the more likely it is to survive.

Ricco's law. The principle that for small areas of the retina (up to about 10′ diameter at the fovea) the perceived brightness and the brightness threshold depend solely on the amount of light delivered, and are independent of how it is distributed within the given area, i.e. $A \times L = K$ where A is area, L luminance and K a constant. For the law governing larger areas *see* PIPER'S LAW.

right and wrong cases, method of. A synonym for CONSTANT STIMULI, METHOD OF.

right-associate learning. An obsolete synonym for PAIRED ASSOCIATE LEARNING.

right-branching tree. A tree in which the rightmost nodes branch more than the leftmost. In generative grammar, 'the door of the house of my father' is a construction based on a right-branching tree.

righting reflex. Any reflex that corrects an organism's balance or turns it the right way up.

rigidity constraint. The assumption that bodies are rigid; it is used in deriving depth from motion.

Ringelmann effect. A synonym for SOCIAL LOAFING.

rise. In PITCH CONTOURS, a rise in pitch in a syllable, such as occurs at the end of a YES–NO QUESTION.

risk aversion. The phenomenon that people tend to accept a higher risk to avoid losses than to make corresponding gains.

risky shift. A decision made by a group that is less cautious than the decisions that would have been made by the group members acting on their own. It is an example of a CHOICE SHIFT. *Compare* CAUTIOUS SHIFT.

Ritalin. The trade name for methylphenidate.

rites de passage, **rites of passage.** Ritual practices used to signal the transition of a person from one stage of life to another, e.g. from boy to man, or from single to married. The expression is also used to indicate rituals that signal the transition of one season of the year to another.

ritualization. (Ethology) The modification in the course of evolution of a behaviour pattern originally serving some other end to a communication signal; e.g. the threat posture of the male three-spined stickleback is thought to have evolved from the posture it uses in sand-digging.

ritualized behaviour. (Ethology) Behaviour resulting from RITUALIZATION.

rivalry. *See* BINOCULAR RIVALRY.

RMS. An abbreviation for ROOT MEAN SQUARE.

RNA. An abbreviation for RIBONUCLEIC ACID.

robotics. The study of how to make machines (under the control of a computer or special-purpose computer-like device) perform skilled tasks, particularly mechanical ones, formerly performed only by people.

ROC curve. An abbreviation for RECEIVER-OPERATING CHARACTERISTIC CURVE.

rod and frame test (RFT). A test in which a subject has to set to vertical a rod within a rectangular frame whose orientation changes from trial to trial (a further variation is, in addition, to place the subject on a chair that can be tilted in different directions). The test is used to measure FIELD DEPENDENCE: field-dependent people tend to set the rod at an angle tilted away from the true vertical in the same direction as that in which the frame is tilted.

rod monochromatism. *See* MONOCHROMATISM.

rods. The receptors for SCOTOPIC VISION. They differ from CONES in several respects: (i) rods are absent from the fovea, but predominate in the periphery; (ii) they have a lower threshold than cones; (iii) they only have one photopigment (rhodopsin); (iv) a large number of rods are connected to a single ganglion cell. Hence the periphery has high sensitivity in dim light, but no colour vision and poor acuity.

rods of Corti. A synonym for PILLARS OF CORTI.

Rolandic fissure. A synonym for CENTRAL FISSURE.

role. The part a person chooses to play in a social setting, or the part that society expects him to adopt. It is a cant word in psychotherapy and sociology, often used either with little meaning or derogatorily: one might be proud to be called a rebel, but not to be told one was playing the role of a rebel. The implication behind the use of the word in psychology tends to be that people always copy someone else's mode of behaviour.

role conflict. Disturbance induced by having two or more conflicting roles (or aims), e.g. a father may wish to be kind to his children but also feel it necessary to discipline them.

role confusion. Uncertainty about what role to play, particularly uncertainty about whether to behave in a masculine or feminine way.

Role Construct Repertory Test. A personality test devised by Kelley, which was the forerunner of the REPERTORY GRID TECHNIQUE. It uses the way in which the testee describes events or people of importance to him to exhibit his PERSONAL CONSTRUCTS, i.e. the concepts he habitually uses in viewing the world such as anger, dependence, or frustration.

role deprivation. The denial of a sought-for role or of status, e.g. through discrimination against minorities or compulsory retirement.

role discontinuity. A sudden change in a person's position in life, e.g. becoming unemployed.

role distancing. Deliberately presenting a front without being taken in by it oneself and without becoming like the people who behave like that naturally.

role-enactment theory. A theory of hypnosis postulating that the hypnotized person has consciously or unconsciously adopted the role of complying with the hypnotist's suggestions. It puts the phenomenon of hypnotism in other words, but does nothing to explain it.

role model. A person on whom another models his behaviour.

role playing. Deliberately playing the role of another, a technique used in psychotherapy, management training, etc. to help the participants gain insight.

role reversal. A counselling or psychotherapeutic technique in which two people each play the role of the other.

role set. A group as determined by the roles its members play within it.

role shift. A synonym for ROLE REVERSAL.

rolfing. A deep massage technique, purportedly beneficial, invented by Rolf.

ROM. An abbreviation for READ-ONLY MEMORY.

Romberg's sign. Swaying when standing with eyes shut and feet together, a sign of LOCOMOTOR ATAXIA.

root. 1. (Linguistics) A single morpheme that has lexical meaning, e.g. the root of 'unwashed' is 'wash' (the 'un-' and the '-ed' have no lexical meaning). 2. (Mathematics) A number that when raised to a particular power yields a given number; thus 3 is the cube (or third) root of 27. 3. (Neuroanatomy) *See* SPINAL ROOT.

root conflict. In dynamic psychology, the underlying conflict, usually thought to go back to infancy, that is producing psychological disorder. *Contrast* ACTUAL CONFLICT.

rooting reflex. A reflex, present in infants, in which in response to a gentle touch of the cheek the head moves in the direction of the touch, thus aiding the infant to find the nipple.

root mean square (RMS). $\sqrt{(\Sigma X^2/N)}$, where X is each raw score and N the number of scores. When X is the deviation of each score from the mean, it is the STANDARD DEVIATION.

root mean square amplitude. *See* AMPLITUDE (2).

Rorschach test. A projection test in which ten symmetrical patterns resembling ink blots, some of which are achromatic and some coloured, are presented to a person, who is asked to say what he sees in them. There are elaborate scoring systems for assessing personality from the responses, but, although widely used, there is no evidence that the test has any validity.

Rosenthal effect. The distortion of an experimental result or other outcome caused by the experimenter's expectations, i.e. a kind of self-fulfilling prophecy. Rosenthal demonstrated the effect in experiments, but it applies equally to the grades of someone whom a teacher expects to do well (or badly) etc.

Rosenzweig Picture Frustration Study. *See* PICTURE FRUSTRATION TEST.

rostral. (Anatomy) Pertaining to the front (or ANTERIOR) end of the body, or nearer to that end than some other structure. When used of the brain in an upright species, it means towards the top. *Contrast* CAUDAL.

rotary pursuit meter. A synonym for PURSUIT ROTOR.

rotating room test (RRT). A test of FIELD DEPENDENCE in which an upright room is rotated in a circle in the horizontal plane, producing a centrifugal force on the testee. When asked to set his chair to straight the field-independent person sets it straight in terms of the room, while the field-dependent person is more influenced by the centrifugal force.

rotation. 1. (Statistics) In factor analysis, the rotation of the factors (and hence of the axes used to represent them) to find orientations that account for the maximum variance, or that are in line with theoretical expectations. 2. *See* MENTAL ROTATION.

rote learning. 1. The learning of comparatively meaningless material, e.g. lists of nonsense syllables or disconnected words. 2. Learning material merely by repeated exposure to it or rehearsal of it, without any attempt to impose meaning upon it. Even the apparently meaningless material presented in rote learning (1) experiments does not force the subject to learn purely by rote (2) – he may attempt to impose meaning or structure on it.

round. In an experiment, the performance of one trial (or sometimes one set of trials) by each organism in the experiment, or by each of a group of organisms.

rounded vowel. (Phonetics) A speech sound produced with the lips in a rounded position, e.g. the 'w' in 'water'.

round window. An opening, covered by a membrane, at the base of the SCALA TYMPANI in the COCHLEA. Its function is to reduce the pressures caused by the vibration of the OVAL WINDOW.

RP. An abbreviation for RECEIVED PRONUNCIATION.

R–R conditioning. The conditioning of one response to another.

RRT. An abbreviation for ROTATING ROOM TEST.

R–S interval. In SIDMAN AVOIDANCE CONDITIONING, the time interval between the organism making an avoidance response, and the time when shock will be delivered unless a further response is made.

r strategy. (Genetics) An evolutionary strategy in which many offspring are produced. It occurs in many animal groups, e.g. fish; this strategy obviates the need to protect the young closely. *Compare* K STRATEGY.

RT. An abbreviation for REACTION TIME.

R technique. A factor analysis based on the correlations between tests that attempts to derive a limited number of factors underlying the correlations. *Contrast* Q TECHNIQUE.

Rubin's figure. A reversible figure in which the parts seen as figure and as ground alternate; either two faces or a vase are perceived.

Rubin's figure

rubrospinal tract. The efferent nerve from the red nucleus to the spinal cord.

Ruffini corpuscle. A spindle-like skin receptor, once thought to be sensitive to warmth but now thought to be sensitive to touch.

Ruffini end organ, Ruffini ending, Ruffini papillary ending. Free nerve endings just beneath the skin, probably sensitive to pressure.

rule of inference. (Logic) A rule that permits the deduction of one expression from one or several other expressions. *Compare* MODUS PONENS and MODUS TOLENS.

rumination. (Psychology) 1. A preoccupation with particular thoughts, usually of a highly distressing kind. It is common in depression and other mental disorders. 2. The chewing and swallowing of food that a person has regurgitated.

rumour intensity formula. The principle put foward by Allport and Postman that the strength of a rumour depends on its importance multiplied by the difficulty of falsifying it.

run. 1. To perform an experiment or part of an experiment. 2. A consecutive series of identical items (e.g. five heads in a row when a coin is tossed) occurring as part of a sequence containing a mixture of items.

running memory recognition. A task in which the subject is shown a series of items and is asked to discriminate between new items and ones that have occurred earlier in the series.

runs test. A statistical test that evaluates whether the pattern of RUNS (2) in a sequence differs significantly from chance expectation.

runway. A straight alley down which an organism moves, usually to obtain reinforcement.

S

S. An abbreviation for 1. STIMULUS 2. SUBJECT; 3. STANDARD STIMULUS; 4. sentence.

S+. An abbreviation for POSITIVE STIMULUS.

S−. An abbreviation for NEGATIVE STIMULUS.

S$_c$. A rare abbreviation for CONDITIONED STIMULUS.

S$_d$. An abbreviation for DRIVE STIMULUS.

S^D, S△. An abbreviation for DISCRIMINATIVE STIMULUS. In Skinnerian terminology S^D is used to mean S+ and S△ to mean S−.

S$_G$. Hull's abbreviation for GOAL STIMULUS.

S$_U$. A rare abbreviation for UNCONDITIONED STIMULUS.

s. An abbreviation for the STANDARD DEVIATION of a sample.

s$_G$. Hull's abbreviation for FRACTIONAL ANTEDATING GOAL STIMULUS.

s$_2$. An abbreviation for the VARIANCE of a sample.

SAAST. An abbreviation for SELF-ADMINISTERED ALCOHOLISM SCREENING TEST.

SAC. An abbreviation for STIMULUS AS CODED.

saccade. A flick of the eye made to change fixation; the movement is ballistic and lasts approximately 20–100 msec. Because the reaction time for a saccade is about 200 msec, not more than five can be made a second, which limits reading speed. A **primary saccade** is the first saccade made in order to fixate a new or displaced target; a **secondary** saccade is any further saccade made to correct any error in the primary saccade. A **catch-up saccade** is a saccade made to bring the eye into alignment with a moving target behind which a SMOOTH FOLLOWING MOVEMENT is lagging.

saccadic suppression. The suppression of vision or a rise in brightness threshold during a SACCADE when caused by a central process not merely by blur induced by movement of the visual image.

saccule. One of two sacs in the VESTIBULAR SYSTEM, located near the AMPULLAE, and having a MACULA (a flat body lying in the vertical plane, containing hair cells, the receptor cells, whose tips touch the OTOLITHS). *See also* UTRICLE and SEMICIRCULAR CANALS.

sacral nerves. *See* SPINAL NERVES.

SAD (seasonal affective disorder). A hypothetical form of depression said to occur in the winter months because of lack of sunlight. It is probably as likely to be caused by anticipating or looking back on the miseries of the Christmas season.

sadism. *See* ALGOLAGNIA.

SAE. An abbreviation for STANDARD AMERICAN ENGLISH.

safety signal. (Animal learning) A signal indicating that no punishment will be delivered when punishment has previously occurred in that situation.

sagittal axis. A synonym for PUPILLARY AXIS.

sagittal fissure. The fissure separating the cerebral hemispheres.

sagittal plane. The vertical plane running from front to back of an organism that splits it into two symmetrical (right and left) halves.

sagittal section. (Anatomy) A section made in a vertical plane parallel to the plane that divides the body into two equal left and right halves.

SAI. An abbreviation for SOCIAL ADEQUACY INDEX.

salience. The prominence or attention-catching properties of a stimulus or of a stimulus dimension.

Salpêtrière school. *See* PARIS SCHOOL.

saltation. 1. (Evolution) The sudden appearance of a new species, said to occur in PUNCTUATED EQUILIBRIUM. 2. *See* SENSORY SALTATION.

saltatory conduction. The leap of a nerve impulse from one NODE OF RANVIER to the next in myelinated fibres.

same–different paradigm. A psychophysical procedure for establishing a difference threshold; the subject is presented on each trial with one of four pairs of stimuli AA, BB, AB, or BA, and must say whether the members of each pair are the same or different.

sample. Part of a population, usually randomly selected to be representative of the whole population on which data are gathered. *See* POPULATION.

sample bias. Any way in which a sample is not representative of the population from which it was drawn. It is usually caused by non-random sampling.

sample mean (M, X̄). (Statistics) The mean of a set of values obtained from a sample. *Contrast* POPULATION MEAN.

sample statistic. A statistic compiled from a sample, as opposed to one applying to the population from which the sample was drawn. *Contrast* PARAMETER (2).

sampling distribution. The theoretical distribution of all possible values of a statistic computed from samples randomly drawn from a specified population. The location of a sample statistic in its sampling distribution is used to accept or reject the null hypothesis.

sampling error. The difference between any value of a statistic obtained from a sample of a population and the value in the whole population. Some sampling error is bound to arise from chance, but some may be caused by bias. *See also* STANDARD ERROR.

sampling population. The population from which a sample is drawn.

sampling theory. 1. The principles that govern the selection of representative samples. 2. The theory of the distribution of sample statistics drawn from specified populations.

sampling validity. The extent to which a test appears to sample those traits, and only those traits, underlying whatever it purports to measure.

sampling without replacement. Sampling from a finite population without replacing the items sampled so that they cannot be sampled again.

sampling with replacement. Sampling from a finite population while replacing each item sampled so that it is available for sampling again.

Sander parallelogram. The geometric illusion shown below. The diagonal of the small parallelogram appears shorter than that of the large parallelogram although they are the same physical size.

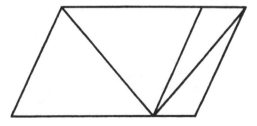

Sander parallelogram

sanguine. *See* HUMOUR (2).

Sanson images. A synonym for PURKINJE–SANSON IMAGES.

SAP. An abbreviation for SPECIFIC ACTION POTENTIAL.

Sapir–Whorf hypothesis. A synonym for WHORFIAN HYPOTHESIS.

SAT. An abbreviation for SCHOLASTIC APTITUDE TEST.

satanophobia. A morbid fear of the devil.

satiation. In Köhler's mistaken theory of figural aftereffects, the increase in resistance to the flow of electrical current in the brain (*see* ELECTROTONUS) that causes figural aftereffects by distorting the flow of current. The term is often extended to mean the fatiguing of any high-level perceptual process, which results in an alternative process taking over. E.g. the alternation in the way a reversible figure is seen is sometimes said to be caused by the satiation in turn of the processes underlying each way of seeing it. The explanation sounds good, but is of course empty.

satiety centre. The VENTROMEDIAL NUCLEUS OF THE HYPOTHALAMUS, stimulation of which stops the organism eating.

satisficing. Taking a decision that is good enough but may not be optimal in order to avoid taking more thought.

satisfier. Thorndike's term for a pleasurable stimulus or reinforcer.

saturation. 1. (Vision) The subjective dimension of the richness or purity of a colour; in general the more white light is present, the less saturated (paler or more **desaturated**) is the colour. 2. (Factor analysis) The extent to which a test correlates with a given factor.

satyriasis. A man's abnormally strong lust for women.

savings method. A technique for studying memory by measuring how much less time (or fewer trials) is required to relearn the material (or task) as compared with original learning.

S–B. An abbreviation for STANFORD–BINET SCALE.

scala media. One of three canals in the COCHLEA; it lies between the SCALA TYMPANI and SCALA VESTIBULI, and contains the ORGAN OF CORTI.

scalar. A quantity that has magnitude only. *Contrast* VECTOR.

scala tympani. One of three canals in the COCHLEA, separated from the SCALA MEDIA by the BASILAR MEMBRANE, and joined at the apex of the cochlea to the SCALA VESTIBULI; at its base is the ROUND WINDOW.

scala vestibuli. One of three canals in the COCHLEA, separated from the SCALA MEDIA by REISSNER'S MEMBRANE, and joined at the apex of the cochlea to the SCALA TYMPANI; it contains the OVAL WINDOW, which transmits sound vibrations to it.

scale. (Psychometry) Any ordering or method of ordering a series of items along a dimension. The term 'nominal scale' is a misnomer, since on such a 'scale' terms are placed in unordered categories. *See* BALANCED SCALE, INTERVAL SCALE, IPSATIVE SCALE, NOMINAL SCALE, ORDERED METRIC SCALE, ORDINAL SCALE, and RATIO SCALE.

scaling. *See* GUTTMAN SCALING, KRUSKAL–SHEPARD SCALING, PSYCHOPHYSICAL SCALING METHODS, and SCALE.

scalloping. A scalloped pattern produced by a CUMULATIVE RECORDER, normally caused by fixed interval reinforcement, under which the organism's response rate drops after each reinforcement, but increases to a peak just before the next reinforcement becomes available.

scalogram. A synonym for GUTTMAN SCALING.

scanning. A strategy for deducing a concept from successive exemplars of it by basing a hypothesis on some feature of an exemplar and changing it when a disconfirming exemplar occurs, while taking into account what can be remembered of previous exemplars. *Contrast* FOCUSING.

scanning speech. Abnormal speech that is slurred, ataxic, or spoken in a monotone or a sing-song; it can occur in multiple sclerosis.

scapegoat. Someone blamed (and usually abused) for a group's problems or miseries. Scapegoats are often to be found in encounter groups.

scatophobia. A morbid fear of faeces.

scatter. (Statistics) A synonym for VARIABILITY.

scatter diagram. A synonym for SCATTER PLOT.

scattering. A schizophrenic thought disorder, in which many irrelevant associations occur resulting in incoherent speech.

scatter plot. A plot in which points represent the values of items on two dimensions; from the dispersion of the points, a rough estimate of the relationship between the two variables may be obtained, e.g. of how closely a value on one dimension can be predicted from a knowledge of the value on the other.

scedacity. (Statistics) The extent to which the variance of different samples is the same. In **homoscedacity** the variability is homogeneous; in **heteroscedacity** the variability is heterogeneous. It is used especially of the variability about regression lines.

scene. The three-dimensional visual environment.

scene analysis. (AI) The theory and its implementation in computer programs of how to reconstruct a model of a 3-D scene from pictorial cues only; in practice the scenes used have usually been limited to opaque polyhedra (sometimes with shadows), and the input to the programs has made explicit the visible edges of the polyhedra (and the boundaries of the shadows). The main cue used has been the VERTEX TYPE of the two dimensional projection of a 3-D corner.

Schafer–Murphy effect. The alleged phenomenon that when subjects are rewarded for seeing an ambiguous figure in one way, they are more likely to see it in that way in future.

Schedule for Affective Disorders and Schizophrenia. A structured interview for assessing the presence, nature, scope and severity of a mental disorder.

schedule-induced behaviour. Irrelevant responses such as licking, drinking, or aggression occurring at times when the probability of reinforcement is low during an appetitive reinforcement schedule.

schedule-induced polydipsia (SIP). The drinking of excessive amounts of water (up to half the animal's body weight) when small amounts of food are periodically (e.g. once a minute) made available for a very brief period; the phenomenon has been demonstrated in several animals, particularly rats.

schedule of reinforcement. *See* REINFORCEMENT SCHEDULE.

scheduling theory. The mathematical theory of how to optimize the sequence and timing of the large number of operations needed to carry out a complex task.

Scheffé test. An A POSTERIORI TEST to determine whether specific differences between means and their combinations are significant, made after an analysis of variance has yielded significant results.

schema. An organized mental model of anything (e.g. of a class of objects or of a class of linked events), which makes it possible to interpret new data in terms of existing knowledge, to make inferences, and to plan. The term is vague and much abused, since psychologists often use it in explanation without specifying the nature of the relevant schema. *Compare* FRAME and SCRIPT.

scheme. Largely synonymous with SCHEMA, but Piaget used the term to refer only to conscious cognitive representations or plans.

schismatic family. A family in which the parents treat one another with contempt.

schizoaffective disorder. (DSM-III) A mental disorder which combines some of the symptoms of schizophrenia with those of manic-depressive illness.

schizoid. A term used in several related ways, but sense (1) is the most common technical use. 1. A synonym for SCHIZOID PERSONALITY DISORDER. 2. Pertaining to characteristics or symptoms like those of schizophrenia. 3. Pertaining to or having symptoms or traits suggestive of incipient schizophrenia, particularly where there is a family history of schizophrenia. 4. Eccentric.

schizoid disorder of childhood or adolescence. (DSM-III) A putative disorder in children or adolescents, marked by extreme withdrawal from others and absence of interest in them.

schizoidism. 1. A synonym for SCHIZOTHYMIC PERSONALITY. 2. The aspects of schizophrenia that are thought to be hereditary.

schizoid personality disorder. (DSM-III) A personality disorder marked by an inability to form social relationships, by withdrawal, coldness, and by a lack of sensitivity to the feelings of others.

schizophrasia. Incoherent speech, like that of schizophrenics.

schizophrenia. A psychosis that begins before about 45 years of age, and is marked by a great variety of symptoms, including hearing voices; feeling one's thoughts, actions, and emotions are controlled by an outside agency; delusions; and flatness or inappropriateness of affect. In schizophrenic episodes there is severe deterioration of mental abilities, and speech may become wholly incoherent. Schizophrenia is divided into the following five main categories: CATATONIC SCHIZOPHRENIA, HEBEPHRENIC SCHIZOPHRENIA, MIXED SCHIZOPHRENIA, PARANOID SCHIZOPHRENIA, and SIMPLE SCHIZOPHRENIA. *See also* ACUTE SCHIZOPHRENIC EPISODE, AMBULATORY SCHIZOPHRENIA, BORDERLINE SCHIZOPHRENIA, CHILDHOOD SCHIZOPHRENIA, DISORGANIZED SCHIZOPHRENIA, INDUCED SCHIZOPHRENIA, LATENT SCHIZOPHRENIA, POSTEMOTIVE SCHIZOPHRENIA, PROCESS SCHIZOPHRENIA, PSEUDONEUROTIC SCHIZOPHRENIA, REACTIVE SCHIZOPHRENIA, and RESIDUAL SCHIZOPHRENIA.

schizophrenic spectrum. All conditions that seemingly resemble schizophrenia. They are divided into the **hard schizophrenic spectrum**, which includes PROCESS SCHIZOPHRENIA, ACUTE SCHIZOPHRENIA, ACUTE SCHIZOPHRENIC EPISODE, BORDERLINE SCHIZOPHRENIA and the **soft schizophrenic spectrum**, which includes PARANOIA, PARANOID PERSONALITY DISORDER, SCHIZOID PERSONALITY, and INADEQUATE PERSONALITY DISORDER. Even within either of the two major classifications, it is doubtful whether the subclasses have the same aetiology. Thus there is no genetic relationship between acute schizophrenic episodes and true schizophrenia.

schizophreniform disorder. An episode of schizophrenia lasting between two weeks and six months, and having a good prognosis.

schizophrenogenic. Pertaining to any factor, genetic or environmental, that predisposes to schizophrenia.

schizotaxia. A genetic predisposition to schizophrenia.

schizothymic personality, schizothymia. A personality that exhibits some schizophrenic characteristics, particularly extreme introversion and withdrawal. It is one of the personality types in KRETSCHMER'S CONSTITUTIONAL THEORY; he thought it was associated with an ASTHENIC physique.

schizotypal personality disorder. (DSM-III) An abnormal personality, in which comparatively mild schizophrenic symptoms appear such as ideas of reference, withdrawal, or paranoia.

Scholastic Aptitude Test (SAT). Standardized tests for aptitude at particular subjects, e.g. mathematics, used especially in the USA.

Schroeder staircase. An ambiguous figure that is seen either as a staircase the right way up or as one upside-down. *See* figure.

Schumann square. A square rotated through 45°, i.e. a diamond; Schumann pointed out that such a figure looks larger than a square of the same dimensions.

schwa. (Phonetics) A vowel that is pronounced with the tongue relaxed, as in the

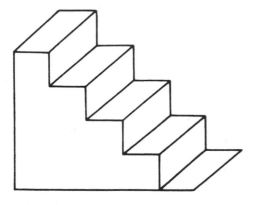

Schroeder staircase

first syllable of 'asleep' or 'ago'. The vowels in 'a' and 'and' and those in many other words are often (though not always) pronounced in this way.

Schwann cell. A cell that provides the membrane (the NEURILEMMA) that covers the myelin sheath of axons in the peripheral nervous system and that guides regenerating axons after damage. *Compare* OLIGODENDROGLIA.

sciascope. An alternative spelling for SKIASCOPE.

SCID. Short for STRUCTURED CLINICAL INTERVIEW.

scientism. Unjustifiable reliance on science.

scierneuropsia. Scieropia of psychological, not physical, origin.

scieropia. A visual defect in which objects appear to be in shadow.

scintillating scotoma. The illusory appearance of a shimmering zigzag cloud, usually a prelude to a migraine attack.

sclera. The white membrane that covers the outside of the eyeball; it joins the CORNEA at the front of the eye.

sclerophobia. A morbid fear of bad people or criminals.

sclerotic coat, sclerotic layer. Synonyms for SCLERA.

scope. (Linguistics) The range of words in a sentence affected by the meaning of a given word; e.g. in 'She wore black stockings and boots', 'black' could be taken to modify both 'stockings' and 'boots', or it could modify only 'stockings'.

scopolagnia. A synonym for VOYEURISM.

scopolamine. An alkaloid that is ANTICHOLINERGIC; small doses are sedative, large ones arousing. In large doses it is hallucinogenic; witches are reported to have rubbed it on their broomsticks so that when they straddled them it was absorbed through the genitalia, thus producing a sensation of flying.

scopophilia. The derivation of sexual excitement from looking at one's own or another's body.

scopophobia. A morbid fear of being seen by others.

scoptophilia. A synonym for SCOPOPHILIA.

scoterythrous. Being insensitive to long-wavelength light. *See* PROTANOMALY and PROTANOPIA.

scotoma. Loss or impairment of vision for light falling on a particular part of the retina. *See also* PHYSIOLOGICAL SCOTOMA.

scotomata. Plural of SCOTOMA, but also used to mean the visual hallucinations preceding a migraine attack, such as zigzag patterns of light, etc.

scotomization. (Psychoanalysis) A defence mechanism in which anything (e.g. a memory or an unconscious wish) that threatens the ego is ignored.

scotophilia. A synonym for 1. SCOPOPHILIA; 2. NYCTOPHILIA.

scotophobia. A morbid fear of the dark.

scotophobin. A hypothetical substance which, it was claimed, when taken from the brain of a rat that had been conditioned to fear the dark and subsequently injected into mice, made them also fear the dark – one of the most outrageous myths in neuroscience.

scotopic luminosity curve. *See* LUMINOSITY CURVE.

scotopic vision. Vision in dim light, when it is subserved by rods; such vision is marked by increased sensitivity to dim light, decreased acuity, and loss of colour vision. *Contrast* PHOTOPIC VISION.

scotopsin. The OPSIN in rods.

SCR. An abbreviation for SKIN CONDUCTANCE RESPONSE.

scratch-pad memory. (Computing) A small high-speed memory store used for the temporary retention of data currently being processed.

screen defence. (Psychoanalysis) A defence mechanism in which a memory, fantasy, dream, or train of thought is unconsciously used to prevent threatening material in the unconscious emerging into consciousness.

screen memory . (Psychoanalysis) The recall of a comparatively non-threatening and insignificant experience, usually from early childhood, unconsciously used to block the recall of more significant and threatening events.

script. 1. A stored representation of the events likely to occur and the relationships between them in a particular situation, such as having a meal at a restaurant. It is needed to understand any reference to that situation and also to plan what to do in it. The term is not unlike SCHEMA, but refers to a framework that is extended over time. 2. (Transactional analysis) The role a person has decided to play in life or to take in relation to another person, which, it is alleged, is always based on games and fantasies.

sculpting. A psychotherapeutic technique in which family members or close associates place one another in positions that represent their feelings towards one another (e.g. defensive or aggressive) in the (unvalidated) hope that this will give them insight into their relationships.

SD. An abbreviation for STANDARD DEVIATION.

SDT. An abbreviation for signal detection theory.

SE. An abbreviation for STANDARD ERROR.

search image. (Ethology) An animal's representation of a particular kind of prey or food that it will seek out. E.g. crows, on encountering food under one kind of shell, tend to search beaches only for that kind of shell, and ignore all others.

Seashore tests. A set of tests of auditory and musical ability.

seasonal affective disorder (SAD). *See* SAD.

sebaceous glands. Tiny glands in the skin that secrete an oily substance to lubricate the skin and hair.

secondary advantage. A synonym for EPINOSIS.

secondary attention. Attention that is directed and sustained endogenously rather than externally through the salience of the stimulus, e.g. the attention needed to read this entry. *Contrast* PRIMARY ATTENTION.

secondary auditory cortex. An auditory area receiving a tonotopic projection comprising parts of Brodmann's areas 22, 42, and 52; *see* Appendix 3.

secondary circular reaction. Piaget's expression for any repetitive action, occurring from about four months of age, that indicates the infant is trying to make something happen; the infant mechanically repeats any action that was followed by a reinforcement in the past with no understanding of the causal connections. *See also* PRIMARY CIRCULAR REACTION and TERTIARY CIRCULAR REACTION.

secondary colour. Any colour produced by an additive mixture of PRIMARIES (1).

secondary conditioning. A synonym for HIGHER-ORDER CONDITIONING.

secondary control. Coping with reality by changing one's own attitudes and goals. *Contrast* PRIMARY CONTROL.

secondary deviance. Deviance or emotional

disturbance caused by society, e.g. by parental upbringing.

secondary drive. A learned drive, e.g. the drive to make money. *Contrast* PRIMARY DRIVE.

secondary elaboration. (Psychoanalysis) The tendency to remember dreams as more coherent than they were.

secondary extinction. The weakening of a response as a result of the extinction of a learned response that followed it; e.g. if rats, trained to run an alley, are placed in the goal box and not fed, the tendency to run from the start box is weakened.

secondary function. Any effects of a stimulus occurring after its withdrawal, e.g. an afterimage or a memory of it. *Contrast* PRIMARY FUNCTION.

secondary gain. A synonym for EPINOSIS.

secondary group. Any group to which someone belongs but to which he does not give his main allegiance. *Contrast* PRIMARY GROUP.

secondary identification. (Psychoanalysis) Incorporating the traits of another person into the self after the stage of identification with the parental figures, an allegedly pathological process.

secondary integration. Freud's term for the integration of the libidinal elements of the PREGENITAL STAGE with the elements of the GENITAL STAGE to form a consistent adult personality.

secondary memory. A synonym for LONG-TERM MEMORY.

secondary motor cortex (M3). A newly discovered area of the frontal lobe layers deep in the cingulate sulcus; it is the oldest motor cortex and is thought to be implicated in very simple actions.

secondary narcissism. *See* NARCISSISM.

secondary need. A learned NEED (often used to mean learned DRIVE).

secondary personality. A second self, with its own goals and traits, that develops in MULTIPLE PERSONALITY.

secondary position. (Vision) Any position of

the eyes that can be reached by a horizontal or vertical movement from the PRIMARY POSITION.

secondary process. (Psychoanalysis) Any activity of the ego, i.e. any conscious process.

secondary punisher. A stimulus that is aversive to an animal because it has previously been followed by a PRIMARY PUNISHER.

secondary punishment. 1. A synonym for SECONDARY PUNISHER. 2. The process by which a SECONDARY PUNISHER has its effect.

secondary quality. (Philosophy) A quality of an object which is not intrinsic to it, but which is due to an interaction between the object and the observer, e.g. colour or taste, as opposed to size or shape, which are allegedly primary qualities. The distinction is insecure, e.g. colour depends on the reflective qualities of the surface which must be a primary quality. *Contrast* PRIMARY QUALITY.

secondary reinforcer. A stimulus that reinforces an action because that action has previously been followed by reinforcement.

secondary reinforcement. 1. A SECONDARY REINFORCER. 2. The process by which a secondary reinforcer has its effect.

secondary relationship. A relationship with anyone to whom there is little or no emotional commitment; such relationships are often governed largely by conventions, e.g. those between teacher and pupil, or customer and shopkeeper.

secondary repression. *See* REPRESSION.

secondary reward. A synonym for SECONDARY REINFORCEMENT (1).

secondary saccade. *See* SACCADE.

secondary scaling. *See* PRIMARY SCALING.

secondary sex characteristics. *See* SEX CHARACTERISTICS.

secondary somatosensory cortex. Brodmann's area 5 and part of 7; *see* Appendices 3 and 4. It receives a somatosensory projection through the CORPUS CALLOSUM. It may be implicated in the sensation of pain.

secondary symptoms. *See* FUNDAMENTAL SYMPTOMS.

secondary territory. Territory used mainly by one or more members of a species, but with some access allowed to others (e.g. a classroom).

secondary thought process. A synonym for SECONDARY PROCESS.

secondary traits. Allport's term for traits or attitudes that affect only a narrow range of a person's behaviour. *Compare* CARDINAL TRAIT and CENTRAL TRAITS.

second cranial nerve. A synonym for OPTIC NERVE.

second messenger. (Neurophysiology) Any substance (e.g. CYCLIC ADENOSINE MONOPHOS-PHATE) that is released in a postsynaptic cell as a result of the reception of NEUROTRANS-MITTER molecules and that plays a role in changing the potential across the cell's membrane.

second moment. *See* MOMENT.

second-order conditioning. A synonym for HIGHER-ORDER CONDITIONING.

second-order factor. (Statistics) In factor analysis, a factor that accounts for some of the correlation between the first-order factors.

second-order schedule. A CHAINED SCHEDULE in which each component is the same (e.g. FI1, FI1, FI1), and the transition from one component to the next is marked by a brief stimulus (e.g. a flash of light). Reward is received only after all components have been completed.

second rank symptoms. Any symptom of schizophrenia thought to derive from FIRST RANK SYMPTOMS, e.g. incoherence.

second signal system. Pavlov's term for internally generated signals that can act as stimuli to the organism producing them; Pavlov largely confined them to language, but this was the thin end of the wedge, and nowadays anything goes as a stimulus in some quarters. *Compare* FIRST SIGNAL SYSTEM. *See also* MEDI-ATION THEORY, the successor of the second signal system.

section. (Anatomy) A slice of tissue cut for examination under a microscope.

sedative. Any drug that reduces anxiety or its physical symptoms and also reduces irritability, restlessness, or excitement. A large dose of a sedative may act as a hypnotic. *See also* MAJOR TRANQUILLIZERS and MINOR TRAN-QUILLIZERS.

segmental phonology. That part of phonology that studies the individual segments (phonemes) of speech.

segmental reflex. A spinal reflex in which the afferent and efferent fibres involved enter and exit from the same segment of the spinal cord.

segregation. 1. (Sociology) The splitting of people into discrete groups. 2. (Gestalt psychology) The tendency of a shape or part of a shape to split from the rest and become a figure with the rest of the scene as background.

seizure. A synonym for CONVULSION.

selaphobia. A morbid fear of a flash.

selected group. A group (e.g. unemployed males under 25) selected from a larger population according to a criterion that excludes some members of the population, usually for the purpose of experimenting on or investigating that group.

selection index. A measure of how far a test (or test item) discriminates between the people for whom the test was designed.

selection task. *See* WASON SELECTION TASK.

selective adaptation. Adaptation to one stimulus that leaves sensitivity to some other related stimuli unimpaired.

selective amnesia. A synonym for PSY-CHOGENIC AMNESIA.

selective answer test. Any multiple choice or true–false test.

selective attention. Concentration on one stimulus, or type of stimulus, to the relative exclusion of others. *See also* ATTENUATION THEORY and FILTER THEORY.

selective exposure. (Social psychology) The tendency of people to expose themselves primarily to information that is consistent with their own attitudes.

selective inattention. Ignoring good aspects of a situation and concentrating on the bad ones. The expression is used of depressives by cognitive therapists.

selective learning. Learning to make a very specific response (as a result of similar responses not being reinforced).

selective listening. Selectively attending to one category of auditory input, e.g. listening to only one ear when different words are fed to each ear, or listening to one voice when several people are talking.

selective serotonin reuptake inhibitors. *See* SSRI.

self-actualization. The full development and use of all one's talents and potentialities; in practice, only potentialities for good are included and a highly successful bank-robber would not be considered to be self-actualized. Maslow thought the desire for self-actualization is present in everyone, but there is unfortunately no evidence for this.

Self-Administered Alcoholism Screening Test (SAAST). A questionnaire used to diagnose alcoholism.

self-attitude. A synonym for SELF-CONCEPT.

self-attribution theory of emotion. Schachter's theory that emotion depends on the interpretation of the signals of bodily arousal in the light of the situation the person is in.

self-concept. The way someone sees himself.

self-concept distress. The loss of self-esteem that may be experienced by an evil-doer. *Compare* RETALIATIVE DISTRESS.

self-control training. A psychotherapeutic method for dealing with anxiety or other distressing emotions. The client is taught that on encountering a stressful stimulus he should shout 'Stop' to his thoughts, then relax, and finally give himself some covert reinforcement.

self-correlation. The correlation between the scores from different questions in the same test, or between different administrations of the same test, or between different versions of the same test.

self-demand feeding. Giving an animal or child access to food whenever it shows signs of wanting to be fed.

self-desensitization. A behaviour therapy technique in which a person is taught to use desensitization on his own; e.g. when he encounters a phobic stimulus in everyday life.

self-directed search. A questionnaire administered by the testee to himself, the results of which are intended to provide guidance on what vocation to adopt.

self-dynamism. Sullivan's expression for all the influences, both social and biological, that form the personality or self-system.

self-efficacy. A person's beliefs about his ability to cope in different situations.

self-embedding. (Linguistics) In a generative grammar, the embedding within a string of symbols of the constituent from which the string is derived, e.g. S → NP+(S)+VP where S is a sentence, NP is a noun phrase, and VP is a verb phrase. This yields constructions like: 'The man who wore the hat wanted a drink'. There is no fixed limit to the depth of the embeddings, but if there are too many the sentence is not acceptable, e.g. 'The dog that the cat that the rat bit scratched was a beagle'.

self-extinction. Horney's term for living vicariously through others with little identity of one's own, a form of neurotic behaviour.

self-instructional training. A technique in cognitive behaviour modification, in which the client is taught to make positive statements about himself and then to make these statements on the appropriate occasions. E.g. a shy person might be taught to say to himself 'I have nothing to lose by going up to strangers at this party'.

self-inventory. Any personality test on which the subject indicates the traits he thinks he possesses.

selfish gene. An expression capturing the idea that evolution is governed not by the survival of individual organisms or groups of organisms but by the survival of genes. *See* SOCIO-BIOLOGY.

self-managed reinforcement. Reinforcing oneself according to a predetermined plan in the hope of helping oneself to do or not to do something, e.g. giving oneself a double whisky for every two hours of not smoking.

self-perception theory. The doctrine that the way a person sees himself stems from his observations of his own behaviour, and that therefore if his behaviour can be changed, his self-perception and emotions will also change.

self-psychology. Any system of psychology that focuses on the self and the way in which internal and external events are interpreted by the self.

self-rating scale, self-report inventory. Synonyms for SELF-INVENTORY.

self-serving bias. Any bias in thought that reflects false credit on oneself or falsely abrogates blame, e.g. the belief that one is a better driver than one is or that a car accident was not one's own fault when it was.

self-stimulation. The performance of a response that causes a shock to be delivered to a 'pleasure centre' in the brain.

self-system. Sullivan's expression for the system of thinking and behaving that has been developed in response to the demands of the parents and other important figures. He thought that although the self-system protects a person from anxiety, it could omit desirable characteristics that might have appeared under other circumstances.

self-terminating search. A search that stops when the correct item is found. *Contrast* EXHAUSTIVE SEARCH.

semantic. Appertaining to meaning.

semantic coding. 1. A mental concept of objects, events, etc. based on listing their properties, as opposed to classifying by forming a prototype or a visual image. 2. More generally, storing the meaning of a word, usually in contrast to storing merely the phonemic pattern of the word.

semantic component. (Linguistics) The part of a grammar that deals with meaning as opposed to syntax.

semantic conditioning. Learning to associate a word with its referent. Sometimes also used to mean learning to make the responses to the word that are appropriate to its referent.

semantic confusion. Any confusion based on similarity of meaning, e.g. remembering 'cat' for 'dog'. *Contrast* ACOUSTIC CONFUSION.

semantic congruity effect. The phenomenon that in a COMPARATIVE JUDGEMENT task subjects are faster if both the stimuli fit the quality to be judged than if both do not. E.g. subjects are faster at deciding which is the larger stimulus with two large stimuli than with two small stimuli, and vice versa.

semantic differential. A technique invented by Osgood in which people are asked to rate an item on a set of seven-point scales, where each scale is a dimension having polar opposites (e.g. 'rough–smooth', with 1 signifying very rough, 7 very smooth). Osgood claimed that the results of such ratings could be explained in terms of three underlying dimensions – activity, potency, and value.

semantic dispersion. A form of SEMANTIC DISSOCIATION in which speech is ungrammatical and has little or no meaning.

semantic dissociation. Any mistaken association between symbol and referent, a type of error to which schizophrenics are prone. It includes ENLARGED SEMANTIC HALO, SEMANTIC DISPERSION, SEMANTIC DISSOLUTION, and SEMANTIC DISTORTION.

semantic dissolution. A form of SEMANTIC DISSOCIATION in which speech loses all meaning.

semantic distortion. A form of SEMANTIC DISSOCIATION in which speech contains NEOLOGISMS and PARALOGISMS.

semantic feature. (Linguistics) Any defining aspect of the meaning of a word, e.g. being male and being married are semantic features of a husband. *See also* SEMANTIC MARKER.

semantic feature hypothesis. The theory that the order in which words are acquired by children reflects their progress in mastering the relevant semantic features.

semantic field. A set of related words which can only be defined in relation to one another, e.g. the domain of colour which includes the words 'colour', 'saturation', 'blue', 'yellow', etc.

semantic generalization. Generalization of a learned response to another stimulus, based not on similarity of the properties of the stimuli, but on similarity between their meanings or associations (e.g. generalizing from 'hammer' to 'nail').

semantic jargon. A form of WERNICKE'S APHASIA in which syntax is preserved but the wrong content words are used.

semantic marker. (Linguistics) The position of a word on one of several dimensions into which its meaning can be decomposed; e.g. 'boy' might be assigned the markers +animate, +male, +young, etc. The markers restrict the range of contexts in which the word can be meaningfully used, e.g. 'The boy was in his old age'. The attempt to account for meaning in terms of semantic markers is disputed.

semantic memory. 1. Memory for anything meaningful. 2. Tulving used the expression in a more restricted sense to mean memory for anything that did not directly form part of an episode in a person's life, e.g. memory for historical or public events, mathematical formulae, etc. *Contrast* EPISODIC MEMORY.

semantic network. A method of storing information about the world in a computer program and, some think, in the brain; it is based on a series of labelled nodes connected by labelled arrows to other nodes. The labels represent objects, properties, and relations. Although they are not words, they are usually (confusingly) written as words. Thus the node for 'dog' might be labelled 'dog' and have the following arrows and nodes (the word before the arrow is the label of the arrow and the word after is the label of the node to which it points). Dog: subordinate of → mammal; subordinate of → pet; property → barking.

semantic paralexia. An aphasic syndrome in which words are misread and a semantically similar word is substituted, e.g. 'cat' for 'dog'.

semantic paraphasia. ·A form of aphasia in which one word (often a related one) is substituted for another, e.g. 'Open the wall' for 'Open the window'.

semantic priming. The facilitation of the recognition or retrieval of a word by the prior presentation of a semantically related word (e.g. 'knife' followed by 'fork').

semantic primitive. Any general concepts into which the meaning of a content word can be decomposed, e.g. 'bachelor' can be defined in terms of the more primitive concepts 'adult', 'male', and 'unmarried'. Decomposing words in this way can reveal the semantic role they can play in a sentence, e.g. because a bachelor is a person, the word can be agentive, i.e. it can represent the agent of an action word such as 'buying'. Some think that all content words can be decomposed into a set of semantic primitives, but no one has yet decided how many are needed, and there are no clear criteria for selecting primitives.

semantics. The study of meaning.

semantic satiation. The loss of meaning of a word which occurs when it is repeated internally or externally many times in succession.

semantic space. Any organization of words, particularly in memory, according to their meanings, e.g. by superordinate and subordinate, by antonyms and synonyms, etc.

semantic therapy. A form of psychotherapy in which the therapist corrects faulty use of words and distorted ideas, and emphasizes clarity of thinking and expression.

semasiography. A system of symbols in which each is a natural representation of its meaning, e.g. road signs or the signs on the doors of public lavatories.

semasiology, semeiology. Synonyms for SEMIOTICS.

semicircular canals. Three canals each forming an incomplete circle in the LABYRINTH, and almost at right angles to one another. They are filled with ENDOLYMPH. Each widens at the UTRICLE end into an AMPULLA. They record, through their HAIR CELLS, changes of pressure in the endolymph and hence the direction and strength of accelerating and decelerating movements of the head. *Compare* VESTIBULAR SACS.

semi-interquartile range. A synonym for QUARTILE DEVIATION.

semiotics, semiology. 1. The study of all aspects of the use of signs or symbols, recently extended to include communication by eating, dancing, bathing, etc. 2. The study of the symptoms of illness.

semipermeable membrane. A membrane allowing some substances to pass through it but not others; e.g. the membrane of a nerve cell.

semi-vowel. (Phonetics) A speech sound of shorter duration than a vowel, in which air is passed through the vocal cavity with less obstruction than in a normal consonant, but with more than in a vowel, e.g. the 'w' in 'wet' and the 'y' in 'yet'.

senile dementia. A progressive syndrome starting in old age with no clear cause, in which intellect, memory, and judgement are impaired; it is often accompanied by apathy or irritability.

sensate focus therapy. An aspect of Masters and Johnson's therapy aimed at overcoming sexual dysfunction; clients build up to sexual intercourse over a period of days, during which they massage and fondle one another, while making their activities progressively more erotic.

sensation. An uninterpreted conscious experience based on the stimulation of receptors. Although pain is a sensation in this sense, it is rare for visual stimulation not to be interpreted; all that can be said is that the less the interpretation, or the more the experience corresponds to what is on the retina rather than to the real world, the more tempting it is to use the word 'sensation'. The existence of two words ('perception' and 'sensation') is misleading; Helmholtz went so far as needlessly to postulate 'unconscious sensations' to provide a mental entity corresponding to the physical processing occurring at the retina. *See also* SENSE DATA.

sensationalism. A synonym for EMPIRICISM.

sensation level (SL). (Sound) The SOUND PRESSURE LEVEL, measured in decibels, at an individual listener's threshold for audibility.

sensation threshold. A synonym for ABSOLUTE THRESHOLD.

sensation type. *See* FUNCTION TYPES.

sense. (Logic) The properties of an object or idea signified (a) by an expression or (b) by a speaker in the course of a speech act. Some authorities limit the meaning to (b), but it is often used in sense (a). The sense of 'the morning star' is a star visible in the morning, but its REFERENT is Venus.

sense data. Sensations. The expression was until recently in vogue with philosophers who thought sense data were incorrigible and provided the only certain knowledge of the world. It has now been realized that almost all perception involves interpretation and hence that incorrigible sense data are extremely rare. *See also* SENSIBILIA.

sense ratio method. A psychophysical scaling method in which a subject is presented with three stimuli, A, B, and C, and adjusts a fourth, D, so that the ratio between C and D appears to equal the ratio between A and B.

sensibilia. (Philosophy) All SENSE DATA, including ones that could be sensed but are not. The term was coined by Russell when he believed objects were merely collections of sense data.

sensing type. *See* FUNCTION TYPES.

sensitive period. (Ethology) A synonym for CRITICAL PERIOD. The expression emphasizes that the boundaries of the critical period are very ill-defined, and learning of the relevant kind may often occur outside what would normally be regarded as the critical period.

sensitive zone. Any part of the body particularly sensitive to stimulation.

sensitivity training. Interaction in a group, with or without a leader, that is intended to promote greater awareness of oneself, of others and of the nature of social interactions.

sensitization. 1. (Psychology) In general, the process of coming to make a given response to a stimulus or situation, without external reinforcement being provided. E.g. repeated exposure to fearful stimuli can cause the anxiety response to be sensitized. 2. (Psychology) More particularly, the process of coming to respond more strongly to a benign stimulus that has been preceded by a painful one. 3. (Pharmacology) The process of coming to respond more strongly to a drug after repeated doses.

sensor. Anything that responds to a stimulus, e.g. a RECEPTOR (1); nowadays often used to mean an artificial device for sensing, such as a strain gauge or a photoelectric cell.

sensorimotor. An alternative spelling for SENSORY–MOTOR.

sensorimotor aphasia. A synonym for GLOBAL APHASIA.

sensorimotor cortex. The somatosensory and motor cortex, which are separated by the CENTRAL FISSURE.

sensorimotor rhythm. A 12–14 Hz EEG rhythm that emanates from the sensorimotor cortex.

sensorineural deafness, sensorineural hearing loss. Impairment of hearing caused by damage to the inner ear or nervous system.

sensorium. All the brain areas responsible for perception and sensation, but sometimes used more broadly to mean 'consciousness'.

sensory. Pertaining to the senses or to sensation.

sensory aphasia. A synonym for WERNICKE'S APHASIA.

sensory apraxia. A synonym for IDEATIONAL APRAXIA.

sensory area. A synonym for SENSORY CORTEX.

sensory ataxia. Ataxia caused by dysfunction of the sensory system, particularly of proprioception.

sensory awareness group. Any group gathered together for the purpose of increasing their awareness of their own and others' feelings, e.g. by cuddling one another, giving vent to their emotions, etc.

sensory conditioning. A synonym for SENSORY PRECONDITIONING.

sensory cortex. Any area of the cortex that receives an input from afferent neurons, or, more loosely, any area of cortex that is primarily devoted to the analysis of data from a particular sense.

sensory deprivation. The reduction of stimulation to a minimum, e.g. by placing someone in warm water, in the dark, and in a soundproof room. Sensory deprivation may lead to hallucinations, delusions, and panic; it is sometimes used as a technique in brainwashing.

sensory discrimination. *See* DISCRIMINATION.

sensory epilepsy. A form of epilepsy marked by PARAESTHESIA.

sensory enrichment. The rearing of an animal (or person) in a complex, enriched environment; there is some evidence that this can produce greater dendritic branching, more spines, and larger synapses in the cortex.

sensory extinction. Inability to report one or other of two stimuli simultaneously presented in the same modality; it is caused by brain damage.

sensory homunculus. The HOMUNCULUS (2) that consists of a mapping of the regions of the body. It is in the somatosensory cortex. In it each region of the body is mapped in an area adjacent to its representation in the MOTOR CORTEX.

sensory information store (SIS), sensory memory. A very brief (not more than a few seconds at most) memory, in which stimuli are coded in much the same way that they are coded at the lower levels of a sensory system. For examples, *see* ECHOIC MEMORY and ICONIC MEMORY.

sensory–motor. Pertaining to any activity in which the main task is to coordinate sensory input with motor ouput; thus, tennis is (largely) a sensory–motor skill, chess is not.

sensory–motor stage. The first of PIAGET'S STAGES of development, lasting from birth to about two years of age, in which children have no proper concepts, but learn in an *ad hoc* way to make motor responses to objects in their immediate environment; the concept of OBJECT PERMANENCE develops towards the end of this stage.

sensory neglect. A synonym for UNILATERAL NEGLECT.

sensory preconditioning. The learning of a connection between two stimuli presented successively (S1 followed by S2) without reinforcement that results in a response subsequently conditioned to S2 being elicited by S1. To make sure sensory preconditioning has occurred, it is necesary to run a control group in which the two stimuli are not paired to show the result is not due to SENSITIZATION.

sensory projection area. An area of the brain innervated by afferent fibres from one of the senses. *Compare* SENSORY CORTEX.

sensory register. A synonym for SENSORY INFORMATION STORE.

sensory relay nuclei. Thalamic nuclei that relay sensory information to the sensory areas of the cortex.

sensory root. Any dorsal root of the spinal cord, which is the path by which all sensory information enters the cord.

sensory saltation. A tactile illusion in which when two nearby points on the skin are tapped in alternation, the person senses an illusory third tap between the two points being tapped.

sensory suppression. An inability to perceive a stimulus when another stimulus is applied at the contralateral locus, and when the stimulus would have been perceived if the second stimulus had not been present. It is caused by unilateral brain damage.

sensualists. A school, originating in France in the 18th century, that believed every action occurred in response to a stimulus.

sentence completion test. A test of verbal intelligence in which the person has to supply a missing word or phrase; also a projective test in which he has to complete an unfinished sentence in any way he wishes.

separable stimulus dimensions. Dimensions of a stimulus that are perceived as distinct and do not interact, e.g. colour and shape. *Compare* INTEGRAL STIMULUS DIMENSION.

separation anxiety. The anxiety caused in a young child by separation from its mother or surrogate mother, and by extension the anxiety caused by separating from anyone dear to one.

separation anxiety disorder. A disorder of childhood marked by excessive anxiety caused by separation or fear of separation from the person (usually the mother) to whom the child is primarily attached.

separation-individuation. The process by which the young child separates itself psychologically from its mother and acquires its own identity.

separation of systems. Johannson's expression for the phenomenon that a single motion on the retina may be seen as made up of separate component motions. E.g. the motion described by a point on a rolling wheel can be seen as made up of a translatory forward motion and a circular motion of the point about its hub, provided the hub is visible.

septal region, septal area. A subcortical part of the LIMBIC SYSTEM, located immediately below the CORPUS CALLOSUM (*see* Appendix 2). It receives an input from most other limbic areas; stimulation often produces euphoria, and ablation produces hyperexcitability and rage.

sequela. Any abnormality caused by an illness that has ended.

sequence preference. The tendency of an organism to prefer one sequence of responses to another, e.g. to alternate left and right turns.

sequential analysis. A statistical analysis to discover whether at a given point in an experiment enough data have already been collected to test a hypothesis at a predefined probability of Type I and Type II errors.

sequential statistical test. Any statistical test of a hypothesis carried out using the methods of SEQUENTIAL ANALYSIS.

serial anticipation method. *See* ANTICIPATION METHOD.

serial association. Any association between two items perceived consecutively in time; it is applied particularly to the process underlying SERIAL LEARNING (1).

serial behaviour. A series of responses carried out in a fixed order, regardless of whether they are run off ballistically. *See also* CHAIN REFLEX.

serial exploration, method of. A synonym for LIMITS, METHOD OF.

serial learning. 1. Learning to recall items in a list in the same order in which they are presented. 2. Discrimination learning in which the discriminanda are periodically replaced with new ones, e.g. a REVERSAL SHIFT, a NON–REVERSAL SHIFT, or the GENERALIZED ODDITY PROBLEM, etc. Many species take less time to learn to discriminate a new set of stimuli after repeated shifts, and some learn to solve the generalized oddity problem.

serial monogamy. A synonym for SERIAL POLYGAMY (believe it or not).

serial non–reversal shift learning. Discrimination learning in which a series of NON–REVERSAL SHIFTS are presented; many organisms learn new pairs of stimuli more quickly after a sufficient number of shifts.

serial polygamy. A marriage system in which a man has only one wife at a time, but can have more than one in succession.

serial position curve. A graph of SERIAL LEARNING (1), showing the sequence of items to be learned on the horizontal axis and the probability of recalling each on the vertical axis.

serial position effect. The phenomenon that, in SERIAL LEARNING (1), items towards the beginning and end of the list tend to be learned more rapidly than those in the middle, thus producing a U-shaped SERIAL POSITION CURVE.

serial processing. (Computing) The processing of information in consecutive steps as opposed to PARALLEL PROCESSING, in which many different operations are conducted simultaneously.

serial recall. The recall or attempted recall of a series of items in the same order in which they were presented.

serial reversal learning. Discrimination learning in which a series of REVERSAL SHIFTS are presented; many organisms learn each reversal more quickly after a sufficient number of shifts.

serial search. A search through memory, human or computer, in which one item or block of items is examined at a time.

serotonergic. Activated or controlled by serotonin (e.g. of a synapse).

serotonin. 5-hydroxytryptamine (5-HT), a NEUROTRANSMITTER with an inhibitory action; it is widespread in the body and brain. It is probably implicated in the control of sleep, being present in the RAPHE NUCLEUS, and it may play a role in manic-depressive disorders.

servomechanism, servo. Any device which ensures that a given state is achieved or maintained by monitoring the effects of its output on the environment, and adjusting further output accordingly, usually by negative FEEDBACK. *Contrast* BALLISTIC MOVEMENT.

set. 1. (Psychology) A temporary disposition to behave, think or perceive in a particular way. 2. (Mathematics) Any collection of items comprising a CLASS.

set point. The state that a servomechanism is set to attain; depending on the size and direction of the difference between the existing state and the set point, the system will vary its behaviour in such a way as to bring it closer to it. Innate drives appear to have set points; obesity may be largely due to the set point governing eating being wrong.

set theory. The mathematics of sets developed from an axiomatic system, particularly the formalization of the relationships between sets, including infinite sets.

SEU. An abbreviation for SUBJECTIVE EXPECTED UTILITY.

seven plus or minus two. George Miller's term for the number of CHUNKS that can be simultaneously held before the mind, as determined by studies on short-term memory and such findings as that in many sensory dimensions a stimulus can be accurately assigned to only about seven exclusive divisions of the dimension.

seventh cranial nerve. A synonym for FACIAL NERVE.

severe mental retardation. The possession of an IQ of between 25 and 39. *See* MENTAL RETARDATION.

sex anomaly. Any considerable departure of the sex organs from normality.

sex assignment. The gender assigned to a person at birth.

sex characteristics. The genetically-determined physical traits that differentiate the sexes. **Primary sex characteristics** are those directly associated with reproduction and fostering (e.g. the penis or mammary gland), while **secondary sex characteristics**

play no direct role in these activities (e.g. distribution of body hair, shape of buttocks).

sex chromosomes. The paired chromosomes that determine a person's sex, XX in a female, XY in a male. *See also* HETEROSOME.

sex differences. Statistical differences between the traits exhibited by men and women (largely excluding differences in SEX CHARACTERISTICS); much heat but little light has been generated by the attempt to discover how far these differences are genetic or acquired.

sex limited character, sex influenced character. An inherited trait that is expressed only in one sex, e.g. baldness.

sex linking. (Genetics) The transmission of a trait by a gene on the X-chromosome. Because there are no corresponding genes on the Y-chromosome, men are more prone to traits governed by recessive genes on the X-chromosome than women. A man (XY) can only receive such a gene from his mother and can only transmit it to his daughters (XX).

sexology. The systematic study of sex and sexual relations.

sex rivalry. (Psychoanalysis) The child's alleged competition with, and jealousy towards, its parent of the same sex.

sex role. A synonym for GENDER ROLE.

sex role inversion. A synonym for TRANSSEXUALISM.

sex role stereotyping. The traits and attitudes thought to be peculiar to a given sex by the community.

sex typing. Any behaviour towards a male or female which a person performs because he thinks it is appropriate for their sex, e.g. opening doors for women, but not for men.

sexual anomaly. A polite term for sexual perversion.

sexual instincts. 1. (Psychoanalysis) Drives that arise directly or indirectly from the libido: apart from the sex drive, they include hunger, thirst, smoking, painting, reading, and anything else you care to think of. 2. (Psychology) The drive to engage in sexual activity.

sexual response cycle. The four stages through which men and women normally pass before and after intercourse, namely: (i) **appetitive phase** – sexual desire; (ii) **excitement phase** – sexual arousal including erection in the male and vaginal lubrication in the female; (iii) **orgasmic phase** – ejaculation in the male, orgasm in the woman; (iv) **resolution phase** – relaxation and a sense of well-being, and, for a time, inability to have a further erection or orgasm.

sexual selection. The development of secondary sexual characteristics as a result of organisms mating selectively with members of the opposite sex who have desirable characteristics.

S-factor. A synonym for SPECIFIC ABILITY.

shadow. One of Jung's archetypes, derived from man's animal ancestors; it represents the opposite tendencies to those of which the person is consciously aware. If growth is to be satisfactory, it must ultimately be incorporated into the person's personality.

shadowing. The continuous repetition of words spoken by another person; shadowing has been used in experiments on dichotic listening, and also as a means of occupying most of a person's attention, e.g. to prevent rehearsal of recently-presented material.

shallow living. Horney's expression for engaging in many shallow activities in order to deal with underlying conflicts; it is a form of neurotic resignation, unless of course you genuinely like shallow things.

sham drinking. *See* SHAM FEEDING.

sham feeding. The extraction of food from an animal's oesophagus through an implanted fistula, so that what is eaten never reaches the stomach; the procedure has been used in the study of hunger. The same technique applied to drinking is **sham drinking**.

sham operation. A control operation performed to make sure that the effects of an experimental operation were not merely caused by the anaesthetic and the trauma of the operation.

sham rage. Undirected rage in an animal caused by interference with its brain, e.g. by stimulating some parts of the hypothalamus or by removing the cortex.

shape constancy. The tendency for a surface to be seen as approximately its correct shape, regardless of the angle through which it is tilted with respect to the observer. If the observer has no previous knowledge of the shape, shape constancy is often far from perfect.

shape from motion. The means by which the three-dimensional shape of an object is unconsciously inferred from its changing appearance when it moves relative to the observer's eye.

shape-tilt invariance hypothesis, shape-slant invariance hypothesis. The hypothesis that judgements of shape and tilt are dependent on one another, so that any mistake about tilt should result in a corresponding mistake about shape. Experiments suggest there is in fact little correlation between mistakes about tilt and mistakes about shape.

shaping. An OPERANT CONDITIONING technique in which the subject is at first rewarded for making a response (e.g. approaching a bar) that resembles the response to be learned (pressing the bar), and on subsequent trials is rewarded only for responses approximating more and more closely to the one to be learned, until eventually it makes only that one.

shared paranoid disorder. Paranoid beliefs, usually persecutory, shared by two people in a close relationship.

sharpening. The tendency over time for some details of an event to become highlighted and exaggerated in memory. *Contrast* LEVELLING and ASSIMILATION (8).

Sheldon's constitutional theory. A theory developed by Sheldon relating body type to temperament, with three classifications of body type (ENDOMORPHY, MESOMORPHY, and ECTOMORPHY) and three corresponding classifications of temperament (VISCEROTONIA,

SOMATOTONIA, and CEREBROTONIA); he extended his theory to embrace mental illness and delinquency.

shifted checkerboard figure, shifted quadrilateral. Synonyms for the MUNSTERBURG ILLUSION.

shock phase, shock reaction. *See* GENERAL ADAPTATION SYNDROME.

shock–shock interval. In SIDMAN AVOIDANCE CONDITIONING, the interval between the delivery of one shock and the next when the animal fails to make the avoidance response.

shock treatment, shock therapy. The treatment of mental disorder by rendering the patient unconscious through electroconvulsive shock or a drug like insulin.

short-circuit appeal. A technique of persuasion in which an appeal is made to the emotions rather than the reason.

short-range motion system. A low-level uniocular system that can detect apparent motion with a short time pause (less than about 80 msec) between exposures and a short space (less than 15° of arc). *Contrast* LONG-RANGE MOTION SYSTEM.

short-term store (STS), short-term memory (STM). A memory store having limited capacity (about seven items), which lasts only for a few seconds unless maintained by REHEARSAL (2). Its capacity is usually measured by DIGIT SPAN. The terminology in this area of psychology is chaotic – *see* PROCESSING MEMORY, IMMEDIATE MEMORY, WORKING MEMORY and CENTRAL EXECUTIVE, all of which may or may not be identical to short-term memory: take your pick.

short-wavelength cone. *See* CONE.

SHRDLU. (AI) A by now classic program written by Winograd that can carry out instructions on a simulated microworld of toy blocks; the program 'understands' a fragment of English, and in rearranging the blocks on command has an ability to plan and to explain to an interrogator why it is acting as it is at any particular moment.

shuttle box. An experimental box divided in two halves, in which, at a signal (e.g. light onset), an animal is trained to move from one side to the other, usually to avoid shock.

shwa. An alternative spelling for SCHWA.

SI. An abbreviation for **Système Internationale**, a metric system of measurement based on metres, grams, seconds, amperes, etc.

sibilant. (Phonetics) A fricative sound produced by passing air through a groove made by pressing the top of the tongue against the alveolar ridge, e.g. the 's' in 'sit'.

sibling. A brother or sister.

sibship. All the brothers and sisters in a family.

side effect. An unintended and usually adverse effect of a drug.

Sidman avoidance conditioning. An avoidance conditioning procedure in which the organism receives a periodic shock (e.g. every 30 sec) unless it performs an avoidance response in the interval; any response resets the time counter to zero. The crucial difference from other forms of avoidance schedule is that the organism receives no external signal preceding shock onset.

sighting line, sight line. Synonyms for VISUAL AXIS.

sight method. A synonym for WHOLE WORD METHOD.

sight vocabulary. All the words that a person, particularly a person learning to read, can read 'on sight', i.e. without having to recognize them by translating them into a series of phonemes.

sigma (σ). A symbol for 1. MILLISECOND; 2. the STANDARD DEVIATION of a population distribution.

sigma score. A synonym for STANDARD SCORE.

signal anxiety. (Psychoanalysis) An anxiety response that alerts the ego to an internal or external threat and that may help it to ward off PRIMARY ANXIETY.

signal detection theory (SDT). A normative mathematical model of how stimuli are detected in the presence of internal or external NOISE (1). The theory assumes that over trials the intensity of the noise is normally distributed, and that around threshold there is an overlap between the resulting distribution for the strength of the noise and that of the signal plus noise (*see* figure below). The difference between the peaks of the two distributions (measured in standard deviations) is known as **d'** (a measure of discriminability). The point on the axis of strength of stimulation above which the observer says the stimulus is present is known as the RESPONSE CRITERION (β). This is not permanently fixed and can be varied by varying the experimental conditions, e.g. by giving higher rewards for spotting the stimulus when present than for correctly reporting that it is absent. Both d' and β can be calculated from the distribution of a subject's HITS and FALSE ALARMS when the conditions are manipulated to yield results for different (though as yet undetermined) values of β. The method is a more sophisticated way of calculating thresholds than others, since it takes into account the setting of the subject's response criterion. *See also* RECEIVER-OPERATING CHARACTERISTIC CURVE.

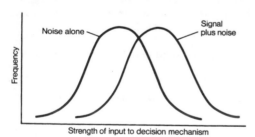

signal detection theory

signalling system. *See* FIRST SIGNAL SYSTEM and SECOND SIGNAL SYSTEM.

signal-to-noise ratio (s/r). The ratio of the power of a signal to that of any NOISE (1) that may mask it.

signature. An abbreviation for LOCAL SIGN.

sign Gestalt. Tolman's expression for the learned expectancy for what will follow a given stimulus or what will follow a response given to that stimulus.

significance level (p). (Statistics) The probability of rejecting the null hypothesis if it is true (TYPE I ERROR). The probability chosen is conventionally set at 0.05 or 0.01. The expression is also sometimes taken to mean the probability, under the null hypothesis, of obtaining the observed or more extreme value of a test statistic. *Compare* ALPHA LEVEL.

significant other. Sullivan's expression for anyone (e.g. a parent) who has a strong influence on a person's values and attitudes.

sign language. Communication, usually with or between the deaf, by visible signs made by the hands or other parts of the body.

sign learning. Tolman's expression for what he thought was the main kind of learning, namely, learning what is likely to follow a particular stimulus or response in a given situation.

sign stimulus. (Ethology) A synonym for RELEASER: there is no clear distinction between the two expressions.

sign test. (Statistics) A non-parametric test for determining the significance of the difference between two paired sets of observations. The number of differences between the scores of each pair in one direction (i.e. either positive or negative) is compared with the number expected by chance, using the binomial distribution. It is less powerful than the WILCOXON TEST since it does not take into account the size of the differences.

silver stain. (Neuroanatomy) A histological dye containing a silver salt that is absorbed by neurons, and hence makes them visible against the surrounding tissue.

similarity, law of. 1. A law of association postulating that similar items will be associated. 2. A law of Gestalt psychology postulating that the more similar are elements in the perceptual field the more likely they are to be grouped together.

similarity paradox. A synonym for SKAGGS–ROBINSON PARADOX.

simile. A figure of speech in which an analogy is drawn between two things. In simile the analogy is made explicit by the use of words like 'like'. *Compare* METAPHOR.

simple cell. A cell in the visual system responding to bars or edges in a particular orientation and position on the retina; it will only respond either to a white or a black bar, or, if it is an edge detector, to an edge with the brighter part on a given side. It differs from COMPLEX CELLS in that it responds only to one type of bar or edge, and the stimulus must be in exactly the right position to produce the maximum response; moreover, its receptive fields can be mapped by using a point of light. *Compare* BAR DETECTOR and EDGE DETECTOR.

simple eye. An eye having a single lens, e.g. the vertebrate eye.

simple phobia. A phobia for a specific object or situation, excluding agoraphobia and the social phobias.

simple reaction time. The REACTION TIME taken to respond to a stimulus when only one stimulus can be given and only one response made. *Contrast* COMPLEX REACTION TIME.

simple schedule, simple reinforcement schedule. A REINFORCEMENT SCHEDULE that does not contain two or more component schedules (e.g. FIXED RATIO SCHEDULE, FIXED INTERVAL SCHEDULE, VARIABLE RATIO SCHEDULE, VARIABLE INTERVAL SCHEDULE, DIFFERENTIAL REINFORCEMENT OF HIGH RESPONSE RATES, and DIFFERENTIAL REINFORCEMENT OF LOW RESPONSE RATES). *Contrast* HIGHER-ORDER SCHEDULE.

simple schizophrenia. A form of schizophrenia marked by apathy and blunting of affect; thought is severely impaired and the patient becomes extremely withdrawn.

simple structure. (Statistics) In factor analysis, a pattern of factor loadings, favoured by Thurstone, in which there are as many zero loadings as possible, and no negative ones.

simple tone. A synonym for PURE TONE.

simplicity principle. The principle, upheld by the Gestaltists, that people interpret stimuli in such a way as to perceive the simplest external situations that could have given rise to them. *Contrast* LIKELIHOOD PRINCIPLE (2).

simulation. The physical instantiation of a model explaining a set of phenomena. *See* COMPUTER SIMULATION.

simultanagnosia. An inability, due to brain damage, to perceive or to integrate stimuli presented simultaneously to different parts of the visual field, e.g. a picture depicting a scene.

simultaneous conditioning. CLASSICAL CONDITIONING in which the conditioned and unconditioned stimuli are presented at the same time.

simultaneous contrast. A change in the appearance of one stimulus away from the appearance of that of another, where both stimuli are presented simultaneously, e.g. BRIGHTNESS CONTRAST and the SIMULTANEOUS TILT EFFECT.

simultaneous discrimination training. DISCRIMINATION TRAINING in which the discriminanda (usually two) are all present on each trial and the organism has to choose between them. *Contrast* SUCCESSIVE DISCRIMINATION TRAINING.

simultaneous tilt effect. The displacement of the apparent orientation of a line or grating away from the orientation of a neighbouring line or grating when both are viewed together. *Compare* TILT AFTEREFFECT.

sine wave. A periodic waveform in which the amplitude at each point is proportional to the sine of the PHASE ANGLE; sine waves produce PURE TONES.

sine wave grating. A SPATIAL FREQUENCY GRATING in which the distribution of light intensity forming the bars is sinusoidal.

single-blind procedure. An experiment in which the experimenter knows in which condition each subject is, but the subjects do not.

Compare DOUBLE-BLIND PROCEDURE and OPEN STUDY.

single-case design. An experimental design using only one subject. It is sometimes used in outcome studies of psychotherapy: the effects on a single subject of systematically varying psychotherapeutic procedures are examined.

single-cell recording. Recording with microelectrodes the firing pattern of a single cell.

single frame task. A VISUAL SEARCH task in which all the stimuli, including DISTRACTORS, are presented simultaneously. *Contrast* MULTIFRAME TASK.

single unit. A single neuron.

sinistral, sinistrad. Pertaining to the left, or toward the left of the body.

sinistrality. A preference for using the left side of the body.

sinusoid. A synonym for SINE WAVE.

SIP. An abbreviation for SCHEDULE-INDUCED POLYDIPSIA.

SIS. An abbreviation for SENSORY INFORMATION STORE.

sitophobia. A morbid fear of food.

situational. Arising from the temporary situation in which someone is placed, used particularly with terms indicating psychiatric disorders.

situational analysis. The study of psychological phenomena occurring in natural situations.

situational approach. An approach to leadership, based on the belief that it will depend very much on the situation who will make the best leader; the approach is colloquially known as **horses for courses**.

situational attribution. Ascribing one's own or another's behaviour to external rather than endogenous factors.

situational conditions. (Educational psychology) All the external factors that influence how well a pupil learns, e.g. physical environment, size of class, teaching methods.

situational homosexuality. Temporary homosexuality arising from the situation, e.g. from being in a single-sex school or in prison.

situationalism. The doctrine that behaviour is largely determined by the immediate environment, and that a person's traits and mental make-up play little part in determining what he does. *Contrast* INTERACTIONAL PSYCHOLOGY.

situational orgasmic dysfunction. *See* ORGASMIC DYSFUNCTION.

situational psychology. A synonym for SITUATIONALISM.

situational psychosis. A synonym for BRIEF REACTIVE PSYCHOSIS.

situational semantics. A theory of meaning in which the truth or falsity of a statement is said to depend on the context in which it is made.

situational specific erectile dysfunction. Failure to obtain an erection on some but not all of the occasions when a man might reasonably expect to have one.

situational test. A test in which a person is put in a situation (with or without knowing it), which is as close as possible to that for which he is being assessed.

situation dependent learning. The phenomenon that recall is impaired if attempted in a different situation (e.g. a different room) from that in which the learning took place.

situationism. The tendency to explain behaviour in terms of the situation rather than in terms of the attributes of the person. Many believe this tendency has gone too far in social psychology.

Sixteen Personality Factor Questionnaire. Cattell's personality inventory, whose results split into 16 traits under factor analysis.

sixth cranial nerve. A synonym for ABDUCENS NERVE.

size constancy. The tendency for objects to be seen as being their correct size, regardless of variations in their retinal size caused by changes in distance.

size distance invariance hypothesis. The hypothesis that apparent size and apparent distance vary proportionately for all physical extents subtending the same visual angle, i.e. as/ad = k where as is apparent size and ad is apparent distance. The hypothesis holds good under most circumstances, but breaks down in some e.g. in the MOON ILLUSION.

size–weight illusion. The tendency, when asked to judge the weight of an object, to be influenced by its size, so that objects of the same weight are judged to be heavier the smaller (and hence the denser) they are.

Skaggs–Robinson paradox. The apparent paradox that proactive and retroactive interference are least when the material to be learned in different blocks of trials is identical, become greater as the material becomes less and less similar, and decrease effectively to zero as the material becomes even more dissimilar.

skeletal muscles. The muscles that move parts of the skeleton; they are all STRIATED MUSCLES and are usually arranged in pairs – EXTENSOR and FLEXOR muscles.

2½D sketch. *See* TWO-AND-A-HALF-D SKETCH.

skewed family. A family in which one parent completely dominates in an uncaring way the other parent and the rest of the family.

skewness. The extent to which a frequency distribution is asymmetrical. *See* MOMENT.

skiascope. A synonym for RETINOSCOPE.

skill. A learned ability to carry out a task, whether motor or cognitive.

skin conductance response (SCR). A synonym for GALVANIC SKIN RESPONSE.

Skinner box. An experimental apparatus devised by Skinner, consisting of a box containing a manipulandum, a means of delivering food automatically, and often a means of delivering stimuli; it also incorporates a device to record the animal's responses automatically and to schedule the availability of reward. Its success was due to its automatic nature, which meant no subjective element could enter into the recording of responses, and which freed the experimenter to do what he chose while the experiment was running. The original Skinner box has been modified for use with many species, and may contain more than one manipulandum.

Skinnerian. Pertaining to RADICAL BEHAVIOURISM.

SL. An abbreviation for SENSATION LEVEL OF SOUND.

slant. 1. The direction and extent of the inclination of a surface relative to the viewer. 2. (Computer vision) The angle between the surface normal and the line of sight. In other words, the angle through which a surface is rotated about the axis of TILT (3).

slave system. A specialized system (e.g. the REHEARSAL LOOP) under the control of a higher system (e.g. the CENTRAL EXECUTIVE).

SLD. An abbreviation for SPECIFIC LEARNING DISABILITY.

sleep. A state in which a person is largely insensitive to stimuli, and has relaxed muscles and a reduced metabolism. There are four stages of progressively deeper sleep: **stage I**: no DELTA WAVES (long, slow EEG waves); **stage II**: delta waves for up to 20 per cent of the time; **stage III**: delta waves up to 50 per cent of the time; **stage IV**: delta waves over 50 per cent of the time. It usually takes more than an hour to reach stage III or IV sleep. These four stages are called NON-REM SLEEP, but having reached stages III or IV the sleeper usually goes into a different kind of sleep, REM SLEEP in which there are rapid eye movements and erratic breathing, and in which delta waves disappear. REM sleep is strongly associated with dreaming, but dreams can also occur in non-REM sleep. There are no good hypotheses about the purpose of sleep, dreaming, or REM sleep.

sleep centre. An area in the HYPOTHALAMUS, thought – probably erroneously – to control sleep.

sleep deprivation. Lack of sleep, which if prolonged may produce hallucinations and disorientation; it is used as a brain-washing technique.

sleep epilepsy. A synonym for NARCOLEPSY.

sleeper effect. The phenomenon that the full change in attitudes produced by a perceived message often only occurs some time after the message has been received, particularly if it comes from a doubtful source.

sleep spindles. A short (about 1 sec) burst of fast (10–14 Hz) EEG waves, occurring in light sleep, particularly in stage II.

SLI. An abbreviation for SPECIFIC LANGUAGE IMPAIRMENT.

slip of the tongue. An unintended error in talking. Freud thought slips of the tongue were caused by repressed wishes; they are now studied by psycholinguists to infer how speech is organized in the mind before being delivered.

slots. In a SCHEMA or SCRIPT blank entries that can be filled by a concept (a FILLER) not fully determined by the schema. E.g. in a restaurant script the exact nature of a starter (soup, prawns, oysters) would not be specified, but might be supplied on an occasion when the script was used.

slow learner. A child who learns slowly, particularly one having an IQ of between 80 and 95.

slow potential. A synonym for GRADED POTENTIAL.

slow-wave sleep (SWS). Stage III or stage IV SLEEP, which is characterized by the appearance of much slow-wave (delta) activity in the EEG.

SMA. An abbreviation for SUPPLEMENTARY MOTOR AREA.

small group. A group of between about three and ten people.

small-sample theory. The theory of how to make valid inferences about a population from a small sample.

smell prism. A synonym for ODOUR PRISM.

SmI. An abbreviation for PRIMARY SOMATOSENSORY CORTEX.

smooth curve. A curve that does not change direction suddenly.

smoothed curve. A curve whose sudden or apparently random changes in direction have been smoothed out.

smooth eye movement. An eye movement that, unlike a SACCADE, is smooth, controlled by feedback, and slow. There are three kinds: COMPENSATORY EYE MOVEMENTS, SMOOTH FOLLOWING MOVEMENTS, AND VERGENCE.

smooth following movement. A SMOOTH EYE MOVEMENT in which the eyes fixate on an object moving smoothly, and preserve fixation on it by following it; smooth following movements cannot be made across a stationary scene. *Compare* PURSUIT MOVEMENT.

smooth muscle. Muscle in which the actin and myosin overlap, and which therefore does not appear striped under a microscope; it has short fibres and contracts slowly, but can stay contracted for long periods. Smooth muscles control the internal organs (except the heart), the iris, and the erection of hair cells; they operate mainly involuntarily. *Contrast* STRIATED MUSCLES.

smooth pursuit movement. A synonym for SMOOTH FOLLOWING MOVEMENT.

s/n. An abbreviation for SIGNAL-TO-NOISE RATIO.

Snellen chart. Rows of letters, with the size of the letters varying systematically from one row to the next, used as a rough test of visual acuity by discovering which rows a person seated at a fixed distance can read. The chart is usually placed 6 metres from the testee.

Snellen fraction. A measurement of acuity by means of the SNELLEN CHART. The numerator gives the distance (in feet or metres) at which the testee viewed a Snellen chart and the denominator the distance at which someone with normal vision (taken to be a minimum separable of one minute of arc) would be able to read the smallest row of letters read by the testee. Thus a fraction that is 1.0 indicates normal vision (e.g. 6/6 in metres or 20/20 in feet). Again 10/20 indicates that the testee's minimum separable is twice the normal since a normal person would read the smallest row read by the testee at twice the distance.

snowball effect. The phenomenon that when there is disagreement within a group, changes in the expressed beliefs of one member will shift the beliefs of some other members, and that such shifts are cumulative.

snowball sampling. A technique for identifying the members of a large group. A few people are asked who are members, the people they name are asked for further members, etc., until no new names are forthcoming

SOA. An abbreviation for STIMULUS ONSET ASYNCHRONY.

SOAR. A decision-making computer program based on productions but incorporating means–ends analysis to solve problems or to achieve a goal. It contains analogues of working memory and long-term memory.

sociability rating, sociability index. Any systematic assessment of how sociable a person is.

sociacousis. Hearing impairment caused by an ecological factor, e.g. by listening to loud pop groups.

social adequacy index. A measure of how impaired a person is in understanding and speaking, based on tests of hearing and articulation.

social adjustment theory. The systematic study of attitude change as a method of social adjustment. *See* ADAPTATION LEVEL THEORY and ASSIMILATION CONTRAST CHANGE.

social anchoring. Basing one's beliefs and attitudes on those of a reference group, rather than making up one's own mind.

social anthropology. A synonym for CULTURAL ANTHROPOLOGY.

social breakdown syndrome. A syndrome caused by being institutionalized, e.g. in a prison or mental hospital, where the person may become apathetic, withdrawn, and passive.

social class. A social category defined by wealth, breeding, education, common habits and attitudes, and even accents. The expression usually carries the implication that different classes can be rank ordered in terms of superiority.

social comparison theory. The doctrine that people assess their attitudes, abilities, etc. by comparing them with those of others.

social contagion. The spread throughout a group of attitudes, ideas, or feelings.

social Darwinism. The doctrine, first put forward by Spencer, that in society the weakest go to the wall, often with the implication that this is a good thing.

social decrement. An impairment in performance caused by a person being in the presence of others. *Contrast* SOCIAL INCREMENT.

social desirability bias. The tendency for people to respond to questionnaires not with their own opinions but with the answer they think will meet with most approval from others.

social determinism. A synonym for CULTURAL DETERMINISM.

social diad. An alternative spelling for SOCIAL DYAD.

social dilemma. Doubt over whether to do something to help oneself when it would have bad consequences for society if everyone did it, e.g. hoarding sugar during a shortage.

social disability syndrome. A synonym for SOCIAL BREAKDOWN SYNDROME.

social distance. The extent to which members of different groups or classes within a society stay apart from one another or reject one another.

social distance scale. A measure of the SOCIAL DISTANCE between a person and members of other groups or classes; the respondent answers questions like 'Would you marry a person from such and such a group/class?'

social dyad. Any two people who interact.

social dynamics. The processes that underlie social change or the study of these processes.

social ecology. The study of the effects of the environment on organisms and vice versa.

social entropy. The doctrine that as societies change, the energy for further change is reduced so that eventually they become static.

social exchange theory. The doctrine that social interactions are based on expectations that benefits given, whether material or emotional, will be returned; a theory more commonly known by the less pretentious expression 'one good turn deserves another'.

social facilitation. The facilitation of behaviour by the presence of conspecifics, e.g. both chickens and people tend to eat more in the presence of conspecifics who are also eating, and applause helps actors and athletes to do their best. Social facilitation does not apply to certain complex tasks, like compiling dictionaries.

social feedback. Letting a person know what you think of him, e.g. by not smiling at a bad pun.

social fission. The splitting apart of a group.

social identity. A person's sense of what he is like when derived from the group to which he belongs.

social immobility. The inability of the members of a society to move between classes or between other large groups.

social impact theory. The theory has two propositions. (a) The larger the number of people influencing someone in the same direction, the more important they are and the more immediate their influence, then the greater their influence will be. (Compare nervousness when giving a lecture to 10 with that when giving it to 1,000 people.) (b) Influence will decrease the more other people are subjected to it, the more important those people are and the less immediate the influence. (Compare nervousness when giving a solo recital with that when a member of an orchestra.)

social increment. An improvement in carrying out some function, e.g. keeping clean, caused by the presence of others. *Contrast* SOCIAL DECREMENT.

social indicator. (Sociology) A statistic about a society that reveals something about its members collective behaviour, e.g. divorce rate or number of boiled sweets eaten.

social inhibition. Impaired performance or restraint caused by the presence of others. E.g. in some societies people do not urinate in public.

social insects. Insects, like bees and ants, that live in communities, and whose survival depends on individuals taking on highly specialized roles within the community. The ideas of SOCIOBIOLOGY were in part derived from the study of such insects.

social instinct. The desire to interact with others.

social intelligence. *See* INTELLIGENCE.

socialization. The process by which a person, starting in infancy, learns how to behave towards other people. It is sometimes claimed that unless at a very early age the infant forms an attachment to the mother or to a mother-figure, socialization is never satisfactory.

socialized-aggressive conduct disorder. *See* CONDUCT DISORDER.

socialized-non-aggressive conduct disorder. *See* CONDUCT DISORDER.

social learning theory. 1. A theory put forward by Bandura and Walters, postulating that much of a person's behaviour (particularly his social behaviour) is learned by copying that of 'models' whom he respects; the theory led to a new technique in behaviour therapy in which the patient tries to model his behaviour on that of the therapist. *See* MODELLING. 2. More generally, any theory of social behaviour that emphasizes the role of learning and reinforcement as the determining factors; e.g. N.E. Miller and Dollard attempted to show how social drives could arise as secondary drives from the primary drives.

social loafing. The phenomenon that some people make less effort when working together at the same task than when working alone, e.g. in a tug-of-war.

social mobility. The extent to which the members of a society do or can move between social classes or between other large groups.

social motive, social need. Any secondary motive acquired as a result of interaction with others, e.g. the achievement drive, though it is hard to be certain that this and many other social motives do not also have some innate basis.

social norm. Any behaviour, belief, attitude, or emotional reaction held to be correct or acceptable by a given group or society.

social penetration. The process by which people get to know each other better through self-revelation.

social perception. The process by which people assess social aspects of others (e.g. their personality, emotions, motives) by making inferences from their appearance, behaviour, speech, etc.

social phobia. (DSM-III) Any phobia based on fear of doing something in public, e.g. speaking, using a public urinal, eating in a restaurant.

social psychiatry. The study of the effect of social relationships on the production and alleviation of mental illness, and the attempt to alleviate mental illness by altering the patients' attitudes to their relationships or by altering the relationships.

social psychology. The branch of psychology that studies social interactions of all kinds, including their origins and their effects on the individual.

social pyramid. The distribution of members of a society by class, which, if the lowest and most numerous class is placed at the bottom, and the highest and smallest at the top, would have the shape of a pyramid.

Social Readjustment Score. A score that measures the amount of stress to which an individual has been subjected. Judges assess the severity of a number of stressful events to provide a score for each. The testee notes each stressful event that has occurred in his life and its frequency; his score is the sum of the scores for each event multiplied by its frequency.

social reality. The conventions and beliefs of a society or group as used as the basis for a person's own attitudes, which may in consequence depart from objective reality (e.g. a belief in witchcraft or in radical behaviourism).

social reinforcement. Any behaviour of a conspecific that can act as a reinforcer, e.g. praise.

social scale. Any method of assigning people to different social categories.

social science. The systematic study of interactions between people. Anthropology, economics, politics, sociology, and social psychology are thought to be social sciences, but although the adjective is appropriate the use of the noun is tendentious.

social selection. The influence of social factors on the survival of individuals or of their genes.

social self. 1. Those aspects of the self that are important for or are influenced by social relations. 2. A person's outward demeanour and behaviour, which may be a front. 3. The way a person sees himself as behaving towards others.

social skills training (SST). A therapy for shy or socially maladept people in which an attempt is made to train them to behave towards others with confidence and grace, e.g. by ceasing to interrupt or by learning how and when to make eye contact.

social stratification. The division of a society into hierarchical classes.

social stress theory. The doctrine that over-crowding induces stress in organisms.

social universal. Any social drive or trait that exists in all human societies, e.g. aggression, sexuality, or speech.

social workers. People who have been through a recognized training course and are employed to supply advice to people in trouble. In practice they spend most of their time not in giving advice, but in committees where they discuss with one another how best to give it. The range of troubles dealt with is wide, and includes poverty, unemployment, loneliness, senility, physical or mental disability, poor housing, children playing truant, marriage breaking up, and mental illness. Social workers may also work with local groups, e.g. youth groups. They often play a role in psychiatric team work, particularly that of liaising with the patient's family.

sociobiology. The systematic attempt to explain innate social behaviour in organisms by demonstrating its precise evolutionary value. Sociobiology is based on the idea that it is the survival of the gene, and not the individual organism or group that determines evolution. Its hypotheses are tested mathematically where possible, mainly by the use of payoff matrices for different innate behaviours. It arose partly from studies of social insects, which posed the problem of how it comes about that some castes never reproduce. For some of its concepts *see* ALTRUISM (1), EVOLUTIONARILY STABLE STRATEGY, and EVOLUTIONARY STRATEGY.

sociocentrism. The acceptance by a person of the norms and values of his group as the standard by which to judge everything.

sociocultural anthropology. A synonym for CULTURAL ANTHROPOLOGY.

sociodrama. A synonym for PSYCHODRAMA.

socioeconomic state (SES). A ranking of a person's standing in society based on indices like wealth, class, and education.

sociofugal space. An area designed to minimize social interaction, e.g. booths in restaurants.

sociogenic. 1. Caused by social factors. 2. Pertaining to the origins of society.

sociogram. A means of representing the relations between members of a group; each member is represented by a node and arrows between nodes denote liking or disliking of other members. It has been extended to represent other relationships between people.

sociolect. (Linguistics) The dialect of any division of a society whose speech is similar but different from that of other divisions. *Contrast* IDIOLECT.

sociolinguistics. The study of the effects of variations in language on social relations and vice versa. It is particularly concerned with social class, variations in dialect, and the role of gestures in communication.

sociological determinism. A synonym for CULTURAL DETERMINISM.

sociology. The study of groups, institutions, and societies, using observational rather than experimental methods. It puts less emphasis on processes within the individual than does social psychology.

sociometric cleavage. In a sociometric test, the relative absence of interaction between the members of one or more sets of individuals within the population studied. It is an indication that the population is split into separate groups.

sociometric clique. The presence of a large number of interactions in a sociometric test between a subset of individuals, which indicates that they form a tightly knit group.

sociometrics. Any attempt to quantify aspects of interpersonal relationships.

sociometric test. A test in which each member of a group is asked questions concerning e.g. which other members of the group he likes, which he would like to work with, go on holiday with, etc. The results can be displayed as SOCIOGRAMS.

sociometry. Moreno's method of arriving at aspects of social relations through sociometric tests and of displaying the results in a SOCIOGRAM.

sociopathy. A snappier, but unfortunately outmoded, synonym for ANTISOCIAL PERSONALITY DISORDER.

sociopetal space. An area designed to encourage social interaction, like a rugby team's communal bath.

sociotaxis. Any social stimulus, e.g. a voice or a gesture.

sociotechnical model. The doctrine that social organizations are produced by an interaction between the social habits and the artefacts of a society.

sociotherapy. Any therapy emphasizing the role of interpersonal relations in mental disorder.

sodium amytal. A short-acting barbiturate, sometimes used in psychotherapy to relax patients and free them from inhibition.

sodium pump, sodium potassium pump. The mechanism that pumps sodium ions from the inside to the outside of the membrane of a cell. When an action potential occurs, sodium ions are transmitted to the inside of the membrane; they must be pumped out to restore and maintain the RESTING POTENTIAL. The same mechanism actively brings potassium ions from the outside to the inside of the membrane.

soft data. Data based only on an observer's impressions.

soft palate. The soft part of the palate, which lies to its rear, and which when elevated prevents sound vibrations passing from the vocal cords into the nasal pathway. *See also* NASAL.

soft schizophrenic spectrum. *See* SCHIZOPHRENIC SPECTRUM.

soft sign. A physical sign suggesting but not proving the existence of an organic condition, particularly minimal brain damage or childhood schizophrenia. Difficulty in tapping regularly is an example of such a sign.

software. Any computer program or system of programs as opposed to the physical components of a computer (the HARDWARE) on which programs are run, and by extension, the connectivity of the nervous system, particularly in so far as it can be changed so that different 'programs' can be run on it. Since their theories do not normally go down to the level of the nervous system, psychologists are said to work on the software of the brain, i.e. its connectivity viewed in a highly abstract way.

solipsism. (Philosophy) The doctrine that all that exists is oneself.

solitary nucleus. A nucleus in the MEDULLA that is a relay station between the taste receptors and the CEREBRAL CORTEX.

solitary play. The first stage of play, in which the child is not influenced by the presence of other children playing. *Compare* PARALLEL PLAY.

solubility. The extent to which a substance dissolves in a solvent.

solution learning. A synonym for TRIAL AND ERROR LEARNING.

solvent. A substance, usually a liquid, that can dissolve another substance.

soma. 1. The whole body. 2. All the cells in the body except the GAMETES. 3. A synonym for CELL BODY.

somaesthesis, somaesthesia. All senses reporting information about the parts of the body, both external (e.g. pressure and temperature), and internal (e.g. kinaesthesis and the visceral senses).

somaesthetic cortex. A synonym for SOMATOSENSORY CORTEX.

somasthenia. Persistent bodily weakness.

somatic. Pertaining to the body.

somatic area. A synonym for SOMATOSENSORY CORTEX.

somatic compliance. The expression of a psychological disturbance through malfunctioning of bodily parts or organs, as in CONVER-SION HYSTERIA.

somatic disorder. 1. An organic disorder. 2. A rare expression for a disorder not having a neurological cause.

somatic marker. Damasio's expression for the brain's representation of the autonomic and somatic feedback from emotional responses; it can also be activated by the brain bypassing the peripheral route.

somatic nerves. All nerves conveying information from the body (excluding the internal organs) or controlling the skeletal muscles (in contrast to nerves subserving the autonomic system).

somatic nervous system. That part of the PERIPHERAL NERVOUS SYSTEM that controls the skeletal muscles and receives information from the bodily senses (excluding the internal organs). *Contrast* AUTONOMIC NERVOUS SYSTEM.

somatic receptors. The sensory receptors of the SOMATIC NERVOUS SYSTEM.

somatic sensory area. A synonym for SOMATOSENSORY CORTEX.

somatic system. A synonym for SOMATIC NERVOUS SYSTEM.

somatic therapy. Treatment by physical methods (e.g. drugs, ECT) rather than by psychological ones.

somatization. The organic expression of a mental disorder, as in asthma or peptic ulcers.

somatization disorder. (DSM-III) A form of CONVERSION HYSTERIA in which there is a recurrence over a period of time of multiple physical symptoms that have no discernible organic cause; among the symptoms are breathlessness, vague pains, palpitations, and difficulty in swallowing.

somatoform disorder. A group of disorders in which involuntary physical symptoms appear with no discernible organic cause; it includes CONVERSION HYSTERIA, PSYCHOGENIC PAIN, and

HYPOCHONDRIA. *Compare* FACTITIOUS DISORDER and PSYCHOSOMATIC DISORDER.

somatogenic. Originating from the body.

somatognosia. Awareness of one's own body.

somatoparaphrenia. (Neuropsychology) A person's delusory belief that one of his limbs does not belong to him; it can be caused by brain damage.

somatopsychic. A synonym for PSYCHOSOMATIC.

somatopsychosis. 1. Any psychosis in which one of the main symptoms is delusions about the parts of the body. 2. A psychosis associated with disease or malfunctioning of the viscera.

somatosenses. A synonym for SOMAESTHESIS.

somatosensory. Pertaining to SOMAESTHESIS.

somatosensory association cortex. A synonym for SUPPLEMENTARY SOMATOSENSORY CORTEX.

somatosensory cortex. The areas of the brain receiving a somatosensory projection excluding the motor cortex. *See* PRIMARY SOMATOSENSORY CORTEX, SECONDARY SOMATOSENSORY CORTEX, and SUPPLEMENTARY SOMATOSENSORY CORTEX.

somatosensory system. The receptors, pathways, and areas of the brain mediating somaesthesis.

somatostatin. A peptide in the brain that inhibits the release of growth hormone from the pituitary.

somatotonia. A personality type (aggressive, robust) in SHELDON'S CONSTITUTIONAL THEORY; it is said to be associated with MESOMORPHY.

somatotopic projection. The topological layout on the cortex of the motor system and the somatosensory system; in both the motor and sensory cortex, neighbouring parts of the body are represented by neighbouring points in the cortex. *See also* HOMUNCULUS (2).

somatotrophic hormone. A synonym for GROWTH HORMONE.

somatotype. Any category of body type that is thought to be related to personality.

somatotypology. The classification of people by body build (usually to establish a link with temperament). *See also* CONSTITUTIONAL TYPE.

somesthesia. A synonym for SOMAESTHESIS.

somesthesis. An alternative spelling of SOMAESTHESIS.

somesthetic cortex. A synonym for SOMATOSENSORY CORTEX.

somnambulism. Walking while asleep.

sonant. Any voiced speech sound.

sone. The unit used in ratio scales of loudness: one sone is the apparent loudness of a 1,000 Hz tone 40 dB above threshold.

soporific. A sleep-inducing drug.

sororate. The custom, practised in some societies, of the deceased wife's widower marrying her sister.

S–O–R theory. Any theory that allows for the role of internal (organismic) factors in determining behaviour. The 'O' stands for organism. *Contrast* STIMULUS–RESPONSE THEORY.

sorting test. Any test in which a person is asked to sort items into categories.

soul image. Jung's expression for the ANIMUS and ANIMA.

sound. 1. (Physics) Travelling changes in pressure within a medium, caused by vibrations. 2. (Psychology) The sensation induced by sound waves reaching the ear.

sound cage. A cubicle used to test the ability to localize sound.

sound intensity. The power flow of a sound wave per unit area. The SI unit of measurement is watts per square centimetre. Sound intensity (I) is related to SOUND PRESSURE by the formula $I = p^2/dc$ where p is RMS sound pressure, d is the density of the medium, and c is the speed of sound in the medium. The subjective correlate of sound intensity is loudness.

sound level meter. A device for measuring the intensity of sound, either directly or after giving different weightings to sounds of different frequencies that correspond to the sensitivity of the ear at each frequency, thus yielding a measurement that corresponds approximately to LOUDNESS.

sound localization. A synonym for AUDITORY LOCALIZATION.

sound perimetry. Testing the accuracy with which sounds coming from each direction can be localized.

sound pressure. The extent to which the pressure of a sound wave deviates from the static pressure of air, usually measured as the root-mean-square of the deviations in pressure from the static pressure (e.g. in dynes per square centimetre). *See* SOUND INTENSITY.

sound pressure level (SPL). The physical intensity of a sound measured in DECIBELS relative to the STANDARD REFERENCE PRESSURE LEVEL.

sound shadow. Any region in which the intensity of a sound is reduced because its passage is blocked by an object. AUDITORY LOCALIZATION is in part based on the sound shadow produced by the head for high-frequency sounds.

sound spectrograph. *See* SPECTROGRAPH.

sour. One of the four primary taste qualities.

source trait. A deep-seated trait (like extraversion or introversion) that gives rise to more superficial traits (**surface traits**); ideally source traits should show little correlation with one another.

spaced practice. A synonym for DISTRIBUTED PRACTICE.

space error. In psychophysics, a CONSTANT ERROR induced by the spatial positions of the stimuli. The expression is also used more widely to refer to any error arising from spatial factors, e.g. a position habit.

space factor. A unitary factor hypothesized to underlie the range of spatial abilities.

spacing. (Ethology and Social psychology) The physical distance maintained between any members of the same species. *Compare* PROXEMICS.

spacing effect. The improvement in learning that occurs as the interval between repetitions of the material to be learned is increased.

span of apprehension, span of attention. The maximum number of items (or CHUNKS) that can be immediately recalled after a brief exposure to a set of items.

span of consciousness. An obsolete term for the maximum number of items that a person can simultaneously hold in consciousness.

spasm. A sudden involuntary muscular contraction, as in hiccups or a convulsion. *See* CLONIC PHASE and TONIC PHASE.

spasmophemia. Stuttering or any speech disorder caused by spasms of the vocal tract.

spasticity. Resistance to the movement of a joint, created by the simultaneous discharge of antagonistic muscles. The condition is caused by damage (sometimes peripheral) to the motor system.

spastic paralysis. Paralysis with tenseness of the muscles; it can be caused by damage to the motor cortex.

spatial ability. The ability to perform tasks requiring manipulation of spatial relations, e.g. map reading, solving a maze, mental rotation. It is often thought to be one of the two most important specific factors underlying intelligence, the other being VERBAL ABILITY.

spatial discrimination. The minimum distance apart that two points or edges touching the body must be in order for the subject to determine that he is being touched in two separate places.

spatial disorder. Any disorder of spatial perception or ability; it can be caused by parietal lobe lesions.

spatial dysfunction. An apraxic syndrome in which the patient is uncertain of the location of the parts of his body. It can be caused by lesions in the parietal cortex.

spatial frequency channel. A hypothetical channel in the visual system tuned to respond to a particular range of spatial frequencies in the retinal image (i.e. to sinusoidal gratings with a specific and limited range of wavelengths). There is some evidence for discrete spatial frequency channels (most workers postulate about six), but the literature is vast and inconclusive.

spatial frequency grating. A grating of parallel light and dark bars of equal frequency, usually formed by a sinusoidal distribution of light.

spatially selective enhancement effect (SSEE). Increased firing of cells in the visual system caused by the organism attending to the region of space to which they respond.

spatial neglect. Pathological inability to sense anything, using any of the senses, in a particular region of space relative to the body; it is caused by brain damage. *Compare* UNILATERAL NEGLECT.

spatial summation. The summation on the membrane of the postsynaptic cell of graded potential changes, caused by its receiving, more or less simultaneously, many inputs from presynaptic cells. Several such inputs may produce an ACTION POTENTIAL, where one or two would not. *Compare* TEMPORAL SUMMATION.

spatial threshold. A synonym for SPATIAL DISCRIMINATION.

spatiotopic. Pertaining to a topological projection of a sensory system onto an area of the brain.

speaker state signal. The non-verbal and paralinguistic cues that indicate that someone wants to speak.

Spearman–Brown formula. A method of estimating the reliability of a test from the known reliability of a portion of the items comprising it.

Spearman rank order correlation, Spearman rho coefficient. A rank order correlation between two variables, based on the differences between their paired ranks using the formula:

$$\frac{6 \sum\limits_{i=1}^{N} D_i^2}{N\,(N^2 - 1)}$$

where D is the difference between a pair of ranks and N is the number of pairs. *Compare* KENDALL'S TAU.

special child. A euphemism for a child with a problem, whether mental, physical, or emotional.

special education. Education directed specifically at the SPECIAL CHLID.

special factor. A SPECIFIC FACTOR thought by some to underlie intelligence, either on its own or in combination with a GENERAL FACTOR. Special factors are invoked only if they account for a reasonable proportion of the variance on several tests. Spatial ability and verbal ability are examples.

special senses. The senses in the head, i.e. vision, hearing, smell, and taste (and, according to taste, the vestibular sense).

speciation. The development of a new species.

species. *See* TAXONOMY.

species-specific behaviour. Behaviour shown by all normal members of a species under given circumstances, regardless of the contribution of heredity and environment to its origin.

specific ability. Any ability to which GENERAL ABILITY makes a comparatively small contribution; often used as a synonym for SPECIAL FACTOR.

specific action potential (SAP). (Ethology) Any instinctive drive that gives rise to a FIXED ACTION PATTERN.

specific developmental disorder. A disorder of childhood that is highly specific and not caused by some more general disorder like mutism or mental retardation, e.g. DEVELOPMENTAL DYSLEXIA or specific arithmetic disorder.

specific developmental dyslexia. An unnecessarily lengthy synonym for DEVELOPMENTAL DYSLEXIA.

specific energy doctrine. The doctrine, advanced by Müller and since proven, that the attributes of sensation are determined by which receptor or receptors are stimulated, and not by the nature of the proximal or distal stimulus.

specific factor. A factor based on only one test item or small set of closely-related test items.

specific hunger. A hunger for a specific dietary component, e.g. salt or thiamine. In practice there is probably only a specific hunger for salt, though animals deprived of a substance they need may learn to eat a food containing it because it makes them feel better.

specificity theory. (Skin senses) The hypothesis that, in the skin senses, different receptors respond selectively to different stimulus continua, particularly those of touch, temperature, and pain. *Contrast* PATTERN THEORY.

specific language impairment. Failure to acquire language properly with no obvious cause, i.e. when hearing, intelligence, upbringing etc. are normal.

specific learning disability. Impairment in a child's ability to learn a specific intellectual skill, like arithmetic or reading, not caused by any general deficit like epilepsy or low intelligence.

specific nerve energy doctrine. A synonym for SPECIFIC ENERGY DOCTRINE.

specific reaction theory. The hypothesis that it is the autonomic system's reactions to stress that produce psychosomatic symptoms.

specific transfer. Transfer between two tasks caused by their having elements in common.

specious present. The small period of time within which any stimulus that occurs seems to be in one's immediate consciousness and to be occurring in the present moment. *See also* PSYCHOLOGICAL MOMENT.

spectator role. Masters and Johnson's expression for observing one's own sexual performance; this may create worries about its adequacy and inhibit spontaneous sexual behaviour.

spectator therapy. Therapy in which some members of a group watch the therapy given to others, from which it is hoped they will benefit.

spectral absorption curve. A curve showing the amount of incident light absorbed by a substance at each wavelength; in vision the curve describes the absorption characteristics of the visual pigments.

spectral colour. A synonym for SPECTRAL HUE.

spectral emisson curve. A curve showing the relative amount of light emitted by a light source at each wavelength.

spectral hue. Any hue that can be produced by monochromatic light. The spectral hues with the approximate wavelengths (in nm) that give rise to them are as follows. Violet, 380–450; blue, 450–480; blue–green, 480–510; green, 510–550; yellow–green, 550–570; yellow, 570–590; orange, 590–630; red, 630–750. *See also* EXTRASPECTRAL HUE.

spectral luminous efficiency function. *See* LUMINOUS EFFICIENCY FUNCTION.

spectral sensitivity curve. A curve showing the sensitivity of a sensor or a sensory system to stimuli of different wavelengths. In vision, it depicts the sensitivity of the retina, i.e. the absolute threshold for seeing at different wavelengths; separate curves are derived for photopic and scotopic vision. In hearing, the absolute threshold for each audible frequency is plotted.

spectrogram. A graphic representation of a sound wave, much used in the analysis of speech. Usually, time is plotted along the horizontal axis and frequency along the vertical axis; the intensity of the sound at each frequency is represented by the darkness of each point in the graph.

spectrograph. A device for producing a SPECTROGRAM.

spectrophotometer. A device for determining the absorption spectrum of a semitransparent pigment by measuring how much incident light at each wavelength it transmits. *See also* MICROSPECTROPHOTOMETER.

spectrum. A range of physical wavelengths or the range of subjective effects produced when they are used as stimuli. Thus, 'visual spectrum' may refer either to the range of visible wavelengths or to the range of hues; similarly the auditory spectrum refers either to the range of audible frequencies or to the corresponding range of pitches.

spectrum theory. (Psychiatry) The discarded theory that all mental illness lies on a continuum, especially a continuum of anxiety and methods for coping with it.

specular. A posh synonym for GLOSSY.

speech act. (Linguistics) An utterance that executes a purposeful act (as almost all utterances do); speech acts are classified by the intention behind the utterance, e.g. DIRECTIVES, COMMISSIVES, DECLARATIONS, EXPRESSIVES, and REPRESENTATIVES.

speech area. A synonym for BROCA'S AREA.

speech block. A temporary inability to speak or to continue speaking.

speech-retarded child. A child who learns speech slowly (but who may ultimately be completely normal).

speech synthesizer. A device (usually a computer) that produces intelligible speech according to rules.

speech therapy. Any therapy to correct a speech disorder.

speed accuracy trade-off. The phenomenon that in many tasks people make more errors the faster they go, and can to some extent regulate their speed to keep errors down to a given level.

speed reading. Reading faster, often much faster, than 500 words a minute, which is roughly the theoretical maximum if every word is to be read, given that not more than five fixations can be made a second, and not more than three words can be read at each fixation. Speed reading largely consists of skipping with a resulting loss of knowledge of detail and general comprehension.

speed test. An ability test whose result depends on how many correct responses a person can make in a given time. *Contrast* POWER TEST.

Spence theory. A theory explaining PEAK SHIFT by positing an excitatory generalization gradient around the positive stimulus and an inhibitory one around the negative stimulus; the peak of the positive stimulus is shifted as a result of the asymmetrical reduction in excitation caused by the inhibitory gradient.

spermatophobia. A morbid fear of sperm.

spheraesthesia, spheresthesia. Synonyms for GLOBUS HYSTERICUS.

spherical aberration. The production of blur in an optical image, caused by the fact that a lens of spherical curvature does not form a perfect image.

sphincter morality. (Psychoanalysis) Attitudes associated with the precursor of the SUPEREGO. They result from the child introjecting the demands made on it in toilet training.

spicy. One of the six so-called primary odours of the ODOUR PRISM, reminiscent of the smell of nutmeg. It is also one of the four odours of the ODOUR SQUARE.

spider cell. A synonym for STELLATE CELL.

spike. The record of a nerve impulse, which shows a sudden change in membrane potential rising rapidly to a spike; the term is also used to mean the nerve impulse itself.

spike-and-dome discharge. The presence in the EEG of a spike followed by a low-amplitude slow wave, recurring at a frequency of about 3 Hz; it occurs in *petit mal* epilepsy.

spinal accessory nerve. A synonym for ACCESSORY NERVE.

spinal animal. A synonym for SPINAL PREPARATION.

spinal canal. The cavity containing the spinal cord and the spinal fluid that bathes it; at the lower end it extends beyond the spinal cord.

spinal column. The spine.

spinal cord. The tube of nervous tissue running from the base of the brain through the spinal column. *See also* SPINAL NERVES.

spinal fluid. The part of the CEREBROSPINAL FLUID that is in the spine.

spinal ganglia. Ganglia on the dorsal root of each spinal nerve, composed of the cell bodies of somaesthetic fibres.

spinal gate control theory. *See* GATE CONTROL THEORY.

spinal lemniscus. The continuation of the lateral spinothalamic tract through the hindbrain and midbrain to the thalamus.

spinal nerves. The pairs of peripheral nerves that are connected to the spinal cord in two branches: the afferent component is attached to the dorsal root and the efferent component to the ventral root (*see* SPINAL ROOT). In man there are 31 pairs: 8 pairs of **cervical nerves** (connected in the region of the neck), 12 pairs of **thoracic nerves** (connected in the region of the chest), 5 pairs of **lumbar nerves** (connected in the region just below the chest), 5 pairs of **sacral nerves** (connected in the lower back region), and 1 pair of coccygeal nerves (connected at the lowest vertebra). *Compare* CRANIAL NERVES.

spinal preparation. An animal in which for experimental purposes the spinal cord has been severed from the brain.

spinal reflex. A reflex, like the knee jerk, that is mediated by connections at the spinal level; the strength of such reflexes may be influenced by current activity in the spinal cord, which in turn can be affected by descending signals from the brain.

spinal root. The two short pathways into which each spinal nerve divides as it approaches the spinal cord: the **dorsal root** (composed of sensory fibres) enters towards the back of the cord; the **ventral root** (composed of efferent fibres) towards the front.

spindle cell. A synonym for FUSIFORM CELL.

spindle layer. A synonym for FUSIFORM LAYER.

spindle wave. Any high-amplitude spiky wave, particularly those that appear in the electroencephalogram of people asleep. They become more prominent as the sleeper passes from stage I of sleep to stage IV.

spine. (Neuroanatomy) Short for DENDRITIC SPINE.

spinoreticulothalamic tract. Another name for the SPINOTHALAMIC TRACT, but emphasizing that many of the pathways end not in the thalamus but in the reticular formation.

spinospinal tracts. Short tracts carrying information between and within the levels of the spinal cord.

spinothalamic tracts. Tracts that conduct afferent information about pain and temperature (the **lateral spinothalamic tract**), and probably touch and pressure (the **anterior spinothalamic tract**), through the dorsal columns of the spinal cord towards the thalamus.

spiral aftereffect. The MOTION AFTEREFFECT produced by a rotating spiral. If an observer fixates it, he sees circles continuously moving inwards or outwards, depending on the direction of rotation; when it stops moving, he sees movement in the opposite direction.

spiral ganglion. The ganglion in the wall of the COCHLEA where the cell bodies of the ganglion cells innervating the HAIR CELLS are located.

spiral lamina. *See* OSSEOUS SPIRAL LAMINA.

SPL. An abbreviation for SOUND PRESSURE LEVEL.

splanchnic. Pertaining to the viscera.

splenium. The rearmost part of the CORPUS CALLOSUM.

split brain. A brain in which the CORPUS CALLOSUM (and sometimes other commissures and the optic chiasm) has been cut or in which the corpus callosum is congenitally absent. Animals and people with split brains have been extensively studied to examine problems of laterality, and of the transfer of information from one hemisphere to another.

split-half correlation, split-half reliability. The correlation between scores on two halves of a test, which is a measure of its reliability.

split litter method. The systematic assignment of litter mates to different experimental groups to minimize the effects of genetic variability.

split personality. A synonym for MULTIPLE PERSONALITY.

split span paradigm. An experimental technique, first used by Broadbent, on which two lists of items, e.g. digits, are simultaneously presented, one list to each ear. Subjects tend to recall all the items sent to one ear and then those sent to the other, rather than recalling them in their temporal order.

spontaneity test. A way of acquiring insight into people's relationships by observing them interacting in a naturalistic situation.

spontaneity therapy. A technique invented by Moreno, in which the client spontaneously acts out his problems through PSYCHODRAMA, in the hope that this will either be cathartic or will provide insights either directly or through others' comments.

spontaneous alternation. The tendency for animals, particularly rats, when faced with a choice point, systematically to change the choice made from trial to trial. In the learning of mazes, this tendency may for many trials overcome the effects of reinforcement being provided for a particular choice.

spontaneous discharge, spontaneous firing. The firing of a neuron without its having been stimulated.

spontaneous phenomena. (Parapsychology) Psychic phenomena that occur naturally and with no premeditation on anyone's part, i.e. not in a seance or laboratory, etc.

spontaneous recovery. The phenomenon that a learned response that has been partly extinguished increases in strength over an interval in which no further extinction trials are given. *Compare* SPONTANEOUS REGRESSION.

spontaneous regression. 1. (Learning) A decrease in response strength occurring between the end of one training session and the beginning of the next. *Compare* SPONTANEOUS RECOVERY. 2. The alleged return of a hypnotized person to speaking and acting in the way he had done at a former age, or to reliving events from a former age. It is alleged that he can behave in ways for which he has no conscious memory.

spontaneous remission. REMISSION of an illness not caused by treatment. The expression 'spontaneous recovery' is not used in this context since doctors are loath to admit that anyone could recover without medical treatment.

Spoonerism. The transposition of the initial sounds of two words in a sentence, a phenomenon studied to reveal how speech elements are structured in the mind in order to produce speech. The phenomenon is named after Spooner of Oxford whose legendary transpositions are said to have resulted in such sentences as 'I'll fight the liar' for 'I'll light the fire'.

spotlight model. The hypothesis that people can pay visual attention at any one time to any given area of the visual field but not to two or more separated areas.

spreading activation. The spread of activity over adjacent parts of a network, whether neural or theoretical.

spreading depression. The inhibition of the activity of neurons caused by applying a salt solution (usually potassium chloride) and the spread of the inhibition away from the point of application to neighbouring tissue.

spread of effect. Thorndike's expression for his hypothesis that reinforcement strengthens (and punishment weakens) the connection between responses made not merely to the immediately preceding stimuli but to stimuli slightly removed in time, and also to stimuli similar to the initial stimulus (generalization).

spurious correlation. A correlation between two variables that is not due to any direct causal or other connection between them, but which is caused by other variables affecting them both in the same way. It is frequently found when correlating time series, e.g. in a German town the number of children born correlated for many years with the number of storks there.

SQ3R method. A method of studying written material, based on (in sequence) *S*urveying the material, formulating *Q*uestions about it, *R*eading it with the questions in mind, *R*eciting the main points, and finally *R*eviewing it.

squeeze technique. A method of preventing premature ejaculation, in which the partner squeezes the head of the penis until the urge to ejaculate stops.

squint. A synonym for STRABISMUS.

S–R learning. An abbreviation for STIMULUS–RESPONSE LEARNING.

S–R theory. An abbreviation for STIMULUS–RESPONSE THEORY.

SS. An abbreviation for STANDARD SCORE.

SSEE. An abbreviation for SPATIALLY SELECTIVE ENHANCEMENT EFFECT.

S-shaped curve. A synonym for OGIVE.

S–S learning. Stimulus–stimulus learning, i.e. learning the associations between stimuli, and in particular that one stimulus is closely followed by another. *Compare* SENSORY PRECONDITIONING.

S sleep. An abbreviation for SLOW-WAVE SLEEP.

SSRI. Any **selective serotonin reuptake inhibitor**. They are used as antidepressants and are thought to have a more specific action on neurotransmitters than the TRICYCLICS or MAOIS. The two main SSRIs are **fluvoxamine** and **fluoxitine**: the trade name for the latter is **Prozac**, which has given rise to much hype and controversy in the US.

SST. An abbreviation for 1. STIMULUS SAMPLING THEORY; 2. SOCIAL SKILLS TRAINING.

s-structure. An abbreviation for SURFACE STRUCTURE.

St. An abbreviation for STANDARD STIMULUS.

stabilimeter. A device for measuring body sway, usually while the subject is blindfolded.

stability of the visual world. The phenomenon that the visual world does not appear to move when the image it produces is swept across the retina as a result of eye movements.

stabilized image. A retinal image which remains stationary on the retina even when the eyes move; the effect can be achieved by having the subject wear a contact lens with a small mirror, and reflecting the pattern to be viewed off that mirror and by way of others on to a plain surface so that the pattern moves in synchrony with the eye. Because of adaptation, stabilized images become difficult or impossible to see after a few seconds' viewing.

stack. (Computing) A temporary store from which the items are withdrawn in the opposite order to that in which they were inserted, i.e. the last item in is the first out, etc. Hence it is sometimes known as a **push-down stack**. *Contrast* RANDOM ACCESS MEMORY.

stages of sleep. *See* SLEEP.

staircase illusion. A synonym for SCHROEDER STAIRCASE.

staircase method. A psychophysical method for determining thresholds in which, in the case of absolute thresholds, the intensity of the stimulus is increased when the subject fails to perceive it, and decreased when he does perceive it. For difference thresholds the size of the difference is changed in the same way. The method is a variation on the METHOD OF LIMITS, and is highly efficient since it ensures that all readings are taken near threshold and therefore not wasted.

standard (S). Short for STANDARD STIMULUS.

Standard American English (SAE). The language of white Americans.

standard candle. A synonym for INTERNATIONAL CANDLE.

standard chromaticity diagram. A figure having along its horizontal and vertical axes the proportion of X and Y primaries under the XYZ SYSTEM of colour specification, and containing a COLOUR TRIANGLE in which the sides representing spectral colours are bowed outwards. The edge of the triangle represents saturated hues and the interior desaturated hues. The triangle is normally shown in colour so that the approximate colour specified by any combination of the X and Y primaries can be read from it.

standard deviation (SD, s, σ). A measure of the dispersion of a set of values about the mean given by the formula $SD = \sqrt{(\Sigma(X_i - \bar{X})^2/N)}$, where X_i is the ith value, $\bar{X}$ the mean and N the number of values. In a normal distribution, the interval between one standard deviation above and below the mean includes about 68 per cent of values, and that between two standard deviations above and below the mean includes about 95 per cent. The standard deviation of a sample is commonly symbolized by s, and that of a population mean by σ.

standard difference. The difference between two means divided by the STANDARD ERROR of that difference.

standard error (SE). The STANDARD DEVIATION of the theoretical sampling distribution of a statistic. E.g. the standard error of the mean of normal samples is $\sigma/\sqrt{N}$ where σ is the population standard deviation and N is the sample size. *See also* STANDARD ERROR OF THE MEAN.

standard error of estimate. The standard deviation of the distribution of the differences between a set of values and the fitted values from a regression line.

standard error of the mean (σ_x, σ_m). The standard deviation of the theoretical sampling distribution of the sample mean. An approximate value is obtained by dividing the standard deviation of the sample by the square root of the number of items sampled. It can be used to assess how closely a sample mean is likely to approximate to the population mean.

standardization. (Psychometrics) The establishment of population norms for a test; it can include making the test reliable and ensuring its validity.

standardized score. A synonym for STANDARD SCORE.

standard observer. A hypothetical observer whose sensory system is completely normal. *Compare* IDEAL OBSERVER.

standard ratio. A synonym for STANDARD DIFFERENCE.

standard reference pressure level. The pressure level at the ear which normally forms the reference point for measurements of sound intensity in DECIBELS. It is a notional absolute threshold of a 1,000 Hz sound and is 0.0002 dyne per square centimetre.

standard score. A synonym for Z-SCORE.

standard stimulus (S, St). In psychophysics, the stimulus presented to the observer, which he is asked either to match by selecting another stimulus that appears equal to it, or to use as a basis for a magnitude estimate, e.g. by setting another stimulus to appear half as loud, half as bright, etc.

standard theory. (Linguistics) Chomsky's 1965 theory which postulated transformations on the deep structure to form the surface structure, with the additional hypothesis (now thought to be false) that the meaning of the sentence resides in the deep structure, not the surface structure.

standing wave. A wave occurring in a medium (e.g. an elastic string) such that each part of the medium moves a given amount, but the wave does not travel along it. Points at which there is no displacement are called **nodes**, and points of maximal displacement **antinodes**.

Stanford–Binet Test. An intelligence test for children and adults, derived from the Binet Scale, but considerably changed. It yields a mental age, which can be divided by chronological age to produce an IQ score.

stapedes. The plural of STAPES.

stapedius. A muscle in the middle ear which when contracted helps to reduce movement of the OSSICLES, and hence prevents the ear from being damaged by intense sound.

stapes. A small stirrup-shaped bone in the middle ear, one of the OSSICLES, which transmits sound vibrations to the OVAL WINDOW of the COCHLEA.

star cell. A synonym for STELLATE CELL.

startle reflex, startle response, startle reaction. A largely innate reaction to an unexpected and threatening stimulus, in which there is arousal, flexion of the extremities, and an increase in heartbeat and respiration, with attention being directed towards the stimulus.

stasibasiphobia. A morbid fear of standing upright and walking.

stasiphobia. A morbid fear of standing up.

stasis. (Evolution) A period in which a species' genes show little change.

state anxiety. Anxiety that depends on a person's situation and varies with it. *Contrast* TRAIT ANXIETY.

state dependent learning. The phenomenon that learning transfers incompletely when the organism is in a new internal state. E.g. recall of material learned after a drug has been administered can be impaired if attempted in the absence of the drug.

static reflex. Any reflex that maintains posture or balance.

static response. A synonym for STATIC REFLEX.

static sense. The sense of balance.

station point. A synonym for VIEWPOINT.

statistical artefact. An incorrect conclusion caused by errors in the collection or statistical analysis of data, e.g. through using an A PRIORI TEST that was not planned.

statistical attenuation. The reduction in the size of a correlation, caused by errors in measuring one or both of the variables.

statistical contamination. The effect of an unrecognized independent variable that works either in the same or the opposite direction to an independent variable under test. Since the contaminating variable is only recognized after the study, it is not normally possible to apportion the effects found between it and the variable under test.

statistical controls. The correction of raw data by statistical methods to make allowance for the existence of biases that could not be controlled in the experimental design.

statistical dependence. A correlation between two or more variables; the expression emphasizes that the correlation need not be due to a direct connection (e.g. a causal one) between the variables.

statistical error. Any error in sampling or in the analysis of data, such as using the wrong tests or misinterpreting their outcomes.

statistical inference. The drawing of conclusions about populations from the statistical analysis of sample data.

statistical interaction. A synonym for INTER-ACTION.

statistical law. Any generalization that is usually but not always applicable.

statistical learning theory. The attempt to describe the process of learning (and particularly the shape of the learning curve) by mathematical models, in which the state of the organism changes from trial to trial according to a probabilistic process.

statistical prediction. Making a prediction, diagnosis, etc., not by intuition but by incorporating the relevant knowledge into a rigorous and explicit framework, and where appropriate using statistical techniques. E.g. in medical diagnosis each symptom or combination of symptoms could be assigned a weight as indicative of a given illness, and the most probable illness could be arrived at on this basis. *Contrast* CLINICAL PREDICTION.

statistical regression. A synonym for regression to the mean.

statistical significance. A synonym for SIGNIFICANCE LEVEL.

statistics. The branch of applied mathematics that deals with the collection, analysis, and interpretation of data, and makes inferences about populations from samples. *See* DESCRIPTIVE STATISTICS, INFERENTIAL STATISTICS, NON–PARAMETRIC STATISTICS, and PARAMETRIC STATISTICS.

statoacoustic nerve. A synonym for VESTIBULOACOUSTIC NERVE.

statocyst. The organ of balance in some invertebrates including crustacea and molluscs. It consists of a vesicle containing **statoliths** (particles of sand, lime, etc.), which stimulate receptors when the animal moves.

statokinetic response. Any response that preserves the body's balance while it is in motion.

statolith. *See* STATOCYST.

stat rat. An imaginary rat or other subject, whose behaviour over a series of trials in a learning experiment is simulated, usually by computer. Where it is hypothesized that the effects of a trial on a subject are probabilistic, or that its choices are probabilistic, such simulation is needed to discover how a group of subjects will behave according to the theory. *See also* STATISTICAL LEARNING THEORY.

status validity. A synonym for CONCURRENT VALIDITY.

steady state. Any state of a system that remains stable, usually because negative feedback is correcting deviations from it.

stellate cell. A type of GOLGI TYPE II CELL with richly branching (star-like) dendrites and a single short axon; it is found in both cerebellar and cerebral cortex, particularly in layers II and IV of the latter. *See also* BASKET CELL and GRANULE CELL.

stem. A synonym for ROOT.

step-down test. A test in which an animal is shocked if it steps down from a platform; it is later replaced on the platform to discover if, as a result of learning, the latency of stepping down will increase. The test is particularly useful for measuring the effects of ECT on memory, since if the ECT acts as a punishment, the animal should have an increased rather than a reduced latency, as compared with a control subject not receiving ECT. In fact, animals given ECT after the first trial often show lower latency than controls, thus demonstrating the effects of ECT on learning.

step function. Any function which changes discontinuously, i.e. in steps.

step interval. The range of values grouped together in a frequency distribution (e.g. in a HISTOGRAM).

stepping reflex. A reflex stepping movement present in the first two weeks of life when the infant is held with his feet touching a surface and is moved forward.

step tracking. A TRACKING task in which the target moves in discrete jumps rather than continuously.

steradian. A unit of solid angle, being the angle having its vertex at the centre of a sphere and demarcating an area of the sphere's surface equal to the square of the radius. The area is $1/4\pi$ of the total area of the sphere.

stereoacuity. A synonym for STEREOSCOPIC ACUITY.

stereochemical theory of odour discrimination. The theory that different odorous molecules bind to different receptor sites in the olfactory epithelium, and that there are a limited number of different sites. At present there are thought to be seven, corresponding to ethereal, camphoraceous, musky, floral, minty, pungent, and putrid smells.

stereocilia. *See* HAIR CELL.

stereognosis. Knowledge about an object derived through touch, particularly recognition of the object.

stereogram. A pair of two dimensional pictures which when viewed stereoscopically are seen in three dimensions. *See also* RANDOM DOT STEREOGRAM.

stereokinetic effect. An illusion produced by viewing a slowly rotating disc on which interlocking rings or ellipses are drawn: the figures are seen in depth.

stereopathy. Pathologically persistent and stereotyped thinking.

stereopsis. A cue to depth, based on differences in the images of the left and right eyes; it is caused naturally by the difference in their viewpoints, and artificially by designing stereograms containing systematic differences. *See* BINOCULAR DISPARITY.

stereoscope. A device for projecting two pictures, one to each eye, by means of mirrors or prisms.

stereoscopic acuity. The minimum BINOCULAR DISPARITY sufficient to produce an impression of a difference in depth. It is as low as 2″ of arc.

stereoscopic vision. Depth vision obtained through STEREOPSIS.

stereotaxic atlas. A series of charts showing the 3-D coordinates of the different parts of the brain for a particular species, for use with a STEREOTAXIC INSTRUMENT.

stereotaxic instrument. A device in which an organism's head can be accurately positioned by rods inserted into the outer ears, and which through a 3-D coordinate reference system enables an experimenter or surgeon to locate accurately any point in the brain.

stereotropism. Any orienting response to a solid object.

stereotype. (Social psychology) A grossly oversimplified view of the characteristics of the members of a group (usually but not always derogatory), in which the characteristics thought to be prevalent in the group are attributed to each member, regardless of individual differences. The stereotype a person has of his own group is an **autostereotype**, that of other groups a **heterostereotype**.

stereotyped behaviour. Inflexible behaviour following a fixed pattern without adjustment to changing circumstances.

stereotyped movement disorder. Any disorder in which the main symptom is the repetition of a movement, e.g. a tic. *Compare* TOURETTE'S DISORDER.

stereotypy. Prolonged pathological repetition of movements or speech sounds, common in autism and catatonic schizophrenia. Sometimes also applied more loosely to nonpathological but inflexible and repetitive behaviour.

steroids. Hydrocarbon compounds containing 17 carbon atoms. Different steroids have very different properties: they range from some hormones to toad poisons.

Stevens's law, Stevens's power law. Synonyms for POWER LAW.

sthenometer. Any device for measuring muscular strength.

sticky fixation. (Neuropsychology) Difficulty or inability to alter the direction of a fixation; it is caused by brain damage.

Stiles–Crawford effect. The phenomenon that light entering the eye through the centre of the pupil appears brighter than light entering the eye near its edge; the effect is only obtained in photopic vision. It has been suggested that the cones act as LIGHT GUIDES, and that light striking them obliquely may pass straight through them rather than being reflected down them.

Stilling test. A test for colour blindness, in which dots of different hues but the same brightness are arranged to form numbers.

stimulant. Any drug that increases activity and alertness, e.g. amphetamine or caffeine. Most such drugs appear to work by directly increasing the activity in arousal centres (e.g. the reticular activating system), but some drugs (e.g. alcohol or nicotine) appear to have both a depressant and a stimulant effect.

stimulation. The production of a sensation, or the excitation of a neuron.

stimulation-produced analgesia. Analgesia produced by electrical stimulation of the brain.

stimulus. 1. Any pattern of physical energy, whether of external or internal origin, that impinges on the organism's receptors, and that can be detected by the organism. 2. The part of the pattern of such physical energies to which the organism responds. *See* PROXIMAL STIMULUS. 3. Any class of stimuli (2) that the organism (or experimenter) groups together as signifying the same external object, event, or class of objects or events. 4. The external object or event that gives rise to stimulus (1). *See* DISTAL STIMULUS. 5. Any mental event (e.g. a memory) that triggers a response. This use is confusing and was introduced by the behaviourists in an attempt to save stimulus–response theory. 6. Any event that excites or inhibits a neuron. *See also* CONDITIONED STIMULUS, DISCRIMINATIVE STIMULUS, NEGATIVE STIMULUS, POSITIVE STIMULUS.

stimulus as coded (SAC). The central representation of a stimulus; e.g. the visual image is not normally coded as a two-dimensional image but as a three-dimensional representation of the object from which the light in the image was reflected.

stimulus attitude. A synonym for STIMULUS SET.

stimulus barrier. (Psychoanalysis) A postulated process whereby the infant defends itself from being overwhelmed by stimuli, particularly threatening ones.

stimulus bound. 1. Pertaining to a personality that is inflexible, and that responds automatically and without thought to the immediate situation. 2. Pertaining to perceptions that are determined largely by the physical nature of the stimulus, with little interpretation of it.

stimulus continuum. Any dimension along which a stimulus of a given type can vary, e.g. light intensity or sound frequency.

stimulus differentiation. 1. The process of learning to discriminate between the members of a set of similar stimuli. 2. (Gestalt psychology) The emergence of structural elements in an initially amorphous perceptual field.

stimulus dimension. A synonym for STIMULUS CONTINUUM.

stimulus element. A small (and wholly undefined) part of a stimulus array postulated by Estes in his STIMULUS-SAMPLING THEORY.

stimulus equivalence. The capacity of two or more stimuli to elicit the same response, particularly when not determined by the physical similarity of the stimuli. E.g. the same response may be made to an actual fire and a cry of 'fire'.

stimulus error. Titchener's expression for a failure to introspect correctly one's immediate experience through taking other considerations into account. Someone accustomed to judging light intensities might correctly judge that one light was twice as intense as another, but he would be committing the stimulus error, since apparent brightness increases approximately logarithmically with intensity.

stimulus field. A modern and otiose expression for DISTAL STIMULUS.

stimulus generalization. See GENERALIZATION (2).

stimulus intensity dynamism (V). Hull's term for the fact that in general the stronger the stimulus the stronger the response of the organism. See HULLIAN THEORY.

stimulus object. A synonym for DISTAL STIMULUS.

stimulus onset asynchrony (SOA). The time between the onset of one stimulus and another (e.g. a TARGET and a MASK), which may be positive or negative according to which stimulus comes first.

stimulus overload. The presence of so many attention-compelling stimuli that they cannot all be processed, a situation thought to provoke stress.

stimulus–response compatibility. The ease with which a person can make a given response to a given stimulus array. E.g. a task in which a subject has to move a lever to the left when the left hand of two lights comes on and to the right when the right hand one comes on has more stimulus–response compatibility than one in which the subject has to move the lever in the opposite direction to the light that is lit. Somewhat surprisingly, almost all appliances from ovens to aircraft cockpits are designed to minimize stimulus–response compatibility.

stimulus–response learning. Learning to attach a response to a stimulus, once misguidedly thought to be the basis of all learning.

stimulus–response theory. Any theory in which all learning is viewed simply as a process of attaching responses to stimuli.

stimulus-sampling theory. A mathematical learning theory proposed by Estes. He thought that on each trial the organism samples a proportion of the STIMULUS ELEMENTS present, and that if reinforcement occurs the response made is attached to all elements sampled. Whether the response is made on a given trial depends on the proportion of stimulus elements sampled on that trial that have been conditioned. Learning curves can often be simulated by the model, but it gives little insight into the learning process, and the notion of a stimulus element is vague.

stimulus set. 1. In REACTION TIME experiments, a set to pay attention to the stimulus rather than to the response. *Contrast* RESPONSE SET (1). 2. More generally, a preparedness to react to a particular stimulus or kind of stimulus.

stimulus–stimulus learning. *See* s–s LEARN-ING.

stimulus substitution theory. A theory of classical conditioning hypothesizing that the conditioned stimulus 'substitutes' for the unconditioned stimulus, thus producing the same response.

stimulus suffix effect. In free recall of auditory material, reduced retention of the last item or two in the list, caused by presenting an item not to be recalled after the end of the list (the suffix). This procedure presumably impairs echoic memory for the immediately preceding items.

stimulus trace. A representation of a stimulus that decays rapidly with time, postulated to explain TRACE CONDITIONING and the occurrence of instrumental learning when there is an interval between the discriminative stimulus and the reinforcement.

stimulus variable. An independent variable that consists of changes in the stimulus.

stirrup. A synonym for STAPES.

STM. An abbreviation for SHORT-TERM MEMORY.

stochastic process. A temporal series of events, none of which can be predicted with certainty, but each of which can be assigned a probability of occurring, where the probability of an event at a given time may be influenced by the occurrence of previous events. Trial by trial performance in learning is often regarded as a stochastic process. *Compare* MARKOV PROCESS.

Stockholm syndrome. The emotional bond that sometimes develops between captives and captors.

stocking anaesthesia. Loss of sensation in the area normally covered by a stocking, a form of conversion hysteria. *Compare* GLOVE ANAESTHESIA.

stooge. A person who in collaboration with the experimenter pretends to be a subject in an experiment, usually so that he can manipulate the genuine subjects in some way.

stop consonant. (Phonetics) A consonant in the production of which part of the vocal tract is briefly closed, e.g. the 'b' in 'beer' and the 'k' in 'kiss'.

stopped image. A synonym for STABILIZED IMAGE.

storage. Memory, used particularly of computer memory. This scientific-sounding term has been extended to human memory in order to give psychologists the illusion that they are scientists.

strabismus. Incorrect alignment of the two eyes, normally caused by a disorder of the extraocular muscles that is large enough to produce double images. Hence, there is no binocular fusion. The condition often arises in childhood, and unless treated may produce AMBLYOPIA.

strain. (Biology) A group of organisms within a species that arise from inbreeding and have characteristics that distinguish them from other members of the species.

strange-hand sign. A disorder in which a person cannot recognize his own hand by SOMAESTHESIS; it can be caused by a defect in the corpus callosum.

strategy. 1. A systematic plan of action for solving a problem or performing a task. Psychologists often use the term to refer to unconscious strategies. One of the difficulties confronting cognitive psychology is that different people use different strategies to perform the same task. 2. (Sociobiology) Any means of aiding survival and reproduction, whether behavioural or physiological, and whether common to a species or specific to some of its members. *See* EVOLUTIONARILY STABLE STRATEGY and EVOLUTIONARY STRATEGY.

stratification. The division of society into social classes that systematically differ in status.

stratified sampling. Selecting a sample by taking a specified number of cases from each stratum of the population.

streaming. (Education) Dividing children into classes according to their ability.

stream of consciousness. 1. James's expression for the continuous flow of the contents of the mind, emphasizing that it is not made up of discrete static elements. 2. Writing or talking based on random associations with little or no system, as in James Joyce.

Street figures. Figures that at first look like a series of blobs, but which after inspection suddenly yield the appearance of an object such as a dog or a face.

strength. (Animal learning) *See* RESPONSE STRENGTH.

strephosymbolia. Mirror-image reversal in reading or writing of letters (e.g. 'b' for 'd') or words ('nip' for 'pin').

stress. 1. (Psychology) The imposition of strain on a person or the effects of the strain on him; both physical and psychological factors can be stressful. Prolonged stress may impair functioning or trigger mental illness. *See also* GENERAL ADAPTATION SYNDROME. 2. (Linguistics) Emphasis on a syllable, carried by loudness and possibly also by variations in pitch and length. Conventionally, only two levels of stress are distinguished, but most linguists think there are more. *See also* CONTRASTIVE STRESS, LEXICAL STRESS, and TONE GROUP.

stressed syllable. In a word, a syllable on which the STRESS normally falls. The vowel in a stressed syllable is never reduced.

stress inoculation training. A form of cognitive therapy designed to help people cope with a stressful event by exposing them to it under safe conditions, and by persuading them to have faith in their ability to deal with it.

stress interview. An interview in which the interviewee is deliberately stressed in order to discover whether he would withstand such stress in real life situations.

stressor. An event that causes stress.

stress reaction. Any of the reactions to stress, particularly maladaptive ones such as panic or disordered thinking. *See* GENERAL ADAPTATION SYNDROME.

stress test. Any test designed to assess a person's reaction to either psychological or physiological stress, by putting him in a stressful situation of the sort that might occur in real life.

stretch receptor. A PROPRIOCEPTOR in muscles or tendons that respond to tension.

stretch reflex. The reflexive contraction of a muscle in response to its being stretched; it helps to maintain the position of the parts of the body.

striate body. A synonym for CORPUS CALLOSUM.

striate cortex (V1). Brodmann's area 17; *see* Appendix 3. The rearmost part of the occipital cortex, one of the retinotopic areas; it receives a direct visual input.

striated muscle. Muscle that looks striped under a microscope because it is composed of alternating bands of MYOSIN and ACTIN; all SKELETAL MUSCLES are striated. Striated muscles contract faster than SMOOTH MUSCLES, but cannot sustain contraction for so long.

stria terminalis. A fibre bundle connecting parts of the AMYGDALA with the HYPOTHALAMUS.

striatum. The part of the developing FOREBRAIN that becomes the basal ganglia.

strident. (Phonetics) A high-frequency speech sound produced by a complex stricture in the vocal tract, e.g. the 'f' in 'fish' and the 's' in 'sing'. *Contrast* MELLOW.

striped muscle. A synonym for STRIATED MUSCLE.

stripes therapy. A form of group therapy in which the participants converse with bare backs; a horizontal stripe is painted on a person's back each time the group, by majority vote, deems that he has misbehaved.

stroboscope. A device for turning a light on and off repeatedly, usually with an adjustable frequency.

stroboscopic effect. A synonym for STROBO-SCOPIC MOTION.

stroboscopic illusion. The illusion, produced by intermittently illuminating the spokes of a rotating wheel, that the wheel is stationary, rotating at the wrong speed, or rotating backwards; more generally, any form of STROBOSCOPIC MOTION.

stroboscopic motion. Any form of apparent motion perceived when the observer is presented with discrete exposures of identical (or similar) stimuli in different positions. *See* OPTIMAL APPARENT MOTION.

stroke. Sudden damage to the vascular system in the brain, caused by the rupture or blockage of a blood-vessel and usually resulting in impairment or loss of some psychological functions.

strong AI. The view that an appropriately programmed computer would have a mind of its own and might be conscious. **Weak AI** holds on the contrary that no matter how much computers might simulate mental activities, they would never have minds.

Strong–Campbell Interest Inventory. An inventory designed to discover in what vocations a person would be happy: it is a development of the STRONG VOCATIONAL INTEREST BLANK.

strong law of effect. The law that reinforcement is both a necessary and sufficient condition for learning to occur; this is a modification of Thorndike's EFFECT, LAW OF in which reinforcement was only a sufficient condition.

Strong Vocational Interest Blank. An inventory designed to discover in what vocations a person would be successful and happy.

Stroop task. A task in which the subject is asked to name the colour in which each of a series of words is printed. If the words are colour names printed in colours that differ from the colour named (e.g. the word 'Red' printed in green) performance is worse than if the words are not colour names (e.g. 'Pen' printed in green) – which is the **Stroop effect**. There are many variations on this task.

structural ambiguity. Ambiguity in a sentence that has more than one meaning because it can be syntactically decomposed in different ways, e.g. 'They are cooking apples'. *See* diagram below. *Compare* LEXICAL AMBIGUITY.

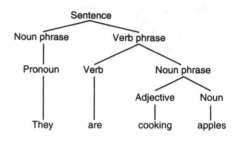

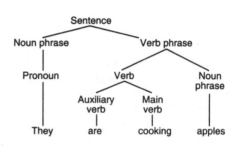

structural analysis. The analysis of a task to be taught into its components, particularly into the rules that must be learned to perform it, and the specification of when they are to be used. After such an analysis the pupil can be gradually taught the rules, using a series of progressive exercises. Moreover, analysis of his performance will show at each point in such **structured learning** exactly what aspects of the rules etc. he has failed to grasp, and his failures can be remedied.

structural description. A model of the structure of something. For example, in vision a model cast in terms of entities (e.g. edge, region), properties (e.g. vertical, elongated), and relationships (e.g. intersecting). Such models can form a useful abstract description for the purpose of recognition; they are often formulated as DIRECTED GRAPHS.

structural group. A psychotherapeutic group whose members have been chosen for their capacity to produce beneficial changes in one another.

structuralism. 1. An extinct approach to psychology, based on the belief that all conscious processes are made up from combinations of single elements whose specification through introspection is psychology's prime task. This approach was pursued by Wundt and Titchener from about 1880 to 1910. 2. Piaget's approach to psychology, in which the structure of mental representations and of the processes operating upon them is sought, and an attempt made to investigate how these structures change in the course of time. 3. An approach to anthropology, associated with Lévi-Strauss, which has spread to other social sciences and to literature. In it the structure of different aspects of a society, ranging from religion to eating, are analysed into an underlying network of relationships. There is particular stress on oppositions and hierarchical structures, and on assigning meaning (often tendentiously) to the structure in the light of hypothesized general principles of thought, either within a given society or of a universal nature. For many, it is a relief that we are now in the poststructuralist era. 4. *See* STRUCTURAL LINGUISTICS.

structural linguistics. 1. Generally, the analysis of language in terms of interrelated constituents, including both surface and underlying constituents (e.g. verb phrase, phoneme). The approach was started by Saussure, who pointed out that a linguistic symbol (or a concept) cannot be defined in its own right, but only in relation to other symbols (or concepts). 2. More specifically and more commonly, Bloomfield's approach to linguistics, which stressed the segmentation and classification of the surface features of an utterance, but neglected the underlying structures and the meaning.

structural psychology. A synonym for STRUCTURALISM (1).

structural therapy. A therapy for autistic children in which they are placed in a rich but structured environment in an attempt to stimulate them.

Structured Clinical Interview (SCID). A more up-to-date version of the SCHEDULE FOR AFFECTIVE DISORDERS AND SCHIZOPHRENIA.

structured interview. An interview conducted according to a preassigned plan which may include the topics to be covered and even the questions to be asked. *Contrast* UNSTRUCTURED INTERVIEW.

structured learning. See STRUCTURAL ANALYSIS.

structure from motion. A synonym for DEPTH FROM MOTION.

structure of intellect model. Guilford's model of the intellect, based on factor analysis, in which the mind has different intercommunicating capacities (e.g. visual, semantic), each of which can operate in different ways (e.g. evaluatively, divergently) and produce different outputs. The model is too vague to be helpful.

structure word. A synonym for FUNCTION WORD.

STS. An abbreviation for SHORT-TERM STORE.

Student's test, Student's t-test. Synonyms for T-TEST.

stylus maze. A maze run by a person by guiding a stylus through its pathways, either under visual or tactile control.

subarachnoid space. The region between the ARACHNOID LAYER and the DURA MATER, which contains cerebrospinal fluid.

subception. A synonym for SUBLIMINAL PERCEPTION.

subconscious. A loose term used in a variety of ways. 1. A synonym for PRECONSCIOUS. 2. The material on the fringe of consciousness that can rapidly be brought to mind. 3. The Freudian PRECONSCIOUS and UNCONSCIOUS together.

subcontrary. A proposition that is related to another proposition in such a way that they can both be true but cannot both be false (e.g. 'It is not a lion' and 'It is not a tiger'). *Compare* CONTRARY.

subcortical. Pertaining to those parts of the brain below the level of the cortex.

subculture. Any group within a larger society that has habits, values, and attitudes that distinguish it from the rest of society.

subcutaneous. Beneath the surface of the skin, but not necessarily beneath all the layers of skin.

subdural. Beneath the DURA MATER, the outer membrane of the meninges.

subictal epilepsy. A form of epilepsy without seizures but with involuntary twitches or muscle movements, accompanied by anxiety or depression.

subitization. The perception at a glance of the number of items present, without counting them successively; the maximum number of items that can be counted in this way is about five.

subject (S). Any person (more often than not a college student) or animal on whom an experiment is conducted.

subjective attribute. The way in which a quality is perceived; red is a subjective attribute, having a surface reflecting predominantly long wavelength light is a physical attribute.

subjective colours. The illusory appearance of a HUE when only achromatic light is present. *See also* BENHAM'S TOP and FECHNER'S COLOURS.

subjective contour. Usually a synonym for KANIZSA CONTOUR, but sometimes used to mean any contour not directly produced by brightness contrast across the contour.

subjective expected utility (SEU). A person's estimate of the EXPECTED UTILITY of the outcome of an option.

subjective probability. A person's intuitive estimate of the probability of something happening.

subjective sensation. A sensation (e.g. a PHOSPHENE) produced in the absence of the normal stimulus.

subjective test. Any test, such as the RORSCHACH TEST, that has no rigorous procedure for scoring, and whose scores depend on the tester's intuitions.

subjectivism. (Philosophy) An approach to ethics based on the idea that all morality is simply a reflection of subjective tastes and preferences, whether of the individual or of the society.

subject–object differentiation. Piaget's expression for the child's recognition that it is an entity distinct from the world around it.

subjunctive. (Linguistics) A mood of a verb used in certain subordinate clauses, and to express uncertainty, e.g. 'If she *were* here, I *would* kiss her'.

sublimation. (Psychoanalysis) The expression of repressed wishes in acceptable form, usually by the pursuit of hobbies or work; e.g. painting a forest may, according to Freud, be an expression of childhood curiosity about the mother's pubic hair.

subliminal. Below the threshold whether of perception or of consciousness.

subliminal learning. Learning without the person being aware that he is learning.

subliminal perception. Perceiving a very faint stimulus without being conscious of it; the fact that it has been perceived is demonstrated by subsequent behaviour, e.g. it has been claimed that if subliminal scenes depicting extreme heat are shown in a cinema, the patrons will rush to buy ice-cream. The extent, and even the existence, of subliminal perception is in dispute. *See also* PERCEPTUAL DEFENCE.

submissive behaviour. (Ethology) Species-specific ritual behaviour exhibited by an individual that is losing a fight with a conspecific, in order to signal acknowledgement of defeat, at which point the other stops fighting; the behaviour has evolved to prevent serious injury to members of the species. E.g. a wolf losing a fight will offer its neck to its opponent.

subordinate clause. *See* CLAUSE.

subsidiation. The achievement of a subgoal.

substance. (Medicine) A chemical or drug.

substance abuse. Drug abuse.

substance-induced. Pertaining to any mental illness, disorder, abnormality or symptom that has been caused by excessive consumption of any substance, e.g. alcohol.

substance P. A PEPTIDE that acts as a NEURO-TRANSMITTER. It is found in the cerebral cortex, hypothalamus, basal ganglia, and autonomic system. It is thought to be implicated in the pain pathways since it is secreted in the dorsal roots by nociceptive afferents.

substantia gelatinosa. A mass of tissue at the internal tip of the dorsal horn on the spinal cord; it may play a part in the control of pain.

substantia nigra. Part of the EXTRAPYRAMIDAL MOTOR SYSTEM lying in the PONS and connected to the NEOSTRIATUM; malfunction of its dopaminergic projection is probably implicated in Parkinson's disease.

substantive universal. See LINGUISTIC UNIVERSAL.

substitute formation. (Psychoanalysis) The redirecting of a repressed impulse into another path that is more acceptable to the EGO or SUPEREGO, e.g. by switching to a related but more innocuous goal or by the formation of neurotic symptoms.

subthalamic nuclei. Groups of cells at the base of the THALAMUS, forming part of the extrapyramidal system and having an input from the GLOBUS PALLIDUS and PEDUNCLE and an output to the BASAL GANGLIA.

subthreshold. Below threshold.

subthreshold potential. A change in the membrane potential of a neuron that is not large enough to trigger an impulse.

subtraction method. A method of estimating the duration of a psychological process by measuring the reaction time for a task thought to need process A, measuring the reaction time for a task thought to need processes A + B, and then subtracting the first time from the second to yield the time for

process B. The method was first used by Donders e.g. to obtain the difference between a simple reaction time and a choice reaction time. The method depends on the questionable assumption that the two processes are carried out independently and in series.

subtractive colour mixing. See COLOUR MIXING.

successive aperture viewing. The viewing of an object when it is moving behind a smaller hole or slot, so that the parts of the object are exposed successively. See ANORTHOSCOPE.

successive approximation, method of. A synonym for SHAPING.

successive contrast. A change in the appearance of a stimulus, in a direction away from the appearance of one immediately preceding or succeeding it in time. Where the stimulus inducing the effect is the first one, the term AFTEREFFECT is usually used rather than 'successive contrast'. Compare e.g. TILT AFTEREFFECT.

successive discrimination training. Discrimination training in which only one discriminandum is present on each trial and the subject has to learn to make different responses to the different discriminanda, e.g. the responses of approaching one and avoiding another. Contrast SIMULTANEOUS DISCRIMINATION TRAINING.

successive intervals, method of. A psychometric scaling method in which stimuli are presented successively and the subject indicates their position on the scale either by marking a point on a line or by assigning a number to each, thus producing a RATIO SCALE.

successive reproduction method. A method for investigating learning and memory in which the subject has to reproduce at intervals the material he has learned.

sufficient condition. A condition that if fulfilled will lead to the occurrence of a given event. Contrast NECESSARY CONDITION.

sufficient statistic. (Statistics) A statistic that

uses all the relevant data sampled to estimate a population parameter.

suffix. (Linguistics) A bound morpheme at the end of a word, e.g. '-ed' in 'kicked'.

suffix effect. A synonym for STIMULUS SUFFIX EFFECT.

sulcus. A groove in the surface of the cortex. FISSURE is usually used of large grooves, sulcus of smaller ones.

sulcus principalis. The fissure running between the two cerebral hemispheres.

Sullivan's interpersonal theory. *See* INTERPERSONAL THEORY.

summation. 1. (Neurophysiology) *See* SPATIAL SUMMATION and TEMPORAL SUMMATION. 2. (Perception); *See* BINOCULAR SUMMATION and BINAURAL SUMMATION.

summation curve. The plot of a CUMULATIVE DISTRIBUTION.

summation test. A way of determining whether there is inhibitory conditioning to a stimulus. The conditioned excitatory response to a positively conditioned stimulus is measured in the presence and in the absence of the conditioned inhibitor: the difference in the strength of the CR is a measure of its strength.

summation tone. One kind of combination tone, namely, a faint tone that is the sum of the frequencies of the two tones presented; e.g. if tones of 500 Hz and 800 Hz are presented, the summation tone heard will be of 1,300 Hz.

sunk costs error. The mistake of continuing with a project because one has already made an investment (of time, money etc.) in it when one will only incur further costs that outweigh any possible benefits. Almost everyone makes this mistake, but ministries of defence do so on a spectacular scale.

superego. (Psychoanalysis) The part of the mind into which the attitudes of the parents and possibly other important figures have been introjected, and which constitutes a person's conscience by barring the ID from gratifying itself in unacceptable ways.

superego lacuna. (Psychoanalysis) A failure of the SUPEREGO to forbid a class of immoral acts, particularly in psychopaths.

superego resistance. (Psychoanalysis) Resistance to therapy caused by the SUPEREGO producing guilt feelings and masochistic behaviour that the therapist cannot overcome.

superior. (Anatomy) Towards the upper part of an organ or of the body. *Contrast* INFERIOR.

superior colliculi. The anterior of two pairs of nuclei in the brainstem lying just below the pineal gland. In mammals they receive an input from the eyes and project to the pulvinar; they are implicated in the control of eye movements. In lower vertebrates lacking a cortex, they play a much larger role in vision.

superior frontal gyrus. *See* Appendix 1.

superior frontal sulcus. *See* Appendix 1.

superior intelligence. An IQ of above 120, which is possessed by 15 per cent of people.

superior oblique. An extraocular eye muscle that pulls the eye downward and slightly towards the nose.

superior olive, superior olivary nucleus. A nucleus in the PONS, receiving a sensory input relayed via the COCHLEAR NUCLEUS from both ears.

superior parietal lobule. *See* Appendix 1.

superior rectus. An extraocular eye muscle that pulls the eye upward and slightly towards the temples.

supernormal stimulus. (Ethology) An exaggerated version of a SIGN STIMULUS to which an animal gives a stronger response than to a normal sign stimulus; e.g. some birds retrieve abnormally large artificial eggs in preference to their own.

superposition. A synonym for INTERPOSITION.

superpositional models. Theories that hold that no explicit concepts are formed and that a concept consists merely of all the exemplars of it that have been memorized and that can be examined to determine whether a new instance belongs to that concept.

superstitious behaviour. In general, behaviour motivated by superstition. In particular, an analogue of superstitious behaviour that is exhibited by pigeons (and other animals) on random reinforcement schedules; certain behaviour, e.g. turning the head to one side, may be accidentally reinforced, making it more frequent, and hence more likely to be reinforced in future. Random schedules can therefore produce a number of 'superstitious' habits. *Compare* ADVENTITIOUS REINFORCEMENT and CROSS CONDITIONING.

supervalent. Pertaining to an intense and obsessive preoccupation with a topic, as found e.g. in sexual jealousy, arising according to Freud because it has its roots in repressed material.

supplementary motor cortex (M2). The mesial part of Brodmann area 6 (*see* Appendix 4); thought to be implicated in motor SYNERGISM.

supplementary somatosensory cortex. Brodmann's area 43; *see* Appendix 3.

supportive psychotherapy. Therapy whose aim is to reassure the patient or build up his self-confidence, but which does not attempt to probe deep problems; it can be used simply as a method of helping someone endure a bad patch or an episode of mental illness.

suppression. 1. (Psychoanalysis) The conscious putting out of mind of an idea, or wish, as opposed to putting it out of mind unconsciously (REPRESSION). 2. Short for BINOCULAR SUPPRESSION. 3. Short for SENSORY SUPPRESSION. 4. Short for CONDITIONED SUPPRESSION.

suppressor variable. In a battery of tests, a test that increases the efficiency of the remaining tests by measuring an irrelevant variable which contributes together with a relevant variable to scores on some of the tests; by deducting scores on the suppressor variable from those on the other tests, the predictive validity may be improved.

suprachiasmatic nucleus. A nucleus of the hypothalamus lying above the chiasm; it is thought to be implicated in circadian rhythms.

supraliminal. Above threshold.

supramarginal gyrus. Brodmann's area 40; *see* Appendices 1 and 3. It lies in the INFERIOR PARIETAL LOBULE, and borders, with the angular gyrus, on the primary receptor areas for vision, hearing, and somaesthesis. It is involved in cross modality associations including those needed to transpose writing into speech and vice versa.

supraoptic nucleus. A nucleus of the hypothalamus, lying above the optic chiasm, that secretes antidiuretic hormone and oxytocin into the posterior pituitary, and that produces drinking when stimulated by salt or electric current.

supraordinate stimulus. In instrumental conditioning, a stimulus that indicates which aspects of the situation are relevant for obtaining reinforcement.

suprarenal gland. A synonym for ADRENAL GLAND.

suprasegmental. (Linguistics) Pertaining to a vocal effect, such as pitch or stress patterns, that extends over two or more phonemes.

suprasegmental phonology. (Linguistics) That part of phonology that studies features of the speech sound that extend over more than one phoneme, e.g. INTONATION.

suprasegmental reflex. A reflex that is coordinated by the brain, unlike the SEGMENTAL REFLEX and the INTERSEGMENTAL REFLEX.

suprasylvian gyrus. A cortical area in carnivores, possibly equivalent to the inferior parietal gyrus in primates. In cats it contains some visual associative cortex.

suprathreshold. Above the absolute threshold.

surdity. Deafness.

surface colour. The appearance of colour when it is seen as belonging to a surface, i.e.

extended in space at a particular distance from the observer. *Contrast* FILM COLOUR.

surface dyslexia. A form of ACQUIRED DYS-LEXIA in which a person can read out the sound of words (e.g. by using GRAPHEME–PHONEME CORRESPONDENCE RULES), but has difficulty recovering their meaning; e.g. he might read 'flower' as 'flour'.

surface normal. The line intersecting a surface at an angle of 90° in all directions. *See* SLANT.

surface structure (s-structure). (Linguistics) The phrase structure tree formed after trans-formations have been applied to the DEEP STRUCTURE. It includes TRACES.

surface trait. *See* SOURCE TRAIT.

surgency. Effectively a synonym for EXTRA-VERSION.

surrogate therapy. Sex therapy in which the patient has intercourse with the therapist (or more usually with someone supplied by the therapist) in the hope of improving his sexual performance.

surroundedness, law of. The Gestalt principle that where one figure surrounds another the surrounding figure is likely to be seen as background and the enclosed figure as figure.

survivor syndrome. A syndrome caused by surviving a disaster in which others perished; it is marked by anxiety, apathy, guilt, etc.

sustained call. A synonym for X CELL.

sustentacular cells. Cells that provide struc-tural support for other cells, e.g. the pillars of Corti.

SVIB. An abbreviation for STRONG VOCA-TIONAL INTEREST BLANK.

Swindle's ghost. A synonym for PURKINJE AFTERIMAGE.

SWS. An abbreviation for SLOW-WAVE SLEEP.

syllabary. A form of writing in which each symbol stands for a syllable.

syllable. (Linguistics) A segment of speech containing only one vowel sound that may be bounded at the beginning or end or both by consonant sounds.

syllogism. Sometimes called **propositional syllogism** in contrast to LINEAR SYLLOGISM. A valid or invalid deductive inference from two premises to a conclusion that relies on the use of QUANTIFIERS, e.g. 'All men are mortal. Socrates is a man. Therefore Socrates is mortal.' One term (the **middle term**) must appear in both premises; the subject of the conclusion is the **minor term** and appears in the **minor premise**; the object of the conclu-sion is the **major term** and appears in the **major premise**. Classically 256 kinds **(moods)** of syllogism have been distin-guished, since they vary according to whether the middle term is subject or object in each premise (four **figures**), and according to whether the subject and object in each pre-mise is quantified as universal (all) or par-ticular (some). Thus there are four ways in which the quantifiers can be distributed in each premise and therefore $4^3 = 64$ combi-nations taking both the premises into ac-count. Since each combination can appear in four figures, there are 256 (4 × 64) moods. The conclusion is invalid in many of these moods. Unless trained in logic, most people have great difficulty in drawing the correct conclusions, e.g. they may wrongly infer from 'Some X are Y' and 'Some Y are Z' that 'Some X are Z'. *See also* ATMOSPHERE HYPOTHESIS.

syllogistic model of attitude organization. A theory that describes attitudes to objects in terms of syllogisms where the premises are: (i) the **belief premise**, which states beliefs about what characteristics are possessed by the object of the attitude; (ii) the **evaluation premise**, which states the person's attitudes towards these characteristics.

Sylvian fissure. A synonym for LATERAL SULCUS.

symbiosis. 1. (Biology) A close association between two species that is beneficial to both, e.g. ants obtain food by keeping aphids, and the aphids are protected by being kept. 2. (Social psychology) A com-plementary relationship, often pathological, between people, e.g. that between a sadist and a masochist, or between a dominant person and a dependent one.

symbiotic psychosis. A psychosis occurring between two and five years of age, in which the child shows complete emotional dependence on the mother, panics if any separation is threatened, and is developmentally retarded.

symbol-digit test. A type of CODE TEST.

symbolic computational architecture. A synonym for CLASSICAL COMPUTATIONAL ARCHITECTURE.

symbolic distance effect. The phenomenon that, when a subject has to gauge from memory the relative position of two items on a dimension (e.g. length), the smaller the difference between the two items on the dimension, the longer is the subject's reaction time. It occurs even when both differences are large – e.g. it takes longer to decide whether a dog is bigger than a mouse than whether an elephant is bigger than a mouse.

symbolic logic. A formal system of symbols, AXIOMS, and RULES OF INFERENCE, in which theorems may be derived. The predicate calculus and the propositional calculus are branches of symbolic logic, as is much of mathematics.

symbolism. A synonym for SYMBOLIZATION.

symbolization. (Psychoanalysis) The unconscious process by which repressed wishes or other material are changed into a symbolic form that enables them to enter consciousness.

symbolophobia. A morbid fear of symbols and particularly of other people interpreting one's words or actions in ways one does not intend.

symbol substitution test. A synonym for CODE TEST.

symmetry, law of. The Gestalt principle that in perception a figure will be grouped in as symmetrical a way as possible.

Symonds Picture Study Test. A projective test for adolescents in which they tell stories about pictures shown them.

sympathectomy. Ablation of or sectioning of part of the SYMPATHETIC SYSTEM.

sympathetic apraxia. Apraxia in the left side of the body, particularly an inability to respond to commands, caused by damage to the corpus callosum preventing signals from the left hemisphere reaching the right motor cortex.

sympathetic chain. The chain of SYMPATHETIC GANGLIA.

sympathetic division of autonomic nervous system. A synonym for SYMPATHETIC SYSTEM.

sympathetic ganglion. Any of the clusters of cells of the SYMPATHETIC SYSTEM. They lie outside the spinal cord, and are interconnected to form a chain.

sympathetic system, sympathetic nervous system. One of the two divisions of the AUTONOMIC NERVOUS SYSTEM; it has a chain of connected sympathetic ganglia lying just outside the spinal cord, which are innervated from all segments of the thoracic part of the spinal chord and the first and second of the lumbar part. It mainly serves an arousal function, dilating the pupils, reducing salivation, dilating the lungs, inhibiting bladder contraction, and increasing heart rate, blood sugar levels, and the secretion of EPINEPHRINE and NOREPINEPHRINE.

sympathomimetic agent. Any drug that stimulates the SYMPATHETIC SYSTEM.

sympatric species. A species having the same habitat as another.

symptomatic psychosis. A synonym for ORGANIC PSYCHOSIS.

symptomatic treatment. Psychotherapy directed at removing or alleviating a patient's symptoms, rather than at changing the underlying dynamic processes thought by some to underlie the symptoms.

symptom bearer. A person with psychiatric

symptoms who is a member of a badly adjusted family, and who is bearing most of the stress caused by the family's interactions.

symptom choice. The unconscious selection by a person of a particular set of psychiatric symptoms which express underlying conflicts (or so it is alleged).

symptom formation. (Psychoanalysis) The process of developing a neurotic or psychosomatic symptom, which, although it may in part satisfy a repressed wish, is maladaptive and often anxiety-provoking.

symptom substitution. (Psychoanalysis) The alleged tendency for one neurotic symptom to be replaced by another unless the unconscious conflicts producing the symptoms are reduced; psychoanalysts have claimed that for this reason behaviour therapy, which tackles symptoms, could not work, but the evidence suggests that symptom substitution is a myth, and that reducing any one symptom tends to reduce all others.

synaesthesia. The perception of a quality normally belonging to one sensory modality when another sensory modality is stimulated, e.g. hearing a tone as hard.

synapse. The point at which one nerve cell influences the firing or the membrane potential of another, or at which it changes the state of a muscle or gland. **Type 1 synapses** have round synaptic vesicles and are usually excitatory. **Type 2 synapses** often have elliptical vesicles and are usually inhibitory. *See also* CHEMICAL SYNAPSE and ELECTRICAL SYNAPSE.

synaptic button, synaptic bouton. The enlarged end of an axonal branch of a presynaptic cell that is separated from the postsynaptic cell by the SYNAPTIC CLEFT, and that contains the SYNAPTIC VESICLES.

synaptic cleft. The unbridged gap between the presynaptic and postsynaptic cells in a chemical synapse: it is about 40 nm wide, much bigger than a BRIDGED GAP. NEURO-TRANSMITTERS pass across it.

synaptic knob. A synonym for SYNAPTIC BUTTON.

synaptic transmitter. A synonym for NEURO-TRANSMITTER.

synaptic vesicle. Small capsules in the terminals of a presynaptic cell, which contain neurotransmitter substances and which release them into the synaptic cleft when the cell fires.

synaptosome. A collection of nerve endings including synapses that are separated out from other material by centrifuging part of a brain. While they are still chemically active they can be used e.g. to measure the effects of adding a given substance (e.g. SSRI) on the reuptake of a given neurotransmitter.

synchronic. Pertaining to the study of the state of a system at one point in time, used particularly of language. *Contrast* DIACHRONIC.

synchronization. Of EEG waves, the presence of a large-amplitude, regular rhythm.

syncope. Brief fainting caused by inadequate blood supply to the brain.

syncretism. 1. (Linguistics) In the history of language the merging into the same form of words originally having different inflections. 2. (Linguistics) The use of the same form for different uses of a lexeme. E.g. 'were' as an auxiliary verb can stand both for the subjunctive and for the past tense. 3. Piaget's term for the construction of poorly differentiated schemata through the assimilation of elements.

syndrome. A cluster of symptoms all thought to be produced by the same illness.

synectics. A brainstorming technique based on the generation of many (often bizarre) analogies.

synergism. The coordinated action of different elements to achieve a common end, e.g. the contraction and relaxation of several muscle groups to produce a particular movement, or the combined effect of two drugs that influence an organism in the same way.

synergist. (Physiology) A muscle that pulls in the same direction as another.

synesthesia. An alternative spelling for SYN-AESTHESIA.

synkinesis. An involuntary muscle movement occurring when an attempt is made to make another movement, particularly the involuntary movement of a part of the body occurring when attempting to move the corresponding but paralysed part on the opposite side.

synonym. A word with the same meaning as another.

syntactical aphasia. A form of aphasia in which individual words can be understood, but in which the ability to interpret or form grammatical constructions is lost or severely impaired.

syntactic category. A synonym for PART OF SPEECH.

syntagmatic. (Linguistics) Pertaining to the relations a linguistic constituent can have with other constituents; e.g. 't' can appear in 'tip', 'wit', 'at'; 'the' can only appear at the start of a noun phrase, etc. The role of a constituent can be defined in terms of its syntagmatic and PARADIGMATIC relations with other constituents.

syntagmatic association. An association to a word based on what frequently or naturally precedes or follows the word in a sentence, e.g. 'drink – beer'. *Contrast* PARADIGMATIC ASSOCIATION.

syntax. The rules governing the sequence in which words and morphemes can legitimately be combined to make a sentence, but usually disregarding the meaning of content words; thus 'colourless green ideas sleep furiously' is a grammatically correct but meaningless sentence, whereas 'green sleep ideas furiously colourless' is not even grammatical.

syntaxis. Sullivan's term for thought processes that are objective and open to corroboration. *Compare* PARATAXIS (2).

synthetic language. (Linguistics) A language in which syntax is expressed mainly by inflections. *Contrast* ANALYTIC LANGUAGE.

synthetic perspective. *See* PERSPECTIVE.

synthetic speech. Speech produced according to rules by a machine. *Compare* RESYNTHESIZED SPEECH and SPEECH SYNTHESIZER.

syntonia. A tendency to overreact emotionally to the environment.

systematic desensitization. A technique of behaviour therapy used to reduce the power of a thought or event to disturb. The patient is exposed to the least disturbing aspect of the item (usually while relaxed) and is slowly exposed to successively more disturbing aspects of it until the item loses its power to disturb. The technique is commonly used in the treatment of phobias. *Contrast* IMPLOSION THERAPY.

systematic error. A synonym for CONSTANT ERROR.

systematic sampling. Any sampling from a population based on a rule, e.g. sampling every tenth house.

Système Internationale. *See* the abbreviation, SI, which is in more common use.

systemic. Distributed throughout an organism.

systems analysis. The attempt to analyse a complex system, particularly an organization, usually undertaken with a view to improving it, and usually involving mathematical analysis of the data and the application of the techniques of operational research.

Szondi test. An unvalidated projection test in which a person has to choose the faces he most and least likes from a set containing photographs of psychiatric patients with different mental disorders.

T

T. A symbol for the WILCOXON TEST statistic.

t. *See* T-TEST.

ₛtᵣ. Hull's abbreviation for LATENCY, *see* HULLIAN THEORY.

TA. An abbreviation for TRANSACTIONAL ANALYSIS.

tabes dorsalis. Degeneration of neurons in the spinal cord, caused by syphilis.

table look-up. (AI) Looking up in a computer or in the mind the stored value of a function with a given argument, rather than finding the value by calculation. E.g. multiplication tables could contain values for pairs of multipliers up to much higher numbers than 12. The procedure is usually faster than calculation but demands more storage space.

tabula rasa. The mind of the newborn containing, according to empiricists, no innate ideas.

tachistoscope. An instrument for exposing visual stimuli for brief (e.g. 20 msec) and accurately timed periods; the duration is usually determined by electronic timing (or by a shutter) and can be varied by the experimenter.

tachylalia, tachyphasia, tachyphresia. Abnormally rapid speech.

tachyphylaxis. A synonym for ACUTE TOLERANCE.

tacit knowledge. Knowledge used by a person without his knowing he is using it. In some cases (*see* COGNITIVE PENETRABILITY) he may be conscious of the knowledge but not know he is using it, in others he may use knowledge that he is unaware of, e.g. in producing grammatical sentences.

tact. A term invented by Skinner which he defined as 'A verbal operant in which a response of a given form is evoked (or at least strengthened) by a particular object or property of an object or event'. Make of this definition what you will.

tactile. Pertaining to the sense of touch.

tactile circle. A small region of skin within which two simultaneously presented tactile stimuli are felt as one.

tactile corpuscle. A synonym for MEISSNER'S CORPUSCLE.

tactile menisci, tactile discs. Skin receptors that end on shallow cup shaped discs and are probably sensitive to touch. Also called **Merkel's discs.**

tactual. A synonym for TACTILE.

tactual egocentre. *See* EGOCENTRE.

Tadoma method. A method to enable people who are both blind and deaf to understand speech; it involves placing the fingers on the mouth and neck of a speaker.

tag question. A question placed at the end of a declarative sentence, e.g. 'He's not here, *is he?*'

tail. (Statistics) The extreme part of a distribution, which when represented graphically looks like a tail.

tail-flick test. A test used to assess the efficacy of pain-killing drugs, in which a rat's tail is heated until the rat flicks it; the amount of heat needed to produce a tail-flick is a measure of the power of a pain-killer.

Talbot–Plateau law. The law that when a light flickers at a rate above the critical fusion threshold its apparent brightness is determined by its intensity averaged over time.

talion dread. (Psychoanalysis) Fear of retaliation in kind for real or fantasized injuries to others, e.g. fear of castration by one's father for wishing to possess one's mother.

talking cure. The alleviation of mental disorder through any form of psychotherapy that is based entirely on conversations between therapist and patient, and does not involve training the patient in new habits (as does behaviour therapy); the term is used, usually derogatorily, particularly of psychoanalysis.

tandem reinforcement schedule. A COMPOUND SCHEDULE in which two (or more) simple schedules (e.g. FR10, VI30) are given in succession. No reward is given for completing any but the last simple schedule, but on completion of one schedule, the next automatically begins. No signal is given to indicate which schedule is operating. *Compare* CHAINED SCHEDULE.

tanyphonia. An abnormally thin, tinny-sounding voice.

tapetum. A reflecting layer at the back of the retina found in some nocturnal animals (e.g. cats); it increases the number of quanta absorbed by the photopigments because the quanta that reach that layer may be absorbed after being reflected.

taphephilia. A synonym for TAPHOPHILIA.

taphephobia. A synonym for TAPHOPHOBIA.

taphophilia. A morbid love of cemeteries.

taphophobia. A morbid fear of graves or of being buried alive.

tapping test. A psychomotor test in which a person taps at a regular rhythm.

tarantism. A form of mass hysteria in which people dance excitedly for prolonged periods.

taraxein. A protein sometimes thought to be found only in the urine of schizophrenics, though whether it is produced by a metabolic defect or by a dietary deficiency is uncertain.

Tarchanoff method. A method of recording the GALVANIC SKIN RESPONSE by measuring changes in the potential difference between two points on the skin. *Compare* FERE METHOD.

tardive dyskinesia. Involuntary stereotyped movements of the face, mouth, and tongue, which can be caused by the prolonged administration of neuroleptics.

target. 1. (Psychology) Any item sought, e.g. from memory or in perception. *Contrast* DISTRACTOR (2). 2. (Vision) The point on which someone is trying to fixate. 3. (Physiology) The locus or cell at which a particular substance acts or to which an axon is growing.

Tartini's tone. A synonym for DIFFERENCE TONE.

task demands. A synonym for DEMAND CHARACTERISTICS.

taste aversion. *See* LEARNED TASTE AVERSION.

taste bud. An organ containing about 200 taste receptors arranged in the shape of a flask; in man, there are about 10,000 taste buds located on the tongue, palate, and tonsils, and in the pharynx and larynx. Traditionally, their sensitivities are divided into sweet (tip of tongue), bitter (back of tongue), sour (sides of tongue), and salty (widely scattered).

taste tetrahedron. A graphic representation of taste, with the four basic tastes (sweet, sour, salty, and bitter) at the corners of a tetrahedron, and with intermediate tastes represented by other points in the shape.

TAT. An abbreviation for THEMATIC APPERCEPTION TEST.

tau (τ). *See* KENDALL'S TAU.

tau effect. An illusion produced by flashing three lights successively at three different positions; if the positions are separated by the same spatial interval, but one pair is separated by a larger time interval than the other, then that pair is seen as spaced further apart than the other. *Compare* KAPPA EFFECT.

taurine. An amino acid thought to be an inhibitory NEUROTRANSMITTER.

tautophone. A device for playing jumbled and random speech sounds, which a person is asked to interpret as a projective test.

taxis. (Ethology) Moving the body in a direction relative to a stimulus, usually towards it (**positive taxis**) or away from it (**negative taxis**); the term is usually used only when the action is innate or common to all members of a species. *See also* CHEMOTAXIS, GEOTAXIS, KLINOTAXIS, MENOTAXIS, TELOTAXIS, and TROPOTAXIS. *Compare* TROPISM.

taxonomy. The biological study of the classification of organisms or the classification itself. The principal subdivisions recognized are, from the broadest to the narrowest: **kingdom** (animals), **phylum** (chordates), **class** (mammals), **order** (primates), **family** (Hominidae), **genus** (*Homo*), **species** (*Homo sapiens*).

Taylor Manifest Anxiety Scale. A questionnaire used to measure consciously felt anxiety by asking subjects to check those statements about anxiety that apply to them.

TCA. An abbreviation for TRICYCLIC ANTIDEPRESSANT.

T-data. Data obtained from a mental test. *Compare* L-DATA and Q-DATA.

teacher unit. (Connectionism) A unit with a predetermined level of activation that determines the change in weights of other units in order to achieve a given level of activation in an output unit. *Compare* BACK-PROPAGATION.

teaching machine. A device used to provide PROGRAMMED INSTRUCTION.

tectorial membrane. A membrane in the ORGAN OF CORTI, in which the tips of its HAIR CELLS are embedded.

tectum. The roof of the MIDBRAIN, which contains the SUPERIOR COLLICULUS and INFERIOR COLLICULUS. *See also* OPTIC TECTUM.

tegmentum. The ventral and largest portion of the PONS, which contains sensory pathways proceeding to the THALAMUS, part of the RETICULAR FORMATION, the LOCUS COERULEUS and INFERIOR OLIVE, some cranial nerve nuclei, and the periventricular grey matter.

telaesthesia. (Parapsychology) Obtaining knowledge about something or somebody without the use of the senses by paranormal means.

teleception. A sense that detects things at a distance (e.g. vision or audition).

telegnosis. (Parapsychology) Knowledge gained by extrasensory perception.

telegraphic speech. The speech of infants from about 18 months to three years old, which consists of short utterances of a few words, usually with function words omitted. *Compare* HOLOPHRASIS.

telekinesis. A synonym for PSYCHOKINESIS (1).

telemetry. A method for studying physiological responses (e.g. heart rate, blood pressure, or galvanic skin response) in a real-life situation. The subject wears a small transmitter which radios responses from an array of electrodes on his body.

telencephalon. Phylogenetically the most recent part of the brain, comprising the cerebral cortex, basal ganglia and olfactory bulb; together with the DIENCEPHALON it makes up the FOREBRAIN.

teleoception. An alternative spelling of TELECEPTION.

teleology. The study of ends, purposes, or goals, and in philosophy the study of the ultimate purpose of the universe (if any).

teleonomy. A genteel synonym for TELEOLOGY, used by those who wish to make the concept sound scientifically respectable.

teleopsia, teleoreceptor. A visual disorder in which objects are seen as much further away than they are.

telepathy. (Parapsychology) Direct knowledge of some of the contents of another's mind gained without the use of the senses.

telephone theory. (Hearing) A synonym for FREQUENCY THEORY.

teleplasm. (Parapsychology) Any non-material but visible stuff, like ectoplasm, emanating from a medium.

telereceptor. A receptor responsive to distant stimuli, e.g. auditory or visual receptors.

telestereoscope. A stereoscope whose optical system is adjusted to give an exaggerated impression of depth.

telesthesia. An alternative spelling for TEL-AESTHESIA.

teletactor. A device for converting sound waves to vibration on the skin, used to help the deaf.

telodendria. The very fine terminal branches of an axon.

telotaxis. (Ethology) A taxis controlled by receptors that can instantaneously determine the direction of the controlling stimulus without the need for successive exposures to it. *Contrast* KLINOTAXIS.

temperature. In a PARALLEL DISTRIBUTED PROCESSING system, the range of uncertainty as to whether units will turn on or off when receiving a given input. The uncertainty is introduced to prevent the system settling in a local minimum. *See* ANNEALING.

temperature spot. *See* COLD SPOT and WARM SPOT.

template matching. A theory of recognition (mainly of visual recognition) holding that patterns are recognized by matching them to a stored pattern of the same shape. As a general account of pattern recognition, the theory fails, since what is important is the structure of a pattern, not how well it fits a pre-existing mould. *See* STRUCTURAL DESCRIPTION.

temporal conditioning. Conditioning in which the unconditioned stimulus occurs at regular (usually short) intervals with no overt conditioned stimulus. Organisms can learn to make the conditioned response at the appropriate time after the last occurrence of the unconditioned stimulus. *Compare* TRACE CONDITIONING. *See also* SIDMAN AVOIDANCE CONDITIONING.

temporal lobe. The lobe occupying the lower middle part of the CORTEX, *see* Appendices 1 and 2. It lies behind the FRONTAL LOBE, below the PARIETAL LOBE, and in front of the OCCIPITAL LOBE. It contains several auditory areas and some language areas; one part (the IT area) is implicated in visual recognition.

temporal lobectomy. The removal of some or all of a TEMPORAL LOBE; epileptic foci are commonly excised from it.

temporal lobe epilepsy. Epilepsy caused by a focus in the temporal lobe, which can produce PSYCHOMOTOR EPILEPSY or GRAND MAL attacks.

temporal maze. A maze in which there is no physical cue signalling which way to turn, but which can only be solved by remembering what sequence of turns to make. E.g. a rat can be run in a maze containing only one choice point to which it keeps returning and be required to make the sequence of turns right, right, left, left in order to obtain reward.

temporal modulation transfer function (TMTF). The amount of amplitude change needed to detect loudness changes in a given sound wave as a function of the temporal frequency of the changes.

temporal pole. The anterior tip of the TEMPORAL LOBE.

temporal summation. The addition, on the membrane of the postsynaptic cell, of graded potential changes, caused by repeated inputs from presynaptic cells which are spread out over a short period of time. *Compare* SPATIAL SUMMATION.

temporary threshold shift (TTS). A temporary raising of a threshold; e.g. someone deafened by a loud sound will have a temporary rise in his auditory threshold.

tendon. A band of strong fibrous tissue joining a muscle to a bone.

tendon reflex. A spinal reflex in which, when a tendon is stretched, receptors in the MUSCLE SPINDLE are fired and cause the muscle to contract, thus restoring the joint to its previous position.

tense. (Linguistics) Any modification to the form of a verb (performed by inflexion or by auxiliary verbs) that indicates the time when the action occurs (past, present, or future) with reference to the present or to some other point in time.

tension reduction hypothesis (TRH). The hypothesis that alcohol is drunk because it reduces tension.

tensor network theory. The systematic mapping of vectors of one coordinate system into those of another; the theory has been applied to such physiological systems as the vestibulo-ocular reflex (it is hypothesized that a given vectorial output from the vestibular system is mapped onto instructions to the extraocular muscles) and the cerebellum (which may take as input an instruction to touch an object with certain spatial coordinates and then map these coordinates onto motor commands).

tensor tympani. A muscle in the middle ear which when contracted helps to reduce the movement of the OSSICLES, hence protecting them from being damaged by intense sounds.

tenth cranial nerve. A synonym for VAGUS NERVE.

teratophobia. A morbid fear of monsters, or of having a deformed child.

Terman McNemar Test of Mental Ability. A group intelligence test for 13–18 year olds.

terminal bouton, terminal button, terminal bulb, terminal knob. Synonyms for SYNAPTIC BUTTON.

terminal stimulus. The most extreme stimulus along a dimension to which an organism can respond.

Ternus phenomenon. The phenomenon that if a line of three equally spaced dots is shown briefly, and is replaced by a second line of three dots displaced by the interval between a pair of dots, all three dots are seen to move smoothly even though on the second exposure the first and second dots occupy identical positions to the second and third dots in the first exposure, and therefore have not moved. The phenomenon is known as **group movement**. With very short inter-stimulus intervals, the first dot of the first exposure is seen to jump across to become the third dot in the second exposure, with the other two dots remaining stationary (**element movement**).

territorial aggression. (Ethology) Aggressive behaviour in defence of territory; in many species it is ritualized and rarely leads to a physical fight, e.g. the singing and display of a male robin.

territoriality. The tendency of organisms to preserve a space of their own into which conspecifics are not allowed to enter. *Compare* TERRITORIAL AGGRESSION, PRIMARY TERRITORY, PUBLIC TERRITORY, and SECONDARY TERRITORY.

tertiary circular reaction. Piaget's expression for the repetitive manipulation of objects occurring with some alterations: the alterations are thought to give the child a chance to develop new psychomotor schemata. This behaviour is said to occur towards the end of the SENSORY–MOTOR STAGE. *See also* PRIMARY CIRCULAR REACTION and SECONDARY CIRCULAR REACTION.

tertiary position. Any position of the eye other than a PRIMARY POSITION or SECONDARY POSITION, i.e. any position that cannot be reached by a vertical or horizontal movement from the primary position.

tessellation. Distortion in the shape of an image when it is transduced into activity in discrete elements (PIXELS). E.g. if pixels are arranged in rows and columns, a line just off horizontal will stimulate a short row of pixels, but a little further along it will come to stimulate pixels in an adjacent row. The distortion occurs even if pixels are arranged randomly.

test age. A score in years allocated on the basis of a test result; the score is the average age at which children give the raw score of the testee.

Test Anxiety Questionnaire. A questionnaire that measures how worried people are at doing poorly on a test.

test bias. A test on which different groups having the same ability in the skill being measured score differently because the questions favour one group. E.g. the inclusion of questions on cosmetics on an intelligence test would bias it against males (and these days against many females).

testing effect. The effect of taking a test on the opinions and attitudes of those who take it.

testosterone. The most active ANDROGEN hormone. It is produced by the testes in the male, in small quantities by the ovaries in the female, and by the adrenal cortex in both sexes. It stimulates the development of the male reproductive organs and of male secondary sex characteristics like body hair and strong muscles. It also raises the sexual drive in males, and increases aggression in some species, probably including man.

test–retest coefficient. The correlation between the scores of the same subjects on the same test or different versions of the same test taken on separate occasions; it is a measure of the test's reliability.

test stimulus. 1. A synonym for STANDARD STIMULUS. 2. Any stimulus used to test whether another stimulus has affected perception. *Contrast* INSPECTION STIMULUS.

tetanic. Pertaining to the frequently repeated stimulation of a neuron or group of neurons.

tetanizing shock. An electric shock strong enough to cause TETANUS (1).

tetanus. 1. Prolonged muscle spasm. 2. An infectious disease causing TETANUS (1).

tetrachoric correlation. (Statistics) The correlation between two continuous variables, each of which has been artificially dichotomized, e.g. the correlation between people with lower than average and above average IQ and reaction time also dichotomized. If only one variable is genuinely dichotomous, the POINT BISERIAL CORRELATION should be used, if both are genuinely dichotomous, the PHI COEFFICIENT should be used.

tetrachromatic theory. A synonym for OPPONENT PROCESS THEORY OF COLOUR VISION.

textons. Julesz's term for the limited number of kinds of elements that can be used to distinguish at a glance between two textures having the same overall brightness. They include the orientation, length, and thickness of the lines and perhaps properties like the number of intersections and free ends.

texture gradient. Gibson's term for the changes in the retinal sizes of the elements in a textured surface that provide a cue to its orientation. The cue is present even in a texture whose elements vary randomly in physical size, e.g. a ploughed field, since their average retinal size decreases with distance.

TGA. An abbreviation for TRANSIENT GLOBAL AMNESIA.

TGG. An abbreviation for TRANSFORMATIONAL GENERATIVE GRAMMAR.

T-group. A group formed with the intention of increasing its members' awareness of themselves and others, and of improving the way they react to others. The expression is used mainly of groups consisting of members of the same or similar organizations (e.g. a business) and tends to connote less deep interpretations of behaviour than occur in an ENCOUNTER GROUP.

thalamic theory of emotion. A synonym for CANNON–BARD THEORY.

thalamus. The largest structure (in man, about the size of a golf ball) in the DIENCEPHALON. It lies beneath the corpus callosum and above the hypothalamus. It contains nuclei for relaying information from all the senses, except olfaction, to the cortex, and for relaying information from the motor cortex to the spinal cord. It also communicates with the association cortex, cerebellum, basal ganglia, reticular formation and midbrain. *See* Appendix 5. *See also* ANTERIOR THALAMIC NUCLEUS, CENTROMEDIAL THALAMIC NUCLEUS, DORSOMEDIAL NUCLEUS, INTRALAMINAR NUCLEI, LATERAL DORSAL NUCLEUS, LATERAL GENICULATE NUCLEUS, MEDIAL GENICULATE NUCLEUS, PULVINAR, VENTRAL ANTERIOR THALAMIC NUCLEUS, VENTRAL LATERAL THALAMIC NUCLEUS, and VENTRAL POSTERIOR THALAMIC NUCLEUS.

thalassophobia. A morbid fear of the sea.

thanatology. The study of dying from any aspect.

thanatomania. A compulsion to commit murder or suicide.

thanatophobia. A morbid fear of death or the dead.

Thanatos. (Psychoanalysis) The instinct to die, a concept postulated by Freud late in life; it combats Eros.

Thematic Apperception Test (TAT). A projective test, in which people are shown ambiguous pictures and asked to make up stories based on them.

theomania. The delusion, common among politicians and professors, that one is God or inspired by God.

theophobia. A morbid fear of God.

theorem. A proposition that can be proved within a formal system of logic.

theoretical horopter. A synonym for the VIETH–MULLER CIRCLE.

therapeutic community. Any community containing people with mental disorders, and set up with the intention that its activities and the interactions between its members should ameliorate mental disorder. A hospital ward or a day-care centre can function as therapeutic communities. In such communities it is common to have a semblance of democracy, but despite the numerous meetings, decisions are usually taken by staff, and not by patients.

therapeutic group. A group of mentally disordered people, usually under the direction of a therapist, brought together in order to improve their mental health or emotional state.

therapeutic impasse. The point in psychotherapy at which the therapist decides he cannot be of any further assistance to the patient. The therapist ascribes the impasse to the patient's resistance, the patient to the therapist's inadequacy.

therapeutic matrix. In marital therapy, the way in which the partners and the therapists are organized, e.g. each being seen separately by different therapists, or all four meeting together.

therapeutic window. The range of plasma levels of a drug within which optimal therapeutic effects are obtained; below the range the drug has too little beneficial effect, while too high concentrations may either produce serious side effects or reduce the therapeutic effect.

therapy. Any treatment for an illness or disorder undertaken with the intention of ameliorating or curing it.

thereness-thatness box. A box containing two corridors at right angles to one another. Usually one corridor is viewed normally and the other either normally or with depth cues reduced (e.g. with monocular vision or through a reduction screen). The apparatus is used in size-constancy experiments in which the subject judges the size of a standard stimulus, seen under a variety of viewing conditions in terms of a comparison stimulus viewed normally.

theriomorphism. The ascription to people of animal characteristics, or the depiction of people as beasts.

thermalgesia, thermanalgesia. Hypersensitivity to heat, in which warmth causes pain.

thermistor. A device for measuring temperatures, using the effects of temperature on the electrical resistance of semiconducting materials; it can be miniaturized and implanted in a neuron.

thermoalgesia. A synonym for THERM-ALGESIA.

thermoanaesthesia, thermoanalgesia, thermoanesthesia. Insensitivity to temperature stimuli.

thermocouple. A device for measuring temperature that is based on the different rate of current flow through a wire at different temperatures.

thermophobia. A morbid fear of heat.

thermoreceptors. Sensory receptors sensitive to temperature.

thermoregulation. The control of the body's temperature: the main regulating centre is in the HYPOTHALAMUS, which contains THERMORECEPTORS and can control vasodilation, sweating, etc.

thermostatic hunger hypothesis. The hypothesis that food intake is governed by body temperature, increasing as it drops.

thermotropism, thermotaxis. Orientation or movement regulated by the ambient temperature, e.g. movement towards a warm spot.

theta waves. EEG waves with a frequency of 4–7 Hz; they occur in stage I and stage II sleep. They can also be recorded from the HIPPOCAMPUS in awake animals and are thought by some to be implicated in memory.

thiamine. Vitamin B1, a deficiency of which damages the nervous system.

thinking type. See FUNCTION TYPES.

thinning. In operant conditioning, gradually reducing the frequency of reinforcement, or gradually increasing the time intervals between reinforcements.

thiopental. A very short-acting BARBITURATE.

thioridazine. One of the PHENOTHIAZINES.

thioxanthines. A group of drugs which resemble the PHENOTHIAZINES and are MAJOR TRANQUILLIZERS.

third cranial nerve. A synonym for OCULOMOTOR NERVE.

third moment. See MOMENT.

thirst. The drive that regulates water balance in the body. See also OSMOMETRIC THIRST and VOLUMETRIC THIRST.

thoracic nerves. See SPINAL NERVES.

thoracico-lumbar division. A synonym for the sympathetic division of the autonomic nervous system, which emanates from the thoracic and lumbar segments of the spinal cord.

Thorndike–Lorge word count. A list of English words tabulated by their frequency of use in printed matter.

Thorndike puzzle box. See PUZZLE BOX.

thought control. Control over the direction of one's thoughts, particularly distressing ones, as taught to clients by some cognitive therapists.

thought experiment. A synonym for GEDANKEN EXPERIMENT.

thought stopping. A behaviour therapy technique in which patients are instructed to stop their thoughts whenever they become emotionally undesirable; this is done in the hope that they will learn to use this procedure on their own.

thought transference. A synonym for TELEPATHY.

Thouless ratio. The BRUNSWIK RATIO calculated after taking the logarithm of each term.

thread experiment. An experiment performed by Wundt to test the accuracy of depth vision on monocular and binocular vision. The subject sees a portion of a single vertical thread which is successively exposed at two different distances, and has to judge on which exposure the thread is nearer.

three-colour theory. A synonym for the YOUNG–HELMHOLTZ THEORY.

three-component model of attitude. A theory that regards attitudes as made up of cognitive, behavioural, and emotional dispositions.

three-needle experiment. An experiment designed by Helmholtz to test STEREOACUITY. Two needles are placed at the same distance from the subject, who has to judge whether a third is in line with them.

threshold. 1. The value of a physical stimulus at which it becomes detectable (ABSOLUTE THRESHOLD), or the minimum difference in the values of two stimuli lying on the same dimension at which they can be discriminated (DIFFERENCE THRESHOLD). Within limits the value assigned to a threshold is arbitrary: it is usually taken to be that at which the stimulus (or the difference between two stimuli) is detected on 50 per cent of presentations. The lower the threshold, the better the performance. *See also* ADJUSTMENT, METHOD OF CONSTANT STIMULI, METHOD OF, and LIMITS, METHOD OF. 2. The minimum amount of stimulation needed to fire a neuron.

threshold of feeling. (Hearing) The minimum sound pressure level at the external auditory meatus that provides a sensation, even though the sensation is different in kind from the sensation of hearing.

threshold shift. A change in the value of a threshold. E.g. in auditory masking, the threshold shift is the difference between the threshold for a tone when not masked and for the same tone when masked.

Thurstone scale. A scale to measure the direction and strength of an attitude towards an item. It is contructed as follows. (i) A large number of statements about the item are drawn up, ranging from very favourable to very unfavourable, e.g. 'I despise anyone who is not an atheist', 'I would not let my son marry an atheist'. (ii) These statements are then rated on an 11-point scale by judges who are instructed to make the differences between successive points equal (a difficult if not impossible task). (iii) The scale value of each item is then calculated as the mean of the judges' ratings of it. (iv) A number of statements covering the whole range of attitudes (from 1 to 11) are selected from the original statements. The selected statements are ones on which the judges' ratings are in agreement. These statements can now be administered to subjects who are asked to indicate for each one whether they agree or disagree with it. Their score on the attitude scale is the mean of the score for all items they have endorsed.

thymine. One of the four nucleotide bases of DNA; in RNA the corresponding base is URACIL.

thymoleptics. Drugs that alter mood, particularly those that ameliorate depression.

thymus. A gland below the THYROID that produces white blood cells and influences immunological responses: it is important in early life, but shows involution after adolescence.

thyroid. An endocrine gland at the base of the neck, which regulates growth and metabolism. With excessive secretion, **hyperthyroidism**, the metabolic rate is too high, and excitability and anxiety occur. With too little secretion, **hypothyroidism**, the metabolic rate is too low, and the person is often sluggish and tired.

thyroid-stimulating hormone (TSH), thyrotrophic hormone, thyrotropic hormone, thyrotropin. A hormone secreted by the PITUITARY that stimulates the THYROID gland. *See also* HYPOTHALAMIC-RELEASING FACTORS.

thyroxine. The hormone secreted by the thyroid, which promotes growth in immature organisms and increases metabolic rate in periods of increased activity.

tied image contour. The part of a SUBJECTIVE CONTOUR that extends over parts of the figure where there is no abrupt change in brightness to indicate a contour, as e.g. in a KANIZSA CONTOUR.

tiefenlocalization. (Neuropsychology) Difficulty in judging depth caused by brain injury.

tight junction. (Neurophysiology) An ELECTRICAL SYNAPSE in which the outer (PHOSPHOLIPID) layers of the pre- and postsynaptic cells' membranes are fused together.

tilde. (Logic) The name of the symbol for negation, which is written '∼'.

tilt. 1. The orientation of a line. 2. The SLANT (1) of a surface (a usage best avoided). 3. (Computer vision) The angle of the axis measured clockwise from vertical in the frontal-parallel plane around which a surface is rotated. *See* SLANT (2).

tilt aftereffect. The displacement of the apparent orientation of a line or grating away from the orientation of a previously inspected line or grating. The effect is maximal when the inspection and test gratings differ from one another by only a few degrees. *Compare* SIMULTANEOUS TILT EFFECT.

timbre. The property of an auditory sensation by virtue of which two sounds having the same pitch and loudness may appear dissimilar. It depends upon such properties of the stimulus as its spectrum, temporal characteristics, and waveform. Although all sounds have a timbre, the term is characteristically used of musical instruments and the human voice.

time and motion study. The analysis, usually in an industrial setting, of the time required to carry out different activities, undertaken with a view to reorganizing them in order to foster efficiency.

time binding. The capacity to delay gratification in the light of future expectations.

time domain. (Hearing) The description of a sound in terms of its variation in amplitude across time. *Contrast* FREQUENCY DOMAIN.

timed test. A synonym for SPEED TEST.

time error. Any consistent error made as a result of the presentation in time of the standard and comparison stimuli, particularly in psychophysical experiments in which the point of subjective equality is being determined. *See* NEGATIVE TIME ERROR and POSITIVE TIME ERROR.

time out (TO). In operant conditioning, a period of time during which reinforcement is unavailable, whether because it is no longer presented or because the operant response can no longer be made (e.g. as a result of withdrawing the manipulandum). Time out is used as a technique in behaviour therapy, e.g. someone prone to anger at home might be instructed to withdraw to the garage whenever he becomes angry.

time point sampling. Recording a subject's behaviour at fixed intervals, e.g. every half hour.

time samples. Data obtained at several selected times.

time score. A score based on how much time is needed to complete a task.

time series. Data tabulated by the times at which successive observations are made.

time sharing. (Computing) The division of a computer's time between several users or between several peripherals, achieved by rapidly switching from one to another.

tinnitus. Constant noises in the head, like ringing or buzzing, with no external origin; it can be caused by damage to almost any part of the auditory system.

tip of the tongue phenomenon (TOT). Inability to produce a word that one knows one knows, often accompanied by the ability to recall certain aspects of it, e.g. its first phoneme or its stress pattern.

tissue need. A synonym for PHYSIOLOGICAL NEED.

Titchener circles. A geometric illusion produced by inspecting two circles of the same size, one surrounded by smaller circles and the other by bigger circles. The former circle looks larger than the latter.

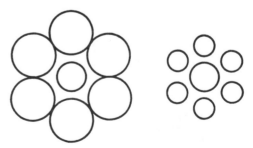

Titchener circles

tit-for-tat. An EVOLUTIONARILY STABLE STRATEGY in which an animal cooperates on the first encounter with another member of its species and thereafter does whatever the other animal did on the previous encounter.

titration. 1. (Chemistry) The addition of one substance to another until a reaction between them is complete. 2. (Generally) Determining how much of anything is needed to offset a fixed amount of something else. This technique can be used in psychological experiments, e.g. ascertaining how much red light must be added to a green light of a given intensity in order to produce an achromatic colour.

T-junction. A VERTEX TYPE in the two-dimensional projection of a polyhedron. It is shaped like the letter T, but includes cases where the lines meet obliquely, rather than at right angles. Except for the rare occurrence of such a junction being produced by ACCIDENTAL ALIGNMENT, it signifies that the surface sharing an edge represented by the stroke is occluding the edge represented by the tail. It is thus the main cue for INTERPOSITION.

TM. An abbreviation for TRANSCENDENTAL MEDITATION.

T-maze. A maze in the shape of a letter T; usually an animal is started from the end of the tail and is rewarded at the end of one or the other arm of the stroke.

TMR. An abbreviation for TRAINABLE MENTALLY RETARDED.

TNR. An abbreviation for TONIC NECK REFLEX.

TO. An abbreviation for TIME OUT.

token. (Linguistics and Philosophy) An instance of an expression or sound. Thus a given instance of the use of the word 'Dog' would be a token, whereas the word itself is the **type**, which can have many different tokens.

token economy. A behaviour therapy technique, in which people in an institution are rewarded for good behaviour with tokens that can be exchanged for privileges. E.g. a mental patient might be rewarded for bodily cleanliness by tokens that he can exchange for a period of watching television.

token identity theory. (Philosophy) The theory that individual psychological events can be identified with individual brain events. It differs from TYPE IDENTITY THEORY in that the latter makes the further assumption that a given type of psychological event can be identified with a given type of brain event. According to token identity theory the neural events underlying the same mental state may be different in different people and even in the same person at different times. Hence the token identity theory denies reductionism and is often held by functionalists.

token nodes. See TYPE NODES.

token reward. 1. A physical object of no value in itself, which can be exchanged for something that is rewarding. 2. In CHAINED SCHEDULES, a stimulus that indicates that the animal has completed one component of the schedule, and hence is closer in time to obtaining a reward.

tolerance. (Medicine) The reduction in the effects of a drug, occurring as a result of usage, which necessitates increased dosage to restore the original effects. Tolerance develops to most addictive drugs. See also ACUTE TOLERANCE, CHRONIC TOLERANCE, CROSS TOLERANCE, DRUG DISPOSITIONAL TOLERANCE, PHARMACODYNAMIC TOLERANCE, and PHARMACOKINETIC TOLERANCE.

tolerance of ambiguity. Ability to tolerate uncertainty, a hypothesized character trait; the AUTHORITARIAN PERSONALITY is supposed to have low tolerance for ambiguity.

tomography. Any non-invasive technique that yields information about the different spatial parts of the brain, particularly about successive slices through it, e.g. COMPUTERIZED AXIAL TOMOGRAPHY or POSITRON EMISSION TOMOGRAPHY.

tomomania. A compulsive urge to undergo an operation.

tonal attribute. Any attribute of a tone, e.g. pitch, loudness, tonal volume, or tonal brightness.

tonal bell. A bell-shaped space on which the different tonal attributes may be plotted; it is the auditory analogue of the colour pyramid in vision.

tonal brightness. The extent to which a tone sounds bright, which depends largely on whether its harmonics are mainly of high or of low frequency. *Contrast* TONAL DENSITY.

tonal chroma, tonal colour. Synonyms for TIMBRE.

tonal contour. A synonym for PITCH CONTOUR.

tonal density. The extent to which a tone sounds dull, i.e. the inverse of TONAL BRIGHTNESS.

tonal dimension. A synonym for TONAL ATTRIBUTE.

tonal gap. A region of the sound frequency spectrum over which a person's sensitivity is reduced.

tonal island. A range of sound frequencies that lies between two TONAL GAPS and within which sensitivity is preserved.

tonality. The frequency distribution of the notes in a given musical language or the kind of sound produced by that distribution.

tonal pencil. A diagram exhibiting the relationship between pitch and volume.

tonal range, tonal scale. The range of sound frequencies that are audible to a person with normal hearing.

tonal volume. The apparent volume of space a sound seems to occupy, which probably depends mainly on the number of echoes; in most closed environments sounds of low frequency produce more echoes than sounds of high frequency.

tone. 1. Any periodic sound. 2. A sound sensation having pitch. *Contrast* NOISE (2). *See also* COMBINATION TONE, COMPLEX TONE, DIFFERENCE TONE, FUNDAMENTAL, INTERRUPTION TONE, PARTIAL TONE, PURE TONE, and SUMMATION TONE.

tone colour. A synonym for TIMBRE.

tone deafness. An abnormally poor ability to discriminate different acoustic frequencies.

tone group, tone unit. A series of syllables (usually a clause) over which a pitch contour is organized. The **nucleus** of the pattern contains a rise or fall (or both) in pitch; at the **head** (the beginning) of the pattern the pitch is usually level or contains a small fall. In English, pitch contours are used, among other things, to convey which information is new and which is given, to make contrast, and to make syntactic distinctions. *See also* FALL, FALL–RISE, HIGH RISE, and LOW-RISE.

tone variator. A device for producing pure tones.

tonic. Pertaining to any prolonged state of contraction of a muscle, whether normal (e.g. a closed jaw) or abnormal (e.g. a prolonged spasm caused by epilepsy).

tonic convulsion. *See* CONVULSION.

tonic immobility. A synonym for FREEZING.

tonic neck reflex (TNR). A reflex in which the foetus extends its arm and leg on the side to which its head is turned and flexes them on the opposite sides of its body. It starts about 28 weeks after conception and is the first postural reflex.

tonic phase. The phase of an epileptic seizure during which the muscles are continuously contracted. *Contrast* CLONIC PHASE.

tonic reflex. An increase in MUSCLE TONUS in specific muscles throughout the body made in preparation for an action; e.g. the tension produced in certain muscles when someone prepares to stand up.

tonometer. 1. A device that measures MUSCLE TONUS. 2. A device that measures the pitch of a tone.

tonoscope. A device for converting sound waves into a pattern of light.

tonotopic map, tonotopic projection. A mapping of different frequencies onto the auditory cortex with neighbouring frequencies being represented in neighbouring regions.

tonus. The continuous slight tension in a muscle not in direct use.

topagnosia, topagnosis. Inability to localize the site of a tactile stimulus.

topalgia. A pain localized in a small area, usually of hysterical origin.

top-down processing. Processing in which incoming information is not merely processed through successively higher levels but in which the operations at one level are affected by information supplied from a higher level. E.g. if in order to extract visual contours, a hypothesis is made about the object being inspected and some contours are recovered using information generated by that hypothesis, then top-down processing would be taking place. *Contrast* BOTTOM-UP PROCESSING.

topectomy. The removal of selected small portions of tissue from the frontal lobe, performed in the hope of ameliorating mental illness.

topic. (Linguistics) In a sentence, the entity about which a statement is being made; it is usually the grammatical SUBJECT, though not always, e.g. 'There's my *house*'.

topicalization. (Linguistics) The movement of a constituent of a sentence to the beginning in order to emphasize it and make it the topic, e.g. 'John you'll never meet'.

topographagnosia. An abnormal inability to deal with spatial relationships in finding one's way around, reading maps, drawing plans etc. It is caused by brain damage, especially to the parietal lobes.

topographical map. A synonym for TOPOLOGICAL MAP.

topographical psychology. An approach to psychology based on dividing the mind into component parts, particularly Freud's division into the id, ego, and superego.

topography. *See* RESPONSE TOPOGRAPHY.

topological map. The mapping of a set of points laid out in space in such a way that neighbouring points in space are represented by neighbouring points in the map though the map may be distorted by being stretched in places. Compare the distortion that occurs when a sheet of rubber is stretched. *Compare* RETINOTOPIC, SOMATOTOPIC PROJECTION, and TONOTOPIC MAP.

topological psychology. Lewin's theory. He thought the mind centred on tensions (needs), valences (the value of objects in a person's LIFE SPACE), and the equilibrium between the person and his environment. These so-called forces were said to interact as vectors.

topology. The branch of mathematics that studies the properties of a surface or space that remain constant when it is distorted without separating neighbouring points, e.g. by stretching or knotting but not cutting. Some of the concepts have been used very loosely by Lewin and by Piaget in his account of the development of children's ideas about space.

topophobia. A morbid fear of a particular place.

torpillage. The treatment of hysteria by the application of painful electric shock to a part of the body.

torsion. (Vision) Rotation of the eyeball about a front-to-back axis. Rotation of the upper cornea in an arc towards the nose is INTORSION, rotation towards the temple is EXTORSION.

TOT. An abbreviation for TIP OF THE TONGUE PHENOMENON.

total internal reflection. The reflection produced in a thin transparent tube with a refractive inner surface. Light hitting the surface at a large angle of incidence is reflected back into the tube. The principle is used in OMMATIDIA and in fibre optics.

Total Quality Management (TQM). A doctrine advocating among other things that all levels of an organization should be involved in decision making; that the key to success in business is establishing and meeting the needs of the customer; that where within a company a department supplies a service to another department, the first department should regard the second as a customer, etc. In Britain TQM is honoured more in its absence than in its presence.

totem. Any physical object (usually an animal or a plant, or their symbolic representations) that has mystical significance for a society; often totems are associated with different families or clans, and form the basis for rituals. Freud thought totems symbolized the primal father.

TOTE unit. A hypothetical unit in the mind that *T*ests the state of something, *O*perates on it to bring it into the desired state, *T*ests to find whether it is in the desired state, and if it is, *E*xits.

touch spot. Any small patch of skin that is particularly sensitive to touch.

Tourette's disorder, Tourette's syndrome. A neurological disorder, marked by tics and repetitive involuntary movements, grunts, and other noises. It is often accompanied by a compulsion to utter obscenities.

Tower of Hanoi problem. The problem of shifting a stack of numbered discs, initially ordered from 1 on top successively down to *n* at the bottom, to another position stacked in the same order. There are only three possible positions on which the items can be stacked, and there is a constraint that in repositioning a disc, it cannot be placed on top of one with a lower number. The Tower of Hanoi has been extensively used in studies of problem solving, because of the recursive structure of the problem space.

toxicomania. A morbid desire to consume poisons.

toxicophobia. An alternative spelling of TOXO-PHOBIA.

toxicosis. 1. The state of having been poisoned. 2. A synonym for LEARNED TASTE AVERSION.

toxic psychosis. Any psychosis caused by being poisoned.

toxophobia. A morbid fear of being poisoned.

TQM. An abbreviation for TOTAL QUALITY MANAGEMENT.

trace. 1. The activity in, or change in, the nervous system that underlies the storage of information either in short-term or long-term memory. 2. (Linguistics) The formal means of marking the original place of a constituent in a sentence (as derived by a phrase-structure grammar) when the constituent has been moved to another place in the surface structure. E.g. in 'The man whom I hate is here', there is a trace for the object of the subordinate clause ('the man') after 'I hate'. The trace and the word in the new position ('whom') are said to show COINDEX-ING. 3. (Chemistry) To use a labelled chemical to follow a chemical reaction. *See* RADIO-ACTIVE TRACERS.

trace conditioning. A classical conditioning procedure in which there is a considerable interval (e.g. 15 sec) between the offset of the conditioned stimulus and the onset of the unconditioned stimulus. *See also* INHIBITION OF DELAY, and *compare* DELAYED CONDITIONING and TEMPORAL CONDITIONING.

tracer. Any compound that after injection is taken up by neurons and transported along their axons and whose traces can be used to discover neuronal pathways. For example, *see* RADIOACTIVE TRACERS and HORSERADISH PEROXIDASE.

tracking. 1. Following a moving target, with the eyes, hands, a pointer, etc. *See also* COMPENSATORY TRACKING, PURSUIT TRACKING, and STEP TRACKING. 2. A synonym for STREAMING.

tract. A bundle of nerve fibres, usually within the central nervous system. *Compare* NERVE, the term for such bundles in the peripheral nervous system.

trainable mentally retarded (TMR). A retardate with an IQ of 40–55, who cannot benefit from a formal education but can be trained in some ways. *Compare* EDUCABLE MENTALLY RETARDED.

training analysis. A psychoanalysis given with the primary purpose of teaching the analysand how to analyse others; in theory it gives him insight into himself which is needed to stop him projecting his own problems on to his patients. It also teaches the principles of analysis.

trait. Any persistent characteristic of an organism, whether learned or inherited, and whether physical or mental.

trait anxiety. A person's characteristic overall level of anxiety. *Contrast* STATE ANXIETY.

trait validity. The extent to which a test measures each of the traits underlying whatever it is supposed to measure. *Contrast* NOMOLOGICAL VALIDITY.

trance. A sleep-like state in which awareness is reduced or circumscribed; it can occur e.g. under hypnosis.

tranquillizer. Any drug that relieves tension. *See* MAJOR TRANQUILLIZERS and MINOR TRANQUILLIZERS.

transactional analysis (TA). A form of group therapy devised by Berne, in which interactions are used to reveal what role (e.g. that of parent or child) a person is unconsciously playing, his unconscious goals, and the tricks ('games people play') he habitually uses in his dealings with others.

transactional theory. (Perception) An approach to perception adopted by Ames and Ittelson that stresses knowledge gained by interaction with the environment and the use of this knowledge to interpret further stimuli.

transcendental meditation. Meditation based on Eastern mysticism, usually involving the repetition of a mantra.

transcortical aphasia. Aphasia caused not by damage to the cortical speech areas but by damage to the pathways connecting them.

transcortical motor aphasia. An EXPRESSIVE APHASIA with good comprehension retained, caused by a lesion in the frontal lobe near Broca's area.

transcortical sensory aphasia. A RECEPTIVE APHASIA with speech retained, which can be caused by a lesion at the junction of the parietal, occipital, and temporal lobes.

transcription. 1. (Generally) Changing a message from one code into another, e.g. changing spoken to written English. 2. (Genetics) The copying of the base sequence of DNA into the corresponding base sequence of RNA, a stage in protein synthesis. *See also* TRANSLATION.

transcription factors. Proteins that switch genes on or off.

transducer. A device that receives a signal in one physical form and outputs it in another; e.g. sensory receptors signal the stimulus received by a change in their membrane potential.

transductive reasoning. Piaget's expression for reasoning at the preoperational stage, which centres on concrete examples, and in which neither true INDUCTION nor DEDUCTION occurs.

transection. (Neuroanatomy) Cutting across an axon, nerve, or tract, or severing one part of the nervous system from another.

transfer. The effect of learning one task on performance on another (**transfer of training**), or the effects of one experience on the way something else is experienced. **Positive transfer** occurs when the learning of one task assists performance on another, **negative transfer** when it impairs performance on another. Not all transfer involves learning, e.g. an AFTEREFFECT can transfer from one eye to the other. Transfer can be of many kinds, *see* e.g. BILATERAL TRANSFER, INTERAURAL TRANSFER, INTERHEMISPHERIC TRANSFER, INTERMODAL TRANSFER, INTEROCULAR TRANSFER, NON–SPECIFIC TRANSFER, and SPECIFIC TRANSFER.

transfer along a continuum. The phenomenon that organisms trained to discriminate on stimuli having a large difference on a continuum (e.g. black versus white) master a discrimination between stimuli having a small difference (e.g. neighbouring shades of grey) better and in a smaller total number of trials than do organisms trained from the outset on the difficult discrimination.

transference. (Psychoanalysis) The tendency for the analysand to treat the analyst as a parent (or some other important figure) and to project onto him feelings about that parent. **Positive transference** occurs when the patient shows liking for the analyst, **negative transference** when he shows hostility. According to psychoanalytic dogma, transference helps to uncover the analysand's repressed feelings towards the important figures in his life. *See also* COUNTERTRANSFERENCE.

transference neurosis. (Psychoanalysis) A neurosis caused by the repressed wishes released in transference, which can replace the original neurosis suffered by the patient. For the patient to regain mental health the transference neurosis must itself be cured.

transference resistance. A patient's use of transference to avoid remembering the past, or to avoid facing the anxiety generated by the prospect of the analysis ending.

transfer function. The function that specifies the relationship between the input to a system and its output.

transfer of training. *See* TRANSFER.

transfer RNA. *See* RIBONUCLEIC ACID.

transfer test. A test to discover whether learning one task affects performance on another. The expression is most commonly used where the test is intended to provide information about what was learned in the original task. E.g. an animal originally trained to discriminate between a square and a triangle might be shown a diamond to discover whether it treats it as a square (four sided figure) or as a triangle (point at the top).

transformation. 1. (Logic and Mathematics) The replacement of one expression or equation by another that is formally equivalent. 2. (Psychoanalysis) The alteration of a repressed wish to a form in which it may enter consciousness. 3. (Linguistics) *See* TRANS-FORMATIONAL RULE.

transformational grammar, transformational generative grammar. Any grammar containing TRANSFORMATIONAL RULES. These rules can be added to other generative rules, such as those of a PHRASE-STRUCTURE GRAMMAR. Transformational grammars can exhibit correspondences between different sentences (e.g. between active and passive, affirmative and negative, declarative and interrogative forms), by deriving them all from the same deep structure, while a pure phrase-structure grammar has to derive them from different deep structures. It has been shown that without extra constraints, transformational grammars are equivalent in computational power to a Turing machine. Without such constraints they cannot delimit LINGUISTIC UNIVERSALS from other formal systems.

transformational rule. (Linguistics) A rule that governs the alteration of the order of symbols in a phrase marker and the addition or deletion of symbols, e.g. the rule $(NP_1 - V - NP_2) \rightarrow (NP_2\ be - V - by - NP_1)$ transforms an active to a passive sentence (as in 'John writes books' $\rightarrow$ 'Books are written by John').

transformed score. Any score that has been changed from the raw score in a systematic way, e.g. by taking its logarithm or expressing it in units of standard deviation.

transient. (Hearing) A sudden rise or fall in air pressure at the ear, such as may occur at the onset of a sound or in a click.

transient agnosia. Short-lasting agnosia; it can be caused by a stroke.

transient cell. A synonym for Y CELL.

transient disparity. A synonym for ENVELOPE DELAY.

transient evoked response. An evoked response produced by stimuli given at large enough intervals to allow the effects of one stimulus to dissipate before the next is given.

transient global amnesia (TGA). A sudden and temporary loss of memory, involving both RETROGRADE AMNESIA and ANTEROGRADE AMNESIA; it can be caused by ischaemia in the hippocampus or fornix.

transient situational personality disorder. A brief neurosis caused by stress.

transient structural disturbance. A synonym for ADJUSTMENT DISORDER.

transient tritanopia. Mollon's expression for the phenomenon that the threshold for a blue stimulus is higher after a yellow adapting field is turned off than in the presence of the adapting field.

transitional cortex. The area of cortex lying between the archicortex and neocortex or between the palaeocortex and neocortex. It is on the medial surface of the temporal lobe, in the region of the hippocampus. Its anatomical characteristics suggest that it developed before the neocortex but after the archicortex and palaeocortex – hence 'transitional'.

transitional object. An object used by a child to comfort itself, e.g. a teddy bear or favourite blanket.

transition network. An AUTOMATON that can be implemented in a computer program and that can be used for parsing some sentences. The program parses from left to right, and moves through labelled arcs from one state to another, depending on the information it receives at each point. Thus if a program has just received the word 'the' its state will be 'In the middle of a noun phrase, expect noun or adjective'. If an adjective is received, it will return to the same state since another adjective may follow. If a noun is received and the noun phrase was the first in the sentence, it will go to a state where (among other things) it is expecting a verb or an auxiliary verb. *See also* AUGMENTED TRANSITION NETWORK.

transition probability. The probability that a specific state (event etc.) will be followed by another specific state. In psychology the term is commonly used of the probability of a word following another word or following a string of words.

transitive. 1. (Linguistics) Pertaining to a verb (e.g. 'hit') that can take a direct object as opposed to an **intransitive** verb that cannot take a direct object, e.g. 'go'. 2. (Logic) Pertaining to a relationship such that if A has the relationship to B and B has it to C, then A has it to C (e.g. the relationship 'higher than'). Relationships of which this is not necessarily true are **intransitive** (e.g. 'next to').

translation. (Genetics) The production of sequences of amino acids by the attachment

of TRANSFER RNA to MESSENGER RNA. *Compare* TRANSCRIPTION (2).

translocation. A MUTATION consisting of the transfer of part of a chromosome to another part of that chromosome or of a different chromosome.

transmethylation. The addition of a methyl group to an existing compound, e.g. norepinephrine is changed to epinephrine by transmethylation. It is hypothesized that schizophrenia is caused by errors in the transmethylation of the BIOGENIC AMINES.

transmitter. Short for NEUROTRANSMITTER.

transmuted score. A synonym for TRANSFORMED SCORE.

transneuronal degeneration. A synonym for TRANS-SYNAPTIC DEGENERATION.

transorbital lobotomy, transorbital leucotomy. A form of FRONTAL LOBOTOMY invented by Freeman, in which an instrument is thrust through the orbit of the eye and then swung through the frontal lobes; the operation was originally often performed without an anaesthetic and sometimes with the use of an ice-pick.

transpersonal psychology. A movement that studies phenomena thought to go beyond the limits of the individual person. They include awe, ecstasy, mystical experiences, and other ALTERED STATES OF CONSCIOUSNESS. The movement starts where HUMANISM leaves off: one can only wonder what next.

transport. (Physiology) The movement of substances in the body, e.g. across a membrane or down an axon.

transport autoradiography. A radiographic technique in which a radioactive substance is injected in the region of a cell body. It is taken up by the cell body and transported down the axon. Hence it reveals the destination of the axon.

transposition, transpositional learning. In discrimination learning, generalizing according to the relative values of the stimuli (rather than their absolute values); e.g. having learned to select a 6-inch rod and avoid a 3-inch one, an animal or person tested with a 9-inch and a 6-inch rod may select the 9-inch one.

transposition of affect. A synonym for DIS-PLACEMENT OF AFFECT.

trans-sexualism. A persistent and overpowering desire to belong to the opposite sex, usually accompanied by a wish to acquire the anatomy of that sex, a desire that modern surgery can sometimes partially fulfill.

trans-sexuality. A psychosexual disorder in which it is believed that one is a man trapped in a woman's body, or a woman trapped in a man's body.

trans-situationality principle. The false principle that a reinforcer that is effective in one situation will be as effective in all.

trans-synaptic degeneration. Degeneration in a neuron caused by damage to another neuron with which it synapses.

trans-synaptic filament. A synonym for GROWTH CONE.

transverse section. (Anatomy) A SECTION made in a plane perpendicular to the longest axis of an organ or of the body. *See also* CORONAL SECTION and FRONTAL SECTION.

transverse temporal gyrus. A synonym for HESCHL'S GYRUS.

transvestism, transvestitism. Dressing as a member of the opposite sex in order to obtain sexual pleasure, but without wishing to become a member of that sex; this sexual deviation is largely confined to males.

trapezoid body. A nucleus in the PONS receiving an input relayed from the COCHLEAR NUCLEUS and projecting fibres to the SUPERIOR OLIVARY NUCLEUS on both sides of the brain stem.

trapezoidal window. A synonym for AMES WINDOW.

trauma. A severe physical or psychological injury.

traumatic neurosis. A synonym for POST-TRAUMATIC STRESS DISORDER.

traumatophobia. A morbid fear of being injured.

travelling wave. (Hearing) The wave that travels down the BASILAR MEMBRANE (from the OVAL WINDOW to the APEX) when an auditory stimulus is received. The wave has its greatest amplitude near the oval window (the stiffest part of the membrane) for high frequencies, and towards the apex of the cochlea for low frequencies.

treatment variable. A synonym for INDEPENDENT VARIABLE.

T1 receptor, T2 receptor. *See* CUTANEOUS RECEPTORS.

tree diagram. Any structure of branching nodes, usually with several layers, emanating from a single node, with each node dividing into two or more branches until a set of terminal nodes is reached. Trees are a convenient way to exhibit hierarchical structures, which can be represented less perspicuously by nested brackets. Some search procedures can be represented by a tree, as can a phrase-structure grammar, where the terminal nodes represent words. In diagrams the origin of the tree is conventionally placed at the top.

tremograph. A device for recording body TREMOR (1).

tremor. 1. Any trembling movement of a part of the body. 2. (Vision) *See* PHYSIOLOGICAL NYSTAGMUS.

trend analysis. (Statistics) The analysis of data to detect consistent trends, sometimes with a view to extrapolating them to predict further events. *Compare* JONCKHEERE TEST.

treppe. The increase in the contraction of a muscle when it is repeatedly or constantly stimulated.

TRH. An abbreviation for 1. TENSION REDUCING HYPOTHESIS; 2. THYROTROPHIC RELEASING HORMONE.

triad. 1. (Social psychology) A group of three people. 2. (Experimental psychology) *See* TRIADS, METHOD OF. 3. *See* COGNITIVE TRIAD.

triads, method of. Any experimental procedure in which the subject is shown three stimuli, of which he has to select one, according to a rule such as 'the odd one'.

triage. (Medicine) The division, after a disaster, of the sick or injured into three groups: (i) those who will die regardless of medical intervention; (ii) those who will live regardless of medical intervention; (iii) those who will live only if they receive medical care. Where resources are scarce, they can be concentrated on the last group.

trial. In a psychological experiment, a single performance by a subject of a task (e.g. running a maze, or responding to the presentation of a stimulus in a psychophysical experiment). The response made on each trial is usually recorded.

trial-and-error learning. Learning to perform a task by making a series of random actions, and eliminating those that are errors; early behaviourists thought all learning was of this kind, but although trial-and-error learning plays a role, insight is also important.

triangle of conflict. (Psychotherapy) A person's deep feelings, his defences against recognizing unacceptable feelings, and the anxiety that such recognition produces.

triarchic theory. An exceptionally woolly hypothesis, put forward by R. J. Sternberg, positing among other things that intelligence involves (a) one's internal world; (b) one's external world; (c) one's experience, which mediates between the first two.

tribadism. The rubbing together of the genitals of two women.

trichaesthesia, trichesthesia, trichoesthesia. The sensation produced by the movement of a hair on the skin.

trichopathophobia. A synonym for TRICHOPHOBIA.

trichophagy. Persistent biting at or eating of one's own hair.

trichophobia. A morbid fear of hair.

trichromacy. Colour vision in which any mixture of wavelengths can be matched by mixing three primary colours (*see* METAMERIC MATCHING); it is based on having three separate cone pigments. Normal colour vision is trichromatic, though some trichromats have anomalous colour vision.

trichromatic theory. The theory put forward by Young and Helmholtz that there are three separate colour processes and that the colour seen depends on the relative excitation of each. *Contrast* OPPONENT PROCESS THEORY OF COLOUR VISION.

trichromatism, trichromatopsia. Synonyms for TRICHROMACY.

tricyclics, tricyclic antidepressants. A group of drugs that have an antidepressant action. They may work, at least in part, by preventing the reuptake of NOREPINEPHRINE through the membrane of the presynaptic cell.

tridimensional theory of feeling. Wundt's view that all feeling can be accounted for in terms of three dimensions: pleasant unpleasant, tense relaxed, and excited depressed.

trigeminal lemniscus. The part of the LEMNISCAL SYSTEM, carrying fibres from the TRIGEMINAL NERVE to the THALAMUS.

trigeminal nerve. The fifth CRANIAL NERVE, which has three main parts. The **ophthalmic nerve** carries afferent fibres from the scalp and forehead, the nasal cavity, the cornea, and conjuctiva. The **maxillary nerve** serves the upper teeth and gums, part of the nose, and the parts of the cheek lying to the side of the eye and nose. The **mandibular nerve** supplies the lower jaw, lower teeth, lower lip, and the masticatory muscles.

trigeminal nuclei. Nuclei in the medulla from which the TRIGEMINAL NERVE originates.

trigger zone. The part of the postsynaptic cell which when stimulated most readily initiates an axon potential.

trigram. A sequence of three letters, usually not making a word and usually made up of consonant vowel consonant; it has been much used in experiments on rote learning.

trimetric projection. A form of ORTHOGRAPHIC PROJECTION in which three orthogonal faces of an object have the same shape as one another on the surface to which they are projected.

triple X condition. A chromosomal anomaly, in which a woman has three X chromosomes, sometimes but not always associated with mental retardation.

triskaidekaphobia. A morbid fear of the number 'thirteen'.

trisomy. The possession of three chromosomes at a particular site instead of the normal two. When 'trisomy' is followed by a number, the number indicates which chromosome is anomalous. Thus in trisomy-21, there are three members of the 21st chromosome, the condition that produces Down's syndrome.

tritan. A person who is tritanomalous or tritanopic.

tritanomalous. A person with TRITANOMALY.

tritanomaly. A mild form of colour blindness in which although there is trichromacy, there is a decreased sensitivity to blue light, probably caused by an inadequacy in the short wavelength (blue) cone system.

tritanope. A person with TRITANOPIA.

tritanopia. A very rare form of DICHROMATISM in which the blue cones appear to be non-functional; it is characterized by an inability to discriminate different blues or blues and greens. See also TRANSIENT TRITANOPIA.

triune brain. Maclean's speculative and mis-leading hypothesis that the human brain is made up of a **reptilian brain** (hindbrain and midbrain), a **visceral brain** which is a primitive mammalian brain (the limbic system), and the newly evolved NEOCORTEX. The older parts of the brain, according to him, carry forward traits, such as aggression, which are not appropriate to man's condition.

trochlear nerve, trocular nerve. The fourth CRANIAL NERVE; see EXTRAOCULAR NERVES.

troilism. Sexual activity with three participants.

troland. A unit of measurement of retinal illuminance, defined as the photometric intensity of the light falling on the retina when an extended source of luminance of one candela per square metre is viewed through a pupil of area 1 mm^2.

trophallaxis. The exchange of regurgitated food between members of the same species, common in colonies of social insects.

trophic hormones. Anterior pituitary hormones that affect the amount secreted by other endocrine glands, e.g. FOLL-ICLE-STIMULATING HORMONE, LUTEINIZING HORMONE, and INTERSTITIAL CELL-STIMULAT-ING HORMONE.

trophotropic process. Hess's outmoded expression for the neural processes mediating arousal. Contrast ERGOTROPHIC PROCESS.

tropia. A misalignment of the two eyes when both are fixating a point. If large enough to produce double images, it is called STRABISMUS. Contrast HETEROPHORIA.

tropism. The turning of a plant or animal towards (**positive tropism**) or away from (**negative tropism**) a source of stimulation. The meaning is very similar to that of TAXIS, though some think that taxis should be used of animals and tropism of plants.

tropotaxis. A taxis in which movement proceeds in a direct path towards the controlling stimulus. Contrast KLINOTAXIS.

trouble-shooting. 1. (Managerial psychology) The detecting and rectifying of bad interactions, poor channels of communication, etc. within an organization. 2. A synonym for FAULT FINDING.

Troxler's effect. The phenomenon that with sustained fixation, visual stimuli falling on the periphery of the eye disappear. Peripheral stimuli may disappear before central ones because receptive fields are larger in the periphery, and the eye movements made in physiological nystagmus may not be extensive enough to sweep the peripheral stimuli across a receptive field.

true mean. A synonym for POPULATION MEAN.

true self. The underlying self which, so Horney alleges, has many unrealized potentials and which is considered by optimistic psychotherapists to be always good.

true variance. The actual variance in a population, as opposed to the variance observed in a selected sample.

truncated distribution. (Statistics) A frequency distribution in which one or both tails have been cut off either deliberately or as an artefact of the way a sample is selected.

truth conditional semantics. A theory of meaning postulating that the meaning of a sentence is the state of affairs in the world that must obtain for it to be true. *Compare* MODEL THEORETIC SEMANTICS.

truth table. A method of deciding whether a formula of the propositional calculus is true; it depends on constructing a table listing all possible combinations of truth values for the component propositions and evaluating the logical connectives. E.g. the truth value for $p \supset q$ ('p implies q') is:

p	q	$p \supset q$
T	T	T
T	F	F
F	T	T
F	F	T

tryptamines. A group of drugs resembling SEROTONIN, some of which are psychedelic.

tryptophan. An essential amino acid which is a precursor of SEROTONIN.

T-scope. An abbreviation for TACHISTOSCOPE.

T score. A transformed score with a mean of 50 and a STANDARD DEVIATION of 10.

TSH. An abbreviation for THYROID STIMULATING HORMONE.

t-test. (Statistics) A parametric test for assessing hypotheses about population means. It is most commonly used when the null hypothesis is that two populations have the same mean value on some variable of interest. The form of the test used in this case depends on whether independent samples are drawn from each population, or whether the samples are matched in some way (e.g. by having the same subjects each perform under two conditions). Though the test is based on assumptions of normality and homogeneity of population variances, it is relatively robust against departures from these assumptions.

TTR. An abbreviation for TYPE TOKEN RATIO.

TTS. An abbreviation for TEMPORARY THRESHOLD SHIFT.

tufted cell. A nerve cell in the olfactory bulb to which olfactory nerve cells are connected.

Tukey test. (Statistics) An *a posteriori*, multiple-comparison test for the difference between two or more means. It is similar to the NEWMAN–KEULS test, but less likely to err by making a TYPE I ERROR.

tuning curve. A plot of the responses of a system to a series of points along a dimension. E.g. orientation detectors in the visual cortex respond most strongly to bars or edges in a particular orientation, and they respond less strongly to bars and edges lying to either side of that orientation. Tuning curves are often specified in terms of their **half height**, i.e. the distance along the dimension from the point of maximal response at which the response is half of the maximal response.

tuning fork. A metal fork with two tines that emits a pure tone when struck.

tunnel effect. Short for ACOUSTIC TUNNEL EFFECT.

tunnel vision. Vision limited to the central region of the retina, a condition that can be produced by disease, injury, or hysteria.

Turing machine. Turing's specification of an abstract automaton. It consists of a head to read and write either of two symbols, a tape, and a set of internal states. At each step, according to its internal state and the symbol just read, the computer will leave the tape where it is or move it one step to the left or right, write or not write on the tape, and change (or not) its internal state in a specific way. The idea of this automaton was important, since, despite its simplicity, Turing was able to show that it could compute any computable function.

Turing test. A hypothetical test, devised by Turing, for whether a computer system can think in the same way as a person. A person interrogates another person or a computer, each hidden from him: the test is whether he can find out to which he is connected.

Turner's syndrome. A disorder caused by the absence of one or both of the X chromosomes in a woman; it is characterized by a tendency to low IQ, short height, and sterility.

T-vertex. A synonym for T-JUNCTION.

twelfth cranial nerve. A synonym for HYPO-GLOSSAL NERVE.

twilight sleep. Extreme drowsiness with re-duced awareness of the external world; it may be caused by drugs, including alcohol, barbiturates, or scopolamine.

twilight state. A temporary restricted state of consciousness in which, although complex acts may be carried out, a person is unaware of much of his surroundings; it can occur in dissociative hysteria, epilepsy, and under the influence of alcohol.

twilight vision. A synonym for SCOTOPIC VISION.

twisted cord illusion. A variant on Fraser's spiral illusion, shown below. The horizontal and vertical lines of the letters appear tilted in the direction of their black and white strands.

two-and-a-half D sketch. Marr's expression for a representation of the visual world, consisting of the distance and tilt of each surface at each point relative to the view-point. Because such a representation changes with viewpoint, and because it lacks structure, Marr argued that it cannot be directly used for recognition, which needs a more abstract representation. The expres-sion is unfortunate, since the two-and-a-half D sketch contains full 3-D information.

two-by-two table. A CONTINGENCY TABLE with two categories each having two values.

two-factor learning theory. An account of AVOIDANCE LEARNING proposed by Mowrer, in which it is assumed two different things are learned. First, fear is learned as a response to the conditioned stimulus by CLASSICAL CON-DITIONING; second, the animal learns to make the avoidance response through IN-STRUMENTAL CONDITIONING (with fear reduc-tion as reinforcement). More generally, two-factor learning theorists believe that differ-ent mechanisms underlie classical and in-strumental conditioning.

two-factor theory of intelligence. Spearman's theory of intelligence, which posits that it is

twisted cord illusion

composed of a GENERAL FACTOR and several specific factors.

two-factor theory of memory. Any theory of memory that maintains that separate processes underlie EPISODIC MEMORY and SEMANTIC MEMORY.

two-point threshold. The minimum distance between two points on the skin needed to yield a sensation of two separate stimuli when they are both touched simultaneously.

two-process learning theory. A synonym for TWO-FACTOR LEARNING THEORY.

two-process theory of motion. Braddick's theory that there are two motion detecting systems, an automatic one operating over short intervals and spatial extents, the other operating over a wider range of intervals and extents, and involving inference-like processes. *See* SHORT-RANGE MOTION SYSTEM and LONG-RANGE MOTION SYSTEM.

two-rod test. A test of stereoscopic acuity in which a rod is presented at a distance of 20 feet, and the observer has to adjust another rod to appear the same distance away. The rods are very thin and all but the central section of each is hidden by a screen containing an aperture.

two-tailed test. A statistical test of a null hypothesis whose regions of rejection are placed at both ends (or tails) of the distribution of the test statistic, e.g. when the alternative to the null hypothesis is that the mean of one population differs from that of the other, regardless of whether it is higher or lower. *Contrast* ONE-TAILED TEST.

tympanic canal. A synonym for SCALA TYMPANI.

tympanic cavity. A synonym for MIDDLE EAR.

tympanic membrane. A synonym for EAR-DRUM.

tympanic reflex. A reflex of the muscles controlling the ossicles, in which they contract in response to loud sounds, thus reducing the amplitude of vibration at the oval window, and protecting the inner ear from damage.

tympanum. A synonym for EARDRUM.

type. (Linguistics and Philosophy) *See* TOKEN.

type A personality. The personality of someone who is very competitive, impatient, always in a hurry, and tries to do different things at once (e.g. shaving while driving); it is thought to be positively correlated with proneness to coronary disease.

type B personality. The personality of someone who is relaxed, easy-going, not too competitive, and not prone to feeling frustrated; it is thought to be negatively correlated with coronary heart disease.

type C personality. A personality in whom strong emotions are suppressed, thought by some to be predisposed to cancer.

type I conditioning. A synonym for CLASSICAL CONDITIONING.

type II conditioning. A synonym for IN-STRUMENTAL CONDITIONING.

type I error. (Statistics) Rejection of the null hypothesis when it is in fact true.

type II error. (Statistics) Acceptance of the null hypothesis when it is in fact false.

type I synapse, type II synapse. *See* SYNAPSE.

type fallacy. The tendency to view people as occupying extreme positions on a dimension (e.g. lumping together all extraverts or all introverts) rather than making allowance for the fact that most dimensions of personality are continuous.

type identity theory. (Philosophy) The theory that a given type of psychological event can be identified with a given type of brain event. *Contrast* TOKEN IDENTITY THEORY.

type nodes. In semantic networks, the representation of a class of items (e.g. 'cats'); **token nodes** represent individual items (e.g. 'my cat') and are connected to the appropriate type node by a relationship such as 'is a'.

type R conditioning. A synonym for IN-STRUMENTAL CONDITIONING.

type S conditioning. A synonym for CLASSICAL CONDITIONING.

type token ratio (TTR). The ratio of the number of words (tokens) to the number of different words (types) used in a corpus of language; the higher the ratio, the greater is the diversity of the words used.

typology. Any systematic classificatory scheme. *See also* CONSTITUTIONAL TYPE.

tyrosine. An amino acid that is a precursor of adrenergic transmitters, e.g. EPINEPHRINE and NOREPINEPHRINE.

U

U. The test statistic in the MANN–WHITNEY U TEST.

U curve. A synonym for U-SHAPED CURVE.

UCR. An abbreviation for UNCONDITIONED RESPONSE.

UCS. An abbreviation for UNCONDITIONED STIMULUS.

UCs. An abbreviation for UNCONSCIOUS.

UG. An abbreviation for UNIVERSAL GRAMMAR.

ultradian rhythm. Any biological rhythm with a period of less than a day.

ultrasonic. Pertaining to sound waves above the upper frequency (about 20,000 Hz) that can be heard by people.

ultraviolet. Pertaining to light below the lowest wavelength (about 380 nm) that can be seen be people.

Umweg **problem.** A synonym for DETOUR PROBLEM.

Umwelt. 1. (Biology) Von Uexküll's term for those aspects of the environment (including conspecifics) with which an organism interacts, e.g. by perceiving or moving. Since a snail's drives and its sensory and motor apparatus are very different from a rat's, the animals' *Umwelt* would be very different, even if they were both in the same place. 2. (Existentialism) A person's way of relating to his physical environment. *Compare* EIGENWELT and MITWELT.

unbiased estimate. A sample estimate whose mean value in repeated random sampling is equal to that of the population parameter being estimated.

unbridged junction. A synonym for SYNAPTIC CLEFT.

unconditional positive regard. Rogers' expression for a therapist's attitude of warmth and acceptance towards a patient, which he thought was essential for therapeutic success and which – oddly – he believed could be genuinely provided regardless of how nasty the patient was. *Contrast* CONDITIONAL POSITIVE REGARD.

unconditional response. A synonym for UNCONDITIONED RESPONSE.

unconditional stimulus. A synonym for UNCONDITIONED STIMULUS.

unconditioned response. *See* UNCONDITIONED STIMULUS.

unconditioned stimulus (US). In a CLASSICAL CONDITIONING experiment, a stimulus that innately produces a response that is characteristic of the species (the **unconditioned response (UR)**); learning consists of attaching to the conditioned stimulus the response evoked by the unconditioned stimulus.

unconscious. 1. The part of the mind containing all the mental processes of which a person in unaware, including e.g. memories of which a person is not currently conscious. 2. (Psychoanalysis) The part of the mind containing the ID and parts of the SUPEREGO, and all the material that a person cannot bring to consciousness because it has been repressed. *Compare* PRECONSCIOUS.

unconscious inference. Helmholtz's expression, used to stress his belief that perceptual processes are complex, involve learning, and are akin to inference; thus he thought the visual system unconsciously learned to infer depth from the various depth cues.

uncrossed disparity. *See* BINOCULAR DISPARITY.

uncus. A cortical structure in the limbic system, which is the thickened cephalic end of the parahippocampal gyrus. *See* Appendix 2.

undergeneralization. Generalizing too little, particularly when first learning a word, e.g. a child may use 'doggy' to refer only to its own pet dog. *Contrast* OVERGENERALIZATION (1).

undersocialized aggressive conduct disorder. (DSM-III) A conduct disorder marked by aggression, violence, and antisocial acts.

undersocialized non-aggressive conduct disorder. (DSM-III) A conduct disorder in which antisocial acts are persistently committed but without violence.

undifferentiated schizophrenia. A synonym for MIXED SCHIZOPHRENIA.

undistributed middle. A fallacy in syllogistic reasoning of the form:

Given	All X are Y	(All bees are insects)
	All Z are Y	(All hornets are insects)
Therefore	All X are Z	(All bees are hornets)

Here Y is the middle term, but in the syllogism it is not distributed, that is, no assertion is made about all Ys; if it were distributed in the second premise (All Y are Z), it would be legitimate to conclude that 'All X are Z'. In more complex examples, many people make this fallacy.

undoing. (Psychoanalysis) A defence mechanism in which a person does something to remove or allay upsetting thoughts, e.g. the washing rituals of an obsessive–compulsive which are assumed to remove guilt or to obliterate a previous desire to be unclean.

unfilled pause. A silent gap in speech.

unfinished business. In Gestalt psychotherapy, any event in a person's past with which he has never come to terms.

uniaural. A synonym for MONAURAL.

unicellular. Single-celled (of organisms).

unidextrous. Having a preference for one hand.

unidimensional. Pertaining to or having only one dimension. *Contrast* MULTIDIMENSIONAL.

uniform distribution. A frequency distribution in which all classes or values have the same frequency or probability.

unilateral. Pertaining to one side of the body or one hemisphere of the brain.

unilateral neglect. A neurological symptom, in which the patient ignores one side of the external world and one side of his body; he may feel that his limbs on the neglected side do not belong to him. The symptom can be produced by damage to the parietal lobe. *Compare* SPATIAL NEGLECT.

unimodal. Of a distribution, having only one mode, which, if the data are represented graphically, corresponds to there being only one peak.

uniocular. A synonym for MONOCULAR.

uniovular twins. A synonym for MONOZYGOTIC TWINS.

unipolar cell. A neuron with only one primary process (the axon) leaving the soma.

unipolar manic-depressive disorder. *See* MANIC-DEPRESSIVE DISORDER.

unipolar neuron. A synonym for UNIPOLAR CELL.

unique factor. A synonym for SPECIFIC FACTOR.

unique hue. Those hues (red, green, yellow, and blue) that do not appear to be a mixture of any other hues.

uniqueness constraint. The assumption that an object can be in only one location at one time, so that each feature in the left eye image matches one and only one feature in the right eye image. Without this constraint, the

CORRESPONDENCE PROBLEM in stereopsis could not be solved.

unit. 1. A standard quantity in which something is measured, e.g. decibel, sone, or wavelength. 2. Short for SINGLE UNIT.

unitary stimulus dimension. A synonym for INTEGRAL STIMULUS DIMENSION.

unit character. A trait genetically transmitted as a whole, i.e. one that does not vary continuously but is either present or absent.

unit formation. A relationship between the cognitive elements that enter into BALANCE THEORY.

unit hypothesis. The hypothesis that the amount of generalization along a continuum decreases with the number of test stimuli that lie between the training stimulus and a given test stimulus (and increases with the number that lie beyond it). Thus generalization from a vertical line to a 30° line might be greater if the test stimuli were lines at 30°, 60°, and 90° than if they were lines at 10°, 20°, and 30°.

unitization. The process by which a group of units comes to be perceived as a whole although they were initially perceived as separate units. E.g. the process by which letter recognition develops into word recognition.

univariate. Having only one variable.

universal. (Logic) A proposition that asserts that something is true of all members of a given class.

universal grammar. The abstract rules to which the syntax of all human languages are hypothesized to conform; it is thought that unless the types of possible grammar were constrained, it would be impossible for any language acquisition device to learn a given grammar from the examples to which a child is exposed.

universalizability. (Philosophy) The doctrine that all particular moral judgements (e.g. about an action performed by someone) imply and can only be supported by moral principles that are of general applicability.

universal machine. A putative machine that can compute anything computable and can therefore simulate any possible manipulation of symbols, including any such manipulations made by the brain. *See* TURING MACHINE.

universal proposition. A synonym for UNIVERSAL.

universal quantifier. *See* QUANTIFIER.

universal symbol. (Psychoanalysis) A symbol that has the same meaning for everyone. *Contrast* INDIVIDUAL SYMBOL.

unlearning. A reduction in the tendency to make a previously learned response, whether through extinction, forgetting, or the learning of a different response.

unmarked. *See* MARKEDNESS.

unobtrusive measure. (Social psychology) Any way of recording behaviour that the subject is unaware of (or is only dimly aware of), e.g. observation through a one-way mirror. *Compare* OBTRUSIVE MEASURE.

unpaired comparison test. Any statistical test used to compare groups when the members of different groups cannot be matched in pairs. *Contrast* PAIRED COMPARISON TEST.

unplanned comparison test. A statistical test for the significance of differences in the results of different conditions that is applicable where no prior hypothesis has been postulated.

unreadiness, law of. Thorndike's principle that conduction across a 'conduction unit' is unpleasant if the unit is not ready to conduct. *See* READINESS, LAW OF.

unspaced practice. Learning a task with only short intervals between trials or blocks of trials.

unspecified mental retardation. (DSM-III) A state of retardation in which the person's intelligence cannot be evaluated by any standard tests.

unstressed. (Linguistics) Not accentuated (of a syllable).

unstructured interview. An interview in which the material to be covered has not been decided in advance. *Contrast* STRUCTURED INTERVIEW.

unstructured stimulus. A stimulus with little inherent organization that can be perceived in different ways (e.g. a Rorschach inkblot).

unsupervised neural network. A neural network that learns (e.g. to make a discrimination or to generalize) without being taught by back-propagation.

unvoiced consonant. (Phonetics) A consonant in which there is no VOICING, e.g. the 'p' in 'pin' or the 't' in 'tin'. *See* VOICE-ONSET TIME.

up-and-down method. A synonym for STAIRCASE METHOD.

upper threshold. The maximum point along a physical dimension at which a stimulus can be sensed or the maximum point at which it can be sensed without damage to the receptors, e.g. a sound frequency of about 20,000 Hz is the upper frequency threshold for hearing.

UR. An abbreviation for UNCONDITIONED RESPONSE.

uracil. One of the four nucleotide bases in RNA; in DNA the corresponding base is THYMINE.

uranophobia. A morbid fear of heaven or the sky.

urolagnia, urophilia. A morbid interest in urine, particularly the derivation of sexual excitement from watching someone else urinate or from being urinated upon.

US. An abbreviation for UNCONDITIONED STIMULUS.

use, law of. A synonym for FREQUENCY, LAW OF.

U-shaped curve. Any graph of a distribution that is shaped like a U.

U-test. *See* MANN–WHITNEY U-TEST.

utilitarianism. (Philosophy) Bentham's doctrine that the ultimate moral end is the greatest happiness of the greatest number.

utility. In economics, psychology, and sociology the value to an individual or organization of a particular outcome. *See also* SUBJECTIVELY EXPECTED UTILITY.

utility theory. A normative theory of decision taking in which the decision maker puts a numerical value (the UTILITY) on all the possible outcomes of each option. The utility of each outcome is then multiplied by its probabliity of occurrence giving its EXPECTED UTILITY. The expected utility of an option is the sum of the expected utilities of its possible outcomes. In theory, the option with the highest expected utility should be chosen.

utricle. One of two sacs in the VERTIBULAR SYSTEM. It is located near the ampullae; its floor is horizontal and is thickened laterally to form a MACULA containing hair cells, whose microvilli are moved by otoliths when the head moves.

utrocular. Pertaining to the ability to detect on which eye a given stimulus is falling when both eyes are open and the stimulus only falls on one.

uvula. A flap of tissue at the back of the throat that is an extension of the soft palate.

uvular. (Phonetics) Pertaining to a consonant articulated with the back of the tongue against the uvula as in the French pronunciation of /r/.

V

V. An abbreviation for 1. VARIABLE STIMULUS; 2. VOLT; 3. VOLUME; 4. STIMULUS INTENSITY DYNAMISM; 5. VERB; 6. VERBAL ABILITY.

V1. Brodmann's area 17 (*see* Appendix 3), the STRIATE CORTEX, which contains a direct visual projection forming a retinotopic map.

V2. Brodmann's area 18 (*see* Appendix 3), which contains a retinotopic map.

V3. Brodmann's area 19 (*see* Appendix 3), in which there are several retinotopic maps.

V4. An area on the fringe of Brodmann's area 19; *see* Appendix 3. Many of its cells are thought to code for colour.

V5. A synonym for MT.

vacuum activity. (Ethology) A fixed action pattern occurring in the absence of any RELEASER, presumably because the level of the appropriate drive or action-specific energy is very high. *Contrast* DISPLACEMENT ACTIVITY and REDIRECTED ACTIVITY.

vagina dentata. (Psychoanalysis) The fantasy that the vagina is a mouth with teeth that can castrate the male; this fantasy is alleged to occur in members of both sexes.

vagus nerve. The tenth CRANIAL NERVE, which supplies the muscles of the pharynx and larynx, and which is distributed widely throughout the viscera, thus forming part of the PARASYMPATHETIC SYSTEM.

VAKT procedure. An acronym for the **multi-sensory method**, that is, teaching reading using all the senses – *v*ision, *a*udition, *k*inaesthesis, and *t*ouch; the latter two senses are brought into play by having the child trace the letters of any word it does not know.

valence. Lewin's term for the extent to which anything (e.g. an event, object or person) attracts (**positive valence**) or repels (**negative valence**) a person. *See also* CHROMATIC VALENCE.

validation. The process of establishing that a theory or test is valid.

validity. 1. (Psychology) The extent to which a test or experiment genuinely measures what it purports to measure. *Contrast* RELIABILITY. *See also* A PRIORI VALIDITY, COEFFICIENT OF VALIDITY, CONCURRENT VALIDITY, CONGRUENT VALIDITY, CONSENSUAL VALIDITY, CONSTRUCT VALIDITY, CONTENT VALIDITY, CONVERGENT VALIDITY, CRITERION VALIDITY, DEFINITIONAL VALIDITY, DIFFERENTIAL VALIDITY, DISCRIMINANT VALIDITY, EMPIRICAL VALIDITY, FACE VALIDITY, FACTORIAL VALIDITY, INCREMENTAL VALIDITY, NOMOLOGICAL VALIDITY, PREDICTIVE VALIDITY, SAMPLING VALIDITY, TRAIT VALIDITY. 2. (Logic and Mathematics) The property of a proof that renders it correct.

value. 1. (Mathematics, Logic, and Computing) The numerical value or the symbol string taken by a FUNCTION (2, 3) when it has been assigned an ARGUMENT (1). 2. (Statistics) Any point, interval, or class in a category; the term is not limited to categories in which the values are numerical. Thus the category 'sex' has two values – male and female. *Compare* LEVEL.

vanishing cues. A method of teaching people (especially neurological patients) the meaning of terms (especially computer terms) by presenting the definition and then spelling out the word letter by letter until the person can say it; the procedure is repeated until the person can respond correctly when no letters are presented.

vanishing point. The point in a picture or scene at which all horizontal lines parallel in the scene to the optical axis of the putative viewer converge: this point lies at the centre of the horizon. The term is sometimes used for the point at which any given set of parallel lines converge.

vantage point. A synonym for VIEWPOINT.

variability. (Statistics) The spread of scores in a sample or the extent to which they differ from the mean.

variable. 1. (Psychology) A factor manipulated by the experimenter (INDEPENDENT VARIABLE) or any aspect of the results recorded (DEPENDENT VARIABLE). *See also* INTERVENING VARIABLE, PREDICTOR VARIABLE. 2. (Mathematics) A symbol in a mathematical or logical expression (e.g. x) that can take different values.

variable control problem. The problem of how successive movements of parts of the body are integrated over time and of how the choice is made of a particular trajectory of all the possible ones that will achieve the result aimed at.

variable error. In psychophysics, any errors of judgement that are due to chance factors and have no systematic bias (*contrast* CONSTANT ERROR). More generally, any errors that appear to be random and unsystematic.

variable interval schedule (VI). A SIMPLE REINFORCEMENT SCHEDULE in which the organism is reinforced for the first response made after a random interval has elapsed since the previous reinforcement, but where the average length of the intervals is usually fixed. The average interval length used is given in seconds by a number following VI, e.g. VI30. *Compare* FIXED INTERVAL SCHEDULE and VARIABLE RATIO SCHEDULE.

variable ratio schedule (VR). A SIMPLE REINFORCEMENT SCHEDULE in which the organism is reinforced for the nth response after it was last reinforced, with n varying at random but with the average number of responses fixed. The average ratio used is given by the expression VRn, e.g. VR10 (reinforcement occurring on average every 10 responses).

Compare FIXED RATIO SCHEDULE, VARIABLE INTERVAL SCHEDULE.

variable stimulus. A synonym for COMPARISON STIMULUS.

variance. (Statistics) The square of the standard deviation. *See also* ANALYSIS OF VARIANCE, BETWEEN-GROUP VARIANCE, ERROR VARIANCE, INTERACTION VARIANCE, and TRUE VARIANCE.

variate. A synonym for VARIABLE.

vascular accident. A synonym for STROKE.

vasoconstriction. The contraction of a blood-vessel.

vasodilation. The dilation of a blood-vessel.

vasomotor. Pertaining to the motor control of the diameter of blood-vessels.

vasopressin. A synonym for ANTIDIURETIC HORMONE.

VECP. An abbreviation for VISUALLY EVOKED CORTICAL POTENTIAL.

vector. In mathematics a quantity having both magnitude and direction, which can be used to characterize forces. *Contrast* SCALAR. The term has often been loosely used of hypothesized mental forces (e.g. by Lewin), but – needless to say – with no attempt at quantification.

veg. The unit of perceived weight in terms of which subjective heaviness scales are constructed.

vegetative neurosis. A synonym for VISCERAL NEUROSIS.

vegetative system. Hess's expression for those parts of the nervous system regulating organic functioning, as opposed to the ANIMAL SYSTEM.

velar. (Phonetics) Pertaining to a consonant (e.g. the 'c' in 'cap', the 'g' in 'gown') produced with the tongue against the soft palate towards the back of the mouth.

velocity. A vector representing the speed and direction of a moving object. *See also* DERIVATIVE.

velocity constancy. The phenomenon that objects appear to move at approximately their real speed despite variations in the speed of their projection in the retinal image (caused by variation in their distance from the observer).

velum. A synonym for SOFT PALATE.

venerophobia. A morbid fear of venereal disease.

Venn diagrams. A more sophisticated version of EULER CIRCLES, in which class inclusion relations are represented by overlapping circles, and shading of parts of circles are used to denote the null class. Thus 'All A are B' would be represented by two overlapping circles with shading on that part of circle A that lies outside circle B.

ventral. (Anatomy) On or towards the front of the body; when used of the brain in an upright species, it means towards the base. *Contrast* DORSAL.

ventral anterior thalamic nucleus. A thalamic nucleus receiving fibres from the globus pallidus and projecting to the frontal cortex.

ventral lateral thalamic nucleus. A thalamic nucleus receiving fibres from the CEREBELLUM, projecting to the MOTOR CORTEX and subserving motor functions.

ventral noradrenergic bundle. A noradrenergic tract running from the brainstem to the hypothalamus.

ventral posterior thalamic nuclei. Thalamic nuclei receiving fibres from the MEDIAL LEMNISCUS, projecting to the primary somaesthetic cortex and subserving somaesthesis.

ventral ramus. *See* RAMUS.

ventral root. *See* SPINAL ROOT.

ventral tegmental area (VTA). Part of the pons on which some MEDIAL FOREBRAIN fibres end; when it is injected with morphine, reinforcement occurs.

ventricle. (Anatomy) 1. Any of the four cavities in the brain; they communicate with the spinal cord and contain cerebrospinal fluid. 2. Either of the two posterior cavities of the heart; they are fed by the AURICLES (2).

ventrobasilar complex. A group of nuclei in the thalamus that relay somatosensory information to the cortex.

ventromedial frontal cortex. A synonym for ORBITAL CORTEX.

ventromedial nucleus of the hypothalamus (VMH). A nucleus of the hypothalamus, damage to which may cause overeating, obesity, and aggressive behaviour.

verb. The part of speech that refers to the occurrence of an action, e.g. 'to take', 'to erupt'. *Compare* VERB PHRASE.

verbal. Pertaining to words whether written or spoken. *Contrast* ORAL (2).

verbal ability. The ability to use words, e.g. to complete analogies. It is often thought to be a special factor in intelligence.

verbal alexia. Impairment of the capacity to recognize words, with little or no loss of the capacity to recognize letters.

verbal aphasia. A synonym for EXPRESSIVE APHASIA.

verbal loop. A hypothetical immediate memory in which a few words (between about 7 and 10) can be stored by being consciously circulated through the system, thus refreshing the memory for each in turn.

verbigeration. Repetitive and meaningless speech.

verbochromia. The experiencing of colours when certain words are heard or thought of. A form of SYNAESTHESIA.

verbomania. A synonym for LOGORRHEA.

verb phrase (VP). (Linguistics) The PREDICATE of a sentence, i.e. that part of a sentence that makes a statement about the SUBJECT (2).

vergence. The turning of the eyes in synchrony inwards (CONVERGENCE) or outwards (DIVERGENCE) in order to adjust for changes in the distance of the point fixated. The degree of vergence is the difference in the position of the two eyes, which will decrease with the distance of the fixation point. Distinguish from VERSION.

vergence disparity. Any error of VERGENCE made while fixating.

Verhoeff apparatus. An apparatus for testing stereoscopic acuity.

veridical perception. Perceiving the world as it really is.

verification time. The time taken to decide whether a proposition is true or false (often with respect to some scenario presented by the experimenter); this technique has been much used in an attempt to discover how information is stored and accessed.

vermis. The median lobe of the cerebellum.

vernier acuity. Visual acuity for the displacement between two lines or bars that are nearly but not quite collinear; under optimal conditions, the threshold is about 2″ of arc.

version. The average direction of the position of the two eyes. It will be zero if the eyes are fixated straight ahead (even if they are converged) and will depart from zero in opposite directions for fixation on objects to one or other side. Distinguish from VERGENCE.

vertex type. A classification of vertices into ell, arrow, fork, etc., used by workers in artificial intelligence. If the vertex represents a corner of a three-dimensional polyhedron, the type of vertex constrains the type of 3-D corner, e.g. an arrow vertex cannot be generated by a corner in which three concave lines meet.

vertical décalage. See DECALAGE.

vertical disparity. A form of BINOCULAR DISPARITY in which the image of a point in space is displaced vertically on one retina with respect to the other. It occurs when objects are nearer to one eye than to the other, i.e. when they lie to the left or right of the fixation point.

vertical group. A group whose members come from at least two different social classes.

vertical mobility. The extent to which in a society people move up or down the social scale within a lifetime.

vertical oblique projection. See OBLIQUE PROJECTION.

vertical sampling. The selection of samples from different social classes.

vertigo. Dizziness and the feeling of a spinning head; it is caused by a disturbance to the labyrinth or by brain damage.

vesania. An obsolete term for insanity.

vesicle. Any fluid-filled sac in the body. See SYNAPTIC VESICLE.

vestibular apparatus. The semicircular canals and vestibular sacs.

vestibular canal. A synonym for SCALA VESTIBULI.

vestibular membrane. A synonym for REISSNER'S MEMBRANE.

vestibular nerve. The branch of the VESTIBULOACOUSTIC NERVE serving the vestibular system whose hair cells terminate upon it. It runs to the vestibular nuclei in the medulla, but has branches to the cerebellum, reticular formation, and visceral nuclei.

vestibular nuclei. The nuclei in the medulla on which the vestibular nerve terminates; they send axons to the spinal cord, cerebellum, and cortex (particularly to the ECTOSYLVIAN GYRUS and SUPRASYLVIAN GYRUS).

vestibular nystagmus. NYSTAGMUS driven by the vestibular system. E.g. if someone is accelerated around a vertical axis in the dark, he will show nystagmus.

vestibular sacs. Two sacs, the UTRICLE and the SACCULE, in the vestibular system located near the AMPULLAE. They record translatory motions of the head through changes in the pressure of the otoliths on the hair cells.

vestibular sense. The sense of balance; it determines through PROPRIOCEPTION the felt position and acceleration of the head. It is based on the SEMICIRCULAR CANALS and VESTIBULAR SACS.

vestibular system. The system that controls balance, made up in man of the SEMICIRCULAR CANALS, the VESTIBULAR SACS, the vestibular nerve, the vestibular nuclei, and the parts of the cortex to which the latter project.

vestibule. The middle part of the inner ear; it contains the UTRICLE and SACCULE. The term is sometimes used more broadly as a synonym for VESTIBULAR APPARATUS.

vestibuloacoustic nerve. The eighth CRANIAL NERVE, which conveys information from the vestibular system and the ear.

vestibulo-ocular reflex (VOR). A reflex motion of the eyes activated by movements of the head and controlled by the vestibular system; the reflex ensures that the eyes continue to fixate an object despite head movements.

vestibulospinal pathway. A neural pathway running from the vestibular system down the length of the spinal cord.

VIB. An abbreviation for VOCATIONAL INTEREST BLANK.

vibration receptor. The skin receptor that responds to vibration, thought to be the Pacinian corpuscle.

vicarious extinction. A reduction in the strength of a response caused by watching someone else being extinguished on it.

vicarious function. The hypothesized taking over of the function of one part of the brain by another when the former is damaged or destroyed.

vicarious reinforcement. The process of increasing the strength of a response by getting the subject to watch somebody else while he performs the response and is reinforced for it.

vicarious trial and error (VTE). Mentally trying out possible courses of action in order to decide which to take. The expression is particularly used of the behaviour of rats, which, when faced with a simultaneous discrimination, often look repeatedly at each of the discriminanda before making a choice.

Vienna circle. A group of philosophers and logicians (including Carnap, Gödel, and Reichenbach) who met in the 1920s and 1930s. They were the founders of logical positivism.

Vierordt's law. The principle that short intervals are overestimated and long ones are underestimated.

Vieth–Müller circle. A circle passing through the fixation point and the nodal points of each lens. If CORRESPONDING POINTS lay equal distances out from the fovea on the temporal and nasal hemiretinas it would correspond to the HOROPTER: hence, it is sometimes known as the theoretical horopter. In fact the empirically determined horopter is much less concave than the Vieth–Müller circle.

viewer-centred description. (Vision) A description of an object based on coordinates that are relative to the observer's viewpoint. E.g. the position of each point on a surface can be described in terms of its distance and direction from the eye relative to the line of sight. *Compare* TWO-AND-A-HALF-D SKETCH and *contrast* OBJECT-CENTRED DESCRIPTION.

viewing angle. The angle between a surface being fixated and the observer's eye.

viewpoint. The point from which an object (or scene) is viewed; it changes with movements of the observer or object.

vigilance. Altertness or the extent to which in a given situation, a person can respond quickly to any stimulus calling for a response. There are many tests for vigilance, most involving responses to a brief and infrequent stimulus that is difficult to detect; with repetitive tasks of this nature vigilance declines over time.

Vigotsky Test. A test of concept formation in which the subject is asked to sort blocks differing in colour, shape, height, and width into categories (e.g. tall thin ones); the subject is not told the categories in advance but can discover if he is correct by examining, after sorting each block, a nonsense word written underneath it – blocks having the same word belong to the same category.

Vincent curve. A procedure for plotting group learning curves that takes into account the difference in the number of trials taken to reach criterion by different subjects. Basically, each subject's scores are split into constant fractions of the number of trials each took to criterion; the group learning curve is made up of the performance of all the animals on successive fractions, e.g. the first tenth of the number of trials to criterion, second tenth, etc.

Vineland Social Maturity Scale. A test of the capacity to function well socially, based on a questionnaire administered to the respondent's acquaintances; when compared with established norms the results yield a social quotient.

violet. *See* SPECTRAL HUE.

viraginity. A woman's exhibition of or desire to possess male qualities.

virilism. The presence of male secondary sexual characteristics in a woman; it can be caused by an excess of androgen.

virtual address. (Computing) An address used in a program that does not specify the ABSOLUTE ADDRESS; the system's program or compiler maps the virtual address onto an absolute address automatically allocated.

virtual machine. The way in which a computer operates according to a given program. Different kinds of computer can be programmed to be the same virtual machine.

virtual reality. A computer technique in which the proximal stimuli presented to an observer are so similar to those he would receive from some part of the real world that he feels he is interacting with it. Virtual reality can involve vision (e.g. using stereopsis and motion parallax to create an impression of depth), binaural hearing and touch (e.g. the observer may wear a glove and be given the appropriate tactile stimuli to

the hand when he grasps a virtual object). Virtual sexual intercourse between separated partners has not yet been attained.

viscera. The body's internal organs, particularly the abdominal organs.

visceral brain. *See* TRIUNE BRAIN.

visceral drive. A synonym for PHYSIOLOGICAL DRIVE.

visceral learning. Learning to control at will the operation of any internal organ (e.g. blood pressure). *See* BIOFEEDBACK.

visceral neurosis. A neurosis that causes a pathological disturbance to the VISCERA (e.g. a duodenal ulcer).

visceroceptor. An INTEROCEPTOR in the VISCERA.

viscerogenic drive. A synonym for PHYSIOLOGICAL DRIVE.

visceroreceptor. A synonym for VISCEROCEPTOR.

viscerotonia. A personality type (relaxed, pleasure-loving) in SHELDON'S CONSTITUTIONAL THEORY, said to be associated with ENDOMORPHY.

VI schedule. An abbreviation for VARIABLE INTERVAL SCHEDULE.

visible spectrum. A synonym for VISUAL SPECTRUM.

visibility coefficient. A synonym for LUMINOSITY COEFFICIENT.

visibility curve. A synonym for LUMINOSITY CURVE.

visible speech. A synonym for SPECTROGRAM.

visile. A person with a strong preference for the visual modality and with much visual imagery.

visual acuity. The capacity to detect fine detail in vision, which can be measured in several ways. *See* e.g. LANDOLT CIRCLE,

MINIMUM SEPARABLE, STEREOSCOPIC ACUITY, VERNIER ACUITY.

visual agnosia. Impaired ability for visual recognition, with other visual capacities largely intact (e.g. intact ability to use vision to guide the manipulation of objects). It is caused by brain damage, particularly to the inferotemporal lobe or parietal lobe.

visual allaechesthesia, visual allechesthesia. (Neuropsychology) A rare condition, sometimes resulting from parietal–occipital damage, in which the person sees a stimulus falling on one hemisphere of the retina in the position it would be seen if it fell on the opposite hemisphere, i.e. objects on the left are seen on the right and vice versa; it is often accompanied by PALINOPSIA.

visual angle. The angle, measured in degrees of arc, subtended by the distance between two points in space at the nodal point of the lens; it is also convenient to measure retinal distances in terms of visual angle, e.g. the diameter of the fovea is about 5°, that of a cone is about 20″.

visual aphasia. A synonym for ALEXIA.

visual association cortex. The areas of the cortex in which there is a RETINOTOPIC projection, other than the PRIMARY VISUAL CORTEX. Some of these areas have several projections. They comprise Brodmann's areas 18–21; *see* Appendices 3 and 4. *See also* V2, V3, V4, MT, and IT.

visual–auditory association cortex. Brodmann's area 37 (*see* Appendices 3 and 4), which has both visual and auditory inputs, and is implicated in reading.

visual aura. Hallucinations of flashes of light, zigzag lines, etc., which sometimes precede a GRAND MAL seizure.

visual axis. The line passing from the fixation point through the nodal point of the lens to the centre of the foveola. *Contrast* OPTICAL AXIS.

visual capture. The phenomenon that when visual information differs from that supplied by another modality, it is the visual information that is (unconsciously) accepted. E.g. if a subject runs his fingers up and down a vertical rod which is viewed through prisms that make it appear tilted, he will feel his fingers moving in the direction in which the rod is seen.

visual cliff. An ingenious apparatus devised by E. J. Gibson to test the existence of depth perception. It consists of two horizontal surfaces, one considerably below the other. The surfaces are covered by a continuous sheet of glass that rests on the upper surface. The subject is either placed on a platform running along the divide between the two surfaces to discover on to which surface it steps down, or it is placed alternately on the glass above the higher surface and on that above the lower to discover whether it shows more fear when over the latter. The apparatus has been extensively used with very young animals, most of which give clear evidence of depth perception.

visual completion. The failure to see any gap in a regular or familiar figure, part of which falls on a blind part of the retina, i.e. on the OPTIC DISC or on a SCOTOMA. Provided enough of the figure falls outside the blind part, the remainder is supplied in perception and it is seen as complete.

visual cortex. Any area of the cortex receiving a retinotopic projection. *See* PRIMARY VISUAL CORTEX and VISUAL ASSOCIATION AREA.

visual egocentre. *See* EGOCENTRE.

visual field. All the points in the external world that fall on the eyes at one moment in time. The binocular visual field is roughly circular with a diameter of 120° of visual angle. Directions in the retinal image are the reverse of those in the visual field because the image is inverted.

visual field defect. Blindness or impairment of vision in a part of the visual field, caused by damage to the visual system.

visual illusion. Any illusion occurring in vision. *See* e.g. GEOMETRIC ILLUSION and MACH BANDS.

visual image. A visual mental image; it can arise through perception, but the term is more commonly applied to internally generated images. There has been much recent work demonstrating the ways in which they can and cannot be formed and transformed.

visual induction. Any effect of a stimulus falling on one point of the retina on a stimulus falling on an adjacent part, e.g. brightness or colour contrast.

visualization technique. A method of inducing hypnosis, in which the subject is asked to imagine visual scenes of a soothing or relaxing nature.

visually evoked cortical potential (VECP), visually evoked potential. An evoked potential caused by a visual stimulus.

visual masking. Reducing the visibility of a brief visual stimulus by presenting another stimulus in close temporal and spatial proximity. There are several kinds of masking: see BRIGHTNESS MASKING, METACONTRAST, PARACONTRAST, PATTERN MASKING BY NOISE, and PATTERN MASKING BY STRUCTURE.

visual–motor coordination. The ability to execute skilled motor movements under visual control.

visual–motor Gestalt test. A synonym for BENDER–GESTALT TEST.

visual persistence. A synonym for ICONIC MEMORY.

visual photopigment. The photopigment in the rods and cones, which is made up of OPSIN and RETINENE. The reception of a quantum of light by a photopigment molecule causes isomerization of the retinene (the restructuring of the atoms in a carbon chain), which bleaches the pigment and initiates hyperpolarization of the membrane of the receptor cell. Further chemical changes result in the opsin and retinene separating. The retinene is subsequently deisomerized by enzymes in the pigment epithelium and reunites with the opsin to form an unbleached pigment. The terminology attached to the different retinal pigments is extremely confusing, largely thanks to Wald. RHODOPSIN is a single rod pigment which looks red (i.e. reflects red light) but has maximal absorption at wavelengths around 500 nm (blue–green). Wald discovered a second rod pigment present in certain species, which on the analogy of

rhodopsin he named PORPHYROPSIN. He went on to name two cone pigments IODOPSIN and CYANOPSIN. Criticizing Wald, Walls wrote that there was 'no excuse' for such terms. First, as Dartnall discovered, Wald often worked on a mixture of pigments mistaking them for a single pigment. Second, if a new name were given to every new pigment discovered, one would soon run out of names. Third, Wald's terms describe the colour of the pigment, whereas it is more natural and useful to use terms describing the hue at which its peak absorption occurs (*see* e.g. CYANOLABE). *See also* RETINAL.

visual purple. A synonym for RHODOPSIN.

visual routine. A series of operations performed on the PRIMAL SKETCH or on the TWO-AND-A-HALF-D SKETCH to identify certain global properties, e.g. whether a line forms a closed curve, or whether a point is inside or outside a closed curve.

visual search. The search for a particular stimulus or stimuli (e.g. the letter z) in a display, a task much used to investigate PREATTENTIVE PROCESSING.

visual span. A synonym for READING SPAN.

visual spectrum. The range of wavelengths (approximately 380 nm to 740 nm) that can be seen by someone with normal vision.

visual suppression. A reduction in visual sensitivity that occurs before, after and during a saccade or eyeblink. It has the effect of partially suppressing the perception of new stimuli occurring at that time.

visual tracking. A synonym for PURSUIT MOVEMENT.

visual world. J. J. Gibson's term for that part of one's physical environment – 3-D edges, surfaces etc. – that can be perceived visually.

visual yellow. A synonym for XANTHOPSIN.

visuo-motor ataxia. Inability to combine correctly the visual input with motor output.

visuospatial agnosia. Impaired ability to localize correctly objects in the visual field; it can be caused by brain damage, particularly to the parietal cortex.

visuospatial scratch pad. A hypothetical SHORT-TERM STORE for visual information.

visuotopic. A synonym for RETINOTOPIC.

vital force. *See* VITALISM.

vitalism. The doctrine that a vital force of a non-material nature underlies all life.

vitamin. Any organic substance (excepting the essential amino acids) that cannot be internally synthesized, and must therefore be obtained from the environment; small quantities are needed to maintain health. Most vitamins are thought to play a part in enzyme reactions.

vitamin A. An alcohol from which RETINENE is formed by oxygenation. It has two forms: RETINAL is based on vitamin A1 and 3-dehydroretinal on vitamin A2.

vitamin B1. A synonym for THIAMINE.

vitreous chamber. The part of the eye lying between the lens and the retina.

vitreous humour. The transparent jelly lying between the lens and the retina.

vividness, law of. The principle that the more salient an item is, the more readily an association is formed to it.

VMH. An abbreviation for VENTROMEDIAL NUCLEUS OF THE HYPOTHALAMUS.

vocal cords. Two sets of ligaments in the larynx that vibrate when air is expelled from the lungs and hence produce voiced sounds.

vocality. The extent to which a sound resembles a vowel sound.

vocalization. 1. The production of sounds by the vocal tract that are not part of language, e.g. the babbling of a baby. 2. The production of any sound by the vocal tract, including speech sounds.

vocal tract. The cavities and associated structures used to produce speech, including the larynx, pharynx, nasal cavities, tongue, mouth, lips, etc.

vocational aptitude test. Any test for determining how good a person will be at a particular job.

vocational counselling, vocational guidance. Guidance on what sort of job a person is most suited for.

Vocational Interest Blank. *See* STRONG VOCATIONAL INTEREST BLANK.

vocative. The case of a noun or pronoun used to address someone, e.g. '*George*, come here'.

voice. A grammatical category used of verbs, clauses, and sentences based on differences in the relationship of the subject and object to the verb. In English there are two voices: the ACTIVE VOICE (e.g. 'The dog bit him') and the PASSIVE VOICE ('He was bitten by the dog').

voiced consonant. A consonant (e.g. the 'b' in 'big', the 'd' in 'dig') in which VOICING begins almost as soon as the first release of air from the mouth. *See* VOICE-ONSET TIME.

voice key. A switch that is turned on by a voice, often used to record the reaction time from the presentation of a stimulus (or question) to the beginning of a vocal response.

voice-onset time (VOT). The time interval between the first release of air in pronouncing a consonant and the beginning of VOICING. It is much shorter in voiced consonants (e.g. [b], [d]) than in unvoiced (e.g. [p], [t]). *See also* CATEGORICAL PERCEPTION.

voiceprint. The spectrogram of a person's voice, particularly when used to identify the speaker.

voice-stress analyser. A device used to detect small changes in the voice (e.g. a change in pitch) occurring when a person is under stress; it is sometimes used as a lie detector.

voicing. The sound produced by vibration of the vocal cords. Voicing occurs in all vowels and some consonants (e.g. the 'z' in 'zip' is voiced, whereas the 's' in 'sip' is not). *See also* VOICE-ONSET TIME.

vol. The unit used to measure the subjective dimension of auditory volume.

volley. The simultaneous firing of a number of neurons.

volley theory. (Hearing) A theory of frequency detection which holds that although individual neurons in the auditory nerve cannot fire in synchrony with high pitched sounds, different sets of neurons fire to different wave peaks; hence, although each fibre would fire at a lower frequency than the sound frequency, the frequency of volleys would correspond to the sound frequency, and could be used to detect pitch. It is likely that volleys play a part in pitch discrimination with sounds having a frequency below 4,000 Hz (though place of maximal stimulation on the basilar membrane may also contribute). For higher frequencies the place of maximal distortion of the basilar membrane is probably the only determinant of pitch perception. *See* PHASE LOCKING; *contrast* FREQUENCY THEORY and PLACE THEORY.

volt (v). *See* OHM'S LAW.

volume. 1. A subjective property of sound, which corresponds roughly to the amount of space it seems to occupy; high-pitched sounds in general have less volume than lower-pitched ones. 2. Loudness.

volume colour. A synonym for FILM COLOUR.

volume receptor. A receptor sensitive to blood volume; it is believed to exist in the heart and kidneys. It is thought to trigger thirst, partly through intermediary hormones, when blood plasma level is low.

volumetric thirst. Thirst caused by a decrease in the volume of extracellular fluid. *Compare* OSMOMETRIC THIRST.

voluntarism. The obscure philosophical doctrine (espoused by Schopenhauer among others) that the will is the only true reality.

voluntary admission. Any admission to a psychiatric institute made of the patient's own free will and not under any legal sanction.

voluntary muscles. Those muscles that can be voluntarily controlled; they are mainly STRIATED MUSCLES.

volunteer bias. A sampling error based on selecting volunteers, who, simply because they are volunteers, may not be representative of the population from which they are drawn.

von Restorff effect. The phenomenon that when a list of items is being learned, any item that is distinctive from the others (e.g. a green nonsense syllable in a list of black ones) is learned faster and better.

VOR. An abbreviation for VESTIBULO-OCULAR REFLEX.

VOT. An abbreviation for VOICE-ONSET TIME.

vowel. A speech sound produced without any part of the vocal tract being sufficiently constricted to cause audible friction. Different vowels are produced by small differences in tongue position and by whether air is expelled only through the mouth, or through mouth and nose. Acoustically they are differentiated by the position of their FORMANTS.

voyeurism. Obtaining sexual pleasure from observing others engaged in sexual activities or nude or undressing.

VP. An abbreviation for VERB PHRASE.

VR schedule. An abbreviation for VARIABLE RATIO SCHEDULE.

VTA. An abbreviation for VENTRAL TEGMENTAL AREA.

VTE. An abbreviation for VICARIOUS TRIAL AND ERROR.

Vygotsky test. An alternative spelling for VIGOTSKY TEST.

W

W. An abbreviation for 1. WEBER FRACTION; 2. coefficient of concordance; 3. work done in a response, *see* HULLIAN THEORY.

w. An abbreviation for 1. WILL FACTOR; 2. weight; 3. amount of food reward, *see* HULLIAN THEORY.

Wada technique. A test for language laterality, in which sodium amytal is injected into the left or right carotid artery; if the speech centres are on the side injected, the person becomes dysphasic for a short time.

wagon wheel illusion. The illusion that a rotating wheel viewed stroboscopically is going backwards. It occurs because during the interval between successive exposures each spoke has moved closer to its neighbour than to its original position. Hence movement is seen in the wrong direction. *Compare* OPTIMAL APPARENT MOTION.

WAIS. An abbreviation for WECHSLER ADULT INTELLIGENCE SCALE.

WAJDA technique. A synonym for WADA TECHNIQUE.

waking centre. A hypothesized brain centre responsible for determining when someone wakes; there is unlikely to be any one centre since damage both to the reticular activating system and to the posterior hypothalamus can produce excessive sleep.

Wald–Wolfowitz runs test. A test to determine whether in a sequence containing two types of events, the uninterrupted runs of one type exceed what would be expected by chance.

Wallerian degeneration. A synonym for ANTEROGRADE DEGENERATION.

wallpaper experiment. An old-fashioned way of measuring the effects of changes in convergence on apparent size and apparent distance by having a subject fixate a wallpaper with a repeating pattern; it is possible to fixate it at different degrees of convergence without introducing binocular disparity.

warm spot. A small area of skin that is especially sensitive to warm stimuli.

warm-up period. A period at the start of the performance of a task in which performance improves through non-specific factors like increases in motivation or attention.

Washoe. A chimpanzee who, so it was claimed, learned American Sign Language. Although she mastered a fair number of gestures, her syntax was sadly deficient.

Wason selection task (Wason four-card problem). A task in which the subject is shown the faces of four cards, two bearing numbers and two letters. He is told that each card has a number on one side and a letter on the other and is asked to select the cards that would prove a rule such as 'Any card with an A on one side has a 3 on the other'. When shown a set like 'A D 3 7' most subjects fail to select the card that might disprove the rule ('7') and select an irrelevant card named in the rule ('3').

watchkeeping task. A task in which the subject has to monitor a display continuously in order to detect occurrences of an infrequent event; such tasks are used to measure VIGILANCE.

waterfall illusion. A synonym for MOTION AFTEREFFECT.

500

water jar problems. Problems in which the subject has to decide how to measure out a given amount of water starting with jars of known size. E.g. given three jars holding respectively 3, 21, and 127 pints, how can exactly 100 pints be measured out?

watt. A measure of power, equal to one joule per second; it is the power dissipated by a current of one ampere flowing across a potential difference of one volt.

wave. A disturbance that carries energy, and is propagated through a medium or space by a travelling local displacement of the medium or a change in its physical properties. Where there are a series of waves of similar form, their spacing can be measured either as WAVELENGTH (as is usual for light) or as the temporal FREQUENCY with which successive waves traverse a point (as is usual for sound waves).

waveform. The shape of a wave, normally represented by plotting its amplitude against time.

wavelength (λ). Usually the peak to peak distance of a sine wave, but sometimes used to indicate the distance between repetitions of any periodic waveform. Wavelength is velocity divided by frequency ($\lambda = v/f$).

waxing flexibility. A synonym for CATALEPSY.

Waxman–Geswind syndrome. A synonym for INTERICTAL SYNDROME.

WAY technique. An abbreviation for WHO ARE YOU? TECHNIQUE.

W cell. A poorly defined class of retinal ganglion cells that have slow conducting axons and that cannot be clearly classified as either X CELLS or Y CELLS.

WDW normalization. Arranging the proportions of the PRIMARIES in such a way that the individual observer sees an achromatic hue when those proportions are presented. These proportions are then used as the reference values for other mixtures.

weak AI. *See* STRONG AI.

weak law of effect. A synonym for EMPIRICAL LAW OF EFFECT.

weaning aggression. Aggression by parents to offspring who do not want to be weaned or who are too dependent on them.

Weber fraction. *See* WEBER'S LAW.

Weber's law. The generalization that the just noticeable difference (ΔI) is proportional to the magnitude of the stimulus, i.e. $\Delta I/I = K$, where I is the intensity of the standard stimulus. $\Delta I/I$ is known as the **Weber fraction.** The law is a reasonable approximation for most stimulus dimensions, except at the lower and upper ends of the range of intensities. *Compare* FECHNER'S LAW.

Weber–Fechner law. A synonym for FECHNER'S LAW.

Wechsler Adult Intelligence Scale (WAIS). An intelligence test for adults based on the Wechsler Scale, comprising six verbal tests (e.g. comprehension, vocabulary) and five performance tests (e.g. picture arrangment, block designs). It is well validated and in common use.

Wechsler–Bellevue Scale. A scale going back to 1929, containing both verbal and performance items; it was revised to form the WECHSLER ADULT INTELLIGENCE SCALE.

Wechsler Intelligence Scale for Children (WISC). An intelligence test for children aged 5–15, which is similar in construction to the WECHSLER ADULT INTELLIGENCE SCALE.

Wechsler Memory Scale (WMS). A psychometric scale purporting to measure memory which includes seven sub-tests such as digit-span and paired-associate learning.

Wechsler Memory Scale Revision (WMS-R). An improved version of the Wechsler Memory Scale, which includes additional tests particularly ones for long-term memory.

Wechsler Preschool and Primary Scale of Intelligence (WPPSI). An intelligence test for children between 4 and 6.5 years of age, containing both verbal and performance items.

Weigh–Goldstein–Scheerer Test. A concept formation test in which a person has to sort blocks according to colour and shape, and to switch between different methods of categorization; it has been used to assess the effects of brain damage.

weight. 1. (Mathematics) A constant usually a fraction used to modify the strength of the contribution of one variable to another. 2. (Connectionism) The strength of the connection between two units; if positive, the first unit will increase the activation of the second, if negative, it will decrease it. Learning is achieved by changing weights. 3. *See also* STATISTICAL PREDICTION, DELTA RULE and MULTIATTRIBUTE UTILITY THEORY.

well-formed formula (WFF). Any expression in mathematics or formal logic that is correctly written according to the formation rules of the system.

Weltanschauung. A person's outlook on the world, or the sum of all his beliefs.

Wernicke–Korsakoff syndrome (WKS). A combination of Wernicke's dementia and the Korsakoff syndrome, both of which are thought to be caused by a thiamine deficiency.

Wernicke's aphasia. A primarily RECEPTIVE APHASIA caused by damage to the posterior region of the first temporal gyrus, usually of the left hemisphere.

Wernicke's area. A region in the posterior temporal gyrus of the dominant hemisphere. It mainly comprises Brodmann's areas 39 and 40; *see* Appendix 3. Damage to it causes aphasia, particularly receptive aphasia, though other aphasic symptoms are usually also present. It connects with, among other regions, Broca's area, the auditory cortex, and the frontal lobes.

Wernicke's dementia, Wernicke's encephalopathy, Wernicke's syndrome. A brain disorder caused by lack of thiamine and niacin and marked by clouding of consciousness and ataxia; it can be caused by alcoholism.

Westphal's sign. Absence of the knee jerk reflex, a sign of tabes dorsalis.

Wever–Bray effect. A synonym for the COCHLEAR MICROPHONIC.

w factor. An abbreviation for WILL FACTOR.

WFF. An abbreviation for WELL-FORMED FORMULA.

WGTA. An abbreviation for WISCONSIN GENERAL TEST APPARATUS.

wh-word. An abbreviation for an interrogative word or a relative pronoun, e.g. 'who', 'why', 'what', 'how'.

white. The (achromatic) colour produced by a matt, strongly reflecting achromatic surface.

white commissure. *See* ANTERIOR WHITE COMMISSURE.

white matter. Those parts of the central nervous system containing mainly myelinated fibres, which appear white; e.g. the myelinated fibres of the cortex which run below the grey matter.

whiteness constancy. *See* BRIGHTNESS CONSTANCY.

white noise. A signal (usually an acoustic signal) having both random frequency and amplitude, with equal power per unit bandwidth. *Compare* PINK NOISE.

white ramus. *See* RAMUS COMMUNICANS.

Who Are You? technique. A projection test in which a person has to give three written replies to the question 'Who are you?'

whole method of learning. Learning material *en bloc* by going through all of it repeatedly, rather than learning one part at a time. In the **modified whole method of learning**, difficult or important parts of the task or the material to be learned may be given extra practice. *Contrast* PART METHOD OF LEARNING.

whole object. (Psychoanalysis) Anything to which a person responds as a whole, rather than responding to a particular aspect of it. *Compare* PART OBJECT.

whole report method. A technique in which the subject is asked to report all items on a display, usually one that is exposed only briefly. *See* PART REPORT METHOD.

whole word method. A technique for teaching reading in which children are taught to recognise whole words rather than starting by learning the sounds of each letter. *Contrast* PHONICS METHOD.

Whorfian hypothesis. The hypothesis that perception, concepts, and thought processes are influenced by one's native language. There is little support for it; thus, people from cultures having only a small number of colour terms classify and discriminate colours in the same way as do Westerners.

wh-question. An interrogation beginning with an interrogative pronoun, e.g. 'which', 'when', 'how'. *Contrast* YES–NO QUESTION.

Widrow–Huff rule. A synonym for DELTA RULE.

Wilcoxon signed ranks test. A synonym for WILCOXON TEST.

Wilcoxon test. A non–parametric PAIRED COMPARISON TEST to determine whether there is a significant difference between two sets of matched scores. It is based on ranking the absolute differences between the two sets of paired scores, and applying to the ranks the sign of the differences. It is a non–parametric equivalent of a T-TEST for related samples, and is more powerful than the SIGN TEST. *Compare* FRIEDMAN TEST.

Wild Boy of Aveyron. A boy who had lived in the wild without human contact (as far as is known) until he was found at the age of 7.

will factor. A factor extracted by factor analysis from a test battery which corresponds to determination or persistence.

Williams syndrome. A congenital condition characterized by verbal precocity, but with severe intellectual (and sometimes visual) deficits.

will therapy. Rank's therapy, which encourages the patient to exert will-power

and to become independent, particularly from the influence of his mother.

will to power. Adler's term for the need, particularly strong in males, to be superior and to dominate.

win–stay, lose–shift strategy. The tendency of animals and people to stick to the same response (or hypothesis) so long as they receive reward for it, and to change the response when they do not; the expression is applied particularly to serial discrimination learning.

WISC. An abbreviation for WECHSLER INTELLIGENCE SCALE FOR CHILDREN.

Wisconsin Card Sorting Test (WCST). A test in which the testee is shown cards bearing forms that differ in colour, shape and the number of items present. He has to learn to sort them according to a rule (e.g. in four piles according to which of four colours is present). When he has learned how to sort them, the rule is changed (e.g. to sorting by shape) and he has to learn the new rule. Patients with frontal lesions have great difficulty in learning new rules.

Wisconsin General Test Apparatus (WGTA). An apparatus for testing monkeys in their home cage. A tray is placed just outside the cage and the animal selects one of the stimuli. The reward is usually placed underneath the positive stimulus. The apparatus can be hidden by a shutter in the intertrial interval while the position of the discriminanda is changed.

wish fulfillment. (Psychoanalysis) The gratification of the desires of the id, which because of the superego often has to take place in disguised form, e.g. through dreams, sublimation, projection, etc.

withdrawal reaction. Avoidance of social contact and refusal to face problems at home or at work, a reaction that can be pathological, e.g. in schizophrenia.

withdrawal symptoms. The unpleasant symptoms that are caused by ceasing to take a drug of addiction. The symptoms vary with the drug but may include restlessness, inability to concentrate, irritability, insomnia, depression, nausea, and delirium.

within-group variance. The amount of variance caused by differences within a group. *Contrast* BETWEEN-GROUP VARIANCE.

within-subjects design. An experimental design in which each subject goes through all conditions; it has the advantage over a BE-TWEEN-SUBJECTS DESIGN of reducing the effects of variations between subjects, but it has the disadvantage that undergoing one condition may affect a subject's performance on conditions subsequently administered.

WKS. An abbreviation for WERNICKE–KORSAKOFF SYNDROME.

WMS, WMS-R. Abbreviations for WECHSLER MEMORY SCALE and WECHSLER MEMORY SCALE REVISION.

wolf child. A synonym for FERAL CHILD.

Wolf Man. One of Freud's most famous cases, a man who had a phobia of wolves; despite the weight Freud placed on the case, the man was never cured.

Woodworth–Matthews Personal Data Sheet. A personality inventory for children and adolescents, designed to screen for neurosis; it contains 116 questions, mainly on common complaints about life.

word approximation. The misuse of words or the use of new words that seem to make some sense (e.g. 'brunch').

word association test. A test in which a person presented with a word has to respond rapidly with another, often used as a projective test by e.g. Jung.

word blindness. A synonym for ALEXIA.

word-building test. A test in which a person is given a set of letters and has to construct as many words from them as he can.

word configuration. The overall shape of a word, as determined by its length, pattern of ascending and descending letters, etc. It is not known how far word configuration is used in word recognition.

word count. The specification of the frequency with which each word is used in a text or texts, e.g. in Shakespeare's plays or an elementary reading primer.

word deafness. A synonym for AUDITORY APHASIA.

word-length effect. The phenomenon that the longer it takes to sound a string of words to a subject, the fewer words are preserved in short-term memory. The fact that phonological length determines what is remembered suggests that a phonological store is being used.

WordNet. An electronic thesaurus being developed by George Miller in which words and the relationships between them are stored. E.g. for nouns the relations 'part of' and 'kind of' would be stored.

word salad. Incoherent and unintelligible speech often containing neologisms, such as may be produced by schizophrenics or aphasics.

word superiority effect (WSE). The phenomenon that a letter is more readily recognized if it forms part of a word than if it is presented on its own. E.g. a subject told that either A or O will appear in a brief exposure will perform better if he is presented with either 'WARD' or 'WORD' than if shown either 'A' or 'O'. Since letters must presumably be identified in order to recognize words, the finding appears paradoxical. *See also* OBJECT SUPERIORITY EFFECT.

work (W). 1. (Psychology) A theoretical concept in Hull's theory. According to him all responses are accompanied by work (effort) and the work generates REACTIVE INHIBITION, to which conditioned inhibition is conditioned. *See* HULLIAN THEORY. 2. (Physics) The measurement of a force multiplied by the distance moved by the point of application of the force in the direction of the force. The SI unit is the JOULE.

work decrement. A decline over time in the speed of efficiency with which work is carried out.

working. Pertaining to something assumed or approximated, e.g. 'working hypothesis'.

working memory. The current contents of consciousness, a temporary store in which items from long-term memory or from perception may be placed, and in which they may be manipulated. *Compare* SHORT-TERM STORE.

working through. (Psychoanalysis) The hypothetical process by which the patient obtains insight into his motives and conflicts and, with luck, comes to master them.

working vocabulary. A synonym for ACTIVE VOCABULARY.

work therapy. Work carried out by patients (e.g. basket making) to alleviate boredom, to increase self-respect, and to prevent their withdrawing into themselves.

WPPSI. An abbreviation for WECHSLER PRESCHOOL AND PRIMARY SCALE OF INTELLIGENCE.

WSE. An abbreviation for WORD SUPERIORITY EFFECT.

Wundt's area illusion. The geometrical illusion illustrated right. The upper figure appears larger, possibly because its long side is compared with the neighbouring short side of the lower figure.

Wundt's figure. The geometrical illusion illustrated right, in which the two physically horizontal lines appear bowed towards one another. It is a variant of the HERING ILLUSION.

Wurzburg school. A group headed by Kulpe

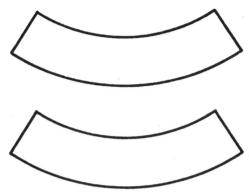

Wundt's area illusion

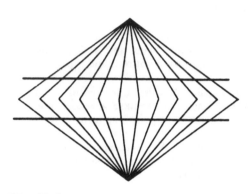

Wundt's figure

around 1900, which favoured introspection but reacted against the straightforward approach of Wundt and concentrated on thoughts and mental attitudes; they discovered imageless thought.

X

X. A raw score from a group of scores.

X̄. The arithmetic mean.

x. A value of the ABSCISSA.

xanthocyanopsia. A type of colour blindness, in which blues and yellows can be discriminated but not reds and greens.

xanthopsia. A visual impairment in which everything seems to have a yellow tinge; it can be caused by poisoning or by jaundice.

xanthopsin. A synonym for 3-HYDROXY-RETINAL, which is a yellow-coloured chromophore.

x-axis. The horizontal axis on a graph.

X-bar grammar notation. (Linguistics) A notation in phrase-structure grammar that makes it explicit which constituent is the head of a larger constituent. In this notation, the head of a constituent is the constituent that appears at the highest level; levels are marked by bars above the names of constituents. In the example shown the whole clause is a noun phrase (NP), an adjective and a noun is also a noun phrase (N̄), and a noun is a noun phrase (N). The head of the noun phrase is therefore 'building'. The term 'X-bar' is derived from the bars placed over a syntactic category to indicate its level in the hierarchy.

X cell. A ganglion cell in the retina or lateral geniculate, which responds linearly to stimulation of on- and off-regions of its receptive field. It exhibits sustained firing to a stimulus and has small receptive fields. It forms part of the PARVOCELLULAR SYSTEM.

X chromosome. One of the two chromosomes determining sex; females have two X chromosomes, males an X and a Y. *Compare* Y CHROMOSOME.

x coordinate. A value on the horizontal axis of a graph.

xenoglossophilia. A tendency to use rare or foreign words.

xenoglossophobia. A fear of foreign languages, a characteristic of English tourists.

xenophobia. A morbid fear of strangers.

XOR. An abbreviation for 'exclusive or'. *See* DISJUNCTION.

X-O test. An early test of attitudes.

XXX syndrome. A synonym for TRIPLE X CONDITION.

XXY syndrome. A synonym for KLINEFELTER'S SYNDROME.

XYY syndrome. A chromosomal anomaly that can occur in males; it was at one time thought to predispose to violent or criminal behaviour, but this is now in doubt.

XYZ system. A system of describing colours

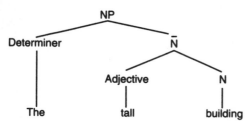

set up by the COMMISSION INTERATIONALE D'ECLAIRAGE; it specifies three primaries that are a mathematical abstraction from the RGB system and which obviate the need for using negative numbers when specifying colour in terms of primaries. In practice if only hue and saturation are to be specified, it is only necessary to specify the proportion of two of the primaries (X and Y) since this determines the proportion of the third.

Y

y. A value of the ordinate.

Yates correction. (Statistics) A correction for small samples in the calculation of chi-square in a 2-by-2 table, in which 0.5 is deducted from each figure exceeding expectation, and 0.5 is added to each figure that is less than the expected value. Assuming fixed marginal totals, which is rarely appropriate, the effect is to bring the distribution of the calculated chi-square nearer to the continuous distribution from which the usual chi-square tables are derived. *Compare* CORRECTION FOR CONTINUITY.

y-axis. The vertical axis on a graph.

y cell. A ganglion cell in the retina or lateral geniculate, with a large receptive field, which does not respond linearly to stimulation of on- and off-regions of its receptive field. It forms part of the MAGNOCELLULAR SYSTEM.

Y chromosome. One of the two chromosomes that determine sex, the other being the X CHROMOSOME; the XY pairing yields a male phenotype.

y coordinate. A value on the vertical axis of a graph.

yellow. *See* SPECTRAL HUES.

yellow–green. *See* SPECTRAL HUES.

yellow spot. A synonym for MACULA LUTEA.

Yerkes–Dodson law. The principle that performance on a task is an inverted U-shaped function of arousal (or motivation).

yes–no question. A question requiring a yes or no answer. *Contrast* WH QUESTION.

yes–no technique. A technique in which a signal (or two different signals) is presented and the subject has to say 'Yes' if he perceives the signal (or the difference between the two signals) and 'No' if he does not. Data obtained this way can be analysed by SIGNAL DETECTION THEORY.

yoga. A school of Hindu philosophy whose adherents practise mental and physical exercises to bring them into contact with some kind of ultimate reality. The exercises include contemplation and curious bodily postures; they are sometimes practised in the West to obtain relaxation and self-control.

yoked control. An experimental procedure in which the control and experimental subjects are paired. Within each pair the control subject receives the same stimuli, reinforcement, or punishment as the experimental subject, but without being allowed to make responses.

Young–Helmholtz theory. A theory of colour vision that is an early version of TRICHROMACY THEORY.

Z

z-band. *See* EXTRAFUSAL FIBRES.

Zeigarnik effect. The tendency for tasks that have not been completed to be better remembered than tasks that have been.

Zeitgeber. Any external cue to a bodily rhythm, such as light and dark for the circadian rhythm.

Zeitgeist. The direction in which social norms are changing in a society.

zelophobia. A morbid fear of being made to feel jealous.

Zen Buddhism. A form of Buddhism whose adherents try to reach a transcendental stillness of the spirit by meditation and other methods.

Zener cards. A deck of 25 cards each bearing one of five symbols (e.g. a circle or a star) used in parapsychological experiments on extrasensory perception.

zero crossing. The point at which a mathematical function changes sign (i.e. passes through zero). One method of detecting edges in the visual image is to perform a CONVOLUTION of the grey-level image with DIFFERENCE OF GAUSSIANS operators and then find the positions at which these operators pass through zero, or in physiological terms pass from excitation to inhibition or vice versa.

zero-order correlation. A correlation performed on the raw data without first removing the effects of any related variables. *Compare* PARTIAL CORRELATION.

zero-sum game. (Game theory) A game in which the pay-offs to one player are balanced by the losses to the other (or others): i.e. the game is wholly competitive.

Zipf's law. As applied to language, the principle that there is a negative correlation between word length and frequency of usage.

Zöllner illusion. The geometric illusion that when neighbouring parallel lines are alternately crossed by short oblique lines running in opposite directions to one another, the parallel lines appear to diverge from one another. It is an instance of the SIMULTANEOUS TILT EFFECT.

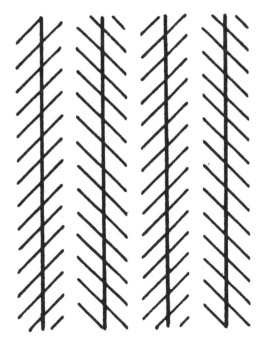

Zöllner illusion

zone of proximal development. The difference between the level of intellectual ability

509

at a given age and the level that could have been reached after systematic instruction.

zooerasty. Sexual excitement obtained by a person from an animal.

zoolagnia. Sexual attraction to an animal.

zoomorphism. The attribution of animal traits to people or to inanimate objects.

zoophilia. A preference for obtaining sexual excitement from animals rather than people.

zoophobia. A morbid fear of animals.

zoopsia. Hallucinatory images of animals, e.g. snakes; it can occur in delirium tremens.

z-process. A method of helping children (particularly autistic ones) to gain attachment to a parental figure. It is hypothesized that children who have not become attached cannot sustain eye contact. They are held close to a parental figure for long periods of time to encourage them to do so.

z-score. A score expressed as the number of units of standard deviation above or below the mean, according to the formula, $z = (X-M)/SD$, where X is the score, M the mean, and SD the standard deviation. It has the following properties: (i) its sum is zero; (ii) its standard deviation is 1.0. Where the population mean and standard deviation are known, the z-score may be used to determine whether the obtained mean of a selected sample is significantly different from the population mean (e.g. in IQ testing). It is also used to render different methods of scoring comparable, and plays a part in most significance tests.

z-transformation. *See* FISHER'S Z-TRANS-FORMATION.

zygosis. The union of two GAMETES.

zygosity. The classification of twins into MONOZYGOTIC TWINS or DIZYGOTIC TWINS.

zygote. The cell formed by the union of two gametes (the ovum and the spermatozoon).

Appendices

Appendix 1

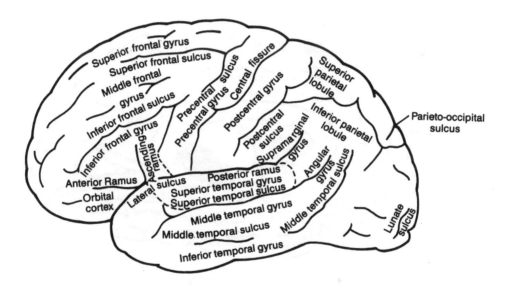

Sulci and gyri of the lateral surface of the cerebral cortex.
(Based on Fig 7. 111A of *Gray's Anatomy* 35th edition)

Appendix 2

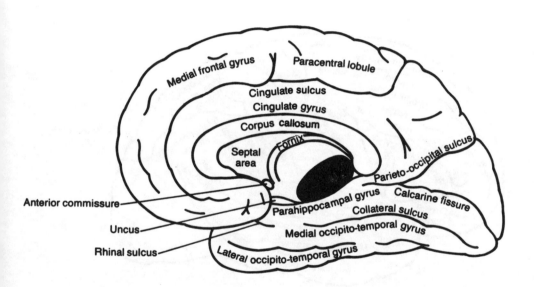

Sulci and gyri of the medial surface of the cerebral cortex.
(Based on Fig 7. 114A of *Gray's Anatomy* 35th edition)

Appendix 3

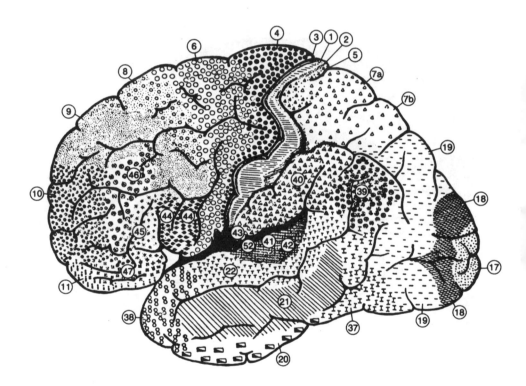

Brodmann's areas of the lateral surface of the cerebral cortex.

Appendix 4

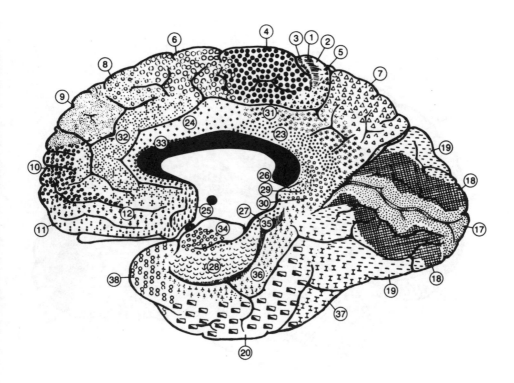

Brodmann's areas of the medial surface of the cerebral cortex.

Appendix 5

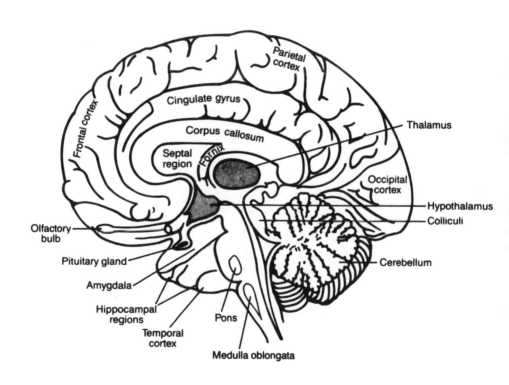

Medial view of the brain.

UCC - PSYCHOLOGY DEPT.